ROLEX
ROLEX

THE WORLD OF PROFESSIONAL GOLF
2021

Editor: Andy Farrell
Writers: Peter Dixon, Doug Ferguson, Donald "Doc" Giffin, Lewine Mair, Marino Parascenzo
Guest contributors: Andrew Cotter, Alastair Johnston, Meghan MacLaren, Dr Andrew Murray
Managing Editor: Sarah Wooldridge
Photography: Getty Images
Producer, official video: Sian Bayliss

First published 2021

Designed and produced by TC Communications Ltd.

ISBN 978-0-9914858-7-1

Printed and bound in England

ROLEX

PRESENTS

THE WORLD OF PROFESSIONAL GOLF 2021

Founded By Mark H McCormack

IMG

To view the official video of
The World of Professional Golf 2021,
which reviews the highlights of the 2020 year in golf,
please go to:
www.rwopg2021.com and enter the password: **Rolex2021**

Contents

THE TOURS

Preface

If ever a year could have done with a mulligan it was 2020. Professional golf does not usually deal in "do-overs", but while the game was affected by the coronavirus pandemic like everything else, it returned to provide more indelible memories to add to the sport's rich history — from Bryson DeChambeau's triumph at the US Open and Dustin Johnson at the Masters, to Korea's Sei Young Kim finally claiming a first major title and Sophia Popov, 304th on the Rolex Rankings, winning the AIG Women's Open. And much, much more.

Recording these deeds is the purpose of this annual, since 2006 titled Rolex Presents *The World of Professional Golf.* Without the co-ordinated efforts of the game's organising bodies to re-start competition on most, if not all, tours, the 2021 edition would have been rather slim. Things were a little different, with fans largely absent and highlights such as The Open Championship and the Ryder Cup held over for 12 months, but in the end there was plenty to celebrate in the way the late Arnold Palmer suggested when *Mark H McCormack's Golf Annual* was founded in 1967. That this annual continues for a 55th edition is due to the generous support of Arnaud Laborde of Rolex.

Every tournament has its own cast of characters and often multiple plot lines. To draw out those stories more powerfully, this edition has been fully revised and re-designed thanks to the outstanding efforts of Tim Leney and his team at TC Communications. For easy reference, scores are presented alongside reports, while there is greater use of photography and added historical context for the major championships, both men's and women's. An enhanced focus on women's golf includes expanded coverage of the Korea LPGA Tour, a breeding ground for new major champions.

Doug Ferguson continues to provide his definitive review of the year in golf, while reflecting the unique nature of the 2020 season, there are additional features from our guest contributors on the measures necessary to provide a tournament "bubble", a player's view on the creation of the Rose Ladies Series, as well as tributes to Mickey Wright and Peter Alliss.

For more than three decades, the annual was compiled and designed by Jan and Bill Davis, with Jan taking over as editor from the late, great Bev Norwood. Their encouragement and assistance has been invaluable and their well-deserved retirement comes with grateful thanks. This edition also continues the longstanding contributions of Marino Parascenzo, who has written beautifully for the title for more than four decades, and Doc Giffin, who has had a hand in all 55 editions to date.

Compiling this book would not be possible without the dedicated work of the communications, media and digital teams at all the leading organisations and tours. Thank you. It is also right to acknowledge the inestimable contribution of the broadcasters, reporters and photographers who provide coverage of professional golf — often under extraordinary circumstances in 2020.

For this edition particularly, thanks are due to: Alexandra Gasser, Melanie Roux and Julie Wittig of Rolex; Neil Ahern, Vanessa O'Brien and Dr Andrew Murray of the European Tour; Sian Bayliss; Tom Benbow; Colin Callander; Chuah Choo Chiang and Laury Livsey of the PGA Tour; Andrew Cotter; Vicky Cuming; Peter Dixon; Doug Ferguson; Mary Flanagan and Mike Woodcock of The R&A; Sasha Forster of the OWGR; Tony Greer; Sean Harry and Andrew Reddington of Getty Images; Ross Hallett; Laura Healey; Alastair Johnston; Tim Lacy; Meghan MacLaren; Lewine Mair; Michele Mair; Amy Mills of the LPGA; Adrian Mitchell; Jonathan Montague; Elliott Platts of the LET; Justin Ray and Dan Zelezinski of 15th Club; Yoshiko Tsukamoto of the JLPGA; and Sarah Wooldridge.

Andy Farrell
Editor
February 2021

Foreword

It has long been my feeling that a sport as compelling as professional golf is deserving of a history, and by history I do not mean an account culled years later from the adjectives and enthusiasms of on-the-spot reports that have then sat in newspaper morgues for decades waiting for some patient drudge to paste them together and call them lore. Such works can be excellent when insight and perspective are added to the research, but this rarely happens. What I am talking about is a running history, a chronology written at the time, which would serve both as a record of the sport and as a commentary upon the sport in any given year — an annual, if you will ...

When I embarked on this project two years ago (the first of these annuals was published in Great Britain in 1967), I was repeatedly told that such a compendium of world golf was impossible, that it would be years out of date before it could be assembled and published, that it would be hopelessly expensive to produce and that only the golf fanatic would want a copy anyway. In the last analysis, it was that final stipulation that spurred me on. There must be a lot of golf fanatics, I decided. I can't be the only one.

And then one winter day I was sitting in Arnold Palmer's den in Latrobe, Pennsylvania, going through the usual motions of spreading papers around so that Arnold and I could discuss some business project, when Arnold happened to mention that he wanted to collect a copy of each new golf book that was published from now on, in order to build a golf library of his own.

"It's really too bad that there isn't a book every year on the pro tour," he said.

"Ah," I thought. "Another golf fanatic. That makes two of us."

So I decided to do the book. And I have. And I hope you like it. If so, you can join Arnold and me as golf fanatics.

Mark H McCormack
Cleveland, Ohio
January 1968

Clive Brunskill/Getty Images

Mark H McCormack 1930—2003

In 1960, Mark Hume McCormack shook hands with a young golfer named Arnold Palmer. That historic handshake established a business that would evolve into today's IMG, the world's premier sports and lifestyle marketing and management company — representing hundreds of sports figures, entertainers, models, celebrities, broadcasters, television properties, and prestigious organisations and events around the world. With just a handshake Mark McCormack had invented a global industry.

Sean McManus, President of CBS News and Sports, reflects, "I don't think it's an overstatement to say that like Henry Ford and Bill Gates, Mark McCormack literally created, fostered and led an entirely new worldwide industry. There was no sports marketing before Mark McCormack. Every athlete who's ever appeared in a commercial, or every right holder who sold their rights to anyone, owes a huge debt of gratitude to Mark McCormack."

Mark McCormack's philosophy was simple. "Be the best," he said. "Learn the business and expand by applying what you already know." This philosophy served him well, not only as an entrepreneur and CEO of IMG, but also as an author, a consultant and a confidant to a host of global leaders in the world of business, politics, finance, science, sports and entertainment.

He was among the most-honoured entrepreneurs of his time. *Sports Illustrated* recognised him as "The Most Powerful Man in Sports". In 1999, ESPN's Sports Century listed him as one of the century's 10 "Most Influential People in the Business of Sport".

Golf Magazine called McCormack "the most powerful man in golf" and honoured him along with Arnold Palmer, Gerald Ford, Dwight D Eisenhower, Bob Hope and Ben Hogan as one of the 100 all-time "American Heroes of Golf". *Tennis* magazine and *Racquet* magazine named him "the most powerful man in tennis".

Tennis legend Billie Jean King believes, "Mark McCormack was the king of sports marketing. He shaped the way all sports are marketed around the world. He was the first in the marketplace, and his influence on the world of sports, particularly his ability to combine athlete representation, property development and television broadcasting, will forever be the standard of the industry."

The London *Sunday Times* listed him as one of the 1,000 people who influenced the 20th century. Alastair Cooke on the BBC said simply that "McCormack was the Oracle; the creator of the talent industry, the maker of people famous in their profession famous to the rest of the world and making for them a fortune in the process ... He took on as clients people already famous in their profession as golfer, opera singer, author, footballer, racing car driver, violinist — and from time to time if they needed special help, a prime minister, or even the Pope."

McCormack was honoured posthumously by the Golf Writers Association of America with the 2004 William D Richardson Award, the organisation's highest honour, "Given to recognise an individual who has consistently made an outstanding contribution to golf".

Among McCormack's other honours were the 2001 PGA Distinguished Service Award, given to those who have helped perpetuate the values and ideals of the PGA of America. He was also named a Commander of the Royal Order of the Polar Star by the King of Sweden (the highest honour for a person living outside of Sweden) for his contribution to the Nobel Foundation.

Journalist Frank Deford states, "There have been what we love to call dynasties in every sport. IMG has been different. What this one brilliant man, Mark McCormack, created is the only dynasty ever over all sport."

Through IMG, Mark McCormack demonstrated the value of sports and lifestyle activities as effective corporate marketing tools, but more importantly, his lifelong dedication to his vocation — begun with just a simple handshake — brought enjoyment to millions of people worldwide who watch and cheer their heroes and heroines.

That is his legacy.

ROLEX

In 2020, the world of sport, like the rest of society, faced unprecedented challenges. To their immense credit, the athletes, and the organizations who administer their disciplines, showed tremendous determination and innovation to maintain competition schedules despite the restrictions placed before them. Throughout this difficult year, Rolex remained committed to its sporting partners, supporting the vision of these individuals and institutions in their pursuit of excellence.

Against this complex backdrop, golf was a role model for the global sports industry, the first to resume tournament activity and eventually completing about 75 per cent of its events across all tours.

Rolex has been part of the fabric of golf for more than 50 years. It began in 1967 when we formed our seminal collaboration with Arnold Palmer, joined by fellow members of The Big Three, Jack Nicklaus and Gary Player. As part of this long-standing association, we continue to support all aspects of the sport, including the game's custodians, The R&A and the USGA, along with the elite professional men's and women's tours and tournaments, and junior, amateur and senior ranks worldwide.

It is a relationship that continues to grow and flourish. From 2021, Rolex is proud to re-establish a partnership with the PGA of America, one that incorporates The Ryder Cup and the PGA Championship. With the latter alliance, Rolex now partners all Majors.

Last year, players had to adapt like never before but still provided many towering performances. Highlights of 2020 included triumphs by several Rolex Testimonees. American Bryson DeChambeau broke through to claim his first Major at the U.S. Open, his fellow countryman Justin Thomas won the WGC-FedEx St. Jude Invitational, while Spain's Jon Rahm took the BMW Championship in a playoff. On the European Tour, Englishman Matt Fitzpatrick held his nerve to claim victory at the DP World Tour Championship, Dubai, the Rolex Series season-ending event.

There were also outstanding results posted by some of our younger Testimonees. In winning the Vivint Houston Open, Carlos Ortiz became the first Mexican to claim a PGA TOUR title in 42 years, while Matt Wolff of the United States and Chile's Joaquín Niemann played with style and consistency to continue their rise up the rankings. Both players, already PGA TOUR winners, are part of the Rolex New Guard, the emerging stars ready to assume the mantle of excellence from the game's legends.

Despite the disruptions, players managed to produce many magical moments out on the course, captured here in *The World of Professional Golf*, which Rolex has been presenting since 2006.

Jean-Frédéric Dufour
Rolex SA
Chief Executive Officer

Rolex and Golf

Rolex supports the most prestigious events, players and organizations in golf and also encourages the development of the game worldwide through its involvement in amateur and junior ranks. The brand is a key presence at men's and women's Majors and at leading team events, namely The Ryder Cup, the Solheim Cup and the Presidents Cup. Its contribution to excellence in golf is based on a rich heritage stretching back more than 50 years, starting in 1967 with Arnold Palmer, joined by members of The Big Three, Jack Nicklaus and Gary Player. After this legendary trio blazed a trail by popularizing the game globally, modern-day legend Tiger Woods has successfully followed in their footsteps and helped the sport soar to new heights. Today's champions and fellow Major winners Brooks Koepka, Jordan Spieth and Lexi Thompson, among other Testimonees, have maintained this legacy of excellence, while members of the New Guard, represented by the likes of Joaquin Niemann and Maria Fassi, have the qualities to do likewise when their time comes. Throughout this enduring partnership, Rolex has championed both innovation and respect for the traditions and spirit of the ancient game.

Jamie Squire/Getty Images

Bryson DeChambeau, winner of the U.S. Open

Andy Lyons/Getty Images

Jon Rahm, winner of the BMW Championship

Jed Jacobsohn/Getty Images

Bernhard Langer, winner of the Cologuard Classic

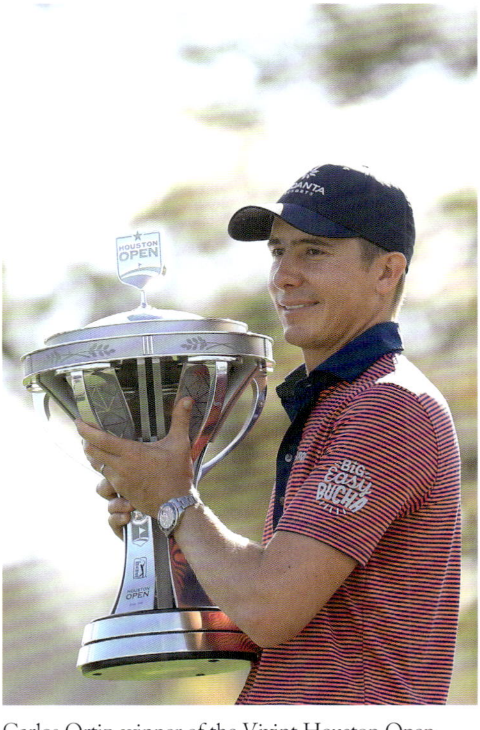

Carmen Mandato/Getty Images

Carlos Ortiz, winner of the Vivint Houston Open

Ronald Martinez/Getty Images

Daniel Berger, winner of the Charles Schwab Challenge

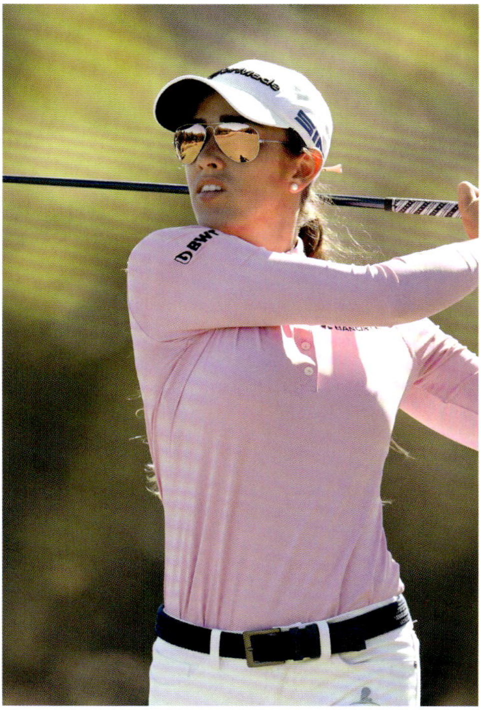

Micheal Reaves/Getty Images

Maria Fassi — Cooper Communities NWA Classic

Brett Carlsen/Getty Images

Phil Mickelson — Schwab Series at Ozarks National

Chris Trotman/Getty Images

Adam Scott, winner of the Genesis Invitational

Ross Kinnaird/Getty Images

Matt Fitzpatrick — DP World Tour Championship

Andy Lyons/Getty Images

Justin Thomas, winner of the WGC — FedEx St. Jude Invitational

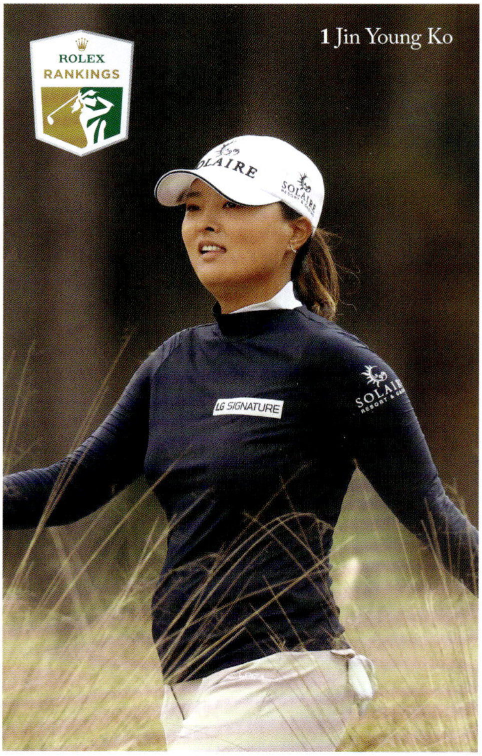

1 Jin Young Ko

Micheal Reaves/Getty Images

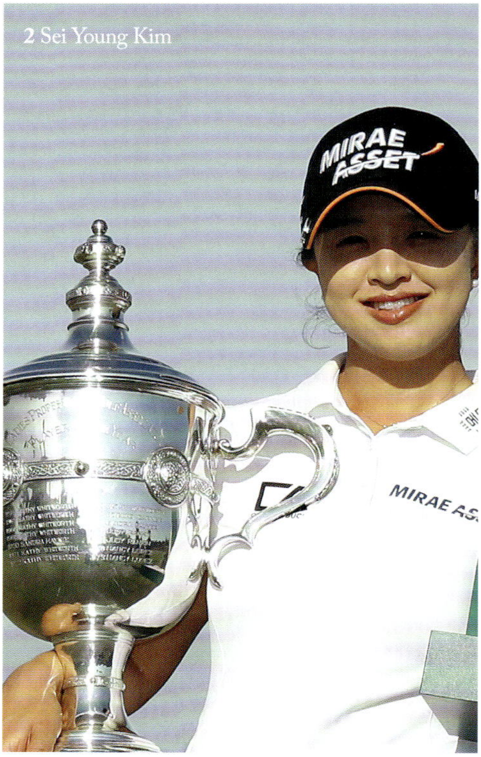

2 Sei Young Kim

Patrick Smith/Getty Images

5 Danielle Kang

Mike Comer/Getty Images

6 Brooke Henderson

Christian Petersen/Getty Images

3 Inbee Park

Sue McKay/Getty Images

4 Nelly Korda

Micheal Reaves/Getty Images

7 Nasa Hataoka

Atsushi Tomura/Getty Images

8 Minjee Lee

Mark Runnacles/Getty Images

Kevin Cox/Getty Images

Rolex's contribution to excellence in golf is based on a rich heritage stretching back more than 50 years, starting in 1967 with Arnold Palmer, joined by members of The Big Three, Jack Nicklaus and Gary Player.

The Year In Prospect

Francois Nel/Getty Images

The Open returns in summer of riches

By Lewine Mair

In quiet corners, such as the sand dunes of Sandwich, life goes on. Whatever else happens at Royal St George's this summer, asparagus and wild orchids will be everywhere apparent on the links. It is reassuring to have something to depend on in 2021.

Once, little more than a year ago, not being able to depend on The Open lighting up the summer's golf would have been unthinkable. Then came 2020 and its pandemic.

Now The R&A are planning to stage the 149th championship 12 months on from when it was originally scheduled. They are having to make contingencies from having a full crowd to none at all, and points in-between, but having it back in its rightful place in the calendar will be no less comforting than the return of a springtime Masters.

With similar caveats, other events postponed from 2020 will hope to proceed. If it all goes ahead, and it remains an "if" at the time of writing, what golfing riches there will be — not just a full complement of men's and women's major championships, but both the Ryder and Solheim Cups, plus the Olympics in Tokyo. What a joy that would be.

Spectators at Sandwich, however many get to attend, are in for another touch of the unexpected. For the first time this year, it is highly possible there could be a second crop of the asparagus coinciding with Open week.

It is all down to climate change.

To give another example of what is happening on the ecology front, a visiting scientist could scarcely contain his excitement when, not so long ago, he saw lady's bedstraw and yellow rattle thriving in the rough. Apparently, their appearance has provided living proof that Royal St George's is doing all the right things.

Paul Larsen, who started in his role as head greenkeeper at the links in 2011, is transfixed by his course and has revelled in going down the environmentally friendly route. When he first arrived, the club had never been given a "favourable" mention in Natural England's rating of Sites of Special Scientific Interest. However, in what was the quickest turnaround those environmental officials have ever known, the links were "in recovery" by 2015 and have since been accorded the prized "favourable" label.

Not everyone will be aware that drought-like conditions in the spring have made for intermittent problems in this little corner of the UK. Back in 1922, for instance, there was a letter in *The Times* suggesting that that year's Open might not, after all, go ahead. "Last year," said the writer, "the drought played havoc with the greens. As a result, their recovery has been so slow and partial that only the most favourable weather can bring them on sufficiently."

The favourable weather came and that year's Open was pronounced a great success. Meanwhile, what Peter Dawson said at The R&A's pre-championship press conference of 2011 will be entirely at odds with what most people remember from Darren Clarke's winning week. Said Dawson, "We had no rainfall here to speak of between the end of February and the end of May. At that time, we were looking at the prospect of having a championship with very little rough indeed." Yet what stands out above all else from that Open was the wind-tossed rain on the Saturday. Clarke, the linksland equivalent of an old sea dog, did not have to cope with the worst of the weather for too long into his Saturday 69, but the 61-year-old Tom Watson negotiated it all the way in his 72. At the end, he passed on some wise words to those younger men he had seen trying to whack the ball as hard as they could to beat the elements. "Swing with ease into the breeze," was the time-honoured message he delivered.

Royal St George's was thrice blessed in having its own answer to the accelerating drought problem. It lay in the clay-based field which belonged to the club and was sitting directly opposite the clubhouse. They were able to transform it into a reservoir and, over the last few years, it has made the world of difference in terms of keeping the course well and inexpensively hydrated.

At the same time, it has added to the points accrued for the aforementioned SSSI, as, indeed, has the club's virtual elimination of fertilisers. Larsen, who was fifth overall in the latest European Turf awards but number one among greenkeepers, speaks with pride of how they now use "hardly any".

2021 SCHEDULE

January 21-24	Abu Dhabi HSBC Championship	Abu Dhabi GC
February 25-28	WGC Workday Championship	The Concession
March 11-14	Players Championship	TPC Sawgrass
March 24-28	WGC Dell Technologies Match Play	Austin CC
April 1-4	ANA Inspiration	Mission Hills
April 8-11	Masters Tournament	Augusta National
April 29-May 2	HSBC Women's World Championship	Sentosa
May 20-23	PGA Championship	Kiawah Island
May 27-30	KitchenAid Senior PGA Championship	Southern Hills
June 3-6	US Women's Open	Olympic Club
June 17-20	US Open	Torrey Pines
June 17-20	Korea Women's Open	TBC
June 24-27	KPMG Women's PGA Championship	Atlanta AC
July 8-11	ASI Scottish Open	The Renaissance Club
July 8-11	US Senior Open	Omaha CC
July 15-18	The 149th Open	Royal St George's
July 22-25	Amundi Evian Championship	Evian
July 22-25	The Senior Open presented by Rolex	Sunningdale
July 29-Aug 1	Olympics Men	Kasumigaseki
July 29-Aug 1	US Senior Women's Open	Brooklawn
August 4-7	Olympics Women	Kasumigaseki
August 12-15	Trust Golf Women's Scottish Open	Dumbarnie
August 19-22	AIG Women's Open	Carnoustie
August 5-8	WGC FedEx St Jude Invitational	TPC Southwind
August 19-22	The Northern Trust	Liberty National
August 26-29	BMW Championship	Caves Valley
August 27-29	Senior LPGA Championship	French Lick
September 2-5	Tour Championship	East Lake
September 4-6	Solheim Cup	Inverness
September 9-12	BMW PGA Championship	Wentworth
September 24-26	Ryder Cup	Whistling Straits
October 28-31	WGC HSBC Champions	Sheshan International
November 18-21	DP World Tour Championship	Jumeirah Golf Estates
November 18-21	CME Group Tour Championship	Tiburon
November 25-28	Andalucia Costa del Sol Open de Espana	TBC

Never mind what it has done for the well-being of the course itself, it has had a breathtaking affect on the wildlife. "If anyone says anything to you about golf courses not being good for the environment, send them to me," he suggests.

Barn owls are now being sighted on a regular basis and, for another species to have made the news in 2020, what of the women professionals? Though the links have hosted as famous a women's amateur matchplay event as the Curtis Cup, they held what was their first women's professional tournament — it was part of the Rose Ladies Series — last summer. The women could not have been more complimentary about what lay in wait. "It's just so special to be the winner at such a great and prestigious course," said Scotland's Emma Dryburgh, who finished one ahead of Charley Hull and Georgia Hall. "The course's condition was immaculate."

That event took place in the week before what would have been the men's Open Championship. As for the week of The Open itself, the club held an Open of its own. When the Secretary, Tim Checketts, and Larsen first discussed the idea — and what a grand idea it was on the part of Chris Healy, the Chairman of Greens — they thought they might get 30 members playing at most. Instead, more than 200 signed on and the links were jam-packed on all four days. As in so many of the best of Opens, there were three glorious days followed by a horror. The members who picked up the much-coveted prizes were Jeremy Dixon (handicap) and Jack Shipton (scratch).

"The tournaments we had were good preparation for us," said Larsen. "The course had to be as good for members as it would have been for Dustin Johnson, Shane Lowry and the rest because that's how we always try to present it."

Larsen and his men had not spent too much time fretting once they learned from The R&A that The Open was not going to happen in 2020. "To be honest, it was out of most of our minds in the months that followed," he said. "Our thoughts were focussed on staying healthy and on keeping the course in good shape with the handful of men we had in the team at that point. We'd heard rumours that the championship might get played in September but that was never going to work. There wouldn't have been enough daylight down here."

A SECOND COUNTDOWN

The opening weeks of 2021, when the country was in lockdown mode once again, presented renewed issues for Larsen and his staff. "Before Christmas," he said, "we were taking it for granted that The Open would be played in front of a full crowd and what we're doing now is to continue to prepare as if that's how it's going to be. We all want a full crowd. The members, when you meet them walking their dogs across the course at the moment, say the same. Myself, I'm longing for people to see how good we've got the links looking."

He and his team never adopted a weary, "We've got to go through all this again" as they started on their second countdown to the championship. "None of the men wanted to go through the latest lockdown sitting at home; they're always desperate to be out on the links." Which, he says, more or less sums up why they chose to become greenkeepers in the first place.

At the start of 2020, there were a few areas of slightly patchy rough which Larsen wanted to refine ahead of last July, while he was also preparing to freshen up the bases of a handful of bunkers. Some 25 bunkers were rebuilt just over four years ago with a view to having them 100 per cent right for 2020. Twelve months on from there and they are all in perfect shape, if hardly prompting a "can't wait to be in them" feeling among more ordinary golfing mortals. (Back in the winter of 2003, when Ben Curtis took his parents and in-laws to see the scene of his victory, the entire party was forced to sit down in a bunker at the second by way of sheltering from the elements. "We were so cold," he explained. "Really cold.")

Meanwhile, heading into 2021, the greens, as the bunkers, have become ever more faultless. To borrow from the SSSI rating terminology, they're not just "favourable" but outstandingly so. Everyone has been drooling over them. "I can safely say that the course is better now than it was a year ago," said Larsen.

Open links are updated all the time. In 2003, for example, any number of ball spotters were positioned to see Tiger Woods off to a safe start, only for the world number one to lose his drive in the right rough.

They widened that narrow fairway ahead of Clarke's Open though, to my way of thinking, the demands of that opening hole have always had most to do with that cosily thatched little starter's hut and outbuildings. What with the asparagus and the orchids, too much is too civilised to alert a player to the troubles in store. Some Women & Golf years ago, a visitor from East Asia, maybe desperate for a few more in the way of homely touches, knocked his second at the fourth into the bath of the member who lives behind the fourth green.

Of course, the 2020 Open was not alone in having to wait another 12 months. Precisely the same happened with the Amundi Evian Championship, where Jin Young Ko was the equivalent of Shane Lowry in being able to hang fast to her trophy for twice the usual time span without having to hit a shot.

It is the sounds of the Evian which stir the memory as much as anything else; the silences and the cheers greeting the mixed fortunes of those playing the short 16th just above the clubhouse, and the sirens sounding on Lake Geneva as the ferries set out on their 30-minute crossing to Lucerne.

Still on the subject of sounds, we can only hope to hear the excited crowd reaction in golf mad Japan to the delightful Hinako Shibuno should the Tokyo Olympics go ahead with spectators and the 2019 AIG Women's Open champion qualifies to represent the home nation. "Golf is a giggle" ran the headline in *Women & Golf* as this golfing sprite laughed her way to victory at Woburn.

Olympic Golf is perhaps the event the game did not realise it missed in 2020. As successful as the return to the Games in Rio was, it should make a rather greater impact this time around. "For the sake of golf, even if I'm not there, I'd love it to go ahead," said Justin Rose, the 2016 Gold Medal winner. "It was a great spectacle last time and I think, I'm biased of course, golf came out pretty well. Japan being an established golfing nation, I think hosting the golf would be fantastic."

To defend his title in 2021, Rose still had plenty of work to do to move up the rankings. "You have to earn your way back," he said. He will have to do as Inbee Park did in 2020. The women's champion from Rio knew she had to start the year in good form to make sure she was one of the top-four Koreans in the world in order to tee up in Japan. Among all sports, the bar is never higher than in qualifying for the Korean women's Olympic golf team.

Meanwhile, Rose and others on both sides of the Atlantic of either gender will also be playing their hearts out to finalise a place for the Ryder and Solheim Cups. With no prospect of playing in front of the usual boisterous crowd in 2020, the Ryder Cup in Wisconsin was delayed by 12 months. All of which suggests the greenkeeping team at Whistling Straits will have given a knowing nod to the kind of work Larsen has been doing at Royal St George's.

Had Ian Poulter been the European captain rather than Padraig Harrington, he might have made a case for switching the uniforms to something more up to date than the 2020 version. Harrington, though, will be thinking that he has enough on his plate without such considerations. Barely can he have cleared his head of all the partnership permutations he would have been mulling over for 2020 than he would have had to start working anew on at least some of what he had in mind.

It was hardly the best news for the women, whose 2021 Solheim Cup was already scheduled for September at Inverness, that some of their thunder could go a-missing amid the build-up to the men's match. After the drama of Catriona Mathew's European team winning at Gleneagles in 2019 with the final putt of the final match, their contest deserves a focus of its own.

Yet if anyone is going to bring a sensitive ear to bear on what was never going to be an entirely comfortable situation, it is Harrington. It was back in 2016 that he turned up unannounced to watch the women of Great Britain and Ireland on their way to winning the Curtis Cup at Dun Laoghaire. If that is anything to go by, you doubt that he would give the go-ahead for any full-scale Ryder Cup activities during the immediate build-up and playing of the Solheim.

No less than Royal St George's ecologically friendly greenkeeper, the 2021 Ryder Cup captain is right for his job and right for the times.

Lewine Mair is a senior European writer for Global Golf Post

The Year In Retrospect

A Lim Kim — US Women's Open champion

Jamie Squire/Getty Images

Golf still thrives in year unlike any other

By Doug Ferguson

The year in professional golf began with Justin Thomas making birdie to win the Sentry Tournament of Champions. It ended 350 days later with Jin Young Ko, the number one player in the Rolex Women's World Golf Rankings, making birdie to win the CME Group Tour Championship. Along the way, the PGA Tour staged 37 tournaments that enabled 91 players to earn $1 million or more. The European Tour offered 35 tournaments held in 17 countries and concluded with Lee Westwood at the top of the list. The majors introduced new champions in Bryson DeChambeau, out of nowhere winners like Sophia Popov and a familiar one in Dustin Johnson. The numbers alone would suggest a normal year in the world of golf.

Far from it.

There was no golf anywhere in the world for two months. There were no roars for the last nine months, with no clear idea when that would return. No one was introduced as the "champion golfer of the year" for the first time since 1945. Absent were the sing-song chants of "Ole, ole, ole, ole!" and the throaty cheers of "USA! USA!" on the final weekend of September. Hugs gave way to fist-bumps. And a new phrase was introduced into the vernacular of tournament golf: The bubble.

Golf certainly was not immune to Covid-19, the deadliest pandemic in a century. The LPGA Tour was the first to feel the effects. Coming off two tournaments in Australia, it was headed to a three-week Asia swing when tournaments in Thailand, Singapore and China were cancelled. The European Tour, which along with the Asian Tour already had cancelled a pair of co-sanctioned events in Malaysia and China, postponed the Magical Kenya Open. What followed was a week in March on the PGA Tour that began on a lucrative note and ended with a future that has never been more muddled.

PGA Tour Commissioner Jay Monahan was making the rounds on television shows in New York to promote the tour's new media rights deal when he was asked about any concerns about the new coronavirus.

The Players Championship, with the richest purse in golf at $15 million, began on Thursday as a normal tournament. By the middle of the day, the tour announced the gates would be closed and no fans would be allowed for the next month over concerns of the outbreak. By the end of the day, the PGA Tour went from having no fans to having no players and no tournaments. Rory McIlroy and others showed up the next morning to clean out their lockers. Bernd Wiesberger was in the biggest hurry as he tried to catch the last flight out to Austria that evening. No one knew when they would return, or even if they would. "We did everything possible to create a safe environment for our players. But at this point, and as the situation continues to rapidly change, the right thing to do for our players and our fans is to pause," Monahan said.

The next month was an exercise in salvaging a golf season. It was a reminder that while the week-to-week tours are the backbone in golf, the majors are the heart of the sport. Nothing could move forward without the six largest organisations in golf working together — the PGA Tour, European Tour and LPGA Tour, along with the PGA of America (Ryder Cup, PGA Championship, KPMG Women's PGA), The R&A (The Open Championship, AIG Women's Open), USGA (US Open, US Women's Open) and Augusta National (Masters). Monahan effectively served as moderator for daily calls and it slowly came together.

As an example of how fluid the situation had become, the USGA contemplated holding the US Women's Open and US Open on consecutive weeks in December. Mike Davis, the chief executive of the USGA, realised the PGA Championship would lead off the major season in August. He figured The Open Championship could go no later than September because of weather and daylight. The Masters had penciled in November. A draft of the press release was being prepared for a US Open at Riviera Country Club in Los Angeles when The R&A realised it had no real option other than to cancel. That sent the US Open back to Winged Foot, to be held in September. That was but one piece of so many moving parts that made this year in golf more challenging than any other. An individual sport never required so much teamwork.

Of course, there were challenges in so many other ways. First and foremost was developing a plan built around "health and safety", a phrase that rolled off the tongue as easily as "birdies and bogeys". There were protocols to follow, testing that was required upon arrival and the need to make sure golf wasn't taking away from the well-being of each community in which it played. It led to consecutive tournaments on one golf course on the PGA Tour, new tournaments on the European Tour that were held at the same golf course in successive weeks on two occasions — Celtic Manor in Wales and Aphrodite Hills in Cyprus — and LPGA events with sponsors who cancelled but still offered financial support to other tournaments.

Golf returned in a staggered fashion. The PGA Tour was the first of the main circuits to come back at the Charles Schwab Challenge at Colonial in Texas on June 11-14. The European Tour returned a month later with consecutive weeks in Austria, followed by a novel plan that limited travel. It featured a six-week "UK Swing" and then three weeks on the Iberia peninsula. The LPGA Tour started up at the end of July with one of two new tournaments, this one at Inverness Club in Ohio, site of the 2021 Solheim Cup. The Japan Golf Tour returned in September but only had four more events for the year. The Asian Tour never played after March.

On the golf course, the shots that were played, the scores and the winners made it look like any other year. That was to ignore the deafening silence. Colonial was so empty for the first tournament back that carts used to ferry players to the practice range or to transport TV crews became a nuisance. Players often had to wait for carts that were in their line of sight. Typically, those carts would be behind a wall of spectators. And then there was Sung Kang making a hole-in-one on the first round at Colonial at the 13th hole. He didn't even know it until he was 50 yards from the green. "I'm like, 'Wow, it's in the hole'. It wasn't really crazy. Nobody was really up there, only a few people out there just clapping a little bit," Kang said. Phil Mickelson made a birdie and instinctively pinched the bill of his cap to acknowledge the gallery, until remembering there was no gallery.

JIN YOUNG KO

Lotte Cantata Ladies Open	45T
Kia Motors Korea Women's Open	6
Jeju Samdasoo Masters	20T
Autech Carrier Championship	3T
KB Financial Group Star Championship	2
Hana Financial Group Championship	8T
Pelican Women's Championship	34T
Volunteers of America Classic	5
US Women's Open	2T
CME Group Tour Championship	WON

Dustin Johnson missed the cut at Colonial and felt tenderness in his knee, a concern because he had surgery on his knee the past winter. This was more a case of trying to practice too much to get ready to complete again, first at a made-for-television charity event at Seminole Golf Club in Florida and then a real tournament. He was hard to figure at the onset. Johnson would win at the Travelers Championship, and then post a pair of 80s at the Memorial, shoot 78 and withdraw from the 3M Open in Minnesota. And a few weeks later, he looked like he might never lose. Johnson ended the year by winning or finishing runner-up in six of his last seven tournaments. He captured the FedEx Cup and its $15 million bonus, a relief to the world number one because he had come close before and desperately wanted his name on the list of winners.

Jon Rahm also missed the cut at Colonial and went on to two more victories, including at the Memorial Tournament that elevated him to number one in the world for the first time. It didn't last long. Rahm reached the top of the ranking twice, both times for two weeks. Whether it was the stop-and-start nature of the season or the increasing depth at the top of golf, this was the first time since the Official World Golf Ranking began in 1986 that five players reached number one in a calendar year. It started with Brooks Koepka, who never got on track from a number of nagging injuries. Rory McIlroy, who did everything except win, replaced Koepka during a week off in February. He stayed at number one until July — the ranking was frozen for 12 weeks during the shutdown — before it went to Rahm, Justin Thomas for one week, Rahm again and then Johnson for the rest of the year.

Europe lost some of its lucrative Rolex Series events — only four for the abbreviated season — but CEO Keith Pelley managed to put together a schedule that included five new events as part of the "UK Swing" that the tour funded with €1 million for prize money at each tournament and a bonus pool of £500,000. The bubble was strict, with players staying at host hotels, such as Celtic Manor. Sam Horsfield, of England, won two of them, the Hero Open at Forest of Arden and the Celtic Classic at Celtic Manor. He earned a spot in the US Open through his performance in the UK Swing, only to have to withdraw because of a positive test for Covid-19. The virus was relentless as it was random. Even limited in schedule, Europe delivered some feel-good moments, such as Tyrrell Hatton winning the BMW PGA Championship, the tournament he once attended as a young boy, and Lee Westwood capping off the year by capturing the Race to Dubai at age 47, his third time to be Europe's number one.

Danielle Kang emerged from the shutdown by winning back-to-back in Ohio on the LPGA Tour, one of those victories at the expense of Lydia Ko as the former teen prodigy made gains in working her way out of a slump. In some respects, the LPGA Tour looked like it did some 30 years ago. The fields were dominated by American players with some emerging European stars, but largely lacking South Korea, the biggest force in women's golf. Most of the players chose to stay home, and they played occasionally on the Korean LPGA Tour. That list included Jin Young Ko, who swept all the major awards in 2019 to reach number one in the Rolex Women's World Golf Rankings. Her plan was to rest in the offseason, missing the LPGA events in Florida and Australia, and start up in Asia. And then Asia was cancelled, and Ko never left home. She didn't return to the LPGA Tour until November for two tournaments ahead of the US Women's Open. She was runner-up at the US Women's Open and won the CME Group Tour Championship to capture the Race to the CME Globe. And while her number one ranking was under threat by Kang, Nelly Korda and Sei Young Kim, Ko ended the year at number one.

Kim and DeChambeau fit the bill as players whose next step was winning a major, so their victories were not a surprise. DeChambeau attracted most of the attention because he was so hard to miss. He began a project to add muscle and mass (some 40 pounds) to swing harder and faster and hit the ball farther. He overpowered Detroit Golf Club in winning the Rocket Mortgage Classic and always seemed to be on the first page of the leaderboard. So it was no surprise to see him hoist the US Open trophy. Kim hit the richest putt in women's golf at the end of 2019, a 25-footer for birdie to win the CME Group Tour Championship with its $1.5 million prize. She was on the rise and capped it off with a distant victory in the KPMG Women's PGA Championship at Aronimink, outside Philadelphia. For the women, it was the first time since 2009 the majors were won by players who had never captured a Grand Slam event. The men had two newcomers in DeChambeau and 23-year-old Collin Morikawa at the PGA Championship.

Even so, this was a year defined more by what wasn't played. Not since the end of World War II had The Open Championship not been played. It was cancelled, returning to Royal St George's in England in 2021, with the return to St Andrews for the 150th Open pushed back a year further. Shane Lowry will end up holding onto that silver claret jug for another year. The Ryder Cup had more circumstances to consider.

Golf could be played without spectators, and it was. But the Ryder Cup? That was the decision facing the PGA of America, the host organisation with the match scheduled for America. Is it a Ryder Cup without partisan cheering, or no cheering at all? It was the last big event to decide what to do, and most telling was a development that got the attention of Jay Monahan. The Warrens Cranberry Festival in Wisconsin was cancelled, an event that draws some 45,000 people. Who would ever link golf with cranberries? In this case, given the festival was some 150 miles from Whistling Straits and scheduled for the same weekend, it was ominous. And it was postponed. Monahan was involved because that meant pushing the Presidents Cup back a year, too. Now the Ryder Cup is back to odd-numbered years, as it was before the matches were postponed in 2001 by the September 11 terrorist attacks.

During the discussion to postpone, one PGA of America official raised an interesting question. What if it gets pushed back to 2021 and it still can't have spectators? The answer was if that turned out to be the case, there would be far greater issues than the Ryder Cup.

So what really was different about 2020 in professional golf? The Masters in November stands out. The US Open had been played in September, though not since 1913. The PGA Championship in August? That's where it used to be. World wars and weather have cancelled tournaments. No spectators? There has been the odd tournament without them, such as a microburst of wind that felled trees at Congressional in 2012 during the AT&T National that Tiger Woods won. One could almost make the case there has been testing, although it was for performance-enhancing drugs, not a virus that created a pandemic.

One of the biggest changes was time off. Injury aside, most of the world's best had never been away from competition for so long. Depending on where they lived, some players didn't even have access to their own golf course. Kevin Na was cleaning out his locker at The Players Championship when his caddie found a banana in his bag, which was put in there for a second round that was never played. "If he hadn't pulled that banana out, that banana would have been in there for a long time," Na said. McIlroy was among those who didn't bother practising because there was no purpose. No one knew when — or if — golf would resume.

Sophia Popov found out the Cactus Tour in Arizona was still playing with health regulations, and then she saw an entry list that included former major champion Anna Nordqvist and Linnea Strom. Popov wound up winning three times, a sign of what was to come. Also in Arizona, the field for the local Scottsdale Open was so full that a PGA Tour player, Scott Harrington, only got in at the last moment. To be sure, players were itching to get back to work. The soft opening came in the form of TV exhibitions. Rory McIlroy, Dustin Johnson, Rickie Fowler and Matthew Wolff played an exhibition at Seminole, the first time the fabled Florida course was shown on TV. Then it was Tiger Woods and Phil Mickelson and their teammates — NFL legends Peyton Manning and Tom Brady — at the Medalist. Both were geared toward raising money and showing golf could be safe amid a pandemic.

The Charles Schwab Challenge was the ultimate test. Caddies were given sanitised wipes for bunker rakes and pins. There was a host hotel for players, though not mandatory. This bubble was efficient, but not airtight. And the first event back was a rousing success. No one tested positive for Covid-19. The quality of golf was evident in the scoring. Daniel Berger won a playoff over Collin Morikawa, both at 265. Bryson DeChambeau, Xander Schauffele and Justin Rose were among those who finished one shot behind. There was a false sense of security, for the following week at Hilton Head Island along the South Carolina shores, the island was packed with tourists and players tested positive. Nick Watney earned a footnote in history as the first. Moving on to Connecticut for the Travelers Championship, the caddies for Brooks Koepka and Graeme McDowell tested positive, and both players (along with Chase Koepka) withdrew as a precaution. Two other players tested positive. "The snowball is getting a little bit bigger," McDowell said on his drive home to Florida, signalling an ominous warning. That prompted Monahan to say the percentage remained low, even though every number mattered. "It's pretty clear that this virus isn't going anywhere," Monahan said.

They played on, without interruption, until every tour completed their season. That in itself was remarkable.

As for the time off, no one took greater advantage than DeChambeau, who treats golf like science and has never been afraid of letting his mind take him places no one imagined. He introduced the single-length irons, with all the shafts roughly the length of a seven-iron. He speaks of standard deviation and spatial awareness. He once described his lower back pain as his *quadratus lumborum* not working. For his latest experiment, it was all about distance. He teased about it going into

BRYSON DECHAMBEAU

Abu Dhabi HSBC Championship	MC
Omega Dubai Desert Classic	8T
Waste Management Phoenix Open	52T
Genesis Invitational	5T
WGC Mexico Championship	2
Arnold Palmer Invitational	4
Charles Schwab Challenge	3T
RBC Heritage	8T
Travelers Championship	6T
Rocket Mortgage Classic	WON
Memorial Tournament	MC
WGC FedEx St Jude Invitational	30T
PGA Championship	4T
The Northern Trust	MC
BMW Championship	50
Tour Championship	20
US Open	WON
Shriners Hospitals for Children Open	8T
Masters Tournament	34T

the offseason at the end of 2019 that he was going to return a different person. "You're going to see some pretty big changes in my body, which is going to be a good thing. Going to be hitting it a lot further." He lived up to his word. His diet was said to be as much as 6,000 calories a day. He drank protein shakes the way some players drank water. He worked out harder than ever to build muscle and mass that would allow him to swing the club as hard and as fast as his body could tolerate.

BRYSON RETURNS AS THE INCREDIBLE BULK

Throw in a three-month break from golf, and he returned as the Incredible Bulk. His goal was to generate ball speed of 200 mph leaving his club. Even for power players, that number was already around the mid-180s.

The timing was interesting because The R&A and the USGA in February — one month before the pandemic put a halt to golf — released their "Distance Insights Project" that was two years in the making, and the results surprised no one. Players were hitting it farther than ever, steady gains for more than 100 years, with an average gain of about 30 yards by elite players in the last 25 years alone. The reasons cited were modern clubs and golf balls, improved athleticism and training, swing techniques geared toward hitting it longer and course conditions with tightly mown fairways that allowed for extra roll. It was just beginning to collect feedback when the project was halted. For those who thought the problem was equipment alone, DeChambeau proved otherwise, and he did it at tough Winged Foot with the USGA looking on at the US Open.

The results, though, were immediate. He was a putt away from the playoff at the Charles Schwab Challenge. McIlroy played with him in the final round and couldn't believe what he was seeing. The next week, DeChambeau drove over the green on a reachable par four at Harbour town with a three-wood during the RBC Challenge, where he tied for eighth. He nearly drove a par four over water that was not meant to be reached off the tee at the TPC River Highlands in the Travelers Championship. And he reduced Detroit Golf Club to a pitch-and-putt with his enormous power at the Rocket Mortgage, his first victory of the year. Golf has always been more about "how many" than "how", though DeChambeau brought attention to the latter. He finished in Detroit with a 367-yard drive, and it was only his fourth-longest of the week. In the four tournaments since the resumption of the PGA Tour schedule, DeChambeau hit 29 tee shots of 350 yards or longer. In the final round, facing the 399-yard 13th hole, he waited for the green to clear before blasting away.

Players who made fun of his weight gain began to pay homage, not so much to the method but the discipline it required, and how DeChambeau delivered on what he said he would do. He often talks about leaving bread crumbs so he can find his way back to what was working if the experiment failed. This one did not. He became the talk of golf, must-see television. His pre-shot routine was reminiscent of an Olympic weightlifter huffing and puffing and psyching himself out right before the lift, clean and jerk. At the Shriners Hospitals for Children Open in Las Vegas, DeChambeau took practice swings so hard that he generated a light breeze. And then he walked over to his bag and used a wrench to tighten the screws in his driver. He drove the 300-yard 15th hole at the TPC Summerlin with a four-iron. And it all started with him watching the World Long Drive Championship and asking a question. "If I could do that and hit it straight, what would happen?" he said. "That was the question that inspired me to go down this road."

The crowning moment was the US Open at Winged Foot, where in five previous championships going back to 1929 only two players had broken par — Fuzzy Zoeller and Greg Norman at 276 in 1984. DeChambeau finished at six-under 274 for a six-shot victory. He used his power, sure, but he used his brain. DeChambeau realised the fairways were so narrow that no one was going to be playing from the short grass a majority of the time. So he blasted away, trying to get as close as possible, even from the rough. He usually had no more than wedge and let his irons and putting take care of the rest. He outsmarted the USGA by exposing a flaw in the design. "They just made the fairways too small this week to have it be an advantage for guys hitting the fairway," he said.

DeChambeau became the betting favourite to win the Masters in November. He talked about using a 48-inch driver to hit it farther than anyone imagined. He didn't, and he didn't hit irons very well or putt very well.

Golf remains more about the long ball. Even so, DeChambeau had everyone watching, talking and thinking. And he had a daunting message for the governing bodies as they contemplated the effect on distance. "It's tough to rein in athleticism," he said. "We're always going to be trying to get fitter, stronger, more athletic. And Tiger inspired this whole generation to do this, and we're going to keep going after it."

JOHNSON THE STAR OF THE SHOW

As much of a side show as DeChambeau became, Dustin Johnson became the star of the show. His year began with no small measure of uncertainty based on how the previous year had ended, with eight consecutive tournaments and nothing better than a tie for 20th to show for it. He was last against the 30-man field at the Tour Championship. And then he had knee surgery to repair cartilage and didn't play until the Presidents Cup, where he went an uninspiring 2-2. He had one reasonably good showing in the Saudi International. And then the pandemic hit and Johnson was on the verge of being overlooked. He returned at the Charles Schwab Challenge and missed the cut. That seems so long ago.

His victory in the Travelers Championship meant he had won at least one PGA Tour event in all but one of his 12 years as a pro. But right when it looked as though he was on his way back, Johnson turned in a pair of 80s at the Memorial and withdrew from the next event after a 78 and complaints of soreness in his back. It bore notice because as good as Johnson is, his consistency is always what made him great. His career was starting to become more about what went wrong than what went right, and the narrative went to another level when he took a one-shot lead into the final round of the PGA Championship at Harding Park and finished two shots behind. It was his second straight year as a runner-up in the PGA Championship. He already had achieved the Grand Slam of silver medals having finished second in all the majors. It was his third runner-up finish in the last five majors. That doesn't include the mishaps such as a three-putt par from 12 feet in the 2015 US Open at Chambers Bay to go from a putt to win to a par and a second-place finish, or the time he grounded his club in sand without realising it was a bunker in the 2010 PGA Championship at Whistling Straits, costing him a spot in the playoff.

For so much misfortune, no other player of his generation allows it to roll off him so phlegmatically. "I've done a good job taking the punches and keep right on rolling," he said. This roll was among his best. The sting of the PGA Championship still fresh, he won by 11 shots and became only the third player in PGA Tour history to finish 30 under or lower over 72 holes when he destroyed the field at The Northern Trust to start the tour's FedEx Cup postseason. A week later, he had a tie for the lead going into the last round and came to the final hole needing a birdie to force a playoff with Jon Rahm. Johnson faced a 45-foot birdie putt he had to aim across the green and down a ridge to the hole. He hit it perfectly, and gave a slow, windmill fist pump when it fell. That's a lot of emotion for him. Just his luck, Rahm made a similar putt from just outside 65 feet in the playoff to win the BMW Championship at Olympia Fields outside Chicago. From blessing to curse, as only can happen to Johnson.

The FedEx Cup is often seen as a cash giveaway by the golfing public, now $15 million to the winner. Johnson simply wanted his name on the trophy because of the players who have achieved it already — Woods twice, Henrik Stenson, Rory McIlroy twice, Jordan Spieth, Justin Thomas. Before the pandemic, he had planned to skip the Tokyo Olympics so he wouldn't be overly tired when he reached the FedEx Cup Playoffs. He had the advantage of starting with a two-shot lead at 10 under

DUSTIN JOHNSON

Sentry Tournament of Champions	7T
Saudi International	2
AT&T Pebble Beach Pro-Am	32T
Genesis Invitational	10T
Charles Schwab Challenge	MC
RBC Heritage	17T
Travelers Championship	WON
Memorial Tournament	MC
3M Open	WDN
WGC FedEx St Jude Invitational	12T
PGA Championship	2T
The Northern Trust	WON
BMW Championship	2
Tour Championship	WON
US Open	6T
Vivint Houston Open	2T
Masters Tournament	WON

par as the number one seed and he kept his nose in front the entire way to win. Xander Schauffele had the lowest score and was rewarded with first-place ranking points. The official tally by the tour was Johnson at 21 under (including the 10-under start) for a three-shot victory. It would have been reason for him to take the money (and the trophy) and run to south Florida to spend time on his boat.

Except that this year, he still had two majors ahead of him. One of them, the US Open, fell to DeChambeau. Johnson was gearing up for the Masters when he flew to Las Vegas and tested positive for the coronavirus, costing him starts at the CJ Cup at Shadow Creek and the Zozo Championship at Sherwood, where he is a member when he's in California. That proved to be a detour. The consolation prize was not having to be tested for Covid-19 for 90 days. The bonus was that it did nothing to slow his momentum.

Most telling about his five-shot victory in the Masters was that Johnson became the first Masters champion to earn three crystal vases awarded to the low round of the day. That spoke to his dominance — a 65 in the first and third rounds, a 68 in the closing round. He also showed how much it meant by not saying anything at all. It wasn't by choice. He simply couldn't get the words out of his mouth during his interview on the putting green. Much of that was location. He grew up in South Carolina and the Masters is the major any golfer from the South wants to win. A big part was redemption. Johnson knew he should have won more majors by now. He was aware the golf world was starting to doubt his ability to close out the big ones. He answered a lot of questions that day and restored himself as the best in golf.

Johnson returned to number one in the world with his victory at the TPC Boston in The Northern Trust. By the end of the year, his gap at number one was the largest since it belonged to McIlroy at the end of 2014. Johnson also had the distinction of having been number one longer than anyone except Tiger Woods and Greg Norman since the ranking began in 1986. Finally, it was time to relax on his boat. He was a happy man. "Masters champion Dustin Johnson. It's got a nice ring to it," he said.

FOUR MORE WORLD NUMBER ONES

Jon Rahm is still looking for his first major with time on his side. He has been a large presence since turning pro after the 2016 US Open at Oakmont — Johnson's first major — both on the PGA Tour and the European Tour, along with a Ryder Cup debut in 2018 in which he took down Woods. Rahm has yet to seriously contend in the majors, at least in the final hour. At age 26 and with just over four years of professional golf under his belt, it is too early to judge him with that measure.

But the fiery Spaniard ticked off one box in the summer when he reached number one in the world for the first time. He got there with a wild ride at Muirfield Village to win the Memorial, leading by eight shots at the turn, watching it shrink to three shots with three holes to play, and then holing a tough flop shot out of deep rough for birdie on the 16th hole. That birdie turned into a bogey because of a two-shot penalty for causing his ball to slightly move before the shot. No matter. He still won and shared a fist-bump — the Covid-19 version of a handshake — with Jack Nicklaus. He joined his idol, Seve Ballesteros, as the only Spaniards to reach number one in the world. He also captured the BMW Championship with that magnificent birdie putt in a playoff to beat Johnson. That was as far as he got. It's still progress. It was his fourth consecutive year of at least two victories around the world.

Justin Thomas has been to number one. His problem is staying there. He first rose to number one in 2018 and lasted four weeks. In 2020, he won the WGC FedEx St Jude Invitational — his second World Golf Championship title — over Brooks Koepka and stayed there all of one week. But he has staying power. Thomas never fell out of the top five all year, and it was his fourth consecutive season of at least two victories on the PGA Tour. No one since Woods a decade ago has put together such a streak. Even so, there was reason for Thomas to feel disappointed as he looked back on his year at what was within his reach. He had the 18-hole lead at the US Open and he shared the 36-hole lead at the Masters, both times faltering on the weekend. He was in Sunday position at five other tournaments — he had the lead in three of them — without converting. "I've got to figure that out," he said. Nothing burned him more than losing a three-shot lead with three holes to play in the Workday Charity Open at Muirfield Village and losing to Collin Morikawa in a playoff.

It wasn't all bad. He took advantage of a three-putt par by Xander Schauffele on the 72nd hole of the Sentry Tournament of Champions to get into a playoff, twice hit a hook with his three-wood in the playoff and somehow escaped with a victory. His victory at the WGC FedEx St Jude Invitational included a wild tee shot that missed a hazard by hitting a cart path and turned a potential bogey into a tournament-winning moment. As his game matures, his expectations rise. The PGA Tour stopped giving out a trophy for the leading money winner as it has become all about FedEx Cup points. It used to be the Arnold Palmer Award, and now that goes to the rookie of the year. It's still worth noting that Thomas finished at number one on the PGA Tour money list at just over $7.3 million, not a bad total considering three months were lost to the schedule. It was the third time in the last four years Thomas has led the PGA Tour's money list. He also won the points-based award from the PGA of America as player of the year, mainly because the standings ended before the last two majors were played.

The forgotten number one for 2020 was McIlroy, and an argument can be made that no one was hurt more by the pandemic. When he tied for fifth at the Arnold Palmer Invitational, it was his seventh consecutive top five around the world, which included a victory in the WGC HSBC Champions at the tail end of 2019. McIlroy contended every week he played, and he returned to number one for the first time in nearly five years in February. He didn't win in the four chances he had at the start of the year, and his year ended the same way. Coming out of the pandemic, McIlroy was poised to keep right on going. He was in the mix at the Charles Schwab Challenge only to close with a 74. And so began a streak of a different variety. McIlroy went eight straight tournaments without a top 10, and he finally let on that he was having a difficult time adjusting to the quiet, spectator-free environments.

Simply put, he found himself going through the motions. "That's partly to do with the atmosphere and partly to do with how I'm playing. I'm not inspiring myself, and I'm trying to get inspiration from outside sources to get something going," he said. McIlroy also had plenty on his mind off the course as his wife, Erica, gave birth to a daughter they named Poppy. He had a pair of top 10s in the majors to close out the year but number one in the world looked farther away at the end of the year than it was at the beginning. More troublesome for McIlroy is another year without a major. He now has gone six years without.

Brooks Koepka, who began the year at number one, was among those who effectively were missing in action. Koepka was coping with injuries to his left leg and hip during an offseason that kept him from playing in the Presidents Cup. He didn't return until two tournaments in the Middle East, the Abu Dhabi HSBC Championship and the Saudi International, and neither were inspiring. It was like that when he returned to American soil. And then the pandemic arrived, costing him more time off he neither wanted nor needed. By then, Koepka was in danger of missing out on the FedEx Cup postseason for the first time since he joined the tour, and he found some form when it was too late. He had a chance to defend his title in the WGC FedEx St Jude Invitational until hitting his drive on the 18th hole in the water.

And he was full of confidence — or sounded that way — at the PGA Championship when he was trying to become the first player to win three successive years in strokeplay. Positioned nicely just two shots behind Johnson going into the final round at Harding Park, he surveyed the leaderboard and said he liked his chances, with a dig at his one-time friend Johnson. "When I've been in this position before, I've capitalised. He's only won one. I'm playing good. I don't know, we'll see." It was a rare dose of trash talk, and it backfired. Koepka shot 74 and tied for 29th. He missed the cut in the Wyndham Championship the following week, and at 97th in the FedEx Cup, withdrew before the opening playoff event and his season was over. Koepka ended the year at 12th in the world, the first player since Jason Day in 2017 to start the year at number one and finish outside the top 10.

Rickie Fowler fell out of the top 50 for the first time since 2014 and faces being left out of certain majors. Francesco Molinari also was a no-show. The Italian had not been the same since losing the lead on the back nine at Augusta National in 2019. A year devoted to pulling himself out of a slump turned into a year at home. Molinari decided during the pandemic to move from London to Los Angeles. He played four times before the pandemic and three times after golf returned. He started the year at 18th in the world and ended it at 112th. Three-time major champion Jordan Spieth kept searching and kept spinning his wheels. He remained winless since The Open Championship victory at Royal Birkdale in 2017. Spieth showed flashes when golf returned from the pandemic, but not for long. He ended 2020 closer to falling out of the top 100 than moving back into the top 50.

The other absentee was Tiger Woods, whose future gets more tenuous with each passing year. The question going into 2020 was more about when he would break the PGA Tour's career victory record he now shares with Sam Snead at 82. By the end of the year, the pulse was leaning more toward "if". The Masters he won in 2019 really was a crowning moment in so many ways. His first major in 11 years. His fifth green jacket, and first Masters title in 15 years. The comeback from four back surgeries and the fallout from medication. And his two children were there to witness what they previously had only known from video highlights. Throw in another classic Woods victory in the Zozo Championship in Japan — wire-to-wire, soft course, giving no one else chasing him reasonable hope — and closing out the year with perhaps his crispest golf in a playing-captain victory at the Presidents Cup, and he was primed. And then just like that, he wasn't.

A CURIOUS YEAR FOR TIGER

Woods hasn't won at Torrey Pines since 2013, before the first of his back surgeries. The course is long, the rough is thick and wet, the Pacific air is cold. He broke par all four days in the Farmers Insurance Open, and while he was never seriously in contention and finished six shots behind, he still tied for ninth. It was his next start at Riviera for the Genesis Invitational where he is tournament host that his season began to look curious. Woods has never won at Riviera, even in his prime. In early 2000, when he won or was runner-up in 10 out of 11 official PGA Tour events he played, the exception was Riviera. He tied for 18th. This time, it was a 76-77 weekend in cold air and a last-place finish among those who made the cut. He said he felt stiff all week. No one would have guessed then he would not play again until July.

Woods skipped the WGC Mexico Championship. And then he chose to sit out the Arnold Palmer Invitational as an eight-time winner at Bay Hill, saying his back and neck needed rest. Another dagger was The Players Championship, which he had missed only four previous times, all injury-related. The tour shut down after the first round, the Masters was postponed, golf was postponed and Woods was out of the public view. He did join Jim Nantz during a re-airing of the previous year's Masters. He was shown having his own Masters dinner while wearing his green jacket on what would have been Tuesday at the Masters. Golf resumed. Woods stayed home. It wasn't until the Memorial that he returned and was never a factor.

It was like that all year. Woods played twice before the pandemic. In the seven tournaments he played after the return, he finished a combined 107 shots out of the lead in the six events he made the cut. At the Masters, he generated a buzz with a 68 in the opening round and was well out of it when he made a 10 on the 12th hole of the final round. "My body just has moments where it just doesn't work like it used to," he said after the Masters. "No matter how hard I try, things just don't work the way they used to, and no matter how much I push and ask of this body, it just doesn't work at times. Yes, it is more difficult than others to be motivated at times. Yes, because things just ache and have to deal with things that I've never had to deal with before."

His year ended on a high note. Playing with 11-year-old son Charlie in the PNC Championship, they finished seventh and Woods was a proud dad. Two days before Christmas, he had a fifth surgery on his lower back, this one the maintenance variety. All that did was lead to more questions about his future.

Another player moving closer to the twilight of his career sure didn't play like it. Lee Westwood tied for fourth in The Open Championship at Royal Portrush in 2019 and took particular delight in knowing it would get him back to the Masters the following year. He had fallen out of the top 100 in the world near the end of 2018 until winning the Nedbank Challenge in South Africa. He was still well outside the top 50 before Portrush. But then he started 2020 with a victory in the Abu Dhabi HSBC Championship, his second title in a Rolex Series event, and he suddenly had reason to feel much younger than his 46 — soon to be 47 — years. Such is the staying power of Westwood that his victory gave him a European Tour title in each of the last four decades, and it was the 25th career title on the European Tour. Just like that, he was back among the elite. Coming over to America for the run-up to the Masters, he tied for fourth in the Honda Classic before golf shut down. Westwood thought he had played the Ryder Cup for the last time at Hazeltine, and now it was on his mind again. "I really enjoyed watching everybody else suffer in the last one. Now I give myself a chance to play," he said. That was put on hold, but not his season.

The Race to Dubai was so disjointed because of the pandemic. It began with 11 events dating to the autumn of 2019, though there was only one Rolex Series event, one World Golf Championships event in Mexico and two other events that offered a regular allotment of points in Dubai and Saudi Arabia. Throw in another World Golf Championship and majors in August and September, and the race to be Europe's number one had a red, white and blue tone to it. Patrick Reed was the leader for much of the season; Reed plays a global schedule and has been a big supporter of the European Tour for years. Right there with him was Collin Morikawa, who had never played on European soil or even taken part in a regular European Tour event. He moved up the standings primarily due to his PGA Championship victory. But the 23-year-old American came over for the DP World Tour Championship, as did Reed. In a most exciting finish to a most unusual year, Reed made enough mistakes over the final holes in Dubai that Matt Fitzpatrick won the tournament and Westwood captured the Race to Dubai.

Even in such a moment of glory, Westwood turned his thoughts to the real winner of the year. He sits on the Players' Committee on the European Tour. He was in the meetings. He was helping with the decisions. "It didn't look good for a period of time there, and we played every week pretty much. That's a phenomenal achievement with what's going on to get those tournaments on," Westwood said. He considered the protocols and the bubbles, the masks and the refrain from socialising so valuable on the tour. Everyone bought into the plan Pelley and his staff laid out. "To actually play tournaments and play a full tour this year has been an incredible job by everybody at the tour, and Keith deserves a pat on the back."

Westwood was number one in Europe for the third time, but he wasn't the best in England. That fell to Tyrrell Hatton, who came into his own with two big victories. One of them was all about timing. Tommy Fleetwood had a chance to win the Honda Classic in Florida and came up short. Paul Azinger, still regarded as "Captain America" for leading his US team to a rare Ryder Cup victory in 2008, was handling the television commentary. He said Fleetwood had a chance to prove he had what it takes to win. "You can win all you want on that European Tour or in the international game and all that, but you have to win on the PGA Tour," he said. It was a stinging comment — particularly the use of THAT European Tour — and Westwood and past Ryder Cup captain Thomas Bjorn were quick to call him out. Fleetwood wasn't listening and wasn't bothered. But it was only fitting that the following week at the Arnold Palmer Invitational, Hatton closed with seven straight pars in some of the toughest conditions of the year for a one-shot victory, his fifth worldwide and first in America.

TYRRELL HATTON

WGC Mexico Championship	6T
Arnold Palmer Invitational	WON
RBC Heritage	3T
Rocket Mortgage Classic	4T
WGC FedEx St Jude Invitational	69T
PGA Championship	MC
The Northern Trust	25T
BMW Championship	16T
Tour Championship	7
US Open	MC
BMW PGA Championship	WON
The CJ Cup	3T
Zozo Championship	28T
Vivint Houston Open	7T
Masters Tournament	MC
The RSM Classic	23T
DP World Tour Championship	8T

That was only the start for Hatton. Bay Hill turned out to be the last tournament for three months on the PGA Tour, even longer in Europe. The time off did not hurt Hatton, however, as he made a bold move at the RBC Heritage and tied for third, added a tie for fourth in the Rocket Mortgage Classic and then won the next best thing to a major. He used to attend the BMW PGA Championship as a child. He even recalls the time he was at Wentworth as a five-year-old with his father and was nearly struck by the tee shot of Vijay Singh. And here he was, at the flagship event of the European Tour, the only player to post scores in the 60s all four rounds for a four-shot victory. Even against a stronger field and tougher course conditions he faced at Bay Hill, this was his signature victory.

"This was a goal of mine, to win this tournament in my career," he said. Another goal was to reach the top 10 in the world, and he achieved that the same week. The next target are the majors, and that could stand some improvement. One year after he made the cut in all four majors, he was among six players who missed the cut in all three majors played in 2020. No matter. It was a very good year.

It was a great year for the women, too, considering what they were up against. LPGA Tour Commissioner Mike Whan felt he had loads of momentum going into 2020 with a schedule of 34 official tournaments and 10 years of hard work and good sponsorship that created a reserve fund for a tour that for more than a half-century has been on its own. Whan even led a unique joint business venture with the Ladies European Tour with hopes of strengthening women's golf worldwide. The LET was able to boost its schedule to 24 events with a $5 million increase in total prize funds. The pandemic cost them the Asia Swing in March, the popular West Coast Swing through Arizona, California and Hawaii in the late spring to general concern how much of a financial blow it would be to women's golf. Whan was quick to shut down the tour and slow to return, with no apologies. He preached caution, and it paid off. Danielle Kang won back-to-back in Ohio, staking her claim as America's best on a tour where Americans are easily lost. Stacy Lewis won the Scottish Ladies Open. And then the winner's circle was filled with one great story after another.

Those three Cactus Tour events in Arizona that Sophia Popov won were only a precursor. She went from caddieing for a friend to getting into a tournament in Ohio, and she did well enough to earn a spot in the AIG Women's Open at Royal Troon, where she had the week of her life to capture her first LPGA title and her first major. She had to miss the next one, the ANA Inspiration, because much like the Masters, the field had been set as if it were being played in April. Mel Reid, a fierce athlete and sympathetic figure while coping with her mother's death in a car accident that derailed her promising career in England, broke through with her first victory in the ShopRite LPGA Classic. Austin Ernst and Ally McDonald added their first titles.

SEI YOUNG KIM DOMINATES

The majors contained one big surprise after another, except for one. Popov, Mirim Lee at the ANA Inspiration and A Lim Kim at the US Women's Open were all first-time major champions. So was Sei Young Kim, though she was hardly a surprise. She already had won 10 times on the LPGA Tour when she dominated the field at Aronimink in the KPMG Women's PGA Championship. Kim added a second title in the Pelican Women's Championship, a new tournament that was salvaged by moving to October. Kim and Kang were the only multiple winners in a season that still managed to squeeze in 18 tournaments and crown a Race to CME Globe champion in Jin Young Ko, the number one player in women's golf.

Ko stayed mostly out of sight during the pandemic except for six appearances on the Korean LPGA — four top 10s, no victories. It was a time for her to be home. And then there was Emily Kristine Pedersen, once a rising star from Denmark who benefited greatly from the shutdown. Pedersen made her Solheim Cup debut in 2017 in Iowa at age 21 and it proved to be a tough week for her and for Europe. She lost all three of her matches and so went her confidence. She struggled to make cuts and lost her LPGA Tour card. She fell out of the top 500 in the Rolex Women's World Rankings. "I sat down with my coach in March and he said, 'How are we getting through this lockdown better than everyone else?' And that motivated me. If I hadn't had my struggles, I don't think I would have learned." She learned, and she won — a lot. Pedersen won the Tipsport Czech Ladies Open for her first title in five years. And then she closed out the LET season with three in a row — the Saudi Ladies International, the Saudi Ladies Team International and the Andalucia Costa del Sol Open de Espana.

There was golf on the PGA Tour Champions, but no conclusion. While the PGA Tour managed to crown a FedEx Cup champion (helped by a season that began last

SEI YOUNG KIM

Diamond Resorts Tournament of Champions	7T
Gainbridge LPGA	5
KLPGA Championship	46T
Lotte Cantata Ladies Open	2
Kia Motors Korea Women's Open	4T
Is Dongseo Busan Open	6T
Walmart NW Arkansas Championship	5T
ANA Inspiration	18T
ShopRite LPGA Classic	18T
KPMG Women's PGA Championship	WON
Pelican Women's Championship	WON
US Women's Open	20T
CME Group Tour Championship	2T

September), it decided the PGA Tour Champions would have one season wrapped into one year. Bernhard Langer won again, because that's all the German does. He captured his 41st career title on the PGA Tour Champions and by the end of the year — but not the season — he was leading the Charles Schwab Cup points race. Four-time major champion Ernie Els won for the first time in the last event before the pandemic at the Hoag Classic, and the Big Easy won again late in the year. He was among four multiple winners in the 15 tournaments that were held. The other was Miguel Angel Jimenez, and then two rookies to the 50-and-older circuit.

Jim Furyk and Phil Mickelson were born a month apart in 1970 and made their Champions debuts at different times. Furyk started at the Ally Challenge at Warwick Hills in Michigan, one of his favourite places when it held the Buick Open on the PGA Tour. He won on his debut, and then he won again on another familiar course, Pebble Beach, at the Pure Insurance Open. Mickelson played more out of desperation. He failed to advance beyond the first week of the FedEx Cup Playoffs, which presented a problem. Mickelson had no tournament to play for the next two weeks with the US Open in September approaching. He entered the Charles Schwab Series at Ozarks National in Missouri, shot 22 under par in the 54-hole event and won on his debut. He played again in the Dominion Energy Charity Classic and won that event, too. Two starts, two victories, $755,000. That was about half of what he earned in 16 starts on the PGA Tour the previous season. Mickelson thought about playing the Charles Schwab Cup Championship in Arizona as his tune-up for the Masters, and then changed his mind and went to the Vivint Houston Open. He missed the cut and then beat only four players at Augusta National. The PGA Tour Champions probably hasn't seen the last of him.

Every year, golf keeps getting younger because players keep getting better. They are ready to win. Gone are the days of any feeling that some apprenticeship must be served. Collin Morikawa graduated from the University of California at Berkeley in 2019. Within two months, he was a winner at the Barracuda Championship, and then he backed it up in 2020 with victories at the Workday Charity Open and the PGA Championship. Matthew Wolff left Oklahoma State after his sophomore year and was a winner within a month. He contended on the back nine at the PGA Championship and US Open, losing out to Morikawa and DeChambeau. By the end of 2020, 14 of the top 20 players in the world were in their 20s, and 20 out of the top 50. And more, undoubtedly, were on the way.

EMILY KRISTINE PEDERSEN

Australian Ladies Classic	50T
Women's NSW Open	37T
Investec SA Women's Open	7T
ASI Ladies Scottish Open	2T
AIG Women's Open	11T
Tipsport Czech Ladies Open	WON
VP Bank Swiss Ladies Open	3T
Lacoste Ladies Open de France	15T
Omega Dubai Moonlight Classic	41T
Aramco Saudi Ladies International	WON
Saudi Ladies Team International	WON
Andalucia Costa del Sol Open de Espana	WON
US Women's Open	MC

With age comes experience, however, and golf lost a foursome of rules and tournament knowledge that covers over 160 years. On the European Tour, chief referees John Paramor and Andy McFee decided to retire. They have been the voice and often the logic of rules on the European Tour for some 40 years each. Once frustrated over being summoned for the most simple of rulings, they established a policy in which players who called for a ruling they should have known — relief from a cart path, for example — they had to watch a special rules DVD that McFee and Paramor created before entering their next event. In America, the PGA Tour announced the retirement of Mark Russell and Slugger White, each with some 40 years of experience, who had served as vice presidents of rules and competition.

The world lost some powerful figures in golf. The older crowd will remember the smooth swing of Peter Alliss, an eight-time Ryder Cup player and Europe's best player in the 1960s whose 23 victories did not, sadly, include The Open Championship. Old and young alike will know the voice — distinctively British, raw opinions, often humorous, always honest. Small wonder Alliss became known as the "Voice of Golf" for his work on the BBC in Britain and ABC in America, along with other countries who had the pleasure of hearing him. He was three months shy of his 90th birthday when he died on December 5. "Pure madness" is how he described Jean Van de Velde playing the 72nd hole at

Carnoustie when he carelessly threw away a chance to win The Open Championship. On the day Tiger Woods was going for the third leg of the Grand Slam and shot 81 in the raging wind off Muirfield, Alliss said, "It's like turning up to hear Pavarotti sing and finding out he has laryngitis."

The golf should not be overlooked. He was proud of of his 1-0-1 singles record against Arnold Palmer in the Ryder Cup. He won the Vardon Trophy as the leading player on the British PGA, the precursor to the European Tour, in 1964 and 1966. He represented England 10 times in the World Cup. Alliss was inducted into the World Golf Hall of Fame in 2012 for his golf, for his voice, for a little bit of everything.

Mickey Wright was all about golf, considered by many to be the greatest woman player in history. Kathy Whitworth won more tournaments. Babe Zaharias had more flair. But any conversation about the best female golfer starts with Wright, who died on February 17 at age 85. She won 82 times and 13 majors, and perhaps her lasting legacy is that Ben Hogan once said she had the finest swing he ever saw. For all the attention heaped on Woods, Wright might have had it worse. During the early years of the LPGA Tour, she averaged 30 tournaments a year between 1962 and 1964 because sponsors who put up money expected her to play. From 1960 to 1964, she averaged 10 victories a year. She retired from full-time competition in 1969 at age 34.

It was only fitting the USGA began awarding the Mickey Wright Medal to the US Women's Open winner. Wright was a four-time winner. The USGA also dedicated a separate room in its museum to Wright, an honour only otherwise bestowed on Bobby Jones, Arnold Palmer and Hogan. She donated some 200 mementos to the USGA, along with a synthetic mat from which she hit balls onto the fairway from her back porch to feel the sensation of a properly hit shot. Kathy Whitworth once said, "I've had the privilege of playing with Sam Snead and Jack Nicklaus and Arnold Palmer and all of them. And some of our ladies had wonderful swings. But nobody hit it like Mickey, just nobody."

Others whom golf lost in 2020 were Doug Sanders, who brought a flamboyance to golf fashion ahead of his time, a colourful character known as much for the 20 times he won on the PGA Tour as the majors that got away. That included a short putt he missed on the final hole at St Andrews, losing the next day to Jack Nicklaus in 1970. "If I was a master of the English language, I don't think I could find the adjectives to describe how I felt when I missed that short one," Sanders said. Pete Dye left behind some of the most clever and "Dye-a-bolical" designs in golf, most notably the TPC Sawgrass and Crooked Stick. His objective was to make golfers feel uncomfortable at what they saw, and he often succeeded.

For the rest of golf, it was mainly about survival. The Open Championship was lost for the year, and so was the Evian Championship on the LPGA Tour. The major tours froze their membership rolls so that no one lost a job, even if that meant a holding period for those next in line. But they kept playing. For every PGA Tour event Jay Monahan attended, the commissioner had to test negative for Covid-19 and receive a vinyl bracelet around his wrist. He kept every one, a reminder that another tournament was in the books and the next one was on the horizon.

Dustin Johnson became a footnote in history twice without even realising it. He can say he is the first Masters champion to have had to recover from the coronavirus. And because the Masters was played in November, he only gets to keep the green jacket for 141 days before the next Masters. There's a long list of oddities like that.

"I know 2020 has been a really strange year," Johnson said. "But it's been good to me."

Doug Ferguson is golf correspondent of the Associated Press

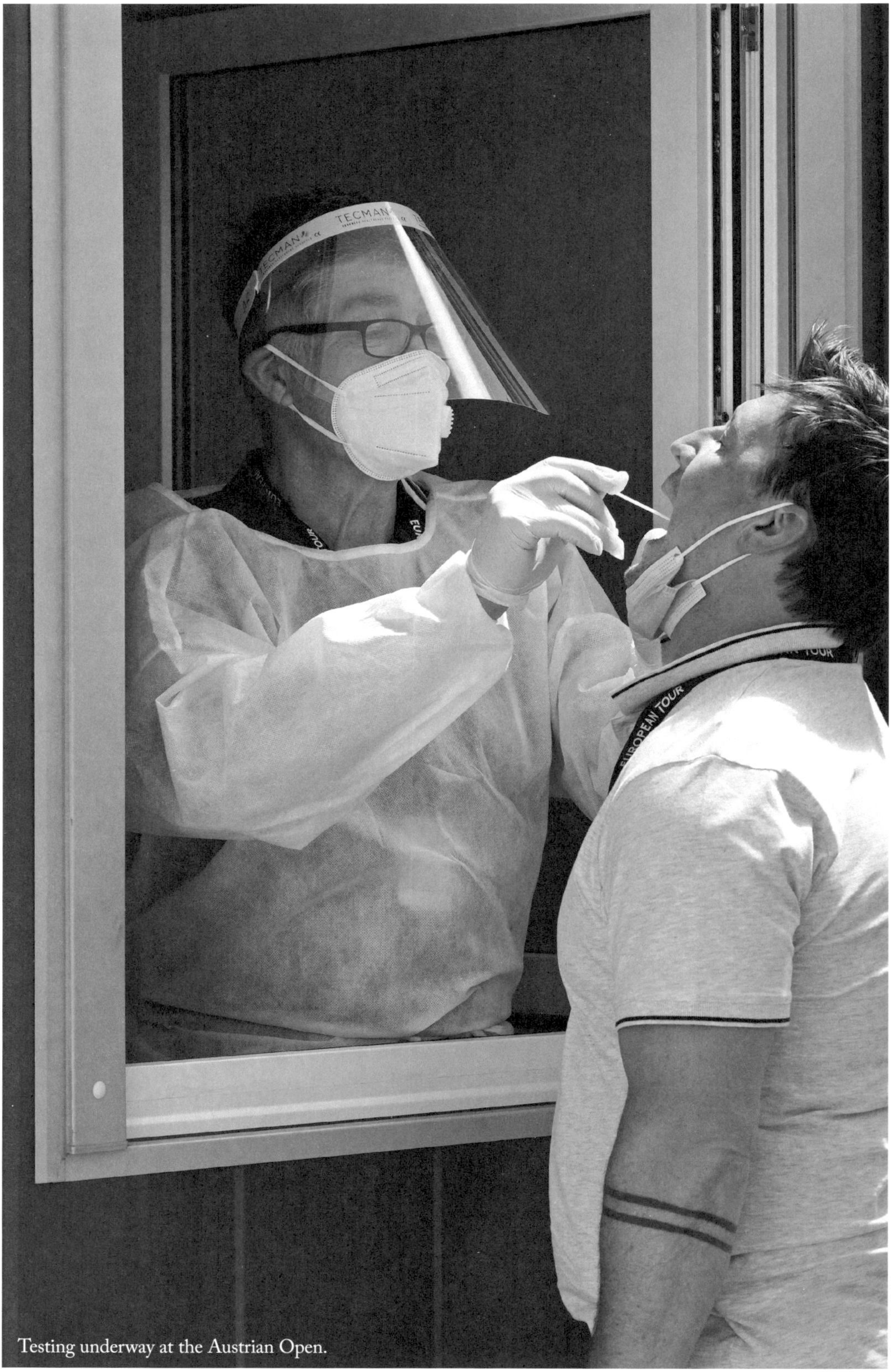

Testing underway at the Austrian Open.

Stuart Franklin/Getty Images

Inside golf's tournament bubble

By Dr Andrew Murray

I love working for the European Tour. We have some fantastic people and put on fantastic events globally. We have a wide range of physios, doctors and other health professionals that support our players with anything to do with illness or injury. The start of 2020, of course, seemed to be like any other. I was looking forward to working with the great colleagues I have in great locations. The Rolex Series events in Abu Dhabi, Dubai and the UK are always huge events I look forward to.

Then a new coronavirus emerged.

I used to work for the Scottish Government in Physical Activity and Sport Policy. When spread started beyond China in January, I spoke to a few colleagues in government in Scotland and England, and it was evident this really could be a truly global public health problem. It started dominating everything from the time spread was more evident in Italy, Spain and the UK.

For a sport with so many health benefits, the irony was that we were spending all our time working out how to stage professional golf tournaments safely in the middle of a pandemic. Playing golf is actually one of the best things that you can do for your health. It was the subject of my PhD, and golfers live longer than non-golfers, with golf providing a range of physical and mental health benefits.

We also know that golf can be played with relative safety in a Covid-19 world, if golfers socially distance, use hand sanitiser and take other appropriate precautions. As a doctor, I'd certainly encourage my patients to play golf and I know The R&A is starting some great work on "Golf on Prescription".

For professional golf, it is not so much the golf course activity that is the issue, but the fact that even for a behind-closed-doors event, we are bringing 500 persons together, when essential players, caddies, staff and TV are considered. Travel has been massively disrupted during the pandemic, as have ways of accommodating everyone. Absolutely every aspect has to be planned to make sure you have a secure bubble.

We have done our very best to provide a safe environment and playing opportunities, and the players, caddies and staff have been great with doing their level best to decrease risk to themselves and in turn the event.

We worked with the World Health Organisation and their guidelines to develop safe protocols for male and female elite golf. The principles are fairly simple, but as everyone has learned during these times, they are not easy, because as humans we love social connection and this is the very thing the virus loves.

The key points since the we returned in mid-2020 have been:

Doing the right things consistently
Keeping two metres apart from others
Wearing a mask inside and, where possible, outside
Cleaning hands and not sharing stuff
Minimising social contacts
Reporting symptoms and isolating

The hardest thing is recognising we work globally, and each country has their own protocols that we work with and apply. We have our overriding principles, but are careful to respect and apply all local guidelines. Finding consistency for players has been a challenge throughout, but we do our best. Generally, the same things work wherever you are but we had to tweak each week depending on the host national government regulations, much in the same way as you adjust to different driving rules when driving a car in different countries.

At the European Tour, CEO Keith Pelley clearly prioritised health and welfare each step of the way. It is a fantastic team and I am constantly amazed by how good everyone is. Before any tournament we do a risk assessment in line with the WHO guidelines along with Stephen McCarron and his team at Fairhurst, a Health and Safety consultancy service. Championship Director Mark Casey, our Covid-19 officers and tournament directors will then speak with our event promoters, and with the host national government and the nation's public health authority. We then get on with the detailed planning. Absolutely every aspect of a tournament is broken down into its individual components and analysed through the Covid-19 lens before putting everything back together in a bio-secure way.

As you can imagine, there have been absolutely no shortage of Microsoft Teams and Zoom conversations. There have been conversations that no one predicted we would be having, especially as traditions are so valued in golf. Players signing their own scorecards, whether we could open the locker rooms, or ask players to arrive at the course ready to go straight to the tee, whether bananas needed to be separated into single bananas to minimise handling by different players (not because bananas need to socially distance!) — each day brings interesting questions.

Sharing information during this time has been vital. As well as keeping in touch with medical colleagues in the UK and around the world, I regard myself as lucky to have worked in professional football, rugby, athletics, and Olympic sports. I chaired a group that includes fellow Chief Medical Officers from the International Olympic Committee, FIFA, World Rugby, ATP tennis, Formula 1, and cricket. We aim to be consistent and learn from each other. There are a lot of similarities between tennis, Formula 1 and international golf with the regular travel and volume of people in a bubble.

We also work very closely with the medical and Covid-19 teams from the PGA Tour, the LPGA, and the Ladies European Tour, who are all terrific. Dr Tom Hospel, from the PGA Tour, and I were speaking each week as our tours prepared to resume play during 2020. We have lots of similarities — the key difference is that the PGA Tour play mainly in the USA, with less international and cross-border travel, and have more consistency of public health regulations each week.

HOME AND ON-SITE TESTING

Testing has been a vital part of the process, both before and at tournaments. Testing prior to travel means that the vast majority of persons with Covid-19 are identified prior to travel and can at least isolate at their home. We had a great service with LetsGetChecked, our pre-travel home testing kit providers. Our testing providers at events, Cignpost and Professor Denis Kinane, have been off-the-charts good — very good in picking up all cases, and closely checking all the results. Ourselves and the PGA Tour provided the fastest testing in sport — over 90 per cent of results delivered in less than four hours on site — faster than Formula 1, and even professional football in the UK typically took 24-48 hours in 2020.

Temperature checks and symptom screening took place daily. Typically we have two doctors on site, a local doctor expert in public health and a European Tour doctor, with myself on hand over the telephone or at the event. Along with Covid-19 issues, we support players with any other illness, injury, anti-doping enquiries and also help maximise performance.

The players both on the European Tour and the Ladies European Tour have been absolutely excellent. Not perfect all the time, but really, really good. Each step of the way we've tried to provide education, engagement and support. We can't pretend with Covid-19 that our decisions are always going to be popular, but we've tried to be fair and provide as safe an environment as possible.

We have asked a lot of them, not just with all the testing and the basic protocols laid out above, but maintaining the bubble each week by remaining either at the golf course or their designated hotel, and travelling directly between the two. It has not always been easy but the players have helped enormously by positively promoting the key health messages. Along the way we have been grateful for important feedback from the players which has helped us tweak our protocols where necessary.

Players at the Aberdeen Standard Investment Ladies Scottish Open and the AIG Women's Open were no less impressive at handling all the protocols. As a father of two girls and as a Scotsman, I just love these events. We had fantastic winners, even if the celebrations were very different. They were probably the first big global female sporting events to return — and where you have IMG, The R&A, the LET, LPGA and Visit Scotland involved you'll always get great events.

Scotland was more cautious coming out of the first lockdown than England, but the local public health authorities were very supportive and the high level of collaboration between all the bodies was outstanding. As at the European Tour, the leadership shown in prioritising the health and safety, and well-being, of everyone involved is something I have been proud to play a part in supporting.

A PLAYER'S VIEW

"After three weeks in the European Tour's bubble, I am so thankful to everyone at the Tour who has worked so hard to keep us playing golf. The effort that now goes into making events safe for players, caddies and support staff is unbelievable. It's a hell of an operation. We basically have a mobile medical lab at every tournament turning around PCR tests for Covid-19 every few hours. Daily health questionnaires and temperature checks are part of everyday life on tour. It's crazy when you see the scale of the operation. The whole thing is led by Dr Andrew Murray, who I think might be a superhero. Despite having a young family of his own back in Scotland, the Doc has been doing an incredible job leading the Tour through the madness of Covid. He's one of those people who makes you feel calm and at ease no matter what the circumstances. As soon as you talk to him, you feel assured and factually aware of the current situation. So a huge thanks to Doc Murray, as well as all the people working on our events for making them such a safe environment for everyone!"

— Tommy Fleetwood's social media post

It is incredibly difficult operating big sporting events during Covid, particularly with the travel involved. The protocols were very robust, and people have followed them. Our aim will not change whatever happens from here — to provide tournaments when and where it is safe to do so, and to have appropriate protocols in place for as long as they are needed.

We look forward to seeing fans return to our events whenever it is safe and appropriate. The health benefits of golf are not just about playing it but extend to attending a tournament, too. We found at events in Scotland spectators take an average of 11,000 steps. As Nelson Mandela said, "Sport has the power to change the world." It's got the power to inspire. It can bring folk together. It can speak to folk. It can create hope. It can provide great sporting theatre. I've really missed it, as a sports fan myself.

But, I have to say, I enjoyed the last putt going down in Dubai in December at the DP World Tour Championship. It was a thrilling finale with Lee Westwood and Matt Fitzpatrick taking the respective Race to Dubai and DP World Tour Championship prizes in dramatic fashion, and I thought it was fitting with Lee having hosted the Betfred British Masters at the restart in 2020. To see the season completed was very satisfying.

After a year none of us will forget, I will also remember my daughters Nina, six, and Fran, four, getting enthusiastic about the Ladies Scottish Open and the AIG Women's Open, and Nina offering over Zoom to lend her plastic club to one of the players! It showed me golf and our players have the capacity to inspire.

My nose also remembers each of the 50 swabs I've had during the year!

Dr Andrew Murray is Chief Medical Officer of the European Tour and, pandemics allowing, plays his golf at Craigmillar Park in Edinburgh. Information on the health benefits of golf are available at www.golfandhealth.org and on The R&A website.

Charley Hull
and Kate Rose

David Cannon/Getty Images

Back to the future with the Rose Series

By Meghan MacLaren

Is this actually happening?" A message sent in early June that could represent almost anything during the chaos of 2020. In this instance though, while it was bewilderment, it was bewilderment dressed up in positivity.

During the summer I was part of a WhatsApp group of fellow UK based female professional golfers. It was set up originally to discuss the pros and cons of playing on the 2020 Pro Tour, a newly formed mini tour in the north of England, boasting one of the first gender-equitable policies of play. Topics of conversation were primarily whether the course setup and tee differences between men and women were fair, and how welcoming the male players had been.

Personally, I'd been fairly ignorant to the mini-tour scene before 2020. In the UK, I was aware of the EuroPro Tour and that was about it. America — which seemed a world away as we hit balls into nets in our gardens and dreamed of adrenaline-fuelled tournaments in distant lands during April and May — had given me a small sampling of its mini-tour scene when I first turned professional. I spent a month or so in Florida one February, finally isolated from my cocoon of college golf, playing a handful of two-day events to prepare for the season ahead. My overriding memory is just of extortionate entry fees. Having been through that process of cutting my teeth, including on the Ladies European Tour's feeder tour (LET Access), stepping down a few tiers of professional golf did not feel like something I would experience again. I think most players feel like they move beyond that.

But the landscape of 2020 put mini tours on the map for many professional golfers — maybe for fans too. As the world tried to find its feet amid a crushing pandemic, financially bigger sporting entities quietly found their way back to function. Meanwhile smaller tours, particularly the European-based ones such as the LET and the Challenge Tour, struggled to find a start date. There were too many variables that insufficient funds could not yet navigate. But golf in the UK had finally been given the green light. So a group of professional golfers, united by their location, constraints, and drug of choice (golf tournaments) turned with unrestrained enthusiasm to anything and anywhere offering that drug.

The fact that hotels remained closed did not matter. Driving hundreds of miles there and back for a practice round before driving hundreds of miles there and back again for a competitive round became perfectly acceptable. Gratitude for the pure essence of golf and those willing to provide it for us blinded any logistical issues. Playing alongside men went from an unsure necessity to a refreshing norm (and enjoyable learning experience) — at least for myself and other female pros I spoke to. Young amateurs being grouped around tour winners and Ryder and Solheim Cup players drew a throwback to an era when pro-ams were a part of golf's ecosystem; one of the otherwise lost advantages of a sport unlike any other.

Both the 2020 ProTour and the Clutch Tour did a phenomenal job at creating those opportunities — providing an equitable platform for female golf professionals, in particular. I am not sure they will ever realise the magnitude of that for us.

In the midst of scrawling the internet for more tours and more tournaments, there were whispers of something "big" for female golfers. It started with a conversation between LET professional Liz Young and the head pro, Jason McNiven, at their golf club, Brokenhurst Manor. McNiven also happens to be an incredibly renowned club-fitter trusted by many of us. He has long championed the cause of women's golf and recognised the disparity we face in both opportunity and resources. But recognition and action are two ends of a spectrum not many people are willing to bridge.

Together, Liz and Jason planned an event at Brokenhurst for UK female professionals. Its location (probably closer to the Isle of Wight than to the homes of anyone who actually played) again caused a usually quite precious group of people no grumblings at all. It was another hit, another chance to do what we love. To many of us who originally "entered" that lone event — merely an email to Liz — that is all it was. Little did we know what a bit of smart marketing was going to do to our summer.

I am not sure even Liz knows how that event turned into the Rose Ladies Series. But it did. A summer comprising of seven one-day events at some stellar golf courses around the UK, culminating in a three day grand final — finishing just in time for the resumption of the LET season. More than just a chance to earn some money (each winner received a £5,000 cheque) and get ready for "real" tournaments again, was the significance of the name behind the series.

So the story goes, Justin Rose and his incredible wife, Kate, saw a piece in *The Telegraph* (by the wonderful Kate Rowan) about the struggles of female professional golf amidst Covid. And so they opened their chequebooks, and more importantly their mouths — by acknowledging our reality. They said all the things we feel daily as female professional golfers, without having the resources to do anything about. The words were simple, yet stated something no one close to the stature of Justin Rose — a major champion, former world number one, Olympic gold medallist, Ryder Cup stalwart, (golfing) household name — had publicly recognised before. As the PGA Tour got on with business, reducing their enforced lay-off to three months, the Ladies European Tour went five months between tournaments. The Roses decided to do something about that … and it changed everything.

And so my WhatsApp message, "Is this actually happening?", was sent.

It was surreal. The media were all over us. Prominent companies, notably American Golf and Computacenter, followed the Roses' lead and added financial backing that enabled the series to become both structured and meaningful. We turned up at that first event at Brokenhurst, with rusty games and new shoes, with more cameras and attention than at 95 per cent of the tour events we play. A lot has been made of the gender pay-gap in recent years, not just in golf but across all sports and business. I for one think it is a significant step forward that there is even a conversation happening. But as I said, to turn that conversation into action and opportunity … courses such as Royal St George's, intended destination for the 2020 Open Championship, and Wentworth, home of the European Tour, had never hosted female professional events before.

"Is this actually happening?" It was.

A WAVE OF EMOTION

I was lucky enough to win the second event of the Rose Series at Moor Park Golf Club. On the hottest day of the year to that point, I experienced every fluctuating wave of emotion only golf can provide. As did my sister, who became instrumental to my enjoyment of the summer by caddieing for me each week (and posing for the never-actually-candid candid photos taken by the wonderful David Cannon at every opportunity). A surprisingly simple birdie on the first, walking in a 40-footer for eagle, a satisfying two on the 10th to get to five under — internal pleasure reflected in an external smile at the reminder of just how at ease stress-free golf can make you feel.

But golf always manages to be golf, doesn't it? I managed to play the wrong ball on the next hole — something I can't remember ever doing before, and yet in doing so it seemed like a remarkably easy occurrence — leading to a disorientating double bogey. My conscious brain shook it off with an ironic smile, but my unconscious brain was rattled, adding two more "real" bogeys in quick succession. Seeing a leaderboard calmed me, knowing that that all-consuming notion of winning was still in my grasp. Several bursts of adrenaline and a lengthy post-round wait later — including a trip to the nearest petrol station to buy cautionary celebratory ice creams — I was a tournament winner again.

Winning breeds confidence, no matter the level. I learnt that lesson in college, becoming a different player with a different mindset after my four years and eight victories at Florida International University. Like every golfer, I had experienced some struggles with my game, and so Moor Park taught me that lesson once again, when I really needed it. Mini tours provide a glimpse of it. And Sophia Popov accelerates that understanding to a whole different stratosphere.

Much was made of Popov's heart-warming major win at the AIG Women's Open on a brutally tough Royal Troon, primarily due to her lack of LPGA/LET status at the time. She had snuck her way into the event with some good form at the right time, taking advantage of extra opportunities in a still Covid-minded world. The narrative is one of relentless grinding; believing but never knowing when your Cinderella story might await. But an often missed chapter to this particular tale is that of Popov winning multiple times on the Cactus Tour in the months preceding her "breakthrough" win.

To compare the Cactus Tour (a US west coast-based mini tour for female professional golfers) and one of the most prestigious events in all of women's golf would be redundant. But to fail to acknowledge its relevance would be equally so. There will never be a formula for winning a major (or any tournament at all, for that matter). Golf, and the human condition, have too many variables. But mini tours provide a chance to put your game under competitive strain and competitive emotions. Mini tours provide a chance to gain comfort with swing changes, or clean up strategic sloppiness, or to exorcise some demons — every golfer rides these waves and so many more throughout their careers. No practice session can replicate that.

Most of all, mini tours provide a chance to embrace winning. To not be afraid of it; to learn how your mind and body react to this oh-so-tantalising prospect. To realise how much you want it.

So after the strangest year of all our lives, I have embraced a new fact of golf. As a member of the LET, I have not left mini tours behind. None of us ever have. When it is appropriate and when the opportunities exist, you can move along any of the tiers you want. After all, for most players apart from a very privileged few, the main tours cannot fill every week of the calendar and nor should they. There is no reason why full and mini tours should not co-exist and thrive alongside each other. And after the wildfire that brought a sudden, scary and premature end to the Grand Final of the Rose Series at Wentworth, it feels as if there is unfinished business. I hope it returns. There are a whole lot of players whose careers would benefit from it.

A mini tour provided Sophia Popov with a platform to write her name in history. Would she have done so without it? We will never know.

But because of 2020, we do know this: it can actually happen.

Meghan MacLaren is a two-time winner (so far) on the Ladies European Tour. A report of the Rose Series Grand Final appears in chapter 19.

A champion with a lifelong love of the game

By Lewine Mair

I had my first fleeting glimpse of Mickey Kathryn Wright on the pro-am day ahead of the 1976 Colgate Dinah Shore, an event which she had won three years earlier. She was hurrying round the side of the clubhouse in Palm Springs in her trademark tennis shoes. As I had never seen her play before, my American friends suggested I go and watch one of the game's greatest champions while I could, and what an amazing experience it turned out to be.

When I think about that very first sighting today, she was probably not in any kind of a hurry at all. Far more likely was that this basically shy soul did not want to get caught up in conversation on her way to the first tee.

Wright died from a heart attack on February 17 at the age of 85. Her love of golf was as robust as it had ever been but, following a nasty fall, she had never been well enough to leave hospital. Yet no further back than 2017, when she had undergone a couple of surgeries, she had been back playing in no time at all. Indeed, in an interview with *Golf Digest's* Guy Yocum, she talked animatedly of how she had hit five wedge shots the previous day in the heat of the Florida afternoon. "I went out and picked up the balls like I always do," she told him. Then she turned interviewer to ask, "How many 82-year-old women do you know who have been out hitting balls in 95-degree weather?"

She knew how far she had hit those shots too — between 100 and 110 yards. "Much the same distance as when I was playing the tour," she told Yocum.

The reason Wright retired from full-time golf at the relatively early age of 34 had nothing to do with golf itself. Rather, it was to do with the pressures inseparable from trying to keep up with everything that was expected of her. As a 12-year-old child, she had loved having her shots admired but, after a run in the 60s in which she won 44 LPGA tournaments in the space of four years, it all became too much.

Mike Whan, when he started out in his role as the CEO of the LPGA some 11 years ago, had studied the extent to which the players of Wright's generation had given of themselves to make their tour a success. What is more, he was so impressed by the founders' approach that, in announcing his retirement for this coming summer, he advised the present generation that the old-timers' ways could not be bettered. "Never stop Acting Like Founders!" he told them in the last line of the letter he sent round.

Whan always makes a point of giving the players details of their pro-am partners by way of making for easy conversation on the day and, by the same token, he asks that they send thank-you notes to the golfers concerned. Has it contributed to the healthy schedules the LPGA have enjoyed during Whan's reign? Of course it has.

Wright cared about the success of the tour no less than she cared about her own play and, for two years during her extraordinary winning spree, she served as the LPGA's president. In the course of that period, she attended all the cocktail parties and rotary meetings which that entailed. "The sum of trying to meet the expectations of my coach, the LPGA, my father and the public exhausted me physically and emotionally," she told Yocum. "I developed an ulcer and had all kinds of anxiety. It wasn't the years, it was the mileage. It was a lot of pressure to be in contention week after week for five or six years."

Kathy Whitworth said of her great friend and rival, "She had to play almost every week for the tour to survive. Sponsors threatened to cancel their tournaments if she didn't play. And, knowing that if they cancelled, the rest of us wouldn't be able to play, Mickey always did."

Back in 2000, in an interview with *Golf World*, Wright herself elaborated on her predicament: "I guess they call it burnout now, but it wore me out. Unless you're a golfer, you can't understand the tension and pressure of tournament play." And it was the expectations. When she did not win, she would be deluged with questions along the lines, "What's wrong with your game? Are you coming apart?" As she would explain to *Golf World*, "Second or third isn't bad, but it feels bad when you've won 44 tournaments in four years."

She soldiered on until 1969 when, with as many as 81 of her 82 LPGA titles under her belt, of which 13 were majors, she sprained her ankle for a second time.

At that, she gave up on the serious stuff and made an abortive attempt to return to university.

Back in 1954, she had done a year at Stanford. She studied psychology for a year before dropping out in 1955 to pursue a professional golf career. Years later she spelt out that decision as follows: "I've earned my own version of a master's degree in psychology in study and experience, trial and error, on golf courses throughout the United States. Psychology is as integral a part of good golf as an efficient swing."

Second time around, she repaired to Southern Methodist University where one semester was more than enough. She could not get her head around "New Maths" but still contrived to get an "A" before returning to her world of golfing problems.

To her, solving problems was part of golf's fun. In truth, she was a bit of a Padraig Harrington in that she always liked to be working on something, with that something usually based around such fundamental issues as grip and stance.

"THE FINEST GOLF SWING I EVER SAW"

Among the female golfing fraternity, only Joyce Wethered, the English golfer who won all five of the English championships in which she played in the 1920s and four of her six British championships, received the same glowing tributes from the men as she did.

Bobby Jones was among those to have described Wethered's swing as the best he had seen, regardless of gender. Not only that, but he owned to the feeling that he had been "outclassed" by her. Ben Hogan said pretty much the same of Wright.

"She had the finest golf swing I ever saw, man or woman," said Hogan. Byron Nelson was another to sing her praises, describing her fundamentals as unmatched. Speaking in 2015, Whitworth agreed with all of that. "I've had the privilege of playing with Sam Snead and Jack Nicklaus and Arnold Palmer and all of them. And some of our ladies had wonderful swings. But nobody hit it like Mickey, just nobody."

It was a pity that Wright and Wethered were 34 years apart for their rivalry might have aroused a touch of the same interest as that, say, of Jack Nicklaus and Tom Watson. Though Wethered was still using hickory where Wright had steel-shafted Wilson clubs, so much about them was so similar. And not least in terms of the attitudes they brought to bear.

Wethered had this capacity to disappear into what she called "a cocoon" of concentration; Wright, meantime, could feel herself vanishing into a fog. "Winning," she said, "really never crossed my mind that much. It's trite, but I knew if I did it as well as I could, I would win." She was that confident that her best was better than other people's best.

Yet each of Wethered and Wright had come about her much-feted swing in her own way. For Wethered, the game was all about imitation. Wright, in contrast, had many teachers, starting with Johnny Bellante.

In her first lesson at the La Jolla Country Club, he broke off a branch from a eucalyptus tree and asked her to swish it "and make it sing". It was one of the best lessons she ever had, teaching her as it did the sensation "of swinging through the ball rather than at it". Yet Harry Pressler was the man who taught her the most and, as the years wore on, the more she referred to her swing as Pressler's.

Both Wethered and Wright, incidentally, shared the same view about the importance of developing the kind of muscle memory which would lead to swings repeating under pressure and thereby doing away with the temptation to fiddle around on the course.

Towards the end of their lives, these two greats of the game were both asked to talk about the main changes which had taken place since their days at the helm. Wethered commented on clothes and how she felt more than a touch envious of the moderns in their short skirts or slacks: "In my day there was no alternative to the ghastly long skirts." Wright, for her part, did not mind saying that she was not impressed with modern teaching and what it was doing to the players' bodies. She died before Tiger Woods had what was a fifth surgery on his back but she felt that too many of them looked like patchwork quilts with strips of plaster covering their latest injuries.

The only injury she ever sustained from playing the amount of golf she did had its origins in a cyst in a wrist. And, though people put down the tennis shoes she eventually wore on the tournament scene to golf's wear and tear, they were in fact down to her acute sense of duty. Conscious of the need to dress up for every one of the cocktail parties which were part and parcel of her LPGA presidency, she would don high heals and the two sprained ankles mentioned earlier were down to them.

Those tennis shoes of hers took everyone aback. My own feeling was that she was lucky to have played on her side of the Atlantic. It would have been a matter for any number of women's committee meetings had she appeared in such footwear anywhere in the UK and, so well known were some of those committee ladies of old for their intransigence, that you had to doubt whether they would have let it happen. Only in the last 20 years or so would Wright have got away with what the old-school would have called, "This departure from the norm". (That was what they said about Gloria Minoprio when she appeared in trousers for a first time in 1933.)

To pick out just a few of the most salient points about Wright's career, her first tournament win came in 1956 in Jacksonville, Florida and, by 1961, she was dominating the tour, winning at least 10 tournaments annually from 1961 to 1964. Among her major wins were four US Opens and four LPGA Championships. In 1958 she became the first to win both in the same year, indeed the same month, June. She did that double again in 1961, the year she won three of the four LPGA majors. Then, when she won the Titleholders and the Western Open in 1962, she held all four major titles at the same time. Wright's last tournament victory came four years after leaving the tour full-time, at the 1973 Colgate-Dinah Shore Winner's Circle.

She moved to Stuart, Florida, in 1974, where she lived the rest of her life, surviving breast cancer along the way.

In 2012, the *Stuart News* reported that Wright spent most days gardening, fishing, playing the stock market and doing crossword puzzles. For golf, she hit wedges off a practice mat on her patio onto the 14th fairway of an adjoining course, while you would imagine that any spare time was spent preparing the 200 items she donated in 2012 to the United States Golf Association. On her death, she left all her remaining possessions to the USGA, who dedicated the US Women's Open winner's medal in her name. A Lim Kim became the first recipient in December at Champions in Houston.

The one "first" you would never have associated with Mickey Wright was that she was the first member of the LPGA to be fined. She had been playing in a round-robin event and struggled to accept how, when she had won more than anyone else, she had not been the winner.

She made a fuss, and who can blame her. In all her years at the top, she had thrived on the belief that she only had to play well to win. That week, she had played distinctly well, only to have her long-held theory turned on its head.

For just about the only time in her life, golf's quiet problem-solver was stumped.

Lewine Mair is a senior European writer for Global Golf Post

MICKEY WRIGHT'S MAJOR VICTORIES

1958	LPGA Championship, US Women's Open
1959	US Women's Open
1960	LPGA Championship
1961	Titleholders Championship, US Women's Open, LPGA Championship
1962	Titleholders Championship, Western Open
1963	Western Open, LPGA Championship
1964	US Women's Open
1966	Western Open

Golf's voice of warmth and comfort

By Andrew Cotter

It's not an easy task, to try and sum up Peter Alliss.

On the surface it appears quite simple and, indeed, you could attempt to do so in a single phrase — the one which often immediately followed his name. He was "Peter Alliss — the Voice of Golf".

But you also have to understand *why* he had that grand title. What made his the voice of the game?

Well, firstly, he had the qualification of having been on the stage himself. Three times a PGA champion among his many titles and eight times a Ryder Cup player. It gave him an understanding of the highs and lows, the joy and the torture, of this wonderful game.

Of course, a fine playing career on its own is never enough. Many are the great exponents of a sport who do not make outstanding commentators. Yet there has never been, in any sport, somebody who moved quite so well from playing to talking. In fact, it always seemed to me that Peter was a broadcaster who could play golf, rather than the other way round.

This is what was spotted — or overheard — by a BBC producer, Ray Lakeland, on a flight back from Ireland in 1960. The ability to tell a story which, coupled with his golfing knowledge, gave him the opportunity to wield both clubs and a microphone for a few years — learning, as he did so, beside the great Henry Longhurst.

It was a seamless transition and one that seemed so natural because, outstanding though his golf career was, his talents for describing the game were even more obvious.

He had all the gifts — apart from the warm and comforting voice itself and the fact that he was a such a great raconteur, he had a feel for the timing required in television commentary. He was the perfect accompaniment to the pictures, never smothering them with his own grandstanding or a desire to be heard, but walking hand in hand with them. What we saw on the screen and the noises we heard from the event itself — they were the most important thing and he just steered them along with a choice phrase or exclamation.

He understood the power of a silence. He knew that sometimes the quiet close-up on the eyes of a player cannot be improved upon, or that with the roar of a crowd nothing more needs to be said. So wait for the moment. Use your words wisely.

And in that elegant style he provided the soundtrack to so many of golf's iconic moments — capturing perfectly the varying fortunes and faces of the game. The joy in the voice which matched Seve's smile on the 18th at St Andrews, the exasperation in the tones as Van de Velde rolled up his trousers and stepped down into the Barry Burn. He expressed simply and eloquently what we all felt.

But if he was there for the big shots and decisive putts, he was also there for all the incidental things. And this is when the true broadcasting ability comes through, because during the long days and hours of coverage of a golf tournament is when you need to have more than a pile of facts at your fingertips.

You see, perhaps Peter's greatest talent was that he was a gifted observer — not just of golf, but of life. There were shots which we used to show that were only meant for him. On one memorable occasion it was the elaborate warm-up routine of Miguel Angel Jimenez. But on others it would be something more mundane which brought out his brilliance. "Here you are, Peter ..." the director would say as, on our screens, appeared a cheerful, wandering dog which had escaped from its owner, or an amorous couple sheltering under an umbrella, or a heavily-lunched man dozing in the rough ... Ordinary life — observed and so sharply and beautifully described.

If you watched golf over the past decades you may well, at some point, have chuckled at one of these scenes. You might also have heard in the background his friend and sidekick the late Alex Hay, or, in more recent years, Ken Brown, reduced to helpless laughter as the words came from the great man. And perhaps that is the best tribute I can pay Peter. Listening to him, or working alongside him, was *fun*.

There were serious and dramatic moments, of course, and we gave them due reverence. But there was a sense of mischief as well — as there should be in a sport which is always both light and shade. You only have to watch Peter's acceptance speech at his induction into the World Golf Hall of Fame to see his timing and delivery in action. And to see him holding a room with a twinkle in his eye, ready to cut through some of the grandiosity that golf can often deliver.

His style perhaps grated with a different audience. One that craved the stats and the spin-rates — and there is certainly a place for that. But he was broadcasting to a wider audience on the BBC, so he painted with a broader brush and provided something that could be understood by everyone and entertain more than just the golf fans among us.

But above all he was simply your companion as you watched golf. That is what he was for me as I grew up, obsessed with the game. And it's why one of my greatest thrills in broadcasting was to work with him.

Now, I often prefer to recall not the moments when we were commentating on the back nine of a major Sunday — hugely enjoyable though those times were. I think instead of when the microphones went down and when we all sat for a while in the box at Loch Lomond or Wentworth, Augusta or St Andrews, chatting about the world.

I am so glad that he was at least commentating until close to the end, when we covered The Masters in November. Of course it was in odd circumstances — Peter at his home in Surrey, the rest of us in a studio in Salford. The logistical and technical effort required to make sure that he would still be able to commentate was enormous. But there was never any doubt that he should be. He had to be. If there was golf on the BBC and he was able to commentate, then he would be doing so.

Yes, the highlights format was frustrating for him, as it is sport stripped back to a few shots and bare facts — sport without the colour. And Peter always provided the colour. But it is instead the thousands of hours of coverage for decades before that we will remember.

Such was his presence it is still rather strange to think that he is gone. But, like all the great broadcasters and figures who have an effect on our lives, there is an echo that carries on.

So you can watch those moments again and Peter Alliss — "the Voice of Golf" — will always be there. Or, simply close your eyes and picture the scenes and the shots. And you can hear it still.

Andrew Cotter is a broadcaster who has been a member of the BBC television golf commentary team since 2004, and is author of Olive, Mabel & Me

IN MEMORIAM

Among those professional golfers who died in 2020 were:

Mickey Wright, 85, February 17

One of the greatest woman golfers of all time. Dominated the LPGA for a decade in the late 1950s and early 1960s. She won 13 major championships, and 82 titles in all, with a powerful and elegant swing. In 1961, she won 10 times, including four in a row, and her score of 69 in the US Women's Open on a severely testing course at Baltusrol was considered one of the greatest rounds ever played.

John O'Leary, 70, March 26

Hugely popular member of the European Tour for two decades, who was also a director of the tour for 34 years. A Ryder Cup player in 1975, O'Leary won twice. Famously, he became the third Irishman to win the Irish Open at Portmarnock in 1982 — by one stroke from Maurice Bembridge and against a field including Nick Faldo, Bernhard Langer and his roommate, Sam Torrance. It took 25 years for another Irishman to claim the title with a delighted O'Leary presenting the trophy to Padraig Harrington in 2007.

Doug Sanders, 86, April 12

"There but for the grace of God," intoned Henry Longhurst as Sanders missed a putt from 30 inches to win the 1970 Open at St Andrews. Lost to Jack Nicklaus in a playoff, one of four runner-up finishes in majors. He won 20 times on the PGA Tour, the first as an amateur at the Canadian Open in 1956, the last in 1972. He won five times in 1961 and played in the 1967 Ryder Cup. A stylish, colourful and flamboyant dresser, he was affectionately known as the "Peacock of the Fairways".

Peter Gill, 89, April 23

English club professional who finished one stroke outside a playoff on each of his first two appearances in the PGA Seniors Championship in 1981-82 and was then the runner-up, nine strokes behind, in 1983. Christy O'Connor Sr won the title on each occasion.

Billy Farrell, 84, May 8

Son of Johnny Farrell, the 1928 US Open champion, Billy was a journeyman member of the PGA Tour but better known as the longtime club professional at the Stanwich Club in Connecticut. Reached the green at the par-five 17th hole at Baltusrol in two strokes during the 1967 US Open, 26 years before John Daly achieved the same feat.

Ernie Gonzalez, 59, May 15

Became only the third left-hander to win on the PGA Tour, after Sam Adams and Bob Charles, with his only victory at the Pensacola Open in 1986. In an event plagued by bad weather, the Californian finished his second round on Saturday, with an eagle and five birdies over the back nine, before Sunday's rescheduled 36-hole finale was entirely washed out.

Steve Spray, 79, May 15

Won the San Francisco Open Invitational in 1969 at Harding Park for his only PGA Tour title, having finished fifth at the US Open the previous year. Spent three decades as the head pro at St Louis Country Club.

Gordon J Brand, 65, August 11

Runner-up to Greg Norman at the 1986 Open at Turnberry, Brand was part of the European Tour for more than two and a half decades making over 450 appearances. His only victory came at the 1989 Belgian Open. He was a prolific winner on the Safari Tour, played in the Ryder Cup in 1983, represented England in the World Cup and the Alfred Dunhill Cup. Brand won five times on the European Senior Tour, including the 2008 PGA Seniors Championship after a six-hole playoff against his namesake Gordon Brand Jr.

Mike Joyce, 81, August 28

A club professional from Long Island whose tour career started after he turned 50. He mainly played part-time on the Seniors circuit in the 1990s, only going full-time for a couple of years after winning the GTE Northwest Classic in 1992.

Peter Alliss, 89, December 5

Followed his father Percy as a Ryder Cup competitor, playing eight times as a leading British player of the 1950-60s. He won the PGA three times and, in successive weeks in 1958, the Opens of Italy, Spain and Portugal. A club professional and course designer, his six-decade career as a television commentator earned him the epithet as the "Voice of Golf".

Mike Ehrmann/Getty Images

Celebrating the perfect family game

By Alastair Johnston

Watching Tiger Woods playing alongside his son Charlie at the PNC Championship in December brought back memories of a moment 23 years ago.

Back in 1997, Tiger and I were next-door neighbours at Isleworth. After his momentous victory at the Masters that year, when he returned home I offered him my congratulations. However, I did not reference his amazing performance at the Masters. Instead, I advised him that as a newly minted major champion, he had now qualified to participate in the Father/Son Challenge! Not surprisingly, this left him somewhat bemused at the time.

Over two decades later, after making his debut with his 11-year-old son, it is safe to say Tiger gets it. As a worldwide television audience saw — with only limited spectators allowed on site, of course — the pair had the time of their lives. With both dressed in Tiger's traditional Sunday red, there was Charlie twirling the club just like his dad and, from his own special forward tee, signalling a thumbs up to the back tee when he hit a good one. Most of them were "good ones".

For Tiger, who spent most of this career thinking only of winning, his mission now was very different: making sure Charlie had a good time. "Memories we'll have for our entire lives," Tiger said after the pair finished seventh. "He's not going to appreciate this at 11 years old. I didn't when I was with my dad. As the years go by, you start appreciating it more."

One day he will. And I hope Charlie also appreciates at some point that thousands of kids watching at home will have been inspired to want to play golf with their dads. That is the message I tried to tell him at the end of their dream weekend.

Having Tiger make his debut in the event in the year we changed the name to the PNC Championship was ideal timing. This was the 23rd tournament since it started in 1995 and it had long since become a family affair, not just about fathers and sons.

But that is how it started. I was in the locker room one year at the Senior Players Championship, and there were three players who had completed their own rounds engrossed in conversations on their phones. Each of them was talking to their respective sons who concurrently were playing in junior golf tournaments back home. They were Dave Stockton, Ray Floyd and Jack Nicklaus.

It struck me that we could create an event where the fathers could play with their sons as partners in a fully fledged major tournament, including television coverage and all the facilities that would be consistent with a PGA Tour standard competition.

How unique and compelling that could be, I thought. I approached Jon Miller at NBC to explore whether or not his network would have an interest in co-venturing on such an initiative. Ultimately, we were able to put together a protocol that made this happen.

We started off with 10 champions, with Ray Floyd and his son Ray Jr winning for the first three years. Then it was Bob and David Charles and, in 1999, Jack and Gary Nicklaus, before Ray Floyd won twice more but with younger son Robert. The winners receive the Willie Park trophy, twin belts in the style of the original award for The Open Championship. Willie Park won the first Open and four in all. His son Willie Park Jr also won The Open twice. The Open belt was retired as a trophy when Young Tom Morris won it three years in a row, leading to the creation of the Claret Jug. Old Tom and Young Tom each won The Open four times. Fathers and sons go right back to the start of recognised golf championships.

Players who have won majors or the Players Championship are eligible to compete. Putting together the field every year has always been a rewarding experience. Not so enjoyable have been the times when I have had to advise players that for one reason or another they are not being invited back in any given year. I can empathise with the emotions of disappointment this precipitates. As far as the professionals themselves are concerned, they are all hardened career athletes and have resilience to such eventualities. But imagining them having to tell their son or daughter that they would not be receiving an invitation is a conversation that is not enviable.

What keeps bringing them back is how the event is embraced by all the family, with siblings and other relatives acting as caddies or enjoying the occasion as a supporter. Lee Trevino has played in every single tournament, which has been wonderful to see.

I have been humbled on many occasions by a pro telling me that because of the opportunity that the tournament has provided to allow him to play with one of his kids has emphasised or in some cases rekindled their personal relationship in a most unique way. Not only were they playing together in the event, but it gave them every reason to spend time together practising and sharing aspirations, and, subsequently, the memories of such an experience.

With the format being a scramble, mutual encouragement and understanding during the round are the keys to a successful partnership given that — usually — there is such a gulf in golfing ability. Ultimately, the tournament has rarely been won by more than one or two strokes

It was Fuzzy Zoeller in 2005 who broke away from the father-son model by inviting his daughter Gretchen to play in the tournament. Bernhard Langer has won twice with each of his sons, Stefan and Jason, but has also played with his daughters, Jackie and Christina. Arnold Palmer and Jack Nicklaus have both played with their grandsons.

Then, in 2019, we welcomed Annika Sorenstam to the tournament, playing with her father Tom. It was significant because we wanted to be able to demonstrate inclusivity in an evolving world where sports have been enhanced by embracing a broader constituency of participants. It was important for everyone involved with the tournament that we provided that recognition for professionals from the female ranks. There could be no better ambassador than Annika as a 10-time major champion, her status as a role model, along with so many other compelling personal attributes.

Now our professional champions can play with any family member as their partner. Among the debutants in 2020, Bubba Watson played with his father-in-law Wayne Ball and Justin Thomas with his father Mike. Justin has not had any other coach in his career than Mike, a PGA professional who has worked extensively with juniors at home in Kentucky, as well as a certain recent winner on the kids circuit in Florida, namely Charlie Woods.

So it could not have worked out better that it was Mike who holed the winning putt on the 18th green as he and Justin finished one stroke ahead of Vijay and Qass Singh. A quarter of a decade after the tournament was first played, it was another fine celebration of golf as the perfect family game.

Alastair Johnston is Vice Chair of IMG and founder of the PNC Championship. A report of the 2020 tournament appears in chapter 8.

The Rankings

Jin Young Ko

Michael Reaves/Getty Images

Rolex Rankings

All year Jin Young Ko held her place at the top of the Rolex Rankings but in the very last tournament Sei Young Kim had the chance to depose her compatriot. The pair duelled over a December weekend at the CME Group Tour Championship when Ko, the runner-up at the US Women's Open the previous week, eventually prevailed. The two-time major winner had played little in 2020 due to the pandemic but performed superbly when it mattered. Finishing second in her only major appearance in Houston enabled her to qualify for the LPGA's season-ending event and the high first prize there meant she also retained the circuit's money title.

Kim had the considerable consolation of being the Rolex LPGA Player of the Year following her maiden major victory at the KPMG Women's PGA Championship and a win at the Pelican Championship. Former world number one Inbee Park moved up from 14th at the end of 2019 to third with a string of strong major results and victory at the Australian Open. Americans Nelly Korda and Danielle Kang completed the top five, with Canadian Brooke Henderson, Japan's Nasa Hataoka and Australia's Minjee Lee following. Hyo Joo Kim rose four places to ninth although she only competed at home in Korea, while Sung Hyun Park dropped from second to 10th.

There were some impressive leaps on the rankings in 2020. Sophia Popov jumped from 344th to 26th thanks to her incredible AIG Women's Open victory, Yuka Saso, of the Philippines, from 282nd to 45th due to strong play in Japan, and Korea's Hae Ran Ryu from 122nd to 17th. Emily Kristine Pedersen's four victories on the Ladies European Tour took the Dane from 509th to 71st and Australian rookie Stephanie Kyriacou moved from 1,184th to 142nd.

Since the Women's World Golf Rankings began in 2006, Ko became the fourth player to sit all year in top spot, following Lydia Ko, Yani Tseng and Lorena Ochoa, who did so in both 2008 and 2009. Due to the pandemic, the rankings were at first frozen until play resumed and then temporarily amended so that a player's individual points average did not decay as normal over the two-year cycle, but was only updated after they had competed. This amendment was revoked early in 2021.

The Rolex Rankings — developed at the World Congress of Women's Golf in May 2004 — is sanctioned by the main professional women's tours: the Ladies Professional Golf Association (and Symetra Tour); the Ladies European Tour (and Access Series); the Japan LPGA Tour (and Step Up Tour); the Korea LPGA Tour; the WPGA Tour of Australasia; the China LPGA Tour; and the Chinese Taipei LPGA Tour; as well as The R&A and the United States Golf Association.

The Rolex Rankings are updated and released weekly. The major golf tours developed the rankings and the protocol that governs it, while R2IT, an independent software development company, was retained to develop the software and maintain the rankings on a weekly basis.

Official events from all the tours are taken into account and points awarded according to strength of field, with the exception of the five major championships on the LPGA Tour, which have a fixed points distribution. The players' points averages are determined by taking the number of points awarded over a 104-week rolling period, with points awarded in the most recent 13-week period carrying a strong value, and then dividing by the number of tournaments played, with a minimum divisor of 35.

MOST WEEKS AT NUMBER ONE BY YEAR

			Weeks				Weeks
2006	Annika Sorenstam	SWE	45	2014	Inbee Park	KOR	31
2007	Lorena Ochoa	MEX	37	2015	Lydia Ko	NZL	29
2008	Lorena Ochoa	MEX	52	2016	Lydia Ko	NZL	52
2009	Lorena Ochoa	MEX	52	2017	Lydia Ko	NZL	23
2010	Jiyai Shin	KOR	19	2018	Shanshan Feng	CHN	16
2011	Yani Tseng	TPE	46	2019	Jin Young Ko	KOR	35
2012	Yani Tseng	TPE	53	2020	Jin Young Ko	KOR	52
2013	Inbee Park	KOR	38				

Final 2020 Rolex Women's World Golf Rankings

				Average Points	Events	Total Points
1	(1)	Jin Young Ko	KOR	**9.05**	52	470.61
2	(5)	Sei Young Kim	KOR	**7.77**	55	427.49
3	(14)	Inbee Park	KOR	**6.56**	44	288.57
4	(3)	Nelly Korda	USA	**6.34**	47	297.77
5	(4)	Danielle Kang	USA	**6.32**	49	309.51
6	(8)	Brooke M Henderson	CAN	**5.73**	53	303.49
7	(6)	Nasa Hataoka	JPN	**5.51**	51	281.03
8	(9)	Minjee Lee	AUS	**5.08**	55	279.33
9	(13)	Hyo Joo Kim	KOR	**4.90**	51	249.68
10	(2)	Sung Hyun Park	KOR	**4.67**	47	219.58
11	(10)	Lexi Thompson	USA	**4.48**	44	197.05
12	(7)	Jeongeun Lee[6]	KOR	**4.27**	55	234.95
13	(11)	Hinako Shibuno	JPN	**3.90**	54	210.56
14	(18)	So Yeon Ryu	KOR	**3.84**	47	180.40
15	(16)	Carlota Ciganda	ESP	**3.77**	51	192.18
16	(82)	Ayaka Furue	JPN	**3.71**	35	129.76
17	(122)	Hae Ran Ryu	KOR	**3.59**	32	125.80
18	(22)	Hannah Green	AUS	**3.51**	51	178.77
19	(51)	Jennifer Kupcho	USA	**3.31**	33	115.71
20	(32)	Ha Na Jang	KOR	**3.30**	54	178.05
21	(12)	Ariya Jutanugarn	THA	**3.28**	55	180.22
22	(15)	Ai Suzuki	JPN	**3.21**	54	173.26
23	(17)	Jessica Korda	USA	**3.14**	40	125.52
24	(21)	Mi Jung Hur	KOR	**3.13**	46	144.16
25	(27)	Hye Jin Choi	KOR	**3.10**	62	192.09
26	(344)	Sophia Popov	GER	**3.03**	42	127.31
27	(25)	Hee Jeong Lim	KOR	**3.03**	50	151.54
28	(85)	Mirim Lee	KOR	**2.98**	49	145.90
29	(40)	Lydia Ko	NZL	**2.92**	52	152.05
30	(68)	A Lim Kim	KOR	**2.88**	59	169.72
31	(23)	Shanshan Feng	CHN	**2.87**	46	131.97
32	(63)	Austin Ernst	USA	**2.87**	47	134.75
33	(19)	Lizette Salas	USA	**2.84**	48	136.50
34	(26)	Charley Hull	ENG	**2.80**	48	134.45
35	(59)	Ally Ewing (McDonald)	USA	**2.80**	53	148.14
36	(101)	Stacy Lewis	USA	**2.79**	37	103.18
37	(24)	Jiyai Shin	KOR	**2.79**	61	169.91
38	(41)	Georgia Hall	ENG	**2.70**	49	132.41
39	(102)	Melissa Reid	ENG	**2.64**	45	118.71
40	(65)	Amy Olson	USA	**2.63**	53	139.54
41	(50)	Min Ji Park	KOR	**2.63**	56	147.17
42	(33)	Marina Alex	USA	**2.61**	47	122.46
43	(38)	Moriya Jutanugarn	THA	**2.56**	55	140.77
44	(20)	Amy Yang	KOR	**2.51**	53	133.11
45	(282)	Yuka Saso	PHI	**2.47**	24	86.45
46	(105)	Yealimi Noh	USA	**2.47**	33	86.28
47	(28)	Brittany Altomare	USA	**2.46**	54	132.74
48	(29)	Seon Woo Bae	KOR	**2.46**	63	154.69
49	(44)	Megan Khang	USA	**2.33**	51	118.73
50	(30)	Da Yeon Lee	KOR	**2.30**	50	115.18

Figure in brackets indicates final position of 2019

				Average Points	Events	Total Points
51	(37)	Caroline Masson	GER	**2.26**	54	122.10
52	(76)	Angela Stanford	USA	**2.25**	47	105.90
53	(52)	So Mi Lee	KOR	**2.24**	43	96.32
54	(89)	Anna Nordqvist	SWE	**2.15**	54	116.21
55	(95)	Hyun Kyung Park	KOR	**2.10**	45	94.69
56	(56)	Gaby Lopez	MEX	**2.10**	54	113.52
57	(58)	Celine Boutier	FRA	**2.06**	60	123.85
58	(36)	Yu Liu	CHN	**2.01**	58	116.85
59	(45)	Kristen Gillman	USA	**1.97**	41	80.96
60	(35)	A Yean Cho	KOR	**1.94**	51	98.80
61	(118)	Madelene Sagstrom	SWE	**1.88**	49	92.31
62	(48)	In Gee Chun	KOR	**1.86**	50	93.15
63	(54)	Mone Inami	JPN	**1.85**	45	83.34
64	(34)	Eun-Hee Ji	KOR	**1.85**	50	92.45
65	(46)	Min Young Lee[2]	KOR	**1.84**	65	119.86
66	(49)	Mi Hyang Lee	KOR	**1.82**	56	102.19
67	(57)	So Young Lee	KOR	**1.82**	59	107.57
68	(31)	Bronte Law	ENG	**1.78**	52	92.70
69	(43)	Azahara Munoz	ESP	**1.77**	60	106.39
70	(104)	Ashleigh Buhai	RSA	**1.75**	60	105.03
71	(509)	Emily Kristine Pedersen	DEN	**1.75**	42	73.40
72	(61)	Momoko Ueda	JPN	**1.74**	59	102.86
73	(131)	Jasmine Suwannapura	THA	**1.74**	64	111.27
74	(39)	In-Kyung Kim	KOR	**1.73**	32	60.71
75	(103)	Jennifer Song	USA	**1.71**	50	85.69
76	(67)	Nanna Koerstz Madsen	DEN	**1.67**	54	90.39
77	(42)	Angel Yin	USA	**1.65**	51	83.96
78	(86)	Jodi Ewart Shadoff	ENG	**1.64**	51	83.79
79	(72)	Sakura Koiwai	JPN	**1.60**	74	118.6
80	(202)	Na Rin An	KOR	**1.58**	57	90.14
81	(79)	Cheyenne Knight	USA	**1.53**	53	81.20
82	(115)	Katherine Kirk	AUS	**1.51**	54	81.37
83	(70)	Ji Yeong Kim[2]	KOR	**1.46**	60	87.86
84	(74)	Jenny Shin	KOR	**1.45**	53	76.64
85	(47)	Sun Ju Ahn	KOR	**1.43**	48	68.85
86	(319)	Yuna Nishimura	JPN	**1.43**	34	50.04
87	(55)	Su Oh	AUS	**1.42**	55	77.85
88	(99)	Erika Hara	JPN	**1.40**	69	96.50
89	(100)	Song Yi Ahn	KOR	**1.36**	55	74.92
90	(53)	Morgan Pressel	USA	**1.36**	49	66.51
91	(230)	Mina Harigae	USA	**1.30**	44	57.25
92	(69)	Minami Katsu	JPN	**1.30**	68	88.33
93	(62)	Yui Kawamoto	JPN	**1.29**	62	80.17
94	(107)	Brittany Lincicome	USA	**1.27**	30	44.52
95	(71)	Chae Yoon Park	KOR	**1.27**	57	72.18
96	(75)	Chella Choi	KOR	**1.25**	55	68.60
97	(94)	Anne van Dam	NED	**1.22**	53	64.78
98	(123)	Xiyu Lin	CHN	**1.22**	53	64.53
99	(110)	Cristie Kerr	USA	**1.21**	45	54.59
100	(73)	Eri Okayama	JPN	**1.19**	62	73.89

				Average Points	Events	Total Points
101	(78)	Nicole Broch Larsen	DEN	**1.19**	54	64.12
102	(77)	Ji Hyun Kim	KOR	**1.16**	57	66.14
103	(262)	Perrine Delacour	FRA	**1.15**	44	50.80
104	(66)	Mamiko Higa	JPN	**1.15**	68	78.46
105	(113)	Alena Sharp	CAN	**1.14**	50	57.05
106	(126)	Min Sun Kim[5]	KOR	**1.12**	56	62.53
107	(83)	Jing Yan	CHN	**1.06**	52	55.24
108	(64)	Annie Park	USA	**1.04**	52	54.25
109	(97)	Ga Young Lee	KOR	**1.04**	45	46.65
110	(182)	Hee Young Park	KOR	**1.04**	41	42.44
111	(208)	Lauren Stephenson	USA	**1.03**	35	36.14
112	(60)	Jeong Min Cho	KOR	**1.02**	58	59.15
113	(145)	Sayaka Takahashi	JPN	**1.01**	63	63.66
114	(87)	Lala Anai	JPN	**1.01**	73	73.63
115	(142)	Sarah Schmelzel	USA	**1.00**	53	53.23
116	(88)	Ah-Reum Hwang	KOR	**1.00**	65	65.07
117	(485)	Lindsey Weaver	USA	**1.00**	35	34.99
118	(797)	Andrea Lee	USA	**0.99**	16	34.77
119	(98)	Jung Min Lee	KOR	**0.99**	56	55.45
120	(117)	Ji Hyun Oh	KOR	**0.97**	53	51.65
121	(221)	Cydney Clanton	USA	**0.97**	45	43.66
122	(189)	Linnea Strom	SWE	**0.96**	53	51.12
123	(108)	Mi-Jeong Jeon	KOR	**0.94**	64	60.36
124	(246)	Stephanie Meadow	NIR	**0.93**	49	45.74
125	(96)	Wei-Ling Hsu	TPE	**0.92**	61	56.13
126	(109)	Bo Ah Kim	KOR	**0.91**	58	52.94
127	(92)	Ji Young Park	KOR	**0.91**	56	50.90
128	(112)	Erika Kikuchi	JPN	**0.91**	65	59.03
129	(111)	Jane Park	USA	**0.90**	42	37.93
130	(132)	Esther Henseleit	GER	**0.90**	34	31.61
131	(84)	Teresa Lu	TPE	**0.90**	65	58.67
132	(81)	Pornanong Phatlum	THA	**0.90**	54	48.60
133	(138)	Maria Fernanda Torres	PUR	**0.90**	52	46.76
134	(91)	Jaye Marie Green	USA	**0.89**	52	46.53
135	(124)	Jin Seon Han	KOR	**0.89**	59	52.54
136	(146)	Bo Mee Lee	KOR	**0.89**	54	47.87
137	(120)	Ji Hee Lee	KOR	**0.87**	58	50.33
138	(300)	Maria Fassi	MEX	**0.86**	28	30.22
139	(125)	Caroline Hedwall	SWE	**0.86**	49	42.28
140	(137)	Ye Rim Choi	KOR	**0.85**	57	48.50
141	(217)	Da Been Heo	KOR	**0.84**	54	45.61
142	(1184)	Stephanie Kyriacou	AUS	**0.84**	15	29.50
143	(116)	Gerina Piller	USA	**0.84**	36	30.29
144	(411)	Kelly Tan	MAS	**0.84**	47	39.28
145	(144)	Saki Asai	JPN	**0.83**	62	51.66
146	(141)	So Yi Kim	KOR	**0.83**	56	46.47
147	(114)	Asuka Kashiwabara	JPN	**0.83**	68	56.41
148	(90)	Ryann O'Toole	USA	**0.82**	50	41.04
149	(133)	Kana Mikashima	JPN	**0.81**	66	53.61
150	(-)	Bianca Pagdanganan	PHI	**0.81**	11	28.28

			Average Points	Events	Total Points
151	(232)	Woo Jeong Kim	KOR	**0.80**	43	34.37
152	(135)	Pajaree Anannarukarn	THA	**0.80**	49	39.03
153	(240)	Han Sol Ji	KOR	**0.79**	56	44.50
154	(158)	Saki Nagamine	JPN	**0.79**	67	53.01
155	(287)	Christina Kim	USA	**0.78**	46	35.99
156	(80)	Misuzu Narita	JPN	**0.77**	61	46.89
157	(121)	Ju Young Pak	KOR	**0.77**	57	43.79
158	(156)	Pernilla Lindberg	SWE	**0.76**	53	40.44
159	(200)	Brittany Lang	USA	**0.76**	43	32.81
160	(408)	Yu Jin Sung	KOR	**0.76**	36	27.40
161	(127)	Jeong Eun Lee	KOR	**0.76**	45	34.14
162	(152)	Patty Tavatanakit	THA	**0.75**	28	26.42
163	(128)	Seo Jin Park	KOR	**0.75**	43	32.41
164	(148)	Mika Miyazato	JPN	**0.74**	43	32.03
165	(405)	Ayaka Watanabe	JPN	**0.73**	60	43.76
166	(119)	Hee-Kyung Bae	KOR	**0.73**	63	45.83
167	(106)	Mo Martin	USA	**0.72**	31	25.05
168	(168)	Harukyo Nomura	JPN	**0.71**	36	25.72
169	(199)	Na-Ri Lee	KOR	**0.71**	55	39.06
170	(93)	Seung Yeon Lee	KOR	**0.70**	50	35.22
171	(186)	Min Kyung Choi	KOR	**0.70**	54	37.65
172	(143)	Aditi Ashok	IND	**0.68**	55	37.66
173	(130)	Sakura Yokomine	JPN	**0.68**	59	40.22
174	(150)	Chae-Young Yoon	KOR	**0.67**	59	39.57
175	(201)	Yoon Kyung Heo	KOR	**0.66**	34	23.08
176	(214)	Miki Sakai	JPN	**0.66**	72	47.34
177	(254)	Leona Maguire	IRL	**0.65**	55	36.02
178	(163)	Olivia Cowan	GER	**0.64**	36	23.12
179	(472)	Ji Sun Kang	KOR	**0.63**	24	22.03
180	(159)	Chie Arimura	JPN	**0.62**	59	36.42
181	(171)	Yuka Yasuda	JPN	**0.61**	27	21.46
182	(280)	Julia Engstrom	SWE	**0.61**	44	26.97
183	(149)	Shiho Oyama	JPN	**0.61**	54	32.96
184	(260)	Robynn Ree	USA	**0.61**	45	27.41
185	(475)	Se Lin Hyun	KOR	**0.61**	20	21.26
186	(210)	Alison Lee	USA	**0.60**	37	22.14
187	(166)	Ha Neul Kim	KOR	**0.59**	51	30.30
188	(643)	Maiko Wakabayashi	JPN	**0.59**	22	20.79
189	(261)	Saiki Fujita	JPN	**0.59**	64	37.71
190	(153)	Marianne Skarpnord	NOR	**0.59**	42	24.75
191	(659)	Julie Kim	KOR	**0.59**	22	20.58
192	(181)	Weiwei Zhang	CHN	**0.59**	38	22.34
193	(139)	Hee Won Na	KOR	**0.59**	62	36.43
194	(372)	Sumika Nakasone	JPN	**0.59**	46	26.92
195	(154)	Hikaru Yoshimoto	JPN	**0.58**	64	37.02
196	(155)	Bo Mi Kwak	KOR	**0.58**	43	24.79
197	(129)	Hina Arakaki	JPN	**0.57**	67	37.99
198	(194)	Mayu Hamada	JPN	**0.57**	64	36.20
199	(140)	Char Young Kim[2]	KOR	**0.57**	56	31.66
200	(134)	So Yeon Park	KOR	**0.56**	57	31.84

				Average Points	Events	Total Points
201	(178)	Emma Talley	USA	**0.56**	54	30.07
202	(223)	Shina Kanazawa	JPN	**0.55**	61	33.37
203	(136)	Rei Matsuda	JPN	**0.55**	67	36.63
204	(270)	Elizabeth Szokol	USA	**0.55**	47	25.67
205	(225)	Nuria Iturrioz	ESP	**0.54**	52	28.30
206	(183)	Pavarisa Yoktuan	THA	**0.54**	46	24.84
207	(243)	Hae Rym Kim	KOR	**0.54**	59	31.82
208	(255)	Minami Hiruta	JPN	**0.54**	58	31.21
209	(264)	Laura Fuenfstueck	GER	**0.54**	44	23.55
210	(-)	Gabriela Ruffels (A)	AUS	**0.54**	9	18.73
211	(1100)	Matilda Castren	FIN	**0.53**	36	19.16
212	(167)	Eun Woo Choi	KOR	**0.53**	50	26.47
213	(239)	Pei-Ying Tsai	TPE	**0.53**	67	35.30
214	(197)	Mariah Stackhouse	USA	**0.53**	48	25.26
215	(157)	Lindy Duncan	USA	**0.53**	53	27.84
216	(147)	Saranporn Langkulgasettrin	THA	**0.52**	54	27.93
217	(245)	Yu-Ju Chen	TPE	**0.52**	31	18.03
218	(160)	Haeji Kang	KOR	**0.51**	49	25.10
219	(164)	Kana Nagai	JPN	**0.51**	71	36.22
220	(169)	Mariajo Uribe	COL	**0.51**	42	21.31
221	(276)	U Ree Jun	KOR	**0.50**	55	27.64
222	(176)	Ritsuko Ryu	JPN	**0.50**	63	31.64
223	(284)	Manon De Roey	BEL	**0.50**	50	25.06
224	(175)	Rumi Yoshiba	JPN	**0.50**	72	35.75
225	(220)	Hiroko Azuma	JPN	**0.49**	67	32.99
226	(162)	Mami Fukuda	JPN	**0.49**	65	31.85
227	(177)	Gyeol Park	KOR	**0.49**	55	26.79
228	(793)	Jeong Mee Hwang	KOR	**0.49**	21	17.02
229	(283)	Gemma Dryburgh	SCO	**0.48**	45	21.63
230	(216)	Pei-Yun Chien	TPE	**0.48**	55	26.37
231	(170)	Serena Aoki	JPN	**0.48**	71	34.04
232	(203)	Momoko Osato	JPN	**0.48**	69	33.07
233	(192)	Min Song Ha	KOR	**0.48**	58	27.65
234	(346)	Luna Sobron Galmes	ESP	**0.47**	45	21.26
235	(172)	Hana Wakimoto	JPN	**0.47**	53	24.99
236	(226)	Charlotte Thomas	ENG	**0.47**	52	24.27
237	(286)	Ayako Kimura	JPN	**0.46**	66	30.57
238	(185)	Ji Hyun Lee[2]	KOR	**0.46**	50	22.87
239	(236)	Ju Yeon In	KOR	**0.46**	55	25.15
240	(188)	Katherine Perry-Hamski	USA	**0.46**	37	16.87
241	(604)	Hye Lim Jo	KOR	**0.46**	20	15.94
242	(174)	Tiffany Joh	USA	**0.45**	50	22.63
243	(180)	Seul Gi Jeong	KOR	**0.45**	56	25.32
244	(252)	Yan Liu	CHN	**0.45**	33	15.79
245	(195)	Paula Creamer	USA	**0.45**	37	16.68
246	(184)	Sarah Kemp	AUS	**0.45**	47	21.10
247	(298)	Sanna Nuutinen	FIN	**0.45**	55	24.67
248	(193)	Mind Muangkhumsakul	THA	**0.45**	39	17.40
249	(161)	Ayako Uehara	JPN	**0.44**	56	24.77
250	(272)	Gi Ppuem Lee	KOR	**0.44**	43	19.01

				Average Points	Events	Total Points
251	(196)	Reika Usui	JPN	**0.44**	44	19.38
252	(209)	Hyun Soo Kim	KOR	**0.44**	52	22.90
253	(212)	Christine Wolf	AUT	**0.44**	42	18.34
254	(213)	Aoi Ohnishi	JPN	**0.44**	56	24.38
255	(207)	Tiffany Chan	HKG	**0.43**	45	19.22
256	(889)	Seung Hui Ro	KOR	**0.43**	18	14.89
257	(247)	Nana Suganuma	JPN	**0.42**	40	16.87
258	(205)	Eun Soo Jang	KOR	**0.42**	55	23.16
259	(277)	Mao Nozawa	JPN	**0.42**	58	24.33
260	(218)	Yeon Ju Jung	KOR	**0.42**	56	23.32
261	(165)	Sandra Gal	GER	**0.42**	41	17.03
262	(-)	Kaitlyn Papp (A)	USA	**0.41**	3	14.50
263	(263)	Na Yeon Choi	KOR	**0.41**	30	14.43
264	(187)	Daniela Darquea	ECU	**0.41**	44	17.97
265	(257)	Babe Liu	TPE	**0.41**	41	16.69
266	(228)	Dana Finkelstein	USA	**0.41**	47	19.07
267	(265)	Ran Hong	KOR	**0.41**	52	21.06
268	(256)	Mohan Du	CHN	**0.40**	26	14.17
269	(400)	Chia Yen Wu	TPE	**0.40**	23	14.16
270	(253)	Daniela Holmqvist	SWE	**0.40**	44	17.78
271	(231)	Carly Booth	SCO	**0.40**	30	14.13
272	(1193)	Yun Ji Jeong	KOR	**0.40**	20	14.02
273	(306)	Yu-Chiang Hou	TPE	**0.40**	30	13.95
274	(619)	Mao Saigo	JPN	**0.40**	23	13.94
275	(229)	Atthaya Thitikul	THA	**0.40**	11	13.91
276	(258)	Hyo Rin Lee	KOR	**0.40**	57	22.57
277	(680)	Seul Ki Lee	KOR	**0.39**	19	13.78
278	(299)	Lee-Anne Pace	RSA	**0.39**	44	17.23
279	(342)	Su Yeon Jang	KOR	**0.39**	55	21.52
280	(237)	Ye Jin Kim	KOR	**0.39**	54	21.03
281	(274)	Akira Yamaji	JPN	**0.39**	44	16.99
282	(724)	Ji Su Kim	KOR	**0.39**	30	13.50
283	(311)	Mizuki Tanaka	JPN	**0.38**	47	17.95
284	(222)	Karis Davidson	AUS	**0.38**	60	22.82
285	(206)	Hsuan-Yu Yao	TPE	**0.38**	62	23.54
286	(190)	Eimi Koga	JPN	**0.38**	60	22.65
287	(310)	Sarah Burnham	USA	**0.38**	30	13.20
288	(669)	Rose Zhang (A)	USA	**0.38**	5	13.20
289	(478)	Hikari Tanabe	JPN	**0.37**	46	17.20
290	(482)	Ruoning Yin	CHN	**0.37**	15	13.04
291	(259)	Yeun Jung Seo	KOR	**0.37**	57	21.23
292	(268)	Meghan MacLaren	ENG	**0.37**	48	17.80
293	(248)	Karolin Lampert	GER	**0.37**	40	14.78
294	(371)	Klara Spilkova	CZE	**0.37**	36	13.29
295	(191)	Su Ji Kim	KOR	**0.37**	56	20.63
296	(233)	Parinda Phokan	THA	**0.37**	37	13.56
297	(179)	Haruka Morita-Wanyaolu	CHN	**0.37**	64	23.43
298	(249)	Su Jin Lee[3]	KOR	**0.37**	30	12.80
299	(849)	Ree An Kim	KOR	**0.36**	18	12.73
300	(219)	Jae-Eun Chung	KOR	**0.36**	61	22.04

YEAR-END TOP 10s

2006	2007	2008	2009	2010
1 Sorenstam	1 Ochoa	1 Ochoa	1 Ochoa	1 Jy Shin
2 Ochoa	2 Pettersen	2 Tseng	2 Jy Shin	2 Kerr
3 Webb	3 Webb	3 Sorenstam	3 Pettersen	3 Pettersen
4 Kerr	4 Sorenstam	4 Creamer	4 Kerr	4 NY Choi
5 Inkster	5 Creamer	5 Pettersen	5 Tseng	5 Tseng
6 A Miyazato	6 Kerr	6 Jy Shin	6 Creamer	6 A Miyazato
7 Creamer	7 Jy Shin	7 Kerr	7 Nordqvist	7 IK Kim
8 J Jang	8 Inkster	8 Alfredsson	8 A Miyazato	8 SJ Ahn
9 Ohyama	9 MH Kim	9 Stanford	9 Stanford	9 SH Kim
10 Hurst	10 Pak	10 Webb	10 Wie	10 Wie

2011	2012	2013	2014	2015
1 Tseng	1 Tseng	1 I Park	1 I Park	1 L Ko
2 Pettersen	2 NY Choi	2 Pettersen	2 L Ko	2 I Park
3 NY Choi	3 Lewis	3 Lewis	3 Lewis	3 Lewis
4 Kerr	4 I Park	4 L Ko	4 Pettersen	4 Thompson
5 Creamer	5 Feng	5 SY Ryu	5 Feng	5 SY Ryu
6 SJ Ahn	6 Pettersen	6 Feng	6 Wie	6 Feng
7 Jy Shin	7 SY Ryu	7 NY Choi	7 SY Ryu	7 SY Kim
8 IK Kim	8 Jy Shin	8 Webb	8 HJ Kim	8 A Yang
9 A Miyazato	9 A Miyazato	9 Thompson	9 Webb	9 IK Kim
10 Lewis	10 M Miyazato	10 IK Kim	10 Thompson	10 Chun

2016	2017	2018	2019	2020
1 L Ko	1 Feng	1 A Jutanugarn	1 JY Ko	1 JY Ko
2 A Jutanugarn	2 SH Park	2 SH Park	2 SH Park	2 SY Kim
3 Chun	3 SY Ryu	3 SY Ryu	3 N Korda	3 I Park
4 Feng	4 Thompson	4 I Park	4 Kang	4 N Korda
5 Thompson	5 Chun	5 Thompson	5 SY Kim	5 Kang
6 SY Kim	6 A Jutanugarn	6 Mj Lee	6 Hataoka	6 Henderson
7 HN Jang	7 Nordqvist	7 Hataoka	7 J Lee[6]	7 Hataoka
8 Henderson	8 IK Kim	8 Hall	8 Henderson	8 Mj Lee
9 SY Ryu	9 L Ko	9 Henderson	9 Mj Lee	9 HJ Kim
10 SH Park	10 Kerr	10 JY Ko	10 Thompson	10 SH Park

Official World Golf Ranking

Although a record five players reached the number one spot on the Official World Golf Ranking in 2020, for the third time in four years Dustin Johnson claimed the McCormack Award as the player who spent most weeks at the top of the ranking. Brooks Koepka, who interrupted Johnson's hold on the trophy in 2019, was followed as the number one by Rory McIlroy, Jon Rahm and Justin Thomas but Johnson ended the year as the dominant player thanks to his FedEx Cup triumph and his second major victory at the Masters Tournament.

While Koepka dropped out of the top 10 after an injury-hit season, four of the top five from the end of 2019 remained at the summit of the ranking. But just below that group there was considerable change. PGA champion Collin Morikawa gained the second most points in the year behind Johnson, jumping from 65th to seventh after his maiden major win in San Francisco.

For the first time ever, four players under the age of 24 were in the top 20, with Morikawa joined by Viktor Hovland, who moved up 79 places, Matthew Wolff, who jumped 102 places, and Sungjae Im. US Open champion Bryson DeChambeau moved from 14th to ninth, while Daniel Berger rose 141 places to 13th.

Among the 13 players who lost most points over the year, nine were former major champions, including Koepka, Tiger Woods, Francesco Molinari and Justin Rose.

Due to the pandemic, the ranking was frozen for 12 weeks before tour golf was able to resume.

The McCormack Award was first presented to Woods in 1998, who kept it to himself for 13 years. The idea to reward the player who spent most weeks as the number one in any given year was proposed by then PGA Tour Commissioner Tim Finchem, with the name recognising the late Mark H McCormack's vision and dedication in establishing and administering the World Ranking system.

The Ranking was launched at the 1986 Masters, since when 24 players have been the number one. Of those, the 14 who have not dominated over an entire year are: Bernhard Langer, Fred Couples, Nick Price, Tom Lehman, Ernie Els, David Duval, Vijay Singh, Lee Westwood, Martin Kaymer, Adam Scott, Jordan Spieth, Thomas, Rose and Rahm.

A forerunner world ranking appeared in *Mark H McCormack's World of Professional Golf* prior to 1986.

MOST WEEKS AT NUMBER ONE BY YEAR

			Weeks				Weeks
1986	Seve Ballesteros	ESP	20	2004	Tiger Woods	USA	35
1987	Greg Norman	AUS	51	2005	Tiger Woods	USA	38
1988	Greg Norman	AUS	44	2006	Tiger Woods	USA	52
1989	Seve Ballesteros	ESP	31	2007	Tiger Woods	USA	52
1990	Greg Norman	AUS	46	2008	Tiger Woods	USA	52
1991	Ian Woosnam	WAL	39	2009	Tiger Woods	USA	52
1992	Nick Faldo	ENG	25	2010	Tiger Woods	USA	43
1993	Nick Faldo	ENG	52	2011	Luke Donald	ENG	32
1994	Greg Norman	AUS	27	2012	Rory McIlroy	NIR	28
1995	Greg Norman	AUS	29	2013	Tiger Woods	USA	41
1996	Greg Norman	AUS	52	2014	Rory McIlroy	NIR	22
1997	Greg Norman	AUS	40	2015	Rory McIlroy	NIR	34
1998	Tiger Woods	USA	43	2016	Jason Day	AUS	41
1999	Tiger Woods	USA	38	2017	Dustin Johnson	USA	46
2000	Tiger Woods	USA	52	2018	Dustin Johnson	USA	35
2001	Tiger Woods	USA	52	2019	Brooks Koepka	USA	33
2002	Tiger Woods	USA	52	2020	Dustin Johnson	USA	19
2003	Tiger Woods	USA	52				

Known as the McCormack Award since 1998

Final 2020 Official World Golf Ranking

				Average Points	Events	Total Points	2020 Points Lost	2020 Points Gained
1	(5)	Dustin Johnson	USA	**12.670**	40	506.80	-247.52	463.54
2	(3)	Jon Rahm	ESP	**9.982**	47	469.15	-256.03	328.72
3	(4)	Justin Thomas	USA	**9.174**	46	421.99	-245.24	334.56
4	(2)	Rory McIlroy	NIR	**7.144**	45	321.47	-289.48	143.43
5	(14)	Bryson DeChambeau	USA	**7.101**	47	333.77	-225.13	313.98
6	(11)	Webb Simpson	USA	**7.018**	41	287.75	-181.14	235.02
7	(65)	Collin Morikawa	USA	**7.008**	40	280.32	-70.04	272.75
8	(9)	Xander Schauffele	USA	**6.899**	47	324.24	-213.38	247.98
9	(7)	Patrick Cantlay	USA	**6.221**	40	248.84	-176.72	149.21
10	(32)	Tyrrell Hatton	ENG	**6.143**	47	288.73	-116.05	247.02
11	(12)	Patrick Reed	USA	**5.865**	52	304.97	-186.06	238.11
12	(1)	Brooks Koepka	USA	**5.332**	42	223.95	-292.96	89.30
13	(154)	Daniel Berger	USA	**4.818**	42	202.36	-61.79	217.07
14	(93)	Viktor Hovland	NOR	**4.659**	42	195.69	-45.47	178.80
15	(117)	Matthew Wolff	USA	**4.610**	40	184.41	-38.53	168.51
16	(25)	Matthew Fitzpatrick	ENG	**4.579**	52	238.12	-131.01	175.67
17	(10)	Tommy Fleetwood	ENG	**4.199**	52	218.36	-187.91	111.55
18	(34)	Sungjae Im	KOR	**4.190**	52	217.90	-109.51	185.23
19	(16)	Tony Finau	USA	**4.105**	52	213.45	-185.03	158.07
20	(21)	Hideki Matsuyama	JPN	**4.097**	52	213.06	-135.13	134.06
21	(13)	Adam Scott	AUS	**4.063**	40	162.51	-144.24	92.97
22	(20)	Louis Oosthuizen	RSA	**3.941**	47	185.23	-129.85	117.94
23	(38)	Abraham Ancer	MEX	**3.677**	52	191.20	-110.60	158.29
24	(15)	Paul Casey	ENG	**3.570**	48	171.34	-151.68	92.94
25	(35)	Kevin Kisner	USA	**3.434**	52	178.59	-108.65	136.87
26	(62)	Jason Kokrak	USA	**3.430**	49	168.05	-69.92	136.92
27	(53)	Cameron Smith	AUS	**3.329**	50	166.47	-97.69	148.12
28	(183)	Harris English	USA	**3.249**	52	168.95	-35.29	156.99
29	(28)	Marc Leishman	AUS	**3.222**	46	148.21	-134.47	118.09
30	(91)	Ryan Palmer	USA	**3.132**	43	134.66	-62.07	126.50
31	(66)	Scottie Scheffler	USA	**3.107**	52	161.57	-52.15	136.21
32	(45)	Victor Perez	FRA	**3.038**	44	133.67	-71.04	86.35
33	(19)	Shane Lowry	IRL	**3.033**	51	154.66	-138.52	70.31
34	(87)	Christiaan Bezuidenhout	RSA	**3.013**	52	156.68	-57.55	129.68
35	(8)	Justin Rose	ENG	**2.989**	48	143.47	-221.49	77.23
36	(59)	Lee Westwood	ENG	**2.889**	46	132.90	-73.15	120.92
37	(24)	Matt Kuchar	USA	**2.872**	49	140.73	-152.89	92.79
38	(27)	Kevin Na	USA	**2.847**	46	130.97	-107.81	75.56
39	(17)	Gary Woodland	USA	**2.807**	49	137.53	-159.55	58.51
40	(22)	Bernd Wiesberger	AUT	**2.742**	47	128.85	-81.10	47.47
41	(6)	Tiger Woods	USA	**2.724**	40	108.96	-173.24	19.08
42	(33)	Billy Horschel	USA	**2.700**	52	140.39	-112.63	100.45
43	(37)	Jason Day	AUS	**2.580**	45	116.09	-97.78	98.80
44	(47)	Bubba Watson	USA	**2.509**	44	110.39	-92.93	98.39
45	(58)	Joaquin Niemann	CHI	**2.495**	52	129.71	-62.74	95.96
46	(39)	Sergio Garcia	ESP	**2.470**	49	121.04	-97.68	82.69
47	(63)	Brendon Todd	USA	**2.427**	46	111.62	-38.38	71.37
48	(43)	Ian Poulter	ENG	**2.292**	50	114.62	-92.82	80.41
49	(264)	Mackenzie Hughes	CAN	**2.268**	51	115.69	-34.73	116.49
50	(30)	Matt Wallace	ENG	**2.248**	52	116.89	-112.25	75.15

Figure in brackets indicates final position of 2019

				Average Points	Events	Total Points	2020 Points Lost	2020 Points Gained
51	(49)	Erik van Rooyen	RSA	**2.198**	52	114.31	-75.48	69.39
52	(122)	Kevin Streelman	USA	**2.182**	52	113.46	-55.36	101.06
53	(23)	Rickie Fowler	USA	**2.159**	43	92.85	-124.52	49.12
54	(60)	Corey Conners	CAN	**2.137**	52	111.14	-66.44	74.48
55	(64)	Robert MacIntyre	SCO	**2.107**	50	105.33	-55.49	59.32
56	(36)	Chez Reavie	USA	**2.086**	52	108.50	-97.10	53.89
57	(222)	Russell Henley	USA	**2.084**	49	102.13	-32.11	95.37
58	(137)	Andy Sullivan	ENG	**2.082**	48	99.91	-42.58	83.82
59	(672)	Will Zalatoris	USA	**2.045**	40	81.82	-11.56	84.41
60	(104)	Sebastian Munoz	COL	**2.032**	52	105.64	-46.34	76.98
61	(142)	Carlos Ortiz	MEX	**2.024**	52	105.25	-34.92	81.15
62	(116)	Adam Long	USA	**2.021**	52	105.08	-50.92	90.97
63	(119)	Lanto Griffin	USA	**2.012**	52	104.61	-44.66	80.42
64	(101)	Joel Dahmen	USA	**1.960**	52	101.94	-59.52	84.16
65	(26)	Henrik Stenson	SWE	**1.957**	42	82.20	-86.86	12.98
66	(70)	Phil Mickelson	USA	**1.947**	41	79.84	-79.01	69.39
67	(29)	Danny Willett	ENG	**1.943**	52	101.06	-97.20	31.89
68	(102)	Dylan Frittelli	RSA	**1.898**	52	98.71	-51.08	72.93
69	(396)	Sami Valimaki	FIN	**1.868**	40	74.73	-15.75	73.08
70	(201)	Lucas Herbert	AUS	**1.866**	40	74.63	-45.65	82.32
71	(78)	Cameron Champ	USA	**1.813**	51	92.44	-61.60	61.56
72	(77)	JT Poston	USA	**1.806**	52	93.90	-59.09	59.49
73	(54)	Tom Lewis	ENG	**1.795**	49	87.94	-78.88	56.58
74	(61)	Chan Kim	USA	**1.768**	40	70.72	-36.28	26.87
75	(42)	Byeong Hun An	KOR	**1.742**	52	90.59	-87.41	49.03
76	(31)	Shugo Imahira	JPN	**1.688**	51	86.09	-87.96	14.23
77	(170)	Aaron Rai	ENG	**1.687**	49	82.68	-34.88	68.58
78	(50)	Adam Hadwin	CAN	**1.678**	46	77.17	-73.54	35.22
79	(125)	Martin Kaymer	GER	**1.667**	47	78.35	-45.92	57.47
80	(121)	Graeme McDowell	NIR	**1.651**	50	82.55	-56.31	74.88
81	(208)	Talor Gooch	USA	**1.645**	49	80.62	-32.80	73.74
82	(44)	Jordan Spieth	USA	**1.645**	47	77.32	-78.68	37.01
83	(118)	Thomas Detry	BEL	**1.632**	52	84.87	-46.91	61.21
84	(82)	Thomas Pieters	BEL	**1.623**	42	68.17	-60.02	37.86
85	(340)	Martin Laird	SCO	**1.620**	43	69.65	-18.61	61.84
86	(86)	Sunghoon Kang	KOR	**1.607**	52	83.54	-63.14	60.53
87	(192)	Rasmus Hojgaard	DEN	**1.585**	45	71.34	-19.27	56.28
88	(40)	Jazz Janewattananond	THA	**1.566**	52	81.43	-82.90	29.66
89	(156)	Doc Redman	USA	**1.555**	43	66.87	-25.96	51.43
90	(464)	Garrick Higgo	RSA	**1.543**	40	61.74	-13.71	61.03
91	(123)	Brian Harman	USA	**1.525**	52	79.32	-45.23	57.32
92	(189)	George Coetzee	RSA	**1.519**	52	79.00	-31.48	65.28
93	(80)	Ryo Ishikawa	JPN	**1.499**	41	61.47	-41.12	21.61
94	(75)	Alex Noren	SWE	**1.492**	52	77.60	-73.57	57.65
95	(97)	Si Woo Kim	KOR	**1.489**	52	77.42	-60.94	58.18
96	(311)	Jim Herman	USA	**1.487**	46	68.38	-17.03	62.67
97	(202)	Zach Johnson	USA	**1.477**	43	63.50	-32.74	59.29
98	(46)	Brandt Snedeker	USA	**1.471**	50	73.53	-88.09	39.64
99	(196)	John Catlin	USA	**1.466**	52	76.22	-34.81	66.65
100	(130)	Max Homa	USA	**1.465**	51	74.72	-48.75	57.65

				Average Points	Events	Total Points	2020 Points Lost	2020 Points Gained
101	(219)	Sam Horsfield	ENG	**1.458**	46	67.07	-32.42	59.19
102	(41)	Rafa Cabrera Bello	ESP	**1.442**	52	75.00	-97.88	33.39
103	(218)	Cameron Tringale	USA	**1.439**	44	63.31	-23.49	47.26
104	(67)	Mike Lorenzo-Vera	FRA	**1.417**	40	56.66	-51.03	21.20
105	(228)	Andrew Landry	USA	**1.413**	50	70.65	-39.68	71.45
106	(240)	Tom Hoge	USA	**1.405**	52	73.06	-30.07	64.85
106	(206)	Michael Thompson	USA	**1.405**	46	64.63	-33.65	59.31
108	(56)	Shaun Norris	RSA	**1.404**	52	72.98	-63.69	27.95
109	(79)	Matthias Schwab	AUT	**1.387**	51	70.71	-50.32	28.90
110	(71)	Lucas Glover	USA	**1.371**	52	71.29	-57.90	38.56
111	(55)	Charles Howell III	USA	**1.368**	52	71.14	-73.94	35.08
112	(18)	Francesco Molinari	ITA	**1.362**	40	54.49	-152.90	5.66
113	(99)	Matt Jones	AUS	**1.359**	52	70.66	-43.73	35.89
114	(106)	Rikuya Hoshino	JPN	**1.359**	44	59.78	-47.62	32.63
115	(246)	Robert Streb	USA	**1.358**	52	70.64	-25.88	59.83
116	(83)	Marcus Kinhult	SWE	**1.356**	47	63.73	-46.02	26.38
117	(100)	Jorge Campillo	ESP	**1.354**	52	70.42	-55.92	47.64
117	(84)	Rory Sabbatini	SVK	**1.354**	52	70.42	-53.43	35.87
119	(88)	Nate Lashley	USA	**1.348**	48	64.71	-43.93	37.35
120	(180)	Antoine Rozner	FRA	**1.346**	50	67.32	-25.93	46.73
121	(139)	Harry Higgs	USA	**1.344**	52	69.86	-34.31	49.74
122	(404)	Brendan Steele	USA	**1.336**	47	62.77	-28.11	70.86
123	(211)	Takumi Kanaya	JPN	**1.334**	40	53.37	-12.99	34.85
124	(111)	Romain Langasque	FRA	**1.308**	48	62.79	-47.28	36.29
125	(113)	Aaron Wise	USA	**1.297**	46	59.65	-52.78	44.10
126	(127)	Branden Grace	RSA	**1.283**	52	66.72	-60.55	61.41
127	(509)	Laurie Canter	ENG	**1.267**	43	54.46	-9.69	48.86
128	(391)	Taylor Pendrith	CAN	**1.256**	40	50.23	-12.33	45.02
129	(52)	Eddie Pepperell	ENG	**1.249**	40	49.96	-76.13	24.51
130	(124)	Harold Varner III	USA	**1.248**	52	64.88	-45.56	43.82
131	(51)	Keegan Bradley	USA	**1.243**	52	64.63	-93.10	39.73
132	(115)	Adri Arnaus	ESP	**1.228**	52	63.87	-49.62	41.85
133	(75)	Kurt Kitayama	USA	**1.225**	45	55.12	-53.27	18.54
134	(305)	Callum Shinkwin	ENG	**1.196**	42	50.22	-14.89	40.34
135	(89)	Benjamin Hebert	FRA	**1.187**	47	55.78	-45.96	21.01
136	(233)	Nick Taylor	CAN	**1.183**	51	60.32	-34.72	56.69
137	(73)	Paul Waring	ENG	**1.179**	40	47.16	-48.39	11.73
138	(200)	Stewart Cink	USA	**1.171**	40	46.85	-32.12	42.32
139	(186)	Mark Hubbard	USA	**1.171**	52	60.87	-29.18	44.21
140	(90)	Danny Lee	NZL	**1.161**	52	60.38	-54.74	31.55
141	(108)	Scott Piercy	USA	**1.160**	48	55.66	-53.19	35.59
142	(207)	Sepp Straka	AUT	**1.149**	52	59.77	-31.68	50.22
143	(269)	Renato Paratore	ITA	**1.142**	52	59.37	-23.31	48.68
144	(158)	Charley Hoffman	USA	**1.137**	51	57.99	-41.87	47.98
145	(69)	Cheng Tsung Pan	TPE	**1.132**	52	58.87	-66.85	25.94
146	(164)	Tyler Duncan	USA	**1.131**	52	58.80	-27.22	36.30
147	(161)	Wyndham Clark	USA	**1.130**	52	58.75	-32.93	40.28
148	(146)	Joachim B Hansen	DEN	**1.129**	52	58.69	-35.23	35.88
149	(157)	Joohyung Kim	KOR	**1.128**	40	45.11	-23.96	28.15
150	(247)	Richy Werenski	USA	**1.110**	52	57.73	-31.03	51.98

			Average Points	Events	Total Points	2020 Points Lost	2020 Points Gained
151	(140)	Troy Merritt	USA	**1.110**	52	57.72	-40.76	40.05
152	(297)	Daniel van Tonder	RSA	**1.099**	44	48.34	-20.42	40.81
153	(193)	Adrian Otaegui	ESP	**1.097**	52	57.07	-39.57	52.13
154	(209)	Sam Burns	USA	**1.082**	48	51.91	-35.52	45.52
155	(120)	Francesco Laporta	ITA	**1.080**	42	45.34	-29.28	14.45
156	(107)	Emiliano Grillo	ARG	**1.074**	52	55.83	-60.12	42.87
157	(287)	Yuki Inamori	JPN	**1.073**	41	44.01	-26.62	39.42
158	(134)	Brad Kennedy	AUS	**1.058**	40	42.31	-34.80	21.66
159	(72)	Justin Harding	RSA	**1.048**	52	54.51	-71.73	28.83
160	(151)	Gunn Charoenkul	THA	**1.036**	45	46.64	-30.00	20.43
161	(1665)	Wilco Nienaber	RSA	**1.033**	40	41.31	-3.81	43.96
162	(177)	Kalle Samooja	FIN	**1.030**	48	49.46	-29.35	32.90
163	(172)	Masahiro Kawamura	JPN	**1.027**	52	53.40	-33.52	39.30
164	(85)	Joost Luiten	NED	**1.019**	52	52.98	-42.26	27.80
165	(251)	Henrik Norlander	SWE	**1.009**	52	52.47	-25.96	42.35
166	(417)	Maverick McNealy	USA	**0.997**	52	51.83	-19.74	50.00
167	(68)	Haotong Li	CHN	**0.995**	49	48.73	-73.84	20.66
168	(283)	Peter Malnati	USA	**0.993**	52	51.63	-24.92	44.46
169	(454)	Jamie Donaldson	WAL	**0.989**	40	39.58	-7.46	32.27
170	(972)	Brandon Wu	USA	**0.985**	40	39.41	-4.51	39.05
171	(96)	Ryan Moore	USA	**0.980**	40	39.19	-49.98	20.09
172	(242)	Min Woo Lee	AUS	**0.979**	40	39.16	-21.01	31.41
173	(169)	Bud Cauley	USA	**0.965**	45	43.43	-29.72	34.43
174	(94)	Junggon Hwang	KOR	**0.964**	40	38.55	-41.96	0.00
175	(159)	Robby Shelton IV	USA	**0.963**	52	50.06	-31.77	29.20
176	(143)	Luke List	USA	**0.961**	52	49.99	-49.81	41.05
176	(166)	Kristoffer Ventura	NOR	**0.961**	42	40.37	-21.83	23.87
178	(175)	JC Ritchie	RSA	**0.958**	40	38.31	-31.03	31.54
179	(512)	Ondrej Lieser	CZE	**0.957**	40	38.28	-8.14	33.49
180	(103)	Vaughn Taylor	USA	**0.957**	51	48.80	-44.85	17.45
181	(131)	Xinjun Zhang	CHN	**0.952**	52	49.49	-39.04	24.71
182	(238)	Dean Burmester	RSA	**0.948**	52	49.32	-32.33	44.86
183	(249)	Wil Besseling	NED	**0.947**	43	40.74	-15.10	27.75
184	(98)	Keith Mitchell	USA	**0.937**	52	48.74	-58.41	28.73
185	(132)	Brian Stuard	USA	**0.928**	52	48.27	-39.17	24.84
186	(149)	Jordan L Smith	ENG	**0.918**	50	45.90	-40.01	28.77
187	(173)	Joakim Lagergren	SWE	**0.918**	47	43.14	-27.20	24.82
188	(281)	Matthew NeSmith	USA	**0.914**	52	47.53	-18.52	38.63
189	(1394)	Marcus Armitage	ENG	**0.911**	43	39.16	-6.57	43.55
190	(266)	Austin Cook	USA	**0.910**	48	43.70	-24.64	34.52
191	(224)	Gavin Green	MAS	**0.907**	51	46.26	-31.61	38.33
192	(273)	Richard Bland	ENG	**0.905**	47	42.55	-17.62	27.07
193	(133)	Mikumu Horikawa	JPN	**0.904**	50	45.18	-36.59	18.42
194	(174)	Matthew Jordan	ENG	**0.902**	47	42.39	-19.82	25.29
194	(426)	Hudson Swafford	USA	**0.902**	40	36.08	-14.99	35.14
196	(213)	Adrian Meronk	POL	**0.900**	46	41.40	-19.16	24.59
197	(135)	Sebastian Soderberg	SWE	**0.898**	49	43.99	-35.85	17.43
198	(48)	Andrew Putnam	USA	**0.897**	50	44.82	-82.02	8.23
199	(195)	Brandon Stone	RSA	**0.894**	52	46.51	-37.08	39.30
200	(145)	Denny McCarthy	USA	**0.888**	52	46.18	-39.05	27.22

			Average Points	Events	Total Points	2020 Points Lost	2020 Points Gained
201	(112) Calum Hill	SCO	**0.883**	45	39.72	-30.17	13.97
202	(171) Brian Gay	USA	**0.881**	52	45.81	-32.33	28.28
203	(109) Guido Migliozzi	ITA	**0.878**	44	38.63	-35.26	12.33
204	(148) Ryan Fox	NZL	**0.855**	50	42.76	-47.03	32.37
205	(57) Jim Furyk	USA	**0.855**	40	34.18	-53.10	4.92
206	(223) Charl Schwartzel	RSA	**0.846**	40	33.85	-27.85	31.29
207	(188) Sebastian Heisele	GER	**0.845**	40	33.82	-17.90	15.20
208	(230) Wade Ormsby	AUS	**0.833**	47	39.13	-28.07	30.35
209	(126) Pat Perez	USA	**0.832**	46	38.25	-37.33	16.90
210	(361) Paul Barjon	FRA	**0.828**	40	33.13	-13.89	27.59
211	(129) Scott Vincent	ZIM	**0.824**	52	42.83	-39.33	14.96
212	(194) David Lipsky	USA	**0.823**	52	42.81	-35.38	33.38
213	(457) Jared Wolfe	USA	**0.822**	44	36.15	-14.58	33.44
214	(152) Andrew Johnston	ENG	**0.817**	40	32.70	-23.99	13.98
215	(226) Ross Fisher	ENG	**0.817**	45	36.77	-30.22	30.97
216	(154) Jhonattan Vegas	VEN	**0.815**	47	38.33	-39.64	24.61
217	(245) Sean Crocker	USA	**0.814**	50	40.68	-23.75	33.22
218	(945) Davis Riley	USA	**0.803**	42	33.72	-9.78	38.30
219	(147) Jason Scrivener	AUS	**0.803**	52	41.74	-34.67	18.62
219	(1107) Marc Warren	SCO	**0.803**	40	32.11	-6.77	34.22
221	(150) Ryuko Tokimatsu	JPN	**0.800**	41	32.78	-34.47	10.36
222	(345) Robert Rock	ENG	**0.799**	40	31.96	-16.91	26.96
223	(453) Hideto Tanihara	JPN	**0.796**	40	31.83	-14.72	27.33
224	(270) Tomoharu Otsuki	JPN	**0.790**	48	37.94	-20.31	24.97
225	(110) Russell Knox	SCO	**0.789**	52	41.01	-56.60	23.24
226	(291) Connor Syme	SCO	**0.785**	50	39.26	-21.04	28.69
227	(144) Matthew Southgate	ENG	**0.784**	51	39.98	-32.60	13.89
228	(822) William Gordon	USA	**0.781**	40	31.22	-7.59	32.25
229	(307) Cameron Davis	AUS	**0.779**	52	40.49	-26.60	36.69
230	(372) Patrick Rodgers	USA	**0.777**	52	40.42	-26.96	44.07
231	(179) Nicolas Colsaerts	BEL	**0.777**	52	40.40	-27.41	20.90
232	(290) Scott Jamieson	SCO	**0.773**	44	34.01	-22.59	26.79
233	(1014) Greyson Sigg	USA	**0.767**	40	30.69	-5.52	31.70
234	(430) Stephan Jaeger	GER	**0.765**	48	36.74	-17.48	33.60
235	(95) JB Holmes	USA	**0.765**	40	30.60	-57.50	15.76
236	(312) Patton Kizzire	USA	**0.748**	50	37.38	-23.31	30.06
237	(187) Ryan Armour	USA	**0.746**	52	38.80	-35.19	28.58
238	(221) Adam Schenk	USA	**0.744**	52	38.70	-28.64	27.63
239	(367) Ryosuke Kinoshita	JPN	**0.744**	40	29.74	-12.82	22.24
240	(237) Scott Brown	USA	**0.736**	52	38.29	-24.92	35.60
241	(398) Darren Fichardt	RSA	**0.730**	48	35.02	-23.31	36.59
242	(237) Steven Brown	ENG	**0.726**	52	37.77	-21.20	21.14
243	(114) Kyle Stanley	USA	**0.724**	51	36.94	-60.51	25.05
244	(136) Sanghyun Park	KOR	**0.719**	47	33.80	-42.11	11.10
245	(256) Scott Stallings	USA	**0.717**	51	36.55	-27.83	28.75
246	(160) Pablo Larrazabal	ESP	**0.716**	51	36.53	-28.66	16.47
247	(141) Mikko Korhonen	FIN	**0.715**	42	30.05	-40.27	14.62
248	(797) James Hahn	USA	**0.708**	40	28.31	-8.34	29.77
249	(74) Andrea Pavan	ITA	**0.705**	52	36.68	-60.08	0.00
250	(198) Seungsu Han	USA	**0.701**	49	34.32	-24.90	15.15

			Average Points	Events	Total Points	2020 Points Lost	2020 Points Gained
251	(227) Jack Senior	ENG	**0.677**	52	35.19	-24.78	21.02
252	(168) Chesson Hadley	USA	**0.677**	50	33.83	-38.56	23.09
253	(764) Mikael Lindberg	SWE	**0.664**	40	26.58	-7.18	25.80
254	(239) Chris Paisley	ENG	**0.659**	48	31.65	-22.73	20.35
255	(399) Richard Mansell	ENG	**0.654**	40	26.15	-10.33	19.20
256	(153) Kazuki Higa	JPN	**0.653**	47	30.68	-28.55	8.06
257	(296) Oliver Farr	WAL	**0.652**	40	26.10	-16.09	14.12
258	(232) Maverick Antcliff	AUS	**0.652**	47	30.64	-20.18	15.68
259	(401) Ross McGowan	ENG	**0.648**	52	33.72	-15.31	26.60
260	(214) Jaco Ahlers	RSA	**0.645**	42	27.10	-22.41	17.48
261	(854) Pep Angles	ESP	**0.644**	40	25.77	-5.05	24.16
262	(293) Chase Seiffert	USA	**0.639**	48	30.68	-17.87	24.56
263	(325) Johannes Veerman	USA	**0.639**	41	26.18	-17.04	20.00
264	(504) Max McGreevy	USA	**0.635**	40	25.40	-10.08	22.29
265	(374) Chris Kirk	USA	**0.635**	40	25.38	-19.01	25.41
266	(234) Hiroshi Iwata	JPN	**0.628**	40	25.12	-22.16	13.74
267	(668) Lee Hodges	USA	**0.622**	46	28.63	-9.50	29.07
268	(414) Dale Whitnell	ENG	**0.618**	40	24.70	-8.62	16.58
269	(278) Justin Walters	RSA	**0.614**	52	31.95	-19.59	18.91
270	(236) Pavit Tangkamolprasert	THA	**0.614**	42	25.79	-20.90	8.96
271	(204) Brice Garnett	USA	**0.608**	52	31.62	-31.92	20.77
272	(300) Kyoung-Hoon Lee	KOR	**0.608**	52	31.60	-25.05	23.12
273	(105) Kiradech Aphibarnrat	THA	**0.608**	48	29.16	-56.71	7.68
274	(497) David Horsey	ENG	**0.607**	45	27.32	-10.52	22.49
275	(526) Jinichiro Kozuma	JPN	**0.605**	40	24.20	-8.20	17.42
276	(673) Chad Ramey	USA	**0.598**	49	29.29	-9.46	27.55
277	(323) Jeff Winther	DEN	**0.593**	42	24.90	-18.37	17.63
278	(377) Tyler McCumber	USA	**0.589**	47	27.66	-17.35	25.26
279	(1650) Hanbyeol Kim	KOR	**0.587**	40	23.49	-1.95	24.27
280	(220) Richie Ramsay	SCO	**0.584**	46	26.85	-20.67	9.59
281	(562) Taehoon Kim	KOR	**0.582**	40	23.29	-8.36	20.11
282	(162) Yuta Ikeda	JPN	**0.580**	41	23.79	-34.40	7.22
283	(419) Niklas Lemke	SWE	**0.572**	47	26.87	-15.83	22.95
284	(505) Joseph Bramlett	USA	**0.569**	51	29.01	-16.42	28.34
285	(178) Alexander Bjork	SWE	**0.568**	45	25.56	-39.45	20.49
286	(182) Beau Hossler	USA	**0.566**	52	29.41	-37.39	20.67
287	(216) Rashid Khan	IND	**0.557**	40	22.29	-19.49	9.12
288	(231) Fabian Gomez	ARG	**0.556**	52	28.91	-21.95	12.40
289	(989) Joel Stalter	FRA	**0.555**	40	22.22	-4.65	22.16
290	(379) Trey Mullinax	USA	**0.554**	40	22.16	-15.35	17.87
291	(383) Oscar Lengden	SWE	**0.553**	45	24.89	-12.42	18.36
292	(255) Louis de Jager	RSA	**0.552**	52	28.68	-25.03	18.62
293	(595) Adrien Saddier	FRA	**0.551**	45	24.79	-10.13	21.76
294	(412) Udayan Mane	IND	**0.544**	40	21.77	-11.85	16.80
295	(295) Soomin Lee	KOR	**0.544**	42	22.84	-18.95	10.62
296	(696) Jaekyeong Lee	KOR	**0.543**	40	21.74	-4.61	17.84
297	(337) Bo Hoag	USA	**0.541**	52	28.12	-16.06	17.47
298	(790) Ben Kohles	USA	**0.540**	43	23.22	-10.90	25.80
299	(315) Phachara Khongwatmai	THA	**0.539**	40	21.56	-16.21	8.49
300	(576) Ollie Schniederjans	USA	**0.538**	50	26.88	-13.16	25.40

AGE GROUPS OF TOP 70 WORLD RANKED PLAYERS

Under 25	**25-28**	**29-32**	**33-36**	**37-40**	**Over 40**
Morikawa (7)	Rahm (2)	McIlroy (4)	D Johnson (1)	Scott (21)	Casey (24)
Hovland (14)	Thomas (3)	Hatton (10)	W Simpson (6)	Oosthuizen (22)	R Palmer (30)
Wolff (15)	DeChambeau (5)	Reed (11)	Kisner (25)	Leishman (29)	Westwood (36)
Sunjae Im (18)	Schauffele (8)	B Koepka (12)	Kokrak (26)	Rose (35)	Kuchar (37)
Scheffler (31)	Cantlay (9)	Fleetwood (17)	Lowry (33)	Na (38)	Woods (41)
Niemann (45)	Berger (13)	Finau (19)	Woodland (39)	Garcia (45)	Watson (44)
McIntyre (55)	Fitzpatrick (16)	Ancer (23)	Wiesberger (40)	Reavie (56)	Poulter (48)
Zalatoris (59)	Matsuyama (20)	English (28)	Horschell (42)		Streelman (52)
Valimaki (69)	C Smith (27)	Hughes (49)	J Day (43)		Stenson (65)
	Perez (32)	Wallace (50)	Todd (47)		Mickelson (66)
	Bezuidenhout (34)	van Rooyen (51)	Sullivan (58)		
	Conners (54)	Fowler (53)	A Long (62)		
	Munoz (60)	Henley (57)	Dahmen (64)		
	Herbert (70)	Ortiz (61)	Willett (67)		
		L Griffin (63)			
		Frittelli (30)			

SIGNIFICANT MOVES IN 2020

UPWARD

	Net Points Gain	Positional Change
Dustin Johnson (1)	216.02	+4
Collin Morikawa (7)	202.71	+58
Daniel Berger (13)	155.28	+141
Viktor Hovland (14)	133.33	+79
Tyrrell Hatton (10)	130.97	+22
Matthew Wolff (15)	129.98	+102
Harris English (28)	121.70	+155
Justin Thomas (3)	89.32	0
Bryson DeChambeau (5)	88.85	+9
Scottie Scheffler (31)	84.05	+35
Mackenzie Hughes (49)	81.76	+215
Sungjae Im (18)	75.73	+16
Will Zalatoris (59)	72.85	+613
Jon Rahm (2)	72.69	0
Christiaan Bezuidenhout (34)	72.13	+53
Jason Kokrak (26)	67.00	+36
Ryan Palmer (30)	64.43	+12
Russell Henley (57)	63.26	+159
Sami Valimaki (69)	58.04	+327
Patrick Reed (11)	52.05	+1

DOWNWARD

	Net Points Gain	Positional Change
Brooks Koepka (12)	203.66	-11
Tiger Woods (41)	154.16	-35
Francesco Molinari (112)	147.24	-94
Rory McIlroy (4)	146.06	-2
Justin Rose (35)	144.26	27
Gary Woodland (39)	101.01	-22
Tommy Fleetwood (17)	76.36	-1
Rickie Fowler (53)	75.40	-30
Henrik Stenson (65)	73.88	-39
Andrew Putnam (198)	73.79	-150
Shugo Imahira (76)	73.73	-45
Shane Lowry (33)	68.21	-14
Danny Willett (67)	65.31	-38
Rafa Cabrera Bello (102)	64.49	-61
Matt Kuchar (37)	60.19	-13

YEAR-END TOP 10s

	1968	1969	1970	1971	1972	1973
1	Nicklaus	Nicklaus	Nicklaus	Nicklaus	Nicklaus	Nicklaus
2	Palmer	Player	Player	Trevino	Player	Weiskopf
3	Casper	Casper	Casper	Player	Trevino	Trevino
4	Player	Palmer	Trevino	Palmer	Crampton	Player
5	Charles	Charles	Charles	Casper	Palmer	Crampton
6	Boros	Beard	Devlin	Barber	Jacklin	Miller
7	Coles	Archer	Coles	Crampton	Weiskopf	Oosterhuis
8	Thomson	Trevino	Jacklin	Charles	Oosterhuis	Wadkins
9	Beard	Barber	Beard	Devlin	Heard	Heard
10	Nagle	Sikes	Huggett	Weiskopf	Devlin	Brewer

	1974	1975	1976	1977	1978	1979
1	Nicklaus	Nicklaus	Nicklaus	Nicklaus	T Watson	T Watson
2	Miller	Miller	Irwin	T Watson	Nicklaus	Nicklaus
3	Player	Weiskopf	Miller	Green	Irwin	Irwin
4	Weiskopf	Irwin	Player	Irwin	Green	Trevino
5	Trevino	Player	Green	Crenshaw	Player	Player
6	M Ozaki	Green	T Watson	Marsh	Crenshaw	Aoki
7	Crampton	Trevino	Weiskopf	Player	Marsh	Green
8	Irwin	Casper	Marsh	Weiskopf	Ballesteros	Crenshaw
9	Green	Crampton	Crenshaw	Floyd	Trevino	Ballesteros
10	Heard	T Watson	Geiberger	Ballesteros	Aoki	Wadkins

	1980	1981	1982	1983	1984	1985
1	T Watson	T Watson	T Watson	Ballesteros	Ballesteros	Ballesteros
2	Trevino	Rogers	Floyd	T Watson	T Watson	Langer
3	Aoki	Aoki	Ballesteros	Floyd	Norman	Norman
4	Crenshaw	Pate	Kite	Norman	Wadkins	T Watson
5	Nicklaus	Trevino	Stadler	Kite	Langer	Nakajima
6	Pate	Ballesteros	Pate	Nicklaus	Faldo	Wadkins
7	Ballesteros	Graham	Nicklaus	Nakajima	Nakajima	O'Meara
8	Bean	Crenshaw	Rogers	Stadler	Stadler	Strange
9	Irwin	Floyd	Aoki	Aoki	Kite	Pavin
10	Player	Lietzke	Strange	Wadkins	Peete	Sutton

	1986	1987	1988	1989	1990	1991
1	Norman	Norman	Ballesteros	Norman	Norman	Woosnam
2	Langer	Ballesteros	Norman	Faldo	Faldo	Faldo
3	Ballesteros	Langer	Lyle	Ballesteros	Olazabal	Olazabal
4	Nakajima	Lyle	Faldo	Strange	Woosnam	Ballesteros
5	Bean	Strange	Strange	Stewart	Stewart	Norman
6	Tway	Woosnam	Crenshaw	Kite	Azinger	Couples
7	Sutton	Stewart	Woosnam	Olazabal	Ballesteros	Langer
8	Strange	Wadkins	Frost	Calcavecchia	Kite	Stewart
9	Stewart	McNulty	Azinger	Woosnam	McNulty	Azinger
10	O'Meara	Crenshaw	Calcavecchia	Azinger	Calcavecchia	R Davis

	1992	1993	1994	1995	1996	1997
1	Faldo	Faldo	N Price	Norman	Norman	Norman
2	Couples	Norman	Norman	N Price	Lehman	Woods
3	Woosnam	Langer	Faldo	Langer	Montgomerie	N Price
4	Olazabal	N Price	Langer	Els	Els	Els
5	Norman	Couples	Olazabal	Montgomerie	Couples	Love
6	Langer	Azinger	Els	Pavin	Faldo	Mickelson
7	Cook	Woosnam	Couples	Faldo	Mickelson	Montgomerie
8	N Price	Kite	Montgomerie	Couples	M Ozaki	M Ozaki
9	Azinger	Love	M Ozaki	M Ozaki	Love	Lehman
10	Love	Pavin	Pavin	Elkington	O'Meara	O'Meara

1998	1999	2000	2001	2002	2003
1 Woods	1 Woods	1 Woods	1 Woods	1 Woods	1 Woods
2 O'Meara	2 Duval	2 Els	2 Mickelson	2 Mickelson	2 Singh
3 Duval	**3** Montgomerie	**3** Duval	3 Duval	3 Els	3 Els
4 Love	4 Love	4 Mickelson	4 Els	4 Garcia	4 Love
5 Els	5 Els	5 Westwood	5 Love	5 Goosen	5 Furyk
6 N Price	6 Westwood	6 Montgomerie	6 Garcia	6 Toms	6 Weir
7 Montgomerie	7 Singh	7 Love	7 Toms	7 Harrington	7 Goosen
8 Westwood	8 N Price	8 Sutton	8 Singh	8 Singh	8 Harrington
9 Singh	9 Mickelson	9 Singh	9 Clarke	9 Love	9 Toms
10 Mickelson	10 O'Meara	10 Lehman	10 Goosen	10 Montgomerie	10 Perry

2004	2005	2006	2007	2008	2009
1 Singh	1 Woods	1 Woods	1 Woods	1 Woods	1 Woods
2 Woods	2 Singh	2 Furyk	2 Mickelson	2 Garcia	2 Mickelson
3 Els	3 Mickelson	3 Mickelson	3 Furyk	3 Mickelson	3 Stricker
4 Goosen	4 Goosen	4 Scott	4 Els	4 Harrington	4 Westwood
5 Mickelson	5 Els	5 Els	5 Stricker	5 Singh	5 Harrington
6 Harrington	6 Garcia	6 Goosen	6 Rose	6 R Karlsson	6 Furyk
7 Garcia	7 Furyk	7 Singh	7 Scott	7 Villegas	7 Casey
8 Weir	8 Montgomerie	8 Harrington	8 Harrington	8 Stenson	8 Stenson
9 Love	9 Scott	9 Donald	9 KJ Choi	9 Els	9 McIlroy
10 Cink	10 DiMarco	10 Ogilvy	10 Singh	10 Westwood	10 Perry

2010	2011	2012	2013	2014	2015
1 Westwood	1 Donald	1 McIlroy	1 Woods	1 McIlroy	1 Spieth
2 Woods	2 Westwood	2 Donald	2 Scott	2 Stenson	2 J Day
3 Kaymer	3 McIlroy	3 Woods	3 Stenson	3 Scott	3 McIlroy
4 Mickelson	4 Kaymer	4 Rose	4 Rose	4 B Watson	4 B Watson
5 Furyk	5 Scott	5 Scott	5 Mickelson	5 Garcia	5 Stenson
6 McDowell	6 Stricker	6 Oosthuizen	6 McIlroy	6 Rose	6 Fowler
7 Stricker	7 D Johnson	7 Westwood	7 Kuchar	7 Furyk	7 Rose
8 Casey	8 J Day	8 B Watson	8 Stricker	8 J Day	8 D Johnson
9 Donald	9 Schwartzel	9 Dufner	9 Z Johnson	9 Spieth	9 Furyk
10 McIlroy	10 W Simpson	10 Snedeker	10 Garcia	10 Fowler	10 Reed

2016	2017	2018	2019	2020
1 J Day	1 D Johnson	1 B Koepka	1 B Koepka	1 D Johnson
2 McIlroy	2 Spieth	2 Rose	2 McIlroy	2 Rahm
3 D Johnson	3 Thomas	3 D Johnson	3 Rahm	3 Thomas
4 Stenson	4 Rahm	4 Thomas	4 Thomas	4 McIlroy
5 Spieth	5 Matsuyama	5 DeChambeau	5 D Johnson	5 DeChambeau
6 Matsuyama	6 Rose	6 Rahm	6 Woods	6 W Simpson
7 Scott	7 Fowler	7 F Molinari	7 Cantlay	7 Morikawa
8 Reed	8 B Koepka	8 McIlroy	8 Rose	8 Schauffele
9 Noren	9 Stenson	9 Finau	9 Schauffele	9 Cantlay
10 B Watson	10 Garcia	10 Schauffele	10 Fleetwood	10 Hatton

Data from World of Professional Golf 1968-1985; World Ranking 1986-2020

World Money Lists

Dustin Johnson led the World Money List for the second time in his career. His on-course earnings of over $9 million took the Masters champion, who also topped the list in 2016, into the top 10 of the Career Money List.

Jin Young Ko, although playing only a limited schedule in 2020, led the women's list for the second consecutive year, while Bernhard Langer returned to the top of the Senior list for the 10th time in 13 years.

The lists are compiled from the results of all the official tournaments on the main tours featured in this book, as well as other events where reliable figures could be obtained. For events to qualify, a minimum of 36 holes and four players are required, while exhibition matches, skins games and skill contests are excluded. Annual performance bonuses such as for the FedEx Cup and the Race to Dubai are also excluded.

In more than five decades that the Men's World Money List has been compiled, the earnings of the player finishing in 200th position have risen from $3,326 in 1966 to $412,978 in 2020. The top-200 players in 1966 earned a total of $4,680,287. In 2020, the comparable total was $304,538,078.

The conversion rates used for 2020 were: Euro = US$1.22; Australian dollar = US$0.77; Japanese yen = US$0.0097; South African rand = US$0.068; Canadian dollar = US$0.78; South Korean Won = US$0.00092.

The Career World Money List, which has been led by Tiger Woods since 2000, is compiled from the regular and senior lists that have been published in all previous editions of this book, as well a table prepared for a companion book, *The Wonderful World of Professional Golf* (Atheneum, 1973). Additional records were taken from official records of major golf associations. The 50 players in this year's list have won $2,733,198,397 in their careers.

MEN'S WORLD MONEY LIST LEADERS

1966	Jack Nicklaus	USA	$168,088
1967	Jack Nicklaus	USA	276,166
1968	Billy Casper	USA	222,436
1969	Frank Beard	USA	186,993
1970	Jack Nicklaus	USA	222,583
1971	Jack Nicklaus	USA	285,897
1972	Jack Nicklaus	USA	341,792
1973	Tom Weiskopf	USA	349,645
1974	Jonny Miller	USA	400,255
1975	Jack Nicklaus	USA	332,610
1976	Jack Nicklaus	USA	316,086
1977	Tom Watson	USA	358,034
1978	Tom Watson	USA	384,388
1979	Tom Watson	USA	506,912
1980	Tom Watson	USA	651,921
1981	Johnny Miller	USA	704,204
1982	Raymond Floyd	USA	738,699
1983	Seve Ballesteros	ESP	686,088
1984	Seve Ballesteros	ESP	688,047
1985	Bernhard Langer	GER	860,262
1986	Greg Norman	AUS	1,146,584
1987	Ian Woosnam	WAL	1,793,268
1988	Seve Ballesteros	ESP	1,261,275
1989	David Frost	RSA	1,650,230
1990	Jose Maria Olazabal	ESP	1,633,640
1991	Bernhard Langer	GER	2,186,700
1992	Nick Faldo	ENG	2,748,248
1993	Nick Faldo	ENG	2,825,280
1994	Ernie Els	RSA	2,862,854
1995	Corey Pavin	USA	2,746,340
1996	Colin Montgomerie	SCO	3,071,442
1997	Colin Montgomerie	SCO	3,366,900
1998	Tiger Woods	USA	2,927,946
1999	Tiger Woods	USA	7,681,625
2000	Tiger Woods	USA	11,034,530
2001	Tiger Woods	USA	7,771,562
2002	Tiger Woods	USA	8,292,188
2003	Vijay Singh	FJI	8,499,611
2004	Vijay Singh	FJI	11,638,699
2005	Tiger Woods	USA	12,280,404
2006	Tiger Woods	USA	13,325,949
2007	Tiger Woods	USA	12,902,706
2008	Vijay Singh	FJI	8,025,128
2009	Tiger Woods	USA	10,998,054
2010	Graeme McDowell	NIR	7,371,586
2011	Luke Donald	ENG	9,730,870
2012	Rory McIlroy	NIR	11,301,228
2013	Tiger Woods	USA	9,490,217
2014	Rory McIlroy	NIR	10,526,012
2015	Jordan Spieth	USA	12,477,758
2016	Dustin Johnson	USA	9,347,352
2017	Justin Thomas	USA	10,300,894
2018	Bryson DeChambeau	USA	9,231,811
2019	Rory McIlroy	NIR	10,820,759
2020	Dustin Johnson	USA	9,385,820

2020 MEN'S WORLD MONEY LIST

1	Dustin Johnson	USA	$9,385,820
2	Justin Thomas	USA	7,273,286
3	Jon Rahm	ESP	7,263,068
4	Bryson DeChambeau	USA	7,162,185
5	Matthew Fitzpatrick	ENG	5,967,223
6	Patrick Reed	USA	5,390,264
7	Collin Morikawa	USA	5,269,713
8	Tyrrell Hatton	ENG	5,183,936
9	Webb Simpson	USA	4,990,562
10	Daniel Berger	USA	4,552,523
11	Xander Schauffele	USA	4,304,987
12	Sungjae Im	KOR	4,204,647
13	Matthew Wolff	USA	4,045,193
14	Viktor Hovland	NOR	4,010,003
15	Harris English	USA	3,955,021
16	Tony Finau	USA	3,622,167
17	Cameron Smith	AUS	3,399,296
18	Abraham Ancer	MEX	3,286,925
19	Patrick Cantlay	USA	3,273,667
20	Jason Kokrak	USA	3,270,835
21	Kevin Kisner	USA	3,048,806
22	Rory McIlroy	NIR	3,024,965
23	Hideki Matsuyama	JPN	2,972,225
24	Marc Leishman	AUS	2,950,006
25	Lee Westwood	ENG	2,939,762
26	Ryan Palmer	USA	2,828,326
27	Mackenzie Hughes	USA	2,776,709
28	Tommy Fleetwood	ENG	2,655,128
29	Kevin Streelman	USA	2,533,239
30	Louis Oosthuizen	RSA	2,372,279
31	Phil Mickelson	USA	2,359,242
32	Adam Long	USA	2,351,748
33	Bubba Watson	USA	2,326,886
34	Billy Horschel	USA	2,277,447
35	Scottie Scheffler	USA	2,262,228
36	Jason Day	AUS	2,217,629
37	Matt Kuchar	USA	2,162,627
38	Joaquin Niemann	CHI	2,146,032
39	Sergio Garcia	ESP	2,142,921
40	Russell Henley	USA	2,129,249
41	Adam Scott	AUS	2,102,862
42	Lanto Griffin	USA	2,056,135
43	Joel Dahmen	USA	2,022,207
44	Carlos Ortiz	MEX	1,984,316
45	Paul Casey	ENG	1,930,261
46	Brooks Koepka	USA	1,914,703
47	Andrew Landry	USA	1,839,365
48	Victor Perez	FRA	1,828,711
49	Talor Gooch	USA	1,806,030
50	Kevin Na	USA	1,787,367
51	Stewart Cink	USA	1,723,364
52	Corey Conners	CAN	1,715,531
53	Brendan Steele	USA	1,696,962
54	Sebastian Munoz	COL	1,696,497
55	Michael Thompson	USA	1,688,771
56	Nick Taylor	USA	1,684,287
57	Brendon Todd	USA	1,668,338
58	Tom Hoge	USA	1,647,798
59	Ian Poulter	ENG	1,633,375
60	Max Homa	USA	1,584,383
61	Aaron Rai	ENG	1,557,908
62	Harry Higgs	USA	1,539,023
63	Christiaan Bezuidenhout	RSA	1,524,761
64	Dylan Frittelli	RSA	1,515,943
65	Martin Laird	SCO	1,484,336
66	Cameron Champ	USA	1,472,433
67	Peter Malnati	USA	1,467,009
68	JT Poston	USA	1,446,154
69	Sung Kang	KOR	1,443,159
70	Alex Noren	SWE	1,419,432
71	Maverick McNealy	USA	1,415,543
72	Jim Herman	USA	1,405,321
73	Robert Streb	USA	1,397,061
74	Chez Reavie	USA	1,379,023
75	Doc Redman	USA	1,357,587
76	Si Woo Kim	KOR	1,357,525
77	Richy Werenski	USA	1,353,026
78	Sepp Straka	AUT	1,347,324
79	Gary Woodland	USA	1,298,661
80	Matt Wallace	ENG	1,292,281
81	Graeme McDowell	NIR	1,290,528
82	Will Zalatoris	USA	1,282,226
83	Zach Johnson	USA	1,277,397
84	Justin Rose	ENG	1,276,977
85	Aaron Wise	USA	1,242,104
86	Shane Lowry	IRE	1,227,311
87	Sam Burns	USA	1,226,679
88	Brian Harman	USA	1,225,622
89	Charley Hoffman	USA	1,220,622
90	Lucas Herbert	AUS	1,210,577
91	Henrik Norlander	SWE	1,175,146
92	Patrick Rodgers	USA	1,164,487
93	Tom Lewis	ENG	1,157,144
94	Wyndham Clark	USA	1,148,483
95	Cameron Tringale	USA	1,128,384
96	Emiliano Grillo	ARG	1,128,073
97	Rickie Fowler	USA	1,125,506
98	Byeong Hun An	KOR	1,121,618
99	Andy Sullivan	ENG	1,095,641
100	Harold Varner III	USA	1,088,755
101	Cameron Davis	AUS	1,076,876
102	Hudson Swafford	USA	1,043,143
103	Troy Merritt	USA	1,031,338
104	Rory Sabbatini	SVK	1,008,965
105	Mark Hubbard	USA	989,595
106	Matthew NeSmith	USA	987,260
107	Sami Valimaki	FIN	973,821
108	Keegan Bradley	USA	971,052

109	Scott Piercy	USA	950,068
110	Brandt Snedeker	USA	929,996
111	Lucas Glover	USA	901,399
112	Matt Jones	AUS	888,121
113	Jordan Spieth	USA	885,513
114	Branden Grace	RSA	883,694
115	Charl Schwartzel	RSA	866,493
116	Nate Lashley	USA	856,287
117	Erik van Rooyen	RSA	855,798
118	Austin Cook	USA	844,798
119	Scott Brown	USA	835,140
120	Brian Gay	USA	826,520
121	Tyler McCumber	USA	819,811
122	Denny McCarthy	USA	816,057
123	James Hahn	USA	814,305
124	Bernd Wiesberger	AUT	805,467
125	Bud Cauley	USA	795,657
126	Robby Shelton	USA	786,400
127	Charles Howell III	USA	780,265
128	Danny Willett	ENG	779,637
129	Tyler Duncan	USA	776,627
130	Luke List	USA	765,632
131	Martin Kaymer	GER	761,946
132	Scott Stallings	USA	761,069
133	Patton Kizzire	USA	759,154
134	Rafa Cabrera Bello	ESP	757,541
135	Danny Lee	NZL	755,651
136	Thomas Detry	BEL	743,502
137	Keith Mitchell	USA	739,379
138	Ryan Armour	USA	736,446
139	Xinjun Zhang	CHN	733,247
140	Adam Hadwin	CAN	722,740
141	Renato Paratore	ITA	699,055
142	Brian Stuard	USA	696,461
143	Robert MacIntyre	SCO	691,953
144	Russell Knox	SCO	680,469
145	Kristoffer Ventura	NOR	678,803
146	Will Gordon	USA	678,073
147	Cheng Tsung Pan	TPE	669,005
148	Robert Rock	ENG	631,937
149	Kyle Stanley	USA	631,193
150	Adam Schenk	USA	613,755
151	John Catlin	USA	609,780
152	Brandon Stone	RSA	600,949
153	Jorge Campillo	ESP	599,294
154	Sam Horsfield	ENG	591,822
155	Adri Arnaus	ESP	590,471
156	Laurie Canter	ENG	585,045
157	Rasmus Hojgaard	DEN	584,701
158	Adrian Otaegui	ESP	583,025
159	Masahiro Kawamura	JPN	569,246
160	Chesson Hadley	USA	568,317
161	Chase Seiffert	USA	558,591
162	Ross Fisher	ENG	556,213
163	Kyoung-Hoon Lee	KOR	555,479
164	Jhonattan Vegas	VEN	555,324
165	Gavin Green	MAS	552,659
166	Beau Hossler	USA	551,523
167	Thomas Pieters	BEL	550,510
168	Bo Hoag	USA	533,872
169	Ryan Moore	USA	530,784
170	Marc Warren	SCO	529,565
171	Dean Burmester	RSA	526,398
172	Sam Ryder	USA	522,141
173	Kalle Samooja	FIN	513,395
174	Joachim B Hansen	SWE	511,759
175	Matthias Schwab	AUT	509,588
176	George Coetzee	RSA	493,009
177	Marcus Kinhult	SWE	489,390
178	Brice Garnett	USA	489,357
179	Eddie Pepperell	ENG	484,636
180	Joseph Bramlett	USA	479,164
181	Shaun Norris	RSA	477,793
182	Jordan Smith	ENG	477,271
183	Doug Ghim	USA	474,131
184	JB Holmes	USA	472,996
185	Sean Crocker	USA	466,552
186	Pat Perez	USA	464,080
187	Antoine Rozner	FRA	462,993
188	Michael Gligic	CAN	444,514
189	Tiger Woods	USA	439,238
190	Scott Jamieson	SCO	437,339
191	Garrick Higgo	RSA	437,040
192	Romain Langasque	FRA	433,855
193	Callum Shinkwin	ENG	433,466
194	Vaughn Taylor	USA	431,848
195	Rob Oppenheim	USA	431,302
196	Wilco Nienaber	RSA	427,749
197	Ollie Schniederjans	USA	424,992
198	Steve Stricker	USA	422,082
199	Taylor Pendrith	CAN	415,910
200	Josh Teater	USA	412,978
201	Rikuya Hoshino	JPN	411,750
202	John Huh	USA	409,494
203	Chan Kim	USA	405,094
204	Haotong Li	CHN	404,149
205	Sebastian Cappelen	DEN	402,649
206	Marcus Armitage	ENG	393,982
207	Yuki Inamori	JPN	393,183
208	Stephan Jaeger	GER	390,506
209	Wade Ormsby	AUS	386,440
210	Chris Kirk	USA	384,419
211	Brandon Wu	USA	382,567
212	Takumi Kanaya	JPN	379,544
213	Joost Luiten	NED	375,448
214	Ryan Fox	NZL	373,136
215	Camilo Villegas	COL	371,379
216	David Lipsky	USA	362,802

217	Ted Potter Jr	USA	361,540	273	Ben Martin	USA	252,393
218	JJ Spaun	USA	360,637	274	Chad Ramey	USA	249,659
219	Hank Lebioda	USA	358,320	275	Tomoharu Otsuki	JPN	249,360
220	Jason Dufner	USA	357,590	276	Mark Anderson	USA	248,810
221	Grant Forrest	SCO	354,412	277	Niklas Lemke	SWE	248,556
222	Matthieu Pavon	FRA	353,171	278	Guillermo Mito Pereira	CHI	248,404
223	Vincent Whaley	USA	352,235	279	Ryo Ishikawa	JPN	244,437
224	Jamie Donaldson	WAL	352,016	280	Ryosuke Kinoshita	JPN	242,683
225	Brandon Hagy	USA	351,952	281	Richie Ramsay	SCO	242,257
226	Justin Harding	RSA	347,696	282	Adrien Saddier	FRA	241,206
227	Sean O'Hair	USA	346,883	283	Jeunghun Wang	KOR	240,945
228	Fabian Gomez	ARG	344,787	284	Ashun Wu	CHN	240,038
229	David Horsey	ENG	337,588	285	Henrik Stenson	SWE	239,502
230	Seamus Power	IRE	335,231	286	Scott Harrington	USA	237,591
231	Davis Riley	USA	333,615	287	Justin Walters	RSA	235,881
232	Joakim Lagergren	SWE	326,864	288	Mikumu Horikawa	JPN	234,778
233	Min Woo Lee	AUS	323,922	289	Brad Kennedy	AUS	234,506
234	Andrew Putnam	USA	322,905	290	Nick Watney	USA	233,397
235	Kevin Tway	USA	321,704	291	Peter Uihlein	USA	232,239
236	Alexander Bjork	SWE	318,454	292	Grayson Murray	USA	228,600
237	Justin Suh	USA	317,658	293	Luke Donald	ENG	227,181
238	Wesley Bryan	USA	317,112	294	Taehee Lee	KOR	225,436
239	Kurt Kitayama	USA	315,151	295	Bronson Burgoon	USA	223,184
240	Anirban Lahiri	IND	313,674	296	Sebastian Heisele	GER	222,542
241	Victor Dubuisson	FRA	312,906	297	Ross McGowan	ENG	222,407
242	Padraig Harrington	IRE	312,902	298	Paul Barjon	FRA	221,216
243	Lee Hodges	USA	304,646	299	MJ Daffue	RSA	220,752
244	Connor Syme	SCO	304,416	300	Ben Kohles	USA	219,737
245	Jared Wolfe	USA	303,547	301	Kevin Chappell	USA	218,671
246	Cameron Percy	AUS	302,648	302	Mikko Korhonen	FIN	217,811
247	Tim Wilkinson	NZL	299,753	303	DJ Trahan	USA	207,562
248	Kramer Hickok	USA	299,637	304	Johannes Veerman	USA	206,819
249	Zac Blair	USA	298,431	305	Curtis Thompson	USA	206,470
250	Nicolas Colsaerts	BEL	289,845	306	Kiradech Aphibarnrat	THA	205,575
251	Scott Hend	AUS	288,269	307	Jason Scrivener	AUS	205,456
252	Jimmy Walker	USA	287,110	308	Maverick Antcliff	AUS	204,928
253	Pablo Larrazabal	ESP	286,012	309	Curtis Luck	AUS	203,047
254	Mike Lorenzo-Vera	FRA	283,014	310	Paul Waring	ENG	200,155
255	Richard Bland	ENG	280,387	311	Chris Paisley	ENG	199,666
256	Steven Brown	ENG	279,653	312	Ryan Brehm	USA	197,304
257	Jeff Winther	DEN	279,101	313	Nick Hardy	USA	196,948
258	David Drysdale	SCO	278,951	314	Max McGreevy	USA	194,411
259	David Hearn	CAN	277,260	315	Brett Drewitt	AUS	193,400
260	Jack Senior	ENG	275,195	316	Shugo Imahira	JPN	190,703
261	Greyson Sigg	USA	274,402	317	Dylan Wu	USA	190,007
262	Roger Sloan	CAN	273,886	318	Seth Reeves	USA	189,688
263	Hanbyeol Kim	KOR	272,575	319	Sebastian Soderberg	SWE	188,595
264	Jazz Janewattananond	THA	272,571	320	Dan McCarthy	USA	186,565
265	Matthew Jordan	ENG	271,709	321	Dawie van der Walt	RSA	185,913
266	Adrian Meronk	POL	269,796	322	Jack Singh Brar	ENG	185,895
267	Wil Besseling	NED	267,685	323	Akshay Bhatia	USA	185,557
268	Jinichiro Kozuma	JPN	265,724	324	Jonathan Byrd	USA	183,355
269	Hideto Tanihara	JPN	264,175	325	David Kocher	USA	183,078
270	Matthew Southgate	ENG	262,743	326	Aaron Baddeley	AUS	182,423
271	Benjamin Hebert	FRA	258,007	327	Dale Whitnell	ENG	180,909
272	Chris Baker	USA	256,918	328	Andrew Johnston	ENG	180,887

329	James Morrison	ENG	180,233	365	Zecheng Dou	CAN	145,971
330	Trevor Simsby	USA	180,000	366	Oliver Farr	WAL	145,452
331	Richard T Lee	CAN	178,185	367	Nacho Elvira	ESP	143,620
332	Francesco Laporta	ITA	177,612	368	Nicholas Lindheim	USA	143,240
333	Seungyul Noh	KOR	175,878	369	Ondrej Lieser	CZE	142,268
334	Taylor Montgomery	USA	174,457	370	Soren Kjeldsen	DEN	141,905
335	Alexander Levy	FRA	174,373	371	Louis de Jager	RSA	140,173
336	Brad Hopfinger	USA	172,858	372	Edoardo Molinari	ITA	137,417
337	Hiroshi Iwata	JPN	168,489	373	Robin Sciot-Siegrist	FRA	137,064
338	Joel Stalter	FRA	168,212	374	Craig Howie	SCO	136,948
339	Shubhankar Sharma	IND	167,970	375	Erik Barnes	USA	136,616
340	Tommy Gainey	USA	167,465	376	Sebastian Garcia Rodriguez	ESP	135,791
341	Scott Vincent	USA	165,493	377	Oscar Lengden	SWE	134,703
342	Roberto Diaz	MEX	165,349	378	Rhein Gibson	AUS	131,438
343	Jonathan Caldwell	NIR	165,269	379	Vince India	USA	131,380
344	Lorenzo Gagli	ITA	165,163	380	Theo Humphrey	USA	130,995
345	Calum Hill	SCO	165,157	381	Jamie Lovemark	USA	127,284
346	John Chin	USA	164,922	382	Alejandro Canizares	ESP	127,110
347	Joohyung Kim	KOR	163,830	383	Alex Smalley	USA	126,156
348	Trey Mullinax	USA	163,103	384	Thorbjorn Olesen	DEN	126,008
349	Fabrizio Zanotti	PRY	163,026	385	Ewen Ferguson	SCO	125,688
350	Gunn Charoenkul	THA	162,003	386	Clement Sordet	FRA	123,519
351	Julien Guerrier	FRA	161,528	387	Ryuko Tokimatsu	JPN	122,277
352	Justin Lower	USA	160,927	388	Callum Tarren	ENG	121,995
353	Brandon Harkins	USA	160,792	389	Cameron Young	USA	121,814
354	Andrew Novak	USA	160,302	390	Paul Haley II	USA	121,626
355	Jimmy Stanger	USA	157,701	391	Zander Lombard	RSA	120,984
356	Wes Roach	USA	157,666	392	Oliver Fisher	ENG	120,898
357	Aaron Cockerill	CAN	156,382	393	Pep Angles	ESP	120,620
358	Hirotaro Naito	JPN	156,213	394	Rikard Karlberg	SWE	118,607
359	Kyle Jones	USA	154,946	395	Darren Fichardt	RSA	118,006
360	Francesco Molinari	ITA	152,850	396	Augusto Nunez	ARG	117,602
361	Marcel Schneider	GER	151,003	397	Satoshi Kodaira	JPN	117,551
362	JC Ritchie	RSA	150,624	398	Sangmoon Bae	KOR	116,564
363	Evan Harmeling	USA	148,859	399	Yuwa Kosaihira	JPN	116,093
364	Jayden Schaper	RSA	148,170	400	Carl Yuan	CHN	115,824

WOMEN'S WORLD MONEY LIST LEADERS

1989	Betsy King	USA	$675,964	2005	Annika Sorenstam	SWE	2,756,540
1990	Beth Daniel	USA	963,578	2006	Lorena Ochoa	MEX	2,656,310
1991	Pat Bradley	USA	763,118	2007	Lorena Ochoa	MEX	4,364,994
1992	Dottie Mochrie (Pepper)	USA	819,895	2008	Lorena Ochoa	MEX	2,763,193
1993	Mayumi Hirase	JPN	757,712	2009	Jiyai Shin	KOR	2,179,908
1994	Laura Davies	ENG	1,006,143	2010	Jiyai Shin	KOR	2,150,256
1995	Annika Sorenstam	SWE	1,043,121	2011	Yani Tseng	TPE	3,806,713
1996	Laura Davies	ENG	1,383,003	2012	Inbee Park	KOR	3,185,020
1997	Annika Sorenstam	SWE	1,460,252	2013	Inbee Park	KOR	2,508,811
1998	Annika Sorenstam	SWE	1,170,898	2014	Stacy Lewis	USA	2,574,039
1999	Karrie Webb	AUS	1,641,959	2015	Lydia Ko	NZL	2,859,771
2000	Karrie Webb	AUS	2,111,213	2016	Ariya Jutanugarn	THA	2,583,428
2001	Annika Sorenstam	SWE	2,105,868	2017	Sung Hyun Park	KOR	2,346,664
2002	Annika Sorenstam	SWE	2,997,812	2018	Ariya Jutanugarn	THA	2,791,449
2003	Annika Sorenstam	SWE	2,159,050	2019	Jin Young Ko	KOR	3,126,955
2004	Annika Sorenstam	SWE	2,746,824	2020	Jin Young Ko	KOR	1,911,762

2020 WOMEN'S WORLD MONEY LIST

1	Jin Young Ko	KOR	$1,911,762
2	Sei Young Kim	KOR	1,473,934
3	Inbee Park	KOR	1,385,297
4	A Lim Kim	KOR	1,172,348
5	Yuka Saso	PHI	1,006,596
6	Nasa Hataoka	JPN	947,716
7	Danielle Kang	USA	897,872
8	Ayaka Furue	JPN	876,965
9	Sophia Popov	GER	822,803
10	Austin Ernst	USA	771,092
11	Amy Olson	USA	763,832
12	Hyo Joo Kim	KOR	732,421
13	Minjee Lee	AUS	724,273
14	Erika Hara	JPN	685,291
15	Lydia Ko	NZL	684,018
16	Hae Ran Ryu	KOR	674,103
17	Brooke M Henderson	CAN	648,604
18	Hye Jin Choi	KOR	637,620
19	Ally Ewing (McDonald)	USA	629,772
20	So Yeon Ryu	KOR	623,228
21	Sakura Koiwai	JPN	609,361
22	Anna Nordqvist	SWE	595,855
23	Jasmine Suwannapura	THA	587,829
24	Angela Stanford	USA	586,321
25	Ayaka Watanabe	JPN	583,913
26	Nelly Korda	USA	575,894
27	Ha Na Jang	KOR	573,792
28	Na Rin An	KOR	569,695
29	Georgia Hall	ENG	551,713
30	Moriya Jutanugarn	THA	551,475
31	Min Ji Park	KOR	545,175
32	Emily Kristine Pedersen	DEN	533,982
33	Jeongeun Lee[6]	KOR	533,240
34	Mirim Lee	KOR	523,690
35	Stacy Lewis	USA	513,863
36	Madelene Sagstrom	SWE	492,083
37	Hyun Kyung Park	KOR	486,139
38	Hee Jeong Lim	KOR	483,355
39	Saki Nagamine	JPN	483,247
40	Carlota Ciganda	ESP	477,707
41	Hinako Shibuno	JPN	473,592
42	Seon Woo Bae	KOR	472,368
43	Jiyai Shin	KOR	465,224
44	Yuna Nishimura	JPN	464,766
45	Hannah Green	AUS	442,843
46	Mel Reid	ENG	441,415
47	Ashleigh Buhai	RSA	429,628
48	Yealimi Noh	USA	418,959
49	Celine Boutier	FRA	410,962
50	Lexi Thompson	USA	404,237
51	Jennifer Song	USA	393,883
52	Momoko Ueda	JPN	391,187
53	Jennifer Kupcho	USA	381,160
54	So Young Lee	KOR	378,017
55	Megan Khang	USA	377,242
56	Min Young Lee[2]	KOR	372,278
57	Gaby Lopez	MEX	371,650
58	So Mi Lee	KOR	369,382
59	Ariya Jutanugarn	THA	368,414
60	Jodi Ewart Shadoff	ENG	356,618
61	Ai Suzuki	JPN	356,367
62	Da Yeon Lee	KOR	353,857
63	Mina Harigae	USA	327,376
64	Charley Hull	ENG	318,987
65	Miki Sakai	JPN	312,303
66	Caroline Masson	GER	311,905
67	Cheyenne Knight	USA	306,519
68	In Gee Chun	KOR	301,686
69	Katherine Kirk	AUS	295,584
70	Linnea Strom	SWE	292,312
71	Mone Inami	JPN	287,412
72	Perrine Delacour	FRA	260,737
73	Ji Yeong Kim[2]	KOR	257,575
74	Na-Ri Lee	KOR	253,222
75	Cydney Clanton	USA	253,035
76	Ayako Kimura	JPN	250,594
77	Yu Liu	CHN	250,472
78	Jenny Shin	KOR	248,596
79	Sayaka Takahashi	JPN	247,547
80	Jessica Korda	USA	246,578
81	Cristie Kerr	USA	243,576
82	Andrea Lee	USA	242,944
83	Kana Mikashima	JPN	239,040
84	Lindsey Weaver	USA	237,952
85	Ji-Hee Lee	KOR	234,574
86	Song Yi Ahn	KOR	232,979
87	Pernilla Lindberg	SWE	229,189
88	Brittany Altomare	USA	228,702
89	Marina Alex	USA	225,882
90	Hee Young Park	KOR	224,002
91	Kelly Tan	MAS	223,397
92	Stephanie Meadow	IRE	222,733
93	Mamiko Higa	JPN	222,237
94	Xiyu Lin	CHN	220,677
95	Mi-Jeong Jeon	KOR	215,100
96	Kristen Gillman	USA	215,042
97	Brittany Lincicome	USA	206,124
98	Azahara Munoz	EPS	205,120
99	Hikari Tanabe	JPN	204,383
100	Bianca Pagdanganan	PHI	203,775
101	Saiki Fujita	JPN	202,468
102	Min Sun Kim[5]	KOR	202,040
103	Mayu Hamada	JPN	201,779
104	Sarah Schmelzel	USA	198,601
105	Da Been Heo	KOR	197,234
106	Maiko Wakabayashi	JPN	196,365
107	Sumika Nakasone	JPN	193,731
108	Mizuki Tanaka	JPN	192,291

109	Lizette Salas	USA	192,024
110	Mi Hyang Lee	KOR	190,083
111	Eri Okayama	JPN	189,848
112	Yui Kawamoto	JPN	189,169
113	Leona Maguire	IRE	188,752
114	Ji Hyun Oh	KOR	187,107
115	Erika Kikuchi	JPN	184,384
116	Anne van Dam	NED	183,484
117	Minami Hiruta	JPN	181,274
118	Mao Nozawa	JPN	179,601
119	Han Sol Ji	KOR	177,764
120	Shina Kanazawa	JPN	175,776
121	Chie Arimura	JPN	175,243
122	Saki Asai	JPN	173,736
123	Mao Saigo	JPN	171,668
124	Amy Yang	KOR	171,438
125	Momoko Osato	JPN	167,321
126	Christina Kim	USA	167,125
127	Ji Hyun Kim	KOR	166,803
128	Woo Jeong Kim	KOR	165,343
129	Nanna Koerstz Madsen	DEN	162,108
130	Lala Anai	JPN	159,283
131	Minami Katsu	JPN	158,425
132	Alena Sharp	CAN	158,084
133	Jung Min Lee	KOR	157,499
134	Pei-Ying Tsai	TPE	154,455
135	Bo Ah Kim	KOR	154,022
136	Lauren Stephenson	USA	153,018
137	Chae Yoon Park	KOR	146,659
138	Emma Talley	USA	146,423
139	Maria Fassi	MEX	145,766
140	So Yi Kim	KOR	144,237
141	Mi Jung Hur	KOR	143,941
142	Min Kyung Choi	KOR	143,680
143	Shiho Oyama	JPN	142,992
144	Jin Seon Han	KOR	142,221
145	Ye Rim Choi	KOR	138,531
146	Yu Jin Sung	KOR	135,810
147	Manon De Roey	BEL	135,801
148	Julie Kim	KOR	135,122
149	Maria Fernanda Torres	PUR	134,799
150	U Ree Jun	KOR	134,687
151	A Yean Cho	KOR	134,350
152	Chella Choi	KOR	134,194
153	Ji Sun Kang	KOR	130,269
154	Mika Miyazato	JPN	128,708
155	Eun-Hee Ji	KOR	127,651
156	Se Lin Hyun	KOR	125,682
157	Hae Rym Kim	KOR	122,343
158	Ju Young Pak	KOR	121,593
159	Hiroko Azuma	JPN	121,274
160	Robynn Ree	USA	120,354
161	Annie Park	USA	118,543
162	Brittany Lang	USA	117,129
163	Hee-Kyung Bae	KOR	116,365
164	Chae-Young Yoon	KOR	114,705
165	Eun Woo Choi	KOR	113,005
166	Matilda Castren	FIN	112,105
167	Hye Lim Jo	KOR	111,384
168	Elizabeth Szokol	USA	110,873
169	Caroline Hedwall	SWE	110,808
170	Ga Young Lee	KOR	110,554
171	Julia Engstrom	SWE	110,394
172	Angel Yin	USA	106,122
173	Bronte Law	ENG	105,803
174	Jeong Mee Hwang	KOR	105,300
175	Sung Hyun Park	KOR	104,115
176	Ji Su Kim	KOR	102,560
177	Ju Yeon In	KOR	100,068
178	Su Yeon Jang	KOR	99,972
179	Ji Young Park	KOR	98,321
180	Yun Ji Jeong	KOR	97,809
181	Ashleigh Buhai	RSA	97,782
182	Su Oh	AUS	97,479
183	Laura Fuenfstueck	GER	96,805
184	Gyeol Park	KOR	96,793
185	Sanna Nuutinen	FIN	96,693
186	Hyo Rin Lee	KOR	96,681
187	Rumi Yoshiba	JPN	96,575
188	Nuria Iturrioz	ESP	95,455
189	Teresa Lu	TPE	95,409
190	Ritsuko Ryu	JPN	94,426
191	Yuting Seki	JPN	92,343
192	Seung Hui Ro	KOR	91,554
193	Mariah Stackhouse	USA	89,463
194	Kana Nagai	JPN	89,339
195	Ree An Kim	KOR	88,868
196	Lindy Duncan	USA	88,492
197	Serena Aoki	JPN	88,109
198	Miyuu Yamashita	JPN	87,586
199	Haru Nomura	JPN	87,092
200	Mami Fukuda	JPN	87,040

2020 SENIOR WORLD MONEY LIST

1	Bernhard Langer	GER	$1,627,854
2	Ernie Els	RSA	1,500,269
3	Kevin Sutherland	USA	1,226,807
4	Miguel Angel Jimenez	ESP	1,197,292
5	Jim Furyk	USA	1,056,022
6	Scott Parel	USA	1,031,908
7	Jerry Kelly	USA	980,978
8	Robert Karlsson	SWE	881,115
9	Woody Austin	USA	876,401
10	Retief Goosen	RSA	775,224
11	Brett Quigley	USA	749,516
12	Fred Couples	USA	689,933
13	Glen Day	USA	655,945
14	Rod Pampling	USA	643,569
15	Darren Clarke	NIR	616,932
16	Paul Broadhurst	ENG	612,436
17	Colin Montgomerie	SCO	606,090
18	Wes Short Jr	USA	546,514
19	Shane Bertsch	USA	541,929
20	Mike Weir	CAN	540,377
21	Vijay Singh	FJI	532,861
22	Kenny Perry	USA	524,180
23	Tim Petrovic	USA	521,655
24	Steve Flesch	USA	500,708
25	Gene Sauers	USA	492,634
26	Brandt Jobe	USA	477,168
27	Doug Barron	USA	470,609
28	Steve Stricker	USA	452,617
29	David Toms	USA	406,877
30	Kirk Triplett	USA	359,885
31	KJ Choi	KOR	358,446
32	Tom Lehman	USA	357,992
33	Marco Dawson	USA	356,879
34	Kent Jones	USA	338,097
35	Stephen Leaney	AUS	319,414
36	Paul Goydos	USA	306,112
37	Chris DiMarco	USA	299,532
38	Jeff Maggert	USA	297,479
39	Bob Estes	USA	291,544
40	Scott McCarron	USA	290,322
41	Rocco Mediate	USA	276,336
42	Stephen Ames	CAN	258,643
43	Tom Byrum	USA	256,756
44	Ken Duke	USA	247,661
45	Mark O'Meara	USA	243,739
46	Joe Durant	USA	235,380
47	Scott Dunlap	USA	234,576
48	David McKenzie	AUS	227,357
49	Tim Herron	USA	224,292
50	Lee Janzen	USA	222,561
51	Duffy Waldorf	USA	222,013
52	Dicky Pride	USA	206,627
53	John Daly	USA	205,110
54	Jay Haas	USA	202,740
55	Jesper Parnevik	SWE	193,557
56	Akira Teranishi	JPN	184,297
57	Ken Tanigawa	JPN	183,555
58	Norio Shinozaki	JPN	179,273
59	Dudley Hart	USA	178,262
60	Hiroo Okamo	JPN	175,956
61	Scott Verplank	USA	174,485
62	Jose Maria Olazabal	ESP	169,696
63	Cameron Beckman	USA	161,218
64	Billy Mayfair	USA	152,550
65	Eiji Mizoguchi	JPN	149,218
66	Toru Suzuki	JPN	146,225
67	Corey Pavin	USA	139,053
68	Fred Funk	USA	130,000
69	Larry Mize	USA	129,690
70	John Huston	USA	126,368
71	Billy Andrade	USA	124,048
72	Masayoshi Nakayama	JPN	118,364
73	Mark Calcavecchia	USA	115,032
74	Tom Gillis	USA	110,205
75	Tom Pernice Jr	USA	106,391
76	Michael Allen	USA	105,061
77	Steve Pate	USA	99,390
78	Yoshinobu Tsukada	JPN	98,600
79	Masayuki Kawamura	JPN	97,642
80	Jeff Sluman	USA	97,636
81	Gregory Meyer	USA	92,148
82	Keiichiro Fukabori	JPN	89,087
83	Taichi Teshima	JPN	85,452
84	Yoichi Shimizu	JPN	84,163
85	Ryoken Kawagishi	JPN	83,677
86	Mark Brooks	USA	81,977
87	Joey Sindelar	USA	81,889
88	Olin Browne	USA	81,718
89	Carlos Franco	PRY	78,337
90	Yoshinori Mizumaki	JPN	75,037
91	Tom Kite	USA	72,294
92	Willie Wood	USA	71,619
93	David Frost	RSA	71,303
94	David Morland IV	USA	69,200
95	Shinsuke Yanagisawa	JPN	68,481
96	Robin Byrd	USA	65,256
97	Masayoshi Yamazoe	JPN	64,718
98	Kiyoshi Murota	JPN	64,259
99	Tsukasa Watanabe	JPN	56,242
100	Lee Trevino	USA	53,625

CAREER WORLD MONEY LIST

1	Tiger Woods	USA	$145,114,169
2	Phil Mickelson	USA	100,943,938
3	Ernie Els	RSA	90,720,838
4	Vijay Singh	FJI	90,097,342
5	Jim Furyk	USA	84,240,636
6	Rory McIlroy	NIR	79,457,342
7	Justin Rose	ENG	77,600,941
8	Sergio Garcia	ESP	77,142,465
9	Dustin Johnson	USA	74,475,334
10	Adam Scott	AUS	69,272,709
11	Lee Westwood	ENG	65,779,698
12	Bernhard Langer	GER	62,885,758
13	Matt Kuchar	USA	59,307,818
14	Retief Goosen	RSA	56,682,734
15	Padraig Harrington	IRE	56,106,317
16	Luke Donald	ENG	55,682,144
17	Davis Love	USA	55,550,059
18	Paul Casey	ENG	53,560,457
19	Steve Stricker	USA	53,274,860
20	Colin Montgomerie	SCO	53,060,694
21	Ian Poulter	ENG	52,467,416
22	Zach Johnson	USA	51,912,637
23	Jason Day	AUS	51,244,189
24	David Toms	USA	49,386,220
25	Kenny Perry	USA	48,160,533
26	Bubba Watson	USA	46,167,831
27	Graeme McDowell	NIR	45,928,679
28	Fred Couples	USA	45,058,159
29	Rickie Fowler	USA	44,836,805
30	Jordan Spieth	USA	44,008,953
31	Stewart Cink	USA	43,896,572
32	Henrik Stenson	SWE	43,497,895
33	Miguel Angel Jimenez	ESP	43,388,699
34	Webb Simpson	USA	43,149,994
35	Charles Howell III	USA	42,457,243
36	Tom Lehman	USA	40,384,888
37	Rory Sabbatini	SVK	39,127,242
38	KJ Choi	KOR	38,535,684
39	Jerry Kelly	USA	38,426,121
40	Francisco Molinari	ITA	38,101,684
41	Nick Price	ZIM	37,899,403
42	Hale Irwin	USA	37,815,229
43	Justin Leonard	USA	37,534,807
44	Mark Calcavecchia	USA	37,468,478
45	Jay Haas	USA	37,187,391
46	Patrick Reed	USA	37,132,534
47	Robert Allenby	AUS	36,974,182
48	Justin Thomas	USA	36,802,185
49	Fred Funk	USA	36,750,433
50	Louis Oosthuizen	RSA	36,558,958

World's Winners of 2020

PGA TOUR

Sentry Tournament of Champions	Justin Thomas
Sony Open	Cameron Smith
The American Express	Andrew Landry
Farmers Insurance Open	Marc Leishman
Waste Management Phoenix Open	Webb Simpson
AT&T Pebble Beach Pro-Am	Nick Taylor
Genesis Invitational	Adam Scott
WGC Mexico Championship	Patrick Reed
Puerto Rico Open	Viktor Hovland
Honda Classic	Sungjae Im
Arnold Palmer Invitational	Tyrrell Hatton
Charles Schwab Challenge	Daniel Berger
RBC Heritage	Webb Simpson
Travelers Championship	Dustin Johnson
Rocket Mortgage Classic	Bryson DeChambeau
Workday Charity Open	Collin Morikawa
Memorial Tournament	Jon Rahm
3M Open	Michael Thompson
WGC FedEx St Jude Invitational	Justin Thomas
Barracuda Championship	Richy Werenski
PGA Championship	Collin Morikawa
Wyndham Championship	Jim Herman
The Northern Trust	Dustin Johnson
BMW Championship	Jon Rahm
Tour Championship	Dustin Johnson
Safeway Open	Stewart Cink
US Open Championship	Bryson DeChambeau
Corales Puntacana Resort Championship	Hudson Swafford
Sanderson Farms Championship	Sergio Garcia
Shriners Hospitals for Children Open	Martin Laird
The CJ Cup	Jason Kokrak
Zozo Championship	Patrick Cantlay
Bermuda Championship	Brian Gay
Vivint Houston Open	Carlos Ortiz
Masters Tournament	Dustin Johnson
The RSM Classic	Robert Streb
TaylorMade Pebble Beach Invitational	Kyle Reifers
Mayakoba Golf Classic	Viktor Hovland
QBE Shootout	Matt Kuchar/Harris English
PNC Championship	Justin Thomas/Mike Thomas

KORN FERRY TOUR

Bahamas Great Exuma Classic	Tommy Gainey
Bahamas Great Abaco Classic	Jared Wolfe
Panama Championship	Davis Riley
Country Club de Bogota Championship	Guillermo Mito Pereira
LECOM Suncoast Classic	Andrew Novak

El Bosque Mexico Championship	David Kocher
Korn Ferry Challenge	Luke List
The King & Bear Classic	Chris Kirk
Utah Championship	Kyle Jones
TPC Colorado Championship	Will Zalatoris
TPC San Antonio Challenge	Davis Lipsky
TPC San Antonio Championship	Davis Riley
Price Cutter Charity Championship	Max McGreevy
Pinnacle Bank Championship	Seth Reeves
WinCo Foods Portland Open	Lee Hodges
Albertsons Boise Open	Stephan Jaeger
Nationwide Children's Hospital Championship	Curtis Luck
Korn Ferry Tour Championship	Brandon Wu
Lincoln Land Championship	Brett Drewitt
Evans Scholars Invitational	Curtis Thompson
Wichita Open	Jared Wolfe
Savannah Golf Championship	Evan Harmeling
Orange County National Championship	Trey Mullinax

MACKENZIE TOUR–PGA TOUR CANADA

Canada Life Series — Bear Mountain (Mountain)	Evan Holmes
Canada Life Series — Bear Mountain (Valley)	Yi Cao
Canada Life Series — TPC Toronto	Albert Pistorius
Canada Life Series Championship	Laurent Desmarchais (A)

LOCALiQ SERIES

Alpharetta Classic	Bryson Nimmer
The Championship — Echelon	Bryson Nimmer
The Classic — Callaway Gardens	Stoney Crouch
The Invitational — Auburn University	Cooper Musselman
Jacksonville Championship	Carson Young
The Challenge — Harbor Hills	Toni Hakula
Classic — Weston Hills	Justin Doeden
LOCALiQ Series Championship	David Pastore

PGA TOUR LATINOAMERICA

Estrella del Mar Open	Alexandre Rocha
Shell Open	MJ Maguire
Puerto Plata Open	Brandon Matthews

EUROPEAN TOUR

Abu Dhabi HSBC Championship	Lee Westwood
Omega Dubai Desert Classic	Lucas Herbert
Saudi International	Graeme McDowell
Oman Open	Sami Valimaki
Commercial Bank Qatar Masters	Jorge Campillo
Austrian Open	Marc Warren
Euram Bank Open	Joel Stalter

Betfred British Masters	Renato Paratore
Hero Open	Sam Horsfield
English Championship	Andy Sullivan
Celtic Classic	Sam Horsfield
ISPS Handa Wales Open	Romain Langasque
ISPS Handa UK Championship	Rasmus Hojgaard
Estrella Damm Andalucia Masters	John Catlin
Portugal Masters	George Coetzee
Open de Portugal	Garrick Higgo
Dubai Duty Free Irish Open	John Catlin
Aberdeen Standard Investments Scottish Open	Aaron Rai
BMW PGA Championship	Tyrrell Hatton
Scottish Championship	Adrian Otaegui
Italian Open	Ross McGowan
Aphrodite Hills Cyprus Open	Callum Shinkwin
Aphrodite Hills Cyprus Showdown	Robert MacIntyre
Golf in Dubai Championship	Antoine Rozner
DP World Tour Championship	Matthew Fitzpatrick

CHALLENGE TOUR

Northern Ireland Open	Tyler Koivisto
Italian Challenge Open Eneos Motor Oil	Hurly Long
Andalucia Challenge de Espana	Ondrej Lieser
Andalucia Challenge de Cadiz	Pep Angles
Challenge Tour Grand Final	Ondrej Lieser

ALPS TOUR

Ein Bay Open	Lars Keunen
Red Sea Little Venice Open	Stefano Mazzoli
Gosser Open	Lukas Nemecz
Cervino Alps Open	Jordi Garcia del Moral
Open de la Mirabelle d'Or	Alejandro Del Rey
Toscana Alps Open	Matteo Manassero
Alps de Andalucia	Lucas Vacarisas
Alps de Las Castillas	Jacobo Pastor Lopez
Italy Alps Open	Jacopo Vecchi Fossa

NORDIC GOLF LEAGUE

Lumine Hills Open	Marcus Helligkilde
Lumine Lakes Open	Mikael Lindberg
Spanish Masters	Jeppe Huldahl
PGA Catalunya Resort Championship	Jeppe Huldahl
Katrineholm Open	Ludvig Aberg (A)
Barseback Resort Masters	Ludvig Aberg (A)
Stockholm Trophy	Mikael Lindberg
PGA Championship Braviken Open	Bjorn Hellgren
SM Match	Martin Eriksson
Landeryd Masters	Robin Petersson
Esbjerg Open	Niklas Norgaard Moller
V Sport Challenge	Joakim Wikstrom

TanumStrand Fjallbacka Open	Pelle Edberg
Ledreborg Palace Masters	Mikael Lindberg
Visby Open	Joakim Wikstrom
Race to Himmerland	Jesper Svensson
Lindbytvatten Tour Final	Lasse Jensen

PRO GOLF TOUR

Red Sea Egyptian Classic	Victor Veyret
Red Sea Ain Sokhna Classic	Jean Bekirian
Open Palmeraie	Thomas Rosenmuller
Open Casa Green	Julien Brun
Open Royal Anfa Mohammedia	Nick Bachem (A)
Open Bahia Beach	Jeremy Freiburghaus
Gradi Polish Open	Julien Brun
Raiffeisen Pro Tour	Ales Korinek
Starnberg Open	Marc Hammer (A)
Altepro Trophy	Thomas Rosenmuller
Schladming Dachstein Open	Thomas Rosenmuller
Haugschlag NO Open	Jeremy Freiburghaus
Castanea Resort Championship	Philipp Mejow

MENA TOUR

Journey to Jordan 1	David Langley
Newgiza Open	Sebastien Gros
Ghala Open	Bailey Gill
Royal Bahrain Open	David Hague
Journey to Jordan 2	Ryan Lumsden

AFRICAN SUNSHINE TOUR

SA Open Championship	Branden Grace
Eye of Africa PGA Championship	Darren Fichardt
Gauteng Team Championship	Jaco Prinsloo/JC Ritchie
Limpopo Championship	JC Ritchie
RAM Cape Town Open	Anton Karlsson
Dimension Data Pro-Am	Christiaan Bezuidenhout
Sunshine Tour Championship	Garrick Higgo
Betway Championship	Darren Fichardt
African Bank Sunshine Tour Championship	Daniel van Tonder
Titleist Championship	George Coetzee
Vodacom Championship Unlocked	Daniel van Tonder
Vodacom Championship Reloaded	Daniel van Tonder
Sun Wild Coast Sun Challenge	Merrick Bremner
Investec Royal Swazi Open	Daniel van Tonder
Time Square Casino Challenge	Ruan Korb
Joburg Open	Joachim B Hansen
Alfred Dunhill Championship	Christiaan Bezuidenhout
SA Open Championship	Christiaan Bezuidenhout

BIG EASY TOUR

Big Easy Road To — Services	Ruan Van Velzen [A]
Big Easy Road To — State Mines	Kyle McClatchie
Big Easy Road To — Reading	Herman Loubser
Big Easy Road To — Centurion	Gerhard Pepler

ASIAN TOUR

Hong Kong Open	Wade Ormsby
SMBC Singapore Open	Matt Kuchar
Bandar Malaysia Open	Trevor Simsby

CHINA TOUR

Volvo China Open	Huilin Zhang

ALL THAILAND GOLF TOUR

Boonchu Ruangkit Championship	Pavit Tangkamolprasert
Singha E-San Open	Phachara Khongwatmai
Thongchai Jaidee Foundation	Thaworn Wiratchant
Singha Pattaya Open	Prom Meesawat
Singha Thailand Masters	Ratchapol Jantavara
Singha Laguna Phuket Open	Pawin Ingkhapradit

PROFESSIONAL GOLF TOUR OF INDIA

Golconda Masters	Udayan Mane
Tata Steel Players — The Golf Resort	Udayan Mane
Bengal Open	Aadil Bedi
Tata Steel Players — Panchkula	Akshay Sharma
Tata Steel Players — Chandigarh	Karandeep Kochhar
Jeev Milkha Singh Invitational	Karandeep Kochhar
Tata Steel Tour Championship	Gaganjeet Bhullar

KPGA KOREAN TOUR

Busan Gyeongnam Open	Jihoon Lee
Gunsan Open	Joohyung Kim
KPGA Open	Soomin Lee
KPGA Championship	Seonghyeon Kim
GS Caltex Maekyung Open	Taehee Lee
Hazzys Open	Hanbyeol Kim
Shinhan Donghae Open	Hanbyeol Kim
Hyundai KJ Choi Invitational	Changwoo Lee
Genesis Championship	Taehoon Kim
Bizplay-Electronic Times Open	Wonjoon Lee
LG Signature Players Championship	Seungsu Han

JAPAN TOUR

Fujisankei Classic	Rikuya Hoshino
Japan Open Championship	Yuki Inamori
Mitsui Sumitomo VISA Taiheiyo Masters	Jinichiro Kozuma
Dunlop Phoenix	Takumi Kanaya
Golf Nippon Series JT Cup	Chan Kim

ABEMA TV TOUR

PGM Challenge II	Daichi Sato
TI Challenge	Keisuke Otawa
Ryo Ishikawa everyone Project Challenge	Ren Takeuchi
Delight Works Challenge	Hideto Kobukuro

ISPS HANDA PGA TOUR OF AUSTRALASIA

ISPS Handa Vic Open	Min Woo Lee
Coca-Cola Queensland PGA Championship	Michael Sim
Isuzu Queensland Open	Anthony Quayle
New Zealand Open	Brad Kennedy
TX Civil & Logistics WA PGA Championship	Jarryd Felton
Nexus Risk WA Open	Hayden Hopewell (A)
Tailor-Made Building Services NT PGA Championship	Aaron Pike

LPGA TOUR

Diamond Resorts Tournament of Champions	Gaby Lopez
Gainbridge LPGA	Madelene Sagstrom
LPGA Drive On Championship	Danielle Kang
Marathon Classic	Danielle Kang
Walmart NW Arkansas Championship	Austin Ernst
ANA Inspiration	Mirim Lee
Cambia Portland Classic	Georgia Hall
ShopRite LPGA Classic	Mel Reid
KPMG Women's PGA Championship	Sei Young Kim
LPGA Drive On — Reynolds Lake Oconee	Ally McDonald
Pelican Women's Championship	Sei Young Kim
Volunteers of America Classic	Angela Stanford
US Women's Open	A Lim Kim
CME Group Tour Championship	Jin Young Ko

SYMETRA TOUR

Florida's Natural Charity Classic	Janie Jackson
Firekeepers Casino Hotel Championship	Ruixin Liu
Founders Tribute	Sarah White
IOA Championship	Fatima Fernandez Cano
Four Winds Invitational	Kim Kaufman
IOA Classic	Laura Wearn
Symetra Classic	Pei-Yun Chien
Mission Inn Resort Championship	Matilda Castren
Carolina Golf Classic	Ana Belac
Symetra Tour Championship	Frida Kinhult

LADIES EUROPEAN TOUR

Rose Ladies Series Grand Final	Alice Hewson
ASI Ladies Scottish Open	Stacy Lewis
AIG Women's Open	Sophia Popov
Tipsport Czech Ladies Open	Emily Kristine Pedersen
VP Bank Swiss Ladies Open	Amy Boulden
Lacoste Ladies Open de France	Julia Engstrom
Omega Dubai Moonlight Classic	Minjee Lee
Aramco Saudi Ladies International	Emily Kristine Pedersen
Saudi Ladies Team International	Emily Kristine Pedersen
Andalucia Costa del Sol Open de Espana	Emily Kristine Pedersen

LET ACCESS SERIES

Flumserberg Ladies Open	Sanna Nuutinen
Amundi Czech Ladies Challenge	Tiia Koivisto
Lavaux Ladies Open	Agathe Laisne (A)
Santander Golf Tour Lerma	Luna Sobron Galmes
Santander Golf Tour Lauro	Agathe Laisne (A)

SUNSHINE LADIES TOUR

Cape Town Ladies Open	Lee-Anne Pace
Supersport Ladies Challenge	Lejan Lewthwaite
Dimension Data Ladies Pro-Am	Lejan Lewthwaite
South African Women's Masters	Jane Turner
Canon Serengeti Par-3 Challenge	Nicole Garcia
Joburg Ladies Open	Monique Smit
Jabra Ladies Open	Ashleigh Buhai
Investec South African Women's Open	Alice Hewson
Investec Royal Swazi Open	Casandra Hall

JAPAN LPGA TOUR

Earth Mondahmin Cup	Ayako Watanabe
NEC Karuizawa 72	Yuka Saso
Nitori Ladies	Yuka Saso
Golf 5 Ladies	Sakura Koiwai
JLPGA Championship Konica Minolta Cup	Saki Nagamine
Descente Ladies Tokai Classic	Ayaka Furue
Japan Women's Open	Erika Hara
Stanley Ladies	Mone Inami
Fujitsu Ladies	Jiyai Shin
Mitsubishi Electric/Hisako Higuchi Ladies	Yuna Nishimura
Toto Japan Classic	Jiyai Shin
Itoen Ladies	Ayaka Furue
Daio Paper Elleair Ladies Open	Ayaka Furue
JLPGA Tour Championship Ricoh Cup	Erika Hara

JLPGA STEPUP TOUR

Rashink Re Syu Ryu/RKB Ladies	Nozomi Uetake
Shizuoka Shimbun & SBS Ladies	Hana Lee
Chugoku Shimbun Chupea Ladies Cup	Seira Oki
Sanyo Shimbun Ladies Cup	Rena Ishikawa
Kanehide Miyarabi Open	Eri Joma
Daikure Ladies Cup	Karin Takeyama
Fundokin Ladies	Hana Lee
Castrol Ladies	Hiromu Ono

KOREA LPGA TOUR

KLPGA Championship	Hyun Kyung Park
E1 Charity Open	So Young Lee
Lotte Cantata Ladies Open	Hyo Joo Kim
Kia Motors Korea Women's Open	So Yeon Ryu
BC Card Hankyung Ladies Cup	Ji Yeong Kim[2]
McCol Yongpyong Resort Open	Min Sun Kim[5]
IS Dongseo Busan Open	Hyun Kyung Park
Jeju Samdasoo Masters	Hae Ran Ryu
Orange Life Champions Trophy	KLPGA
Dayouwinia MBN Ladies Open	Min Ji Park
Fantom Classic	Song Yi Ahn
Autech Carrier Championship	Na Rin An
KB Financial Group Star Championship	Hyo Joo Kim
Huencare Ladies Open	So Mi Lee
SK Networks Seokyung Ladies Classic	Ha Na Jang
Hana Financial Group Championship	Na Rin An
SK Telecom ADT CAPS Championship	Hye Jin Choi

KLPGA DREAM TOUR

Gunsan 1	Jae Hee Kim
Hanse Phoenix 2	Ga Eun Song
Muan All for You 3	Jee Hyun Ahn
Hanse Phoenix 4	Su Bin Lee
West Ocean 5	Jae Hee Kim
Muan All for You 6	Gyeong Rim Baek
Hanse Phoenix 7	Song Yeon Kim
KBC West Ocean 1	Bo Min Shin
Muan All for You 8	Jee Hyun Ahn
West Ocean 9	Ji Yu Jung
Gunsan 10	Se Been Jung
Muan All for You 11	Bo Kyeom Park
West Ocean 12	Hee Ji Kim
Hanse Phoenix 13	Jae Hee Kim
KBC West Ocean 2	Chae Eun Lee[2]
Hanse Phoenix 14	Hye Jung Lee
West Ocean 15	Ji Min Jung
Gunsan 16	Ju Young Park[5]
Gunsan 17	Su Bin An
Muan All for You 18	Ji Won Hong
Grand Final	Ji Min Jung

LPGA OF TAIWAN TOUR

Hitachi Ladies Classic	Yu-Ju Chen
WPG Ladies Open	Chia-Yen Wu
CTBC Ladies Open	Yu-Ling Hsieh
Grin Cup Charity Open	Ho-Yu An (A)
Yichen Future Open	Chia-Yen Wu
Wistron Ladies Open	Cheng-Hsuan Shih
Party Golfers Ladies Open	Min Lee
Taiwan Mobile Ladies Open	Pei-Yun Chien

CHINA LPGA TOUR

Zhuhai Guowei Centre Plaza Hollywood Challenge	Ruoning Yin
Moutai Golf Liquor Zhuhai Golden Gulf Challenge	Ruoning Yin
Mitsubishi Heavy Orient Masters	Ruoning Yin
Beijing Pearl Challenge	Wenbo Liu
Zhangjiagang Shuangshan Challenge	Xiaowen Yin (A)
Hangzhou International Championship	Jienalin Zhang

WPGA TOUR OF AUSTRALASIA

Windaroo Lakes Pro-Am	Laura Fuenfstueck
Findex Yamba Pro-Am	Holly Clyburn
Aoyuan International Moss Vale Pro-Am	Manon De Roey
Ballarat Icons ALPG Pro-Am	Dottie Ardina
ISPS Handa Vic Open	Hee Young Park
ISPS Handa Women's Australian Open	Inbee Park
Geoff King Motors Australian Ladies Classic	Stephanie Kyriacou (A)
Women's NSW Open	Julia Engstrom

PGA TOUR CHAMPIONS

Mitsubishi Electric Championship	Miguel Angel Jimenez
Morocco Champions	Brett Quigley
Chubb Classic	Scott Parel
Cologuard Classic	Bernhard Langer
Hoag Classic	Ernie Els
Ally Challenge	Jim Furyk
Bridgestone Senior Players Championship	Jerry Kelly
Charles Schwab Series — Big Cedar Lodge	Shane Bertsch
Charles Schwab Series — Ozarks National	Phil Mickelson
Sanford International	Miguel Angel Jimenez
PURE Insurance Championship	Jim Furyk
SAS Championship	Ernie Els
Dominion Energy Charity Classic	Phil Mickelson
TimberTech Championship	Darren Clarke
Charles Schwab Cup Championship	Kevin Sutherland

JAPAN PGA SENIOR TOUR

ISPS Handa Corona Ni Katsu!	Shinsuke Yanagisawa
ISPS Handa Corona! Professional Golfer 100th Anniversary	Toru Suzuki
Maruhan Cup Taiheiyo Club Senior	Norio Shinozaki
Japan Senior Open Championship	Akira Teranishi
Japan PGA Senior Championship	Masayoshi Nakayama
Cosmohealth Cup Senior	Yoshinori Mizumaki
Iwasaki Shiratsuyu Senior	Eiji Mizoguchi
Kanehide Senior Okinawa Open	Masayuki Kawamura

MULTIPLE WINNERS OF 2020

4 — Dustin Johnson
Travelers Championship
The Northern Trust
Tour Championship
Masters Tournament

4 — Emily Kristine Pedersen
Tipsport Czech Ladies Open
Aramco Saudi Ladies International
Saudi Ladies Team International
Andalucia Costa del Sol Open de Espana

4 — Daniel van Tonder
African Bank Sunshine Tour Championship
Vodacom Championship Unlocked
Vodacom Championship Reloaded
Investec Royal Swazi Open

3 — Christiaan Bezuidenhout
Dimension Data Pro-Am
Alfred Dunhill Championship
SA Open Championship

3 — Ayaka Furue
Descente Ladies Tokai Classic
Itoen Ladies
Daio Paper Elleair Ladies Open

3 — Jae Hee Kim
Dream Gunsan 1
Dream West Ocean 5
Dream Hanse Phoenix 13

3 — Mikael Lindberg
Lumine Lakes Open
Stockholm Trophy
Ledreborg Palace Masters

3 — Thomas Rosenmuller
Open Palmeraie
Altepro Trophy
Schladming Dachstein Open

3 — Justin Thomas
Sentry Tournament of Champions
WGC FedEx St Jude Invitational
PNC Championship (with Mike Thomas)

3 — Ruoning Yin
Zhuhai Guowei Centre Plaza Hollywood Challenge
Moutai Golf Liquor Zhuhai Golden Gulf Challenge
Mitsubishi Heavy Orient Masters

2 — Ludvig Aberg (A)
Katrineholm Open
Barseback Resort Masters

2 — Jee Hyun Ahn
Dream Muan All for You 3
Dream Muan All for You 8

2 — Na Rin An
Autech Carrier Championship
Hana Financial Group Championship

2 — Julien Brun
Open Casa Green
Gradi Polish Open

2 — John Catlin
Estrella Damm Andalucia Masters
Dubai Duty Free Irish Open

2 — Pei-Yun Chien
Symetra Classic
Taiwan Mobile Ladies Open

2 — George Coetzee
Titleist Championship
Portugal Masters

2 — Bryson DeChambeau
Rocket Mortgage Classic
US Open Championship

2 — Ernie Els
Hoag Classic
SAS Championship

2 — Julia Engstrom
Women's NSW Open
Lacoste Ladies Open de France

2 — Darren Fichardt
Eye of Africa PGA Championship
Betway Championship

2 — Jeremy Freiburghaus
Open Bahia Beach
Haugschlag NO Open

2 — Jim Furyk
Ally Challenge
PURE Insurance Championship

2 — Erika Hara
Japan Women's Open
JLPGA Tour Championship Ricoh Cup

2 — Tyrrell Hatton
Arnold Palmer Invitational
BMW PGA Championship

2 — Alice Hewson
Investec South African Women's Open
Rose Ladies Series Grand Final

2 — Garrick Higgo
Sunshine Tour Championship
Open de Portugal

2 — Sam Horsfield
Hero Open
Celtic Classic

2 — Viktor Hovland
Puerto Rico Open
Mayakoba Golf Classic

2 — Jeppe Huldahl
Spanish Masters
PGA Catalunya Resort Championship

2 — Miguel Angel Jimenez
Mitsubishi Electric Championship
Sanford International

2 — Ji Min Jung
Dream West Ocean 15
Dream Grand Final

2 — Danielle Kang
LPGA Drive On Championship
Marathon Classic

2 — Hanbyeol Kim
Hazzys Open
Shinhan Donghae Open

2 — Hyo Joo Kim
Lotte Cantata Ladies Open
KB Financial Group Star Championship

2 — Sei Young Kim
KPMG Women's PGA Championship
Pelican Women's Championship

2 — Karandeep Kochhar
Tata Steel Players — Chandigarh
Jeev Milkha Singh Invitational

2 — Matt Kuchar
SMBC Singapore Open
QBE Shootout (with Harris English)

2 — Agathe Laisne (A)
Lavaux Ladies Open
Santander Golf Tour Lauro

2 — Hana Lee
Shizuoka Shimbun & SBS Ladies
Fundokin Ladies

2 — Lejan Lewthwaite
Supersport Ladies Challenge
Dimension Data Ladies Pro-Am

2 — Ondrej Lieser
Andalucia Challenge de Espana
Challenge Tour Grand Final

2 — Udayan Mane
Golconda Masters
Tata Steel Players — The Golf Resort

2 — Phil Mickelson
Charles Schwab Series — Ozarks National
Dominion Energy Charity Classic

2 — Collin Morikawa
Workday Charity Open
PGA Championship

2 — Bryson Nimmer
Alpharetta Classic
The Championship — Echelon

2 — Hyun Kyung Park
KLPGA Championship
IS Dongseo Busan Open

2 — Jon Rahm
Memorial Tournament
BMW Championship

2 — Davis Riley
Panama Championship
TPC San Antonio Championship

2 — JC Ritchie
Gauteng Team Championship (with Jaco Prinsloo)
Limpopo Championship

2 — Yuka Saso
NEC Karuizawa 72
Nitori Ladies

2 — Jiyai Shin
Fujitsu Ladies
Toto Japan Classic

2 — Webb Simpson
Waste Management Phoenix Open
RBC Heritage

2 — Joakim Wikstrom
V Sport Challenge
Visby Open

2 — Jared Wolfe
Bahamas Great Abaco Classic
Wichita Open

2 — Chia-Yen Wu
WPG Ladies Open
Yichen Future Open

Chronology of 2020

	CHAPTER
JANUARY	
Justin Thomas wins a three-way, three-hole playoff to open the year at Kapalua	8
Grace rebounds to complete the set with South African Open victory	14
Wade Ormsby claims second win in four years at delayed Hong Kong Open	15
At windy Waialae, from two behind with two to play, Cam Smith wins in playoff	8
Jimenez beats Couples and Els in playoff at PGA Tour Champions opener	23
"Still good enough", 46-year-old Westwood chalks up 25th win in Abu Dhabi	12
Matt Kuchar overcomes final-round triple to beat Justin Rose in Singapore	15
Six up with six to play, tied with two left, Landry birdies the last two at AmEx	8
On Monday, after seven extra holes, Gaby Lopez wins at Diamond Resorts	18
On Australia Day, Herbert wins in Dubai and Leishman in San Diego	12/8
Maiden win for Madelene Sagstrom at the Gainbridge LPGA	18
FEBRUARY	
McDowell beats Johnson by two in Saudi for first European Tour win in six years	12
JC Ritchie successfully defends a title for the second week running in SA	14
Simpson beats Finau in Phoenix with birdies at the 71st, 72nd and 73rd holes	8
Min Woo Lee claims maiden win at Vic Open with sister Minjee watching on	17
Canada's Taylor beats Mickelson and goes wire-to-wire at Pebble Beach	8
Inbee Park's putting back to her imperious best in Australian Open win	22
Sim beats Arnold at fourth extra hole at QLD PGA, still gives him a lift home	17
Bezuidenhout eagles the last at Fancourt for victory in the Dimension Data	14
In his first start of the year, Adam Scott wins at Riviera; Tiger finishes last	8
Amateur Stephanie Kyriacou, 19, wins the Australian Classic by eight shots	22
Left-handed Higgo wins Sunshine Tour Championship to be rookie of the year	14
Patrick Reed claims second WGC title with 45 one-putts in Mexico	8
With a 30-footer at the last, Hovland is the PGA Tour's first Norwegian winner	8
MARCH	
Finland's Sami Valimaki wins his sixth European Tour event in Oman playoff	12
Aussie Brad Kennedy, 45, wins NZ Open for the second time	17
Julia Engstrom, 18, seals first LET win with five-iron to two feet in Dubbo	22
Korea's Sungjae Im impresses with first PGA Tour victory at Honda	8
Langer wins 41st Champions event coming from four behind at Cologuard	23
Drysdale misses out in his 498th event as Campillo wins five-hole playoff	12
Hatton survives Saturday massacre at Bay Hill and claims first win in the US	8
Ernie Els wins on third PGA Tour Champions start at Hoag Classic	23
Players Championship abandoned after one round due to coronavirus	8
Before lockdown, Alice Hewson wins first LET title at South African Open	19
MAY	
Winner Park feted with flower petals in Covid-safe celebration as KLPGA returns	21
JUNE	
Hyo Joo Kim beats Sei Young Kim in a playoff at the Lotte Cantata	21
PGA Tour resumes at Colonial with Berger defeating Morikawa in extra time	8
So Yeon Ryu wins Korea Open and donates entire prize to Covid relief	21
Simpson earns second win of the season at Harbour Town	8
Dustin Johnson wins for the 13th consecutive PGA Tour season at Travelers	8

JULY	CHAPTER
Beefed up Bryson overpowers Detroit for sixth PGA Tour victory	8
Albatross for Lee^6 in Busan as Hyun Kyung Park, 20, claims second win	21
European Tour returns in Austria with first win in six years for Warren	12
Morikawa tops Thomas in playoff in Workday version of Muirfield Village	8
Rahm wins the Memorial proper and is second Spaniard to be world number one	8
Guard of honour for Paratore at behind-closed-doors British Masters	12

AUGUST	
Jimenez passes Torrance with 707th European Tour start, Hero Horsfield wins	12
It's Thomas by three at the WGC FedEx St Jude and now he is number one	8
LPGA resumes after six-month break as Danielle Kang drives on for win	18
Jim Furyk wins on PGA Tour Champions debut at familiar Warwick Hills	23
Sullivan to the Manor born with first win for five years by seven strokes	12
Last round of Rose Series Grand Final cancelled due to wildfire at Wentworth	19
Kang does the Toledo double after Lydia Ko hits wall in Marathon	18
PGA triumph for Morikawa as 23-year-old wins on second major start	1
Bryson Nimmer wins second event in a row in LOCALiQ Series	11
A classic at Celtic Manor, Horsfield goes win-missed cut-win	12
After playoff win in Scotland, Stacy Lewis has first victory as a mother	19
What a weekend for Jim Herman as 61-63 brings Wyndham reward	8
Jerry Kelly holes in one at 12, doubles the last for Senior Players victory	23
China's Yi Cao wins by eight strokes in Canada Life Series at Bear Mountain	10
Romain Langasque claims first win in week two at Celtic Manor	12
Sunshine Tour resumes with Fichardt finishing with 64 for Betway win	14
With a 60 on day two, Johnson scores 30 under and wins Northern Trust by 11	8
An incredible story as 304th ranked Sophia Popov wins at Royal Troon	2
Phil Mickelson debuts on Champions circuit with 61 and four-stroke win	23
Rookie Yuka Saso, 19, wins for second successive event in Japan	20
Rasmus Hogjaard, 19, is the second youngest with two European Tour wins	12
Pedersen eagles the last with monster putt for first win in five years in Czech	19
Brandon Wu comes from five behind for first win at Korn Ferry Tour Championship	9
Rahm holes amazing 66-foot putt to beat Johnson in BMW playoff	8

SEPTEMBER	
From Covid misdemeanour to tour champion for John Catlin at Valderrama	12
Yet another win for George Coetzee on his home course at Pretoria	14
Johnson scoops $15m FedEx Cup bonus with Tour Championship victory	8
From Pretoria to Portugal, Coetzee wins for second week running	12
It took 11 years but 2009 Open champion Stewart Cink is a winner again	8
Inspired Mirim Lee chips her way to ANA glory with playoff victory	3
Akira Teranishi achieves dream Japan Senior Open win by five at Naruo	25
Higgo claims second win of the year and first in Europe at Open de Portugal	12
A hole-in-one on day two helps Sweden's Engstrom to her second victory	19
2018 Open champion Georgia Hall scores first US win in Portland playoff	18
Bryson DeChambeau muscles his way to six-shot win at Winged Foot	4
Furyk becomes second player to win first two Champions starts at PURE	23
A second Sunshine win in three events for unlocked van Tonder	14
Catlin overtakes Rai in Northern Ireland for second win in three starts	12

OCTOBER	CHAPTER
Rai makes up for previous week with Scottish playoff win over Fleetwood	12
Erika Hara takes the Japan Women's Open by four strokes	20
Van Tonder reloads with third win in four, going wire-to-wire at Huddle	14
Atlantic City trip pays off for Mel Reid with emotional maiden LPGA victory	19
With approach to two feet at the last, Garcia closes out Sanderson win in style	8
Boyhood dream comes true for hooded Hatton with PGA win at Wentworth	12
Na Rin An almost loses 10-stroke lead before late rally secures first KLPGA win	21
With a closing 63, Sei Young Kim finally claims first major at Women's PGA	5
Els claims second Champions win with 40-footer at the last green	23
For the second time in three years, nervous Yuki Inamori wins Japan Open	16
Korea's Jiyai Shin wins her 25th Japan LPGA title at Fujitsu	20
Hyo Joo Kim claims KLPGA major by eight for second win for the year	21
Kokrak earns first win in 10th season as CJ Cup moves to Shadow Creek	8
Like Furyk, Mickelson wins first two Champions starts with Dominion title	23
Pike returns home to Palmerston course, beats house guest Sim at NT PGA	17
Unlikely late birdie in Italy helps McGowan to second win after 11-year wait	12
On her 28th birthday, with parents on hand, Ally McDonald has first LPGA win	18
Zozo moves to Sherwood and Cantlay comes from behind for third win	8
Swazi Open victory by 18 points gives van Tonder fourth win for the season	14
NOVEMBER	
In first ever Cyprus event, "one in a million" putt helps Shinkwin to first win	12
Veteran Brian Gay claims playoff win over Clark in Bermuda	8
Darren Clarke claims maiden Champions win, first title since 2011 Open	23
Japan Classic misses LPGA players but Shin wins second in three events	20
Scotland's Robert MacIntyre wins Sunday showdown for maiden victory	12
Minjee Lee holes from 20 feet under floodlights for Dubai Moonlight win	19
Carlos Ortiz is third Mexican, and first for 42 years, to win on PGA Tour	8
Sutherland wins nine-hole playoff against Broadhurst at Champions finale	23
Pedersen defeats Hall in playoff for second victory of the season in Saudi	19
Finally a win at the last for KLPGA Player of the Year Hye Jin Choi	21
A second playoff win of her rookie season for Ayaka Furue in Japan	20
Dustin Johnson wins quiet Masters by five strokes with new record total	6
Takami Kanaya, 22, claims second win and first as a pro at Dunlop Phoenix	16
Japan's Furue, 20, wins for second week in a row and third for the season	20
Nienaber hits 439-yard drive in Joburg but Hansen gets the victory	14
Ondrej Lieser is the first Czech to win the Challenge Tour Grand Final	13
Pedersen at the double: takes individual and team honours at Royal Greens	19
In first start since WPGA victory, Sei Young Kim wins again at the Pelican	18
Streb almost holes approach at second extra hole to beat Kisner at RSM	8
A second win of the season for Bezuidenhout by four strokes at Leopard Creek	14
Erika Hara adds JLPGA Tour Championship to Japan Open title	20
Third win in a row and fourth in all for LET number one Pedersen in Spain	19
DECEMBER	
Back-to-back for Bezuidenhout with SA Open win by five at Sun City	14
Stanford, 43, wins for the first time in her home state of Texas	18
Hovland birdies the 18th again for second win of the year at Mayakoba	8
Little known Korean A Lim Kim birdies the last three holes to win US Open	7
In crazy finish, Fitzpatrick wins DP World, Westwood a third order of merit	12
Rolex number one Jin Young Ko overcomes Sei Young Kim in duel at LPGA finale	18

The Majors

Jamie Squire/Getty Images

Left: Tom Pennington/Getty Images, Middle: David Cannon/R&A, Right: Christian Petersen/Getty Images

Left and Middle: Patrick Smith/Getty Images, Right: Jamie Squire/Getty Images

PGA Championship

Sean M Haffey/Getty Images

Harry How/Getty Images

Harry How/Getty Images

Ezra Shaw/Getty Images

Clockwise from left: Collin Morikawa, 23, celebrates a first major win at misty Harding Park after holding off Brooks Koepka, Paul Casey, Bryson DeChambeau and 54-hole leader Dustin Johnson.

Jan Kruger/R&A

Richard Heathcote/R&A

Andrew Redington/R&A

Matthew Lewis/R&A

Clockwise from left: Tears for a champion, even before Sophia Popov tapped in for victory at Royal Troon; Popov's second at the 18th; runner-up Jasmine Suwannapura; Minjee Lee chips at the Postage Stamp.

Christian Petersen/Getty Images

Jeff Gross/Getty Images

Jeff Gross/Getty Images

Jeff Gross/Getty Images

Clockwise from left: Mirim Lee chips in for eagle at the final hole at Mission Hills before defeating Brooke Henderson and Nelly Korda in a playoff — and then taking the traditional leap into Poppie's Pond.

Jamie Squire/Getty Images

Gregory Shamus/Getty Images

Gregory Shamus/Getty Images

Clockwise from left: A victory salute for Bryson DeChambeau after muscling Winged Foot into submission as never seen before. He won by six strokes from Matthew Wolff and eight from Louis Oosthuizen.

KPMG Women's PGA Championship

Patrick Smith/Getty Images

Andy Lyons/PGA of America

Patrick Smith/Getty Images

Clockwise from left: All smiles for Sei Young Kim after winning her first major at Aronimink. A 63 left Brooke Henderson and Anna Nordqvist in her wake, while Inbee Park was five behind in second.

Masters Tournament

Patrick Smith/Getty Images

Jamie Squire/Getty Images

Jamie Squire/Getty Images

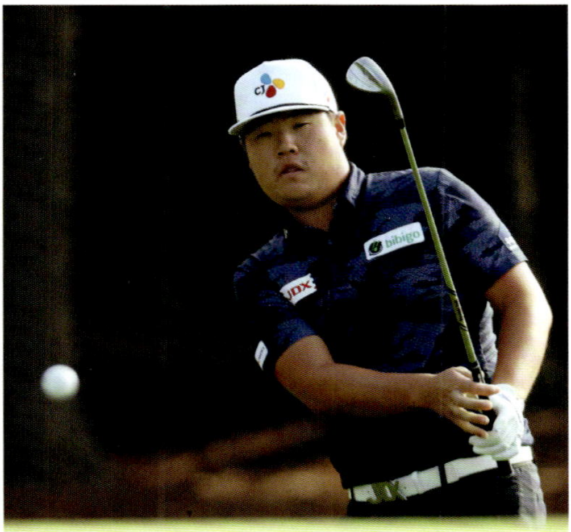

Jamie Squire/Getty Images

Clockwise from left: A quiet fist pump for Dustin Johnson after a five-stroke win; Cam Smith drives to a 17th fairway free of Augusta patrons; he shared second with Sungjae Im; Tiger Woods foundered at the 12th.

US Women's Open

Jamie Squire/Getty Images

Carmen Mandato/Getty Images

Carmen Mandato/Getty Images

Jamie Squire/Getty Images

Clockwise from left: A Lim Kim birdies the 18th at Champions to pip longtime leader Hinako Shibuno, runners-up Amy Olson and Jin Young Ko, and Moriya Jutanugarn, here watching sister Ariya.

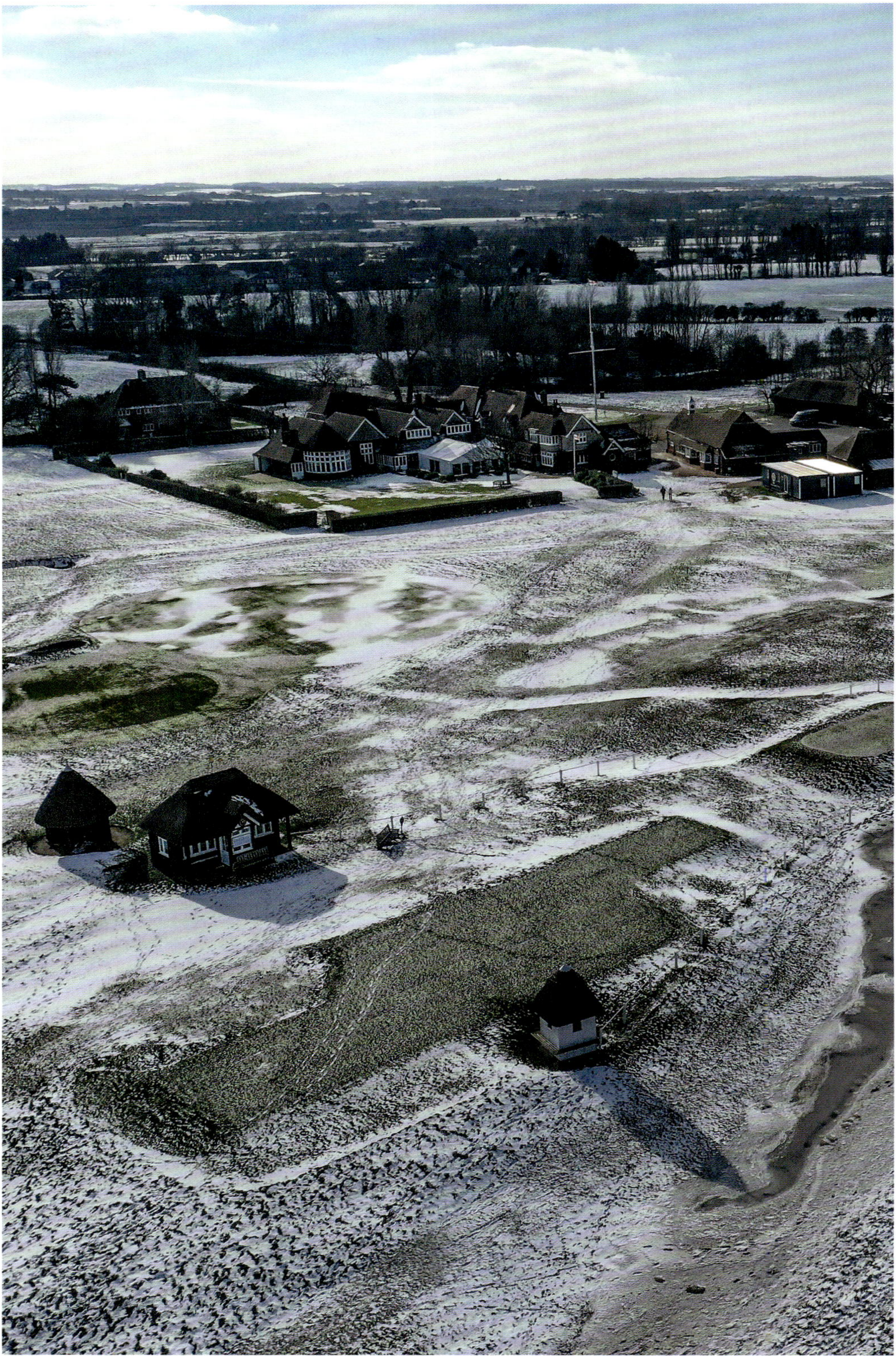

David Cannon/Getty Images

Hope in a bleak midwinter: summer will return with The 149th Open at Royal St George's in 2021.

The Majors

PGA CHAMPIONSHIP

Harry How/Getty Images

Morikawa stamps authority with great drive

And then there were four. With victory at the 102nd PGA Championship at TPC Harding Park, Collin Morikawa joined Jack Nicklaus, Tiger Woods and Rory McIlroy as the only players ever to lift the Wanamaker Trophy at the tender age of 23. And like that great trio, the fresh-faced young American showed he had the talent, the aptitude and the sheer courage to snatch a major championship from underneath the noses of illustrious rivals.

We should have seen it coming. Only four weeks earlier, Morikawa had beaten world number one Justin Thomas in a playoff for the Workday Charity Open at Muirfield Village. And now, when crunch time arrived on this most majestic of public courses in San Francisco, the Californian conjured a piece of golfing magic that will live long in the memory. It's a shame that thanks to the pandemic, there were no spectators to witness it.

Morikawa's drive at the short par-four 16th in the final round will go down as one of the most impressive shots in the history of the championship. It might be matched, but it will probably never be bettered.

Timing is everything and in this instance his timing was perfect. He had just been caught by England's Paul Casey at the top of a packed leaderboard and decided that attack was his best option. In the event his drive finished seven feet from the hole and the subsequent eagle putt that followed gave him a two-shot lead with two to play. He was not about to slip up.

Cameron Champ, his playing partner, was most impressed: "The shot on 16 looked like it was out of a video game," he said. "The way it came off and the way it bounced right up there close, it was awesome."

Casey may have been disappointed not to have secured his first major trophy after almost 20 years of trying, but he had nothing but praise for a player already being spoken of in hushed tones: "I've been around the block, so I know talent when I see it, know when somebody is that good. And Collin was that good," he said.

"We, the veterans, could just tell — he's the one. Even if the media weren't talking about him that's where we were focusing our attention. And we weren't wrong. Instant maturity was probably the one thing that stood out; the way he speaks, the way he plays golf. He's really stamped his authority."

The facts do not lie. A member of the paid ranks for just 14 months, three of which were wiped out by the pandemic, Morikawa's weekend scores of 65 and 64 had never been bettered in the final two rounds of a male major championship. He had now played in two majors and had won one of them. In 27 professional starts, he had three wins under his belt and just one missed cut. Victory at Harding Park — where he was top in driving accuracy, proximity to the hole with approach shots, and strokes gained putting — moved him to number five in the world, a meteoric rise up the rankings.

It is an immense burden to be placed on the shoulders of any young player, but Morikawa had the look of someone who could cope with the expectations about to come flying his way. Comparisons with Woods at the same age seemed inevitable, but with such strength in depth in the modern game could any player dominate in the fashion of Tiger at his best? Morikawa would certainly be giving it a try.

"You know, this is what fans want to see," he said. "They want to see who is going to step up, who is going to hit that really good shot towards the end coming down the stretch. It doesn't stop here. I've got a very good taste of what a major championship is like. The majors are going to be circled in, just like everyone else, but I've got to focus on every single week. I'm trying to win every single week. I'm not trying to come out and just win the majors."

As he hoisted the Wanamaker Trophy above his head the lid fell off and crashed to the ground. It was his only mistake of the weekend and it proved that the serious business was over, the concentration could slip.

The week had started with all the talk focused on Brooks Koepka's chances of winning a third successive PGA Championship and it ended with talk of the new kid on the block. The future of the game suddenly looked to be in very good hands.

FIRST ROUND

And so to TPC Harding Park for the first round of the first major championship to be played in 13 months. It was somewhat ironic that, thanks to Covid-19, the 102nd PGA Championship was back in its August slot just a year after it was moved to May. But no one was thinking about that as a benign day dawned on this princely layout on the shores of Lake Merced. The world's finest players were gathered together once again and poised to challenge for one of the game's most coveted trophies.

As talking points go, it would be fair to say that defending champion Koepka was the topic of conversation leading in to the championship (that's if you don't count a player by the name of Tiger Woods). The young American's recent record in the majors read like a line from Woods' own résumé: played eight, won four. Koepka had won back-to-back US Opens in 2017 and 2018 and repeated the feat in the PGA Championship, lifting the gleaming Wanamaker Trophy above his head in 2018 and 2019. Now he was bidding to become only the fourth man since 1882 to win the same major three years in a row.

With its thick, patchy rough and narrow cypress tree-lined fairways, few observers were predicting a low scoring week at Harding Park, particularly with the heavy air and chilly conditions often brought about by San Francisco's legendary marine layer. Curiosity was also the order of the day. Could Koepka get off to a flying start? What should be expected of Tiger, playing only his fourth event of 2020? Or what about the "Incredible Bulk", Bryson DeChambeau, who came out of lockdown with an extra 40 pounds of muscle and a newfound ability to smash the ball out of sight?

And with the pandemic making this the first major to be played behind closed doors, would the lack of spectators — and reduced intensity — work to the benefit of the new generation of young players itching to take on the established stars? Who knew what lay in store for the likes of Morikawa, Matthew Wolff and Scottie Scheffler?

In the event, the first day was made for low scoring. A course feared and revered in equal measure suddenly resembled a sheep in a wolf's clothing. Leading the way was Australia's Jason Day, the champion in 2015, whose five-under-par morning round of 65 was matched later in the day by Brendon Todd, at 35 a late developer who was suddenly enjoying life among the game's higher echelons.

While delighted with his round, Day was sad that few people were there to witness it. "I actually miss playing in front of fans because you obviously work off that, especially in a major championship," he said. "Usually, it's buzzing and it happens from Monday all the way through to Sunday."

It was certainly buzzing for Todd, for whom two of his three career wins had come in 2019. It was a day when the American, who last played in the championship in 2015, capitalised on a putter that could only be described as hot. "It was lights-out today," he said. "I couldn't have putted any better."

If there were any doubts that day one represented just the opening skirmishes of a major campaign, a look at the players lining up behind the leaders dispelled such thoughts. Nine of them had rounds of 66, among them 2013 US Open champion Justin Rose and the aforementioned Koepka, whose confidence knows no bounds. "I can definitely play a lot better," he said. "I just need to tidy a few things up and we'll be there come Sunday on the back nine. To win three in a row here would be special."

Talking of bragging rights, Woods claimed those in what was widely regarded as the marquee group, made up of himself, Justin Thomas, the world number one, and Rory McIlroy. The four-time champion had a 68, to McIlroy's level-par 70 and Thomas's 72. This was his lowest opening round in a major in eight years. His response? "I'm happy and content," Woods said. For McIlroy, who bogeyed three holes in a row on his front nine before fighting back, it felt like the one that got away. "It was there for the taking today," said the four-time major champion. "I definitely could have been a few shots lower."

The best of the conditions was experienced by the morning starters. With the wind picking up and gusting up to 20mph, the scoring average in the afternoon was nearly a stroke higher. Todd's 65 was the best of them, while DeChambeau came in with a 68, as did Casey. Elsewhere, Jordan Spieth's hopes of completing a career grand slam already seemed scuppered by an opening round of 73, while the supremely talented Dustin Johnson moved nicely into position with a round of 69, the same score as Morikawa.

After 18 holes: 65 (-5) Day, Todd; **66** Scheffler, Kaymer, Schauffele, Cauley, Rose, Steele, Koepka, Lorenzo-Vera, Z Johnson

SECOND ROUND

Ask any of the 156 players at the start of the week who they would expect to be leading the PGA Championship at the halfway stage and it's more than a fair bet they would not have gone for a player from China ranked outside the world's top 100. The player in question, short on confidence and lacking in practice, would have wholeheartedly agreed.

What then was to be made of Haotong Li's position atop the leaderboard after a bogey-free second round of 65 that opened a gap of two strokes over a fearsome chasing pack that included Koepka, Rose, Day and a resurgent Tommy Fleetwood? In its most simple terms, this had been history in the making. No Chinese male player had ever held the lead after any round at a major championship.

Li was in China when the pandemic shut down golf and he only returned to the US in July, three weeks before the re-scheduled PGA. He missed the cut in his first event back and then tied for 75th in a 78-man field at the WGC FedEx St Jude Invitational. If he had been hoping to lull his rivals into a false sense of security, he could not have done a better job. No one could have predicted an opening 36 holes that included a solitary bogey in an eight-under-par total of 132. And no one, it would seem, was more surprised than Li himself, particularly after finding only four fairways in the second round.

"I've got no expectations actually because the last few months I stayed at home in China doing nothing," he said. "I just want to be out here to have fun." If Li proved anything it was the old adage that "form is temporary, class is permanent". In 2017, he revealed the depth of his talent with a stunning final round of 63 at The Open Championship at Royal Birkdale and, a year later, he emerged victorious after going toe-to-toe with McIlroy down the stretch at the Dubai Desert Classic.

The standout score of the day was Fleetwood's 64, a swashbuckling effort from a player who would not look out of place on the set of *Pirates of the Caribbean*. The Englishman had seven birdies and a bogey in his round and was where he wanted to be at the halfway point. After finishing runner-up to Koepka at the 2018 US Open and Shane Lowry at The Open a year later, was he about to go one better?

"Any time you're in contention for a major you learn," Fleetwood said. "And every time these weeks come about you just prepare for it to be your week and today was a great day. Got a weekend of golf left, so let's see. But you can't buy experience and I've been lucky enough to have some of that in the majors. Hopefully it stands me in good stead these next two days."

What Fleetwood would have given for Koepka's experience. In both words and deeds, the defending champion gave the impression that he thought it was just a matter of days before he lifted the Wanamaker Trophy for the third time in three years. If there was a small sign of vulnerability it was the sight of a physio coming out to him three times on the back nine to help loosen a tight hip. But while a score of 68, finished off with a birdie, for six under par was perfectly acceptable he let it be known there was more in the tank.

"I felt like I probably could be 10 under right now," Koepka said. "Hit a lot of good putts, just didn't go in. A couple of them, if I just hit them, they're in. But driving it pretty well. Iron play, I'm pretty pleased with. You know, I like where I'm at." Enough said.

In total 24 players were within five strokes of the lead with two rounds to play. Surprisingly, none of the marquee grouping of Woods (72), Thomas (70) and McIlroy (69) was among them, although they did enough to make the halfway cut, on level par, one over and one under, respectively. As with the previous day, McIlroy was left frustrated after a round that could have been so much better. The Northern Irishman kick-started his challenge with four birdies in succession from the seventh, only to give most of the strokes back after three-putting from seven feet at the 12th for a triple bogey. Woods suffered equally on the greens and paid dearly.

"Once Tiger and I got our tee shots off 18, I just gave him a look like, phew, glad that's almost done," McIlroy said. "We all have an opportunity to post a low one tomorrow and get ourselves back into it."

Among other notable performances there were scores of 67 for Johnson, Casey, Daniel Berger and Mike Lorenzo-Vera. Wolff had a 68, Morikawa a 69, and DeChambeau a 70. Todd, the joint first round leader, had a 70.

After 36 holes: 132 (-8) Li 65, **134** Day 69, Rose 68, Koepka 68, Lorenzo-Vera 68, Berger 67, Fleetwood 64; **135** Todd 70, Casey 67, Champ 64

THIRD ROUND

It's a mantra that could easily have been conceived with Koepka in mind: if you've got it, flaunt it.

It would be fair to say the defending champion was in full flaunting mood at the finish of an enthralling third day. Koepka found himself just two strokes off the lead, after a round of 69 that twisted one way and then the other, and he liked what he could see around and ahead of him.

Leading the way was Johnson, whose imperious 65 had moved the 2016 US Open champion to nine under par, one stroke ahead of two relatively inexperienced yet highly regarded young players in PGA Tour rookie Scheffler (65) and Champ (67). In all, 19 players were within five shots of the lead after a day of low scores and long putts, a day during which eight players had at least a share of the lead at some point.

With four wins in his last eight majors, Koepka had built himself a reputation as a player for the big occasion. By way of contrast Johnson, his friend and fierce rival, had let a few too many majors slip through his grasp when they seemed there for his taking. Perhaps it was time to remind him, to see if he could sleep comfortably on the lead.

"Everything seems like it is coming together," said Koepka. "When I've been in this position before, I've capitalised. He," meaning Johnson, of course, "has only won one. A lot of guys on the leaderboard, I don't think have won a major. I feel very comfortable around the lead in big events. Obviously, we don't have fans here … but I'm looking forward to tomorrow. It should be a fun shootout."

Only time would tell if Koepka had made himself a hostage to fortune in his bid to lift the Wanamaker Trophy for the third successive time. For his part, Johnson was his familiar laid-back self. "I've been in the hunt a bunch of times in a major," he said. "I've got one major, so having that experience is definitely going to be beneficial. I'm still going to have to go out and play really good golf. This is a tough golf course, the greens are getting really firm, they are fast. I think the wind is going to blow again tomorrow, so it's going to play difficult."

Both Johnson and Koepka had their troubles. Johnson threw in a double bogey at the ninth and Koepka's tournament threatened to unravel after bogeys at the 13th, 14th and 15th. He responded, as champions do, with two birdies in the closing three holes. No wonder his confidence was sky high.

Another player not lacking in confidence was DeChambeau, whose unique power-based game was beginning to deliver results. A 66 left the American at six under and well within range of Johnson heading into the final round. "I'm proud of myself that I've been able to change my body, change everything, and give myself a chance to win," he said. "That's something that I think is difficult to do."

Some players went quietly about their business, among them Morikawa, the 23-year-old Californian who was being tipped for great things from the moment he turned professional a year earlier. With two PGA Tour wins already in his locker, his eyes were now looking towards his first major. A 65 that included three birdies in the last four holes moved him to within two strokes of the lead and dreaming big. "Who knows where I'll be by the end of the day," he said. "Hopefully I'll be within striking distance."

Haotong Li, the first player from China to lead after any round at a major, was leading through 12 holes until his tee shot stayed up a tree at the 13th. He made a double bogey, dropped two more shots and finished four strokes off the lead.

Woods' hopes of a 16th major title fell by the wayside with a round of 72 that moved him to two over par and out of the running. The same could be said of McIlroy, his playing partner, who moved to level par for the championship after a 71.

Also among the frontrunners was Casey, whose 68 took him into a share of fourth place with Koepka and Morikawa at seven under, while joining DeChambeau one further back were Day, Rose, Fleetwood, Berger and Tony Finau. Whatever lay in store for the final day, it was not going to be lacking in drama.

After 54 holes: 201 (-9) D Johnson 65; **202** Champ 67, Scheffler 65; **203** Koepka 69, Casey 68, Morikawa 65; **204** Day 70, Rose 70, Berger 70, Fleetwood 70, Finau 67, DeChambeau 66

FOURTH ROUND

Cometh the hour, cometh the man. But which man?

If Koepka was to live up to his own billing then the final round was likely to be a procession towards his own crowning glory as he lifted the Wanamaker Trophy for the third time in three years.

If not Koepka, then who? Johnson? The 2016 US Open champion led by one stroke heading into the final round, but he had the unenviable record of holding the 54-hole lead in three majors over the years and failing to win any of them. A fatal flaw? We were due to find out.

And what of the Young Turks, the likes of Morikawa, Scheffler, Champ and Wolff? Fearless to a man, they might not bow the knee to the established stars but could they handle the intense heat of the final round of a major championship?

Could this be a day for one of the older players, Rose or Casey, perhaps? Rose, who had recently turned 40, was itching to add to his solitary major, the 2013 US Open, while Casey, at 43, was looking to become the oldest first-time winner of a major since Roberto de Vicenzo won The Open Championship in 1967. Both were nicely placed.

One thing was for certain. With 19 players within five shots of the lead this was always likely to be a close-run affair, whatever the defending champion had to say about it.

In the end victory came down to a stroke of genius, a shot that will be spoken about for years to come. It came at the short par-four 16th hole and was delivered by Morikawa, someone we could now see had an old head on very young shoulders.

The American had broken a logjam of seven players at 10 under par when he chipped in for a birdie at the 14th. Now we were truly at the business end of proceedings. In the group ahead of Morikawa, Casey was in complete control of his golf. And when the Englishman got up and down for a brilliant birdie at the 16th to draw level at the top on 11 under par, he could picture victory on the horizon. It was a glimpse, but a fleeting one.

Almost immediately Morikawa, who hadn't even been a professional the last time the championship was played, seized the day. Choosing to drive the 294-yard hole, he hit a perfect tee shot that landed just short of the green, flirted with the bunker on the right and rolled to within seven feet of the hole for an eagle and a lead of two strokes with two to play. "I was hoping for a really good bounce and got it," he said.

Casey was standing on the tee at the par-three 17th and was watching as the ball rolled towards the cup. "Nothing you can do but tip your cap to that," Casey said. "Collin had taken on that challenge and pulled it off. That's what champions do."

Morikawa, who had been drawing plaudits for his clean ball-striking and calm demeanour, closed with a 64 that equalled the lowest final round by a PGA champion in 25 years. With a 13-under-par total of 267, his victory margin was two shots over Casey, who had a 66, and Johnson, who had fallen back to level par for the day with a bogey at the 14th and had two late birdies to thank for his round of 68. A fourth 54-hole lead in a major had gone unconverted.

It did not seem any time at all since Morikawa had still been a student at the nearby University of California-Berkeley, his graduation as a major champion arriving a year after leaving college on his return to the Bay Area.

"When I woke up this morning, I was like, 'This is meant to be. This is where I want to be and I'm not scared of it'," Morikawa said.

A five-strong group in fourth comprised DeChambeau, who made an early charge with four birdies in the first seven holes, Finau, Wolff, Scheffler and Day. Rose was one stroke further back on nine under par, after a 67.

Koepka, meanwhile, was left to rue the day he had been dismissive of his peers and rivals. Golf has a way of bringing players down to earth and the golfing gods were in no mood to spare a four-time major champion. Even so, few could have predicted a round of 74 — there was only one score higher on the final day — that saw him sliding down the field before settling in a tie for 29th.

"It's my first bad round in a major in a while," said Koepka, who nonetheless had nothing but praise for the young champion.

"Hat's off to him," he said of Morikawa. "You see these young guys come out of college now and they are ready to win." Indeed, they are.

TPC Harding Park, San Francisco, California — August 6-9
Par 70 (35-35); 7,251 yards — Purse: $11,000,000

1	**Collin Morikawa**	69	69	65	64	267	$1,980,000
2	**Paul Casey**	68	67	68	66	269	968,000
	Dustin Johnson	69	67	65	68	269	968,000
4	Jason Day	65	69	70	66	270	404,350
	Bryson DeChambeau	68	70	66	66	270	404,350
	Tony Finau	67	70	67	66	270	404,350
	Scottie Scheffler	66	71	65	68	270	404,350
	Matthew Wolff	69	68	68	65	270	404,350
9	Justin Rose	66	68	70	67	271	295,600
10	Cameron Champ	71	64	67	70	272	252,123
	Joel Dahmen	69	68	68	67	272	252,123
	Xander Schauffele	66	70	69	67	272	252,123
13	Daniel Berger	67	67	70	69	273	192,208
	Si Woo Kim	69	68	68	68	273	192,208
	Jon Rahm	70	69	68	66	273	192,208
	Patrick Reed	68	70	69	66	273	192,208
17	Haotong Li	67	65	73	69	274	156,500
	Brendon Todd	65	70	72	67	274	156,500
19	Harris English	69	71	69	66	275	134,000
	Lanto Griffin	68	68	71	68	275	134,000
	Kevin Kisner	67	73	68	67	275	134,000
22	Byeong Hun An	72	69	71	64	276	94,571
	Hideki Matsuyama	70	67	69	70	276	94,571
	Alex Noren	67	69	73	67	276	94,571
	Victor Perez	70	69	69	68	276	94,571
	Ian Poulter	73	68	66	69	276	94,571
	Adam Scott	68	70	70	68	276	94,571
	Brendan Steele	66	71	72	67	276	94,571
29	Tommy Fleetwood	70	64	70	73	277	69,500
	Brooks Koepka	66	68	69	74	277	69,500
	Doc Redman	73	67	70	67	277	69,500
	Harold Varner III	72	66	69	70	277	69,500
33	Dylan Frittelli	70	67	70	71	278	57,500
	Viktor Hovland	68	71	73	66	278	57,500
	Rory McIlroy	70	69	71	68	278	57,500
	Louis Oosthuizen	70	71	70	67	278	57,500
37	Bud Cauley	66	71	73	69	279	45,000
	Russell Henley	71	69	71	68	279	45,000
	Nate Lashley	69	70	70	70	279	45,000
	Webb Simpson	71	68	68	72	279	45,000
	Justin Thomas	71	70	68	70	279	45,000
	Tiger Woods	68	72	72	67	279	45,000
43	Abraham Ancer	69	70	72	69	280	31,594
	Patrick Cantlay	73	68	66	73	280	31,594
	Billy Horschel	69	71	71	69	280	31,594
	Michael Lorenzo-Vera	66	68	72	74	280	31,594
	Keith Mitchell	68	72	68	72	280	31,594
	Ryan Palmer	74	66	76	64	280	31,594
	Cameron Smith	71	69	70	70	280	31,594
	Bernd Wiesberger	68	68	70	74	280	31,594
51	Mark Hubbard	70	71	70	70	281	24,000
	Kurt Kitayama	68	72	70	71	281	24,000
	Luke List	72	69	70	70	281	24,000
	Adam Long	73	68	72	68	281	24,000
	Joost Luiten	71	68	73	69	281	24,000
	Brandt Snedeker	72	66	72	71	281	24,000
	Eric van Rooyen	71	70	74	66	281	24,000
58	Adam Hadwin	68	71	70	73	282	21,338
	Brian Harman	68	71	71	72	282	21,338
	Tom Hoge	72	68	72	70	282	21,338
	Mackenzie Hughes	73	68	69	72	282	21,338
	Denny McCarthy	70	69	70	73	282	21,338
	Charl Schwartzel	73	68	68	73	282	21,338
	Kevin Streelman	69	70	73	70	282	21,338
	Gary Woodland	67	72	73	70	282	21,338
66	Emiliano Grillo	70	70	70	73	283	20,000
	Shane Lowry	68	72	69	74	283	20,000
	Robert MacIntyre	73	67	74	69	283	20,000
	Rory Sabbatini	71	70	72	70	283	20,000
	Sepp Straka	70	71	71	71	283	20,000
71	Danny Lee	69	71	74	70	284	19,350
	Phil Mickelson	72	69	70	73	284	19,350
	Jordan Spieth	73	68	76	67	284	19,350
	Bubba Watson	70	71	73	70	284	19,350
75	JT Poston	67	74	75	70	286	19,050
	Chez Reavie	71	70	75	70	286	19,050
77	Jim Herman	71	69	72	75	287	18,850
	Matt Wallace	71	70	74	72	287	18,850
79	Sung Kang	70	71	76	73	290	18,700

MISSED THE 36-HOLE CUT

Christiaan Bezuidenhout	72	70	142
Jason Dufner	70	72	142
Rickie Fowler	73	69	142
Jim Furyk	71	71	142
Talor Gooch	71	71	142
Ryo Ishikawa	72	70	142
Zach Johnson	66	76	142
Chan Kim	72	70	142
Marc Leishman	70	72	142
Shaun Norris	69	73	142
Carlos Ortiz	72	70	142
Henrik Stenson	70	72	142
Lucas Glover	71	72	143
Tyrrell Hatton	72	71	143
Lucas Herbert	73	70	143
Jason Kokrak	69	74	143
Matt Kuchar	71	72	143
Andrew Landry	74	69	143
Tom Lewis	67	76	143
Sebastian Munoz	71	72	143
Kevin Na	70	73	143
Steve Stricker	72	71	143
Michael Thompson	71	72	143
Richy Werenski	71	72	143
Xinjun Zhang	72	71	143
Alexander Beach	73	71	144
Wyndham Clark	71	73	144
Matthew Fitzpatrick	74	70	144
Sungjae Im	73	71	144
Joaquin Niemann	75	69	144
Cheng Tsung Pan	72	72	144
Scott Piercy	70	74	144
Keegan Bradley	73	72	145
Corey Conners	69	76	145
Tyler Duncan	74	71	145
Max Homa	74	71	145
Jazz Janewattananond	74	71	145
Matt Jones	70	75	145
Troy Merritt	73	72	145
Matthias Schwab	69	76	145
Brian Stuard	72	73	145
Ben Cook	71	75	146
Sergio Garcia	73	73	146
Benjamin Hebert	75	71	146
Graeme McDowell	72	74	146
Andrew Putnam	73	73	146
Bob Sowards	71	75	146
Joohyung Kim	70	77	147
Rob Labritz	71	76	147
David Muttitt	72	75	147
Jimmy Walker	73	74	147
Danny Willett	75	72	147
Rafa Cabrera Bello	72	76	148
Jason Caron	76	72	148

Martin Kaymer	66 82	148
John O'Leary	75 73	148
Michael Auterson	75 74	149
Davis Love III	73 76	149
Shaun Micheel	72 77	149
Jeff Roth	74 75	149
Nick Taylor	76 73	149
Daniel Balin	74 76	150
Rich Berberian Jr	76 74	150
Marty Jertson	74 76	150
Ryan Vermeer	79 71	150
Marcus Kinhult	74 77	151
Ken Tanigawa	78 73	151
Shawn Warren	78 73	151
Justin Bertsch	78 75	153
Jorge Campillo	74 80	154
Jeff Hart	77 77	154
Rich Beem	80 75	155
Rod Perry	75 81	156
Alex Knoll	77 80	157
Judd Gibb	77 84	161
Zach Johnson	82 79	161
Cameron Tringale	73	DSQ

ROLL OF HONOUR

1916	Jim Barnes	Siwanoy
1919	Jim Barnes	Engineers
1920	Jock Hutchison	Flossmoor
1921	Walter Hagen	Inwood
1922	Gene Sarazen	Oakmont
1923	Gene Sarazen	Pelham
1924	Walter Hagen	French Lick Springs
1925	Walter Hagen	Olympia Fields
1926	Walter Hagen	Salisbury
1927	Walter Hagen	Cedar Crest
1928	Leo Diegel	Five Farms
1929	Leo Diegel	Hillcrest
1930	Tommy Armour	Fresh Meadows
1931	Tom Creavy	Wannamoisett
1932	Olin Dutra	Keller
1933	Gene Sarazen	Blue Mound
1934	Paul Runyan	The Park
1935	Johnny Revolta	Twin Hills
1936	Denny Shute	Pinehurst (No 2)
1937	Denny Shute	Pittsburgh Field Club
1938	Paul Runyan	Shawnee
1939	Henry Picard	Pomonok
1940	Byron Nelson	Hershey
1941	Vic Ghezzi	Cherry Hills
1942	Sam Snead	Seaview
1944	Bob Hamilton	Manito
1945	Byron Nelson	Moraine
1946	Ben Hogan	Portland
1947	Jim Ferrier	Plum Hollow
1948	Ben Hogan	Norwood Hills
1949	Sam Snead	Hermitage
1950	Chandler Harper	Scioto
1951	Sam Snead	Oakmont
1952	Jim Turnesa	Big Spring
1953	Walter Burkemo	Birmingham
1954	Chick Harbert	Keller
1955	Doug Ford	Meadowbrook
1956	Jack Burke Jr	Blue Hill
1957	Lionel Hebert	Miami Valley
1958	Dow Finsterwald	Llanerch
1959	Bob Rosburg	Minneapolis
1960	Jay Hebert	Firestone
1961	Jerry Barber*	Olympia Fields
1962	Gary Player	Aronimink
1963	Jack Nicklaus	Dallas Athletic Club
1964	Bobby Nichols	Columbus
1965	Dave Marr	Laurel Valley
1966	Al Geiberger	Firestone
1967	Don January*	Columbine
1968	Julius Boros	Pecan Valley
1969	Raymond Floyd	NCR
1970	Dave Stockton	Southern Hills
1971	Jack Nicklaus	PGA National
1972	Gary Player	Oakland Hills
1973	Jack Nicklaus	Canterbury
1974	Lee Trevino	Tanglewood Park
1975	Jack Nicklaus	Firestone
1976	Dave Stockton	Congressional
1977	Lanny Wadkins*	Pebble Beach
1978	John Mahaffey*	Oakmont
1979	David Graham*	Oakland Hills
1980	Jack Nicklaus	Oak Hill
1981	Larry Nelson	Atlanta Athletic Club
1982	Raymond Floyd	Southern Hills
1983	Hal Sutton	Riviera
1984	Lee Trevino	Shoal Creek
1985	Hubert Green	Cherry Hills
1986	Bob Tway	Inverness
1987	Larry Nelson*	PGA National
1988	Jeff Sluman	Oak Tree
1989	Payne Stewart	Kemper Lakes
1990	Wayne Grady	Shoal Creek
1991	John Daly	Crooked Stick
1992	Nick Price	Bellerive
1993	Paul Azinger*	Inverness
1994	Nick Price	Southern Hills
1995	Steve Elkington*	Riviera
1996	Mark Brooks*	Valhalla
1997	Davis Love III	Winged Foot (West)
1998	Vijay Singh	Sahalee
1999	Tiger Woods	Medinah (No 3)
2000	Tiger Woods*	Valhalla
2001	David Toms	Atlanta Athletic Club
2002	Rich Beem	Hazeltine National
2003	Shaun Micheel	Oak Hill
2004	Vijay Singh*	Whistling Straits
2005	Phil Mickelson	Baltusrol (Lower)
2006	Tiger Woods	Medinah (No 3)
2007	Tiger Woods	Southern Hills
2008	Padraig Harrington	Oakland Hills
2009	YE Yang	Hazeltine National
2010	Martin Kaymer*	Whistling Straits
2011	Keegan Bradley*	Atlanta Athletic Club
2012	Rory McIlroy	Kiawah Island (Ocean)
2013	Jason Dufner	Oak Hill
2014	Rory McIlroy	Valhalla
2015	Jason Day	Whistling Straits
2016	Jimmy Walker	Baltusrol (Lower)
2017	Justin Thomas	Quail Hollow
2018	Brooks Koepka	Bellerive
2019	Brooks Koepka	Bethpage (Black)
2020	Collin Morikawa	TPC Harding Park

**won in playoff*

Contested as match play until 1957

Matthew Lewis/R&A

Popov tells her incredible story

It was one of the shortest putts ever to win a major championship. Yet one of the most emotional. Sophia Popov was already in tears. Having seen her approach putt finish alongside the hole, and while waiting for her playing partner, Minjee Lee, to hole out, Popov sunk her head onto the shoulder of her caddie, and boyfriend, Maximilian Mehles. That's when the tears of joy, and relief, started. Moments later the 27-year-old from Germany, listed at 304th on the Rolex Rankings, tapped in to win the AIG Women's Open.

"I guess it is an incredible story," she said. "That's why I broke down on the 18th hole. It's been something I couldn't have dreamed of just a week ago, and it's incredible that golf allows for these things to happen."

A week before her moment of triumph on the links of Royal Troon, after four days of menacing wind, rain and chill, Popov finished second on the Symetra Tour in the summer heat of Phoenix. A week before that, she qualified for the year's first major — initially scheduled as the last — with a ninth place at the Marathon Classic. The week before that, she was caddieing for her friend Anne van Dam in the LPGA's restart at the Drive On Championship.

Popov only won for the first time as a professional, six years after her last victory while in college, four months earlier on the Cactus Tour in Arizona. She won three times in six starts. In 2019 Popov had contemplated giving up the game. Then at the LPGA's Q Series, she eagled the 17th hole of the final round before missing a six-footer on the 18th, meaning she missed her card on the main circuit by one stroke.

When the tours, and the world, went into lockdown in March, Popov, a dual German-American citizen, worked out her frustration at the probability of not being able to upgrade her Symetra Tour status for another year on improving her game and fitness, both at her base in Florida and at her parents' home in Arizona. Winning, it turns out, changes everything.

"It was definitely different to winning a Cactus Tour event," Popov said at Troon. "I was uber-nervous the whole round and I'm just glad I could get it done. My focus this year was the Symetra Tour, to play in the British Open was a bonus. I got here on Tuesday and said, 'I know my game is in really good shape. I know anything's possible.' I took that belief with me to every round but I never expected this."

Popov added: "It feels amazing. There's a lot of hard work behind it, a lot of struggles that I went through the last six years, especially health-wise. I'm just glad I was able to overcome everything. I almost quit playing last year, so thank God I didn't."

Later Popov described how she first felt ill with fatigue and a myriad of other symptoms in 2015. By then the 2010 European Amateur champion had already recorded two top-10 finishes on the Ladies European Tour. A promising career had barely started. "It took a total of about 20 doctor visits three years later to figure out that I had Lyme disease," she explained.

"At that point it was so chronic, it took so long to pinpoint exactly what was going on. For me to regain all my energy — I lost 25 pounds — and get back to where I was before, it was a struggle that only my inner circle knew about until now.

"Lyme is something that sticks with you. I'm very disciplined as far as my health and my nutrition goes, and working out, and do everything in my power to have as little as possible symptoms."

Like Popov's career, the AIG Women's Open, being hosted at Royal Troon for the first time, almost did not happen. After the men's Open at Royal St George's, scheduled a month earlier in July, was postponed to 2021, Martin Slumbers, the chief executive of The R&A, in their first year of fully operating the championship, was determined that it should go ahead with the 40 per cent increase in prize money that had already been announced.

No spectators were allowed, a minimum number of support staff were on site and they ringed the 18th green as the unexpected but engaging new champion was crowned. Players had to stay in a designated hotel, have contact with only one other person — their caddie in most instances — and travel to the course in their own car. Before signing her winning card, Popov remembered just in time to fetch her mask from her golf bag before entering the scoring hut.

A number of leading Korean players were missing, including the world number one Jin Young Ko, but former champion Inbee Park and Canada's Brooke Henderson played for the first time since the restart. "I was really worried about travelling," said Park, "but I feel really safe at the tournament site and the hotel. They are doing a great job. I thought it wouldn't feel like a tournament without all the people but I was surprised. I came here and saw the atmosphere, and it actually really feels like a championship."

Slumbers explained: "If I'm really honest, it was probably only a month ago that we were really comfortable that we could get this away. It has been an enormous effort by an enormous number of people, and our thanks go to not just to AIG and our partners but the governments in both Scotland and Westminster who have been tireless in helping us make a statement in putting this championship on. When I sit here today on the eve of it teeing off, albeit with some pretty dreadful weather forecast for the next couple days, it was a great decision. There's a wonderful sense of excitement."

FIRST ROUND

Due to the tail end of Storm Ellen, players were greeted with gales gusting over 40mph from the south, meaning it was mainly into their faces going out. It was a rude awaking on a course that had previously tested the best male golfers on nine occasions. Dame Laura Davies, on her 40th appearance in the championship she won in 1986, hit the opening tee shot at 6.30am and did not make a par until the fifth hole. Playing alongside Davies, Alena Sharp hit her first drive out of bounds and took a double-bogey six. "It woke me up a bit," she said. The Canadian with a grandmother who was born 40 miles away in Greenock birdied four of the last eight holes for a level-par 71.

Home favourite Catriona Matthew, the 2009 champion in her 26th appearance, used all her experience of similarly "horrific" days past. The European Solheim Cup captain birdied the 15th, 16th and 17th holes, with putts of 30, 15 and 12 feet respectively, to get under par until a bogey at the last meant a 71. It was not a day when she would have been out at her home club in North Berwick given the choice. "I'd probably sit and look at them and think what idiots they are to go out there," Matthew admitted. "You go out there with the mentality to hang in. You might get the odd bad break, you might get a few good ones. Try and give yourself putts for par."

Popov had played in one Women's Open previously, as an amateur in 2011, and only had time for one practice round after her late arrival. But she had enough experience of British links golf from her amateur career to accept her approach at the first hole from 126 yards needed to be played with a four-iron. "There is no secret other than good ball-striking," Popov said. "I was excited because I haven't done it for a while but I know how to keep the ball low and I know how I'm supposed to be playing out here. It's nice that I went out and was able to pick the right shots out from my memory bank."

After three bogeys and two birdies in her first 13 holes, Popov became the first player to post an under-par round with birdies at the 16th and 17th holes for a 70. "To come off the 18th green shooting one under par, I'm extremely happy," she added. "It honestly ranks as one of my best rounds ever. I shot nine under last week, which score-wise is obviously a better score, but I shot that in perfect conditions and absolute just regular target golf in Phoenix."

Elsewhere, Nelly Korda eagled the 16th in a 72 and Georgia Hall, the 2018 champion, had a 73, as did Ariya Jutanugarn, the 2016 champion. Australia's Lee had a 74, while there were 76s from Danielle Kang, Charley Hull, Stacy Lewis, winner of the Scottish Open the previous week, and Hinako Shibuno, the defending champion.

The Japanese player, who missed the cut at the Scottish, won at parkland Woburn in 2019 but her first experience of an Open links was to suffer three bogeys and a triple-bogey eight in her first five holes. The familiar smile from Woburn only returned with a birdie at the last. Kang, who won the first two tournaments after the re-start in America, was nine over par until she finished eagle-birdie-birdie. There were 77s for Inbee Park and Brooke Henderson, and 78s for In-Kyung Kim and Lexi Thompson.

Anna Nordqvist got to two under par with a birdie from two feet at the 13th but the Swede bogeyed the next two holes and joined those on 71. They also included Dani Holmqvist, Jasmine Suwannapura and Lindsey Weaver. The American did not have a caddie and was using a trolley. But while she was trying to extricate herself from one bunker at the 14th, her trolley trundled into another. It was that sort of day. "My worst nightmare come true," Weaver said. "She's okay. Just had to dust off a lot of sand."

On a day when no one kept an over-par score off their card, Marina Alex had a double bogey at the par-five sixth, where her drive went just 175 yards, but then responded with birdies at the eighth, the 12th and the 17th to join Popov on 70.

Amy Olson bogeyed the third but, like Alex, had no other holes over par. Birdies at the fourth, where she chipped in, the sixth and 11th holes got the American to two under. Unlike Nordqvist, she kept going. Her tee shot at the short 14th finished two feet away and she holed a 20-footer on the 16th. Her 67 was eight strokes better than the average score and gave her a three-stroke lead. "That was the best ball-striking day of my life," said the 28-year-old. "I seriously love major championship golf. It requires every part of your game to be sharp and I love that challenge."

After 18 holes: 67 (-4) Olson; **70** Popov, Alex; **71** Holmqvist, Pace, Iturrioz, Suwannapura, Lopez, Weaver, Pedersen, Matthew, Sharp

SECOND ROUND

Heavy rain soon afflicted the early starters on Friday. Winds of 20mph returned with stronger gusts for good measure. The day's scoring average was again in excess of 75 and a half strokes and at the end of it only one player was left under par.

That player was not the overnight leader Olson. The American scored 14 shots higher than on Thursday, an 81 leaving her on eight over par, one stroke inside the cut line. Alex, who shared second place overnight, matched Olson's outward 41 before returning a 79 to be seven over. For a while Popov was leading at one under par long before having to face the elements.

Of those returning to the clubhouse, Austin Ernst headed the list on level par after a 70 containing three bogeys and four birdies, one of them a chip-in three at the ninth. Lydia Ko bogeyed the first hole but then had 16 pars and a birdie at the 13th as a 71 kept the New Zealander on one over par. Emily Kristine Pedersen, one of those who was in the playoff at the Scottish Open the previous week, had a 72 to tie Ko. The Dane was prepared for the worst, explaining: "My dad is a lawyer and my mum is in risk banking and they sometimes see things a little bit worst-case scenario. I think that mind-set helped me today."

Weaver and Suwannapura also had 72s to be one over. The Thai player produced one of the shots of the day with an eagle at the sixth, the hardest hole on the course for the second day running. She holed a five-iron from 142 yards for her third shot. "It was one bounce and in, though I didn't see it, people said it was in the hole," said Suwannapura, who made a seven at the same hole on Thursday. "Lots of ups and downs, you have to be really patient." Weaver battled the course as well as her decade-old trolley. Not so much raging against the machine but a wistful yearning for a "functioning brake".

Park improved by eight strokes, and 71 places on the leaderboard to four over par, with a 69 capped by a birdie on the 18th green from 30 feet. "I really thought that it was almost impossible to shoot under par on the golf course in these conditions," said the champion from just down the coast at Turnberry in 2015. "It was pretty crazy out there yesterday and today, the toughest conditions I've ever played." England's Bronte Law improved by 10 strokes from 80 to 70 to make the cut.

Among the seven players to break par was Holmqvist, whose 70 put her into the lead at one under par. Twice the Swede got to two under par. The first time she dropped back to level at the turn before birdieing the 13th and 14th holes, followed by a bogey at the 15th. Holmqvist had spent much of 2020, as the previous year, rehabilitating a back injury caused when the cart shuttle she was a passenger in crashed into a wall on a steep hill at a tournament late in 2018. "I'm happy to get in under par," said the 32-year-old, who played at Royal Troon as an amateur in the Helen Holm Trophy. "Every shot is a challenge. So whenever you actually pull a good shot off, you're happy."

Lee, no stranger to the wind growing up in Perth with its "Freemantle Doctor", matched Park for the low round of the day. She got to one over par with a fine run coming home, chipping in at the 11th and then holing 15-footers at the last two holes. Korda had another 72 to be two over, Nordqvist a 74 to be three over and Matthew, missing the magic of Thursday, a 76 to be five over. Kang had a 74 to be eight over and the cut came at nine over par, the highest mark since nine over also made it at Royal Lytham in 2009. Henderson, Thompson, Lewis, Shibuno and Hull all missed out.

Popov did not tee off until 2.22pm. She bogeyed the second, birdied the fourth, then bogeyed the fifth and eighth holes. At that point it was getting late and dark and cold, and retreat might have been anticipated from an unproven contender. Not from Popov, however. Television coverage had ceased for the day, yet as each subsequent par was posted on the online scoring system a tale of resilience unfolded. She made it to the 18th without dropping another shot and finished with a birdie. A 72 put her in a tie with Ernst, one behind Holmqvist.

"It was very steady, just grinding it out on the back nine for a solid score," said the German. "My biggest achievement was the mental part of it. It was totally about patience, one shot at a time and just battling the conditions. I knew my game was there. I just had to get it together in my head."

After 36 holes: 141 (-1) Holmqvist 70; **142** Ernst 70, Popov 72; **143** Minjee Lee 69, L Ko 71, Suwannapura 72, Weaver 72, Pedersen 72

THIRD ROUND

Popov went to the top of the leaderboard with a shot that will also be remembered as long as her victory is recalled. It came at the par-five fourth hole. The worst of the weather had relented and what breeze there was came from the prevailing direction, meaning the outward half of the course was less severe than the first two days. American Kristen Gillman went to the turn in 31, making four birdies in a row from the third and almost holing in one at the Postage Stamp. Gillman's 68 got her to two over par, while Australia's Katherine Kirk matched the lowest score of the week with a 67 to get to three over. Kirk's highlight came when holing a putt of 90 feet at the 15th.

For her second shot at the first par five, Popov had 259 yards to the hole and elected to hit her driver. "It suited my eye. Good lie. I said, 'Alright, I'm just going to go for it'," she said. "I hit it in the perfect spot and it just curled around." The ball finished 12 feet from the hole and the putt fell for an eagle. At two under par, Popov now led by one.

She never lost the lead again over the remaining 32 holes. Spending time around van Dam over the lockdown had infused her with a positive spirit but, in addition, caddieing for her friend the previous month had made her revise her own usually aggressive style of play. "I thought about the course a little bit more from a caddie perspective," she explained. "What is the smart decision to make here? Do you have to go for the pins? No, not really. You can give yourself a lot of chances with safer shots going for the middle of the green."

Popov found every green in regulation in the third round. There were still some dangerous moments. At the ninth, 10th and 11th holes she faced testing putts for par but holed them all. "Honestly, I was surprised how calm I stayed over those because I knew these are the key putts that I have to make during the round. So I'm definitely very proud of those."

Making those putts helped with holing a 15-footer for birdie at the 12th. A bonus was holing from 30 feet for a two at the 17th. Popov's 67 matched Olson and Kirk for the lowest of the week to date and was the only round recorded so far to be devoid of any dropped shots. At four under par she led by three strokes from Lee and Suwannapura. Both had 69s, Lee for the second day running, the Thai player dropping a shot at the last as Popov's lead suddenly grew at the end of the day.

Holmqvist, in the final group, made only one birdie in a 77 to fall to five over par. Her playing partner, Ernst, had a 72 and at one over par was sharing fourth place with Caroline Masson, who scored 68 with a late run of three birdies in a row, and Weaver, who had a 71. Weaver's adventurous week continued when she needed a socially distanced search party to find her ball on a bank in the rough at the 12th. The mission was successful, and although she did not make the green with her recovery, she did then chip in for her par.

A few big names were still lurking but possibly now too far back. Ko had a 72 to be two over and Park a 71 to stay at four over, the same mark as Korda, after a 73. Popov was not denying, however, the new situation she found herself in. "There are going to be a lot of nerves, I would be lying if it wasn't that way," she said. "That's why we play the sport. We do this in order to be in a position like I'm going to be in tomorrow."

After 54 holes: 209 (-4) Popov 67; **212** Minjee Lee 69, Suwannapura 69; **214** Masson 68, Weaver 71, Ernst 72

FOURTH ROUND

Popov was so nervous she could hardly eat breakfast on Sunday morning. Yet outwardly she remained calm, even after she drove into a bunker at the first hole and ended up taking a bogey. It was her first dropped shot since the eighth hole on Friday. "That bogey, actually, to me was not that bad of a thing," she said. It turned out to be her only bogey in a run of 45 holes. By birdieing the next two holes, Popov went four shots clear.

Early in the day there was hardly any wind at all. Ally McDonald had a five-under-par round of 66, both Alex and Kang finished with 67s, while Hannah Green parred all 18 holes. Pars were not going to be enough for the leaders. Not when Park was on a charge, birding four holes in a row from the fifth to the eighth. But Korea's multiple major winner stalled on level par and only with a birdie at the 17th did she get under par for the championship. It was a mighty effort after opening with a 77, 11 strokes higher than her closing round which tied McDonald's for the low score of the week.

"I fought really well because after the first day, I really wanted to give up," said Park after finishing fourth. "I didn't give up and I'm really happy with the round today, especially my putter really worked well."

It was Suwannapura who followed Park's lead, also claiming four birdies in succession, from the fourth to the seventh holes. At that point the Thai was five under par but still one behind Popov, who had birdied the sixth. Two dropped shots were redeemed by holing from 25 feet at the 16th and 15 feet at the 17th. A 67 secured runner-up honours, ultimately two behind the champion, all done with a joyful air.

Five years earlier she broke her back hitting a golf shot and it could have ended her career. "Before I had surgery, my doctor said don't even think about not doing it because you'll be in a wheelchair no matter what. I just go with it and I didn't even think I would play golf again. To be able to win on tour, and now finish second this week, I'm grateful to be here."

As the eighth ranked player in the world, 296 places higher than her final-round playing partner, Lee might have hoped to be the one breaking her major duck. There were birdies at the fifth and sixth holes, as well as a stunning three at the Postage Stamp, where she found sand off the tee and holed from 25 feet for the par. But early on the back nine the Australian was frustrated not to give herself better chances. A third 69 in a row left her on three under par and in third place, her best finish in the British major. "I was a little disappointed with my ball-striking but it was a solid week," she said.

"Sophia played so well pretty much all day. Whenever she looked like she was going to make bogey, she would make a par putt, and she made a lot of birdies out there. I didn't think anybody could have beaten her today."

Of the venue, Lee added: "Everything about this place is really cool. We had such a treat this week. Even with the weather, we got to see all of what links golf is about." Popov enjoyed Troon, too, with her caddie Mehles usefully distracting her with chat about the scenery and the boats in the bay. "Kudos to my boyfriend for keeping me calm," she said.

This was not the Cactus Tour any more, but winning is winning. She holed a crucial 15-footer for par on the 11th and took advantage of her luck in skirting a fairway bunker at the 15th to add a fourth birdie of the day. "That was the moment I knew," Popov said. "If it wasn't my week, that drive would have gone into the bunker, and possibly close to the lip." Another birdie followed at the 16th. "The last two holes, thank God, I could take it in a little bit and I looked around and it's just so beautiful and it's such an amazing course.

"We've been extremely privileged. Honestly, thank you to AIG, to The R&A, to everyone that has played a role this week. Considering everything, the way we were taken care of was just incredible."

Popov joined Bernhard Langer and Martin Kaymer as major winners from Germany. The latter phoned her that night. "It shows that with golf you should never give up on your dreams," Kaymer said. "It was beautiful."

A bogey at the last meant a 68 and a seven-under-par total of 277. She was not taking any chances, laying up with her second and then putting from long range up onto the green. Unaware she had three putts for victory, Popov was waiting to see her score on an electronic scoreboard. Lee told her simply: "You're fine. Just go."

There was still the final tap-in to come but the tears came first. "The last putt was so short, I knew I could hole it whatever. I just let go. It's a level of happiness you can't really describe to people, it's crazy."

Royal Troon Golf Club, Troon, South Ayrshire, Scotland — August 20-23
Par 71 (36-35); 6,648 yards — Purse: $4,500,000

1	**Sophia Popov**	70	72	67	68	277	$675,000
2	**Jasmine Suwannapura**	71	72	69	67	279	407,926
3	**Minjee Lee**	74	69	69	69	281	295,468
4	Inbee Park	77	69	71	66	283	228,194
5	Austin Ernst	72	70	72	70	284	183,349
6	Momoko Ueda	75	75	68	67	285	149,712
7	Andrea Lee	74	73	70	69	286	105,426
	In Gee Chun	72	75	70	69	286	105,426
	Jennifer Song	74	74	68	70	286	105,426
	Caroline Masson	72	74	68	72	286	105,426
11	Ashleigh Buhai	74	73	72	68	287	77,057
	Kristen Gillman	75	72	68	72	287	77,057
	Emily Kristine Pedersen	71	72	72	72	287	77,057
14	Marina Alex	70	79	72	67	288	60,240
	Angela Stanford	73	74	73	68	288	60,240
	Nelly Korda	72	72	73	71	288	60,240
	Cydney Clanton	74	73	68	72	288	60,240
	Lydia Ko	72	71	72	73	288	60,240
19	Lizette Salas	73	74	72	70	289	49,926
	Brittany Altomare	77	72	69	71	289	49,926
	Lindsey Weaver	71	72	71	75	289	49,926
22	Ally McDonald	74	75	75	66	290	41,276
	Haru Nomura	74	70	76	70	290	41,276
	Caroline Inglis	75	71	73	71	290	41,276
	Alena Sharp	71	74	73	72	290	41,276
	Ariya Jutanugarn	73	74	70	73	290	41,276
	Megan Khang	75	70	72	73	290	41,276
	Katherine Kirk	72	77	67	74	290	41,276
29	Alison Lee	72	77	72	70	291	33,556
	Hannah Green	75	72	73	71	291	33,556
	Dani Holmqvist	71	70	77	73	291	33,556
32	Danielle Kang	76	74	75	67	292	27,149
	Mi Hyang Lee	76	71	77	68	292	27,149
	Jing Yan	77	73	71	71	292	27,149
	Elizabeth Szokol	72	74	74	72	292	27,149
	Yealimi Noh	72	73	73	74	292	27,149
	Lee-Anne Pace	71	74	73	74	292	27,149
	Anna Nordqvist	71	74	73	74	292	27,149
39	Stephanie Meadow	75	75	72	71	293	20,326
	Perrine Delacour	75	74	73	71	293	20,326
	Dana Finkelstein	77	71	72	73	293	20,326
	Jodi Ewart Shadoff	73	75	72	73	293	20,326
	Mel Reid	78	73	68	74	293	20,326
	Azahara Munoz	74	75	70	74	293	20,326
45	Pernilla Lindberg	75	75	74	70	294	15,728
	Laura Fuenfstueck	73	78	72	71	294	15,728
	Georgia Hall	73	76	74	71	294	15,728
	Amy Olson	67	81	75	71	294	15,728
	Cheyenne Knight	76	75	71	72	294	15,728
	Anne van Dam	77	72	73	72	294	15,728
51	Amy Yang	73	76	75	71	295	12,702
	Carlota Ciganda	77	74	71	73	295	12,702
	Bronte Law	80	70	72	73	295	12,702
	Celine Herbin	74	75	73	73	295	12,702
	Jenny Shin	77	73	69	76	295	12,702
56	Felicity Johnson	76	74	77	69	296	10,907
	Julieta Granada	77	73	76	70	296	10,907
	Moriya Jutanugarn	77	73	70	76	296	10,907
59	Gaby Lopez	71	80	75	71	297	9,384
	Angel Yin	75	74	77	71	297	9,384
	Morgan Pressel	77	74	71	75	297	9,384
	Catriona Matthew	71	76	74	76	297	9,384
	Nuria Iturrioz	71	74	74	78	297	9,384
64	Dottie Ardina	78	73	76	71	298	8,217
	Maria Fernanda Torres	76	72	79	71	298	8,217
	Nasa Hataoka	74	77	75	72	298	8,217
	Emma Talley	77	73	74	74	298	8,217
	Becky Morgan	74	73	74	77	298	8,217
69	Sandra Gal	74	74	78	73	299	7,544
70	Sarah Jane Smith	78	73	72	78	301	7,321
71	Johanna Gustavsson	73	75	84	70	302	5,546
72	Camilla Lennarth	75	76	78	74	303	5,358
	Stephanie Kyriacou	73	78	78	74	303	5,358
74	Michele Thomson	73	77	80	76	306	5,171

MISSED THE 36-HOLE CUT

Celine Boutier	81	71	152
Manon De Roey	81	71	152
Gabriela Ruffels (A)	79	73	152
Charlotte Thompson	79	73	152
Pei-Yun Chien	78	74	152
Julia Engstrom	78	74	152
In-Kyung Kim	78	74	152
Kendall Dye	77	75	152
Brooke M Henderson	77	75	152
Leona Maguire	77	75	152
Hannah Burke	76	76	152
Haley Moore	76	76	152
Monique Smit	75	77	152
Linnea Strom	75	77	152
Nicole Broch Larsen	74	78	152
Kelly Tan	74	78	152
Gerina Piller	81	72	153
Carly Booth	80	73	153
Esther Henseleit	78	75	153
Meghan MacLaren	78	75	153
Yujeong Son	78	75	153
Lexi Thompson	78	75	153
Christine Wolf	77	76	153
Olivia Cowan	76	77	153
Lindy Duncan	76	77	153
Stacy Lewis	76	77	153
Sarah Kemp	75	78	153
Katja Pogacar	75	78	153
Klara Spilkova	75	78	153
Eleanor Givens	74	79	153
Laura Davies	80	74	154
Caroline Hedwall	79	75	154
Tvesa Malik	79	75	154
Jenny Coleman	78	76	154
Kylie Henry	78	76	154
Madelene Sagstrom	78	76	154
Brittany Lang	77	77	154
Olivia Mehaffey (A)	77	77	154
Hinako Shibuno	76	78	154
Karolin Lampert	75	79	154
Xiyu Lin	75	79	154
Nanna Koerstz Madsen	81	74	155
Luna Sobron Galmes	80	75	155
Cristie Kerr	78	77	155
Charley Hull	76	79	155
Minami Katsu	76	79	155
Su Oh	76	79	155
Yui Kawamoto	75	80	155
Alice Hewson	79	77	156
Aditi Ashok	78	78	156
Mone Inami	77	79	156
Gemma Dryburgh	74	82	156
Marianne Skarpnord	74	82	156
Annie Park	81	76	157
Jennifer Chang	80	77	157
Diksha Dagar	79	78	157
Yu Liu	77	80	157

Lina Boqvist	75 82	157
Maria Fassi	75 82	157
Sanna Nuutinenw	74 83	157
Ursula Wikstrom	81 77	158
Whitney Hillier	78 80	158
Charlotte Thomas	78 80	158
Jennifer Kupcho	78 81	159
Patty Tavatanakit	76 83	159
Christina Kim	80 80	160
Tiffany Joh	76 84	160
Emma Nilsson	76 84	160
Louise Ridderstrom	81 83	164
Tonje Daffinrud	85 81	166

ROLL OF HONOUR

1976	Jenny Lee Smith (A)	Fulford
1977	Vivien Saunders	Lindrick
1978	Janet Melville (A)	Foxhills
1979	Alison Sheard	Southport & Ainsdale
1980	Debbie Massey	Wentworth
1981	Debbie Massey	Northumberland
1982	Marta Figueras-Dotti (A)	Royal Birkdale
1984	Ayako Okamoto	Woburn (Duke's)
1985	Betsy King	Moor Park
1986	Laura Davies	Royal Birkdale
1987	Alison Nicholas	St Mellion
1988	Corinne Dibnah*	Lindrick
1989	Jane Geddes	Ferndown
1990	Helen Alfredsson*	Woburn (Duke's)
1991	Penny Grice-Whittaker	Woburn (Duke's)
1992	Patty Sheehan	Woburn (Duke's)
1993	Karen Lunn	Woburn (Duke's)
1994	Liselotte Neumann	Woburn (Duke's)
1995	Karrie Webb	Woburn (Duke's)
1996	Emilee Klein	Woburn (Duke's)
1997	Karrie Webb	Sunningdale
1998	Sherri Steinhauer	Royal Lytham & St Annes
1999	Sherri Steinhauer	Woburn (Duke's)
2000	Sophie Gustafson	Royal Birkdale
2001	Se Ri Pak	Sunningdale
2002	Karrie Webb	Turnberry
2003	Annika Sorenstam	Royal Lytham & St Annes
2004	Karen Stupples	Sunningdale
2005	Jeong Jang	Royal Birkdale
2006	Sherri Steinhauer	Royal Lytham & St Annes
2007	Lorena Ochoa	St Andrews
2008	Jiyai Shin	Sunningdale
2009	Catriona Matthew	Royal Lytham & St Annes
2010	Yani Tseng	Royal Birkdale
2011	Yani Tseng	Carnoustie
2012	Jiyai Shin	Royal Liverpool
2013	Stacy Lewis	St Andrews
2014	Mo Martin	Royal Birkdale
2015	Inbee Park	Turnberry
2016	Ariya Jutanugarn	Woburn (Marquess)
2017	In-Kyung Kim	Kingsbarns
2018	Georgia Hall	Royal Lytham & St Annes
2019	Hinako Shibuno	Woburn (Marquess)
2020	Sophia Popov	Royal Troon

**won in playoff*

Designated an LPGA major since 2001

ANA INSPIRATION

Jeff Gross/Getty Images

Lee chips in with dramatic finale for first major

There is always an element of luck when a chip shot from off the green finds the hole. But when three of them go in during the final round of a major championship, that can only be ... supreme skill?

"Is chipping the best part of your game?"

"Yes," replied Mirim Lee.

"Has it always been the best part of your game?"

"Not really," she admitted. "I think just today."

If so, and a player who can remember multiple times chipping in twice during a round is perhaps being modest, it was a good day for it to happen. It led to Lee tying for the lead at the ANA Inspiration and then defeating Brooke Henderson and Nelly Korda at the first playoff hole for her first major title.

The first chip-in came at the sixth hole. Playing in the penultimate group, Lee's approach came up just in front of the green. She popped that in for her second birdie of the day to move two behind the lead.

A 30-foot birdie putt at the 12th hole kept Lee two behind but at the 16th came a genius bit of escapology. Left of the green and short of the pin high, Lee had to chip over the edge of a bunker from 30 yards yet the ball irresistibly honed in on the hole.

In any other round, on any other day, it would have been the outstanding highlight. But her last chip-in at the 18th hole proved even more dramatic and changed the whole narrative of the day. Until that moment, the championship appeared to be a duel between Korda, who had led for three days, and Henderson, who moved into a share of that lead on Saturday night.

When Lee bogeyed the 17th, failing to get up and down from a bunker, the Korean was two behind Korda, and one adrift of Henderson. "It was a bit disappointing having the bogey on 17," Lee said. "So my plan for 18 was just to have a birdie and do what I have to do to keep my head up." Having gone over the green in two, she needed to get up and down for a four to claim that birdie. The shot was downhill all the way to the hole and there was not a lot of green behind it before the water loomed. If Lee slightly over did her chip in terms of pace, she got the line spot on. It hit the flagstick and dived straight into the hole for an eagle.

There was, literally, a stunned silence. In years past the grandstands at the 18th green at Mission Hills would have erupted in a deafening roar. But there were no spectators. It was a moment of drama that owed a little to luck and an awful lot to skill. Lee smiled but was as shocked as everyone else. "When the shot went in, I think I was really surprised," she said. "It must have been a bit of luck that helped me."

Lee had set the clubhouse target at 15 under par. Korda had just holed a brave 10-footer for her par at the 17th to stay at 15 under, now tied for the lead. Lee assumed, with the tee forward at the par-five 18th to tempt players to go for the green in two as is traditional on the final day of the ANA, that Korda would get her four and the young American would be the one to claim her first major title.

But Korda pulled her drive into thick rough and could not go for the green. She had to lay up and then pitch to the green. Her third shot was not accurate enough to give her a realistic birdie opportunity. From 30 feet, Korda two-putted for her par.

Henderson, still one behind, did hit a good drive and gave her second shot a characteristic thump. It had no chance of staying on the green and would have scampered into the water behind the green but for a blue advertising wall that had been erected on the bank. It took Henderson's sister, and caddie, Brittany, crawling under the canvas to find the ball but eventually the Canadian was able to take her free drop and then produced her own brilliant chip. It finished inside a foot from the hole and Henderson tapped in for a birdie to make it a trio in the playoff.

What was inevitably dubbed the "Great Wall of Dinah" had been a controversial feature all week but came into play excessively in the closing stages. In recent years a grandstand had been in prime position behind the green, extending back into the pond. In theory the wall was maintaining the status quo. In practice there was a significant difference.

Due to the season being rescheduled, what is usually the first major of the year in April had been moved to September. It is a time of year that is much hotter in Rancho Mirage and the Palm Springs area than in the spring. Ahead of the tournament temperatures where well in excess of 100 degrees Fahrenheit and though they dipped just under the 100 mark for the first couple of rounds, on Sunday it was back up to 105 degrees. Players and caddies were allowed to use carts during the practice rounds and caddies during the tournament. Ice towels were available at every turn and more water coolers supplied. Under foot, the summer Bermuda grasses dominated rather than the winer rye of April and it was much firmer. "The greens are so jumpy," Korda said earlier in the week. "They're very firm and they have a big first bounce. With the longer clubs, they just shoot. A lot of times you hit a really good shot but you end up in the rough at the back of the green. It's very bouncy on this Bermuda and you can't even see your pitch marks. It's that firm. Definitely in April you have to fix pitch marks so this is just really different."

So having a "backboard" behind the 18th green of the Dinah Shore Tournament Course, potentially saving balls running into the pond at the back, was an advantage that players picked up on in the practice rounds. All the players. Certainly not just Lee, who at the 72nd hole had 215 yards left and was between a four-iron that might come up short in the water or a five-wood which might run over the back. She took the five-wood and her ball did just reach the wall, from which she got a free drop. "I definitely thought to utilise the backboard," Lee explained. "When I had practice rounds, I had practised that shot."

She still had to produced an extraordinary stroke to claim her eagle and a place in the playoff. Lee played the 18th in a similar fashion at the first extra hole, although this time her second only just trickled over the green. Korda also provided an action replay, again pulling her drive into the rough and having to lay up, while Henderson's second stuck on the bank at the front of the green. Korda's wedge was again not close enough, while Henderson putted up to 10 feet. Lee hit another fine chip, but this time it came up five feet short of the hole. After Korda, from 20 feet, and then Henderson missed their putts, Lee pounced nervelessly to hole her putt and become a major champion.

For the second major in a row, after Sophia Popov's victory at the AIG Women's Open, the winner was hardly expected. Lee was slightly less unexpected in that she was ranked 94th in the world and had won three times on the LPGA previously. But she had not made a cut all year and had battled injuries and exhaustion in the three years since her last win. No wonder the 29-year-old was dumbfounded.

"Honestly, I can't really believe it right now," Lee said, garbed in the traditional bathrobe after a tentative dip into Poppie's Pond. "I feel like I must be a little crazy for having won this."

FIRST ROUND

Moving the tournament into the second major slot due to the April postponement meant an odd anomaly. Popov was missing from the starting field as her exemption for winning at Royal Troon only began with the 2021 ANA, while her non-member status at the time of her victory meant she was not eligible for qualification via the current money list. Voluntarily absent was the 2019 champion Jin Young Ko, who had elected to remain at home in Korea during the pandemic. Meanwhile, England's Charley Hull flew to Palm Springs and then had to isolate in her hotel room after testing positive for Covid-19, so could only watch on television as her compatriots Georgia Hall and Mel Reid opened with three-under-par 69s. Hall's was the first bogey-free round of the day but at the end of the round all those on that mark were three behind Korda.

Taking advantage of the lack of any appreciable breeze, Korda birdied two of the last three holes for her 66. The four at the 18th sneaked her ahead of In Gee Chun, the two-time major winner, and Sweden's Madelene Sagstrom, who had both posted their 67s in the morning. It would be the last time the 22-year-old from Bradenton birdied the 18th for the week.

There were seven birdies in all and they brought applause from her parents, Petra and Regina, who were walking round with both sisters. The previous week Petra had been in New York at one of his old stamping grounds, the US Open, watching tennis-playing son Sebastian make his senior debut at a grand slam. After playing without galleries since the tour's resumption, Nelly was glad of the support. "It's nice to get some clapping occasionally," she said. After a week off, there was a pleasing birdie at the first hole and a tap-in birdie at the 11th after a fine bunker shot. About the only thing she was going to tweak for Friday was drinking more water. "Be more hydrated," she said. "I really liked my game plan going into today, staying calm, and if I keep doing that, I think it will be good."

Thursday was Henderson's 23rd birthday. She was out early and could look forward to enjoying some cake after a 68, which left her two behind with Danielle Kang, the two-time winner in 2020, Yu Liu, Kelly Tan and Nanna Koerstz Madsen. Henderson, the 2016 KPMG Women's PGA champion, dropped only one shot, a three-putt at the first when she turned, but then added four birdies on her second nine. "I made a lot of pars to start, felt like I was really close to making a lot of birdies, so I was happy when they started to fall," she said. "Happy with four under, it's definitely a solid start, a nice way to spend your birthday."

Sister Brittany was one of the caddies who opted for riding her own cart. "Normally I would never agree to taking carts," Brooke explained, "but definitely under the circumstances with it being so hot out here, and since the LPGA was allowing us to use them, it was an advantage. She was able to zoom along, get to my ball fast, calculate some numbers, really get a feel for all the conditions, and then by the time I arrived she already had everything set out and we could discuss a little bit more specifically. I think we'll continue to do it over the next three days."

Other than one occasion when she had to withdraw at the US Women's Open, Henderson had not missed a cut in a major until the AIG Women's Open at Royal Troon the previous month. Hinako Shibuno, the defending champion, had also missed the cut there but, making her competitive debut in America, opened here with a 70. On the same mark was Lee, who had missed the cut in all three of the tournaments she had played in 2020: the Gainbridge in January, the Korea Women's Open in June and the Walmart NW Arkansas a fortnight earlier. She made three birdies and a bogey but had still not scored in the 60s in 2020.

After 18 holes: 66 (-6) N Korda; **67** Chun, Sagstrom; **68** Kang, Henderson, Liu, Tan, Madsen

SECOND ROUND

Something clicked for Lee on Friday at Mission Hills. She made seven birdies and no bogeys in a 65 which was the best score of the tournament through two rounds. "Truthfully, not a lot has changed," Lee said. "It was nice. Compared to some rounds, I didn't miss a lot of shots, but I still did miss some shots, so I look forward to the next couple rounds."

After going out in three under, Lee holed from 25 feet at the 10th, 10 feet at the short 14th, eight feet at the 16th and then made a four at the last. During the tour's shutdown, Lee was back home in Korea but mainly practising, playing only her national championship, which she had won in 2012. It was a relief to be playing again. "When I was in Korea during the break, all I did was practise," Lee said. "It feels so good to be back out here and playing competitive golf. I think that as long as I keep the feeling and momentum of these past few days, I'll be able to get good scores."

Lee jumped 17 spots on the leaderboard and ended the day in second place, two behind Korda. The American added a 67 to her earlier 66 and at 133, 11 under par, was one stroke outside the tournament's 36-hole record. Telling herself that she is "best putter in the world" was paying off. "Thank God for my putting today," Korda said. She did not drop a shot but might have done on several occasions.

"The thing out here is you hit a solid putt, you think it could go in, and it keeps on going," she explained. "You think it's going to stop and it just keeps on releasing. I had a lot of five- and six-footers for par today." She also got out of position at the second and third holes (at the start of her second nine) but holed from outside 20 feet on each occasion to keep a bogey off her card. "I did not know what I was doing on those two holes," Korda said. Her caddie, Jason McDede, told her to "take a deep breath right now" and the three-time LPGA winner holed each time. "I was happy those two went in," she added. "Golf is just all about momentum, so you roll one in here and there and it just makes it a lot easier."

The big hitter had three of her birdies on the short holes and only one on a par five, finishing her day with gains at the eighth and ninth holes to be four ahead until Lee got within two. Third place was four behind as Madsen and Lexi Thompson got to seven under, followed by Chun and Malaysia's Tan one further back.

Madsen takes a bite out of a lemon to punish herself for poor shots but the Dane only had to do it once, on the first tee, in her bogey-free 69. Thompson matched Korda's 67 after starting the round with three birdies in the first five holes. The previous week the 2014 champion had worked with Jim McLean, an instructor she worked with a lot around the age of 12. "Growing up, he knew my swing better than anybody, so I was like, let's just go back to old Lexi," Thompson said.

"He has a lot of videos, lots of notes. Basically, what I saw is what a lot of people always notice, my foot movement and how I get off the ground. There was no restriction, I just hit it hard and got off the ground and I knew it was going up the right and turning back. I'm getting back to that confidence."

Among those on five under par was Henderson and Gabriela Ruffels, the Australian who had just lost her US Amateur crown to Rose Zhang. Ruffels, who had a practice round with the two Korda sisters and another with compatriots Hannah Green and Su Oh, scored 68 and was one in front of Zhang, who scored 69.

After 36 holes: 133 (-11) N Korda 67; **135** M Lee 65; **137** Madsen 69, Thompson 67; **138** Chun 71, Tan 70

THIRD ROUND

Henderson, after a 71 on Friday, made an impressive charge on Saturday, when the weather remained hot and almost windless. The Canadian eagled the second hole from 15 feet and went out in 30. She started six behind but with a birdie at the 11th went into the lead on her own. She dropped her only shot of the day two holes later but a three at the 16th put her back in front at 12 under par. Her 65 matched Lee for the lowest round of the week.

"I'm definitely really happy with this," Henderson said. "I was just trying to move up as much as I could and put myself in great position going into tomorrow."

It was the sort of move that in past years a Saturday crowd at Mission Hills, including many Canadians who winter in the area, would have loved. "It's definitely really noticeable," Henderson said of the lack of atmosphere. "But the thing about this place is there's so much tradition and history here, it's really special. Even without the fans that we miss a lot, it's still a great place to be."

Having gone seven under for the first 11 holes, she was level par for the rest of the round as her charge stalled. "Being a major championship, you've really got to stay patient and know bogeys are going to happen," she said. "The rough out there is very thick and you're just praying it's sitting up if you hit it in there. You have to expect bogeys and try to make a lot of birdies to counter them."

It appeared to be business as usual for Korda, world number three, as she birdied the third hole but then she three-putted the fifth for her first dropped shot since the fourth on Thursday. And at the sixth, after hitting a five-wood into the rough off the tee, she found the lake with her approach from 118 yards. "We thought since it was growing down grain that wouldn't kill it but it just flew nowhere," Korda said. "The Bermuda rough just absolutely killed that shot and unfortunately it went in the water."

By the turn, Korda's two-shot lead from overnight had turned into a deficit of three strokes. But she had settled by then and, after a four at the 11th, she hit wedge shots to two feet at the 12th and six feet at the 15th. Home in 33, she posted a 71 to join Henderson on 12 under. "It was a disappointing front nine, but I was really proud of the way I fought on the back nine. Never gave up and there's still 18 more holes to be played, so much golf."

Korda, who first started competing against Henderson when the pair were only just teenagers, had now led a major for three days, something she had never done even once before. She added: "It's exciting. It's one of the reasons why you play golf, to play with the top players in the world, and play for a major championship."

Thompson looked as if she would be following Henderson's example when she birdied three of the first five holes. But she would play the rest of the course in level par for a 69 to be two behind at 10 under. On the same mark was Australian Katherine Kirk, who holed from outside 30 feet at the first on her way to a second consecutive 67, and Lee, who scored 71. As Korda was making a mess of the sixth, Lee holed from 18 feet for her second birdie of the day to tie for the lead with Henderson.

Yet the Korean was another to falter when she tangled with the rough at the par-five ninth and took a six. She regained the shot two holes later but bogeys at the 15th and 16th holes were only partially offset by a two at 17. "Although there were some mistakes," Lee said, "I feel at the end of the day, I played a really great round. Honestly, I was feeling a little bit under pressure so I think tomorrow if I have a little bit of that, it will be good."

After 54 holes: 204 (-12) N Korda 71, Henderson 65; **206** Thompson 69, Kirk 67, M Lee 71; **207** Ciganda 67; **208** Lewis 67, Zhang 68, Torres 69, Reid 69

FOURTH ROUND

Lee birdied the second hole on Sunday to get within one of the lead, as did Thompson, one of her playing partners. Thompson bogeyed two holes later and had a stop-start day. The former winner had to birdie two of the last three holes to take fourth place, two shots outside the playoff and one ahead of Stacy Lewis.

Apart from Lee chipping in at the sixth, the attention had switched to the young stars in the final group. Both Korda and Henderson birdied the second, as did the third member of the group, 17-year veteran Kirk, who became more chaperone than challenger with a closing 73. Korda birdied the third, Henderson the fourth, and Korda the sixth from six feet.

One ahead at the eighth, Korda then went bogey-birdie-bogey-birdie-bogey. Henderson appeared the steadier of the two, birdieing the 11th and leading on her own for the first time at the 12th. But on the next hole the Canadian got caught up in the rough and took a double bogey, her only over-par hole of the day. Korda was back ahead and put her tee shot at the short 14th to five feet to go two in front.

It was compelling drama, with only the battle for low amateur a minor distraction. Zhang, with weekend rounds of 68 and 72, took the honours by one over Ruffels, who had a pair of 71s. But while the Australian bogeyed two of the last three, Zhang birdied the last two to finish tied for 11th and set a record total for an amateur of 280. "I just feel so incredibly blessed to play such a prestigious event, one I've watched ever since I started golf," said the Californian high school senior who only a month earlier had won the US Women's Amateur.

What of Lee? She did not birdie the two par fives around the turn, but she did hole a long putt at the 12th. "I definitely thought that I could win this, but I tried to disregard that and just keep playing," she said. Her only dropped shot of the day at the 17th came between those two incredible chip-ins. Her 67 was only bettered in the final round by Lydia Ko's 66. "Of the four rounds, today I struggled the most, but I think I had a bit of luck that helped me," Lee said. "But to be honest, not a lot of my shots were the way that I wanted them."

But some were out of this world and interrupted the private duel in the final group. Korda parred the last four holes. Henderson birdied two of the last three. They both returned 69s to join Lee on a total of 273, 15 under, before sharing runner-up honours.

"I definitely played really well this week, which gives me confidence," Henderson said. "Mirim played great today and so did Nelly. It was fun. It was tough to lose that way. I felt like I missed a lot of putts, especially the final round where I feel maybe it could have been a different story."

Korda, after her best major result, admitted she had no idea what Lee had done ahead of the final group but regretted her drives at the 18th. "I played solid today, kept my calm," she said. "Didn't hit a really good shot on 18 off the tee both times, that's what kind of got me in trouble there. I'll take all the experience I can get. I know my game is trending upward."

Part of why Lee felt it was "crazy" for her to have won was because, for most of the year, she had felt exhausted and lacking motivation to play golf. Her coach in Korea, Song Hee Kim, helped her find a way out of the malaise. Lee said she had not cried after winning before but remembering the tough times brought the tears this time.

Before the playoff, Lee spoke to Kim, a former LPGA player, on the phone. She received reassurance that although her game had not been as she wanted, she could still win the playoff against two of the world's top 10. "I tried not to overthink too much, and I think that's why I was able to win, because I got to play like I normally do. All tournaments, major or otherwise, are the same to me. I didn't treat it any different."

Mission Hills Country Club (Dinah Shore), Rancho Mirage, California — September 10-13
Par 72 (36-36); 6,652 yards — Purse: $3,100,000

1	**Mirim Lee**	70	65	71	67	273	$465,000
2	**Brooke M Henderson**	68	71	65	69	273	245,480
	Nelly Korda	66	67	71	69	273	245,480
	Lee won playoff at first extra hole						
4	Lexi Thompson	70	67	69	69	275	159,679
5	Stacy Lewis	70	71	67	68	276	128,524
6	Lydia Ko	69	74	69	66	278	105,156
7	Minjee Lee	71	69	72	67	279	74,388
	Nasa Hataoka	70	73	67	69	279	74,388
	Mel Reid	69	70	69	71	279	74,388
	Katherine Kirk	72	67	67	73	279	74,388
11	Ariya Jutanugarn	73	71	68	68	280	54,679
	Danielle Kang	68	71	70	71	280	54,679
	Rose Zhang (A)	71	69	68	72	280	
	Maria Fernanda Torres	70	69	69	72	280	54,679
15	Amy Yang	71	72	70	68	281	46,579
	Gabriela Ruffels (A)	71	68	71	71	281	
	Mi Hyang Lee	69	70	70	72	281	46,579
18	Leona Maguire	73	72	68	69	282	39,726
	In Gee Chun	67	71	75	69	282	39,726
	Moriya Jutanugarn	71	70	69	72	282	39,726
	Sei Young Kim	69	70	71	72	282	39,726
22	Jennifer Kupcho	72	72	69	70	283	35,208
	Yu Liu	68	71	70	74	283	35,208
24	Lizette Salas	74	74	67	69	284	30,378
	Xiyu Lin	69	77	67	71	284	30,378
	Kristen Gillman	69	72	71	72	284	30,378
	Ally McDonald	71	69	71	73	284	30,378
	Christina Kim	70	69	72	73	284	30,378
	Carlota Ciganda	70	70	67	77	284	30,378
30	Perrine Delacour	74	69	72	70	285	25,938
	Brittany Altomare	71	71	69	74	285	25,938
	Pajaree Anannarukarn	72	70	74	70	286	22,588
	Caroline Masson	71	73	70	72	286	22,588
	Cristie Kerr	71	70	73	72	286	22,588
	Marina Alex	73	69	71	73	286	22,588
	Linnea Strom	72	69	72	73	286	22,588
37	Inbee Park	73	72	70	72	287	19,162
	Georgia Hall	69	71	74	73	287	19,162
	Kelly Tan	68	70	74	75	287	19,162
40	Alena Sharp	75	71	73	69	288	16,876
	Lei Ye (A)	74	69	76	69	288	
	Austin Ernst	71	73	72	72	288	16,876
	Sung Hyun Park	69	73	72	74	288	16,876
44	Yealimi Noh	75	71	72	71	289	13,843
	Eun-Hee Ji	71	74	73	71	289	13,843
	Celine Boutier	75	71	71	72	289	13,843
	Anne van Dam	70	74	73	72	289	13,843
	Sarah Schmelzel	70	73	71	75	289	13,843
	Anna Nordqvist	70	71	73	75	289	13,843
	Jodi Ewart Shadoff	71	73	68	77	289	13,843
51	Esther Henseleit	74	71	78	67	290	10,827
	Amy Olson	79	68	72	71	290	10,827
	Brittany Lang	70	72	74	74	290	10,827
	Stephanie Meadow	70	71	73	76	290	10,827
	Nanna Koerstz Madsen	68	69	76	77	290	10,827
	Hinako Shibuno	70	75	67	78	290	10,827
57	Annie Park	71	73	76	71	291	9,503
	Madelene Sagstrom	67	74	74	76	291	9,503
59	Gaby Lopez	72	75	69	76	292	8,723
	Megan Khang	70	73	72	77	292	8,723
	Angel Yin	74	67	73	78	292	8,723
62	Ryann O'Toole	71	77	74	71	293	7,946
	Hannah Green	69	74	74	76	293	7,946
64	Caroline Inglis	74	74	71	75	294	7,322
	Angela Stanford	75	72	72	75	294	7,322
	Brittany Lincicome	69	75	75	75	294	7,322
	Patty Tavatanakit	73	72	73	76	294	7,322
	In-Kyung Kim	71	75	71	77	294	7,322
69	Azahara Munoz	75	72	74	74	295	6,777
	Yui Kawamoto	71	74	73	77	295	6,777
71	Maria Fassi	73	72	72	79	296	6,542
72	Emilia Carolina Migliaccio (A)	74	71	75	77	297	
73	Dana Finkelstein	72	76	75	75	298	6,387
74	Olivia Mehaffey (A)	77	71	77	76	301	
	Pernilla Lindberg	76	72	77	76	301	6,232
76	Nicole Broch Larsen	72	76	78	76	302	6,155
	MISSED THE 36-HOLE CUT						
	Jaye Marie Green	77	72			149	
	Morgan Pressel	77	72			149	
	Chella Choi	76	73			149	
	Tiffany Joh	76	73			149	
	Jing Yan	76	73			149	
	Cheyenne Knight	75	74			149	
	Charlotte Thomas	75	74			149	
	Jessica Korda	74	75			149	
	Andrea Lee	74	75			149	
	Jasmine Suwannapura	74	75			149	
	Caroline Hedwall	76	74			150	
	Ashleigh Buhai	75	75			150	
	Gerina Piller	75	75			150	
	Cydney Clanton	74	76			150	
	Haru Nomura	74	76			150	
	Jennifer Song	73	77			150	
	Su Oh	72	78			150	
	Elizabeth Szokol	76	75			151	
	Kaitlyn Papp (A)	73	78			151	
	Hee Young Park	79	73			152	
	Lindsey Weaver	77	75			152	
	Emma Talley	76	76			152	
	Bronte Law	79	74			153	
	Pornanong Phatlum	77	76			153	
	Ayako Uehara	77	78			155	
	Klara Spilkova	75				WDN	
	Dani Holmqvist	80				WDN	
	Jenny Shin					WDN	

ROLL OF HONOUR

1972	Jane Blalock	Mission Hills
1973	Mickey Wright	Mission Hills
1974	Jo Ann Prentice*	Mission Hills
1975	Sandra Palmer	Mission Hills
1976	Judy Rankin	Mission Hills
1977	Kathy Whitworth	Mission Hills
1978	Sandra Post*	Mission Hills
1979	Sandra Post	Mission Hills
1980	Donna Caponi	Mission Hills
1981	Nancy Lopez	Mission Hills
1982	Sally Little	Mission Hills
1983	Amy Alcott	Mission Hills
1984	Juli Inkster*	Mission Hills
1985	Alice Miller	Mission Hills
1986	Pat Bradley	Mission Hills
1987	Betsy King*	Mission Hills
1988	Amy Alcott	Mission Hills
1989	Juli Inkster	Mission Hills
1990	Betsy King	Mission Hills
1991	Amy Alcott	Mission Hills
1992	Dottie Mochrie (Pepper)*	Mission Hills
1993	Helen Alfredsson	Mission Hills
1994	Donna Andrews	Mission Hills
1995	Nanci Bowen	Mission Hills
1996	Patty Sheehan	Mission Hills
1997	Betsy King	Mission Hills
1998	Pat Hurst	Mission Hills
1999	Dottie Pepper	Mission Hills
2000	Karrie Webb	Mission Hills
2001	Annika Sorenstam	Mission Hills
2002	Annika Sorenstam	Mission Hills
2003	Patricia Meunier-Lebouc	Mission Hills
2004	Grace Park	Mission Hills
2005	Annika Sorenstam	Mission Hills
2006	Karrie Webb*	Mission Hills
2007	Morgan Pressel	Mission Hills
2008	Lorena Ochoa	Mission Hills
2009	Brittany Lincicome	Mission Hills
2010	Yani Tseng	Mission Hills
2011	Stacy Lewis	Mission Hills
2012	Sun Young Yoo*	Mission Hills
2013	Inbee Park	Mission Hills
2014	Lexi Thompson	Mission Hills
2015	Brittany Lincicome*	Mission Hills
2016	Lydia Ko	Mission Hills
2017	So Yeon Ryu*	Mission Hills
2018	Pernilla Lindberg*	Mission Hills
2019	Jin Young Ko	Mission Hills
2020	Mirim Lee*	Mission Hills

**won in playoff*

Designated an LPGA major since 1983

US OPEN CHAMPIONSHIP

Gregory Shamus/Getty Images

Bryson's new massacre at Winged Foot

When Bryson DeChambeau won the 2020 US Open at Winged Foot, he received a splendid trophy, the Jack Nicklaus medal, a check for $2.2 million, the disbelieving admiration of his peers and — and here's where the academic and scientist in him surface again — validation.

There were the doubters and the scoffers at his proclamation late in 2019. "I'm going to come back next year and look like a different person," he had said. "You're going to see some pretty big changes in my body, which is going to be a good thing. Going to be hitting it a lot further."

Eye rolls, please.

"There will obviously be people that doubt what I do," DeChambeau said. "That's totally fine. That's fuel for my fire. I appreciate that because it makes me think of how I can get better quicker to show people."

A beefier, stronger DeChambeau emerged. And a longer one. At one tournament, he had to back up on the practice range to create room to hit his driver. After the Covid-19 pause at mid-season, he came back yet another 20 pounds heavier — some 40 all told — and yards longer. Always the crusade for length.

"And I'm not going to stop," he said.

Then there is equipment. "I'm going to be trying a 48-inch driver," DeChambeau said. "We're going to be messing with some head designs and do some amazing things to make it feasible to hit these drives maybe 360, 370, maybe even farther." (That could be a sticking point. The US Golf Association and The R&A had already begun studying the possibility of adjusting equipment rules, including the length of drivers, to deal with the distances golfers were hitting the ball.)

And there is the dedication: Saturday, after his third-round 70, he went to the practice range in a short-sleeved shirt, temperatures in the 40s, under the lights and worked on his driver till past eight o'clock. "So my driver was not performing in the way I wanted it to," he said. "I needed to figure something out, so I could play for tomorrow and be super comfortable because, if I'm comfortable with the driver, I knew I could play golf and shoot under par on this golf course."

Validation: he had proved his point.

And there is history: two US Opens were so distinctive, had such an impact that they became absorbed into the game's fabric.

In 1913, Francis Ouimet, the gangly young amateur and ex-caddie, beat two of the world's top pros, Britain's Harry Vardon and Ted Ray, in a playoff at The Country Club — and golf became an American game.

And in 1960, Arnold Palmer trailed by six going into the final round at Cherry Hills, and rocked the land. He drove the 346-yard first and birdied, birdied six of the first seven and won with the greatest comeback in US Open history.

Will Bryson DeChambeau's Massacre at Winged Foot ever join them? Perhaps it already has.

FIRST ROUND

It sounded as though DeChambeau, former budding physicist and newly re-made man — more pro football linebacker than golfer, it seemed — was contradicting himself in his assessment of Winged Foot for this September US Open. Not really.

"Man, it's a great test," he was saying. "You've got to hit a lot of fairways. You can't be in the rough."

Winged Foot's rough. Terror in green. The Bermuda Triangle of golf. Dante's 10th Circle.

To which the big and thick-muscled and smiling DeChambeau added: "I'm hitting it as far as I possibly can up there. Even if it's in the rough, I can still get it to the front edge or the middle of the greens with pitching wedges or nine-irons. That's the beauty of my length and that advantage. I'm going to be trying to go after it as much as I possibly can."

In the first instance, he was speaking of the safe and regular way to play the unforgiving course, the way others would play it. And in the second, he was telling the world — this is how he, Bryson DeChambeau, is going to beat this monster.

And so DeChambeau was primed and on his way to the US Open Championship.

But there was a lot of ground between the interview chair and the trophy surrender. Starting with a 69, one under par and four behind Justin Thomas' 65.

At the same time, in a gruelling performance, Phil Mickelson, at 50 a sentimental favourite to make the cut, shot 79 — only two players scored higher — and trigged a painful memory. In 2006 at Winged Foot, Mickelson was on the verge of winning the US Open he needed for a career Grand Slam. He came to the final hole leading by one, then bounced his tee shot off a corporate tent, blew to a double bogey, and finished second to Geoff Ogilvy. He missed the 18th fairway again this time, but only bogeyed. "I drove it poorly and I putted poorly," he said. Except for the formality of the second round, his US Open was over.

Thomas made some history with his five-under 65 — the lowest score in six US Opens at Winged Foot. The previous low was 66 by Fuzzy Zoeller in the second round when he won in 1984.

"Yeah, 65 is fun no matter where you play, especially at Winged Foot," Thomas said. "I was in a really good frame of mind, and I was focused, sticking to my routine, playing every shot, as opposed to getting ahead of myself. It's one of those rounds where you make the putt on 18, you're done for the day."

After an early birdie-bogey exchange, he was five under for 13 holes from the sixth, including three straight birdies around the turn. He birdied the par-five ninth off a bump-and-run to eight feet, the 10th from 10 and the 11th from the edge of the green. He closed with a scary 25-foot downhill putt at the 18th.

Thomas said he wasn't surprised at the low scoring — there were 21 rounds in the 60s compared with only 12 in the entire 2006 Open. "The greens are very soft," Thomas said. "I thought they'd be a little firmer, but I also understood that they need to err on this side so they can get them how they want this weekend. Wind wasn't really blowing, so it was good scoring conditions."

Thomas led by one over Patrick Reed, who had to battle back from a double bogey at the fifth for his 66. It included a hole-in-one at the 167-yard par-three seventh, a nine-iron shot that one-hopped into the hole. There was a pause for confirmation. With no spectators, there were no cheers.

"It would have been nuts," he said. "It was unfortunate the fans weren't here because that would have been an awesome experience. But at the same time, an ace is an ace. I'll take it either way."

Korn Ferry Tour leader Will Zalatoris, who opened with a 70, also holed a nine-iron at the seventh and had to wait to be sure. He said he knew, finally, when he saw only one ball on the green and "two people up there started screaming".

Tiger Woods, three-time US Open champion, was in five bunkers through five holes, then began to reverse his game, birdieing the ninth, 10th and 11th. But the glow soon faded. Over the last six holes, he had a birdie, three bogeys and a double bogey at the 18th for a 73. "Well, the middle part of my round, a lot of things went my way," he said. "Didn't finish off my round the way I needed to."

DeChambeau introduced himself to Winged Foot and the US Open with a 385-yard drive into the fairway at the 455-yard first, and birdied. A birdie at the par-three seventh and a long putt for another at the 10th got him to three under and within two of Thomas' lead. Bogeys at 13 and 17 brought him back to 69. "I feel good right now with my driver," he said, "as long as I miss the driver in the right spots."

He hit half of the fairways (seven out of 14) and he averaged 311.1 yards on his drives, a tad below the field average of 312.37.

After 18 holes: 65 (-5) Thomas; **66** Wolff, Reed, Pieters; **67** Oosthuizen, McIlroy, Westwood; **68** English, Schauffele, Kokrak, Cabrera Bello, Niemann, Todd

SECOND ROUND

The honeymoon was not only over, it had come to an end with a crash.

When the second round had ended with the daylight dimming over Winged Foot that Friday, six players were under par. There had been 21 under par after the first day.

Said Patrick Reed of the officials, noting the marked difference in the course, one day to the next: "It's almost like they set it up to ease our way into it and then they showed us what it's supposed to really be like."

A further point of clarification — although six players were under par at the halfway point, only three players broke par in the second round, down from the 21 in the first.

Only one player broke par in both rounds. DeChambeau, with 69-68, and at three-under 137, finished the day a shot behind Reed, who took the lead with a 70. Not that Reed was complaining about the course with his assessment of the change. "I love it when it's hard," he said. "I love the grind. I love getting in there. I love when you have to be creative on all different golf shots." For example, the eight-iron into the wind at his 10th (the first), riding the slope of the green for a tap-in birdie. He battled Winged Foot to a five-birdie, five-bogey draw.

Reed said he was still working to keep his backswing a little shorter, for better control. "Everyone likes to hit driver hard," Reed said, "but at the same time around here, I'd give up 50 yards just to hit the ball in the fairway."

Interestingly enough, that was 180 degrees away from DeChambeau's preference to bash it hard, go find it and bash it hard again. Preferably fairway — "I still want to hit it straight" — but fairway or rough, no matter, he believed his strategy created more birdie opportunities.

DeChambeau brought an amazing symmetry to his 68 in the second round, patiently making a birdie to counter every bogey Winged Foot inflicted upon him. Starting on the back nine, from the 10th, he went bogey-birdie-bogey, then from the 14th, birdie-bogey-birdie. Coming in, he bogeyed the second, birdied the third, then the same for the fifth and sixth. Then came his pièce de résistance, the eagle at the par-five ninth. Said the effusive DeChambeau: "Great drive on six, great drive on eight, great shot on seven, and a great drive on nine that just set me up to be able to attack that flag today."

Number nine was a 575-yard par five. He reached with driver-pitching wedge. (He had "recalibrated" his wedges the night before. "I was flying everything 10 yards long," he explained.) A putt from eight feet. "That was a fun way to finish off," DeChambeau said.

Behind him, the picture was changing rapidly.

Rory McIlroy, two behind after the first round, ran headlong into trouble. He'd birdied the first, then staggered over the next six holes to four bogeys and a double and shot 76. Dustin Johnson had a remarkable round going. He was bogey-free with two birdies through his 15th, then bogeyed the next two, shot 70 and was seven behind.

Thomas, who led the first round with a 65, went five over on a seven-hole stretch, shot 73 and shook it off. "Every single person in this tournament," he said, now two behind, "is going to go through a bad run."

The only other players to break par with DeChambeau were Hideki Matsuyama and Bubba Watson, both with one-under 69s. "The Winged Foot bore its teeth today," said Matsuyama, pointing to pin positions and wind drying out the greens. "It was a lot tougher today than yesterday." He bogeyed his ninth (the 18th), started birdie-bogey coming in, and birdied his last two to be four behind.

Watson, who had a 72 in the first round, was playing under the pressure of knowing that Hurricane Sally had hit his home area in Florida. He birdied three straight from the seventh, had a birdie-bogey exchange, then double-bogeyed the 18th and was five behind Reed at 141. His principal observation: "If boss lady said come home … I'd have been down there as fast as I could."

The cut was made at six-over 146. Thus this Open may be marked almost as much by those who missed the cut as those who made it.

Mickelson, at age 50, was a lock to miss after that opening 79. He closed with a 74. "The penalty for a mis-hit is severe, and I found myself getting a little tight and a little steery," he said. Perhaps also feeling tight was the high-roller, according to a report, who bet $45,000 on Mickelson to win at 75-to-1 odds, a $3.3 million chance.

Woods exited on a crusher. He had a bogey and two doubles on his front nine, then four more bogeys before two late birdies for a 77. "It feels like the way the course is turning, anybody who makes the cut has the opportunity to win this championship. I didn't get myself that opportunity." It was the eighth missed cut in his last 15 majors.

For PGA champion Collin Morikawa, 23, ranked fifth in the world and going for his second major of the year, it truly was the final indignity. He had one last chance to make the cut — an eight-foot birdie putt at the last hole. He missed, shot 71, and missed the cut by a stroke. Justin Rose had a birdie-free 77 framed by double bogeys at the first and last holes, Jordan Spieth closed with a no-birdie 81 and Sergio Garcia, with two triple bogeys, also shot 81.

After 36 holes: 136 (-4) Reed 70; **137** DeChambeau 68; **138** Thomas 73, English 70, Cabrera Bello 70; 139 Kokrak 71; **140** Wolff 74, Pieters 74, Schauffele 72, Todd 72, Matsuyama 69

THIRD ROUND

DeChambeau's sermons on smash-and-bash golf were still thundering at the US Open when young Matthew Wolff stepped forward to enunciate his own manifesto. It came after the third round, in which he took the lead with a five-under 65, matching the record for a major at Winged Foot, a long, punishing course with fearful rough. Hit the fairways or perish, was the byword. His response: who cares?

Wolff's manifesto: "There's a lot of holes out there that maybe people would try to hit it in the fairway or maybe take the safe play because it is a US Open, and they know that pars are a good score, but I don't really like to think of it that way. I like to go out there and do what I feel comfortable with. Rip it and see how it goes from there."

Which was largely what DeChambeau had been saying all along, including one of his more studied statements of intent: "I'm going to be aggressive no matter what."

Both preferred the fairways, but they weren't going to throttle back their games to hit them.

And that was how the US Open took shape in the third round. Wolff shot that 65 and took the lead at five-under 205. DeChambeau shot 70 and was two behind, and Louis Oosthuizen a 68 and was third at one under. They were the only three golfers under par. Five behind, considered hot contenders under the circumstances, there were three at even par: Hideki Matsuyama (70), Xander Schauffele (70) and Harris English (72).

Wolff's 65 was a masterpiece. He had five birdies on the front nine, starting with the first and fourth holes on 15-foot putts, both after missing the fairway. At the par-four sixth, he got up and down out of a bunker, greenside at some 350 yards. He holed a 12-footer at the par-three seventh, and he two-putted the par-five ninth after hitting his second and last fairway of the day. He bogeyed the 16th out of a lie so bad it kept him from reaching the green. And he closed with a jewel of a birdie at the tough par-four 18th — a four-iron off the tee (missing the fairway, of course) then a soaring seven-iron to 10 feet.

What was working well? "Everything," he said. "I think my putting was by far the best it's felt in the last two or three months. I feel like I'm really hitting the ball well. My irons were really good, and even though I only hit two fairways, my driver was — it was just barely off."

Wolff, by the way, beat DeChambeau in the no-fairway derby in the third round. Wolff hit two fairways, DeChambeau three.

"The round today was a huge battle," DeChambeau said. "I was proud of the way I persevered out there. It was difficult. Especially when you're not hitting it straight in the fairway. For me, it felt like I kept myself in it, scrambled really well. Got to do that tomorrow, but I also have to hit some more fairways. I know that. I'm going to work on that tonight and make sure I'm doing that tomorrow."

DeChambeau's theory was simple enough. "If you're able to hit it far enough up there, I feel with wedges you can get it out pretty easy." He made it work.

DeChambeau opened the round with two bogeys, then went 15 holes with three birdies and 12 pars. He had birdied 16 and 17, and then the 18th proved pivotal. "I've just got to hit a better hybrid," he said. "Just started out to the right and didn't draw it back." He missed a short par putt, and Wolff birdied and took a two-stroke margin into the final round.

Given the almost cavalier attitude DeChambeau and Wolff had toward the rough, was it really all that difficult? Reed, who said he'd give up 50 yards to hit the fairway, couldn't. He led by one entering the third round, and made a double bogey and six singles for a 43 on the back nine for a 77.

"I couldn't find a fairway," Reed said. "It was brutal."

Winged Foot claimed two prominent hopefuls in the third round — first-round leader Thomas and Spain's Jon Rahm. Both started the round with three straight bogeys and both shot 76. Thomas came out of the third trailing by nine, Rahm by 12.

McIlroy bounced back, spirits and all, from that second-round 76 with a 68 and refused to believe he was out of the running. "No matter where I am at the end of the day," he said (and that turned out to be six behind), "I feel like I've got a pretty good shot."

So Wolff ended the day with history at his fingertips. "I'm probably going to be a little antsy," he said. "It's the US Open, and I have a lead. I'm going to try to keep my nerves as calm as they can be. I put myself in a really good spot. I did everything that I could do up until this point, and tomorrow, I promise you I'm going to try my best. It would be unbelievable to add my name to a US Open trophy."

He also could make history beyond his own victory. He would be the first to win the US Open on his debut since Ouimet in 1913, and at 21, the youngest to win it since Bobby Jones, also 21, in 1923.

"If I don't hit fairways tomorrow," Wolff said with a grin, "I know I can play well."

After 54 holes: 205 (-5) Wolff 65; **207** DeChambeau 70; **209** Oosthuizen 68; **210** English 72, Schauffele 70, Matsuyama 70; **211** McIlroy 68; **212** Cabrera Bello 74, Hovland 70, Z Johnson 68

FOURTH ROUND

The 2020 US Open was the Second Massacre at Winged Foot.

The first had come 46 years earlier, when Hale Irwin won the 1974 Open at seven over par. Critics insisted that the US Golf Association had the course set-up extra-difficult in retribution for Johnny Miller's lightning-in-a-bottle 63 at Oakmont the previous year. Sportswriter Dick Schaap captured it all in a book titled *Massacre at Winged Foot.*

This time, it wasn't Winged Foot performing the massacre.

This time it was a former budding physicist who had reasoned that if he added more mass to his body, he would get more power into his golf swing, and he would bash courses into submission from anywhere, even the rough. Even at Winged Foot.

And so DeChambeau, all brain and more brawn, playing the final hole, aimed for the fairway again but again found Winged Foot's harsh rough, then dutifully made his par four and stepped off into history. He had just won the 2020 US Open. And nobody had ever won a US Open the way he did.

DeChambeau hit only 23 of 56 fairways. Everyone knows you can't be in the rough that much and win.

"I did it — I did it," DeChambeau said. "As difficult as this golf course was presented, I played it beautifully. Even through the rough, I was still able to manage my game and hit it to correct sides of the greens. My putting was immaculate today."

He shot Winged Foot in 69-68-70-67 for a six-under total of 274 and a six-stroke victory. In taking his first major, and seventh PGA Tour win, he was the only player to break par in the final round, and for the week. Only Fuzzy Zoeller and Greg Norman, who played off in 1984 at 276, had previously finished a US Open at Winged Foot under par.

Wolff, leading at five under, and DeChambeau, trailing him by two, were the final pairing on that September afternoon. Then things were quickly reversed. Wolff bogeyed the third and fifth and DeChambeau birdied the fourth, and DeChambeau had the lead. They matched bogeys at the eighth, and then came a dramatic moment that begged for a thunderous gallery that simply wasn't there. At the par-five ninth, DeChambeau bombed his tee shot 375 yards and Wolff outdid him at 389. Both wedged to the green. DeChambeau rolled in a hooking 38-foot putt for an eagle, and Wolff followed him in from 10 for an eagle of his own.

It looked like the beginning of a classic duel. But troubles began piling up on Wolff.

His tee shot at the par-three 10th, into the collar, forced him to stand in a deep bunker and grip his sand wedge halfway down the shaft. He popped the ball 10 feet past the hole and bogeyed. "And then the second shot that got pin high on 12 and then spun back down the slope?" Wolff said. "I mean, it's just bad breaks. I definitely can say that it just wasn't meant to be."

Wolff hit seven fairways and made five bogeys and one double bogey, shot 75 and finished second at 280, a score that would have won four of the previous five US Opens at Winged Foot. He had now finished fourth (at the PGA) and second in his first two major appearances.

Nobody else really stirred. Oosthuizen had a five-bogey 73 to be third, English double-bogeyed the first on a lost ball and shot 73 and fourth, while Schauffele bogeyed five straight, shot 74 and was fifth, his fourth top-six finish in four US Open appearances.

Players had some final thoughts at what they had just witnessed at Winged Foot.

Was there a defence against DeChambeau? "I don't know what they can do, really," said Oosthuizen, "because he's hitting it so far. He's so strong out of the rough. And he's probably one of the best putters out there. Hats off to him. He went out on this journey, and he's pulling it off."

McIlroy, who won the 2011 US Open by eight shots, observed: "I sort of said, Ok, wait until he gets to a proper golf course. He'll have to rein it in. This is as proper as they come, and look what's happened. Look, he's found a way to do it. Whether that's good or bad for the game, I don't know, but it's not the way I saw this course being played or this tournament being played."

Said Schauffele: "Everyone talked about hitting fairways out here. It's not about hitting fairways. It's about hitting on the correct side of the hole and hitting it far so you can hit a wedge instead of a six-iron out of the rough."

DeChambeau had his own closing thoughts. "My goal in playing golf is to try and figure it out," he said. "I'm just trying to figure out this very complex, multivariable game, and multidimensional game as well. It's very, very difficult. It's a fun journey for me.

"This one's for my parents," he added. After the round, he video-chatted with them, the tears coming.

"Hey, Mom; hey, Dad," he said. "I did it."

Winged Foot Golf Club (West), Mamaroneck, New York — September 17-20
Par 70 (35-35); 7,429 yards — Purse $12,500,000

1	**Bryson DeChambeau**	69	68	70	67	274	$2,250,000
2	**Matthew Wolff**	66	74	65	75	280	1,350,000
3	**Louis Oosthuizen**	67	74	68	73	282	861,457
4	Harris English	68	70	72	73	283	603,903
5	Xander Schauffele	68	72	70	74	284	502,993
6	Dustin Johnson	73	70	72	70	285	424,040
	Will Zalatoris	70	74	70	71	285	424,040
8	Tony Finau	69	73	73	71	286	302,236
	Justin Thomas	65	73	76	72	286	302,236
	Webb Simpson	71	71	71	73	286	302,236
	Zach Johnson	70	74	68	74	286	302,236
	Rory McIlroy	67	76	68	75	286	302,236
13	Lee Westwood	67	76	72	72	287	210,757
	Adam Long	71	74	69	73	287	210,757
	Patrick Reed	66	70	77	74	287	210,757
	Viktor Hovland	71	71	70	75	287	210,757
17	Jason Kokrak	68	71	77	72	288	157,931
	Paul Casey	76	70	69	73	288	157,931
	Lucas Glover	71	71	71	75	288	157,931
	Alex Noren	72	74	67	75	288	157,931
	Hideki Matsuyama	71	69	70	78	288	157,931
22	Sungjae Im	70	75	73	71	289	129,407
23	Erik van Rooyen	70	74	76	70	290	101,797
	Taylor Pendrith	71	74	75	70	290	101,797
	Jon Rahm	69	72	76	73	290	101,797
	Brendon Todd	68	72	75	75	290	101,797
	Thomas Pieters	66	74	73	77	290	101,797
	Joaquin Niemann	68	73	72	77	290	101,797
	Rafa Cabrera Bello	68	70	74	78	290	101,797
30	Charles Howell III	73	72	72	74	291	83,422
31	Lucas Herbert	72	74	74	72	292	75,649
	Renato Paratore	71	72	73	76	292	75,649
	Bubba Watson	72	69	74	77	292	75,649
34	Tyler Duncan	73	71	77	72	293	64,024
	Stephan Jaeger	71	70	79	73	293	64,024
	Romain Langasque	71	74	75	73	293	64,024
	Daniel Berger	73	70	74	76	293	64,024
38	Cameron Smith	71	73	78	72	294	52,074
	Jason Day	72	74	76	72	294	52,074
	Brian Harman	74	72	75	73	294	52,074
	Adam Scott	71	74	74	75	294	52,074
	Billy Horschel	72	70	72	80	294	52,074
43	Shane Lowry	76	70	77	72	295	39,275
	Patrick Cantlay	70	76	76	73	295	39,275
	Bernd Wiesberger	73	72	76	74	295	39,275
	Matt Wallace	70	75	73	77	295	39,275
	Lanto Griffin	71	74	71	79	295	39,275
48	Michael Thompson	70	75	75	76	296	32,254
49	Rickie Fowler	69	77	72	79	297	30,312
	Thomas Detry	71	72	73	81	297	30,312
51	John Pak (A)	69	76	79	74	298	
	Chesson Hadley	73	73	77	75	298	28,563
	Ryo Ishikawa	72	74	74	78	298	28,563
54	Adam Hadwin	72	73	74	80	299	27,720
55	Christiaan Bezuidenhout	70	76	72	82	300	27,720
56	Abraham Ancer	71	75	79	76	301	27,073
	Robert MacIntyre	74	72	76	79	301	27,073
58	Troy Merritt	72	74	78	78	302	26,684
59	Rory Sabbatini	69	76	78	81	304	26,296
	Sebastian Munoz	71	74	77	82	304	26,296
61	Shugo Imahira	71	74	78	82	305	25,901
	Danny Lee	70	75	78		WDN	
	MISSED THE 36-HOLE CUT						
	Chan Kim	71	76			147	
	Matt Fitzpatrick	74	73			147	
	Byeong Hun An	71	76			147	
	Takumi Kanaya (A)	72	75			147	
	Joel Dahmen	73	74			147	
	Martin Kaymer	71	76			147	
	Davis Thompson (A)	69	78			147	
	Collin Morikawa	76	71			147	
	Corey Conners	71	76			147	
	Kurt Kitayama	70	77			147	
	Shaun Norris	69	79			148	
	Ryan Palmer	73	75			148	
	Gary Woodland	74	74			148	
	Andy Ogletree (A)	71	77			148	
	Tommy Fleetwood	74	74			148	
	Keegan Bradley	75	73			148	
	Paul Barjon	77	71			148	
	Andy Sullivan	71	77			148	
	Kevin Streelman	73	75			148	
	Mackenzie Hughes	72	76			148	
	Si Woo Kim	72	77			149	
	Preston Summerhays (A)	72	77			149	
	John Augenstein (A)	74	75			149	
	Paul Waring	72	77			149	
	Matt Kuchar	74	75			149	
	Sandy Scott (A)	75	74			149	
	Jim Herman	73	77			150	
	Mike Lorenzo-Vera	73	77			150	
	Matt Jones	76	74			150	

Adrian Otaegui	71 79	150
Connor Syme	75 75	150
Daniel Balin	73 77	150
Brandon Wu	74 76	150
Jimmy Walker	72 78	150
Jazz Janewattananond	73 77	150
Danny Willett	77 73	150
Victor Perez	76 74	150
Justin Rose	73 77	150
Tiger Woods	73 77	150
Chun An Yu (A)	70 80	150
Marc Leishman	73 78	151
Cameron Champ	73 78	151
Cole Hammer (A)	77 74	151
Curtis Luck	75 76	151
Tom Lewis	74 77	151
Chez Reavie	75 76	151
Henrik Stenson	74 77	151
Steve Stricker	74 77	151
Richy Werenski	73 79	152
Kevin Kisner	76 76	152
Brandt Snedeker	75 77	152
JC Ritchie	74 78	152
Ricky Castillo (A)	73 79	152
Kevin Na	75 77	152
Tyrrell Hatton	74 78	152
Ian Poulter	75 77	152
Phil Mickelson	79 74	153
Lee Hodges	76 77	153
JT Poston	71 82	153
Justin Harding	77 76	153
Dan McCarthy	76 77	153
Branden Grace	75 79	154
Davis Riley	79 75	154
Mark Hubbard	76 78	154
Matthias Schwab	77 77	154
Rasmus Hojgaard	77 77	154
Jordan Spieth	73 81	154
Max Homa	78 76	154
Eddie Pepperell	78 76	154
Sami Valimaki	78 76	154
Sergio Garcia	74 81	155
Ryan Vermeer	78 77	155
Graeme McDowell	76 80	156
Lukas Michel (A)	80 77	157
James Sugrue (A)	78 79	157
Marty Jertson	76 81	157
Scott Hend	74 84	158
Ryan Fox	74 85	159
Greyson Sigg	75 85	160
Sung Kang	74 86	160
Eduard Rousaud (A)	76 85	161
Andrew Putnam	73	WDN

ROLL OF HONOUR

1895	Horace Rawlins	Newport
1896	James Foulis	Shinnecock Hills
1897	Joe Lloyd	Chicago
1898	Fred Herd	Myopia Hunt
1899	Willie Smith	Baltimore
1900	Harry Vardon	Chicago
1901	Willie Anderson*	Myopia Hunt
1902	Laurence Auchterlonie	Garden City
1903	Willie Anderson*	Baltusrol
1904	Willie Anderson	Glen View
1905	Willie Anderson	Myopia Hunt
1906	Alex Smith	Onwentsia
1907	Alex Ross	Philadelphia
1908	Fred McLeod*	Myopia Hunt
1909	George Sargent	Englewood
1910	Alex Smith*	Philadelphia
1911	John McDermott*	Chicago
1912	John McDermott	CC of Buffalo
1913	Francis Ouimet* (A)	Brookline
1914	Walter Hagen	Midlothian
1915	Jerome D Travers (A)	Baltusrol
1916	Charles Evans Jr (A)	Minikahda
1919	Walter Hagen	Brae Burn
1920	Ted Ray	Inverness
1921	James Barnes	Columbia
1922	Gene Sarazen	Skokie
1923	Bobby Jones* (A)	Inwood
1924	Cyril Walker	Oakland Hills
1925	William Macfarlane*	Worcester
1926	Bobby Jones (A)	Scioto
1927	Tommy Armour*	Oakmont
1928	Johnny Farrell*	Olympia Fields
1929	Bobby Jones* (A)	Winged Foot (West)
1930	Bobby Jones (A)	Interlachen
1931	Billy Burke*	Inverness
1932	Gene Sarazen	Fresh Meadow
1933	Johnny Goodman (A)	North Shore
1934	Olin Dutra	Merion
1935	Sam Parks Jr	Oakmont
1936	Tony Manero	Baltusrol (Upper)
1937	Ralph Guldahl	Oakland Hills
1938	Ralph Guldahl	Cherry Hills
1939	Byron Nelson*	Philadelphia
1940	Lawson Little*	Canterbury
1941	Craig Wood	Colonial
1946	Lloyd Mangrum*	Canterbury
1947	Lew Worsham*	St Louis
1948	Ben Hogan	Riviera
1949	Cary Middlecoff	Medinah
1950	Ben Hogan*	Merion
1951	Ben Hogan	Oakland Hills
1952	Julius Boros	Northwood
1953	Ben Hogan	Oakmont
1954	Ed Furgol	Baltusrol (Lower)
1955	Jack Fleck*	Olympic
1956	Cary Middlecoff	Oak Hill
1957	Dick Mayer*	Inverness
1958	Tommy Bolt	Southern Hills
1959	Billy Casper Jr	Winged Foot (West)
1960	Arnold Palmer	Cherry Hills
1961	Gene Littler	Oakland Hills
1962	Jack Nicklaus*	Oakmont
1963	Julius Boros*	Brookline
1964	Ken Venturi	Congressional
1965	Gary Player*	Bellerive
1966	Billy Casper Jr*	Olympic
1967	Jack Nicklaus	Baltusrol (Lower)
1968	Lee Trevino	Oak Hill
1969	Orville Moody	Champions
1970	Tony Jacklin	Hazeltine National
1971	Lee Trevino*	Merion
1972	Jack Nicklaus	Pebble Beach
1973	Johnny Miller	Oakmont
1974	Hale Irwin	Winged Foot (West)
1975	Lou Graham*	Medinah (No 3)
1976	Jerry Pate	Atlanta Athletic Club

1977	Hubert Green	Southern Hills
1978	Andy North	Cherry Hills
1979	Hale Irwin	Inverness
1980	Jack Nicklaus	Baltusrol (Lower)
1981	David Graham	Merion
1982	Tom Watson	Pebble Beach
1983	Larry Nelson	Oakmont
1984	Fuzzy Zoeller*	Winged Foot (West)
1985	Andy North	Oakland Hills
1986	Raymond Floyd	Shinnecock Hills
1987	Scott Simpson	Olympic
1988	Curtis Strange*	Brookline
1989	Curtis Strange	Oak Hill
1990	Hale Irwin*	Medinah
1991	Payne Stewart	Hazeltine National
1992	Tom Kite	Pebble Beach
1993	Lee Janzen	Baltusrol (Lower)
1994	Ernie Els*	Oakmont
1995	Corey Pavin	Shinnecock Hills
1996	Steve Jones	Oakland Hills
1997	Ernie Els	Congressional
1998	Lee Janzen	Olympic
1999	Payne Stewart	Pinehurst (No 2)
2000	Tiger Woods	Pebble Beach
2001	Retief Goosen*	Southern Hills
2002	Tiger Woods	Bethpage (Black)
2003	Jim Furyk	Olympia Fields
2004	Retief Goosen	Shinnecock Hills
2005	Michael Campbell	Pinehurst (No 2)
2006	Geoff Ogilvy	Winged Foot (West)
2007	Angel Cabrera	Oakmont
2008	Tiger Woods*	Torrey Pines
2009	Lucas Glover	Bethpage (Black)
2010	Graeme McDowell	Pebble Beach
2011	Rory McIlroy	Congressional
2012	Webb Simpson	Olympic
2013	Justin Rose	Merion
2014	Martin Kaymer	Pinehurst (No 2)
2015	Jordan Spieth	Chambers Bay
2016	Dustin Johnson	Oakmont
2017	Brooks Koepka	Erin Hills
2018	Brooks Koepka	Shinnecock Hills
2019	Gary Woodland	Pebble Beach
2020	Bryson DeChambeau	Winged Foot (West)

**won in playoff*

KPMG WOMEN'S PGA CHAMPIONSHIP

Kim's special mind for winning

For once, renowned South African globetrotter Gary Player and his wife Vivienne spent the summer in one place, staying with his daughter's family in the Philadelphia area. "I've been here for six months and playing all these magnificent golf courses, what a state," said Player, just shy of his 85th birthday. "I've been playing Merion, I've been playing Pine Valley, I've been playing Aronimink. It's been an absolute privilege."

Player also visited Aronimink during the KPMG Women's PGA Championship, delayed from June to October. It was on the Donald Ross-designed layout that he won the 1962 PGA Championship. "This is a really fine test of golf," Player said of the course that will again host the men's PGA in 2026. "When you leave here, you really learn something about shot-making and using the mind. Today, all we hear about is long hitting. Golf is not a game of long hitting. Yes, it's an asset, but what wins golf tournaments are special minds."

The previous month Bryson DeChambeau had applied his unique golfing mind to overpowering the mighty Winged Foot at the US Open. No one was overwhelming Aronimink with power. Playing every inch of its 6,577 allotted yards in the practice rounds with a distinct chill in the air, the players knew they were in for a challenge. "It's probably one of the longest golf courses I've ever played," said three-time champion Inbee Park.

"It's a beast," said Mel Reid, the Englishwoman who had won the ShopRite Classic at another Donald Ross layout, the Bay course at Seaview, the previous week. Danielle Kang, admiringly, called it "monstrous". "They're calling it the 'lumber yard'," said Cristie Kerr, citing the number of times players used woods for their approach shots. "This is a proper golf course," said 2018 Women's Open champion Georgia Hall. "It's what a major should be."

That only eight players broke par for the week was in line with what a major should be. But the direst predictions about the scoring did not materialise thanks to the sensitive set up by the PGA of America's *éminence grise* of championships, Kerry Haigh. Tees pushed forward when needed, holes cut on the greens to both tempt and tease, opportunities for both triumph and disaster. It was a course not to be dominated but to be unlocked with finesse and Sei Young Kim was the player who solved the puzzle.

Kim, the 27-year-old Korean with a black belt in taekwondo, set a new championship record total of 266, a 14-under-par score that no one had expected at the start of the week. Her 63 in the final round equalled the championship best and it was more of a surprise that her birdie putt on the final green just missed rather than falling in. She had already collected 23 birdies and without it still won by five strokes from Park.

Hoping to tie the late Mickey Wright with a fourth victory in the championship, Park scored a 65 in the final round without dropping a shot and yet kept seeing her young compatriot surging further ahead. There was no better illustration of Kim's assured march to victory. Nasa Hataoka and Carlota Ciganda scored 64 and 65 respectively and tied for third place, seven strokes adrift. Kim's playing partners in the final round, Anna Nordqvist and Brooke Henderson, finished 10 and 11 strokes behind in fifth and sixth places.

"I'm so excited. I'm hiding my tears at the moment," Kim said. As for so many of her compatriots, she was inspired by Se Ri Pak's breakthrough in 1998. "It was a major that I really wanted. I dreamt of winning a major championship after seeing Se Ri winning the first one for our country."

Kim is 5'4", the same height as Ian Woosnam, and plays in a similar "pocket rocket" style. By winning her first major she proved she was not just a good little 'un but a great one. She has the asset of length, without being the longest, and plenty of other attributes. She is that increasing rarity, a skilled chipper around the greens with a 56-degree wedge. On her day, putts fall on command. She and her caddie, Paul Fusco, have been together for six years and have learnt how to plot their way around the most fearsome tracks. Most of all, Kim has Player's "special mind" for winning.

She won five times in two years on her home circuit — the first with an eagle on the final hole, the second with the help of a hole-in-one on the 71st hole that got her into a playoff — before making a stunning entrance onto the LPGA tour in 2015. She won three times to claim the rookie of the year award. The first two of those were in playoffs, the second coming at the LOTTE Championship in

Hawaii where she chipped in to force extra time and then holed out from the fairway with an eight-iron for a winning eagle at the first playoff hole. In 2018 she broke Annika Sorenstam's record for the lowest score on tour with a 31-under-par total of 257 at the Thornberry Creek Classic. And at the end of 2019 she holed a devilish, downhill 25-footer to win the CME Group Tour Championship and a record prize of $1.5 million.

Her 11th LPGA victory in six seasons was the natural next step, elevating Kim out of that dreaded category of best player not to have won a major.

FIRST ROUND

Kim made a slow start on Thursday morning. She bogeyed the first hole and was out in two over par. The wind was from a different direction from the practice days and no one was going low. Her first birdie arrived at the 10th hole, one of the hardest on the course with a pond protecting a highly contoured green, and there were two more on the way home, along with two more bogeys. It added up to a 71, one over par. She would end the day four strokes off the lead but only three behind the 68s of Ciganda, Gabby Lopez and Linnea Strom from the morning starters.

In the afternoon, when scoring was less difficult as the temperature rose, Kang birdied three of her first five holes, starting at the 10th. But it took a fine four-iron to eight feet at the par-three eighth, her 17th, to join those on 68. "My knock-down four-irons go pretty straight, so I just aimed it at the pin and hit it as hard as I could because no matter how hard I hit it, it wasn't going to go long," Kang said. The putt, though not long, had five feet of break. "I was just lagging it as close to the hole as possible, to be honest, and it went in. I really needed that because I missed a lot of putts on the front nine."

As Kang was explaining that "there's a lot of three-putt opportunities" due to the severity of the greens, Lydia Ko did just that at the 18th, turning a potential 67 into a 68. Cydney Clanton also ended up on that mark by birdieing four of her last five holes, finishing on the ninth green.

Kelly Tan also made a fast start from the 10th. The Malaysian golfer birdied three of her first four holes and played the back nine in 31 thanks to some inspired work with the putter. She holed from 25 feet on the 10th, a modest seven feet on the 11th, then from 30 feet from off the 13th green and had another 30-footer at the 18th. Two bogeys and a birdie at the seventh on the other side of the course gave her a 67. "The putter was behaving itself pretty well, so I'm very pleased with that," Tan said. "And my ball-striking was good, that's how I have those birdie chances."

Tan admitted that she did not think there were five birdies in a round on offer when she had a first look at the course on the weekend before the ShopRite. But she was grateful for the extra preparation time. "Aronimink is one of the courses that you want to see it a few times," she said. "There's just so many things to learn." She also learnt from starting well at the ANA Inspiration the previous month. "It definitely gave me a little taste of what being in contention is like. You have to learn about how you react in those situations."

Brittany Lincicome, a two-time ANA winner, was joined by her 15-month-old baby daughter Emery on the course at the start of the week and discovered a spark of form once back to business. "Something finally switched in my mind after missing the cut in Atlantic City," she said. "Today it was trusting my process, being aggressive, don't leave the putts short, just attack the golf course, and it kind of worked, which is really scary because this golf course was not easy."

Wearing a plastic brace to protect a painful left thumb, Lincicome tied Tan with a 67. Luck was on her side. At the 11th, her second, she bladed a wedge which hit the flagstick and finished only five feet away, while at the ninth, her last, a curling putt did a 360 before dropping in. "I was just trying to get it to the hole and it snuck in."

After 18 holes: 67 (-3) Tan, Lincicome; **68** L Ko, Kang, Clanton, Lopez, Ciganda, Strom; **69** Castren, Lindberg, Nordqvist, A Yang

SECOND ROUND

It was less windy on Friday but certainly cold first thing in the morning. Nelly Korda was forced to withdraw after feeling discomfort in her back during an opening 71. Lincicome did not make a birdie in her 72. "I didn't stick to my game plan, if anybody cares," she said. "I wasn't aggressive out of the gate, just lollygagging my way through. Those pins out there today were not very nice."

Tan made an early birdie to get to four under par but a poor run around the turn, including a double bogey at the 12th, dropped her back to two under following a 71. There was a 70 for Dame Laura Davies, days short of her 57th birthday and making the cut on her 32nd appearance in the championship. In Gee Chun scored a 67 and defending champion Hannah Green a 66 after a 79 on Thursday.

But the best round of the week so far came from Jennifer Kupcho with a 65, seven shots better than Thursday. The 23-year-old from Colorado, who turned professional after winning the inaugural Augusta National Women's Invitational in 2019, hit all 18 greens in regulation, made five birdies and did not drop a shot. She holed a putt from 30 feet on the 11th, her second, and a speedy putt from long range at the sixth which hit the back of the cup, jumped in the air and fell in. She was the first to reach the clubhouse at three under par.

"It was really cold, but no wind, and it made the golf course a lot easier," said Kupcho. Relatively. "Honestly, I was still really stressed. I want to play good so badly that it just makes me want to hit good shots, and that is obviously stressful." Although Kupcho needed physiotherapy on her baulky back throughout the week, a new caddie and a return to a set of irons she used in college had proved successful with a runner-up finish at the ShopRite.

Moments later there was another 65 from Bianca Pagdanganan, of the Philippines. The big hitting 22-year-old was playing in her sixth LPGA event and her first major, and had opened with a 77. She said: "When my dad picked me up in the car last night, he just looked at me and said, 'Welcome to the majors'. I was like, 'Thanks, Dad, it's a great welcome'. My dad knows my game pretty well. He told me, 'you've just got to stop thinking'. I agree I do play better when I don't think. I'm not the most mechanical, technical person, I'm all about feel." She birdied three of the last five holes to get to two over par and did not drop a shot.

Birdies at the 12th, from 15 feet, and 16th holes helped Kang to a 69 that enabled the former champion to tie Kupcho at three under. "It's so stressful," she said. "That's the beauty of a challenging course like Aronimink. Walking down the 12th fairway I was doing my putting stats and realised I had missed it short and low for 11 holes in a row. So I decided to hit it long and high, and it went in." Playing partner Henderson also returned a 69 to lie level par, the same mark as Park, who had a 70 for the second day running.

Ciganda got to four under par in the afternoon but a dropped shot at the fourth, her 13th, where she found a bunker for her only missed green of the day, meant a 69 to join those on three under. Sweden's Anna Nordqvist, the 2009 champion, also finished three under thanks to a 68.

Kim, meanwhile, was one of the later starters and bogeyed the 11th and 12th holes, teeing off at the 10th, to be three over par. She got one back at the 16th but television coverage had long since halted by the time she had played the front nine of the course in 29 strokes, equalling the championship record held by two Australians, Karrie Webb and Sarah Kemp. Kim birdied the first and then every hole from the fourth, except the eighth. It was holing a 35-footer at the fourth that got her going and then her approach game caught fire, leaving herself putts of three feet at the fifth, 10 feet at the sixth and three feet at the seventh.

"When we entered the front nine, the wind slowed down and it was easier to attack with my irons," Kim said. "Honestly, I didn't look at the leaderboard. I was in a good momentum so I just wanted to ride on that."

Her 65 not only tied the best score of the day but put her top of the leaderboard at four under par. During the season's hiatus, Kim played four events in her native Korea — Fusco, her caddie, travelled over and isolated in a hotel room for two weeks prior to the first event — three times finishing in the top six. She missed the AIG Women's Open but arrived in America in time to finish fifth at the NW Arkansas Championship and 18th at both the ANA Inspiration and the ShopRite Classic.

Her press interview was conducted through an interpreter but when someone asked whether she was ready to win a major, she replied swiftly in English: "It's always my goal."

After 36 holes: 136 (-4) SY Kim 65; **137** Nordqvist 68, Ciganda 69, Kupcho 65, Kang 69;
138 Stephenson 68, L Ko 70, Buhai 68, Strom 70, Tan 71

THIRD ROUND

Catapulted into the final group for the third round, Kim showed her late run on Friday night was no fluke. This time a 67 extended her lead, a bogey at the last hole denying her a three-shot advantage but at seven under par she was two clear of the field.

Earlier on Saturday morning, Pagdanganan managed to replicate her Friday effort exactly — another 65 without a dropped shot. "I don't think I've done this ever, played two back-to-back rounds bogey-free," she said. "It is definitely an achievement, especially on this course. It's really tough." As one of only a small handful of players to average over 280 yards off the tee, Pagdanganan birdied both the par-fives as well as claiming threes at the second, fourth and 13th holes.

She was just pleased her father, Sam, could watch her play as players were allowed guests on site over the weekend. "This is my first major ever, so I'd be lying if I said I wasn't nervous," said the rookie. "It's been pretty surreal being on this incredible golf course and I'm just trying to learn as much as possible. I've enjoyed the last two rounds, it's been fun, being able to embrace my nerves."

While Pagdanganan got to three under par, Park got to four under with a 66. There were a couple of uncharacteristic miscues on the greens but a run of three birdies in a row to close out the front nine, followed by another at the 11th, sparked an ominous challenge from the seven-time major champion. "The course is getting firmer and faster, so it's getting tougher," said Park, whose last major came in 2015. "I'm really loving it. Playing under contention on the weekend, it's great fun." As for tying Wright with four WPGA titles, Park added: "It's just too crazy to think something big like that, in the history of golf, of this championship. There is maybe a slim chance of it happening to me."

Her chances got better — she ended the day in fourth place, three behind Kim — as others slipped back. Another to move in the right direction was Henderson, who also started at level par and returned a 65 to get to five under. Having joked the previous day that she had got all her bogeys out of the way, the 2016 champion did not drop a shot on Saturday. There were some important par-saves, not least at the first and 18th holes, while she went out in 31 and birdied the 12th before parring home.

"I'm really happy with how today went," said the Canadian, who lost in a playoff at the ANA Inspiration. "It was nice to climb up the leaderboard as much as I did. I'm excited for the opportunity tomorrow."

Of those closest to Kim, it was Nordqvist who made the best progress with a 68 to join Henderson at five under after a bogey at the last. Eleven years on from winning a major in her fifth professional start, a second WPGA was within reach. "It's something that no one can take away from me and obviously one of my most proud moments as a pro," Nordqvist said. "It's a great feeling knowing that my name is on the trophy, but I can't really focus too much ahead. There's a lot of good golfers up there."

Ciganda, who also started at three under par, had a 71 to slip back to two under, as did Kupcho. Kang appeared to struggle with a shoulder issue in her 73. Her challenge was undone by finishing with three bogeys in a row, a run sparked by a six at the 16th when she attempted to putt from long range off the green and did not make the putting surface.

Kupcho and Kang were left behind by playing partner Kim. The Korean again enjoyed the front nine, going out in 32 with a hat-trick of birdies from the fifth. "It felt really good, the same as yesterday," she said. Important birdies at the 15th and 16th holes built a lead that was only slightly dented by taking three putts from 60 feet at the last. "I wouldn't say I'm nervous," Kim said of her two-shot lead. "But I'm also excited about going into the final day. I just want to keep focus and the results will follow."

After 54 holes: 203 (-7) SY Kim 67; **205** Nordqvist 68, Henderson 65; **206** I Park 66; **207** Pagdanganan 65

FOURTH ROUND

Perhaps the biggest miscue Kim made on Sunday, getting to the course half an hour later than she planned, was actually made the previous night when setting her alarm. "I guess I was unconsciously nervous before going to sleep," she smiled.

It would not have mattered but for an early start for the final round. A peculiarity of the championship being rescheduled for October meant that television coverage in America had to finish at 2pm.

There was not enough daylight, even with a two-tee start, to get all the players round before then. So the leaders were not in fact in the final few groups to go out, they were followed by stragglers from the bottom of the leaderboard — Dame Laura got to tee off in the last group on a major Sunday one more time.

It made no difference in practical terms and once Kim had her final-day red trousers on — a homage to Tiger Woods that started as an amateur — there was no stopping her. As the two former champions playing alongside Kim saw first hand. Henderson had her first and only birdie of the day at the short 14th, where she almost holed her tee shot, while Nordqvist had to wait until the 18th green.

Nordqvist, who had been outside the top-100 on the Rolex Rankings in August, finished with a 71 to be fifth, with Henderson having a 72 to be sixth. Kupcho had another 71 to tie for seventh with Charley Hull, while Pagdanganan finished a fairy-tale week not with another low score — she had a 73 — but a first top 10 on tour and the invaluable experience of playing alongside Park in the final round of a major.

Kang's dispiriting finish the night before was a precursor of a closing 76, but Hataoka headed up the leaderboard by holing a five-iron from 188 yards for an eagle at the first. The Japanese player had been disappointed the previous day not to have gone lower than a 68 but by adding four birdies she vaulted into third place after a bogey-free 64. Ciganda, with a 65, caught her at seven under par thanks to an eagle at the 16th, where she holed out from a bunker, and a birdie from long range at the last.

But seven under was the mark Kim started the day. After holing a sizeable putt for par at the second hole, the closest she came to dropping a shot all day, she was determined to go as low as possible. Even someone as dangerous as Park could not exert the sort of pressure that might have made Kim hesitate. "I knew Inbee was going to play well," Kim said. "I know Anna and Brooke didn't play as well as they wanted to, but in the back of my head I knew that Inbee was going to play well. I did not look at the scoreboard once. I knew I had to just focus on my game."

Playing one group ahead, Park holed from eight feet for a birdie at the first to go two behind but was never able to cut the deficit further. You would not have known she had woken up with a sore neck. She made a two at the fifth and birdied the seventh to be out in 32, then birdied the 12th and the 17th, where she holed a long putt across the green. That briefly took her within three of Kim but the margin ended up as five strokes.

"I was three back, so I thought 65 will definitely do it," Park said. "I couldn't ask for a better day. Sei Young was just really untouchable. I'd like to congratulate her. She had a great day. That's how a champion plays a final round, so it was good to see that.

"It was hard to believe that she had never won a major before because it felt like she won a few. She definitely deserves a major win. It was a matter of time. It reminds me of 2015 when we went head-to-head on the final day and it was just the opposite today. It was great to watch."

At the Women's PGA in 2015, Park won for the third successive year with Kim finishing runner-up, five strokes behind. The reversal was not lost on Kim, either. "I'm happy to have Inbee as a fellow competitor and a great sister," she said. "I look up to her, and I feel appreciative that she gave a compliment to me. I look forward to competing against her in many other tournaments."

Of the wait to become a major champion, Kim said: "To be honest with you, I didn't know it was going to take this long. I feel the pressure every week but especially in a major championship. This week I tried to stay composed, focus on my game, not worrying about other factors that might affect my game, and I think that helped overall."

"Today is the first time I saw her own it," her caddie Fusco told *GolfWeek*. "In the past, she'd come to a major and say, 'I really want this,' which is great and normal. But you can't play that way. This is the first week she relaxed and let it come to her."

Kim said of her caddie: "The reason that I have ownership of my game on the course is just knowing the fact that Paul is with me as a friend and as a teammate. That gives me comfort on the course, which I think is why we've had a lot of success together."

Kim earned a record first prize for the championship of $645,000. Not quite the $1.5 million from the 2019 CME but this meant more. "Winning CME was great, it was really thrilling," she said, "but this one, it feels like a dramatic accomplishment."

Aronimink Golf Club, Newtown Square, Pennsylvania — October 8-11
Par 70 (35-35); 6,577yards — Purse: $4,300,000

1	**Sei Young Kim**	71	65	67	63	266	$645,000
2	**Inbee Park**	70	70	66	65	271	388,569
3	**Nasa Hataoka**	72	69	68	64	273	249,967
	Carlota Ciganda	68	69	71	65	273	249,967
5	Anna Nordqvist	69	68	68	71	276	175,511
6	Brooke M Henderson	71	69	65	72	277	143,599
7	Charley Hull	70	71	69	69	279	112,752
	Jennifer Kupcho	72	65	71	71	279	112,752
9	Lauren Stephenson	70	68	74	68	280	83,765
	Brittany Lincicome	67	72	72	69	280	83,765
	Gaby Lopez	68	72	68	72	280	83,765
	Bianca Pagdanganan	77	65	65	73	280	83,765
13	Ally McDonald	71	71	70	69	281	63,820
	Nanna Koerstz Madsen	72	69	69	71	281	63,820
	Kelly Tan	67	71	72	71	281	63,820
	Mina Harigae	74	68	66	73	281	63,820
17	Sung Hyun Park	71	71	69	71	282	55,313
18	Pernilla Lindberg	69	76	70	68	283	49,015
	Eun-Hee Ji	71	72	70	70	283	49,015
	Moriya Jutanugarn	72	68	72	71	283	49,015
	Ashleigh Buhai	70	68	74	71	283	49,015
	Lydia Ko	68	70	74	71	283	49,015
23	Hannah Green	79	66	72	67	284	39,175
	Madelene Sagstrom	72	71	72	69	284	39,175
	Sophia Popov	73	73	68	70	284	39,175
	Matilda Castren	69	77	68	70	284	39,175
	Jasmine Suwannapura	70	74	70	70	284	39,175
	Jeong Eun Lee	70	72	70	72	284	39,175
	In Gee Chun	72	67	71	74	284	39,175
30	Jenny Shin	70	76	70	69	285	32,123
	Mel Reid	74	70	71	70	285	32,123
	Lexi Thompson	70	72	73	70	285	32,123
33	Stacy Lewis	75	71	68	72	286	27,815
	Yealimi Noh	74	68	71	73	286	27,815
	Jennifer Song	72	68	73	73	286	27,815
	Danielle Kang	68	69	73	76	286	27,815
37	Robynn Ree	71	71	76	69	287	22,216
	Cristie Kerr	71	74	72	70	287	22,216
	Celine Boutier	74	71	71	71	287	22,216
	Ariya Jutanugarn	73	72	70	72	287	22,216
	Amy Olson	71	70	74	72	287	22,216
	Cydney Clanton	68	74	72	73	287	22,216
	Amy Yang	69	72	72	74	287	22,216
44	Lindy Duncan	72	72	76	68	288	17,763
	Angela Stanford	73	73	70	72	288	17,763
	Angel Yin	74	71	70	73	288	17,763
	Jennifer Chang	75	67	72	74	288	17,763
48	Xiyu Lin	73	73	74	69	289	14,785
	Chella Choi	75	71	72	71	289	14,785
	Elizabeth Szokol	71	74	73	71	289	14,785
	Alena Sharp	71	73	73	72	289	14,785
	Pornanong Phatlum	73	70	74	72	289	14,785
	Yui Kawamoto	72	70	74	73	289	14,785
54	Katherine Kirk	73	73	74	70	290	12,551
	Sarah Schmelzel	70	76	73	71	290	12,551
	Maria Fassi	73	72	74	71	290	12,551
	Isi Gabsa	70	75	69	76	290	12,551
58	Hinako Shibuno	70	75	76	70	291	10,516
	Minjee Lee	73	71	77	70	291	10,516
	Austin Ernst	73	73	74	71	291	10,516
	Hee Young Park	76	69	73	73	291	10,516
	Georgia Hall	70	74	74	73	291	10,516
	Jessica Korda	73	71	73	74	291	10,516
	Perrine Delacour	74	71	71	75	291	10,516
65	Linnea Strom	68	70	81	73	292	9,254
	Mariah Stackhouse	72	74	72	74	292	9,254
	Haeji Kang	73	72	73	74	292	9,254
	Leona Maguire	73	69	76	74	292	9,254
69	Alison Lee	75	71	74	73	293	8,546
	Anne van Dam	73	73	71	76	293	8,546
	Cheyenne Knight	71	74	70	78	293	8,546
72	Laura Davies	75	70	75	75	295	8,295
73	Haru Nomura	74	72	72	80	298	8,189
74	Patty Tavatanakit	72	73	76	78	299	8,084
	Jodi Ewart Shadoff	72	67	72		WND	7,986

MISSED THE 36-HOLE CUT

Stephanie Meadow	78	69	147
Haley Moore	75	72	147
Sandra Gal	74	73	147
Megan Khang	74	73	147
Brittany Lang	74	73	147
Klara Spilkova	74	73	147
Caroline Masson	73	74	147
Lizette Salas	73	74	147
Caroline Hedwall	71	76	147
Gerina Piller	71	76	147
Pajaree Anannarukarn	70	77	147
Nicole Broch Larsen	77	71	148
Caroline Inglis	77	71	148
Jillian Hollis	76	72	148
Mi Hyang Lee	76	72	148
Maria Fernanda Torres	74	74	148
Su Oh	73	75	148
Stephanie Connelly Eiswerth	78	71	149
Sarah Kemp	77	72	149
Esther Henseleit	76	73	149
Lindsey Weaver	76	73	149
Pei-Yun Chien	75	74	149
Esther Lee	75	74	149
Emma Talley	75	74	149
Albane Valenzuela	75	74	149
Yu Liu	73	76	149
Kristy McPherson	77	73	150
Jing Yan	75	75	150
Kristen Gillman	74	76	150
Christina Kim	73	77	150
Annie Park	72	78	150
Kendall Dye	77	74	151
Brittany Altomare	76	75	151
Ryann O'Toole	76	75	151
Alison Curdt	75	76	151
Julia Engstrom	75	76	151
Azahara Munoz	74	77	151
Morgan Pressel	72	79	151
Sarah Burnham	76	76	152
Dana Finkelstein	76	76	152
Wichanee Meechai	74	78	152
Jaye Marie Green	72	80	152
Kim Kaufman	78	75	153
Dottie Ardina	76	77	153
Bronte Law	75	78	153
Sarah Jane Smith	78	76	154
Tiffany Joh	75	79	154
Jordan Lintz	83	73	156
Andrea Lee	78	78	156
Samantha Morrell	82	77	159
Joanna Coe	79	80	159
Seul-Ki Hawley	80	80	160
Ellen Ceresko	82	79	161
Gemma Dryburgh	81	80	161
Jennifer Borocz	80	81	161
Nelly Korda	71		WND
Mirim Lee	77		RTD

ROLL OF HONOUR

1955	Beverly Hanson	Orchard Ridge
1956	Marlene Hagge*	Forest Lake
1957	Louise Suggs	Churchill Valley
1958	Mickey Wright	Churchill Valley
1959	Betsy Rawls	Sheraton Hotel
1960	Mickey Wright	Sheraton Hotel
1961	Mickey Wright	Stardust
1962	Judy Kimball	Stardust
1963	Mickey Wright	Stardust
1964	Mary Mills	Stardust
1965	Sandra Haynie	Stardust
1966	Gloria Ehret	Stardust
1967	Kathy Whitworth	Pleasant Valley
1968	Sandra Post*	Pleasant Valley
1969	Betsy Rawls	Concord
1970	Shirley Englehorn*	Pleasant Valley
1971	Kathy Whitworth	Pleasant Valley
1972	Kathy Ahern	Pleasant Valley
1973	Mary Mills	Pleasant Valley
1974	Sandra Haynie	Pleasant Valley
1975	Kathy Whitworth	Pine Ridge
1976	Betty Burfeindt	Pine Ridge
1977	Chako Higuchi	Bay Tree
1978	Nancy Lopez	Jack Nicklaus Sports Center
1979	Donna Caponi	Jack Nicklaus Sports Center
1980	Sally Little	Jack Nicklaus Sports Center
1981	Donna Caponi	Jack Nicklaus Sports Center
1982	Jan Stephenson	Jack Nicklaus Sports Center
1983	Patty Sheehan	Jack Nicklaus Sports Center
1984	Patty Sheehan	Jack Nicklaus Sports Center
1985	Nancy Lopez	Jack Nicklaus Sports Center
1986	Pat Bradley	Jack Nicklaus Sports Center
1987	Jane Geddes	Jack Nicklaus Sports Center
1988	Sherri Turner	Jack Nicklaus Sports Center
1989	Nancy Lopez	Jack Nicklaus Sports Center
1990	Beth Daniel	Bethesda
1991	Meg Mallon	Bethesda
1992	Betsy King	Bethesda
1993	Patty Sheehan	Bethesda
1994	Laura Davies	DuPont
1995	Kelly Robbins	DuPont
1996	Laura Davies	DuPont
1997	Christa Johnson*	DuPont
1998	Se Ri Pak	DuPont
1999	Juli Inkster	DuPont
2000	Juli Inkster*	DuPont
2001	Karrie Webb	DuPont
2002	Se Ri Pak	DuPont
2003	Annika Sorenstam*	DuPont
2004	Annika Sorenstam	DuPont
2005	Annika Sorenstam	Bulle Rock
2006	Se Ri Pak*	Bulle Rock
2007	Suzann Pettersen	Bulle Rock
2008	Yani Tseng*	Bulle Rock
2009	Anna Nordqvist	Bulle Rock
2010	Cristie Kerr	Locust Hill
2011	Yani Tseng	Locust Hill
2012	Shanshan Feng	Locust Hill
2013	Inbee Park*	Locust Hill
2014	Inbee Park*	Monroe
2015	Inbee Park	Westchester
2016	Brooke Henderson*	Sahalee
2017	Danielle Kang	Olympia Fields
2018	Sung Hyun Park*	Kemper Lakes
2019	Hannah Green	Hazeltine National
2020	Sei Young Kim	Aronimink

**won in playoff*

Known as the LPGA Championship until 2014

MASTERS TOURNAMENT

Rob Carr/Getty Images

Emotional Johnson looks pretty in green

Few things heighten the senses in golf quite like Augusta National during the Masters Tournament. Not so much smelling the damp pine straw after a rain delay, tasting the cheese pimento sandwiches or even touching the fabric of a certain style of jacket. It is seeing all the colours — from the green of the jacket and the fairways to the vivid blooms of azalea and dogwood — and hearing the sounds. The roars that we know so well. Was there a cacophony more joyful than the one that greeted Tiger Woods' fifth victory in 2019 — unless it was for Jack Nicklaus' sixth in 1986. (Not to mention the clamour accompanying Gene Sarazen's albatross in 1935 that echoed around the pines of the 15th hole to become the "shot heard around the world".)

Woods and Phil Mickelson have their distinctive cheers, as Nicklaus and Arnold Palmer did before them. So will Dustin Johnson in years to come.

But not in 2020. There were no roars, there were no patrons. It was November, not April. No spring brightness to the colour palette, but a hint of autumnal rust thanks to a smattering of maples and other deciduous trees among the grand, evergreen pines. The 84th Masters really was a tradition unlike any other.

"We have done our very best to create a safe environment that allows for the Masters to take place successfully, albeit differently than anyone would have imagined," said club chairman Fred Ridley.

There was no Wednesday Par-Three Contest to curse its winner. Instead, a positive Covid-19 test could rule a player out. Former champion Sergio Garcia and Chile's Joaquin Niemann, due to return for the first time as a professional, had to withdraw at the start of Masters week. Another past winner, Adam Scott, and others including Johnson and Tony Finau, were more fortunate in their timing, having tested positive, quarantined and recovered in enough time still to compete.

Yet however much everything was different, as Johnson said on Tuesday: "It's still the Masters and there's still a green jacket on the line."

One more change from the orthodoxies: this Masters was all but decided before the back nine on Sunday. The crucial moment was a birdie from Johnson at the short sixth hole, having seen his four-stroke overnight lead whittled down to one after successive bogeys. After that the world number one eased away from his pursuers, a hat-trick of birdies in the middle of the inward half merely confirming what would end up as a five-stroke victory. It had been a superb display of attacking golf. Johnson set a new Masters record total of 268 and matched the major record of 20 under par. No Augusta winner had recorded fewer than his four bogeys.

He deserved a huge ovation at the 18th but his quiet fist pump of satisfaction matched the applause of the small gathering around the green. In one sense it felt in keeping with a man who rarely offers a public show of emotion.

Johnson said earlier in the week: "I definitely get excited and I can feel it coming down the stretch because I want to win. It means a lot to me. I get, I don't know, maybe more excited afterwards than I do right there in that moment because I'm so focused on what I'm doing."

At a pre-tournament press conference, Johnson had said his favourite thing about the Masters was the sandwiches. He had to wait until Sunday afternoon to get what he actually wanted most of all — the green jacket that he was helped into by defending champion Woods.

Woods said: "DJ has just an amazing ability to stay calm in tough moments, and in order to win this event. We all know as past champions how hard it is, the emotions we have to deal with out there. There's no one more suited to that, I think, than DJ."

But soon the emotion came in a television interview back on the 18th green with Amanda Balionis of CBS Sports. "It's a dream come true," Johnson started before tears came easier than words. "As a kid, I always dreamed about being a Masters champion ... It's hard to talk ... It's incredible, as you can tell ... I've never had this much trouble gathering myself, on the course I'm OK, but not here ... I've got a great team ..."

A father of two young sons, Tatum and River, with fiancée Paulina Gretzky, Johnson later said: "I had a tough time there speaking with Amanda just because it means so much to me. It means so much to my family, Paulina, the kids. They know it's something that I've always been dreaming about and it's why I work so hard. To finally have the dream come true, I think that's why you see all that emotion."

Johnson grew up little more than an hour away on the outskirts of Columbia, South Carolina, very much within the region that considers the Masters as their home championship. This was his 10th appearance at Augusta. He had been in the top 10 on each of his last four appearances, with a best of second in 2019. He missed the tournament in 2017, having won his three previous starts, due to injury after slipping on steps at his rental house during the practice days.

His form coming into this year was also strong. He had won three times, and in his previous six starts had two wins, three seconds and sixth at the US Open. But at the PGA Championship in August he had lost a 54-hole lead in a major for the fourth time out of four. There had been far more setbacks to set on the ledger against his lone major win at the 2016 US Open.

Here he was again, out in front on the final day. "It was a battle all day, an internal battle with myself," Johnson said. "I proved that I can get it done on Sunday with the lead at a major. There were doubts in my mind because I had been there. I'm in this position a lot. It was like, 'When am I going to have the lead and finish off a major?' I was nervous all day, but I felt I controlled myself very well, controlled the golf ball very well in difficult conditions."

FIRST ROUND

What no one wanted after a seven-month delay was a further wait on Thursday morning. Barely had honorary starts Jack Nicklaus and Gary Player, as well as the first groups on each nine, teed off when light rain became torrential and play was suspended for almost three hours. One of the changes for 2020, due to the reduced hours of daylight in November, was for play to start on both the first and 10th tees. Woods was one of those to go off the 10th and he had soon birdied the 13th, 15th and 16th holes on the way to a 68. It proved to be the lowest, but not the most notable, round of his week.

While Woods had played so seldom in the disrupted 2020 season to be high on the list of contenders, the focus was on Bryson DeChambeau. Two months after his stunning US Open win at Winged Foot, the bulked up DeChambeau reckoned he had added even more length to his driving, although, after much consideration, he ultimately decided against using a 48-inch driver. In Monday's practice round he hit approach shots with such short clubs that it harked back to Woods in 1997. At the uphill par-five eighth he required only a six-iron to find the green.

It was different on Thursday, since he required a hybrid at the same hole but his round, starting at the 10th, had faltered as early as the 13th. On one of the holes he was looking to dominate, he drove through the fairway into the trees on the right and put his second over the green into the flowers. He took a penalty drop and flubbed a chip on the way to a double bogey.

"This golf course, as much as I'm trying to attack it, it can bite back," said DeChambeau. However, at the ninth, his last hole, a drive of 364 yards, followed by a short pitch, produced a birdie for a 70.

With the annual rye over-seed of the course having taken place only weeks before in September, the course was due to play softer than it would in April and the rain did not help. As ever when the course does not play at its firmest, scoring was low. Paul Casey immediately took advantage when the skies cleared by returning a seven-under-par 65, including an eagle at the second where his six-iron approach to five feet stopped dead rather than hopping over the back of the green. "I was not relishing the challenge ahead in the rain this morning," Casey said. "So, to be honest, that was a very good break that I capitalised on because it was a glorious day for golf after that."

When play was suspended at 5.30pm due to darkness, with only half the field having completed their rounds, the Englishman was leading by two from Webb Simpson and Xander Schauffele, with Justin Thomas also five under after 10 holes. Thomas finished off a 66 on Friday morning, as did Masters rookie Sungjae Im, while Cameron Smith moved to five under. But two players joined Casey on 65, Johnson and South Africa's Dylan Frittelli, who was in his second Masters and scored 12 strokes lower than his opening round in 2018.

Before the tournament, Johnson said: "I feel like if I can put myself in position come Sunday, I like my chances, but we've got to get there first." It was a journey made longer by the weather delay. He had soon notched up an eagle at the second hole on Thursday and finished the day three under par for nine holes.

"I thought it was pretty good," Johnson said. "I hit some really nice shots, had some good looks. There was so much rain this morning. We were watching on TV, you could tell the course looked really soft. You needed to come out and take advantage because there wasn't really a whole lot of wind and really soft conditions, you can fire it at the flag."

It was the effortless finish to his round on Friday morning, birdieing four of the last seven holes, that should have had his rivals worried. The run started with a two at the 12th, included a four at the 15th, another two at the 16th and a closing three. He had not dropped a stroke.

After 18 holes: 65 (-7) Casey, D Johnson, Frittelli; **66** Thomas, Im; **67** Simpson, Schauffele, Rose, C Smith; **68** Langer, Champ, Matsuyama, Oosthuizen, Westwood, Reed, Woods, Ancer

SECOND ROUND

Those in the second half of the draw had to turn straight round and go out again. Good news for those who had finished their first round well, except that Frittelli bogeyed three of his first four holes on the way to a 73, and Casey later returned a 74. Johnson, however, followed a par at the 10th, his opening hole of the second round, with three birdies in a row at Amen Corner. Two twos in one day at Augusta's 12th. This was looking ominous. It had taken him 22 holes to get to 10 under par and he appeared to be running away from the rest of the field.

But then golf intervened. At the 14th, Johnson had a speck of mud on his ball for his approach, which stayed on the top plateau of the green. From there down to the hole it was regulation three-putt territory. What might have been a blip became more of a stall when his three-iron second at the 15th came up short of the green in the water. "I hit a good shot," he said. "Just the wind picked up a little bit and it floated on me a hair, came up a couple yards short."

A long run of pars followed, including a 360-degree lip-out at the third, before Johnson birdied the ninth for a 70 to join the lead again at nine under par. "Conditions have been similar each day," Johnson said. "The greens were a little bit quicker today and the wind this afternoon was a little gusty. I'm definitely pleased with how I'm swinging the club and controlling the golf ball right now."

Thomas rallied from a couple of early bogeys to birdie the last four holes of the back nine, then turned to the first and took a double bogey. He ended up with a 69 for nine under, a mark reached by Smith, after a 68, thanks to playing the last four holes three-two-three-three: an eagle and three birdies. "It got a bit scrappy but I hung in there and got the reward at the end," said Smith, who was playing in his fourth Masters.

Abraham Ancer was playing Augusta for the first time and was inspired by his compatriot Carlos Ortiz winning the Vivint Houston Open the previous Sunday to become the first Mexican winner on the PGA Tour for 42 years. Ancer added a 67 to his earlier 68 to make it four on nine under. There were 66s from Danny Willett, despite a double bogey at his opening hole, the 10th, Tommy Fleetwood and Rory McIlroy, among others, while Canada's Corey Conners had a 65. DeChambeau, however, lost a ball when trying to drive the green at the third and took a triple bogey on the way to a 74.

While the cut rule was changed to the leading 50 players and ties, eliminating anyone else who was within 10 strokes of the lead, that did not stop Bernhard Langer setting a new record as the oldest player to qualify. Nor did the fact that it was the lowest ever cut at level par, nor did walking 26 holes on a soft, hilly course, nor hitting much longer clubs than almost any of his junior peers. The 63-year-old double champion beat Tommy Aaron's old record by a month.

"There have been so many great players here before me, from Jack Nicklaus to Gary Player to all the greats that have competed here, and to be the oldest to make the cut, it's certainly an achievement," Langer said.

Among those to have to finish their round on Saturday morning was Jon Rahm, who added a birdie at the 13th and then five pars for a 66. That made a five-way tie at the top. Rahm had had an adventurous week. In a practice round on Monday the Spaniard had holed in one at the fourth. On Tuesday, his 26th birthday, he again made an ace, this time skipping the ball across the pond at the 16th before it climbed up onto the green and curled round to the hole. At the nearby 15th on Saturday morning, Rahm had to chip in to save his par.

"It's the type of shot where I'm really just looking to start it on the right line, and land it on the green, because that ball will get to the hole and hopefully finds it, and it did," he said. "It was huge. A chip-in is always a huge boost of confidence."

Rahm had two top-10 finishes in his three appearances at Augusta. Did he think he was "mastering Augusta"? "Mastering? I think you master it when you become the Masters champion. I'm on my way, I guess." The leaderboard suggested there might be a new champion but it was still a crowded field. "If you're a golf fan," Rahm said, "this weekend is going to be a good one to watch with the course getting better and the leaderboard we have going on."

After 36 holes: 135 (-9) Ancer 67, C Smith 68, D Johnson 70, Thomas 69, Rahm 66; **136** Cantlay 66, Im 70, Pan 66, Matsuyama 68, Reed 68; **137** Willett 66, Fleetwood 66, Rose 70

THIRD ROUND

To think, briefly on Saturday, there were nine players sharing the lead. Johnson soon did something about that. He almost holed his five-iron approach from 222 yards at the second and tapped in for an eagle. He holed from eight feet for a birdie at the third and from 40 feet at the fourth. No one else was sharing the lead again during the 2020 Masters.

"I had a good number and it came out exactly where I wanted it to," Johnson said of his near-albatross at the second. "It landed exactly in the right spot. It's tough to get close to that hole location, but with the soft conditions, I was able to hit a nice shot. So, obviously, get eagle on two, and then birdieing three and four, got off to a great start and was able to continue that through the rest of the day."

Birdies at the seventh, 13th and 15th holes gave Johnson his second bogey-free 65 of the week. Previously, his best score at Augusta had been 67. "I feel every year I've learned something," he said. "Kind of figured out a little bit more about the course, how to play it. You know, when can you attack the golf course and when do you just need to try to make an easy four. The more and more I play it, the more comfortable I get."

This was Johnson's 10th outing. Others were still figuring it out. Thomas's challenge stalled with a 71, coming home in 37, while Rahm had a 72, his challenge fading after a double bogey at the eighth hole when his second shot veered alarmingly off line.

Of the other overnight leaders, Ancer and Smith both scored 69s and ended up four behind in second place, along with Im, who had a 68. Frittelli rallied with a 67 to be fifth, followed by Thomas. At 16 under par, Johnson had tied Jordan Spieth's 54-hole record from 2015.

"Going into tomorrow, I think I've got a good game plan," Johnson said. "I'm not going to change it. I'm going to have to go out and play well. There's a lot of really good players right around me, so as we all know here, if you get it going, you can shoot some low scores. I'm going to need to go out and play a really good round of golf if I want to win tomorrow."

Im won the Honda Classic early in 2020 for his first PGA Tour victory. He spoke to countryman KJ Choi about his first visit to Augusta. "He said that with the baby fade I often hit, my game is well suited for this course. I grew up watching the Masters on television and feel like I know the course very well just from that. It suits my eye and also my game. I can look down the fairway from the tee on each hole and see where I have to hit it."

Im and Ancer played in the Presidents Cup together in Australia in 2019. Im recovered from a late bogey at the 17th by birdieing the last. "I feel very comfortable, and my plan tomorrow is to stay composed and stick to my game plan," Im said. Ancer also only dropped one stroke, while Smith did not have a bogey, birdieing the 13th, 14th and 15th holes to sneak under 70 for the third day running.

"I really just can't wait for tomorrow," Smith said. "We'll obviously need a hot start, and then the back nine has been kind to me all week, so hopefully it can be kind to me one more day."

The 27-year-old Australian was only a toddler when Greg Norman lost a six-shot lead at Augusta in 1996. "I try not to think of that moment. My old man still talks about it now. He missed a day of work because of Greggy, but it happens." With Johnson's unproven record of converting 54-holes in majors, Smith added: "Anyone with a four-shot lead is expected to win. You know, there's going to be plenty of boys firing tomorrow."

After 54 holes: 200 (-16) D Johnson 65; **204** Im 68, Ancer 69, C Smith 69; **205** Frittelli 67; **206** Thomas 71; **207** Munoz 69, Reed 71, Rahm 72

FINAL ROUND

For the second Sunday running at the Masters, players went off early from two tees. This year it was so that the tournament finished prior to CBS's NFL commitments. A notable early grouping featured Langer with Charl Schwartzel and DeChambeau. "I felt in the middle of it," said the German of the big-hitting around him. "It is fun to watch and fascinating how they do it. I was in awe of how they swing and how hard they hit it. I had to tell myself to stop watching and focus on what I want to do."

For the record, Langer and Schwartzel had 71s and DeChambeau a 73. The US Open champion had attempted to overpower Augusta as he had Winged Foot but got a different result. He finished a shot behind a man almost four decades his senior and, on his own estimation of the course as a par 68 for him, at a personal 14 over par. Afterwards he complained of dizziness and added: "I felt I could have a great chance to win the tournament if I just played my game. Shoot, I made enough birdies this week and eagles to have a chance to win. There's no doubt about that. I made way too many mistakes."

The most unexpected mistakes came from Woods, who found Rae's Creek at the 12th hole no less than three times: once from the tee after misjudging the wind (easily done), once from the drop zone (also easily done) and once from the back bunker (again, even for a five-time winner, easily done). He ended up with a 10 before birdieing five of the last six holes for a 76, his highest score as a professional at Augusta.

"I've hit a few too many shots than I wanted to today, and I will not have the chairman putting the green jacket on me," Woods said. "I'll be passing it on."

He passed it on to Johnson but only after an early scare for the leader. While Im birdied the second and the third, Johnson duffed a chip into a bunker and only parred the second, before getting his three at the third. Then he bogeyed the fourth after missing the green and the fifth after finding a fairway bunker. His lead was down to one.

But then came the downhill, par-three sixth. An eight-iron to seven feet was the perfect response for Johnson. Im missed the green and took a four, while Johnson holed for a two and a two-shot swing. At the seventh, Johnson played from the trees to the front bunker and had an easy up and down. Im found a back bunker from the fairway and took five.

Smith still presented a challenge, having made a miraculous escape from the trees at the seventh for a birdie. But Johnson never looked like dropping another shot and birdied the ninth as well as three in a row from the 13th. He added a 68 to get to his record Augusta total, while matching the 20 under par tally of Jason Day at the 2015 PGA and Henrik Stenson at the 2016 Open.

Smith birdied the 15th to post another 69, becoming the first player ever to score four rounds in the 60s in the Masters. "That's really cool," Smith said. "I had no idea starting today that I needed to do that. It would have been cooler to do it and win. I was actually saying that I'd take 15 under the rest of my career here and I might win a couple."

Im also birdied the 15th to tie with Smith for runner-up honours after his own 69. "My initial goal at the start of the week was just to make the cut," said the young Korean. "So to finish tied for second is unbelievable." Thomas finished three further back in fourth place, McIlroy and Frittelli shared fifth, Rahm was in seventh, as was Brooks Koepka, and Ancer dropped down to 13th.

Johnson became the fourth world number one, since 1986, to win the Masters following Ian Woosnam, Fred Couples and Woods. Only Nicklaus (son) and Patrick Reed (brother-in-law) had previously had a family member caddie for the champion. Of younger brother Austin, Johnson said: "I just love experiencing all these moments with him. I wouldn't want it any other way."

He added: "Growing up so close to here, since I've been on tour, since I played my first Masters, it's been the tournament I wanted to win the most. Obviously the first major's the hardest, but then I would say the second one is just as hard. They are all difficult to win. It's just hard to get it done in a major for some reason. I've had the lead a couple times and haven't been able to finish it off, and so it is very nice to have a lead and then play well on Sunday and get the win.

"I couldn't be more happy, and I think I look pretty good in green, too."

Augusta National Golf Club, Augusta, Georgia
Par 72 (36-36); 7,475 yards

November 12-15
Purse: $11,500,000

1	**Dustin Johnson**	65	70	65	68	268	$2,070,000
2	**Sungjae Im**	66	70	68	69	273	1,012,000
	Cameron Smith	67	68	69	69	273	1,012,000
4	Justin Thomas	66	69	71	70	276	552,000
5	Dylan Frittelli	65	73	67	72	277	437,000
	Rory McIlroy	75	66	67	69	277	437,000
7	Brooks Koepka	70	69	69	70	278	358,417
	Cheng Tsung Pan	70	66	74	68	278	358,417
	Jon Rahm	69	66	72	71	278	358,417
10	Corey Conners	74	65	71	69	279	287,500
	Patrick Reed	68	68	71	72	279	287,500
	Webb Simpson	67	73	71	68	279	287,500
13	Abraham Ancer	68	67	69	76	280	215,625
	Marc Leishman	70	72	70	68	280	215,625
	Hideki Matsuyama	68	68	72	72	280	215,625
	Kevin Na	73	68	69	70	280	215,625
17	Patrick Cantlay	70	66	73	72	281	178,250
	Xander Schauffele	67	73	71	70	281	178,250
19	Cameron Champ	68	74	68	72	282	144,325
	Tommy Fleetwood	71	66	71	74	282	144,325
	Sebastian Munoz	70	68	69	75	282	144,325
	Scottie Scheffler	71	68	72	71	282	144,325
23	Louis Oosthuizen	68	70	75	70	283	115,000
	Justin Rose	67	70	76	70	283	115,000
25	Shane Lowry	74	69	68	73	284	91,713
	Ian Poulter	72	71	71	70	284	91,713
	Charl Schwartzel	73	71	69	71	284	91,713
	Danny Willett	71	66	74	73	284	91,713
29	Rickie Fowler	70	70	75	70	285	74,750
	Sung Kang	75	69	71	70	285	74,750
	Bernhard Langer	68	73	73	71	285	74,750
	Chez Reavie	71	72	72	70	285	74,750
	Nick Taylor	72	72	69	72	285	74,750
34	Bryson DeChambeau	70	74	69	73	286	62,100
	Si Woo Kim	70	71	73	72	286	62,100
	Adam Scott	70	72	71	73	286	62,100
	Andy Ogletree (A)	73	70	71	72	286	
38	Christiaan Bezuidenhout	69	73	74	71	287	50,600
	Paul Casey	65	74	71	77	287	50,600
	Tony Finau	69	75	71	72	287	50,600
	Billy Horschel	70	70	72	75	287	50,600
	Lee Westwood	68	74	71	74	287	50,600
	Tiger Woods	68	71	72	76	287	50,600
44	Shugo Imahira	72	70	72	74	288	41,400
	Collin Morikawa	70	74	70	74	288	41,400
46	Matthew Fitzpatrick	74	70	73	72	289	33,672
	Charles Howell III	71	70	74	74	289	33,672
	Victor Perez	70	71	76	72	289	33,672
	Jordan Spieth	74	70	73	72	289	33,672
	Matt Wallace	69	73	70	77	289	33,672
51	Rafa Cabrera Bello	73	71	74	72	290	28,003
	Jazz Janewattananond	69	71	75	75	290	28,003
	Zach Johnson	73	71	73	73	290	28,003
	Mike Weir	71	72	71	76	290	28,003
55	Phil Mickelson	69	70	79	73	291	26,680
	John Augenstein (A)	69	72	75	75	291	
57	Bubba Watson	74	69	71	78	292	26,450
58	Bernd Wiesberger	71	72	78	73	294	26,220
59	Brandt Snedeker	71	71	79	74	295	25,990
60	Jimmy Walker	71	73	76	76	296	25,760
	MISSED THE 36-HOLE CUT						
	Byeong Hun An	72	73			145	
	Adam Hadwin	74	71			145	
	Max Homa	70	75			145	
	Matt Kuchar	70	75			145	
	Graeme McDowell	72	73			145	
	Andrew Putnam	73	72			145	
	Henrik Stenson	71	74			145	
	Gary Woodland	72	73			145	
	Justin Harding	75	71			146	
	Brendon Todd	73	73			146	
	Lanto Griffin	74	73			147	
	Tyrrell Hatton	73	74			147	
	Kevin Kisner	71	76			147	
	Larry Mize	70	77			147	
	Matthew Wolff	70	77			147	
	Jason Day	70	78			148	
	Tyler Duncan	77	71			148	
	Jason Kokrak	71	77			148	
	JT Poston	73	75			148	
	James Sugrue (A)	77	71			148	
	Fred Couples	77	73			150	
	Lukas Michel (A)	76	74			150	
	Francesco Molinari	72	78			150	
	Lucas Glover	77	74			151	
	Nate Lashley	75	76			151	
	Sandy Lyle	78	73			151	
	Yuxin Lin (A)	79	73			152	
	Jose Maria Olazabal	78	80			158	
	Abel Gallegos (A)	79	81			160	
	Andrew Landry	78	82			160	
	Vijay Singh	75				WDN	
	Eric van Rooyen	76				WDN	

ROLL OF HONOUR

1934	Horton Smith	Augusta National
1935	Gene Sarazen*	Augusta National
1936	Horton Smith	Augusta National
1937	Byron Nelson	Augusta National
1938	Henry Picard	Augusta National
1939	Ralph Guldahl	Augusta National
1940	Jimmy Demaret	Augusta National
1941	Craig Wood	Augusta National
1942	Byron Nelson*	Augusta National
1946	Herman Keiser	Augusta National
1947	Jimmy Demaret	Augusta National
1948	Claude Harmon	Augusta National
1949	Sam Snead	Augusta National
1950	Jimmy Demaret	Augusta National
1951	Ben Hogan	Augusta National
1952	Sam Snead	Augusta National
1953	Ben Hogan	Augusta National
1954	Sam Snead*	Augusta National
1955	Cary Middlecoff	Augusta National
1956	Jack Burke Jr	Augusta National
1957	Doug Ford	Augusta National
1958	Arnold Palmer	Augusta National
1959	Art Wall	Augusta National
1960	Arnold Palmer	Augusta National
1961	Gary Player	Augusta National
1962	Arnold Palmer*	Augusta National
1963	Jack Nicklaus	Augusta National
1964	Arnold Palmer	Augusta National
1965	Jack Nicklaus	Augusta National
1966	Jack Nicklaus*	Augusta National
1967	Gay Brewer	Augusta National
1968	Bob Goalby	Augusta National
1969	George Archer	Augusta National
1970	Billy Casper*	Augusta National
1971	Charles Coody	Augusta National
1972	Jack Nicklaus	Augusta National
1973	Tommy Aaron	Augusta National
1974	Gary Player	Augusta National
1975	Jack Nicklaus	Augusta National
1976	Raymond Floyd	Augusta National
1977	Tom Watson	Augusta National
1978	Gary Player	Augusta National
1979	Fuzzy Zoeller*	Augusta National
1980	Seve Ballesteros	Augusta National
1981	Tom Watson	Augusta National
1982	Craig Stadler*	Augusta National
1983	Seve Ballesteros	Augusta National
1984	Ben Crenshaw	Augusta National
1985	Bernhard Langer	Augusta National
1986	Jack Nicklaus	Augusta National
1987	Larry Mize*	Augusta National
1988	Sandy Lyle	Augusta National
1989	Nick Faldo*	Augusta National
1990	Nick Faldo*	Augusta National
1991	Ian Woosnam	Augusta National
1992	Fred Couples	Augusta National
1993	Bernhard Langer	Augusta National
1994	Jose Maria Olazabal	Augusta National
1995	Ben Crenshaw	Augusta National
1996	Nick Faldo	Augusta National
1997	Tiger Woods	Augusta National
1998	Mark O'Meara	Augusta National
1999	Jose Maria Olazabal	Augusta National
2000	Vijay Singh	Augusta National
2001	Tiger Woods	Augusta National
2002	Tiger Woods	Augusta National
2003	Mike Weir*	Augusta National
2004	Phil Mickelson	Augusta National
2005	Tiger Woods*	Augusta National
2006	Phil Mickelson	Augusta National
2007	Zach Johnson	Augusta National
2008	Trevor Immelman	Augusta National
2009	Angel Cabrera*	Augusta National
2010	Phil Mickelson	Augusta National
2011	Charl Schwartzel	Augusta National
2012	Bubba Watson*	Augusta National
2013	Adam Scott*	Augusta National
2014	Bubba Watson	Augusta National
2015	Jordan Spieth	Augusta National
2016	Danny Willett	Augusta National
2017	Sergio Garcia*	Augusta National
2018	Patrick Reed	Augusta National
2019	Tiger Woods	Augusta National
2020	Dustin Johnson	Augusta National

**won in playoff*

US WOMEN'S OPEN

Carmen Mandato/Getty Images

A Lim Kim — a new champion unmasked

Three birdies on the last three holes to win by one stroke. It took one of the greatest finishes to any major championship to grab everyone's attention and it also brought A Lim Kim victory at the 75th US Women's Open.

Previously, the spotlight had been elsewhere. There was Cristie Kerr, in her 25th appearance, battling through the pain of playing with three dislocated ribs. There was Kaitlyn Papp, from the University of Texas, contending as an amateur, as well as Thailand's Jutanugarn sisters, steady Moriya and the erratic genius that is her younger sister Ariya.

At the top of the leaderboard it appeared to be a duel between the exciting Hinako Shibuno, attempting to win on her debut as the Japanese player did at the AIG Women's Open in 2019, and the stoic North Dakotan Amy Olson, leading on the final stretch while dealing with her grief at the unexpected death of her father-in-law. The heartfelt support for Olson was palpable even as most followed the action remotely via television and social media with spectators absent from Champions Golf Club.

And even as it appeared they would miss out on the Harton S Semple trophy this time, the big-name Koreans could not be ignored. Jeongeun Lee[6] tied for sixth place on the defence of her title. Inbee Park had finished early with a 68 that stood for some time as the round of the day until world number one Jin Young Ko matched it with two birdies in the last three holes. Ko had to finish in the top four to qualify for the season-ending LPGA event the following week.

But, suddenly, their lesser known compatriot emerged from the fringe of contention to become the centre of attention. With three perfectly timed birdies, the game's newest champion was umasked.

Wearing a face covering, as she had on the course all week, the 25-year-old Kim arrived at the tee of the par-three 16th hole two behind Olson at level par for the championship. "I've been eyeing the leaderboard throughout the round and I knew how many shots I was back," Kim explained. "That's probably the reason why I tried to hit more aggressive, tried to more attack the pins."

Her five-iron shot at the 16th ran no more than four feet past the hole and she made that putt. One under par and one back. At the 17th, she hit an eight-iron with her approach that stopped just over a foot away. She tapped that in to tie for the lead at two under par.

At the 18th, the longest hitter on the Korean LPGA tour required only a wedge for her second shot. The tee was one of those moved forward for the final round due to be played in stormy conditions on Sunday. As it turned out, play was abandoned early in the day and now it was a freezing cold Monday — 11 days before Christmas — but the wind had not got up. Kim landed her approach just over the bunker guarding the front-right of the green and gave herself a birdie putt of seven feet.

This was her first appearance in America. On her home tour in 2018 Kim took Inbee Park to the final hole in the final of the Doosan Match Play and then won for the first time at the Se Ri Pak Invitational. She won again in 2019 and for the second year running won three points out of three for the KLPGA in their annual match against the LPGA. She had 18 top 10s in those two seasons. Although not quite as successful in 2020, Kim did finish in the top 10 of each of her final four events. Earlier in the year, the Seoul Sisters blog had predicted: "With her length and consistency, it seems she is destined to become a big name sooner or later."

By holing this putt, it would be sooner rather than later. Kim, ranked 94th in the world, clenched her fist when it went in, the smile detectable even under her mask. Then she had to wait. She fielded messages from friends and family watching in the middle of a Korean night, although only after her caddie had upended the golf bag to retrieve her phone. A 67, for a three-under-par total of 281, matched the lowest round of the week, first achieved on the opening day by Olson.

Olson had four holes to play. Going over the back of the 16th green meant a bogey and she dropped two behind. After Olson failed to hole her second shot at the 18th, in the players' lounge Kim was doused in fizz by friends, Lee[6] among them. At least she had a coat on by then. At the presentation Kim became the first recipient of the Mickey Wright medal, named for the late four-time champion.

A birdie at the last put Olson into a share of second place with Ko on two under par. Once she had holed out, Olson could not contain the tears any longer. It was the second time in three years she had been so close to winning a major. A first LPGA victory of any kind remained elusive. But these were not tears for the loss of any golf tournament.

"I really believe the Lord just carried me through — it just makes you realise how much bigger life is than golf," Olson said. In tribute to her father-in-law, Lee Olson, she added: "We had a really special relationship. He's a big, tough, military West Point guy, loved the Army, but had a particular soft spot for the women in his life, particularly his wife and daughter-in-law. And just incredibly generous. Loved to hunt and fish, and we'll have a lot of great memories to take from those activities, doing those with him."

Four days earlier Olson, who was the 2009 US Girls' Junior champion and won 20 times in college, had addressed her lack of professional victories in an uncannily prescient manner. "I would definitely say coming out on tour, I expected to win really early," she said. "It always came easy to me in college.

"Coming out here, the biggest thing I've learned is perspective and what I consider success. At the end of my life, it's not going to be number of tournaments I've won but how I lived. Trying to maintain that perspective is really important for me."

FIRST ROUND

Olson had opened the championship in the grand manner. On the 16th hole of the Cypress Creek course, her seventh of the day, Olson holed out with an eight-iron from 139 yards. "I was pretty excited to be able to do that at the US Open," she said. "I hit a fade to try to hold the wind and it landed two paces short of the flag, had some good spin on it and just trickled in. I definitely allowed myself to enjoy the moment."

Olson was not the only player to have a hole-in-one, as Yu Jin Sung aced the fourth hole of the Creek with a five-iron from 169 yards. But Olson was alone at the top of the leaderboard, just as she was after the first round of the AIG Women's Open in August. The 28-year-old had bogeyed her second hole of the day but followed the ace with birdies at the 17th, the first and the eighth.

With a 67, four under par, Olson was one ahead of Shibuno, who was also playing the Cypress Creek course, as well as Moriya Jutanugarn and A Lim Kim, who both opened their accounts on the Jackrabbit course.

With the US Women's Open being played in December for the first time, the reduced daylight meant one course could not accommodate the starting field of 156 players. The solution for the first two days was to utilise both the layouts at Champions, where 97-year-old Jackie Burke Jr still presides at the club he founded with Jimmy Demaret in 1957. As expected, Cypress Creek, with its greater length and huge greens, played the harder of the two, with 15 of the 23 rounds under par coming on the Jackrabbit.

It was on that layout Kerr returned a 71, level par, having undergone cryotherapy twice a day since being involved in a pre-dawn cart accident at Old American the previous week. Both Kerr and her caddie ended up in hospital after she swerved to avoid an oncoming cart and hit a cement post.

"If you would've told me on Monday that I would be playing today I would have said you were crazy," said the 43-year-old. "Wednesday morning, I really didn't want to get out of bed. But I'm here, and I played, and I was tough today, and I feel like I'm going to keep getting better every day. God darn it, I'm going to do this."

Megan Khang, a member of the 2019 US Solheim Cup team, birdied four of the first five holes on Jackrabbit and then got to five under par with another birdie at the 10th. Her run came to an end at the next while another bogey followed before a double bogey at the last dropped her down to one under. Yuka Saso, from the Philippines, a two-time winner as a rookie on the Japan LPGA Tour in 2020, inherited the lead after going out in four-under 32 on Cypress Creek before coming home in two over for a 69.

Only Moriya Jutanugarn managed to return a bogey-free round. Kim birdied her first hole of US Open golf, the 10th on Jackrabbit, and three of her first five, almost as good as her finale. Two bogeys quickly followed but she regained those shots with birdies at the first and the third for her 68. "I tried my best. Not bad, not good," was her verdict.

After 18 holes: 67 (-4) Olson; **68** Shibuno, M Jutanugarn, AL Kim; **69** Strom, Grant, Tavatanakit, Piller, Hull, Popov, Saso

SECOND ROUND

Over two days, it turned out there was no advantage to starting on one course rather than the other — the 66 weekend qualifiers were spilt evenly between the two rotations. A Lim Kim was slated for the Cypress Creek course for the rest of the championship but got off to a poor start on Friday with a 74. Adapting to the dormant Bermuda grass had been a challenge but when she chipped in a few times in the practice rounds she got a liking for the course. At level par she was far from out of the picture but at the end of the second day she was seven strokes adrift of Shibuno.

Shibuno thrilled the gallery at Woburn in 2019, winning her first tournament outside of Japan. Now 22, she was playing in her first US Open but missed the usual interaction with fans. "I feel strange when I make a birdie and it is totally quiet," she said. She tallied six birdies which would have been cheered in other circumstances but made two bogeys for her 67 on the Jackrabbit course. She admitted finding the rough off the tee more than she would have liked but was still able to find the small greens.

Shibuno had not contended in any of the majors so far in 2020 and it had taken a while for her to adjust to her new status in the game. "I turned from a normal person to a celebrity overnight, and I don't know how to explain it," she said. "In Japan, even though I was wearing a mask, people recognised me. It's more difficult for me to go out to dinner than before."

At seven under par, Shibuno had a three-stroke lead. Lying second after two 69s was a Swedish amateur, Linn Grant, two places better than she was at the halfway stage in 2018. Papp, after a 71 on Thursday, posted the best round of Friday on Cypress Creek with a 68, chipping in for a three at the 17th and also birdieing the last.

Olson holed from 30 feet for a birdie at Jackrabbit's first hole to lead by two shots. But she bogeyed the next two, had a double bogey at the 15th and had to birdie the last for 72. She was at three under alongside Papp and Khang, who had a 69 on Cypress Creek with two birdies and 16 pars. "I'll take that any week, any day, any tournament," said Khang, who was taught golf by her father from *Golf Digest* instruction articles and YouTube videos.

Among those at two under par were the two Jutanugarn sisters, as well as Kerr, who admitted having low expectations was helping her get through her painful ordeal, and Stacey Lewis, who lives at The Woodlands nearby. "It just has a different feel for me this year," said Lewis, who was able to go home to daughter Chesnee and take her mind off the golf by thinking about Christmas presents. "It's just a lot more relaxed than I've been in years past."

After 36 holes: 135 (-7) Shibuno 67; **138** Grant 69; **139** Papp 68, Khang 69, Olson 72; **140** Weaver 70, Schmelzel 69, Buhai 69, Kerr, 69, Lewis 68, A Jutanugarn 70, M Jutanugarn 72, Saso 71

THIRD ROUND

On Saturday, a US Open broke out. This was no time to relax. The Cypress Creek course was softer after half an inch of rain overnight and players had to contend with balls picking up mud. There were 19 players under par after 36 holes and only four after 54. There were only two sub-par scores. Hae Ran Ryu had a 70 and Ji Yeong Kim[2], the only player not to drop a shot all day, equalled the low score for the week with a 67. Her score was almost eight strokes better than the day's average.

After chipping in at the ninth, her final hole, Kim was tied for third place on one under par having jumped from the cut line and a tie for 47th place at three over. "I really didn't expect to be performing so well, I'm just glad to be here," said the US Open debutant. "In the first half of the round I wasn't keeping up, but later as the day went on I did look and I was surprised to see how far I've come up on the scoreboard."

Chella Choi's orange ball, after being struck by a four-hybrid at the 180-yard 12th, disappeared for the third hole-in-one of the week and the 30th in the history of the championship. Lewis holed a putt from 78 feet for a birdie at the ninth to get under par but, in spite of knowing the course better than anyone else in the field, the local three-putted at both the par-five 13th for a bogey and at the next, where she also found the water, for a triple bogey. She ended up with the first of two closing 77s to drop out of contention.

Ariya Jutanugarn, the 2018 champion, stumbled to a 74 and spent more time applauding the good shots of one of her playing partners, older sister Moriya. Despite bunker troubles at the 17th that cost a double bogey, Moriya returned a 72 to be one under and aiming for a second Jutanugarn victory in three years. The only pair of sisters to win the same USGA title was Harriot and Margaret Curtis more than a century earlier.

When final questions were called at Moriya's post-round press conference, Ariya teased her: "How far did your sister hit it past you?"

"Wow," Moriya replied, joining in the general laughter. "I would say 30 to 40 yards today. But I definitely think I hit more greens and maybe made a few more putts."

"Every time after I hit my tee shot," Ariya added, "I look back, she like 30 behind, but she hit closer. And then when I hit on the green, she make the putt and I miss the putt. So it's made me feel like I have to work on a lot of things, I have to improve my game after I play with her."

In the final group, amateurs Grant and Papp started steadily. Two years previously, Grant had been in contention at Shoal Creek but collapsed on the weekend. At the 10th hole here, she suffered a quadruple-bogey eight after twice finding the water. A 78 resulted, while Papp had a 74, only dropping back to level par with bogeys at two of the last three holes. Papp first played golf aged five in Japan when her family moved there for four years. Only being able to remember a few words of Japanese, she was shy of trying them out on Shibuno in the middle of a US Open.

A Lim Kim was in a group at one over par that included Kerr, Ariya Jutanugarn, Jin Young Ko and Sei Young Kim. Although the form player entering the week after her triumph at the KPMG Women's PGA, Sei Young had never settled on the course. A Lim, however, loved Champions.

"I'm in love with the course," she said. "It is very much my type. If I was in better condition I think I would be having a higher performance." She made four birdies, including a two at the 16th, but also five bogeys in a 72. Since this was her first appearance at any international major, her expectations really were modest. "It's more about learning and observing, experiencing the whole tournament," she said.

Everyone was dropping shots as Shibuno, while admitting to nerves in her 74, remained at the top of the leaderboard at four under par. "I feel like it's either a great poker face or she's that smiling assassin," said Lydia Ko. Shibuno's lead briefly rose to four with her only birdie of the day at the par-five fifth but was down to just one after she failed to get up and down from a bunker at the last.

Olson had been six behind after two early bogeys but hit an eight-iron to three feet at the 17th for her third birdie of the day. A 71, the best round of any of those in the final groups, left Olson at three under par and one behind. "I'm really pleased with how I played today. It was such a grind," said Olson.

"Pars were a great score on every single hole. Your mental fortitude and perspective are extremely important. I've definitely had some times of adversity already this week. I'm proud of how I've bounced back and just never given up."

After 54 holes: 209 (-4) Shibuno; **210** Olson 71; **212** M Jutanugarn 72, JY Kim[2] 67; **213** L Ko 72, Noh 72, Khang 74, Papp 74; **214** JY Ko 71, AL Kim 72, HR Ryu 70, SY Kim 73, A Jutanugarn 74, Kerr 74

FOURTH ROUND

Such was the rainstorm on Sunday that the leaders had yet to tee off before play was suspended. By the time of Monday's chilly restart, Olson's husband Grant had already gone home to console his mother and brother after the news of his father's death. Understandably enough, Olson at first retreated on the leaderboard. Bogeys at the second, third and fourth holes left her three behind Shibuno.

"Coming out this morning, I had no idea what to expect," she admitted. "It was such a long day yesterday. I allowed myself to think about what I'm grateful for, and I've got a long list."

She rallied spectacularly by birdieing the fifth from 25 feet and the sixth from five feet to be tied with Shibuno. The Japanese player was relying on her short game, which produced a brilliant chip from over the back of the fifth green, but could not prevent a couple of bogeys.

At the turn they were the only players left under par. Inbee Park's bogey at the last meant she dropped back to two over par, probably too far back.

But her 68 was Park's 24th sub-par round in the US Open, tying with Beth Daniel and Betsy King. "I'm just really happy that I was able to finally conquer this golf course," said the two-time champion.

Khang's 72 got her to one over par and fifth place before Jin Young Ko birdied two of the last three holes to match Park's 68. Her second place finish, at two under par, was her highest at the US Open and ensured her qualification for the CME Group Tour Championship later in what would be a victorious week.

Papp, who chipped in on the seventh for a birdie, struggled on the back nine until she birdied the last. A three over par Papp, was not only the low player from Texas but the low amateur, pipping Gabriella Ruffels and Maja Stark by two strokes. Papp said: "This year the group of ams in the field was really strong, and so to be low amateur in that group really means a lot."

Ariya Jutanugarn tied with Papp in ninth place after a turbulent round that included an outward 37 containing just one par. There were four birdies, three bogeys and a double. Moriya, in the final group with Shibuno and Olson, could only make one birdie, with a tee shot to two feet at the eighth, in a 74 that dropped her into a share of sixth place with Park and Lee[6].

Still lurking on the leaderboard was A Lim Kim, who started with four pars before making three birdies in four holes. At the fifth she holed from just off the green, 30 feet in all. She made a 15-footer at the next, a 10-footer for par at the seventh and a 12-footer for a two at the eighth. Out in 33, Kim bogeyed the difficult 10th and three-putted the 11th. She had briefly been one behind, was now two adrift and it looked to be between Shibuno and Olson.

Shibuno also bogeyed at 10 and 11 but while she had triumphed from two behind with seven to play at Woburn in 2019, now she could only make two birdies, one with a long putt and a rueful smile at the last. Another 74 left her in fourth place. "I have frustration, however, I do not have any regret," Shibuno said. "My approach shots weren't preferable under pressure. I learnt a lot about myself."

Olson's run of nine pars in a row came to an end at the worst possible time. At the 16th tee, a place of joy on Thursday, she was caught between clubs. She thought it was safer to hit a cut hybrid but a gust of wind helped it over the green. A tricky chip led to a bogey. Suddenly she was two behind. "I assumed it was going to be between me and Hinako," she said. "I was definitely surprised to see someone come from behind and put that good of a round together."

Kim had four pars to settle down after her two bogeys and then produced the dream finish, taking aim at the flags while walking away after the swing as if unimpressed with the shot. "I'm very honoured to win the 75th US Women's Open," she said through an interpreter. "Still can't really soak in that I'm the champion. Through Covid-19 we had a lot of difficulties, but I'm glad we had the US Women's Open in Houston. It was a great win. Thank you."

Wearing the mask during play was natural for her. "Every time I practise, I usually wear a mask, so I'm used to it. I'm okay to get positive tests for Covid-19 but I don't want to affect other people, players, a caddie, that's within the group, so that's the reason I wear the mask throughout the round."

Kim got interested in the game by going along when her father played. While Se Ri Pak was an inspiration, Annika Sorenstam became her idol. When Sorenstam popped up on Kim's phone on a video call to offer her congratulations, the newest champion exclaimed: "Thank you. I love you!"

Like Sorenstam in 1995, Kim had come from five strokes behind to win. But no one sitting in ninth place with a round to play had previously won the title. Kim did it by beating the day's average score by 7.43 strokes, the largest margin by a champion in the final round since Meg Mallon in 2004.

Kim was the 10th Korean player to win the US Open since Pak in 1998, the fifth debutant to win and the third player, after Hyo Joo Kim and Shibuno, to win a major at the first attempt in six years. Not since Eun-Hee Ji in 2009 had a player birdied the 18th hole to win by one stroke.

To celebrate, Kim was looking forward to some Korean food. And to getting home, although that would involve undergoing two weeks of self-quarantine. No wonder she would have preferred to stay even longer at Champions.

"I love this golf course, love this environment," she reflected. "I want to actually put a tent up here and stay a few more days."

Champions Golf Club (Cypress Creek), Houston, Texas — December 10-14
Par 71 (36-35); 6,731 yards — Purse: $5,500,000
Jackrabbit (R1&2) par 71 (36-35); 6,558 yards

1	**A Lim Kim**	68	74	72	67	281	$1,000,000
2	**Jin Young Ko**	73	70	71	68	282	487,286
	Amy Olson	67	72	71	72	282	487,286
4	Hinako Shibuno	68	67	74	74	283	266,779
5	Megan Khang	70	69	74	72	285	222,201
6	Inbee Park	71	72	75	68	286	177,909
	Jeongeun Lee[6]	73	69	73	71	286	177,909
	Moriya Jutanugarn	68	72	72	74	286	177,909
9	Ariya Jutanugarn	70	70	74	73	287	143,976
	Kaitlyn Papp (A)	71	68	74	74	287	
11	Sayaka Takahashi	73	72	72	71	288	126,465
	Min Young Lee[2]	74	68	76	70	288	126,465
13	Yuka Saso	69	71	77	72	289	96,800
	Eri Okayama	76	69	72	72	289	96,800
	Gabriela Ruffels (A)	71	72	76	70	289	
	Linnea Strom	69	75	73	72	289	96,800
	Maja Stark (A)	70	72	73	74	289	
	Hae Ran Ryu	72	72	70	75	289	96,800
	Lydia Ko	71	70	72	76	289	96,800
20	So Yeon Ryu	72	73	73	72	290	74,219
	Sei Young Kim	72	69	73	76	290	74,219
	Ally Ewing	73	72	76	69	290	74,219
23	Linn Grant (A)	69	69	78	75	291	
	Sarah Schmelzel	71	69	76	75	291	55,526
	Nasa Hataoka	71	73	75	72	291	55,526
	Jenny Shin	72	70	77	72	291	55,526
	Jessica Korda	72	73	74	72	291	55,526
	Cristie Kerr	71	69	74	77	291	55,526
	Chella Choi	73	72	75	71	291	55,526
30	Madelene Sagstrom	74	71	72	75	292	36,915
	Lauren Stephenson	72	72	74	74	292	36,915
	Jennifer Kupcho	70	72	75	75	292	36,915
	Hye Jin Choi	70	73	76	73	292	36,915
	Bronte Law	73	72	71	76	292	36,915
	Cheyenne Knight	75	69	72	76	292	36,915
	Ashleigh Buhai	71	69	79	73	292	36,915
	Ingrid Lindblad (A)	72	69	74	77	292	
	Charley Hull	69	73	78	72	292	36,915
	Ji Yeong Kim[2]	75	70	67	80	292	36,915
40	Hannah Green	72	73	73	75	293	27,067
	Perrine Delacour	72	71	73	77	293	27,067
	Sophia Popov	69	76	75	73	293	27,067
	Yealimi Noh	72	69	72	80	293	27,067
44	Stacy Lewis	72	68	77	77	294	23,576
	Brooke Henderson	72	73	77	72	294	23,576
46	Brittany Lincicome	70	75	73	77	295	19,570
	Pauline Roussin-Bouchard (A)	70	72	75	78	295	
	Lizette Salas	72	69	75	79	295	19,570
	Lindsey Weaver	70	70	75	80	295	19,570
	Gaby Lopez	74	71	74	76	295	19,570
	Minjee Lee	74	71	75	75	295	19,570
52	Seon Woo Bae	75	68	76	77	296	15,736
	Danielle Kang	72	71	79	74	296	15,736
54	Anna Nordqvist	73	71	75	78	297	13,447
	Azahara Munoz	71	70	78	78	297	13,447
	Mone Inami	73	71	76	77	297	13,447
	Jennifer Song	77	68	76	76	297	13,447
58	Pernilla Lindberg	74	70	75	79	298	12,360
	Mi Hyang Lee	72	73	79	74	298	12,360
60	Yui Kawamoto	73	72	74	80	299	12,131
61	Mamiko Higa	73	72	75	80	300	11,960
	Mina Harigae	70	74	77	79	300	11,960
63	Jodi Ewart Shadoff	70	72	79	80	301	11,731
	Na Rin An	72	72	79	78	301	11,731
65	Kana Mikashima	75	69	80	79	303	11,559
66	Su Oh	75	70	78	81	304	11,445

MISSED THE 36-HOLE CUT

Brittany Lang	73	73	146	4,000
Sarah Jane Smith	76	70	146	4,000
Mi-Jeong Jeon	72	74	146	4,000
Amelia Garvey (A)	70	76	146	
Eun-Hee Ji	74	72	146	4,000
Rose Zhang (A)	73	73	146	
Celine Boutier	73	73	146	4,000
Austin Ernst	75	71	146	4,000
Carlota Ciganda	71	75	146	4,000
In Gee Chun	76	70	146	4,000
Nelly Korda	73	73	146	4,000
Anne van Dam	73	73	146	4,000
Maria Fernanda Torres	75	71	146	4,000
Alena Sharp	75	71	146	4,000
Marianne Skarpnord	76	71	147	4,000
Agathe Laisne (A)	77	70	147	
Cydney Clanton	74	73	147	4,000
Jing Yan	74	73	147	4,000
Nanna Koerstz Madsen	75	72	147	4,000
Momoko Ueda	74	73	147	4,000
Minami Katsu	74	73	147	4,000
Teresa Lu	73	74	147	4,000
Patty Tavatanakit	69	78	147	4,000
Emily Kristine Pedersen	75	72	147	4,000
Brittany Altomare	71	76	147	4,000
Lexi Thompson	74	73	147	4,000
Bianca Pagdanganan	72	75	147	4,000
Ryann O'Toole	73	74	147	4,000
Yuna Nishimura	73	75	148	4,000
Pajaree Anannarukarn	76	72	148	4,000
Gerina Piller	69	79	148	4,000
Angel Yin	75	73	148	4,000
Sung Hyun Park	70	78	148	4,000
Mirim Lee	74	74	148	4,000
Ayaka Watanabe	77	71	148	4,000
Pornanong Phatlum	76	73	149	4,000
Caroline Masson	71	78	149	4,000
Olivia Mehaffey (A)	77	72	149	
Auston Kim (A)	75	74	149	
Katherine Kirk	75	74	149	4,000
Fatima Fernandez Cano	79	70	149	4,000
Xiyu Lin	76	73	149	4,000
Georgia Hall	81	68	149	4,000
Mel Reid	75	74	149	4,000
Jasmine Suwannapura	76	73	149	4,000
Saki Asai	76	73	149	4,000
Kelly Tan	75	75	150	4,000
Meghan MacLaren	77	73	150	4,000
Esther Henseleit	76	74	150	4,000
Ayaka Furue	76	74	150	4,000
Lala Anai	78	72	150	4,000
Yu Jin Sung	76	74	150	4,000
Beatrice Wallin (A)	75	75	150	
Yu Liu	76	75	151	4,000
Annie Park	76	75	151	4,000
Benedetta Moresco (A)	80	71	151	
Caroline Hedwall	76	75	151	4,000
Caterina Don (A)	77	74	151	
Emilia Migliaio (A)	74	77	151	
Morgan Pressel	73	78	151	4,000
Nuria Iturrioz	71	80	151	4,000
Lucie Malchirand (A)	75	76	151	
Nicole Broch Larsen	77	75	152	4,000
Sakura Koiwai	77	75	152	4,000
Ana Belac	76	76	152	4,000

Emma Spitz (A)	75 77	152	
Asuka Kashiwabara	79 74	153	4,000
Heeyoung Park	77 76	153	4,000
Angela Stanford	80 74	154	4,000
Jaye Marie Green	78 76	154	4,000
Jeongeun Lee	79 75	154	4,000
Lei Ye (A)	77 77	154	
Amy Yang	77 77	154	4,000
Ho-Yu An (A)	78 76	154	
Frida Kinhult	78 76	154	4,000
Allisen Corpuz (A)	78 76	154	
Christina Kim	81 74	155	4,000
Heejeong Lim	77 78	155	4,000
Kristen Gillman	79 77	156	4,000
Janie Jackson	74 82	156	4,000
Lily May Humphreys (A)	75 81	156	
Ina Kim-Schaad (A)	73 83	156	
Kim Kaufman	78 79	157	4,000
Maria Fassi	83 74	157	4,000
Christine Wolf	77 80	157	4,000
Erika Hara	83 78	161	4,000
Alessia Nobilio (A)	81 82	163	
Seung Yeon Lee	78 85	163	4,000
Emily Toy (A)	88 82	170	
Mi Jung Hur	78	WDN	4,000

ROLL OF HONOUR

1946	Patty Berg	Spokane
1947	Betty Jameson	Starmount Forest
1948	Babe Didrikson Zaharias	Atlantic City
1949	Louise Suggs	Prince Georges
1950	Babe Didrikson Zaharias	Rolling Hills
1951	Betsy Rawls	Druid Hills
1952	Louise Suggs	Bala
1953	Betsy Rawls*	CC of Rochester
1954	Babe Didrikson Zaharias	Salem
1955	Fay Crocker	Wichita
1956	Kathy Cornelius*	Northand
1957	Betsy Rawls	Winged Foot (East)
1958	Mickey Wright	Forest Lake
1959	Mickey Wright	Churchill Valley
1960	Betsy Rawls	Worcester
1961	Mickey Wright	Baltusrol (Lower)
1962	Murle Lindstrom	Dunes
1963	Mary Mills	Kenwood
1964	Mickey Wright*	San Diego
1965	Carol Mann	Atlantic City
1966	Sandra Spuzich	Hazeltine National
1967	Catherine Lacoste (A)	Virginia Hot Springs (Cascades)
1968	Susie Maxwell Berning	Moselem Springs
1969	Donna Caponi	Scenic Hills
1970	Donna Caponi	Muskogee
1971	JoAnne Gunderson Carner	Kahkwa Club
1972	Susie Maxwell Berning	Winged Foot (East)
1973	Susie Maxwell Berning	CC of Rochester
1974	Sandra Haynie	LaGrange
1975	Sandra Palmer	Atlantic City
1976	JoAnne Gunderson Carner*	Rolling Green
1977	Hollis Stacy	Hazeltine National
1978	Hollis Stacy	CC of Indianapolis
1979	Jerilyn Britz	Brooklawn
1980	Amy Alcott	Richland
1981	Pat Bradley	LaGrange
1982	Janet Alex	Del Paso
1983	Jan Stephenson	Cedar Ridge
1984	Hollis Stacy	Salem
1985	Kathy (Baker) Guadagnino	Baltusrol (Upper)
1986	Jane Geddes	NCR
1987	Laura Davies*	Plainfield
1988	Liselotte Neumann	Baltimore (East)
1989	Betsy King	Indianwood (Old)
1990	Betsy King	Atlanta Athletic Club (Riverside)
1991	Meg Mallon	Colonial
1992	Patty Sheehan*	Oakmont
1993	Lauri Merten	Crooked Stick
1994	Patty Sheehan	Indianwood (Old)
1995	Annika Sorenstam	The Broadmoor (East)
1996	Annika Sorenstam	Pine Needles
1997	Alison Nicholas	Pumpkin Ridge (Witch Hollow)
1998	Se Ri Pak*	Blackwolf Run
1999	Juli Inkster	Old Waverly
2000	Karrie Webb	The Merit Club
2001	Karrie Webb	Pine Needles
2002	Juli Inkster	Prairie Dunes
2003	Hilary Lunke*	Pumpkin Ridge (Witch Hollow)
2004	Meg Mallon	Orchards
2005	Birdie Kim	Cherry Hills
2006	Annika Sorenstam*	Newport
2007	Cristie Kerr	Pine Needles
2008	Inbee Park	Interlachen
2009	Eun-Hee Ji	Saucon Valley (Old)
2010	Paula Creamer	Oakmont
2011	So Yeon Ryu*	The Broadmoor (East)
2012	Na Yeon Choi	Blackwolf Run
2013	Inbee Park	Sebonack
2014	Michelle Wie	Pinehurst (No2)
2015	In Gee Chun	Lancaster
2016	Brittany Lang*	CordeValle
2017	Sung Hyun Park	Trump National (Old)
2018	Ariya Jutanugarn*	Shoal Creek
2019	Jeongeun Lee[6]	CC of Charleston
2020	A Lim Kim	Champions

**won in playoff*

Major Records

MOST VICTORIES
18 Jack Nicklaus; **15** Tiger Woods; **11** Walter Hagen; **9** Ben Hogan, Gary Player; **8** Tom Watson; **7** Harry Vardon, Bobby Jones, Gene Sarazen, Sam Snead, Arnold Palmer

15 Patty Berg; **13** Mickey Wright; **11** Louise Suggs; **10** Babe Zaharias, Annika Sorenstam; **8** Betsy Rawls; **7** Juli Inkster, Karrie Webb, Inbee Park

MOST VICTORIES IN A YEAR
3 Ben Hogan — 1953 (Masters, US Open, Open Championship); Tiger Woods — 2000 (US Open, Open Championship, PGA Championship)

3 Babe Zaharias* — 1950 (Titleholders, Western Open, US Open); Mickey Wright — 1961 (Titleholders, US Open, LPGA Championship); Pat Bradley — 1986 (Nabisco Dinah Shore, LPGA Championship, du Maurier Classic); Inbee Park — 2013 (Kraft Nabisco, LPGA Championship, US Open)
**Zaharias won all three of the LPGA majors contested in 1950*

CONSECUTIVE MAJOR VICTORIES
4 Tiger Woods (US Open, Open Championship, PGA Championship, 2000, Masters, 2001)

4 Mickey Wright (US Open, LPGA Championship, 1961, Titleholders, Western Open, 1962)

VICTORIES IN DIFFERENT MAJORS
4 Gene Sarazen, Ben Hogan, Gary Player, Jack Nicklaus, Tiger Woods; **3** Walter Hagen, Jim Barnes, Tommy Armour, Byron Nelson, Sam Snead, Arnold Palmer, Lee Trevino, Tom Watson, Ray Floyd, Phil Mickelson, Rory McIlroy, Jordan Spieth

5 Karrie Webb; **4** Louise Suggs, Mickey Wright, Pat Bradley, Annika Sorenstam, Inbee Park

MOST VICTORIES IN THE SAME MAJOR
6 Harry Vardon (Open Championship); Jack Nicklaus (Masters)

7 Patty Berg (Titleholders, Western Open)

LOWEST SCORES
62 Branden Grace (R3, Open Championship, Royal Birkdale, 2017)
63 Johnny Miller (R4, US Open, Oakmont, 1973); Bruce Crampton (R2, PGA Championship, Firestone, 1975); Mark Hayes (R2, Open Championship, Turnberry, 1977); Jack Nicklaus (R1, US Open, Baltusrol, 1980); Tom Weiskopf (R1, US Open, Baltusrol, 1980); Isao Aoki (R3, Open Championship, Muirfield, 1980); Raymond Floyd (R1, PGA Championship, Southern Hills, 1982); Gary Player (R2, PGA Championship, Shoal Creek, 1984); Nick Price (R3, Masters, Augusta National, 1986); Greg Norman (R2, Open Championship, Turnberry, 1986); Paul Broadhurst (R3, Open Championship, St Andrews, 1990); Jodie Mudd (R4, Open Championship, Royal Birkdale, 1991); Nick Faldo (R2, Open Championship, Royal St George's, 1993); Payne Stewart (R4, Open Championship, Royal St George's, 1993); Vijay Singh (R2, PGA Championship, Inverness, 1993); Michael Bradley (R1, PGA Championship, Riviera, 1995); Brad Faxon (R4, PGA Championship, Riviera, 1995); Greg Norman (R1, Masters, Augusta National, 1996); Jose Maria Olazabal (R3, PGA Championship, Valhalla, 2000); Mark O'Meara (R2, PGA Championship, Atlanta Athletic Club, 2001); Vijay Singh (R2, US Open, Olympia Fields, 2003); Thomas Bjorn (R3, PGA Championship, Baltusrol, 2005);

Tiger Woods (R2, PGA Championship, Southern Hills, 2007); Rory McIlroy (R1, Open Championship, St. Andrews, 2010); Steve Stricker (R1, PGA Championship, Atlanta Athletic Club, 2011); Jason Dufner, 2013 (R2, PGA Championship, Oak Hill, 2013); Hiroshi Iwata (R2, PGA Championship, Whistling Straits, 2015); Phil Mickelson (R1, Open Championship, Royal Troon, 2016); Henrik Stenson, 2016 (R4, Open Championship, Royal Troon, 2016); Robert Streb (R2, PGA Championship, Baltusrol, 2016); Justin Thomas (R3, US Open, Erin Hills, 2017); Haotong Li (R4, Open Championship, Royal Birkdale, 2017); Tommy Fleetwood (R4, US Open, Shinnecock Hills, 2018); Brooks Koepka (R2, PGA Championship, Bellerive, 2018); Charl Schwartzel (R2, PGA Championship, Bellerive, 2018); Brooks Koepka, (R1, PGA Championship, Bethpage Black, 2019); Shane Lowry, (R3, Open Championship, Royal Portrush, 2019)

61 Hyo Joo Kim (R1, Evian Championship, Evian, 2014)
62 Minea Blomqvist (R3, Women's British Open, Sunningdale, 2004); Lorena Ochoa (R1, Kraft Nabisco, Mission Hills, 2006); Mirim Lee (R1, Women's British Open, Woburn, 2016)

LOWEST TOTALS
264 Henrik Stenson (Open Championship, Royal Troon, 2016); Brooks Koepka (PGA Championship, Bellerive, 2018)
265 David Toms (PGA Championship, Atlanta Athletic Club, 2001)

263 In Gee Chun (Evian Championship, Evian, 2016)
267 Betsy King (LPGA Championship, Bethesda, 1992); So Yeon Ryu (Evian Championship, Evian, 2016); Sung Hyun Park (Evian Championship, Evian, 2016)

LOWEST TOTALS TO PAR
20 under par — Jason Day (PGA Championship, Whistling Straits, 2015); Henrik Stenson (Open Championship, Royal Troon, 2016); Dustin Johnson (Masters, Augusta National, 2020)
19 under par — Tiger Woods (Open Championship, St Andrews, 2000)

21 under par — In Gee Chun (Evian Championship, Evian, 2016)
19 under par — Dottie Pepper (Nabisco Dinah Shore, Mission Hills, 1999); Karen Stupples (Women's British Open, Sunningdale, 2004); Cristie Kerr (LPGA Championship, Locust Hill, 2010); Yani Tseng (LPGA Championship, Locust Hill, 2011); Inbee Park (KPMG Women's PGA, Westchester, 2015)

LARGEST WINNING MARGINS
15 Tiger Woods (US Open, Pebble Beach, 2000); **13** Tom Morris Sr (Open Championship, Prestwick, 1862)

14 Louise Suggs (US Open, Prince George's, 1949); **12** Babe Zaharias (US Open, Salem, 1954); Cristie Kerr (LPGA Championship, Locust Hill, 2010)

OLDEST CHAMPIONS
48 years 4 months 25 days — Julius Boros (PGA Championship, 1968)

45 years, 7 months, 11 days — Fay Crocker (Titleholders, 1945)

YOUNGEST CHAMPIONS
17 years 5 months 3 days — Tom Morris Jr (Open Championship, 1868)

18 years 4 months 20 days — Lydia Ko (Evian Championship, 2015)

THE OPEN CHAMPIONSHIP — ROLL OF HONOUR

1860	Willie Park Sr	Prestwick
1861	Tom Morris Sr	Prestwick
1862	Tom Morris Sr	Prestwick
1863	Willie Park Sr	Prestwick
1864	Tom Morris Sr	Prestwick
1865	Andrew Strath	Prestwick
1866	Willie Park Sr	Prestwick
1867	Tom Morris Sr	Prestwick
1868	Tom Morris Jr	Prestwick
1869	Tom Morris Jr	Prestwick
1870	Tom Morris Jr	Prestwick
1872	Tom Morris Jr	Prestwick
1873	Tom Kidd	St Andrews
1874	Mungo Park	Musselburgh
1875	Willie Park Sr	Prestwick
1876	Bob Martin*	St Andrews
1877	Jamie Anderson	Musselburgh
1878	Jamie Anderson	Prestwick
1879	Jamie Anderson	St Andrews
1880	Bob Ferguson	Musselburgh
1881	Bob Ferguson	Prestwick
1882	Bob Ferguson	St Andrews
1883	Willie Fernie*	Musselburgh
1884	Jack Simpson	Prestwick
1885	Bob Martin	St Andrews
1886	David Brown	Musselburgh
1887	Willie Park Jr	Prestwick
1888	Jack Burns	St Andrews
1889	Willie Park Jr*	Musselburgh
1890	John Ball (A)	Prestwick
1891	Hugh Kirkaldy	St Andrews
1892	Harold Hilton (A)	Muirfield
1893	Willie Auchterlonie	Prestwick
1894	JH Taylor	St George's
1895	JH Taylor	St Andrews
1896	Harry Vardon*	Muirfield
1897	Harold Hilton (A)	Royal Liverpool
1898	Harry Vardon	Prestwick
1899	Harry Vardon	St George's
1900	JH Taylor	St Andrews
1901	James Braid	Muirfield
1902	Sandy Herd	Royal Liverpool
1903	Harry Vardon	Prestwick
1904	Jack White	Royal St George's
1905	James Braid	St Andrews
1906	James Braid	Muirfield
1907	Arnaud Massy	Royal Liverpool
1908	James Braid	Prestwick
1909	JH Taylor	Cinque Ports
1910	James Braid	St Andrews
1911	Harry Vardon*	Royal St George's
1912	Ted Ray	Muirfield
1913	JH Taylor	Royal Liverpool
1914	Harry Vardon	Prestwick
1920	George Duncan	Royal Cinque Ports
1921	Jock Hutchison*	St Andrews
1922	Walter Hagen	Royal St George's
1923	Arthur Havers	Troon
1924	Walter Hagen	Royal Liverpool
1925	Jim Barnes	Prestwick
1926	Bobby Jones (A)	Royal Lytham & St Annes
1927	Bobby Jones (A)	St Andrews
1928	Walter Hagen	Royal St George's
1929	Walter Hagen	Muirfield
1930	Bobby Jones (A)	Royal Liverpool
1931	Tommy Armour	Carnoustie
1932	Gene Sarazen	Prince's
1933	Denny Shute*	St Andrews
1934	Henry Cotton	Royal St George's
1935	Alf Perry	Muirfield
1936	Alf Padgham	Royal Liverpool
1937	Henry Cotton	Carnoustie
1938	Reg Whitcombe	Royal St George's
1939	Dick Burton	St Andrews
1946	Sam Snead	St Andrews
1947	Fred Daly	Royal Liverpool
1948	Henry Cotton	Muirfield
1949	Bobby Locke*	Royal St George's
1950	Bobby Locke	Troon
1951	Max Faulkner	Royal Portrush
1952	Bobby Locke	Royal Lytham & St Annes
1953	Ben Hogan	Carnoustie
1954	Peter Thomson	Royal Birkdale
1955	Peter Thomson	St Andrews
1956	Peter Thomson	Royal Liverpool
1957	Bobby Locke	St Andrews
1958	Peter Thomson*	Royal Lytham & St Annes
1959	Gary Player	Muirfield
1960	Kel Nagle	St Andrews
1961	Arnold Palmer	Royal Birkdale
1962	Arnold Palmer	Troon
1963	Bob Charles*	Royal Lytham & St Annes
1964	Tony Lema	St Andrews
1965	Peter Thomson	Royal Birkdale
1966	Jack Nicklaus	Muirfield
1967	Roberto de Vicenzo	Royal Liverpool
1968	Gary Player	Carnoustie
1969	Tony Jacklin	Royal Lytham & St Annes
1970	Jack Nicklaus*	St Andrews
1971	Lee Trevino	Royal Birkdale
1972	Lee Trevino	Muirfield
1973	Tom Weiskopf	Troon
1974	Gary Player	Royal Lytham & St Annes
1975	Tom Watson*	Carnoustie
1976	Johnny Miller	Royal Birkdale
1977	Tom Watson	Turnberry
1978	Jack Nicklaus	St Andrews
1979	Seve Ballesteros	Royal Lytham & St Annes
1980	Tom Watson	Muirfield
1981	Bill Rogers	Royal St George's
1982	Tom Watson	Royal Troon
1983	Tom Watson	Royal Birkdale
1984	Seve Ballesteros	St Andrews
1985	Sandy Lyle	Royal St George's
1986	Greg Norman	Turnberry
1987	Nick Faldo	Muirfield
1988	Seve Ballesteros	Royal Lytham & St Annes
1989	Mark Calcavecchia*	Royal Troon
1990	Nick Faldo	St Andrews
1991	Ian Baker-Finch	Royal Birkdale
1992	Nick Faldo	Muirfield
1993	Greg Norman	Royal St George's
1994	Nick Price	Turnberry
1995	John Daly*	St Andrews
1996	Tom Lehman	Royal Lytham & St Annes
1997	Justin Leonard	Royal Troon
1998	Mark O'Meara*	Royal Birkdale
1999	Paul Lawrie*	Carnoustie
2000	Tiger Woods	St Andrews
2001	David Duval	Royal Lytham & St Annes
2002	Ernie Els*	Muirfield
2003	Ben Curtis	Royal St George's
2004	Todd Hamilton*	Royal Troon
2005	Tiger Woods	St Andrews

2006	Tiger Woods	Royal Liverpool
2007	Padraig Harrington*	Carnoustie
2008	Padraig Harrington	Royal Birkdale
2009	Stewart Cink*	Turnberry
2010	Louis Oosthuizen	St Andrews
2011	Darren Clarke	Royal St George's
2012	Ernie Els	Royal Lytham & St Annes
2013	Phil Mickelson	Muirfield
2014	Rory McIlroy	Royal Liverpool
2015	Zach Johnson*	St Andrews
2016	Henrik Stenson	Royal Troon
2017	Jordan Spieth	Royal Birkdale
2018	Francesco Molinari	Carnoustie
2019	Shane Lowry	Royal Portrush

**won in playoff*

AMUNDI EVIAN CHAMPIONSHIP — ROLL OF HONOUR

1994	Helen Alfredsson	Evian Resort
1995	Laura Davies	Evian Resort
1996	Laura Davies	Evian Resort
1997	Hiromi Kobayashi*	Evian Resort
1998	Helen Alfredsson	Evian Resort
1999	Catrin Nilsmark	Evian Resort
2000	Annika Sorenstam*	Evian Resort
2001	Rachel Teske	Evian Resort
2002	Annika Sorenstam	Evian Resort
2003	Juli Inkster	Evian Resort
2004	Wendy Doolan	Evian Resort
2005	Paula Creamer	Evian Resort
2006	Karrie Webb	Evian Resort
2007	Natalie Gulbis*	Evian Resort
2008	Helen Alfredsson*	Evian Resort
2009	Ai Miyazato*	Evian Resort
2010	Jiyai Shin	Evian Resort
2011	Ai Miyazato	Evian Resort
2012	Inbee Park	Evian Resort
2013	Suzann Pettersen	Evian Resort
2014	Hyo Joo Kim	Evian Resort
2015	Lydia Ko	Evian Resort
2016	In Gee Chun	Evian Resort
2017	Anna Nordqvist*	Evian Resort
2018	Angela Stanford	Evian Resort
2019	Jin Young Ko	Evian Resort

**won in playoff*

Designated an LPGA major since 2013

RYDER CUP — RESULTS

1927	GB&I	2½–9½	USA	Worcester
1929	GB&I	7–5	USA	Moortown
1931	GB&I	3–9	USA	Scioto
1933	GB&I	6½–5½	USA	Southport & Ainsdale
1935	GB&I	3–9	USA	Ridgewood
1937	GB&I	4–8	USA	Southport & Ainsdale
1947	GB&I	1–11	USA	Portland
1949	GB&I	5–7	USA	Ganton
1951	GB&I	2½–9½	USA	Pinehurst (No 2)
1953	GB&I	5½–6½	USA	Wentworth Club
1955	GB&I	4–8	USA	Thunderbird
1957	GB&I	7½–4½	USA	Lindrick
1959	GB&I	3½–8½	USA	Eldorado
1961	GB&I	9½–14½	USA	Royal Lytham & St Annes
1963	GB&I	9–23	USA	Atlanta Athletic Club
1965	GB&I	12½–19½	USA	Royal Birkdale
1967	GB&I	8½–23½	USA	Champions
1969	GB&I	16–16	USA	Royal Birkdale
1971	GB&I	13½–18½	USA	Old Warson
1973	GB&I	13–19	USA	Muirfield
1975	GB&I	11–21	USA	Laurel Valley
1977	GB&I	7½–12½	USA	Royal Lytham & St Annes
1979	Europe	11–17	USA	The Greenbrier
1981	Europe	9½–18½	USA	Walton Heath
1983	Europe	13½–14½	USA	PGA National
1985	Europe	16½–11½	USA	The Belfry
1987	Europe	15–13	USA	Muirfield Village
1989	Europe	14–14	USA	The Belfry
1991	Europe	13½–14½	USA	Kiawah Island (Ocean)
1993	Europe	13–15	USA	The Belfry
1995	Europe	14½–13½	USA	Oak Hill
1997	Europe	14½–13½	USA	Valderrama
1999	Europe	13½–14½	USA	Brookline
2002	Europe	15½–12½	USA	The Belfry
2004	Europe	18½–9½	USA	Oakland Hills
2006	Europe	18½–9½	USA	K Club
2008	Europe	11½–16½	USA	Valhalla

2010	Europe	14½–13½	USA	Celtic Manor
2012	Europe	14½–13½	USA	Medinah (No 3)
2014	Europe	16½–11½	USA	Gleneagles Hotel
2016	Europe	11–17	USA	Hazeltine National
2018	Europe	17½–10½	USA	Le Golf National

SOLHEIM CUP — RESULTS

1990	Europe	4½–11½	USA	Lake Nona
1992	Europe	11½–6½	USA	Dalmahoy
1994	Europe	7–13	USA	The Greenbrier
1996	Europe	11–17	USA	St Pierre
1998	Europe	12–16	USA	Muirfield Village
2000	Europe	14½–11½	USA	Loch Lomond
2002	Europe	12½–15½	USA	Interlachen
2003	Europe	17½–10½	USA	Barseback
2005	Europe	12½–15½	USA	Crooked Stick
2007	Europe	12–16	USA	Halmstad
2009	Europe	12–16	USA	Rich Harvest Farms
2011	Europe	15–13	USA	Killeen Castle
2013	Europe	18–10	USA	Colorado
2015	Europe	13½–14½	USA	St Leon-Rot
2017	Europe	11½–16½	USA	Des Moines
2019	Europe	14½–13½	USA	Gleneagles Hotel

The Tours

Sam Greenwood/Getty Images

PGA Tour

There was a miracle on the PGA Tour in 2020. Not Bryson DeChambeau stalking the land, outmoding golf courses hither and yon. Not Dustin Johnson finding FedEx Cup and Masters glory. Not a youth movement like Collin Morikawa and Co that did a Dorian Gray on the preceding youth movement before one's very eyes. Not even the golf boom — unexpected, ironic and, under the circumstances, beyond belief.

The miracle was the PGA Tour itself. It was a miracle that it survived and even thrived in 2020, with the US, the entire world in the grip of a ferocious and deadly pandemic — Covid-19.

Golf was a trifling matter in the face of a disease that killed some 300,000 Americans and infected over 25 million by the end of the year, and it would rage on. The best defence against it seemed to be distancing — and so governments attempted to discourage crowds, to halt the transmission of the virus by keeping space between people, and so many sports were cancelled, postponed or moved.

The PGA Tour shut down for three months, from early March to early June, and resumed with no spectators or pro-ams. The PGA Tour said that 13 tournaments were cancelled or postponed. Among those postponed were the PGA Championship, from May to August; the Tour Championship, August to September; the US Open, June to September, and the Masters, April to November. The R&A put off The Open Championship until 2021.

Tournaments were played under various conditions and limitations, most notably without fans and mostly in silence, and the players lived by the tour's Health & Safety Plan, 37 robust pages pretty much dictating their lives from at-home testing to travelling to lodging to on-site access to tournament grounds.

The tour resumed in June with the Charles Schwab Challenge. Tour Commissioner Jay Monahan was asked what would make it a successful tournament. "Getting to next week," Monahan said.

Public golf was also hit. Courses were closed early in 2020. And then, while other businesses sank and perished, and while millions were working from their homes, golf somehow began to flower.

Golf, it developed, was recognised as the ideal sport for the pandemic. It was played outdoors, and so quite safe. It offered exercise and human company in fresh air, and goodness knows social distancing was guaranteed. And it was an escape from the cabin fever of millions keeping sheltered. Then up went the numbers.

According to the National Golf Foundation and Golf Datatech, the amount of golf played in late 2020 saw large spikes compared to 2019. Courses were forced to shut down until early summer, but by October, rounds were up 32.2 per cent over October 2019. Similarly, there were increases of about 14 per cent in June, 20 in July, 21 in August and 26 in September. Overall, 2020 would end with about a 12 per cent increase over 2019, or about 50 million rounds.

Then there was the phenomenon known as Bryson DeChambeau, who could quantify and analyse golf as no one ever before him. First, he was an emerging physicist, a scholarship student, at Southern Methodist University and a member of the golf team. He preferred golf, and so brought the theories and rigours of impact mechanics out of the laboratory and onto the tee.

He acquired the nickname "Scientist" for his analytical approach to the game, beginning with his clubs. His clubs were made to his specifications — the irons all the same length, 37½ inches, with thick grips he could hold in his palms instead of his fingers.

He took himself into the lab, as well, reasoning that if he added more muscle to his body, he could hit farther. Through exercise and diet — notably protein shakes and some 5,500 calories a day — he added 20 pounds in the winter and another 20 during the tour's shutdown, and emerged at some 240 pounds. And yards and yards longer. Some of his drives were well over 350 yards. And he had the other requisite skills to go with that mass.

A big, strong hitter, he'd already won five tournaments, the first in 2017, then four in 2018. Then the new, brawnier DeChambeau won twice in 2020 — the Rocket Mortgage Classic in July and the rescheduled US Open in September, where he slashed his way through mighty Winged Foot, and at six-under 274 was the only player under par.

The specifications of his clubs were one thing, his approach to the game another. As he said after a six-stroke victory: "I'm just trying to figure out this very complex, multivariable game, and multidimensional game as well. It's very, very difficult. It's a fun journey for me."

Every year has its new, young phenoms, but 2020 had a bumper crop, led by Collin Morikawa, 22, a graduate of the University of California, Berkeley. He'd already had a Hall-of-Fame round, when he won his first major, the PGA Championship with a closing 64. It included driving the green at Harding Park's 16th. And his streak of 22 cuts made was second-best only to Tiger Woods.

Matthew Wolff, 21, out of Oklahoma State, posted his first win in 2019, and tied for fourth in his first appearance in a major, the 2020 PGA Championship. He then finished second in the US Open after leading going into the final round.

Viktor Hovland, 23, became the first Norwegian to win on the tour, then the first to win twice, both with clutch putts on the final hole. He won the Puerto Rico Open in February with a 30-footer, then the Mayakoba Golf Classic in December with a 12-footer.

Among others in the movement: Korea's Sungjae Im, 22; Chile's Joaquin Niemann, 22, and Will Zalatoris, 24, who won once on the Korn Ferry Tour but was promoted to the PGA Tour for his play in a handful of starts.

The new crop would bear watching in 2021, but they will have to get past Johnson first. After warming up with a win at the Travelers Championship, the 36-year-old dominated the FedEx Cup Playoffs. He won The Northern Trust by 11 strokes at 30 under par. He only lost at the BMW Championship in a playoff to Jon Rahm's ridiculous 66-foot curling putt. At the Tour Championship Johnson started two strokes ahead of anyone else and won by three to win the FedEx Cup for the first time.

Johnson was not finished there. At Augusta National, he won by five with a record Masters score. He looked fine in his new green jacket.

But the real miracle was the golf happened at all.

2020 SCHEDULE

Sentry Tournament of Champions	**Justin Thomas**	
Sony Open	**Cameron Smith**	
The American Express	**Andrew Landry**	
Farmers Insurance Open	**Marc Leishman**	
Waste Management Phoenix Open	**Webb Simpson**	
AT&T Pebble Beach Pro-Am	**Nick Taylor**	
Genesis Invitational	**Adam Scott**	
WGC Mexico Championship	**Patrick Reed**	
Puerto Rico Open	**Viktor Hovland**	
Honda Classic	**Sungjae Im**	
Arnold Palmer Invitational	**Tyrrell Hatton**	
The Players Championship		*abandoned*
Valspar Championship		*cancelled*
WGC Dell Technologies Match Play		*cancelled*
Valero Texas Open		*cancelled*
Zurich Classic of New Orleans		*cancelled*
Wells Fargo Championship		*cancelled*
AT&T Byron Nelson		*cancelled*
RBC Canadian Open		*cancelled*
Charles Schwab Challenge	**Daniel Berger**	
RBC Heritage	**Webb Simpson**	
Travelers Championship	**Dustin Johnson**	
Rocket Mortgage Classic	**Bryson DeChambeau**	
John Deere Classic		*cancelled*
Workday Charity Open	**Collin Morikawa**	
Barbasol Championship		*cancelled*

Memorial Tournament	**Jon Rahm**	
The 149th Open		*postponed to 2021*
3M Open	**Michael Thompson**	
WGC FedEx St Jude Invitational	**Justin Thomas**	
Barracuda Championship	**Richy Werenski**	
PGA Championship	**Collin Morikawa**	*See chapter 1*
Olympics Men's*		*postponed to 2021*
Wyndham Championship	**Jim Herman**	
The Northern Trust	**Dustin Johnson**	
BMW Championship	**Jon Rahm**	
Tour Championship	**Dustin Johnson**	
Safeway Open	**Stewart Cink**	
US Open Championship	**Bryson DeChambeau**	*See chapter 4*
Ryder Cup*		*postponed to 2021*
Corales Puntacana Resort Championship	**Hudson Swafford**	
Sanderson Farms Championship	**Sergio Garcia**	
Shriners Hospitals for Children Open	**Martin Laird**	
The CJ Cup	**Jason Kokrak**	
Zozo Championship	**Patrick Cantlay**	
WGC HSBC Champions		*cancelled*
Bermuda Championship	**Brian Gay**	
Vivint Houston Open	**Carlos Ortiz**	
Masters Tournament	**Dustin Johnson**	*See chapter 6*
The RSM Classic	**Robert Streb**	
TaylorMade Pebble Beach Invitational*	**Kyle Reifers**	
Mayakoba Golf Classic	**Viktor Hovland**	
Hero World Challenge*		*cancelled*
QBE Shootout*	**Matt Kuchar/Harris English**	
PNC Championship*	**Justin Thomas/Mike Thomas**	
**non-FedEx Cup event*		

Sentry Tournament of Champions

It was the dawn of a new year and the rebirth of golf in the first week of January 2020, in the form of the Sentry Tournament of Champions, a shootout for 34 winners from the previous season on the island paradise of Hawaii. Which ended with a drained and frazzled Justin Thomas.

"I really don't know how I won today," Thomas said wearily. "I was winning, and then I was barely winning, and then I was losing — and then I barely got in a playoff."

There was an element of doubt along the way.

Thomas was shredding Kapalua's toughened par-73 Plantation Course in a birdie rampage in the final round, and had a two-shot lead with three holes to play. Which he then somehow managed to blow. He slipped into a tie with Patrick Reed and defending champion Xander Schauffele. In the playoff at the 677-yard par-five 18th, Thomas won with a birdie on the third visit after a breathtaking wedge to three feet. It was the third victory in his last six PGA Tour starts and his 12th since joining the tour in 2015. The victory may have seemed awkward to some, but as far as Thomas was concerned, "It's always nice, no matter how it's done."

Thomas shot 67-73-69-69 and trailed all the way until late in the final round. In the first, he birdied five of his last eight holes for the 67, a stroke off the lead of Chile's Joaquin Niemann, one of 15 first-time winners on the PGA Tour in 2019. Niemann was bogey-free in his 66, and his game was extremely sharp. He missed one green but saved par, his longest birdie putt was 30 feet, and the other six were from 10 feet and less. Niemann was also fresh from playing in his first Presidents Cup at Royal

Melbourne. He didn't win a match, going 0-3-1, but found it to be a success in another way. "One of my best experiences since I turned pro," he said. "I shared a lot of moments with the best players in the world."

The tough weather arrived in the second round, and despite the rain and the 30mph wind gusts, Schauffele shot a masterful 68 for 137 and a one-stroke lead on Reed and Niemann.

"It's sort of a battle of patience and what the course is willing to give you," Schauffele said.

Thomas bogeyed three straight from the second but birdied his way back, then missed the green at the 17th and bogeyed, and also bogeyed the 18th after a penalty drop from the native area. His 73 left him three behind.

"I felt like I really let a really good one get away from me," Thomas said.

The Thomas-Schauffele battle in the third round was no less stormy than the day, marked by constant wind and bursts of rain. Schauffele began the round leading by one but lost it when Thomas birdied five times on the front nine. Thomas then bogeyed twice coming home, shot 69, and Schauffele birdied twice and two-putted for a par five from 62 feet at the 18th for a 71 to take a one-shot lead to Sunday.

In the final round, Thomas birdied four straight from the eighth and six of eight to come from behind and take the two-stroke lead. Then the scramble.

Reed, who had started four behind Schauffele, posted a flawless 66. Schauffele, needing a birdie, three-putted from 35 feet for a par and a 70. Thomas bogeyed the 16th after driving into a bunker. And at the 18th, after his three-wood second caught heavy vegetation, he had to take a penalty drop, then wedged to eight feet and two-putted for a bogey, a 69 and a tie with Schauffele and Reed at 14-under-par 278.

In the playoff at the 18th, Schauffele bowed out with a par on the first visit, and Thomas and Reed tied in pars on the second. On the third, Reed missed his birdie try from eight feet. "It stings at the end whenever you don't birdie for the win," Reed said. Thomas recovered from a poor shot with a brilliant but dangerous wedge from 113 yards to three feet. And Thomas holed the three-footer.

That was the key — that scary wedge. Thomas' caddie had tried to warn him: Was this the safest shot?

"I need to make birdie," Thomas had answered. "I'm not worried what the safest play is."

Kapalua Resort (Plantation), Maui, Hawaii — January 2-5
Par 73 (36-37); 7,596 yards — Purse: $6,700,000

1	**Justin Thomas**	67	73	69	69	278	$1,340,000
2	**Patrick Reed**	72	66	74	66	278	636,000
	Xander Schauffele	69	68	71	70	278	636,000
	Thomas won playoff at third extra hole						
4	Patrick Cantlay	69	71	73	68	281	378,000
5	Rickie Fowler	68	71	74	69	282	285,000
	Joaquin Niemann	66	72	74	70	282	285,000
7	Dustin Johnson	72	71	71	69	283	206,000
	Collin Morikawa	71	71	70	71	283	206,000
	Gary Woodland	73	69	69	72	283	206,000
10	Jon Rahm	69	73	70	72	284	179,000
11	JT Poston	70	71	71	73	285	162,500
	Matthew Wolff	69	72	71	73	285	162,500
13	Lanto Griffin	71	71	72	72	286	147,000
14	Cameron Champ	73	74	69	72	288	127,333
	Kevin Kisner	72	72	68	76	288	127,333
	Matt Kuchar	68	74	71	75	288	127,333
17	Sebastian Munoz	72	75	72	70	289	106,000
	Ryan Palmer	71	72	75	71	289	106,000
19	Paul Casey	74	72	69	75	290	90,500
	Corey Conners	73	70	74	73	290	90,500
	Tyler Duncan	69	78	68	75	290	90,500
	Nate Lashley	71	71	71	77	290	90,500
23	Adam Long	74	71	75	71	291	80,500
	Graeme McDowell	74	69	76	72	291	80,500
25	Max Homa	75	72	71	74	292	75,000
	Sung Kang	72	73	73	74	292	75,000
27	Jim Herman	73	73	69	78	293	71,000
	Chez Reavie	74	71	73	75	293	71,000
29	Brendon Todd	71	74	74	75	294	69,000
30	JB Holmes	78	71	76	71	296	68,000
31	Dylan Frittelli	72	77	73	75	297	67,000
32	Keith Mitchell	76	72	73	81	302	65,500
	Kevin Na	76	74	77	75	302	65,500
34	Martin Trainer	74	77	77	82	310	64,000

Sony Open

Conditions were absolutely perfect for Cameron Smith in the Sony Open. He'd been battling Brendan Steele. And now it was late in the final round, and although the gusting winds had abated, a steady, nagging rain was falling on Waialae, and he was trailing by two shots with only two holes to play. Winning was pretty much out of the question. "I really didn't think there was much of a shot," he said. What was a golfer to do? Well, this was a prudent and honourable time to coast in to a comfortable and rewarding second-place finish.

Smith, 26, an Australian, had two things to say about that.

First: "I've always been quite good at not giving up," he said.

And then after he'd beaten Steele in a playoff, he noted: "Just hung in there, and what do you know?"

It was Smith's second PGA Tour victory, but his first individual title after the team championship with Jonas Blixt in the 2017 Zurich Classic.

As duels go, it was muted at first. Collin Morikawa, the kid who won the 2019 Barracuda Championship in only his sixth start, led the first round with a five-under 65 in tough winds. "I think the harder conditions, the better for me," he said. "Ball-strikers just want to control everything, and I had complete control today." But he cooled and would finish tied for 21st.

Steele opened the tournament with a 68, Smith a 70, and then the chase was on in the second round. Steele, shooting 66, eagled the 18th (his ninth), then birdied five of his last six, but double-bogeyed the sixth, his 15th. "I made one bad swing," Steele offered. He shared the lead at 134 with Cameron Davis, also an Aussie, who shot 66. "It doesn't feel like I'm playing out of my skin," Davis said, "so I just need to continue doing the same things." Cameron Smith, with only one two-putt in his six birdies, shot 65.

But it was more than a 65 to Smith. Australian golfers had pledged contributions for relief for wildfire victims back home. Smith would give $1,000 per birdie, and with 12 birdies so far, he would contribute $12,000.

With 23 players separated by three shots in the third round, Smith opened sluggishly. "Didn't start with my best golf," he said. "Got into the swing of things on the back nine. Rather than worrying about what I was doing with my swing, I just went ahead and tried to hit some golf shots. It was good to get into that frame of mind before tomorrow." Things brightened coming home. He birdied four of the last five holes, only one of them a two-putt, and shot 66.

Steele lost the lead with two early bogeys, then ignited a hot round with an eagle at the par-five ninth, firing a 210-yard four-iron to eight feet. He birdied five of the last eight holes for a 64 and a three-shot lead on Smith at 12 under.

Steele was going for his fourth tour win, and his first since 2017. He had only two top-10 finishes in 50 events worldwide since then.

The drama of the Sony was compressed into the last two holes, with Steele and Smith in the final grouping. Steele, after two birdies and two bogeys, was 12 under coming to the par-three 17th. He missed the green and two-putted for a bogey. Smith, after three birdies and two bogeys, was 10 under and parred the 17th, two-putting from 33 feet, and picked up a stroke. Steele parred the par-five 18th after a hooked second erased a birdie chance. He shot 71.

"Everything that could go wrong, went wrong today," said Steele.

And Smith blasted out of a greenside bunker to eight feet and birdied for a 68, and tied Steele at 11-under 269. It was the highest winning score at the Sony in 15 years.

"No one was playing good golf today, it seemed like," Smith said.

It was a tough time for a playoff. The wind had fallen, but the rain was steady and the course was soaked. They went to the par-four 10th. Steele wedged over the green, chipped to 15 feet, and missed his par. Smith drove into the rough but hit his second to 10 feet, and with the luxury of a two-putt par, he could say, "Finally ... I've won an event by myself."

Waialae Country Club, Honolulu, Hawaii — January 9-12
Par 70 (35-35); 7,044 yards — Purse: $6,600,000

1	**Cameron Smith**	70	65	66	68	269	$1,188,000
2	**Brendan Steele**	68	66	64	71	269	719,400
	Smith won playoff at first extra hole						
3	**Webb Simpson**	71	66	66	67	270	455,400
4	Kevin Kisner	69	69	64	69	271	277,750
	Graeme McDowell	71	69	67	64	271	277,750
	Ryan Palmer	67	68	68	68	271	277,750
7	Lanto Griffin	71	69	68	64	272	214,500
	Ted Potter Jr	67	69	70	66	272	214,500
9	Cameron Davis	68	66	71	68	273	179,850
	Bo Hoag	70	65	69	69	273	179,850
	Henrik Norlander	71	66	68	68	273	179,850
12	Keegan Bradley	69	66	69	70	274	116,050
	Corey Conners	68	71	69	66	274	116,050
	Joel Dahmen	74	66	68	66	274	116,050
	Tom Hoge	71	68	67	68	274	116,050
	Charles Howell III	72	67	66	69	274	116,050
	Peter Malnati	72	66	68	68	274	116,050
	Hideki Matsuyama	74	67	67	66	274	116,050
	Brandt Snedeker	72	67	69	66	274	116,050
	Vaughn Taylor	75	66	66	67	274	116,050
21	Mark Anderson	72	68	64	71	275	64,350
	Emiliano Grillo	70	69	67	69	275	64,350
	Sungjae Im	69	68	67	71	275	64,350
	Collin Morikawa	65	70	68	72	275	64,350
	Rob Oppenheim	70	65	72	68	275	64,350
	Rory Sabbatini	68	67	70	70	275	64,350
	Brendon Todd	68	70	69	68	275	64,350
28	Zach Johnson	69	68	70	69	276	46,200
	Marc Leishman	68	70	71	67	276	46,200
	Sam Ryder	67	68	73	68	276	46,200
	DJ Trahan	69	68	71	68	276	46,200
32	Brian Harman	68	68	74	67	277	36,850
	Russell Knox	70	65	70	72	277	36,850
	Matthew NeSmith	71	69	69	68	277	36,850
	Alex Noren	69	69	71	68	277	36,850
	Nick Taylor	70	69	67	71	277	36,850
	Tim Wilkinson	68	69	70	70	277	36,850
38	Abraham Ancer	69	71	69	69	278	27,390
	Daniel Berger	70	70	69	69	278	27,390
	Michael Gellerman	69	67	73	69	278	27,390
	Matt Jones	67	71	70	70	278	27,390
	Patrick Rodgers	68	69	69	72	278	27,390
	Chase Seiffert	71	69	71	67	278	27,390
	Michael Thompson	70	69	69	70	278	27,390
45	Joseph Bramlett	73	67	72	67	279	18,497
	Kramer Hickok	72	68	71	68	279	18,497
	Rikuya Hoshino	73	67	71	68	279	18,497
	Jerry Kelly	70	70	71	68	279	18,497
	Ben Martin	73	68	65	73	279	18,497
	Pat Perez	68	73	66	72	279	18,497
	Scott Piercy	70	69	71	69	279	18,497
	Jimmy Walker	70	71	67	71	279	18,497
53	Nate Lashley	70	69	69	72	280	15,609
	Carlos Ortiz	72	69	71	68	280	15,609
	Sepp Straka	70	69	76	65	280	15,609
	Brian Stuard	73	68	72	67	280	15,609
57	Rhein Gibson	70	69	73	69	281	14,916
	Scott Harrington	69	71	71	70	281	14,916
	Harry Higgs	73	68	72	68	281	14,916
	Joaquin Niemann	71	70	71	69	281	14,916
	Andrew Putnam	69	67	73	72	281	14,916
	Hudson Swafford	69	67	75	70	281	14,916
63	Zac Blair	72	67	74	69	282	14,388
	Talor Gooch	70	71	70	71	282	14,388
65	Mikumu Horikawa	73	67	76	67	283	14,190
66	Satoshi Kodaira	69	70	72	75	286	14,058

The American Express

It was merely your average golf nightmare.

Andrew Landry, with his second PGA Tour win at his fingertips, was leading The American Express by six shots on the final nine — and proceeded to blow every bit of it and fall into a tie with two holes to play. He scratched back a one-shot edge at the 17th, and then rather than nurse that slim lead home, he went to the 18th tee and hit just your average heart-in-the-throat drive out over the water.

Whew! is the appropriate expression in such cases. Yes, Landry went on to win, and as comebacks go, this one was a resurrection.

Landry regained his breath and his composure, and noted: "I don't want to be a part of something like that ever again."

Landry, a slight Texan, 5-foot-7 and weighing 150, came to the AmEx at La Quinta looking for anything. He had missed seven of eight cuts in the current tour overlap season, and he'd missed the cut the previous week in the Sony Open. This time in the AmEx, across the three courses, Landry, winner of the 2018 Valero Texas Open, shot 66-64-65-67 for a 26-under-par total of 262 and a two-stroke win over Abraham Ancer.

And Ancer, 28, born in Texas and holder of dual US and Mexican citizenship, and a standout at the University of Oklahoma, came within a whisker of his first tour title. He tied the Stadium Course record with a flawless nine-under 63 in the final round. He owned the par fives, two-putting for birdies from 45, 54 and 63 feet, and one-putting the 16th from five. Ancer, playing two groups ahead of Landry, realised at the 17th that he was tied for the lead. "All right," Ancer told himself, "we got to make two other birdies. I made the putt there on 17, and then just couldn't make it happen on 18."

Phil Mickleson, the tournament host, was making his 2020 debut and marked it with what looked like a wickedly awful hit, but was actually an effort at trailblazing golf. In the first round, he went to the tee at the par-four ninth and walloped a tee shot through two fairways. It was deliberate. He was trying to hit the first fairway for a better angle to the back-right flag.

"Takes the water out of play and I just have a much better angle," he said. At least he parred, and that took some of the sting out of the double bogey back at the eighth. "I feel like I'm ready to go on a tear, Mickelson said after his two-under 70, but he went on to miss the third-round cut at three-under 213.

Landry was a chaser through the first two rounds. He opened with the 66 at the Stadium Course, two behind co-leaders Zac Blair and Grayson Murray. In the second, a 64 at La Quinta left him a stroke behind Rickie Fowler (64) and Scottie Scheffler (64) at the halfway point. Then it looked like a two-man duel when Landry, with a 65 at the Nicklaus Course, and Scheffler, shooting 66 at the Stadium, tied for the third-round lead at 21 under, four ahead of Rickie Fowler. At the 18th, Scheffler watched, breathless, as his over-drawn tee shot headed for the seaside rocks. Then saw it bounce back into the fairway. "I guess," Scheffler would explain, "you take them where you can get them." He would finish third.

In the fourth round, six birdies through the 12th left Landry a heady 27 under. Up ahead, Ancer was churning. He also made six birdies through 11, but he trailed by six. Then came Landry's near-fatal stretch. He bogeyed three straight, three-putting the 13th from 62 feet and missing the next two greens. Ancer birdied 14, 16 and 17.

"On 17, right before I hit my tee shot, I realised I was tied," Ancer said, and he knew he had to birdie both 17 and 18. But he could add only 17.

"But," said Ancer, who finished at 24-under 264, "I played good. I'm proud of how I played."

Landry regained the lead at the 17th, holing a seven-footer for birdie. Then he rode that bold cut drive at the 18th to a birdie from six feet for his 67 and the win.

"Just to be able to get the job done, man," Landry said. "It means a lot to be able to be a winner again."

PGA West (Stadium), La Quinta, California — January 16-19
Par 72 (36-36); 7,113 yards — Purse: $6,700,000
Nicklaus Tournament (R1-3) par 72 (36-36); 7,159 yards
La Quinta CC (R1-3) par 72 (36-36); 7,060 yards

1	**Andrew Landry**	66	64	65	67	262	$1,206,000
2	**Abraham Ancer**	68	67	66	63	264	730,300
3	**Scottie Scheffler**	65	64	66	70	265	462,300
4	Bud Cauley	68	64	71	65	268	301,500
	Sepp Straka	69	65	68	66	268	301,500
6	Sam Burns	71	68	67	63	269	218,588
	Sebastian Cappelen	67	70	64	68	269	218,588
	Tom Hoge	66	70	66	67	269	218,588
	Ryan Moore	68	65	67	69	269	218,588
10	Rickie Fowler	65	64	70	71	270	162,475
	Sungjae Im	67	66	69	68	270	162,475
	Grayson Murray	64	71	69	66	270	162,475
	Andrew Putnam	67	69	65	69	270	162,475
14	Tony Finau	69	62	71	69	271	122,275
	Alex Noren	67	67	68	69	271	122,275
	Adam Schenk	66	69	68	68	271	122,275
17	Talor Gooch	69	71	64	68	272	98,825
	Hank Lebioda	65	71	66	70	272	98,825
	Kevin Na	69	67	69	67	272	98,825
	Matthew NeSmith	68	68	70	66	272	98,825
21	Paul Casey	68	67	67	71	273	63,399
	Cameron Champ	67	71	68	67	273	63,399
	Michael Gligic	69	65	70	69	273	63,399
	Brian Harman	67	67	69	70	273	63,399
	Kyoung-Hoon Lee	68	69	68	68	273	63,399
	Sebastian Munoz	67	68	68	70	273	63,399
	Chase Seiffert	66	67	67	73	273	63,399
	Tim Wilkinson	71	65	66	71	273	63,399
29	Daniel Berger	69	68	69	68	274	41,121
	Cameron Davis	66	67	72	69	274	41,121
	Chesson Hadley	73	67	64	70	274	41,121
	Ben Martin	72	64	71	67	274	41,121
	Doc Redman	68	70	68	68	274	41,121
	Sam Ryder	69	70	68	67	274	41,121
	Nick Watney	67	71	65	71	274	41,121
	Vincent Whaley	71	68	67	68	274	41,121
37	David Hearn	71	68	65	71	275	29,815
	Russell Knox	66	71	70	68	275	29,815
	Maverick McNealy	69	65	71	70	275	29,815
	JT Poston	67	69	69	70	275	29,815
	Ted Potter Jr	70	63	73	69	275	29,815
	Brendon Todd	69	68	65	73	275	29,815
43	Bronson Burgoon	72	66	69	69	276	22,445
	Mark Hubbard	69	71	67	69	276	22,445
	Brendan Steele	70	66	67	73	276	22,445
	Vaughn Taylor	69	74	64	69	276	22,445
	Cameron Tringale	69	69	67	71	276	22,445
48	Brandon Hagy	74	63	69	71	277	16,989
	Max Homa	71	68	63	75	277	16,989
	John Huh	67	69	69	72	277	16,989
	Denny McCarthy	71	68	65	73	277	16,989
	Harris English	71	68	64	74	277	16,989
	Carlos Ortiz	71	70	66	70	277	16,989
	Rory Sabbatini	70	70	67	70	277	16,989
55	Zac Blair	64	70	71	73	278	15,410
	Ryan Brehm	69	67	71	71	278	15,410

	Jason Dufner	67 71 69 71	278	15,410		Wes Roach	68 65 69 78	280	14,338
	Fabian Gomez	69 70 67 72	278	15,410		Patrick Rodgers	69 66 72 73	280	14,338
	Scott Stallings	67 71 67 73	278	15,410	68	Troy Merritt	71 68 68 74	281	13,802
	Jhonattan Vegas	68 69 70 71	278	15,410		Henrik Norlander	75 66 66 74	281	13,802
61	Charley Hoffman	74 63 69 73	279	14,807		Josh Teater	67 70 69 75	281	13,802
	Scott Piercy	67 68 72 72	279	14,807		DJ Trahan	69 69 69 74	281	13,802
	Matthew Wolff	67 69 71 72	279	14,807	72	Brian Stuard	67 70 70 75	282	13,467
64	Tyler Duncan	66 73 67 74	280	14,338	73	Anirban Lahiri	70 70 66 77	283	13,333
	Tyler McCumber	67 71 69 73	280	14,338	74	Matt Every	70 67 68 82	287	13,199

Farmers Insurance Open

It's on the schedule formally as the Farmers Insurance Open. Formal ended there. This was your average wide-open, no-holds-barred, full-throated free-for-all.

No day dawned on the same leader, and none at all on Marc Leishman, the big, affable Aussie, who as the winner, was more like a driven party-crasher in the final round.

"I just wanted to play well ... give myself a chance," he offered.

Until then, he was just part of the scramble in this January frolic at Torrey Pines, overlooking the Pacific. The focus was on Tiger Woods, 44, tied with the legendary Sam Snead for PGA Tour victories at 82. Where better to get that record 83rd than Torrey, where he had won this event seven times (under its various names) along with the 2008 U.S. Open. "I really don't think about it," Woods said.

Keegan Bradley, playing the North Course, and Danish rookie Sebastian Cappelen, on the tougher South tied for the first-round lead at 66.

Bradley, on what went well: "I just played really, really well all day."

For Cappelen: "What wasn't working?"

And said Woods after a 68 on the North, "Overall, I felt like it was a good start."

Woods, at the South in the second round, opened with a four-putt double bogey from 25 feet. Was that record 83rd win on his mind or does he play shot by shot? "Well," said Woods, "shot by shot got me to 82."

Ryan Palmer shied away looking at a scoreboard. "We'll see when we get done," he insisted. When he finally dared to look, he saw he'd shot a 10-under 62 on the North and led by two over Brandt Snedeker (67). Leishman fell six behind with his two-birdie, two-bogey 72.

And come the third round, he still wasn't making a ripple. He trailed by four after a 68, but his putting had perked up. Of his six birdies, two were from 16 feet, one from 23, and he closed with a two-putt from 55 feet at the par-five 18th.

Jon Rahm opened birdie-eagle with a chip-in and a holed-out wedge and shot a no-bogey 65 for a one-stroke lead over Palmer. Rahm cautioned himself: "No matter how good I'm playing, somebody can come and do the same thing."

The fourth round had its share of disappointments. Tiger Woods never got close to scoring that record 83rd victory. He shot 70 and tied for ninth. Palmer, a stroke behind going into the final, shot 77. Rory McIlroy needed a win to return to the world number one ranking, but fell short with a 69 and tied for third.

And then Rahm. He had warned himself that someone could always overrun you, and someone did — Leishman.

Playing a half-hour ahead, Leishman launched an eight-birdie spree with a 42-foot putt at the first, and also made clutch par putts of 20, 12 and eight feet. Then he bogeyed the 17th.

"I think I've led here early in the last round maybe once or twice and let it slip," Leishman said. "I was very determined to not let that happen again."

And with Rahm threatening behind him, Leishman calmly sank a five-footer for a birdie at 18.

Rahm shook off a brutal start, a double bogey and two singles in four holes, and then found himself on the 18th green facing a 50-foot putt for an eagle he thought would win for him. He missed.

"Good try," his caddie said.

"What do you mean?" said Rahm, thinking he had tied Leishman. "We're in a playoff."

"Nope," said the caddie. "He birdied 18."

Rahm posted a 70 for 274, and Leishman's closing birdie gave him a one-stroke win on a 65, a 15-under 273 total and his fifth tour victory.

And his mind was never far from home. He'd won on Australia Day, a national holiday, and huge wildfires were raging there, killing people and animals.

"Just devastating," Leishman said. "So if this can bring them a little bit of joy ..."

Torrey Pines Golf Course (South), San Diego, California — January 23-26
Par 72 (36-36); 7,765 yards — Purse: $7,500,000
North (R1&2) par 72 (36-36); 7,258 yards

1	**Marc Leishman**	68	72	68	65	273	$1,350,000
2	**Jon Rahm**	68	71	65	70	274	817,500
3	**Rory McIlroy**	67	73	67	69	276	442,500
	Brandt Snedeker	69	67	72	68	276	442,500
5	Tom Hoge	71	71	67	68	277	307,500
6	Tony Finau	70	70	68	70	278	253,125
	Patrick Reed	69	69	70	70	278	253,125
	Bubba Watson	67	73	69	69	278	253,125
9	Harry Higgs	70	68	69	72	279	181,875
	Charley Hoffman	69	74	71	65	279	181,875
	Max Homa	73	68	71	67	279	181,875
	Beau Hossler	72	66	73	68	279	181,875
	Patrick Rodgers	70	69	72	68	279	181,875
	Tiger Woods	69	71	69	70	279	181,875
15	Maverick McNealy	71	71	69	69	280	136,875
16	Keegan Bradley	66	72	73	70	281	114,375
	Cameron Champ	71	68	68	74	281	114,375
	Jason Day	73	67	72	69	281	114,375
	JB Holmes	68	69	71	73	281	114,375
	Sung Kang	69	71	67	74	281	114,375
21	Zac Blair	72	66	72	72	282	69,042
	William Gordon	75	68	69	70	282	69,042
	Russell Knox	69	74	69	70	282	69,042
	Jason Kokrak	69	74	69	70	282	69,042
	Collin Morikawa	70	69	74	69	282	69,042
	Matthew Wolff	76	66	71	69	282	69,042
	Sebastian Cappelen	66	71	71	74	282	69,042
	Tyler McCumber	72	68	68	74	282	69,042
	Ryan Palmer	72	62	71	77	282	69,042
30	Mark Anderson	74	66	69	74	283	45,938
	Matthew NeSmith	67	70	76	70	283	45,938
	JJ Spaun	73	67	74	69	283	45,938
	Kevin Tway	67	74	74	68	283	45,938
	Jhonattan Vegas	69	68	75	71	283	45,938
	Jimmy Walker	71	70	70	72	283	45,938
36	Cameron Davis	76	65	69	74	284	32,667
	Jason Dufner	70	71	72	71	284	32,667
	Sungjae Im	67	73	71	73	284	32,667
	Cameron Percy	68	73	74	69	284	32,667
	Robby Shelton	71	72	70	71	284	32,667
	Zack Sucher	70	73	69	72	284	32,667
	Talor Gooch	71	72	72	69	284	32,667
	Luke List	73	70	72	69	284	32,667
	Jamie Lovemark	73	68	69	74	284	32,667
45	Joseph Bramlett	71	70	71	73	285	22,950
	John Huh	70	73	71	71	285	22,950
	Hideki Matsuyama	73	67	74	71	285	22,950
	Kevin Streelman	72	71	68	74	285	22,950
49	Ryan Brehm	70	72	74	70	286	18,700
	Sam Burns	74	69	73	70	286	18,700
	Lucas Glover	73	67	73	73	286	18,700
	Joaquin Niemann	71	70	70	75	286	18,700
	Scott Stallings	71	69	74	72	286	18,700
	Cameron Tringale	68	75	69	74	286	18,700
55	Stewart Cink	68	71	75	73	287	17,025
	Joel Dahmen	67	73	72	75	287	17,025
	Martin Laird	71	71	72	73	287	17,025
	Grayson Murray	70	73	72	72	287	17,025
	Pat Perez	69	74	70	74	287	17,025
	Jordan Spieth	70	70	73	74	287	17,025
	Ben Taylor	71	69	71	76	287	17,025
	Brandon Wu	68	72	71	76	287	17,025
	Xinjun Zhang	67	76	72	72	287	17,025
64	Aaron Baddeley	71	72	69	76	288	16,050
	Denny McCarthy	70	71	73	74	288	16,050
	Doc Redman	70	73	74	71	288	16,050
	Cameron Smith	70	71	74	73	288	16,050
68	Byeong Hun An	67	74	77	71	289	15,600
	Billy Horschel	68	72	80	69	289	15,600
70	Rhein Gibson	69	73	72	76	290	15,375
71	Harris English	72	70	74	75	291	15,150
	Chase Seiffert	71	71	78	71	291	15,150
73	Chris Baker	72	68	74	78	292	14,625
	Dylan Frittelli	76	66	77	73	292	14,625
	Bill Haas	72	70	73	77	292	14,625
	Matt Jones	75	68	73	76	292	14,625
	Richy Werenski	72	68	78	74	292	14,625
78	Trey Mullinax	77	66	75	78	296	14,175
79	Dominic Bozzelli	68	73	78	78	297	14,025

Waste Management Phoenix Open

Webb Simpson came from behind dramatically to make the Waste Management Phoenix Open his sixth career PGA Tour victory — a collection that included the 2012 U.S. Open and the 2018 Players Championship — but this was one of the toughest of all. Not because of the weather or the golf course. It was because when he was lining up that winning 10-foot birdie putt that he made on the first playoff hole, he was drawing a bead on one of his best friends on the tour — Tony Finau.

It didn't help that they were paired together in the last round, and that Finau faltered as Simpson overtook him.

"Yeah, it's hard," Simpson said. "I actually thought about that out there. He's one of my good friends on tour. And so that part's hard. I mean, we're after the same thing. So I hope he doesn't feel bad about today."

"He got the upper hand this time, but I love that guy," Finau said. "And that's one hell of a finish. If you're going to birdie 18 a couple of times, you're probably going to win."

The two friends, though playing in separate groupings for the first three rounds, were on a collision course from the start. Simpson shot 71-63-64-69, and Finau 69-66-62-70 to tie at 17-under 267. In the playoff at the par-four 18th, Finau missed his birdie try from 18 feet, and Simpson holed the winner from 10.

In their head-to-head battle, Finau moved ahead, 69-71, both well off the lead as Wyndham Clark, seeking his first win in his second year on tour, posted a 10-under 61, one of 11 bogey-free cards in the first round. Simpson edged ahead of Finau in the second, 63-66, helped by two great bunker shots that set up birdies — a 60-footer to three feet at his 12th (the third), and a 150-yard shot to two feet at the par-four eighth (his 17th). JB Holmes took the lead with 65 for 13 under par, and Simpson was five behind, Finau six.

The duel came to a peak in the third round. Finau took a one-stroke lead on Simpson with a flawless 62 that included an eagle on a 20-footer at the par-five 13th. "That was the first time he hit a driver into the fairway this week," Finau's caddie Greg Bodine said, with a touch of excess. Simpson shot a two-bogey 64 sparked by a hole-in-one at the par-three 196-yard 12th that he couldn't even enjoy. "I can't really see that well," he said. So he watched the spectators. "And then their hands went up."

The tournament came down to the closing few. Finau was leading by two with two to play. Simpson drove the short par-four 17th and two-putted for birdie and trailed by one, then tied him with a bending 17-footer for birdie at the 18th. Then Simpson holed the 10-footer for birdie at the first hole of the playoff.

"I definitely didn't give him the tournament," Finau said. "Unfortunately, it's how the cookie crumbles ... I love the guy."

Said Simpson: "He is a great friend. You hope you both play well — and you hope you win by one."

TPC Scottsdale, Scottsdale, Arizona — January 30-February 2
Par 71 (35-36); 7,261 yards — Purse: $7,300,000

1	**Webb Simpson**	71	63	64	69	267	$1,314,000
2	**Tony Finau**	69	66	62	70	267	795,700
	Simpson won playoff at first extra hole						
3	**Nate Lashley**	66	67	69	68	270	386,900
	Justin Thomas	68	68	69	65	270	386,900
	Bubba Watson	69	66	69	66	270	386,900
6	Max Homa	72	67	64	68	271	255,500
	Scott Piercy	67	65	68	71	271	255,500
8	Adam Long	66	68	66	72	272	228,125
9	Daniel Berger	69	71	66	67	273	170,768
	Branden Grace	67	67	70	69	273	170,768
	Billy Horschel	63	68	73	69	273	170,768
	Mark Hubbard	69	68	64	72	273	170,768
	Jon Rahm	67	68	68	70	273	170,768
	Byeong Hun An	65	66	70	72	273	170,768
	Hudson Swafford	66	67	66	74	273	170,768
16	Harris English	65	72	68	69	274	97,212
	Brandon Hagy	67	69	69	69	274	97,212
	Matt Kuchar	68	70	67	69	274	97,212
	Hideki Matsuyama	67	74	65	68	274	97,212
	Keith Mitchell	68	67	70	69	274	97,212
	Patrick Rodgers	67	69	70	68	274	97,212
	JB Holmes	64	65	70	75	274	97,212
	Russell Knox	71	67	67	69	274	97,212
	Xander Schauffele	67	67	66	74	274	97,212
25	Bud Cauley	65	72	70	68	275	52,601
	James Hahn	69	67	69	70	275	52,601
	Harry Higgs	70	68	68	69	275	52,601
	Danny Lee	68	69	69	69	275	52,601
	Carlos Ortiz	71	69	67	68	275	52,601
	Tom Hoge	65	71	67	72	275	52,601
	Luke List	70	69	64	72	275	52,601
	Collin Morikawa	69	67	68	71	275	52,601
	Xinjun Zhang	69	72	68	66	275	52,601
34	Wyndham Clark	61	69	74	72	276	39,785
	Sungjae Im	66	72	68	70	276	39,785
	Doc Redman	69	67	71	69	276	39,785
37	Rickie Fowler	74	65	69	69	277	34,675
	JT Poston	70	68	71	68	277	34,675
	Kevin Tway	72	67	68	70	277	34,675
40	Aaron Baddeley	68	70	72	68	278	28,835
41	Adam Hadwin	69	67	72	70	278	28,835
	Charley Hoffman	71	70	67	70	278	28,835
	John Huh	71	66	66	75	278	28,835
	Gary Woodland	70	67	69	72	278	28,835
45	Corey Conners	71	69	71	68	279	23,725
	Andrew Landry	69	72	69	69	279	23,725
47	Sebastian Munoz	70	71	69	70	280	20,951
	JJ Spaun	70	71	68	71	280	20,951
49	Keegan Bradley	67	70	71	73	281	18,810
	Brian Harman	71	68	67	75	281	18,810
	Nick Taylor	70	70	71	70	281	18,810
52	Bryson DeChambeau	70	69	70	73	282	17,593
	Brice Garnett	72	67	72	71	282	17,593
	Sung Kang	67	72	69	74	282	17,593
55	KJ Choi	66	75	71	71	283	16,936
	Martin Laird	72	67	73	71	283	16,936
	Grayson Murray	70	68	73	72	283	16,936
	Sam Ryder	71	66	74	72	283	16,936
59	Chesson Hadley	73	68	68	75	284	16,498
	Denny McCarthy	71	70	72	71	284	16,498
61	Talor Gooch	68	73	69	75	285	16,206
	Patton Kizzire	70	71	74	70	285	16,206
63	Dylan Frittelli	71	70	72	74	287	15,841
	Cheng Tsung Pan	69	66	75	77	287	15,841
	Jimmy Walker	69	71	69	78	287	15,841
66	Beau Hossler	68	72	77	72	289	15,549

AT&T Pebble Beach Pro-Am

The Great Handicapper in the Sky was figuring the odds on Nick Taylor winning the AT&T Pebble Beach Pro-Am at storied Pebble Beach. These were the factors in his considerations:

Taylor, 31, three-round leader, first 54-hole lead. One win in six years on the PGA Tour, the 2015 Sanderson Farms Championship, opposite-field event. Otherwise, mostly in danger of losing his playing privileges. His one-shot lead was on Phil Mickelson, five-time winner, needs no introduction. He would be playing Mickelson head-to-head. So, the odds on Taylor?

Well, with all due respect to the battling Canadian, was there a number lower than zero?

And therein lay an enchanting tale of 2020. Taylor told it in five words.

On making an eagle on his very first hole of the tournament: "Nice start," he said.

And on stepping off the final green with a four-stroke win: "That was amazing."

Taylor shot 63-66-69-70 across the three courses, never lost the lead, and with a robust 19-under-par 268, beat Kevin Streelman by four and not only survived the head-to-head with Mickelson but beat him by five.

"Last couple years," Taylor said, with great relief, "I've been fighting for my card. So things have changed ... awesome."

Taylor's assault on the improbable began at his very first hole, the 10th at the par-71 Monterey Peninsula. He hit a four-iron approach to four feet, made the eagle, then added six birdies for a spotless eight-under 63 and a three-stroke lead. But it was a quiet 63. The attention was on Spyglass, where Mickelson and Dustin Johnson were playing, along with five National Football League quarterbacks. Mickelson shot 68. "I drove it like a stallion," he said. Said Taylor, almost prophetically, "So the game's been solid — it's just kind of been growing."

From there, the tournament became an exercise in waiting for Taylor to crack. He declined.

Jason Day made a move in the second round, a 64 at Pebble, and was two behind Taylor, who birdied four of his last five holes for a 66, also at Pebble. "At 12, that was a really good bogey save ... kept my round together," Taylor said. In the third, a 69 at Spyglass left him one ahead of Mickelson, who shot 67 at Pebble. He hit half of the fairways and greens but needed just 22 putts. "A pretty good day with my short game," he said.

And so Taylor would be facing Mickelson. "I'm sure I won't be the crowd favourite," he said, "so just got to keep my head down."

Streelman, starting six off the lead, launched his final-round 68 with an eagle on a 12-foot putt at the par-five sixth and finished second, four behind. He hadn't been pleased with his West Coast swing, but now, "I'm really proud," he said.

Mickelson had an erratic time of it in the finish. He had four birdies, but the punishment started with a double bogey at the par-four eighth. It took him four to get on. Missing greens hither and yon, he bogeyed nine, 12, 14 and 16.

"It's disappointing, certainly," Mickelson said, "but I got outplayed. He just played some great golf."

Actually, Taylor did start to crack coming in, but he sealed it off and pulled back. He was blistering the front nine, going birdie-birdie-eagle from the fourth — the eagle from 12 feet at the sixth — and after a bogey-birdie exchange, he crashed. Under heavy wind gusts, disaster beckoned. Stray tee shots cost him bogeys at 11 and 12 and a double bogey at 14. His lead was down to two.

But Taylor pulled himself together, chipped in for birdie at 15 and birdied 17 from six feet for his 70, a 268 total and the four-shot win.

Pressure? Compare that with trying to keep your card.

Said Taylor: "I was under way more pressure in that scenario than when I was trying to win today."

Pebble Beach Golf Links, Pebble Beach, California — February 6-9
Par 72 (36-36); 6,816 yards — Purse: $7,800,000
Spyglass Hill (R1-3) par 72 (36-36); 7,035 yards
Monterey Peninsula (R1-3) par 71 (34-37); 6,958 yards

1	**Nick Taylor**	63	66	69	70	268	$1,404,000
2	**Kevin Streelman**	69	67	68	68	272	850,200
3	**Phil Mickelson**	68	64	67	74	273	538,200
4	Jason Day	67	64	70	75	276	382,200
5	Maverick McNealy	72	72	66	68	278	277,388
	Daniel Berger	70	69	70	69	278	277,388
	Matt Jones	68	73	65	72	278	277,388
	Charl Schwartzel	67	66	73	72	278	277,388
9	Jordan Spieth	70	71	71	67	279	220,350
	Lanto Griffin	67	68	71	73	279	220,350
11	Matthew NeSmith	68	71	69	72	280	181,350
	Patrick Cantlay	66	69	72	73	280	181,350
	Peter Malnati	70	69	66	75	280	181,350
14	JB Holmes	71	72	67	71	281	138,450
	Kevin Na	75	67	68	71	281	138,450
	Joel Dahmen	71	73	67	70	281	138,450
	Max Homa	67	69	71	74	281	138,450
18	Joseph Bramlett	71	70	69	72	282	96,219
	Chesson Hadley	71	67	72	72	282	96,219
	Harry Higgs	66	69	74	73	282	96,219
	Wyndham Clark	68	71	70	73	282	96,219
	Zac Blair	69	69	73	71	282	96,219
	Kurt Kitayama	69	69	69	75	282	96,219
	Scott Piercy	68	66	72	76	282	96,219
25	Ben Martin	72	68	70	73	283	58,667
	Chez Reavie	67	69	73	74	283	58,667
	Kevin Chappell	68	67	74	74	283	58,667
	Tim Wilkinson	69	70	70	74	283	58,667
	Aaron Baddeley	68	69	71	75	283	58,667
	Troy Merritt	69	70	73	71	283	58,667
	Henrik Norlander	69	73	70	71	283	58,667
32	Tyler McCumber	71	70	69	74	284	43,550
	Alexander Noren	69	67	74	74	284	43,550
	Keith Mitchell	69	67	76	72	284	43,550
	Dustin Johnson	69	65	72	78	284	43,550
	Alex Cejka	69	73	70	72	284	43,550
	Matt Every	70	66	68	80	284	43,550
38	Beau Hossler	68	72	70	75	285	28,561
	Kevin Kisner	72	68	70	75	285	28,561
	Chris Baker	69	64	76	76	285	28,561
	Stewart Cink	69	72	70	74	285	28,561
	Matt Kuchar	70	71	68	76	285	28,561
	Seamus Power	72	68	71	74	285	28,561
	Viktor Hovland	70	68	70	77	285	28,561
	Vincent Whaley	71	73	67	74	285	28,561
	Brandon Wu	69	66	76	74	285	28,561
	Brian Gay	72	68	68	77	285	28,561
	Rob Oppenheim	68	74	70	73	285	28,561
	Cameron Davis	71	72	69	73	285	28,561
50	Sean O'Hair	73	65	71	77	286	19,204
	Chase Seiffert	66	76	69	75	286	19,204
	Adam Schenk	68	69	74	75	286	19,204
	Lucas Glover	70	76	66	74	286	19,204
	Doc Redman	73	67	72	74	286	19,204
55	Jim Herman	67	73	70	77	287	18,018
	Cameron Champ	71	66	71	79	287	18,018
	Michael Gligic	72	71	69	75	287	18,018
	Luke Donald	72	71	69	75	287	18,018
	Wes Roach	69	73	70	75	287	18,018
60	Matthew Fitzpatrick	71	70	68	79	288	17,472
	Tom Hoge	69	73	69	77	288	17,472
62	Jason Dufner	73	70	68	78	289	17,160
	Aaron Wise	68	74	70	77	289	17,160
64	Paul Casey	71	65	73	81	290	16,770
	Cameron Tringale	71	69	71	79	290	16,770
	Xinjun Zhang	71	74	67	78	290	16,770
67	John Senden	71	71	67	83	292	16,458
68	Ryan Brehm	73	69	68	87	297	16,302

Genesis Invitational

Of the 273 strokes Adam Scott made in winning the Genesis Invitational, 21 were birdies — a healthy figure by PGA Tour standards, especially considering that the tournament was played at Riviera, a course not known for its birdie-friendliness. And interestingly enough, the key to Scott's victory was not a birdie, even the one at the 17th on Sunday, but one of his eight bogeys. Not the bogey itself, but the flop shot he dared to hit that set it up — bold as burglary, elegant as art. And it saved him.

On the card, it was a five-foot putt for a bogey at the par-four 15th. But that's just a number.

"Look," said Scott, the 2013 Masters champion, "the putt on 17 was great because it kept me fairly comfortable, but the shot that stood out was deciding to flop the second chip on 15 after I was plugged in the bunker, and I kind of knifed it across the green. It was in a horrible position then. I stood there and I wanted to maybe bump it into the fringe, but realistically it was going to be 45 feet past probably, and I thought, well, you can maybe win the tournament if you hit a great flop shot here, so I thought I might as well just go for it."

Scott made the five-footer to save bogey, and his lead was down to one. But it was back to two with a birdie from 10 feet at the par-five 17th, and he closed with an untroubled par to win by two. Scott shot Riviera in 72-64-67-70 for a total of 273, 11 under par.

The Genesis was his 14th PGA Tour win and first in nearly four years, and it came just about two months after he won the 2019 Australian PGA late in December.

In a three-way tie for second were Sung Kang, who eagled the first, then had a double bogey and shot 69; Scott Brown came home with bookend birdies at 10 and 18 with pars in between for a 68, and Matt Kuchar, who birdied the first and the 17th, and scattered three bogeys for a one-over 72. "It was one hard day out there," Kuchar said. He led for the first two rounds on 64-69 and tied for the lead in the third with a 70, caught by Scott and Rory McIlroy.

McIlroy was stung in the final round, going triple bogey-bogey at the fifth and sixth. He shot 73 and tied for fifth. Harold Varner, one behind starting the final round, eagled the first, but shot 40 on the back for a 74 and tied for 13th.

Said Scott, recounting his dangerous flop shot: "I had a little bit of that mindset, not just today but the whole week, of 'what have I got to lose?' Give myself a good chance to get back in the winner's circle on the PGA Tour'."

It wasn't that simple for Tiger Woods. Riviera once again proved to be Tiger-proof. Woods was now 0-for-13 (twice as an amateur) at Riviera. This time he started so-so and got successively worse, shooting 69-73-76-77, 11-over 295, finishing solo 68th and last.

"Good news," Woods said. "I hit every ball forward, not backward. A couple sideways."

Riviera Country Club, Pacific Palisades, California — February 13-16
Par 71 (35-36); 7,322 yards — Purse: $9,300,000

1	**Adam Scott**	72	64	67	70	273	$1,674,000
2	**Scott Brown**	71	68	68	68	275	703,700
	Sung Kang	69	67	70	69	275	703,700
	Matt Kuchar	64	69	70	72	275	703,700
5	Joel Dahmen	68	71	66	71	276	318,990
	Bryson DeChambeau	68	70	69	69	276	318,990
	Max Homa	72	69	65	70	276	318,990
	Hideki Matsuyama	71	72	64	69	276	318,990
	Rory McIlroy	68	67	68	73	276	318,990
10	Talor Gooch	70	72	64	71	277	234,825
	Dustin Johnson	72	66	67	72	277	234,825
	Chez Reavie	69	68	71	69	277	234,825
13	James Hahn	68	70	70	70	278	176,700
	Kyoung-Hoon Lee	67	73	69	69	278	176,700
	Vaughn Taylor	69	67	74	68	278	176,700
	Harold Varner III	67	68	69	74	278	176,700
17	Rafa Cabrera Bello	68	69	72	70	279	127,875
	Patrick Cantlay	68	72	71	68	279	127,875
	Wyndham Clark	67	68	72	72	279	127,875
	Russell Henley	67	69	68	75	279	127,875
	Scott Piercy	70	69	70	70	279	127,875
	Jon Rahm	70	68	69	72	279	127,875
23	Sam Burns	73	68	69	70	280	89,745
	Xander Schauffele	72	70	69	69	280	89,745
	Brian Stuard	72	68	69	71	280	89,745
26	Adam Hadwin	71	71	69	70	281	70,680
	Collin Morikawa	73	67	68	73	281	70,680
	Sebastian Munoz	69	69	70	73	281	70,680
	Carlos Ortiz	68	70	71	72	281	70,680
30	JT Poston	69	72	70	71	282	55,734
	Matthew Fitzpatrick	71	70	68	73	282	55,734
	Luke List	71	68	68	75	282	55,734
	Ryan Moore	71	71	69	71	282	55,734
	Patrick Rodgers	71	71	70	70	282	55,734
	Scottie Scheffler	69	72	71	70	282	55,734
	Cameron Tringale	74	69	67	72	282	55,734
37	Paul Casey	69	69	70	75	283	41,385
	Sergio Garcia	70	70	71	72	283	41,385
	Lanto Griffin	71	70	69	73	283	41,385
	Si Woo Kim	69	69	72	73	283	41,385
	Andrew Landry	68	72	70	73	283	41,385
	Denny McCarthy	69	72	70	72	283	41,385
43	Abraham Ancer	76	67	70	71	284	32,085
	Brooks Koepka	69	73	68	74	284	32,085
	Martin Laird	71	71	70	72	284	32,085
	Marc Leishman	70	72	68	74	284	32,085
47	Brian Harman	70	69	74	72	285	25,482
	Pat Perez	73	70	69	73	285	25,482
	Adam Schenk	67	73	71	74	285	25,482
	Martin Trainer	72	71	68	74	285	25,482
51	Joseph Bramlett	74	69	68	75	286	22,487
	Bud Cauley	74	69	70	73	286	22,487
	Tony Finau	72	71	71	72	286	22,487
	JB Holmes	69	69	76	72	286	22,487
	Patrick Reed	68	73	71	74	286	22,487
56	Justin Rose	69	69	74	75	287	21,483
	Steve Stricker	72	71	71	73	287	21,483
	Brendon Todd	73	70	71	73	287	21,483
59	Charles Howell III	77	66	75	70	288	20,832
	Alex Noren	71	70	72	75	288	20,832
	Rory Sabbatini	72	68	74	74	288	20,832
	Jordan Spieth	72	70	70	76	288	20,832
63	JJ Spaun	73	69	73	75	290	20,367
64	Jason Dufner	75	68	76	73	292	19,995
	Tyler Duncan	73	69	79	71	292	19,995
	Kyle Stanley	71	70	78	73	292	19,995
67	Ryan Palmer	71	70	81	72	294	19,623
68	Tiger Woods	69	73	76	77	295	19,437

WGC Mexico Championship

Question of the week to Patrick Reed, on winning the WGC Mexico Championship:

How is it that you putt these greens so well?

"Good question," Reed said. "I don't know."

The mystery solved, it should be noted that the question was raised by Reed's performance on Chapultepec's poa greens — poa annua, a kind of grass that bedevils some golfers.

Across 72 holes of poa greens, Reed one-putted a staggering 45 times.

But that was an item left for the analysts. More practically speaking, Reed broke from a jammed field down the final nine, came from two behind with four holes to play, raced past Bryson DeChambeau with three straight birdies to win by a stroke. Reed shot 69-63-67-67 for an 18-under total of 266, his second WGC and eighth career victory.

And Reed did it under a dark cloud. His sand-brushing violation and penalty in the Hero World Challenge back in December came up again, this time in a Brooks Koepka interview elsewhere.

"All I can control is me and what I do on and off the golf course," Reed said. "I just go out there and try to play the best golf I can."

Reed had to weather some heavy firepower to get this win. After world number one Rory McIlroy led the first round by two with 65, the rush was on. In the second, DeChambeau made seven birdies in an eight-hole stretch in his 63, including a 50-foot putt he was merely trying to lag at the par-three seventh (his 16th). It dropped. "I just threw my hands up in the air," he said. "I mean, come on — who thinks I'm going to make that one." Said his playing partner, Matt Fitzpatrick, "Go get a lottery ticket or something."

DeChambeau led by one over Reed and South Africa's Erik van Rooyen, 30, former University of Minnesota star. Van Rooyen tied the course record with a 62. Reed posted five birdies on his back nine for a 63, to tie for second at 10 under.

The third round had two stars. One was Justin Thomas, who took a one-stroke lead with a 65 to go to 15 under. But Spain's Jon Rahm was the man of the day. He came from 10 behind to set the course and personal record with a 10-under 61, sparked by a hole-in-one, getting to within four. Rahm said he knew something good was happening when he birdied his first four holes. Said Rahm: "I had tap-in, tap-in, tap-in, 10 feet ..."

The final round was just about anybody's. Five players shared the lead, and four were tied heading home. Then van Rooyen double-bogeyed. So did Thomas. McIlroy had only a bogey and a birdie, Rahm two of each. It ended up a Reed-DeChambeau duel. DeChambeau rang up five birdies in six holes from the ninth, but bogeyed the par-three 17th, three-putting from 65 feet. He shot 65 but came up one short.

Reed started his move with a birdie at 12, and passed DeChambeau with three straight birdies from the 15th. Reed had a two-shot cushion playing the 18th and needed it. He drove into the trees and bogeyed but a 67 for 18-under-par 266 was still good for the win.

And about Reed's 45 one-putts on poa. His secret wasn't in the putting, it was in his head, a resignation to the quirky nature of poa.

"You need to have a very short-term memory," he said, "because you're going to hit some great putts that are going to miss and you're going to hit some bad putts that go in."

Club de Golf Chapultepec, Mexico City, Mexico — February 20-23

Par 71 (35-36); 7,355 yards — Purse: $10,500,000

1	**Patrick Reed**	69	63	67	67	266	$1,820,000
2	**Bryson DeChambeau**	68	63	71	65	267	1,150,000
3	**Jon Rahm**	72	69	61	67	269	600,000
	Erik van Rooyen	70	62	67	70	269	600,000
5	Rory McIlroy	65	69	68	68	270	430,000
6	Tyrrell Hatton	69	68	66	68	271	320,667
	Hideki Matsuyama	69	64	71	67	271	320,667
	Justin Thomas	67	66	65	73	271	320,667
9	Billy Horschel	68	71	68	65	272	237,500
	Kevin Na	71	68	65	68	272	237,500
11	Paul Casey	69	68	66	70	273	205,000
12	Abraham Ancer	70	70	67	68	275	182,000
	Gary Woodland	70	69	65	71	275	182,000
14	Sebastian Munoz	71	66	72	67	276	160,000
	Xander Schauffele	72	72	66	66	276	160,000
16	Rafa Cabrera Bello	71	71	67	68	277	143,500
	Carlos Ortiz	75	68	66	68	277	143,500
18	Tommy Fleetwood	70	69	70	69	278	125,500

	Benjamin Hebert	73	70	65	70	278	125,500
	Kevin Kisner	73	69	67	69	278	125,500
	Bubba Watson	67	72	71	68	278	125,500
22	Matt Kuchar	75	67	67	70	279	105,500
	Cameron Smith	73	73	69	64	279	105,500
	Brandt Snedeker	76	69	70	64	279	105,500
	Lee Westwood	69	70	70	70	279	105,500
26	Zander Lombard	73	68	69	70	280	90,000
	Scottie Scheffler	73	70	67	70	280	90,000
	Adam Scott	74	68	68	70	280	90,000
29	Byeong Hun An	75	69	72	65	281	73,500
	Christiaan Bezuidenhout	72	72	70	67	281	73,500
	Ryan Fox	72	68	73	68	281	73,500
	Lanto Griffin	72	69	70	70	281	73,500
	Justin Harding	71	71	67	72	281	73,500
	Sungjae Im	69	72	70	70	281	73,500
	Shane Lowry	72	69	71	69	281	73,500
	Chez Reavie	71	73	67	70	281	73,500
37	Matthew Fitzpatrick	72	70	70	70	282	56,200
	Sergio Garcia	74	72	70	66	282	56,200
	Shaun Norris	75	68	70	69	282	56,200
	Brendon Todd	72	71	71	68	282	56,200
	Bernd Wiesberger	70	76	68	68	282	56,200
42	Branden Grace	71	71	71	70	283	49,500
	Marc Leishman	74	70	68	71	283	49,500
	Robert MacIntyre	76	68	70	69	283	49,500
	Collin Morikawa	72	70	72	69	283	49,500
	Matthias Schwab	71	68	74	70	283	49,500
	Danny Willett	73	68	70	72	283	49,500
48	Dustin Johnson	76	71	67	70	284	45,500
	Zach Murray	71	69	69	75	284	45,500
50	Corey Conners	68	70	72	75	285	44,000
51	Jason Kokrak	73	70	73	70	286	42,500
	Louis Oosthuizen	68	71	76	71	286	42,500
53	Charles Howell III	75	74	68	70	287	39,100
	Jazz Janewattananond	73	73	73	68	287	39,100
	Kurt Kitayama	76	70	72	69	287	39,100
	Francesco Molinari	72	74	71	70	287	39,100
	Victor Perez	81	70	66	70	287	39,100
58	Lucas Herbert	75	70	74	69	288	36,500
	Jordan Spieth	74	73	70	71	288	36,500
	Matt Wallace	74	77	71	66	288	36,500
61	Lucas Glover	71	73	76	69	289	35,000
	Shugo Imahira	74	70	70	75	289	35,000
	Webb Simpson	72	73	74	70	289	35,000
64	Pablo Larrazabal	71	74	70	75	290	34,000
65	Scott Hend	72	75	75	70	292	33,750
66	Michael Lorenzo-Vera	76	73	72	73	294	33,500
67	Jorge Campillo	77	74	69	75	295	33,250
68	Ryo Ishikawa	80	72	73	71	296	33,000
69	Marcus Kinhult	75	74	75	73	297	32,625
	Graeme McDowell	76	74	75	72	297	32,625
71	Sung Kang	76	76	72	75	299	32,250
72	Tae Hee Lee	80	73	74	76	303	32,000

Puerto Rico Open

Thumbnail biography of a most unlikely championship golfer:

He was born and raised in Norway, and was introduced to golf at age 11 by his father, who had picked it up while working in the US. He had available to him a number of courses, a short season and an indoor range. He eventually became quite good, and eventually became an All-American at Oklahoma State University.

Thus from a land of icy mountains, frigid fjords, and breathtaking skiiers emerged — however improbably — Viktor Hovland, 22, the first Norwegian ever to win on the PGA Tour.

And when that final putt dropped, how did it feel to have won the Puerto Rico Open?

"I don't even know," Hovland said, reliving that scary 30-foot birdie on the final hole. "I couldn't quite believe it. I didn't really make that many putts today. I gave it a good rip and thankfully it hit the middle of the cup, because it was going by a little bit. It was some relief and, yeah, a lot of excitement."

As rookie performances go, Hovland's was a masterpiece. He trailed in the first round, tied for the lead in the second and led from there. He shot the par-72 Grand Reserve in 68-66-64-70 for 268, a robust 20 under, won by a stroke, and completed the drama by surviving a rite-of-passage crisis on the final nine.

"It was," Hovland conceded, "certainly a day of lots of ups and downs."

The downs? There was only one and it was almost a killer in the last round.

Before that, Hovland had his share of inspiring golf along the way. In the second round, there was the eagle at the par-five second triggering a six-under-par run across 10 holes to the 66 that tied him for the lead. Then the rampage in the third round, a no-bogey sprint to an eight-birdie 64 for a fingertip lead of one.

The final round started with Hovland, a rookie, chased by two veterans — Martin Laird, a stroke behind, and Jason Teater, two behind. Laird had double-bogeyed the first and eagled the second, but slid from there. That left Hovland and Teater in what boxing used to call a slugfest.

Teater birdied the first, fifth and sixth holes, and tied Hovland, who birdied the fifth. Hovland went back to a two-stroke lead with a wedge hole-out birdie at the 10th against Teater's bogey.

And then came Hovland's crisis. At the par-three 11th, he missed the green, muffed two chip shots, and triple-bogeyed and was tied. Teater, in the pairing just ahead, took the lead with a birdie at the par-five 15th and it lasted as long as it took Hovland to come along to the 15th and chip in for eagle and retake it. Teater birded 17 to tie again, then parred the 18th for a 69 and a 269 total. Hovland's wedge left him a 30-footer for a birdie and the win. And he was afraid he'd leave it short.

"And I just whacked it," Hovland said. "Thankfully, when it was five, six feet out, it was looking pretty good."

And then it looked perfect — the winning birdie. And Hovland had a 70, and the first victory on the tour by a Norwegian.

"Hats off to Viktor," said Teater, thwarted again. "He's a great player and we're going to see it more often."

Hovland's first thought?

"I should probably call my mom or dad," he said.

Grand Reserve Country Club, Rio Grande, Puerto Rico — February 20-23
Par 72 (36-36); 7,506 yards — Purse: $3,000,000

1	**Viktor Hovland**	68	66	64	70	268	$540,000
2	**Josh Teater**	66	68	66	69	269	327,000
3	**Emiliano Grillo**	66	68	69	70	273	159,000
	Sam Ryder	70	65	69	69	273	159,000
	Kyle Stanley	64	70	71	68	273	159,000
6	Martin Laird	67	69	63	75	274	101,250
	Matthew NeSmith	70	71	66	67	274	101,250
	Ted Potter Jr	68	70	67	69	274	101,250
9	Joseph Bramlett	71	67	69	68	275	75,750
	Rob Oppenheim	69	68	69	69	275	75,750
	Wes Roach	67	70	69	69	275	75,750
	Jhonattan Vegas	68	74	71	62	275	75,750
	Vincent Whaley	70	71	69	65	275	75,750
14	Roberto Castro	71	69	70	66	276	50,250
	Kyoung-Hoon Lee	70	69	70	67	276	50,250
	Ben Martin	70	66	69	71	276	50,250
	Adam Schenk	72	65	69	70	276	50,250
	Shawn Stefani	72	65	72	67	276	50,250
	Xinjun Zhang	71	69	66	70	276	50,250
20	Kristoffer Ventura	72	68	70	67	277	31,607
	Tim Wilkinson	69	70	71	67	277	31,607
	Julian Etulain	67	73	67	70	277	31,607
	Brice Garnett	72	68	67	70	277	31,607
	Doug Ghim	69	70	67	71	277	31,607
	William Gordon	70	68	70	69	277	31,607
	Tyler McCumber	70	68	67	72	277	31,607
27	Mark Anderson	68	73	68	69	278	20,119
	Kiradech Aphibarnrat	68	69	72	69	278	20,119
	Cameron Davis	69	71	69	69	278	20,119
	Rhein Gibson	66	70	72	70	278	20,119
	Bill Haas	69	71	69	69	278	20,119
	Maverick McNealy	70	69	67	72	278	20,119
	Robert Streb	69	68	69	72	278	20,119
	Zack Sucher	70	69	69	70	278	20,119
35	Sangmoon Bae	74	67	66	72	279	13,700
	Ryan Brehm	69	73	69	68	279	13,700
	Chris Couch	66	71	69	73	279	13,700
	Bo Hoag	74	67	68	70	279	13,700
	Beau Hossler	72	70	70	67	279	13,700
	George McNeill	69	69	71	70	279	13,700
	Seamus Power	73	69	69	68	279	13,700
	Patrick Rodgers	70	68	66	75	279	13,700
	Johnson Wagner	71	71	68	69	279	13,700
44	Austin Cook	74	67	68	71	280	9,220
	Anirban Lahiri	70	70	70	70	280	9,220
	Nelson Ledesma	70	68	77	65	280	9,220
	Henrik Norlander	66	75	69	70	280	9,220
	Cameron Percy	70	71	70	69	280	9,220
	Peter Uihlein	66	71	73	70	280	9,220
50	Arjun Atwal	73	67	72	69	281	7,620
	David Lingmerth	71	65	69	76	281	7,620
52	MJ Daffue	67	73	70	72	282	7,110
	Derek Ernst	71	71	73	67	282	7,110
	Fabian Gomez	70	70	70	72	282	7,110
	Chase Seiffert	71	69	72	70	282	7,110
	Robby Shelton	68	73	71	70	282	7,110
	DJ Trahan	72	69	68	73	282	7,110
58	Sebastian Cappelen	72	65	74	72	283	6,840
	Michael Gellerman	71	70	72	70	283	6,840
60	Alex Cejka	72	70	74	68	284	6,660
	JJ Henry	69	70	72	73	284	6,660
	Roger Sloan	73	69	68	74	284	6,660
	Bo Van Pelt	71	69	75	69	284	6,660
64	Brendon de Jonge	71	71	72	71	285	6,450
	Brandon Hagy	72	69	74	70	285	6,450
	John Senden	70	70	73	72	285	6,450
67	Scott Brown	67	71	75	75	288	6,300
	Jay McLuen	67	74	72	75	288	6,300
69	Daniel Chopra	69	73	73	76	291	6,210

Honda Classic

That first big win ought to be a time of high spirits and celebrating. Not quite so for Sungjae Im. He wrapped up his first career PGA Tour win in the Honda Classic that Florida day on March 1 after coming from behind in the final round, and his first thought was for his people back home in South Korea and the monster virus now loose on the earth.

"Over in Korea right now," said Im, "I know a lot of people are dealing with the coronavirus. I'm just glad as a Korean player that I can deliver some good news to the countrymen back home."

Im, 21, was growing fast in golf. He'd played on the Japan and Korean tours, was the 2018 Player of the Year on the Web.com Tour (now the Korn Ferry), then Rookie of the Year on the PGA Tour.

The Honda didn't figure to be a young golfer's picnic, not with the strength of its field at the tough par-70 PGA National. The early toll showed as much. Among those missing the cut: Rickie Fowler, Keegan Bradley, Justin Rose and Brooks Koepka.

For Im, meanwhile, who shot 72-66-70 in the first three rounds, the Honda was looking like just another also-ran performance.

Im opened with a scattering of five bogeys in his two-over 72 and was six behind the 66s shot by Tim Lewis and Harris English, both in the tournament on sponsor's exemptions.

In the second round, Im birdied three of his last four holes for the 66 and was three behind Brendan Steele, taking his first lead in nine Hondas at five under with a 67.

And in the windy third round, Im got nowhere with a three-birdie, three-bogey 70 that left him three behind Tommy Fleetwood, who led by one after a 67. Said Fleetwood: "When you look at five under leading after three days, it just shows how tough it is."

The picture changed fast in the final round.

While Fleetwood was faltering, Canada's Mackenzie Hughes and Im, paired a half-hour ahead, crashed the party. Hughes posted four birdies through the 13th, bogeyed 16 and was four under.

Im, after a birdie-par start, birdied three straight from 10, eight and six feet. He scrambled to two more birdies and three bogeys through 15 and was five under. The 17th would be the decisive hole.

"I love being in the mix," said Hughes.

Said Im: "I've been in this spot many times ... I just felt like the experience really helped."

At the par-three, Hughes rolled in a 55-foot downhiller to a thunderous roar. The birdie tied him with Im at five under.

Im broke the tie, calmly rapping in his eight-footer for his own birdie. A par at the last gave him a 66, and a six-under 274 total. He won by one from Mackenzie, who had gone 66-66 over the weekend, when Fleetwood watered his approach at 18 and bogeyed to finish two back.

Im, with his first tour victory after 50 tries, thought of his homeland. "Right now," he said, "all I can do is pray for the best..."

PGA National Resort (Champion), Palm Beach Gardens, Florida — February 27-March 1
Par 70 (35-35); 7,125 yards — Purse: $7,000,000

1	**Sungjae Im**	72	66	70	66	274	$1,260,000
2	**Mackenzie Hughes**	71	72	66	66	275	763,000
3	**Tommy Fleetwood**	70	68	67	71	276	483,000
4	Byeong Hun An	76	66	68	67	277	280,000
	Daniel Berger	69	70	69	69	277	280,000
	Brendan Steele	68	67	71	71	277	280,000
	Lee Westwood	67	69	71	70	277	280,000
8	Cameron Davis	70	67	73	68	278	204,750
	Russell Henley	70	69	70	69	278	204,750
	Gary Woodland	70	67	74	67	278	204,750
11	Wyndham Clark	68	74	71	66	279	145,250
	Luke Donald	70	66	71	72	279	145,250
	Brice Garnett	72	69	72	66	279	145,250
	Mark Hubbard	69	71	69	70	279	145,250
	Maverick McNealy	70	69	71	69	279	145,250
	Robby Shelton	70	69	70	70	279	145,250
17	Harris English	66	74	72	68	280	103,250
	Ryan Palmer	70	72	68	70	280	103,250
	Charl Schwartzel	69	69	70	72	280	103,250
	Richy Werenski	70	68	73	69	280	103,250
21	Patrick Rodgers	69	71	72	69	281	70,583
	Hudson Swafford	70	69	73	69	281	70,583
	Brandon Hagy	70	71	69	71	281	70,583
	Kramer Hickok	73	70	69	69	281	70,583
	Shane Lowry	69	69	73	70	281	70,583
	Jimmy Walker	72	69	70	70	281	70,583
27	Jason Dufner	70	72	68	72	282	46,944
	Adam Long	71	68	74	69	282	46,944
	Jamie Lovemark	69	69	73	71	282	46,944
	Ian Poulter	70	70	72	70	282	46,944
	Sepp Straka	70	67	74	71	282	46,944
	Cameron Tringale	67	72	72	71	282	46,944

	Jhonattan Vegas	70 71 69 72	282	46,944			
	Nick Watney	71 66 73 72	282	46,944			
35	JT Poston	67 69 73 74	283	36,400			
	Rory Sabbatini	71 69 69 74	283	36,400			
	Aaron Wise	71 70 72 70	283	36,400			
38	Talor Gooch	71 69 75 69	284	31,150			
	Beau Hossler	70 71 71 72	284	31,150			
	Kyoung-Hoon Lee	69 71 71 73	284	31,150			
	Matthew NeSmith	71 72 70 71	284	31,150			
42	Chris Baker	70 73 70 72	285	24,850			
	Bud Cauley	70 72 72 71	285	24,850			
	Billy Horschel	73 67 70 75	285	24,850			
	Vaughn Taylor	71 71 71 72	285	24,850			
	Harold Varner III	69 70 76 70	285	24,850			
47	Brian Harman	71 72 74 69	286	18,573			
	Danny Lee	70 73 73 70	286	18,573			
	Matt Jones	70 73 72 71	286	18,573			
	Kurt Kitayama	70 71 71 74	286	18,573			
	Tom Lewis	66 75 71 74	286	18,573			
	Kevin Streelman	69 70 72 75	286	18,573			
53	Stewart Cink	73 69 71 74	287	16,555			
	Grayson Murray	73 68 70 76	287	16,555			
	Sam Ryder	71 71 75 70	287	16,555			
	Scott Stallings	70 72 76 69	287	16,555			
57	Michael Thompson	70 73 75 70	288	16,170			
58	Dylan Frittelli	74 69 72 74	289	15,890			
	Harry Higgs	72 68 72 77	289	15,890			
	Matthew Wolff	72 70 72 75	289	15,890			
61	Mark Anderson	71 72 71 76	290	15,470			
	Austin Cook	72 70 76 72	290	15,470			
	Cameron Percy	69 74 74 73	290	15,470			
64	Sam Burns	69 71 76 75	291	15,120			
	Fabian Gomez	72 69 79 71	291	15,120			
66	Brian Stuard	67 75 77 73	292	14,910			
67	Zach Johnson	67 75 76 75	293	14,770			
68	Patton Kizzire	70 72 74 78	294	14,630			
69	Hayden Buckley	72 70 80 75	297	14,490			

Arnold Palmer Invitational

Arnie Palmer would have shot a thumbs-up and cracked a huge grin. Things were going beautifully at Bay Hill. The wind was whipping, the air chill, the rough thick and the greens were hard and fast. That Saturday Massacre was the toughest day since 1983, and was separating players from their games, some from their poise.

“I don’t normally fist-pump on a Saturday,” said England’s Tyrrell Hatton. But he fired one off automatically after dropping a 30-foot putt for a birdie and the lead. “I don’t think anyone enjoyed today — It was just … it was just so hard.”

Sunday wasn’t much better. “I actually thought I played myself out of it when I made double on 11,” Hatton said. “When I saw the scoreboard … I realised I had a one-shot lead. I’m over the moon.”

Hatton would shake off that double bogey, and to everyone’s surprise — including his own — fight on to win the Arnold Palmer Invitational presented by Mastercard. On a card of 68-69-73-74, a total of four-under 284, a stroke better than Marc Leishman. It was his fifth victory worldwide but first on the PGA Tour.

The Palmer would open with a familiar face, Matt Every, making himself right at home. Every, 37, ranked 309th in the world, had won twice in his 237 starts — the Palmer both times, in 2014 and 2015. And he started the 2020 edition with a 65, leading Rory McIlroy by one. Only 18 players from the 120-man field broke 70 under the tough conditions. But Phil Mickelson, Adam Scott and Henrik Stenson were not among them. All three shot 77.

Hatton would surface in the second round, but not before Bay Hill and the wind had punished the field. Every suffered the rare distinction of going from leading the first round to missing the cut, shooting 65-83. “It kind of happens to me quite a bit,” Every said. Phil Mickelson eagled his 15th (the sixth) to reach the cut number, then double bogeyed the last for a 72 to miss. Henrik Stenson also double-bogeyed 18 and Adam Scott bogeyed, both for 72s, and also missed.

Hatton took the solo lead in the Saturday Massacre, the third round, with that 30-foot birdie at 18 for a 73, triggering a fist pump he hadn’t really intended. “I think it was more shock,” he said.

In the final round, after two bogeys and two birdies on the front, the moment of truth for Hatton came at the par-four 11th. He drove into the water, hit long, chipped short and had to hole a six-footer for a double bogey.

And he patiently parred the last seven holes for his one-stroke win. “So like I say, it’s tough to win and I’m sure everyone’s time comes,” Hatton said. “And thankfully, my time was this week.”

There was another form of success in the weather-battered week. Joel Dahmen closed with a 71 and tied for fifth, which won him a spot in The Open Championship in the summer.

How would he celebrate this?

“I think,” Dahmen said, “maybe just lay on the couch after this one.”

Bay Hill Club & Lodge, Orlando, Florida
Par 72 (36-36); 7,454 yards

March 5-8
Purse: $9,300,000

1	**Tyrrell Hatton**	68	69	73	74	284	$1,674,000
2	**Marc Leishman**	71	69	72	73	285	1,013,700
3	**Sungjae Im**	70	69	74	73	286	641,700
4	Bryson DeChambeau	73	71	72	71	287	455,700
5	Joel Dahmen	72	72	73	71	288	330,731
	Danny Lee	71	67	75	75	288	330,731
	Rory McIlroy	66	73	73	76	288	330,731
	Keith Mitchell	68	75	74	71	288	330,731
9	Harris English	69	70	74	76	289	244,125
	Matthew Fitzpatrick	70	75	75	69	289	244,125
	Sung Kang	69	68	78	74	289	244,125
	Collin Morikawa	70	71	75	73	289	244,125
13	Talor Gooch	67	80	72	71	290	188,325
	Charley Hoffman	70	73	74	73	290	188,325
15	Tom Hoge	70	70	76	75	291	160,425
	Patrick Reed	70	70	80	71	291	160,425
	Scottie Scheffler	67	74	75	75	291	160,425
18	Christiaan Bezuidenhout	68	72	73	79	292	118,885
	Rickie Fowler	71	70	77	74	292	118,885
	Dylan Frittelli	71	72	74	75	292	118,885
	Jason Kokrak	71	75	72	74	292	118,885
	Brendon Todd	68	72	78	74	292	118,885
	Danny Willett	71	71	77	73	292	118,885
24	Max Homa	72	75	70	76	293	72,424
	Beau Hossler	73	72	76	72	293	72,424
	Adam Long	69	74	78	72	293	72,424
	Troy Merritt	71	72	75	75	293	72,424
	Patrick Rodgers	73	70	73	77	293	72,424
	Xander Schauffele	73	74	72	74	293	72,424
	Jimmy Walker	73	69	80	71	293	72,424
	Matt Wallace	69	73	76	75	293	72,424
32	Bud Cauley	71	72	75	76	294	54,289
	Zach Johnson	72	73	74	75	294	54,289
	Graeme McDowell	68	74	76	76	294	54,289
	Ian Poulter	69	77	74	74	294	54,289
36	Zac Blair	74	70	77	74	295	43,323
	Sam Burns	68	72	76	79	295	43,323
	Lanto Griffin	71	73	76	75	295	43,323
	Billy Horschel	72	73	77	73	295	43,323
	Kevin Na	70	72	79	74	295	43,323
	Harold Varner III	70	74	76	75	295	43,323
42	Keegan Bradley	73	72	76	75	296	33,015
	Harry Higgs	72	73	76	75	296	33,015
	Viktor Hovland	74	73	72	77	296	33,015
	Kyoung-Hoon Lee	72	73	72	79	296	33,015
	Steve Stricker	72	74	74	76	296	33,015
47	Stewart Cink	72	70	75	80	297	25,054
	Scott Harrington	71	70	79	77	297	25,054
	Matt Jones	75	68	73	81	297	25,054
	Brooks Koepka	72	73	81	71	297	25,054
	Rory Sabbatini	70	74	74	79	297	25,054
52	Kevin Chappell	72	74	75	77	298	22,274
	Ryan Moore	71	75	82	70	298	22,274
	Matthew Wolff	73	73	81	71	298	22,274
	Xinjun Zhang	70	75	75	78	298	22,274
56	Byeong Hun An	71	76	75	77	299	21,204
	Abraham Ancer	73	74	79	73	299	21,204
	Scott Brown	69	76	79	75	299	21,204
	Hideki Matsuyama	69	73	80	77	299	21,204
	Robby Shelton	72	75	78	74	299	21,204
	Nick Taylor	73	73	74	79	299	21,204
62	Brian Gay	73	72	78	77	300	20,274
	Rod Perry	72	73	79	76	300	20,274
	Doc Redman	73	73	79	75	300	20,274
	Sam Saunders	74	73	78	75	300	20,274
66	Davis Love	72	73	76	80	301	19,809
67	Vaughn Taylor	73	73	77	79	302	19,623
68	Wyndham Clark	74	72	82	80	308	19,437
69	Rob Oppenheim	69	78	83	83	313	19,251

The Players Championship

By March of 2020, the coronavirus pandemic was grinding away worldwide, raging all through life. The world of sports was certainly not immune. The National Basketball Association had just announced it was suspending its season. The NCAA had said it would play its men's and women's tournaments without fans, and then cancelled them outright, along with other winter and spring championships.

The PGA Tour — significantly with the greater freedom of its safer outdoor game — was playing away, and had come to its flagship event, The Players Championship at TPC Sawgrass in Florida. And Commissioner Jay Monahan had said The Players would be played.

Hideki Matsuyama, who played in the morning, went to the interview room after his first round feeling a great satisfaction, and maybe a twinge of anticipation. But not getting ahead of himself. It was just the first round.

Said one golf writer: "You share a record now with Greg Norman, Nick Price, Fred Couples. How does that make you feel?"

The significance wasn't lost on Matsuyama. All three had shot a 63 somewhere in their career. "Those are all major winners," he noted.

He had eagled his final hole, the ninth, with a 25-foot putt for his own jewel of a 63, to the cheers of the fans. He was the leader by two. He was the ninth player to shoot 63 in The Players, and the fifth to do it in the first round. And of those five, three went on to win The Players — Norman, Martin Kaymer and Jason Day.

That could be the stuff of a player's dreams, but that's as far as it would get.

By noon Thursday, Monahan announced that the tournament would continue, but without fans. And still later, he announced it was cancelled. Things had gotten that chaotic.

"We were endeavouring to give our fans a much-needed respite from the current climate," Monahan said. "But as the situation continues to rapidly change, the right thing to do for our players and fans is to pause."

He had the golfers' support.

"I applaud the decisions made and the actions taken by all the sporting organisations and ruling bodies," said Jack Nicklaus, in a statement, "and we hope they produce the intended result, which is simply to keep people safe and not expose them to significant health risks. And until things resume with some normalcy, my friends, please be safe, be smart and stay healthy."

"I believe the tour made the correct decision to both play the event, and then cancel it," said Billy Horschel, a member of the tour's Player Advisory Council. "I have to trust the tour is doing what is best for everyone involved."

"It's the right decision," said Rory McIlroy. "A 100 per cent. If in a few weeks' time, this dies down and everything is okay, it's still the right decision."

"The biggest thing," said Rickie Fowler, "is obviously we don't want this to turn into something bigger than what it is and what it can be."

"I think it's a time to reflect and just really understand, it's just golf," Zach Johnson said. "It's just golf. It's just a sport. So it pales in comparison to what we could be combating at some point."

Foreign members of the tour faced sharper worries.

"I'm pretty scared," said Spain's Jon Rahm, "because there's quite a bit of people in my family with asthma, and my 85-year-old grandma being one of them. And there's nothing I can do because I can't go home, I can't come back."

That night, Monahan announced that the next three tournaments had also been cancelled — the Valspar Championship, the WGC Dell Match Play Championship and the Valero Texas Open. And as things developed, he wasn't done cancelling.

As for returning to normal:

"Whenever the powers that be say it's safe to do so," McIlroy said. "All you can do is follow the guidelines from the CDC and from the people that really know about this thing."

TPC Sawgrass (Stadium), Ponte Vedra Beach, Florida — March 12
Par 72 (36-36); 7,189 yards — Purse: $15,000,000
Abandoned after one round, all players received $52,000

1	Hideki Matsuyama	63	$52,000
2	Harris English	65	52,000
	Christiaan Bezuidenhout	65	52,000
	Si Woo Kim	65	52,000
5	Marc Leishman	67	52,000
	Patrick Cantlay	67	52,000
7	Graeme McDowell	68	52,000
	Daniel Berger	68	52,000
	Webb Simpson	68	52,000
	Jason Dufner	68	52,000
	Rory Sabbatini	68	52,000
	Michael Thompson	68	52,000
	Scottie Scheffler	68	52,000
	Keith Mitchell	68	52,000
	Jim Herman	68	52,000
	Cameron Champ	68	52,000
	Nate Lashley	68	52,000
	Corey Conners	68	52,000
	Rafa Cabrera Bello	68	52,000
	Viktor Hovland	68	52,000
	Collin Morikawa	68	52,000
22	Matthew Wolff	69	52,000
	Victor Perez	69	52,000
	Kiradech Aphibarnrat	69	52,000
	Martin Laird	69	52,000
	Brendon Todd	69	52,000
	Danny Willett	69	52,000
	Jon Rahm	69	52,000
	Adam Long	69	52,000
	Pat Perez	69	52,000
	Tyrrell Hatton	69	52,000
	Adam Hadwin	69	52,000
	Jason Kokrak	69	52,000
	Sepp Straka	69	52,000
	Jimmy Walker	69	52,000
	Sungjae Im	69	52,000

Charles Schwab Challenge

It was welcome back golf with the Charles Schwab Challenge, early in June, a lifetime since the game was shut down by the coronavirus early in March. And a wild welcome it was, with a traffic jam atop the leaderboard, and then a steeplechase down the final stretch, and then Daniel Berger beating Collin Morikawa in a playoff.

But a tournament that ordinarily would have rocked the course was played in silence. Golf had returned, but as in other sports, the fans had been banned in an effort to reduce the spread of the virus.

A tournament without fans? In the first round, Sung Kang made a hole-in-one at the 13th and didn't realise it till he was near the green. "Only a few people, clapping a little bit," he said. "I appreciated it, though." Phil Mickelson made a birdie and pinched the brim of his cap to acknowledge the applause. But it was habit. There was no applause.

Said Ryan Palmer, who hit the first official shot: "I think just being out here is successful ... getting started."

But it was as though Berger had never been away. That final-round 66 was his 28th consecutive round at par or better, dating back eight months to October.

"It was a little different without fans, but it didn't feel like it wasn't a PGA Tour event," said Berger. "You still felt that pressure."

It was the opposite for Morikawa. "It was crazy different," he said. "I think fans bring so much of an energy, so much more excitement to the game."

Neither led through the first three rounds. Berger shot 65-67-67-66, and Morikawa 64-67-67-67 and the pair tied at 15-under 265. In the playoff at the par-four 17th, Berger saved par from behind the green, and Morikawa missed his three-footer for par.

For golfers who hadn't gone at it for three months, they were in mid-season form.

The first round was a proper free-for-all. Harold Varner III and Justin Rose tied for the lead with seven-under 63s. Varner led in the second as well, with a 66 for a career-low 11-under 129. Morikawa was nine under, and Berger eight under, both after 67s. Xander Schauffele joined the youth crew in the third, taking the lead with a 66-197. Morikawa (67) was a stroke back and Berger (67) another shot further back.

It was a wild final round. Eight players led or were tied for the lead, and six were still in the hunt over the final hour.

One of the six, Jordan Spieth, was sidetracked by three quick bogeys on the front nine, shot 71 and tied for 10th. Three others fell short of the playoff by a shot when they didn't birdie the 18th and tied for third at 14-under — Schauffele (69) from 25 feet, Justin Rose (66) from 18 and Bryson DeChambeau (66) from 12. Jason Kokrak (64), who had finished earlier, also just missed a birdie at 18 and was with them in joint third.

And so almost as though it was scripted, the revival of golf came down to a duel between two of the bright, young generation.

Berger came from two shots off the lead and closed with a five-birdie, one-bogey 66. His putting was inspired. After his shortest putt, a seven-footer at the second, the others were from 20, 14, 21 and 10 feet, the last a clutch performance at the 18th.

Morikawa shot a 67 that included two bogeys, and five birdies from three, 11, 21, seven, and a booming 50 feet at the 14th that gave him a share of the lead. He parred in.

On the playoff hole, both were putting for par. Berger holed his two-footer and had his third victory when Morikawa lipped out his three-footer.

Said Berger, of the historic tournament: "I think it went off without a hitch, and everyone did a great job. I'm just very lucky and blessed to be here as the champion."

"It's going to be a little bittersweet," said Morikawa. But of the historic week: "I wanted to just give myself a hug, give my caddie a hug, just the entire week."

"Listen," said PGA Tour Commissioner Jay Monahan, "there is more work to be done, but this is a phenomenal start to our return. I think it's gone about as well as we could have hoped for. I'm proud of our team for that."

There was one final question for Berger. How does he look in a mask?

"About the same I do now," he said. "Gorgeous."

Colonial Country Club, Fort Worth, Texas — June 11-14
Par 70 (35-35); 7,000 yards — Purse: $7,500,000

1	**Daniel Berger**	65 67 67 66	265	$1,350,000
2	**Collin Morikawa**	64 67 67 67	265	817,500
	Berger won playoff at first extra hole			
3	**Bryson DeChambeau**	65 65 70 66	266	366,094
	Jason Kokrak	67 70 65 64	266	366,094
	Justin Rose	63 69 68 66	266	366,094
	Xander Schauffele	65 66 66 69	266	366,094
7	Patrick Reed	68 69 63 67	267	243,750
	Bubba Watson	68 66 68 65	267	243,750
9	Gary Woodland	65 67 66 70	268	219,375
10	Sungjae Im	66 69 67 67	269	181,875
	JT Poston	68 66 67 68	269	181,875
	Jordan Spieth	65 65 68 71	269	181,875
	Justin Thomas	64 68 66 71	269	181,875
14	Abraham Ancer	64 70 66 70	270	129,375
	Cameron Champ	66 71 65 68	270	129,375
	Patrick Rodgers	67 68 70 65	270	129,375
	Rory Sabbatini	68 68 69 65	270	129,375
	Peter Uihlein	69 65 69 67	270	129,375
19	Corey Conners	66 67 67 71	271	95,625
	Joel Dahmen	68 65 70 68	271	95,625
	Branden Grace	66 66 66 73	271	95,625
	Harold Varner III	63 66 70 72	271	95,625
23	Rafa Cabrera Bello	68 67 69 68	272	65,250
	Tony Finau	68 69 67 68	272	65,250
	Lucas Glover	67 70 69 66	272	65,250
	Chesson Hadley	70 68 64 70	272	65,250
	Brian Harman	65 69 70 68	272	65,250
	Viktor Hovland	70 68 68 66	272	65,250
29	Bud Cauley	71 67 67 68	273	51,375
	Kevin Kisner	67 69 68 69	273	51,375
	Ian Poulter	66 70 67 70	273	51,375
32	Keegan Bradley	69 69 67 69	274	41,875
	Matthew Fitzpatrick	68 69 68 69	274	41,875
	Brooks Koepka	68 68 69 69	274	41,875
	Rory McIlroy	68 63 69 74	274	41,875
	Maverick McNealy	69 69 66 70	274	41,875
	Joaquin Niemann	72 65 72 65	274	41,875
38	Bronson Burgoon	68 70 70 67	275	32,625
	Tyler Duncan	65 70 70 70	275	32,625
	Harry Higgs	70 65 71 69	275	32,625
	Billy Horschel	68 68 70 69	275	32,625
	Matt Jones	66 70 69 70	275	32,625
43	Talor Gooch	68 70 69 69	276	24,425
	Adam Hadwin	65 71 68 72	276	24,425
	Mark Hubbard	67 68 67 74	276	24,425
	Zach Johnson	72 66 69 69	276	24,425
	Adam Schenk	66 72 72 66	276	24,425
	Brian Stuard	68 70 74 64	276	24,425
49	Jim Furyk	67 69 67 74	277	18,885
	Charles Howell III	70 67 66 74	277	18,885
	Andrew Landry	68 70 69 70	277	18,885
	Matthew NeSmith	70 67 70 70	277	18,885
	Pat Perez	69 69 70 69	277	18,885
54	Matthew Wolff	67 69 71 71	278	17,775
55	Zac Blair	71 65 75 68	279	17,475
	Louis Oosthuizen	69 69 69 72	279	17,475
	Scottie Scheffler	68 69 69 73	279	17,475
58	Doc Redman	67 70 73 70	280	17,100
	Richy Werenski	72 66 70 72	280	17,100
60	Byeong Hun An	67 71 69 74	281	16,650
	Chris Kirk	68 70 68 75	281	16,650
	Alex Noren	67 71 67 76	281	16,650
	Jhonattan Vegas	64 74 73 70	281	16,650
64	Keith Mitchell	67 71 71 73	282	16,200
	Scott Piercy	67 71 73 71	282	16,200
66	Denny McCarthy	70 68 73 72	283	15,975
67	Jason Dufner	68 69 70 78	285	15,825

RBC Heritage

The RBC Heritage became a kind of anniversary Father's Day victory for Webb Simpson, given a little stretch of the imagination.

He had won on Father's Day in 2012 — the US Open, that is. But for 2020, the US Open was moved to September, in the schedule-juggling due to the Covid-19 pandemic. The Heritage, usually played the week after the Masters, had been cancelled because of the pandemic. But it was revived and inserted into the usual US Open slot. And when he went on a tear down the final nine, beating Abraham Ancer by a stroke, he had his second Father's Day championship and career-seventh win. Simpson, who also won the Waste Management Phoenix Open in February, moved up to number five in the world.

And the yellow shirt on Father's Day was no coincidence.

"I started wearing yellow on Sundays in his honour," Simpson said. "Yellow is his favourite colour. So still feeling my dad all around me from memories. This morning I thought about him, and when I was on the golf course, I thought about him."

To complete the family picture, Simpson won the 2018 Players Championship on Mother's Day.

Simpson won this Heritage against a loaded field. Take the leaderboard going into the final round. Bryson DeChambeau, Brooks Koepka, Dustin Johnson — a powerhouse threesome tied at 12 under par going into the final round — but they were tied for 16th, three shots out of the lead.

The leaderboard was in gridlock. Simpson, Ancer, Ryan Palmer, and Tyrrell Hatton were tied for the lead at 15 under on the par-71 Habour Town. Daniel Berger was in a three-way tie for fifth at 14 under; and tied for eighth at 13 under was a total snarl of eight, including Sergio Garcia and Ian Poulter.

In short, this Heritage was going to need some sorting out. And Simpson did the sorting, but the hard way.

The pursuit was early and furious. Simpson was knocked out of the tie before the turn. He birdied twice on the front, at the two par-fives. But Berger had three, and Ancer and Hatton had four each.

The reversal came on the back nine, after a three-hour rain delay.

"It was a crazy day," Simpson said. "I didn't get it going until 12, and then the putts started going in and I started getting confident."

Simpson caught the rough at 12, but birdied from two feet. He birdied 13 from 22 feet, and the par-five 15th on two putts from 40 feet. He drove into the rough at the par-four 16th, but birdied from 15 feet. And at the par-three 17th, he rolled in from 18 feet, wrapping up his 65-65-68-64 for 262, 22 under. Ancer's first win had flitted away again despite his own 65.

"Yeah, it's tough," Ancer said. "Especially like this week, hitting it even more than enough to win. That's just golf. I'm just going to keep doing what I'm doing, and I think that will eventually happen."

For Simpson, it was a time to remember. He recalled when he called his dad after winning the US Open. "And when he picked up the phone, he just was laughing," Simpson said. "That's kind of what he did when he was happy, he would just laugh. So I'm going to miss that laugh today, for sure."

Harbour Town Golf Links, Hilton Head, South Carolina — June 18-21
Par 71 (36-35); 7,099 yards — Purse: $7,100,000

1	**Webb Simpson**	65	65	68	64	262	$1,278,000
2	**Abraham Ancer**	69	64	65	65	263	773,900
3	**Daniel Berger**	67	69	63	65	264	418,900
	Tyrrell Hatton	71	64	63	66	264	418,900
5	Sergio Garcia	70	65	65	65	265	274,238
	Joaquin Niemann	69	68	63	65	265	274,238
7	Brooks Koepka	67	66	68	65	266	239,625
8	Bryson DeChambeau	67	64	70	66	267	186,375
	Dylan Frittelli	65	69	71	62	267	186,375
	Ryan Palmer	65	67	66	69	267	186,375
	JT Poston	67	69	66	65	267	186,375
	Justin Thomas	72	66	66	63	267	186,375
	Michael Thompson	65	69	66	67	267	186,375
14	Matthew Fitzpatrick	66	66	68	68	268	129,575
	Ian Poulter	64	69	67	68	268	129,575
	Justin Rose	70	67	66	65	268	129,575
17	Harris English	67	70	68	64	269	104,725
	Brice Garnett	65	71	65	68	269	104,725
	Dustin Johnson	68	66	67	68	269	104,725
	Jhonattan Vegas	70	63	69	67	269	104,725
21	Corey Conners	68	63	69	70	270	69,225
	Lucas Glover	69	68	66	67	270	69,225
	Viktor Hovland	65	71	68	66	270	69,225
	Alex Noren	69	66	66	69	270	69,225
	Doc Redman	72	66	65	67	270	69,225
	Rory Sabbatini	70	67	68	65	270	69,225
	Erik van Rooyen	66	68	66	70	270	69,225
28	Christiaan Bezuidenhout	67	69	68	67	271	48,635
	Tyler Duncan	71	63	68	69	271	48,635
	Brian Harman	70	67	69	65	271	48,635
	Sebastian Munoz	65	69	69	68	271	48,635
	Chris Stroud	68	69	63	71	271	48,635
33	Tony Finau	66	68	68	70	272	36,299
	Jim Herman	68	69	69	66	272	36,299
	Mark Hubbard	64	72	68	68	272	36,299
	Andrew Landry	68	67	66	71	272	36,299
	Matthew NeSmith	66	67	73	66	272	36,299
	Carlos Ortiz	69	67	63	73	272	36,299
	Jon Rahm	71	67	66	68	272	36,299
	Sepp Straka	67	71	67	67	272	36,299
41	Jason Dufner	69	66	70	68	273	25,205
	Adam Hadwin	72	65	67	69	273	25,205
	Max Homa	67	69	69	68	273	25,205
	Matt Kuchar	70	66	67	70	273	25,205
	Rory McIlroy	72	65	66	70	273	25,205
	Sam Ryder	69	65	68	71	273	25,205
	Charl Schwartzel	71	67	66	69	273	25,205
48	Joel Dahmen	68	68	63	75	274	18,673
	Ernie Els	67	67	72	68	274	18,673
	Bill Haas	71	66	68	69	274	18,673
	Scott Stallings	70	68	65	71	274	18,673
52	Harry Higgs	69	68	70	68	275	16,827
	Matt Jones	69	69	66	71	275	16,827
	Cheng Tsung Pan	68	68	70	69	275	16,827
	Brian Stuard	68	70	70	67	275	16,827
	Vaughn Taylor	67	69	70	69	275	16,827
	Bubba Watson	69	68	73	65	275	16,827
58	Chesson Hadley	68	68	68	72	276	16,117
	Bernhard Langer	69	67	71	69	276	16,117
	Maverick McNealy	72	66	66	72	276	16,117
61	Branden Grace	69	69	67	72	277	15,833
62	Stewart Cink	68	68	72	70	278	15,620
	Gary Woodland	69	68	71	70	278	15,620
64	Wyndham Clark	68	66	70	75	279	15,194
	Collin Morikawa	68	69	68	74	279	15,194
	Xander Schauffele	72	66	75	66	279	15,194
	Matt Wallace	68	68	66	77	279	15,194
68	Wesley Bryan	69	68	73	70	280	14,768
	Jordan Spieth	66	70	75	69	280	14,768
70	Mackenzie Hughes	66	68	69	78	281	14,342
	Danny Lee	68	67	76	70	281	14,342
	Peter Malnati	71	67	69	74	281	14,342
	Troy Merritt	70	68	72	71	281	14,342
74	Ryan Armour	69	68	71	74	282	13,916
	Chez Reavie	68	70	68	76	282	13,916

Travelers Championship

It wasn't much as golf ovations go. Just a handful of tournament officials, course workers and golf writers behind the 18th green. A representative group in the Covid-19 no-fan days. There were no feverish high-fives and wild whooping. It was just polite applause for a player who earned it.

Dustin Johnson, after struggling in the first two rounds, had just tapped in for par on the final hole to win the Travelers Championship, making 2020 the 13th consecutive season in his career that he'd won.

"I'm definitely proud of myself for continuing the streak," Johnson said, "and I want to keep it going."

And then he noted, "It was a long time between wins, though."

Over a year, actually. This was late June 2020. His previous win was the WGC Mexico Championship in February 2019. He was back in the pack with his first two rounds of 69-64, then surged with 61-67 for a 19-under 261 total to edge Kevin Streelman by a shot.

This Travelers was a scoring festival at the TPC River Highlands, near Hartford, Connecticut. The tournament opened with 106 of the starting field of 156 breaking the par of 70, rivalling the tournament record of 111 in the second round in 2011.

Johnson just managed to break par with a 69, nine off the lead of Canadian Mackenzie Hughes with his career low of 60. His try for a 59 was a 40-footer at his final hole that just pulled up short. He shrugged it off. "I kind of joked ... that 59 wasn't even the record," Hughes said, referring to Jim Furyk's 58 in 2016. Stacked behind Hughes were Rory McIlroy, Xander Schauffele and Viktor Hovland, all with 63s.

Phil Mickelson, in his first tournament since turning 50, leaped into the second-round lead with a 63 to be 13 under. He bombed away with his driver. "But really," he said, "I just want to get it in play and let my wedges take over." He led by a stroke over Hughes (68) and Will Gordon (62).

Johnson surfaced in the third round, as did Brendon Todd, going for his third win of the season. Both shot flawless career-low 61s, with Todd taking a two-stroke lead at 18 under. He noticed Johnson's name on the leaderboards. "I just use it as motivation to go out there and make some more birdies," he said. Just two of Johnson's birdie putts were longer than nine feet — the 18-footer at 10 and the 21-footer at 12.

For all of his fireworks, Johnson was most relieved by his par save with a 10-foot putt at the par-three 11th.

"Probably the most important part of the round," he said, "would have been 11, where I made that really good bunker save because I put myself in just an awful spot with a wedge."

A burst of three straight birdies was the key to his final-round 67 and one-stroke win. At the par-three eighth, he holed a 27-foot putt. It was a five-footer at the ninth, and at the 10th, he chipped in from 24 feet. It was not only his first win in over a year, but his first without fans.

"It was definitely strange," Johnson said. "But you still can feel the pressure, you still can feel how important a golf tournament it is, and you're coming down the stretch — to me it felt the same, whether it was a million fans or zero."

TPC River Highlands, Cromwell, Connecticut — June 25-28
Par 70 (35-35); 6,841 yards — Purse: $7,400,000

1	**Dustin Johnson**	69	64	61	67	261	$1,332,000
2	**Kevin Streelman**	66	66	63	67	262	806,600
3	**William Gordon**	66	62	71	64	263	436,600
	Mackenzie Hughes	60	68	68	67	263	436,600
5	Kevin Na	66	66	65	67	264	303,400
	Ryan Armour	67	66	68	64	265	233,470
	Bryson DeChambeau	65	67	65	68	265	233,470
	Patton Kizzire	66	66	66	67	265	233,470
	Scott Stallings	66	68	64	67	265	233,470
	Brendan Steele	69	62	68	66	265	233,470
11	Patrick Cantlay	66	67	69	65	267	139,983
	Si Woo Kim	68	66	68	65	267	139,983
	Doc Redman	68	67	69	63	267	139,983
	Abraham Ancer	67	65	66	69	267	139,983
	Viktor Hovland	63	69	67	68	267	139,983
	Zach Johnson	68	64	67	68	267	139,983
	Rory McIlroy	63	68	69	67	267	139,983
	Seungyul Noh	64	68	66	69	267	139,983
	Brendon Todd	66	65	61	75	267	139,983
20	Joel Dahmen	67	68	68	65	268	87,320
	Lucas Glover	66	68	71	63	268	87,320
	Xander Schauffele	63	68	70	67	268	87,320
	Brian Stuard	65	67	68	68	268	87,320
24	Wesley Bryan	67	66	67	69	269	57,628

	Sam Burns	68 66 68 67	269	57,628
	Lanto Griffin	66 67 68 68	269	57,628
	Adam Long	67 69 65 68	269	57,628
	Phil Mickelson	64 63 71 71	269	57,628
	Patrick Reed	70 66 69 64	269	57,628
	Kyle Stanley	69 65 65 70	269	57,628
	Jhonattan Vegas	71 65 67 66	269	57,628
32	Paul Casey	69 66 67 68	270	42,254
	Tyler Duncan	64 70 69 67	270	42,254
	Sergio Garcia	64 70 70 66	270	42,254
	Russell Henley	65 69 72 64	270	42,254
	Harold Varner III	66 69 69 66	270	42,254
37	Rafa Cabrera Bello	65 70 72 64	271	34,410
	Tom Hoge	67 68 66 70	271	34,410
	Mark Hubbard	68 66 70 67	271	34,410
	Jon Rahm	66 68 66 71	271	34,410
41	Joseph Bramlett	69 65 71 67	272	27,750
	Charley Hoffman	67 67 65 73	272	27,750
	Hank Lebioda	69 67 66 70	272	27,750
	Henrik Norlander	68 68 68 68	272	27,750
	Brandt Snedeker	67 69 66 70	272	27,750
46	Byeong Hun An	68 68 69 68	273	19,869
	Jason Day	67 69 69 68	273	19,869
	Sung Kang	65 67 70 71	273	19,869
	Louis Oosthuizen	64 70 71 68	273	19,869
	Chez Reavie	70 66 68 69	273	19,869
	Michael Thompson	64 71 70 68	273	19,869
	Richy Werenski	67 68 71 67	273	19,869
	Aaron Wise	68 67 69 69	273	19,869
54	Kevin Chappell	68 68 69 69	274	17,316
	Austin Cook	71 65 69 69	274	17,316
	Jim Furyk	69 65 70 70	274	17,316
	Jordan Spieth	67 69 69 69	274	17,316
58	Sungjae Im	68 68 71 68	275	16,872
	Marc Leishman	66 65 72 72	275	16,872
60	Emiliano Grillo	67 66 71 72	276	16,502
	Shane Lowry	66 69 74 67	276	16,502
	Troy Merritt	68 64 72 72	276	16,502
63	Joaquin Niemann	68 66 68 75	277	16,206
64	Ian Poulter	67 69 73 69	278	16,058
65	Scott Brown	69 66 72 72	279	15,910
66	Roger Sloan	67 69 71 73	280	15,762
67	Greg Chalmers	69 67 75 73	284	15,614
68	Luke Donald	69 65 73 79	286	15,466

Rocket Mortgage Classic

It's almost as if Bryson DeChambeau, with all that new muscle, had just been loosening up, unconcerned that he was trailing through the first three rounds. Then having served his formidable notice, he went out in the final round, thrashed Detroit Golf Club and walked away comfortably with the Rocket Mortgage Classic.

Although some things could ruffle that calm. Like the episode in the first round. He'd made four birdies and an eagle on the back nine, then missed an eight-foot par putt at the 18th, shot 66, and it cost him a share of the lead.

"That really got me a little agitated," he said. "It's going to put a little fire in my belly."

This was DeChambeau — "The Scientist," some labeled him — the former physics student, given to analysing and studying, who had concluded that contrary to the view of many, more muscle and more mass would make him a much better golfer. And so he had devoted himself to gulping down protein nutrition drinks and lifting weights and exercising, and when he came back out after the golf Covid-19 shutdown, he had put on some 20 pounds and weighed about 240, and turned to a power game. His 350-yard drives and breezy escapes from the rough suggested as much.

His scores didn't vary much in the Rocket. He shot 66-67-67 in the first three rounds, and trailed by one, one and three strokes. Then he asserted himself and closed with an eight-birdie, one-bogey 65 for a 23-under 265 total and won by three.

The tournament had been up for grabs, with new leaders in each round, including the fascinating Matthew Wolff, one of the tour's young guns. Wolff shot his second straight 64 for a three-stroke lead in the third round and said he drew his inspiration from, well, the jingle music coming from an ice cream truck.

"I heard an ice cream truck circling the property," Wolff said. "Seemed like every time I heard that, I made birdie or made a putt, so I've got to give a lot of credit to that."

Wolff stumbled in the final round, bogeying five of his first 10 holes. And DeChambeau put on a stunning show of power golf. At the fourth, a par-five of 621 yards, he drove wide-left, then hit his second 276 yards from the rough, over some tall trees, and two-putted from 37 feet for a birdie. And at the 399-yard 13th, he waited at the tee for the green to clear. "I really could have gotten there," he said. He breezed through the final round. He birdied five of his first 10 holes, bogeyed the 14th, then birdied the last three.

"This is a little emotional for me because I did something a little different," he said. "I changed my body, changed my mindset in the game, and I was able to accomplish a win while playing a completely different style of golf. I hope it's an inspiration to a lot of people."

Detroit Golf Club, Detroit, Michigan — July 2-5
Par 72 (36-36); 7,334 yards — Purse: $7,500,000

1	**Bryson DeChambeau**	66	67	67	65	265	$1,350,000
2	**Matthew Wolff**	69	64	64	71	268	817,500
3	**Kevin Kisner**	65	69	70	66	270	517,500
4	Ryan Armour	69	64	67	72	272	300,000
	Adam Hadwin	67	69	69	67	272	300,000
	Tyrrell Hatton	68	67	69	68	272	300,000
	Danny Willett	71	68	67	66	272	300,000
8	Maverick McNealy	68	68	71	66	273	211,875
	Troy Merritt	68	67	67	71	273	211,875
	Webb Simpson	68	64	71	70	273	211,875
	Sepp Straka	68	66	72	67	273	211,875
12	Jonathan Byrd	70	69	67	68	274	131,875
	Cameron Champ	69	68	71	66	274	131,875
	Rickie Fowler	67	71	69	67	274	131,875
	Viktor Hovland	69	67	67	71	274	131,875
	Mark Hubbard	67	66	69	72	274	131,875
	Tom Lewis	68	71	66	69	274	131,875
	Henrik Norlander	67	70	69	68	274	131,875
	Seamus Power	67	66	69	72	274	131,875
	Matt Wallace	66	69	68	71	274	131,875
21	Lucas Glover	67	70	71	67	275	69,042
	Lanto Griffin	70	66	70	69	275	69,042
	Hideki Matsuyama	71	68	65	71	275	69,042
	Doc Redman	65	70	70	70	275	69,042
	Kristoffer Ventura	69	68	68	70	275	69,042
	Richy Werenski	67	66	72	70	275	69,042
	Wesley Bryan	69	69	65	72	275	69,042
	Chris Kirk	67	65	70	73	275	69,042
	Luke List	69	67	67	72	275	69,042
30	Sam Burns	68	69	69	70	276	43,042
	Chris Stroud	66	71	69	70	276	43,042
	Brian Stuard	68	67	73	68	276	43,042
	Hudson Swafford	67	68	72	69	276	43,042
	Cameron Tringale	68	67	72	69	276	43,042
	Harold Varner III	70	67	70	69	276	43,042
	Fabian Gomez	70	68	66	72	276	43,042
	Adam Schenk	68	71	66	71	276	43,042
	JJ Spaun	66	69	70	71	276	43,042
39	Austin Cook	69	70	72	66	277	30,375
	Emiliano Grillo	66	70	71	70	277	30,375
	Brandon Hagy	67	68	73	69	277	30,375
	Scott Harrington	71	66	67	73	277	30,375
	George McNeill	67	71	71	68	277	30,375
	Scott Stallings	65	71	70	71	277	30,375
45	Arjun Atwal	70	69	66	73	278	21,019
	Chris Baker	69	68	68	73	278	21,019
	Keegan Bradley	69	69	73	67	278	21,019
	Michael Gellerman	68	70	68	72	278	21,019
	Rhein Gibson	67	72	68	71	278	21,019
	Kyoung-Hoon Lee	69	69	72	68	278	21,019
	Pat Perez	68	68	70	72	278	21,019
	Patrick Rodgers	69	70	69	70	278	21,019
53	Luke Donald	69	70	69	71	279	17,738
	Tyler Duncan	68	70	70	71	279	17,738
	Tony Finau	69	70	66	74	279	17,738
	Sungjae Im	70	69	70	70	279	17,738
57	Zac Blair	70	68	69	73	280	17,025
	Si Woo Kim	71	67	70	72	280	17,025
	Seungyul Noh	68	71	70	71	280	17,025
	Brendon Todd	68	69	70	73	280	17,025
	Johnson Wagner	67	71	70	72	280	17,025
62	Kevin Chappell	69	69	66	77	281	16,500
	Josh Teater	70	69	72	70	281	16,500
64	Mark Anderson	68	68	73	73	282	16,200
	Michael Thompson	69	68	73	72	282	16,200
66	Ted Potter Jr	68	68	69	78	283	15,975
67	Steve Stricker	70	67	71	76	284	15,825
68	Zack Sucher	69	69	74	73	285	15,600
	Bo Van Pelt	70	69	73	73	285	15,600
70	Harry Higgs	69	70	78	73	290	15,375

Workday Charity Open

It was the Silent Hole-in-One, the signature moment in the Workday Charity Open, marking no-fan golf during the Covid-19 pandemic as few things could. It came in the first round, Keegan Bradley hitting his six-iron tee shot at the par-three fourth. He arrived at the green, fixed his ball mark but couldn't see his ball anywhere.

Five or six people watched silently from behind the green.

"And then," Bradley said, "someone just goes, 'It's in the hole.' Like, really casually. It was just bizarre."

The hole-in-one is probably the loudest event in golf. This one had just been greeted by silence.

The Workday Charity Open itself was a signature event of golf during the pandemic. The Workday was created almost on the spot in May when the tour announced that the John Deere Classic had been cancelled because of the pandemic. A month later, early in June, the Workday was announced as the replacement tournament. It would be played on the John Deere dates, July 9-12, at Muirfield Village, site of Jack Nicklaus' Memorial Tournament the following week. Something over two months from announcement to first tee-time. It would be the first time in 63 years that the tour would have tournaments on the same course in consecutive weeks.

The Workday didn't lack for marquee names — Phil Mickelson, Brooks Koepka, Jon Rahm, Rickie Fowler among them — but the tournament turned into a shootout of the tour's youth movement. Collin Morikawa, 23, Viktor Hovland, 22, and Justin Thomas, 27, though the latter had already played himself well out of the youth movement. Morikawa led through the first two rounds, Thomas the third, and then all three led at one time or another in the final round, with Morikawa winning in a playoff.

They were the final threesome in the last round. Hovland birdied three straight early, but bogeyed twice coming in, shot 71, and finished third by four strokes. "You're always nervous," Hovland said, "so it doesn't come to you naturally just because you've been there before."

Thomas started the final round leading Hovland by two and Morikawa by three, but the edge was gone quickly. Thomas bogeyed the second and third, Hovland notched three birdies and Morikawa birdied twice, then eagled the par-five fifth on a three-foot putt. The game was definitely on.

Thomas went on a putting rampage — 10 straight one-putt greens from the sixth. Four were pars, five were birdies, and then an eagle from 23 feet at the 15th. And he led by three with three holes to play.

Then he missed the green at 16 and bunkered his drive at 18, bogeyed both and shot 69. Morikawa went birdie-bogey-birdie from the 12th, then birdied 17 for a 66 to tie Thomas at 19-under 269.

The first playoff hole, the 18th, was a classic. Thomas holed a 50-foot putt for a birdie. Morikawa faced a 25-footer to tie. Said Thomas: "I just tried to keep my head down and think he's going to make it, but hoping he's not, selfishly. But he did."

They parred the 18th on the next try, and then on the third, at the 10th, Thomas drove behind a tree and bogeyed, and Morikawa two-putted for a par and his second tour win.

"I shot 19 under par on a pretty tough golf course," Thomas said. "But the fact of the matter is I just completely gave it up, so that's just going to hurt for a while."

For Morikawa, a pro for barely a year, it was almost a bittersweet victory. Thomas had befriended him early on. "Justin is an awesome player, awesome dude, as well," Morikawa said. "He made things a lot easier for me. Props to him."

Muirfield Village Golf Club, Dublin, Ohio — July 9-12
Par 72 (36-36); 7,392 yards — Purse: $6,200,000

1	**Collin Morikawa**	65	66	72	66	269	$1,116,000
2	**Justin Thomas**	68	66	66	69	269	675,800
	Morikawa won playoff at third extra hole						
3	**Viktor Hovland**	69	67	66	71	273	427,800
4	Chase Seiffert	68	69	70	67	274	303,800
5	Ian Poulter	68	69	69	70	276	239,475
	Gary Woodland	73	68	66	69	276	239,475
7	Patrick Cantlay	70	72	70	65	277	169,393
	Jason Day	69	71	70	67	277	169,393
	Russell Henley	70	70	70	67	277	169,393
	Charley Hoffman	74	68	68	67	277	169,393
	Billy Horschel	72	69	70	66	277	169,393
	Sam Ryder	70	72	66	69	277	169,393
	Kevin Streelman	70	64	71	72	277	169,393
14	Matt Jones	69	72	67	70	278	113,150
	Xander Schauffele	69	73	66	70	278	113,150
	Sepp Straka	69	70	69	70	278	113,150
17	Sam Burns	69	66	70	74	279	88,350
	Stewart Cink	72	69	68	70	279	88,350
	Talor Gooch	71	68	71	69	279	88,350
	Chez Reavie	70	72	70	67	279	88,350
	Rory Sabbatini	69	68	69	73	279	88,350
22	MJ Daffue	73	69	65	73	280	59,830
	Rickie Fowler	72	69	66	73	280	59,830
	Jerry Kelly	75	67	68	70	280	59,830
	Hideki Matsuyama	67	68	72	73	280	59,830
	Troy Merritt	69	72	67	72	280	59,830
27	Matthew Fitzpatrick	73	69	71	68	281	45,260
	Brian Gay	71	71	68	71	281	45,260
	Jon Rahm	72	70	75	64	281	45,260
	Roger Sloan	68	73	70	70	281	45,260
31	Zach Johnson	67	74	69	72	282	37,898
	Joaquin Niemann	69	72	73	68	282	37,898
	Henrik Norlander	70	69	71	72	282	37,898
	Tim Wilkinson	68	72	72	70	282	37,898
35	Adam Hadwin	66	73	76	68	283	31,543
	Kyoung-Hoon Lee	71	71	74	67	283	31,543
	Graeme McDowell	68	73	70	72	283	31,543
	Richy Werenski	71	67	74	71	283	31,543
39	Keegan Bradley	69	71	74	70	284	23,250
	Corey Conners	71	69	74	70	284	23,250
	Austin Cook	70	70	75	69	284	23,250
	Matt Kuchar	69	69	74	72	284	23,250
	Shane Lowry	69	72	74	69	284	23,250
	Pat Perez	68	72	72	72	284	23,250
	Patrick Reed	68	70	76	70	284	23,250
	Adam Schenk	72	70	71	71	284	23,250
	Matt Wallace	72	70	75	67	284	23,250
48	Mackenzie Hughes	70	68	72	75	285	16,306
	Cheng Tsung Pan	73	69	73	70	285	16,306
	Chris Stroud	71	71	71	72	285	16,306
	Nick Taylor	67	71	76	71	285	16,306
52	Chesson Hadley	73	69	71	73	286	14,849
	Adam Long	68	73	72	73	286	14,849
	JJ Spaun	73	69	73	71	286	14,849
	Brendan Steele	69	70	71	76	286	14,849
56	Jason Dufner	69	72	71	75	287	14,384
	Steve Stricker	69	70	73	75	287	14,384
58	Phil Mickelson	73	69	74	72	288	14,074
	Andrew Putnam	69	73	76	70	288	14,074
	Scott Stallings	74	68	71	75	288	14,074
61	Bronson Burgoon	74	68	69	78	289	13,764
	Carlos Ortiz	74	68	74	73	289	13,764
63	Sungjae Im	72	70	71	77	290	13,578
64	Si Woo Kim	71	71	72	77	291	13,454
65	Peter Malnati	68	72	84	68	292	13,268
	Louis Oosthuizen	68	70	79	75	292	13,268
67	Cameron Champ	70	72	75	78	295	13,082

Memorial Tournament

Jon Rahm was about to win the Memorial Tournament with ridiculous ease. He was leading by eight shots starting down the final nine. Eight — with nine to play. It was all over.

But somewhere, someone was raising the words of the late, great baseball philosopher Yogi Berra: "It ain't over till it's over."

Rahm did win it, finally. After he took three bogeys and a double bogey, he parred the last two holes to post his fourth PGA Tour victory, his 10th overall, and became the second Spaniard, after the late Seve Ballesteros, to rise to number one in the world.

"I'll probably wake up tomorrow morning and still won't have it processed," a baffled Rahm said. "I can't really explain it."

The numbers can't explain it either, merely chart it.

Rahm had already done a remarkable job. In the third round, he birdied four straight from the 13th. And with Ryan Palmer bogeying 16 and 18 and Tony Finau double-bogeying 12 and 17, Rahm went from a four-stroke deficit to a four-stroke lead.

In the final round, Finau knocked himself out of the running with a front nine of 42. And when Rahm birdied twice going out and Palmer bogeyed twice, Rahm led by eight going into the final nine. Then the Memorial got really memorable for Rahm.

— 10th, par four: Rahm drove into the rough, then two-putted from 14 feet. Bogey. Lead down to seven.

— 11th, par five: Rahm drove into the water, took a penalty drop, took three to reach the green and two-putted from eight feet. Double-bogey seven. Lead down to five.

— 12th, par three: Palmer birdied, Rahm parred. Rahm's lead down to four.

— 14th, par four: Rahm's approach caught the greenside bunker. He two-putted from five feet for bogey. Lead down to three.

— 16th, par three: Rahm missed the green, but hit a brilliant flop shot that rolled in for a birdie. But replays showed that his ball had moved when he put his wedge behind it. The two-shot penalty gave him a bogey four. His lead was down to two.

— 17th, par four: Palmer bogeyed after missing the fairway. Rahm's margin was back to three.

But it took more solid play to get that home. Rahm drove into a fairway bunker at the 17th and hit into the rough from there, but finally holed a four-footer for his par. And at the par-four 18th, he missed the fairway and missed the green, but chipped to two feet and saved par for a three-over 75 and a nine-under 279 total, and a three-stroke win.

Rahm spoke of more than golf. He spoke of family back home in Spain, dealing with the pandemic, and of a grandma who helped raise him.

"So it was so easy to get caught up on arbitrary things like the penalty stroke," he said. "It moved; I accept it. It doesn't change the outcome of the tournament. It just puts a little bit of an asterisk in it in the sense of I wish I could just keep that birdie because it was one of the greatest shots of my life, right?"

Palmer's position went from hopeless to just a glimmer. "Grinding, that's all I can say," Palmer said. "I just didn't quite have it, swing-wise. Just a little lazy. Probably, I'm sure, the moment."

Added Rahm: "But still, man, one of the best performances of my life ... finished today with some clutch up-and-downs. And God, I'm glad it happened that way. As a Spaniard, I'm kind of glad it happened that way."

Muirfield Village Golf Club, Dublin, Ohio — July 16-19
Par 72 (36-36); 7,392 yards — Purse: $9,300,000

1 Jon Rahm	69	67	68	75	279	$1,674,000
2 Ryan Palmer	67	68	73	74	282	1,013,700
3 Matthew Fitzpatrick	75	66	74	68	283	641,700
4 Jason Day	73	66	72	73	284	418,500
Matt Wallace	72	70	70	72	284	418,500
6 Mackenzie Hughes	74	66	73	72	285	325,500
Henrik Norlander	74	66	71	74	285	325,500
8 Tony Finau	66	69	73	78	286	290,625
9 Kevin Na	74	69	71	73	287	272,025
10 Luke List	70	68	79	71	288	234,825
Patrick Reed	71	76	70	71	288	234,825
Xinjun Zhang	72	73	70	73	288	234,825
13 Harris English	70	73	74	72	289	171,585
Billy Horschel	76	71	70	72	289	171,585

	Xander Schauffele	78 69 72 70	289	171,585
	Jordan Spieth	70 70 74 75	289	171,585
	Brendan Steele	68 75 71 75	289	171,585
18	Si Woo Kim	73 73 70 74	290	127,875
	Patrick Rodgers	70 72 71 77	290	127,875
	Steve Stricker	73 67 77 73	290	127,875
	Justin Thomas	74 67 75 74	290	127,875
22	Christiaan Bezuidenhout	72 69 78 72	291	78,120
	Corey Conners	73 74 72 72	291	78,120
	Dylan Frittelli	73 68 74 76	291	78,120
	Keith Mitchell	74 71 73 73	291	78,120
	Chez Reavie	71 67 74 79	291	78,120
	Scottie Scheffler	71 73 70 77	291	78,120
	Brendon Todd	75 72 68 76	291	78,120
	Erik van Rooyen	76 69 73 73	291	78,120
	Matthew Wolff	77 68 70 76	291	78,120
	Gary Woodland	68 70 76 77	291	78,120
32	Patrick Cantlay	70 70 73 79	292	51,925
	Sergio Garcia	72 73 73 74	292	51,925
	Matt Kuchar	76 67 76 73	292	51,925
	Rory McIlroy	70 72 72 78	292	51,925
	Bubba Watson	78 68 70 76	292	51,925
	Danny Willett	74 66 70 82	292	51,925
38	Lucas Glover	69 72 74 78	293	43,245
	Carl Pettersson	72 72 79 70	293	43,245
40	Scott Harrington	74 69 76 75	294	37,665
	Marc Leishman	72 75 71 76	294	37,665
	Ryan Moore	70 75 75 74	294	37,665
	Tiger Woods	71 76 71 76	294	37,665
44	Bud Cauley	75 71 73 76	295	30,225
	Jason Dufner	72 73 73 77	295	30,225
	Lanto Griffin	72 73 76 74	295	30,225
	Cheng Tsung Pan	72 74 75 74	295	30,225
48	Jim Furyk	72 68 79 77	296	23,839
	Viktor Hovland	74 66 77 79	296	23,839
	Charles Howell III	69 77 73 77	296	23,839
	Collin Morikawa	76 70 73 77	296	23,839
	Sebastian Munoz	75 70 72 79	296	23,839
	Carlos Ortiz	74 72 70 80	296	23,839
54	Adam Hadwin	76 70 70 81	297	21,762
	Phil Mickelson	72 74 73 78	297	21,762
	Louis Oosthuizen	72 73 73 79	297	21,762
	Kevin Streelman	75 71 78 73	297	21,762
58	Abraham Ancer	72 75 72 79	298	21,111
	Zach Johnson	76 70 75 77	298	21,111
	Denny McCarthy	75 71 76 76	298	21,111
61	Sepp Straka	73 72 79 75	299	20,739
62	Stewart Cink	73 74 74 79	300	20,088
	Bo Hoag	75 67 79 79	300	20,088
	Brooks Koepka	72 75 73 80	300	20,088
	Scott Piercy	72 73 77 78	300	20,088
	Vijay Singh	71 74 78 77	300	20,088
	Jimmy Walker	70 72 81 77	300	20,088
68	Keegan Bradley	73 73 77 78	301	19,158
	Tyler Duncan	75 71 71 84	301	19,158
	William McGirt	76 69 73 83	301	19,158
	Cameron Smith	74 72 76 79	301	19,158
72	Mark Hubbard	70 76 76 80	302	18,693
73	Sung Kang	74 72 78 80	304	18,507
74	Joel Dahmen	75 72 78 81	306	18,321

3M Open

Michael Thompson was swarmed by his family on the 18th green at the 3M Open, but not in the usual championship celebration. In this time of the coronavirus pandemic of 2020, Thompson was at the 18th green at TPC Twin Cities at Blaine, Minnesota, and Rachel and the kids joined him, but on a FaceTime hookup from back home in Sea Island, Georgia. Such was life on the PGA Tour in 2020.

"It is a little sad that there wasn't anybody out there to cheer on some of the great shots that I hit toward the end," Thompson said, "but I know everybody who's rooting for me at least was watching and screaming at their TV."

Thompson, 35, had one previous PGA Tour victory, the 2013 Honda Classic. He was in his 228th career start, and he was in for a toe-to-toe battle in the 3M. He trailed only in the first round, by only a stroke, shooting the par-71 TPC Twin Cities in 64-66-68-67 for a total of 265, 19 under.

Thompson had slugged it out for three rounds with Richy Werenski, 29, a four-year tour veteran seeking his first win, and finally had to outrun Adam Long, who almost stole the show. Long had just barely made the cut, and then he nearly won.

Werenski took the first-round lead with a birdie at the par-five 18th on a wedge to two feet. He made nine birdies and a bogey for an eight-under 63, and Thompson shot a flawless seven-birdie 64. From there, they were tied at 12 under in the second and 15 under in the third.

"There's still a lot of golf left," Werenski said. "I just kind of want to keep hanging around and hopefully something happens."

It could be argued that Thompson won the tournament with that bold par at the par-five 18th in the third round. He'd watered his tee shot and had to take his penalty drop in the intermediate rough, and had 267 yards over the water to the flag. Hit or lay up? "It's time to step up," said his caddie, Damian Lopez. Thompson launched a fairway wood over the water, caught the back bunker, popped it out to within inches and tapped in for his par. "I'm honestly just proud of myself for stepping up," he said.

Meanwhile, another force had stepped in. Long, 33, a one-time winner, had missed three cuts in his previous five starts. He made this cut on the number, with 68-72 for two under. Then he finished 63-64, with 16 birdies and one bogey, for 17 under and found himself waiting nervously for the end. "I'll get something to eat — hang out," he said.

Werenski finished with a 70 and in a nine-way tie for third, three behind.

Long was a happy golfer. "This weekend I had nothing to lose," he said. "I'm in 50th place starting on Saturday morning. So tried to cruise up, and here we are."

Thompson made his way home. A bogey and three birdies left him within reach of the win with three to play. He got the winner at the 16th, where he splashed a bunker shot to two feet. He added the cushion at the 18th on a 14-foot putt for a two-stroke win.

Then came the family reunion — thanks to technology. "This is definitely a win for everybody who supported me throughout the years," Thompson said. "It doesn't diminish the excitement."

TPC Twin Cities, Blaine, Minnesota — July 23-26
Par 71 (35-36); 7,513 yards — Purse: $6,600,000

1	**Michael Thompson**	64	66	68	67	265	$1,188,000
2	**Adam Long**	68	72	63	64	267	719,400
3	**Tony Finau**	65	66	69	68	268	250,800
	Emiliano Grillo	71	68	64	65	268	250,800
	Max Homa	65	72	64	67	268	250,800
	Charles Howell III	71	65	67	65	268	250,800
	Alex Noren	67	69	66	66	268	250,800
	Charl Schwartzel	66	68	66	68	268	250,800
	Robby Shelton	68	68	68	64	268	250,800
	Cameron Tringale	69	70	63	66	268	250,800
	Richy Werenski	63	67	68	70	268	250,800
12	Cameron Davis	67	66	69	68	270	127,050
	Bo Hoag	65	73	69	63	270	127,050
	Ryan Moore	65	70	67	68	270	127,050
	Nick Watney	65	69	68	68	270	127,050
	Matthew Wolff	65	68	70	67	270	127,050
	Xinjun Zhang	65	67	71	67	270	127,050
18	Harris English	70	65	67	69	271	87,450
	Dylan Frittelli	68	67	70	66	271	87,450
	Doug Ghim	70	68	67	66	271	87,450
	Talor Gooch	66	65	72	68	271	87,450
	Sepp Straka	70	67	71	63	271	87,450
23	Aaron Baddeley	66	73	69	64	272	63,690
	Henrik Norlander	70	70	67	65	272	63,690
	Pat Perez	70	69	66	67	272	63,690
26	Brice Garnett	70	67	68	68	273	48,180
	Michael Gligic	72	68	68	65	273	48,180
	Chase Koepka	70	68	72	63	273	48,180
	Hank Lebioda	69	70	65	69	273	48,180
	Danny Lee	67	68	69	69	273	48,180
	Bernd Wiesberger	73	66	66	68	273	48,180
32	Sam Burns	70	69	69	66	274	34,577
	Jason Dufner	68	72	66	68	274	34,577
	Tom Lewis	68	71	67	68	274	34,577
	Luke List	68	72	67	67	274	34,577
	Matthias Schwab	70	67	68	69	274	34,577
	Kyle Stanley	66	74	65	69	274	34,577
	Rafa Cabrera Bello	71	69	70	64	274	34,577
	Denny McCarthy	68	70	64	72	274	34,577
	Patrick Rodgers	66	68	70	70	274	34,577
41	Chris Baker	68	72	69	66	275	24,750
	Bronson Burgoon	66	70	70	69	275	24,750
	Brian Harman	76	64	68	67	275	24,750
	Chris Kirk	66	71	69	69	275	24,750
	Adam Schenk	67	69	72	67	275	24,750
46	Stewart Cink	69	68	70	69	276	17,980
	Brandon Hagy	70	69	68	69	276	17,980
	Tom Hoge	69	67	70	70	276	17,980
	Si Woo Kim	71	65	68	72	276	17,980
	Alex Cejka	70	70	68	68	276	17,980
	Michael Gellerman	70	70	70	66	276	17,980
	Patton Kizzire	69	70	70	67	276	17,980
53	Arjun Atwal	73	67	71	66	277	15,686
	Robert Garrigus	66	71	67	73	277	15,686
	Tim Wilkinson	70	69	67	71	277	15,686
56	Austin Cook	67	70	68	73	278	15,312
	Josh Teater	70	70	69	69	278	15,312
58	Bill Haas	70	69	72	68	279	14,982
	Kramer Hickok	67	70	73	69	279	14,982
	John Merrick	71	69	70	69	279	14,982
61	KJ Choi	71	67	68	74	280	14,718
62	Scott Stallings	71	64	73	73	281	14,520
	Peter Uihlein	70	69	72	70	281	14,520
64	George McNeill	70	70	72	73	285	14,322
65	Bo Van Pelt	66	68	76	76	286	14,190
66	Kyoung-Hoon Lee	70	70	71	76	287	14,058
67	Tommy Gainey	68	72	73	75	288	13,926
68	Matt Every	70	70	75	80	295	13,794

WGC FedEx St Jude Invitational

It was the WGC FedEx St Jude Invitational, but before the first ball could be hit, it had turned into a Number One Derby.

Spain's Jon Rahm was the brand-new world number one and wanted to stay there. And two former number ones could replace him. Justin Thomas had barely dipped his toe in those waters, just for four weeks, and badly wanted to come back. And Rory McIlroy was there so long, it was practically home.

Rahm rose to number one with his victory at the Memorial Tournament two weeks earlier, but in this, his first outing with the honour, things did not go well.

The first round rained scores in the 60s and Brooks Koepka, the defending champion, took a two-stroke lead with an eight-under 62. Against that backdrop, Rahm shot an uninspired 70. "I certainly didn't play like a world number one," Rahm said. "I just didn't have a swing today." Then the race was over for him in the second round. He took three double bogeys, shot 74 and was on his way to a tie for 52nd. His reign as number one had lasted two weeks.

McIlroy, number one for a total of some 100 weeks, was streaking bogeys — three straight from the fourth in the first round, three more from the seventh in the third, and shot 73 both times and tied for 47th.

And Thomas was labouring. He opened with a 66, four off Koepka's lead. With his middle rounds of 70-66, he was seven, then four behind Brendon Todd, who had won the Bermuda Championship and the Mayakoba Classic back-to-back the previous November. Todd shot 65-69, riding a hot putter. He needed just 24 putts in the second round, one of them a 50-foot birdie at the par-three 14th. Going into the final round, he led Byeong Hun An by one and Rickie Fowler by two, and noted that the best players "treat each final round like it's just another day," clearly intending to do the same.

Things brightened for Thomas in the third. "I kind of found something," he said. "It was nice to shoot four under on that back nine."

Still, he didn't sniff the lead till the ninth of the last round, when he got his fourth front-nine birdie and tied Todd at 12 under. Then came the touch-and-go duel down the stretch with Koepka.

Thomas bogeyed the 12th, and Koepka took the lead with a birdie at 13. Thomas tied, dropping a six-foot birdie putt at 15, then locked up the lead at the par-five 16th, holing a three-footer for birdie and going ahead by two when Koepka missed the fairway and bogeyed. Koepka got a stroke back at the 17th with a birdie from 40 feet, but was finished when he watered his tee shot at the 18th and double-bogeyed for a 69. Thomas closed with a 65 and a 13-under 267 total. Koepka finished three behind and tied for second at 10-under 270 with Daniel Berger (65), Tom Lewis (66) and Phil Mickelson (67).

And Thomas won the Number One Derby, returning to the top for the first time since June 2018. Will his stay be longer this time? "I hope so," Thomas said. "I feel like I'm a better player and a more complete golfer now than I was then."

TPC Southwind, Memphis, Tennessee — July 30-August 2
Par 70 (35-35); 7,230 yards — Purse: $10,500,000

1	**Justin Thomas**	66	70	66	65	267	$1,820,000
2	**Daniel Berger**	71	67	67	65	270	695,000
	Brooks Koepka	62	71	68	69	270	695,000
	Tom Lewis	73	70	61	66	270	695,000
	Phil Mickelson	67	70	66	67	270	695,000
6	Jason Day	68	67	69	67	271	268,333
	Xander Schauffele	68	70	67	66	271	268,333
	Matthew Fitzpatrick	70	64	69	68	271	268,333
	Shane Lowry	68	69	67	67	271	268,333
	Louis Oosthuizen	68	67	68	68	271	268,333
	Chez Reavie	66	67	70	68	271	268,333
12	Dustin Johnson	69	68	68	67	272	166,667
	Webb Simpson	69	66	69	68	272	166,667
	Byeong Hun An	68	65	66	73	272	166,667
15	Abraham Ancer	67	75	65	66	273	131,400
	Rickie Fowler	64	67	69	73	273	131,400
	Ryan Palmer	69	69	71	64	273	131,400
	Scottie Scheffler	69	67	69	68	273	131,400
	Brendon Todd	64	65	69	75	273	131,400
20	Christiaan Bezuidenhout	71	69	64	70	274	106,200
	Joel Dahmen	72	67	65	70	274	106,200
	Hideki Matsuyama	68	71	67	68	274	106,200
	Collin Morikawa	70	71	67	66	274	106,200
	Erik van Rooyen	71	70	68	65	274	106,200
25	Cameron Champ	71	68	67	69	275	87,200
	Billy Horschel	70	70	68	67	275	87,200
	Kevin Kisner	70	68	72	65	275	87,200
	Matt Kuchar	66	72	71	66	275	87,200
	Bubba Watson	68	70	71	66	275	87,200
30	Corey Conners	72	68	66	70	276	72,000
	Bryson DeChambeau	67	73	69	67	276	72,000
	Andrew Landry	70	72	66	68	276	72,000
	JT Poston	70	68	70	68	276	72,000
	Jordan Spieth	68	69	68	71	276	72,000
35	Tommy Fleetwood	72	67	73	65	277	56,111
	Patrick Cantlay	73	72	65	67	277	56,111
	Sergio Garcia	67	71	68	71	277	56,111
	Sungjae Im	67	68	69	73	277	56,111
	Graeme McDowell	68	70	70	69	277	56,111
	Kevin Na	72	64	74	67	277	56,111
	Henrik Stenson	69	69	70	69	277	56,111
	Kevin Streelman	71	66	71	69	277	56,111
	Nick Taylor	69	70	67	71	277	56,111
44	Mackenzie Hughes	68	71	70	69	278	49,000
	Sung Kang	65	69	72	72	278	49,000
	Jason Kokrak	69	68	71	70	278	49,000
47	Rory McIlroy	73	66	73	67	279	46,500
	Patrick Reed	71	69	69	70	279	46,500
49	Tyler Duncan	74	70	66	70	280	44,000
	Lucas Herbert	71	73	69	67	280	44,000
	Matthew Wolff	69	74	65	72	280	44,000
52	Keegan Bradley	68	70	70	73	281	40,000
	Max Homa	66	73	72	70	281	40,000
	Marc Leishman	70	69	69	73	281	40,000
	Joaquin Niemann	73	73	68	67	281	40,000
	Jon Rahm	70	74	71	66	281	40,000
57	Michael Thompson	70	74	69	69	282	37,250
	Gary Woodland	71	69	73	69	282	37,250
59	Viktor Hovland	67	75	72	69	283	35,250
	Jazz Janewattananond	75	71	68	69	283	35,250
	Matt Jones	71	72	69	71	283	35,250
	Robert MacIntyre	71	73	69	70	283	35,250
	Cameron Smith	72	72	71	68	283	35,250
	Matt Wallace	72	71	73	67	283	35,250
65	Tony Finau	70	68	72	74	284	33,250
	Victor Perez	73	71	70	70	284	33,250

67	Paul Casey	71 78 69 67	285	32,625		Cheng Tsung Pan	72 74 70 72	288	31,375
	Brandt Snedeker	73 71 72 69	285	32,625	74	Bernd Wiesberger	71 73 75 70	289	31,000
69	Tyrrell Hatton	72 69 73 73	287	32,000	75	Haotong Li	68 73 74 75	290	30,625
	Ian Poulter	73 69 72 73	287	32,000		Shaun Norris	73 76 72 69	290	30,625
	Danny Willett	69 70 74 74	287	32,000	77	Sebastian Soderberg	72 71 75 73	291	30,250
72	Adam Hadwin	73 71 75 69	288	31,375	78	Rafa Cabrera Bello	73 74 76 72	295	30,000

Barracuda Championship

With, of course, apologies to Shakespeare, but would a win by any other score count as sweet?

Actually, yes, by any score to Richy Werenski, who took his first PGA Tour victory in the Barracuda Championship by a score of, well, 39 points. Whatever the score, the win was worth, among other things, berths in the following week's PGA Championship and the US Open in September.

"It's huge," said Werenski, 28, a former Georgia Tech player. "I feel like I've been playing well for the last couple months. But to get a win, that's huge. Now I know I'm good enough."

The Barracuda, at Tahoe Old Greenwood, was played under the modified Stableford system, which was scored in points rather than strokes — eight points for albatross, five for eagle, two for birdie, zero for par, minus-one for bogey and minus-three for double bogey or worse.

Ryan Moore and Adam Schenk tied for the first-round lead with bogey-free 14-point rounds — seven birdies each. Moore, a five-time winner, had missed cuts in his first three starts following the coronavirus break. "I just didn't feel like myself for the first few weeks," he said, "so I homed in on what I felt I needed to do."

Kyle Stanley was puzzled by the scoring system, but there he was with 22 points and leading by two after the second round. "Actually, I'm not sure what I shot," said Stanley (it was a five-under 66). Werenski, with an 11-point day, had 17 points and trailed by five.

In the third, Troy Merritt had a brisk 14-point day, with eight birdies and two bogeys for 33 points and a four-point edge. He took the lead with a birdie at the par-four 16th, then birdied the par-three 17th. Emiliano Grillo, with 11 points, and Maverick McNealy, with 10, tied for second, four behind. Werenski was seven behind at 26.

At the end, there was one very frustrated golfer and one very surprised golfer once he did the math.

Merritt was in that baffled "what-do-you-have-to-do?" stage. He'd entered the final round with the lead, and then noted, "I finished the day with 10 straight pars, and had 10 birdie putts, and just couldn't get one to fall."

Werenski, at 26 points entering the final round, began with a bogey at the first, losing a point. He birdied the third but bogeyed the sixth, then was piling up points from there, with birdies at the seventh, 12th and 14th holes. The birdie at 12 stung. It's a par-five, and his five-point eagle putt lipped out. But the par-four 16th made up for it. His flop shot from in front of the green scooted obediently into the hole for a five-point eagle.

"I wasn't really thinking about where I was in relation to the leader until then," Werenski said. He holed a 15-footer at the 18th for a birdie and a one-point win over Merritt. No matter the scoring — it all added up to his first win.

Tahoe Mountain Club (Old Greenwood), Truckee, California — July 30-August 2
Par 71 (36-35); 7,690 yards — Purse: $3,500,000

1	**Richy Werenski**	6 11 9 13	39	$630,000	12	Ryan Moore	6 11 9 5	31	69,475
2	**Troy Merritt**	8 11 14 5	38	381,500		Adam Schenk	8 4 8 11	31	69,475
3	**Fabian Gomez**	3 7 11 16	37	206,500		Joseph Bramlett	14 2 6 9	31	69,475
	Matthias Schwab	9 11 4 13	37	206,500		Kyle Stanley	14 4 4 9	31	69,475
5	Robert Streb	4 8 11 12	35	135,188		Brandon Hagy	8 14 0 9	31	69,475
	Scott Stallings	11 9 8 7	35	135,188	17	Chesson Hadley	2 9 11 7	29	56,875
7	Maverick McNealy	10 9 10 5	34	118,125	18	Pat Perez	6 3 12 7	28	53,375
8	Aaron Wise	7 3 4 19	33	109,375	19	Kristoffer Ventura	11 2 4 10	27	48,125
9	Alex Noren	10 8 11 3	32	95,375		Patrick Rodgers	4 8 6 9	27	48,125
	Seamus Power	7 8 6 11	32	95,375	21	Beau Hossler	4 10 1 11	26	38,150
	Emiliano Grillo	11 4 10 7	32	95,375		Sam Ryder	8 6 7 5	26	38,150

	Justin Suh	4	8	7	7	26	38,150
	Roberto Castro	8	5	9	4	26	38,150
25	Charley Hoffman	8	4	6	7	25	28,088
	Cameron Percy	9	-2	10	8	25	28,088
	Michael Gligic	8	10	2	5	25	28,088
	Russell Knox	10	8	3	4	25	28,088
29	Rob Oppenheim	7	2	10	5	24	23,975
	Bo Hoag	6	10	5	3	24	23,975
	Tyler McCumber	3	4	7	10	24	23,975
32	Mark Anderson	8	5	4	6	23	20,883
	Denny McCarthy	8	5	3	7	23	20,883
	Cameron Davis	2	11	6	4	23	20,883
35	Zac Blair	3	4	4	11	22	17,430
	Sangmoon Bae	0	6	4	12	22	17,430
	Peter Uihlein	-5	13	4	10	22	17,430
	Wyndham Clark	10	4	0	8	22	17,430
	Kevin Tway	10	8	-2	6	22	17,430
40	Kyoung-Hoon Lee	4	6	-1	12	21	15,225
41	Sahith Theegala	4	7	6	3	20	12,425
	Tim Wilkinson	8	7	-4	9	20	12,425
	Peter Malnati	8	2	5	5	20	12,425
	Si Woo Kim	9	-1	0	12	20	12,425
	Roger Sloan	1	9	6	4	20	12,425
	William Gordon	7	6	0	7	20	12,425
	Brian Gay	3	8	5	4	20	12,425
48	David Hearn	5	4	3	7	19	9,345
	JJ Spaun	8	-1	7	5	19	9,345
	Doug Ghim	10	-2	6	5	19	9,345
51	Bud Cauley	4	4	1	9	18	8,680
	Russell Henley	3	5	2	8	18	8,680
53	Arjun Atwal	6	3	4	4	17	8,278
	Austin Cook	7	3	3	4	17	8,278
	Chris Baker	2	4	0	11	17	8,278
	Brendan Steele	1	5	-2	13	17	8,278
57	Matthew NeSmith	9	3	1	3	16	8,085
58	Lanto Griffin	8	-2	10	-1	15	8,015
59	Robby Shelton	9	-2	2	5	14	7,945
60	Rhein Gibson	5	5	0	3	13	7,875
61	Alex Cejka	5	3	0	4	12	7,770
	Michael Gellerman	7	-1	3	3	12	7,770
63	Brian Davis	3	4	-6	6	7	7,665
64	Dicky Pride	5	5	-4	-2	4	7,595
65	Peter Kuest	3	8	1	-10	2	7,525
66	Omar Uresti	4	2	-10	5	1	7,455
	Branden Grace	10	10			WDN	

Wyndham Championship

Jim Herman had a sudden change of plans. He wouldn't be going fishing or whatever next weekend. Now he was going to be playing in the FedEx Cup Playoffs.

"Just getting through the weekend was what you're looking to do," Herman, 43, was saying of life on the PGA Tour. "Then you never know what can happen on the weekends."

Like winning, which, to his surprise and that of most everyone else, he did in the Wyndham Championship. Herman shot Sedgefield in 66-69-61-63 for 259, 21 under. Playing from behind for all but the last few holes, Herman overcame a four-stroke deficit to beat Billy Horschel by a stroke.

Herman had a good luck charm going for him: President Donald Trump, whom he'd known since his days as an assistant pro at Trump National in New Jersey. "I played with him a few weeks ago," Herman said. "So whenever I play with him, I usually have some good finishes. He's been very supportive of me."

Not much had been happening on Herman's weekends lately. He'd made only seven cuts in 18 starts. His best finish was a tie for 27th in the 34-man Sentry Tournament of Champions, that he'd reached by winning the 2019 Barbasol Championship. Then came the Wyndham win.

"This," Herman said, "was out of the blue."

It was Herman's third tour victory, after the 2016 Houston Open and the 2019 Barbasol. And it was as tough as it was unexpected. Herman was stuck behind logjam leads in the first two rounds. Harold Varner, Tom Hoge and Roger Sloan, all seeking that breakthrough win, tied for the first-round lead at eight-under 62. Herman was four behind. The second round was even more crowded. Hoge (68), Si Woo Kim (65), Talor Gooch (65) and Horschel (64) tied for the lead at 10 under. Herman, who birdied three of his last four holes and made the cut with a 69, was five behind.

And in his flawless third round, nine birdies — five of them in succession from the 13th — gave him a career-best 61, and he gained merely a stroke. He was four behind Kim (62), who was at 18 under.

"Yeah, 61 — it's great anytime you can do that," Herman said. But now the problem: "Win or go home, here in the final week before the playoffs. If I'm not able to, then go home and get ready for the start of the new season."

But he stayed hot in the final round. He caught Kim with birdies at the first and fourth and an eagle — from 59 feet — at the fifth. He birdied the 17th on a three-foot putt to tie Horschel, then had the lead when Horschel bogeyed the 16th behind him. Both parred in, and Herman had his one-shot win.

"A little disappointed," Horschel said. "I had two good looks on the last two holes. I thought I'd make one of them."

Herman had plans for the weekend. Go home and be a dad again. Now he had to get to the playoffs. "My son's probably not going to be too happy about that," Herman said. "But he'll forgive me since I'm bringing home the trophy."

Sedgefield Country Club, Greensboro, North Carolina — August 13-16
Par 70 (35-35); 7,131 yards — Purse: $6,400,000

1	**Jim Herman**	66 69 61 63	259	$1,152,000
2	**Billy Horschel**	66 64 65 65	260	697,600
3	**Si Woo Kim**	65 65 62 70	262	312,400
	Kevin Kisner	69 64 65 64	262	312,400
	Doc Redman	67 64 63 68	262	312,400
	Webb Simpson	66 66 65 65	262	312,400
7	Zach Johnson	70 67 61 65	263	208,000
	Harold Varner III	62 69 67 65	263	208,000
9	Russell Henley	68 68 63 65	264	168,000
	Sungjae Im	69 64 66 65	264	168,000
	Denny McCarthy	67 68 66 63	264	168,000
	Patrick Reed	65 68 67 64	264	168,000
13	Sam Burns	67 68 65 65	265	129,600
	Tyler Duncan	68 64 66 67	265	129,600
15	Bud Cauley	66 68 67 65	266	104,000
	Cameron Davis	71 65 65 65	266	104,000
	Mark Hubbard	67 65 64 70	266	104,000
	Jason Kokrak	69 63 67 67	266	104,000
	Rob Oppenheim	66 66 62 72	266	104,000
20	Chris Baker	71 63 68 65	267	78,400
	Dylan Frittelli	69 65 66 67	267	78,400
	Peter Malnati	68 65 64 70	267	78,400
23	Harris English	64 67 68 69	268	64,320
	Shane Lowry	68 63 70 67	268	64,320
25	Ryan Armour	73 64 65 67	269	54,080
	Talor Gooch	65 65 68 71	269	54,080
27	William Gordon	68 69 64 69	270	46,720
	Brian Harman	65 71 67 67	270	46,720
	Tom Hoge	62 68 72 68	270	46,720
	Seamus Power	68 69 67 66	270	46,720
31	Ryan Brehm	64 69 72 66	271	37,440
	Wesley Bryan	65 70 70 66	271	37,440
	Paul Casey	67 66 69 69	271	37,440
	Jason Dufner	69 65 67 70	271	37,440
	Adam Long	68 65 71 67	271	37,440
	Roger Sloan	62 70 68 71	271	37,440
37	Christiaan Bezuidenhout	71 64 69 68	272	29,120
	Rafa Cabrera Bello	67 67 67 71	272	29,120
	Matt Jones	68 67 72 65	272	29,120
	Kristoffer Ventura	69 68 63 72	272	29,120
	Vincent Whaley	71 66 66 69	272	29,120
42	Scott Brown	66 71 68 68	273	20,416
	Bo Hoag	66 68 67 72	273	20,416
	Andrew Landry	66 65 71 71	273	20,416
	Hank Lebioda	65 71 68 69	273	20,416
	Matthew NeSmith	69 67 70 67	273	20,416
	Joaquin Niemann	70 66 65 72	273	20,416
	Matthias Schwab	67 69 68 69	273	20,416
	Brandt Snedeker	70 67 65 71	273	20,416
	Scott Stallings	70 66 70 67	273	20,416
51	Chesson Hadley	65 69 70 70	274	15,216
	Kramer Hickok	69 67 65 73	274	15,216
	Chris Kirk	66 69 68 71	274	15,216
	Patton Kizzire	66 67 73 68	274	15,216
	Tom Lewis	67 68 70 69	274	15,216
	Davis Love III	69 67 71 67	274	15,216
	Adam Schenk	67 67 67 73	274	15,216
	Brian Stuard	70 66 69 69	274	15,216
59	Matt Every	68 67 70 70	275	14,144
	Tommy Fleetwood	69 64 68 74	275	14,144
	Michael Gligic	67 69 67 72	275	14,144
	Ben Martin	71 66 70 68	275	14,144
	Troy Merritt	67 69 71 68	275	14,144
	Henrik Norlander	67 68 71 69	275	14,144
	Josh Teater	67 70 67 71	275	14,144
66	Sergio Garcia	67 70 72 67	276	13,504
	Luke List	68 67 66 75	276	13,504
	Patrick Rodgers	70 66 67 73	276	13,504
69	Cheng Tsung Pan	68 64 76 69	277	13,120
	Brinson Paolini	71 66 66 74	277	13,120
	Scott Piercy	68 66 74 69	277	13,120
72	Russell Knox	73 64 72 69	278	12,800
	Jordan Spieth	70 67 70 71	278	12,800
74	Austin Cook	69 67 69 76	281	12,480
	Sebastian Munoz	67 67 73 74	281	12,480
	Peter Uihlein	71 65 70 75	281	12,480
77	Nate Lashley	66 69 77 74	286	12,224

The Northern Trust

And who else had a chance at the Northern Trust? Academically speaking, of course.

Well — Harris English, Kevin Streelman, Cameron Davis and Russell Henley.

Tied for the lead in the first round. Shot 64. Seven under.

And then?

And then Dustin Johnson shot 60 in the second round.

Oh.

To be sure, the Northern Trust, the opener of the FedEx Cup Playoffs, was not quite that simple. But almost. Johnson demolished the tournament, shooting 67-60-64-63 for a total of 254, winning by 11 strokes at 30 under par.

"Do you know what the tour record is?" someone asked.

"I have no idea," Johnson said. "What is it?"

"Look it up — 31 under."

"Oh, that's all right," Johnson said. "Next time."

The Northern Trust opened with a field of 122 (there were three withdrawals from the original 125). The top 70 would move on to the next playoff, the BMW Championship the following week, aiming for the grand finale, the Tour Championship and its $15 million first prize.

The Northern got off to a hot start, with the four tied for the lead. Others crowded in. Among them at 65 were Louis Oosthuizen, Charley Hoffman and Scott Piercy. Sebastian Munoz's 65 was a stunner. He birdied the first seven holes, but then double-bogeyed the ninth and made only one other birdie. "It's golf," Munoz said.

Top-seeded Justin Thomas opened at 68. Tiger Woods birdied five of his last 10 holes for a 68. Collin Morikawa, in his first start since winning the PGA Championship, bogeyed two par-fives and shot 71.

After that opening 67, Johnson beat the traffic in the second round with a birdie-eagle-birdie-eagle-birdie start. His first eagle, at the par-five second, was routine — a 41-foot putt. For his second, at the par-four fourth, he drove the green and had a five-footer.

Johnson was 11 under through 11 holes, from where he parred in for his 60. Could have been 59, he said, a bit miffed at himself. He'd hit driver at 18, but a three-wood would have given him a better chance at another birdie.

"So shot 60," he said. "Pretty happy with my position leading into the weekend."

Which was at 15 under par and leading by two over rookie Scottie Scheffler, who upstaged him with a 59, and Cameron Davis. Scheffler was eight under and at the 13th when he realised what he had going. He faced a four-footer at the 18th for the 59. "You don't really get a putt for 59 often," he said. "So I was quite nervous." But he made it five consecutive years that the tour had a 59 or better.

If there was any doubt where Johnson was headed, he cleared it up quickly in the third round, and he widened the gap at the end with a 20-foot birdie putt at the par-three 17th and a 40-footer for eagle at the par-five 18th for a 64. "I like where I'm at," Johnson said, on 22 under and holding a five-stroke lead. "But I'm still going to have to shoot a good score."

Then there was the 63 in the finale. He eagled the second again, with a seven-iron to eight feet. And at the par-four fourth, he just missed the green and chipped to 19 inches and birdied. And so it went for five more birdies, the last at the par-five 18th where he signed off with a four-footer. It was his 22nd tour victory and returned him to number one in the world.

"Something clicked on Wednesday," Johnson said. "I'm looking forward to the rest of the FedEx Cup Playoffs."

TPC Boston, Norton, Massachusetts — August 20-23
Par 71 (36-35); 7,308 yards — Purse: $9,500,000

1	**Dustin Johnson**	67	60	64	63	254	$1,710,000
2	**Harris English**	64	66	66	69	265	1,035,500
3	**Daniel Berger**	66	66	67	67	266	655,500
4	Kevin Kisner	65	66	70	66	267	427,500
	Scottie Scheffler	70	59	67	71	267	427,500
6	Jon Rahm	69	67	67	65	268	332,500
	Webb Simpson	70	64	68	66	268	332,500
8	Russell Henley	64	67	70	68	269	277,875
	Alex Noren	69	68	64	68	269	277,875
	Ryan Palmer	67	67	68	67	269	277,875
11	Brian Harman	67	66	73	64	270	230,375
	Harry Higgs	67	66	66	71	270	230,375
13	Charley Hoffman	65	68	68	70	271	175,275
	Mackenzie Hughes	68	68	66	69	271	175,275
	Jason Kokrak	68	68	70	65	271	175,275
	Louis Oosthuizen	65	65	68	73	271	175,275
	Robby Shelton	66	71	71	63	271	175,275
18	Talor Gooch	66	72	65	69	272	117,189
	Viktor Hovland	68	70	68	66	272	117,189
	Matt Kuchar	69	69	66	68	272	117,189
	Sebastian Munoz	65	71	69	67	272	117,189
	Danny Lee	66	64	69	73	272	117,189
	Cameron Smith	69	68	66	69	272	117,189
	Bubba Watson	65	68	67	72	272	117,189
25	Corey Conners	72	65	69	67	273	76,238
	Tyrrell Hatton	67	71	63	72	273	76,238
	Justin Rose	69	70	67	67	273	76,238
	Xander Schauffele	68	71	67	67	273	76,238
29	Keegan Bradley	68	67	69	70	274	55,860
	Wyndham Clark	68	71	67	68	274	55,860
	Cameron Davis	64	65	72	73	274	55,860
	Tyler Duncan	69	69	69	67	274	55,860
	Mark Hubbard	67	71	68	68	274	55,860
	Kyoung-Hoon Lee	67	68	69	70	274	55,860
	Hideki Matsuyama	70	69	65	70	274	55,860
	Troy Merritt	72	67	70	65	274	55,860
	Scott Piercy	65	70	70	69	274	55,860
	Cameron Tringale	67	72	67	68	274	55,860
39	Si Woo Kim	68	64	70	73	275	39,425
	Kevin Na	71	65	73	66	275	39,425
	JT Poston	71	67	66	71	275	39,425
	Ian Poulter	66	67	73	69	275	39,425
	Adam Schenk	70	66	71	68	275	39,425
44	Tommy Fleetwood	66	69	71	70	276	30,001
	Emiliano Grillo	69	64	73	70	276	30,001
	Charles Howell III	66	70	68	72	276	30,001
	Brendan Steele	68	67	69	72	276	30,001
	Matthew Wolff	65	67	77	67	276	30,001
49	Rickie Fowler	67	70	71	69	277	23,169
	Adam Long	68	67	72	70	277	23,169
	Patrick Reed	68	71	68	70	277	23,169
	Justin Thomas	68	67	71	71	277	23,169
	Paul Casey	70	69	67	71	277	23,169
	Beau Hossler	73	66	66	72	277	23,169

	Zach Johnson	69 69 67 72	277	23,169		Kevin Streelman	64 71 73 71	279	20,995
	Denny McCarthy	69 68 69 71	277	23,169	64	Brendon Todd	70 66 70 74	280	20,615
	Chez Reavie	68 70 67 72	277	23,169	65	Scott Harrington	68 67 76 71	282	20,330
58	Lanto Griffin	68 68 70 72	278	21,565		Rory McIlroy	69 70 74 69	282	20,330
	Adam Scott	66 70 75 67	278	21,565	67	Andrew Landry	69 70 69 75	283	20,045
	Tiger Woods	68 71 73 66	278	21,565	68	Richy Werenski	69 67 75 74	285	19,855
61	Maverick McNealy	67 71 70 71	279	20,995	69	Matt Jones	68 71 76 71	286	19,665
	Keith Mitchell	69 68 72 70	279	20,995	70	Patrick Rodgers	71 67 76 77	291	19,475

BMW Championship

Jon Rahm, leader in the clubhouse at the BMW Championship, second leg of the FedEx Cup Playoffs, was keeping his putter warm on the practice green when he heard that Dustin Johnson was at the 18th looking at a 45-footer for birdie that would tie him and force a playoff.

"I knew he just had to get the ball rolling on the right direction and that putt was in," Rahm said, "and I was expecting nothing else."

Said Johnson: "I knew I needed to make birdie to get into the playoff. I played an unbelievable putt, got in the playoff. And then Jon made an even more ridiculous putt on top of me."

That was in the playoff. Rahm's ridiculous putt was a 66-foot birdie and it won him the BMW. And he won despite a strange penalty.

In the third round, after two birdies, Rahm had hit his approach to the par-four fifth to 43 feet.

And then he picked up his ball — without marking it. "I was thinking of somebody else and something else," he said. He took the penalty and bogeyed.

And had a nagging thought.

"I just hope," Rahm said, "I don't lose by one."

And so went the BMW. Rahm shot the tough Olympia Fields in 75-71-66-64, Johnson in 71-69-69-67, tying at a mere four-under 276.

This second FedEx Cup Playoff at Olympia proved to be a bear. Johnson had breezed through the first leg, the Northern Trust at TPC Boston, 30 under and winning by 11. Olympia Fields, with its firm greens, narrow fairways and plenty of wind, was a different matter.

"I knew this was gonna be one of those courses," said Tony Finau, one of 10 who shot the par of 70 on Thursday. "I prepared for it like a major."

Only three broke par in the first round — Hideki Matsuyama, leading with a 67; Tyler Duncan, 68, and Mackenzie Hughes, 69. Johnson shot 71, Justin Thomas 73, Rahm 75 and PGA champion Collin Morikawa 76. Tiger Woods, hitting just six fairways, shot 73. He would shoot all four rounds over par for the first time since 2010, and tie for 51st at 11 over.

Olympia was a grudging playground. Rory McIlroy, with a 69, and Patrick Cantlay, a 68, tied for the second-round lead at one under. Johnson was a stroke behind, Rahm seven back. Then Rahm closed in with his 66 in the third round, climbing to just three behind the co-leaders, Johnson and Matsuyama, both shooting 69 and tied at one under.

Rahm, playing two groups ahead of Johnson on Sunday, made his way impressively to six birdies, four of them on the back nine. The 30-footer at the 16th gave him a flawless 64, the lowest round of the week, and made him the leader in the clubhouse at four under.

Johnson was rolling — three birdies through four holes. Then two bogeys: at the eighth out of a bunker, at the 10th out of the rough, and soon he was trailing. But he birdied the par-five 15th, two putts from 30 feet. Then he needed a birdie at the 18th to tie Rahm. But it was a 45-footer. The one Rahm figured was good before Johnson even hit it.

Rahm's turn came in the playoff at the par-four 18th. Johnson had a 30-foot putt for birdie, but Rahm had to go first from 66 feet.

Rahm said he was hoping to get within six feet. He read the green like a diamond-cutter reading a gem: "The first two-thirds … left-to-right break … top of that hill, start quick right … at the end … turning left towards the pin."

The ball dropped. And Johnson's 30-footer pulled up just short.

Said Rahm: "I still can't believe what just happened."

Olympia Fields Country Club (North), Olympia Fields, Illinois — August 27-30
Par 70 (35-35); 7,366 yards — Purse: $9,500,000

1	**Jon Rahm**	75	71	66	64	276	$1,710,000
2	**Dustin Johnson**	71	69	69	67	276	1,026,000
	Rahm won playoff at first extra hole						
3	**Hideki Matsuyama**	67	73	69	69	278	551,000
	Joaquin Niemann	72	71	68	67	278	551,000
5	Tony Finau	70	71	73	65	279	384,750
6	Matthew Fitzpatrick	70	75	68	67	280	337,250
	Jason Kokrak	74	71	69	66	280	337,250
8	Sebastian Munoz						285,000
	Brendon Todd	73	68	71	69	281	285,000
10	Lanto Griffin	70	73	70	69	282	247,000
	Mackenzie Hughes	69	73	69	71	282	247,000
12	Byeong Hun An	73	74	68	68	283	192,375
	Patrick Cantlay	71	68	75	69	283	192,375
	Brian Harman	72	73	69	69	283	192,375
	Rory McIlroy	70	69	73	71	283	192,375
16	Paul Casey	73	72	71	68	284	147,250
	Tyrrell Hatton	73	70	71	70	284	147,250
	Bubba Watson	72	70	70	72	284	147,250
	Matthew Wolff	72	71	74	67	284	147,250
20	Joel Dahmen	71	77	71	66	285	106,780
	Collin Morikawa	76	73	68	68	285	106,780
	Scottie Scheffler	75	72	72	66	285	106,780
	Cameron Smith	75	73	68	69	285	106,780
	Richy Werenski	74	72	70	69	285	106,780
25	Daniel Berger	73	74	69	70	286	69,469
	Russell Henley	74	69	70	73	286	69,469
	Kevin Kisner	72	70	70	74	286	69,469
	Louis Oosthuizen	72	69	74	71	286	69,469
	Carlos Ortiz	70	74	72	70	286	69,469
	Xander Schauffele	73	70	74	69	286	69,469
	Adam Scott	72	69	70	75	286	69,469
	Justin Thomas	73	74	71	68	286	69,469
33	Gary Woodland	75	70	74	68	287	49,129
	Abraham Ancer	70	74	70	73	287	49,129
	Corey Conners	76	69	70	72	287	49,129
	Dylan Frittelli	72	75	69	71	287	49,129
	Billy Horschel	70	71	74	72	287	49,129
	Danny Lee	73	72	74	68	287	49,129
	Brendan Steele	72	71	75	69	287	49,129
40	Harris English	75	71	69	73	288	34,200
	Adam Hadwin	74	72	73	69	288	34,200
	Jim Herman	71	72	73	72	288	34,200
	Viktor Hovland	71	73	73	71	288	34,200
	Maverick McNealy	77	70	73	68	288	34,200
	Alex Noren	72	71	73	72	288	34,200
	Ryan Palmer	71	76	74	67	288	34,200
	Patrick Reed	73	71	72	72	288	34,200
48	Tyler Duncan	68	76	77	68	289	25,365
	Charles Howell III	75	75	69	70	289	25,365
50	Bryson DeChambeau	73	70	75	72	290	23,940
51	Mark Hubbard	70	77	69	75	291	22,496
	Kevin Na	72	74	71	74	291	22,496
	Kevin Streelman	76	80	66	69	291	22,496
	Nick Taylor	75	72	73	71	291	22,496
	Tiger Woods	73	75	72	71	291	22,496
56	Harry Higgs	70	74	75	73	292	21,470
	Sungjae Im	77	74	72	69	292	21,470
	Adam Long	72	77	72	71	292	21,470
59	Max Homa	74	72	70	77	293	20,710
	Matt Kuchar	75	76	69	73	293	20,710
	JT Poston	72	77	73	71	293	20,710
	Robby Shelton	75	72	71	75	293	20,710
	Michael Thompson	72	73	72	76	293	20,710
64	Jason Day	76	74	76	68	294	20,140
65	Cameron Champ	77	74	70	74	295	19,760
	Talor Gooch	76	79	71	69	295	19,760
	Tom Hoge	71	73	75	76	295	19,760
68	Andrew Landry	77	75	74	75	301	19,380
69	Marc Leishman	80	78	79	73	310	19,190

Tour Championship

Dustin Johnson has simply got to work on his victory celebrations. You can barely tell them from his non-celebrations.

He'd just holed the winning putt in the Tour Championship, and who knew? He didn't leap, do a dance, didn't thrust his arms into the heavens. If he broke a smile, who saw it? He did give a bit of a fist pump, a little twitch that wouldn't bother a basking butterfly.

And he had just won $15 million.

The scores could be confusing. A handicap system, called "Starting Strokes", was introduced at the 2019 event to help insure that the winner of the Tour Championship would also be the FedEx Cup champion. Previously, sometimes two winners would emerge.

Johnson shot East Lake, a par 70, in 67-70-64-68, a tally of 269, but 21 under par with his starting strokes. He won by three strokes but he didn't have the lowest score. That was shot by Xander Schauffele, who at 265 tied for second at 18 under with Justin Thomas, who, as did Johnson, shot 269.

The field is seeded, based on FedEx Cup points earned. The top seed — Johnson, in this case — started the tournament at 10 under par, with the number two seed at eight under par, and so on. Thus Johnson started the tournament with a two-stroke lead on Jon Rahm.

"It's not like I have a two-shot lead going into the final round," Johnson said.

The scoring system would require some re-thinking by fans. For instance, Rahm shot five-under 65, and with his eight starting strokes was 13 under. Johnson shot three-under 67, and with his 10 starting strokes, tied Rahm for the lead at 13 under. Thomas shot 66 and was two behind, and Rory McIlroy birdied the last three holes for a 64 and was four behind.

In the second round, Johnson went the last 13 holes without hitting a fairway, made four bogeys and four birdies — the last at the par-five 18th — and shot 70. He led by one over South Korea's Sungjae Im.

Johnson solved a nagging driving problem in the third round — stood a little closer to the ball. "When you hit it off the toe," he said, "it does not like to cut." The obedient ball rewarded him with a 64 and a five-stroke lead for the final round.

"This is a tough golf course," he said. "No lead is safe." As Schauffele and Thomas demonstrated. Schauffele, with two birdies, and Thomas, with five birdies and two bogeys, got within three of Johnson on the front. Coming in, Schauffele had three birdies and Thomas two, and each had a bogey, to get within two. They tied for second.

Johnson was crackling early on Sunday, with three birdies through six holes. Then the tournament tightened. He bogeyed the seventh from the rough, then bogeyed eight, a three-putt. But his Great Escape at the 13th just about locked things up.

Johnson and Schauffele were the final pairing, and played the par-four 13th almost identically. Both missed the fairway and the green, and chipped badly, to about 20 feet. Schauffele then two-putted and bogeyed, and Johnson holed his par, and his lead was back to three over both Schauffele and Thomas. And that's where the margin would stay after Schauffele birdied once coming in, and Thomas finished birdie-bogey-birdie, both for 66s, and Johnson birdied the par-five 18th from five feet for a 68, his third win of 2020. And he gave a fist pump — a twitch. And then came the first prize, the $15 million.

Johnson recalled getting through the tour's qualifying school. "I think they gave me like a $25,000 cheque," he said. "I thought I was rich. Now, I'm very thankful for FedEx, but it's not about the money for me. It's more about the trophy."

East Lake Golf Club, Atlanta, Georgia — September 4-7
Par 70 (35-35); 7,346 yards — FedEx Cup bonus pool: $60,000,000

	START		FINISH	
1 **Dustin Johnson**	-10	67 70 64 68	-21	$15,000,000
2 **Xander Schauffele**	-3	67 65 67 66	-18	4,500,000
Justin Thomas	-7	66 71 66 66	-18	4,500,000
4 Jon Rahm	-8	65 74 66 66	-17	3,000,000
5 Scottie Scheffler	-2	71 66 66 65	-14	2,500,000
6 Collin Morikawa	-5	71 65 67 69	-13	1,900,000
7 Tyrrell Hatton	-2	67 66 71 66	-12	1,300,000
8 Rory McIlroy	-3	64 71 70 67	-11	960,000
Sebastian Munoz	-3	71 65 70 66	-11	960,000
Patrick Reed	-3	71 66 70 65	-11	960,000
11 Sungjae Im	-4	68 64 72 70	-10	750,000
12 Harris English	-4	70 69 69 67	-9	682,500
Webb Simpson	-6	70 71 68 68	-9	682,500
14 Mackenzie Hughes	E	70 69 66 67	-8	620,000
15 Daniel Berger	-4	69 71 64 73	-7	582,000
Hideki Matsuyama	-4	70 70 67 70	-7	582,500
17 Tony Finau	-2	68 71 66 71	-6	550,000
18 Abraham Ancer	-1	64 71 69 72	-5	527,500
Lanto Griffin	-2	67 69 69 72	-5	527,500
20 Viktor Hovland	E	69 69 68 70	-4	497,500
Brendon Todd	-3	67 68 70 74	-4	497,500
22 Bryson DeChambeau	-4	72 69 69 71	-3	478,000
23 Kevin Kisner	-1	72 68 69 71	-1	466,000
24 Cameron Champ	E	68 71 70 71	E	445,333
Cameron Smith	E	68 68 73 71	E	445,333
Ryan Palmer	-1	72 72 70 67	E	445,333
27 Kevin Na	-1	69 70 71 72	+1	420,000
Joaquin Niemann	-2	72 72 67 72	+1	420,000
29 Marc Leishman	-1	66 75 73 69	+2	405,000
30 Billy Horschel	E	70 73 71 70	+4	395,000

2019-20 MONEY LIST

1	Justin Thomas	$7,344,040
2	Jon Rahm	5,959,819
3	Dustin Johnson	5,837,267
4	Collin Morikawa	5,250,868
5	Webb Simpson	5,097,742
6	Bryson DeChambeau	4,998,495
7	Daniel Berger	4,439,420
8	Rory McIlroy	4,408,415
9	Sungjae Im	4,337,811
10	Patrick Reed	4,250,060

Safeway Open

Stewart Cink, age 47, had been playing golf for a long time and had gotten advice of all kinds from a lot of people. But this time, just starting the final round of the Safeway Open, it had to be the first time he'd heard that his tangibles were fine and all he had to do was tend to his intangibles.

Clearly, the advice was good and he followed it and was rewarded with his seventh PGA Tour, his first since he won the 2009 Open Championship, beating Tom Watson, then 59, in a playoff at Turnberry. So started, a week after the Tour Championship, the PGA Tour's new 2020-21 season.

Cink's treasured advice was given by his son Reagan, 23, who was caddieing for him at Silverado. Cink had entered the final round two shots behind third-round co-leaders Cameron Percy, Brian Stuard and James Hahn, tied at 16 under par. Further, and amazingly, entering the final round, 35 players were were within six strokes of the lead, and 32 of them were within five. The spread went from former junior star Akshay Bhatia, 18, to Cink.

Cink recalled Reagan's comment when they were leaving the second hole: "Your tangibles are really, really good right now ... your club, your ball, your putting. Let's just take care of the intangibles today."

"He made a great point," Cink said. "To do it with Reagan on the bag, his fourth time caddieing, was about 25 cherries on the top."

It helped that Cink's path forward was cleared. Percy made two double bogeys and a bogey over three holes on the front nine. Hahn bogeyed three of the first six holes. Stuard was one over through the eighth but couldn't catch up and tied for third.

Doc Redman, 22, was the early leader following a remarkable round. He started the day eight behind the leaders and closed with six straight birdies for a 10-under 62 and a two-stroke lead. "I got hot," he said. "It happens, so it was awesome." He tied for third in the end.

Cink marched through the crowd, making seven birdies over 13 holes from the fourth. His three-putt from 50 feet at the 17th was only his second bogey of the tournament, and his lead was cut to one after Harry Higgs eagled the 16th. At the par-five 18th, Cink knocked his second over the green, chipped from the rough to three feet and made his eighth birdie of the round for a 65, and waited for the last three groups to finish. Higgs, who had a 62 in the second round, was still alive with two holes to play, but parred both for a 68 and finished second by two.

Cink won not only with his son on the bag, but with his wife Lisa, in her fifth year of cancer remission, just beyond the ropes.

"I definitely had a lot of emotions out there today," Cink said. "I just was overcome at a few times with a feeling of gratitude, and just feeling like how fortunate I am to be in the position that I'm in. It all just kind of poured together into feeling like, 'Wow, this is really special'."

Silverado Resort and Spa (North), Napa, California — September 10-13
Par 72 (36-36); 7,166 yards — Purse: $6,600,000

1	**Stewart Cink**	67	70	65	65	267	$1,188,000
2	**Harry Higgs**	69	62	70	68	269	719,400
3	**Chez Reavie**	67	71	66	66	270	322,163
	Doc Redman	70	69	69	62	270	322,163
	Kevin Streelman	72	66	65	67	270	322,163
	Brian Stuard	67	67	66	70	270	322,163
7	Sam Burns	64	65	72	70	271	214,500
	Kristoffer Ventura	69	66	66	70	271	214,500
9	Akshay Bhatia	66	72	66	68	272	166,650
	James Hahn	68	65	67	72	272	166,650
	Russell Knox	63	69	70	70	272	166,650
	Pat Perez	65	69	69	69	272	166,650
	JJ Spaun	70	68	66	68	272	166,650
14	Bud Cauley	68	68	69	68	273	100,650
	Doug Ghim	67	66	69	71	273	100,650
	Michael Gligic	70	68	67	68	273	100,650
	Chesson Hadley	70	67	69	67	273	100,650
	David Hearn	69	69	66	69	273	100,650
	Sepp Straka	70	66	68	69	273	100,650
	Sahith Theegala	71	68	64	70	273	100,650
	DJ Trahan	67	65	70	71	273	100,650
	Xinjun Zhang	69	67	67	70	273	100,650
23	Ricky Barnes	69	66	69	70	274	57,420
	Beau Hossler	73	65	69	67	274	57,420
	Nelson Ledesma	69	68	67	70	274	57,420
	Cameron Percy	64	68	68	74	274	57,420
	Charl Schwartzel	68	68	68	70	274	57,420
	Vincent Whaley	69	70	66	69	274	57,420
29	Jason Dufner	70	67	67	71	275	41,391
	Branden Grace	68	71	68	68	275	41,391
	Bo Hoag	64	72	71	68	275	41,391
	Tom Hoge	66	68	70	71	275	41,391
	Brendan Steele	65	70	69	71	275	41,391
	Harold Varner III	67	71	71	66	275	41,391
	Emiliano Grillo	69	68	65	73	275	41,391
36	Mark Anderson	68	69	71	68	276	29,411
	Cameron Davis	71	68	70	67	276	29,411
	Scott Harrington	66	70	70	70	276	29,411
	Anirban Lahiri	74	65	67	70	276	29,411
	Rob Oppenheim	68	66	73	69	276	29,411
	Andrew Putnam	70	68	69	69	276	29,411
	Ben Taylor	69	67	67	73	276	29,411
	Tim Wilkinson	67	68	68	73	276	29,411
44	Si Woo Kim	70	65	77	66	278	22,770
	Phil Mickelson	71	67	70	70	278	22,770
46	Jim Furyk	72	66	71	70	279	18,282
	JB Holmes	70	68	70	71	279	18,282
	Carlos Ortiz	67	70	68	74	279	18,282
	Patrick Rodgers	67	72	70	70	279	18,282
	Kyle Stanley	70	69	68	72	279	18,282
	Nick Watney	72	65	74	68	279	18,282
52	Ryan Blaum	71	67	72	70	280	15,807
	Austin Cook	68	71	71	70	280	15,807
	Joel Dahmen	71	68	71	70	280	15,807
	Jhonattan Vegas	70	68	69	73	280	15,807
56	Kevin Chappell	69	70	73	69	281	15,114
	Charley Hoffman	67	71	71	72	281	15,114
	Jamie Lovemark	69	69	71	72	281	15,114
	Isaiah Salinda	71	68	69	73	281	15,114
	Hudson Swafford	70	68	72	71	281	15,114
61	Jonathan Byrd	69	69	71	73	282	14,520
	William Gordon	72	67	70	73	282	14,520
	Cheng Tsung Pan	69	70	71	72	282	14,520
	Adam Schenk	68	71	71	72	282	14,520
65	Lucas Glover	69	67	74	73	283	14,124
	Luke List	70	69	70	74	283	14,124
67	Brice Garnett	69	70	73	72	284	13,728
	Brandon Hagy	69	70	74	71	284	13,728
	Joohyung Kim	67	72	75	70	284	13,728
	William McGirt	69	69	77	69	284	13,728
71	Andy Zhang	66	72	70	78	286	13,398
72	MJ Daffue	71	65	74	78	288	13,266
73	Rhein Gibson	73	66	76	76	291	13,134

Corales Puntacana Resort Championship

It's a golfer's lament: "Honestly, I hit one bad golf shot all day."

Final round of the Corales Puntacana Resort and Club Championship. Hudson Swafford, who somehow survived some impressive wobbling and went on to win, was standing in the 13th fairway leading by four. But he was tied when he left the 15th green.

The creeping troubles had surfaced earlier. At the par-five 12th, a magnificent escape. He'd pulled his second shot, missed the green, and the ball rolled down a steep bank. He chipped up, and the ball came back down to his feet. He chipped up again. This time it held beautifully. He saved his par. But at the 13th, another chip came back down to him. This time his re-chip left him 12 feet short. He two-putted for a double bogey. Ahead of him, Mackenzie Hughes birdied the par-five 14th, and at the 15th, when Swafford missed the green and bogeyed, he was tied.

The one bad golf shot?

"I was still in my own world, didn't really feel terrible, but I hit one bad shot and it was on 15," Swafford said. "I hit a bad nine-iron. It was a little too much club, but I knew if I got it up into the wind it would be perfect. But I just kind of quit on it."

His tee shot at the par-three 17th made up for it. "A good-flighted six-iron," Swafford said. "Done it 100,000 times. I love hitting that golf shot. It was a good one, and an even better putt." A kick-in birdie, in fact.

Swafford was nearly a wire-to-wire winner. With his 65-67-69-69 performance, he was in a four-way tie for the lead in the first round, then led Tyler McCumber by one through the second. Then he trailed by two in the third when Adam Long, who tied for 13th in the US Open at Winged Foot a week earlier, went on a putting spree. Long one-putted nine of his last 10 holes and took the lead with a 64. But Long faltered in the fourth and Swafford, ever optimistic, returned to the lead.

Swafford, 33, might not have been the odds-on favourite at Corales or anywhere else. He was playing with a major medical extension after a rib injury and foot surgery. Then the hornet sting early in the second round didn't help. He spent several holes trying to ice it down between shots. ("I guess it cleared my mind of the golf thing and just let me focus on something else," he said.)

After his adventures at the 12th, 13th, 15th and 17th, he came to the 18th needing to hole an eight-foot putt for par for his second career victory. It was a fine time to come face-to-face with a debatable putt.

"My caddie Kyle and I, we were talking," Swafford said. "I thought the putt might go a little to the right. He said it might go a little left. He just said, 'Man, just hit a solid putt. You've hit a lot of them. Just hit one more solid putt'."

Said Swafford, after beating McCumber by one stroke: "I hit a great one."

Corales Golf Club, Punta Cana, Dominican Republic — September 24-27
Par 72 (36-36); 7,666 yards — Purse: $4,000,000

1	**Hudson Swafford**	65	67	69	69	270	$720,000
2	**Tyler McCumber**	65	71	69	66	271	436,000
3	**Mackenzie Hughes**	68	67	67	70	272	276,000
4	Nate Lashley	68	71	65	69	273	196,000
5	Adam Long	70	65	64	75	274	164,000
6	James Hahn	68	68	70	69	275	140,000
	Anirban Lahiri	69	72	64	70	275	140,000
8	Will Zalatoris	70	71	70	65	276	117,000
	Cameron Percy	67	70	72	67	276	117,000
	Luke List	69	65	71	71	276	117,000
11	Sebastian Cappelen	69	69	71	68	277	93,000
	Patrick Rodgers	67	69	72	69	277	93,000
	Xinjun Zhang	66	69	68	74	277	93,000
14	Matt Jones	71	69	71	67	278	65,000
	Alex Smalley	70	67	72	69	278	65,000
	Charley Hoffman	69	68	71	70	278	65,000
	Scott Harrington	65	74	69	70	278	65,000
	Kelly Kraft	68	68	70	72	278	65,000
	Justin Suh	67	67	71	73	278	65,000
	Sean O'Hair	67	67	70	74	278	65,000
21	Hank Lebioda	70	71	72	66	279	39,000
	Pat Perez	70	70	71	68	279	39,000
	Robert Streb	68	72	69	70	279	39,000
	Henrik Stenson	70	69	69	71	279	39,000
	Kramer Hickok	69	72	67	71	279	39,000
	Rhein Gibson	71	69	67	72	279	39,000
	Emiliano Grillo	70	68	68	73	279	39,000
28	Sam Burns	69	67	78	66	280	27,400
	Sangmoon Bae	71	68	75	66	280	27,400
	Kyle Stanley	67	72	73	68	280	27,400
	Vincent Whaley	69	71	71	69	280	27,400
	Jonathan Byrd	68	71	70	71	280	27,400
33	Stephen Stallings Jr	69	72	71	69	281	20,450
	Brian Stuard	67	71	73	70	281	20,450
	David Hearn	67	74	69	71	281	20,450
	Thomas Detry	68	69	72	72	281	20,450
	Joohyung Kim	72	69	68	72	281	20,450
	Rob Oppenheim	72	67	69	73	281	20,450
	Sepp Straka	65	70	72	74	281	20,450
	Ryan Brehm	67	72	68	74	281	20,450
41	George McNeill	69	70	75	68	282	12,862
	Kevin Tway	70	70	72	70	282	12,862
	Matthew NeSmith	69	71	72	70	282	12,862
	Joseph Bramlett	66	70	75	71	282	12,862
	Ricky Barnes	67	73	70	72	282	12,862
	Chase Seiffert	71	70	69	72	282	12,862
	Peter Malnati	69	69	71	73	282	12,862
	Patton Kizzire	71	67	71	73	282	12,862
	Denny McCarthy	68	71	70	73	282	12,862
	Fabian Gomez	70	69	70	73	282	12,862
	Beau Hossler	70	71	68	73	282	12,862
52	Ben Martin	68	71	75	69	283	9,580
	Sam Ryder	70	70	73	70	283	9,580
	DJ Trahan	72	69	72	70	283	9,580
	Kristoffer Ventura	72	69	70	72	283	9,580
56	Matthias Schwab	69	72	75	68	284	9,160
	Adam Schenk	68	69	73	74	284	9,160
	JJ Spaun	71	67	72	74	284	9,160
	Scott Brown	69	69	72	74	284	9,160
	Dominic Bozzelli	70	67	71	76	284	9,160
61	Keith Mitchell	70	70	77	68	285	8,800
	Tim Wilkinson	70	71	75	69	285	8,800
	Cheng Tsung	71	70	73	71	285	8,800
	Brice Garnett	70	71	71	73	285	8,800
65	JJ Henry	70	71	73	72	286	8,440
	Willy Pumarol	73	68	71	74	286	8,440
	Martin Laird	69	69	73	75	286	8,440
	Jamie Lovemark	67	71	72	76	286	8,440
	Mark D Anderson	68	71	71	76	286	8,440
70	Kiradech Aphibarnrat	70	71	77	69	287	8,120
	Zac Blair	68	73	70	76	287	8,120
	Arjun Atwal	73	68	69	77	287	8,120
73	Roberto Diaz	70	71	72	75	288	7,920
	Tommy Gainey	71	68	72	77	288	7,920

Sanderson Farms Championship

Sergio Garcia was twitting himself a bit.

"We love to make every putt we look at — or not look at, in this case," he said at the Sanderson Farms Championship.

Garcia had walked into his first Sanderson not with his eyes wide open, but — in this case — closed.

Putting, that is.

Even on the final putt, a 30-incher for birdie on the final hole for his first victory on the PGA Tour since the 2017 Masters. And then he was surprised that his eyes-closed putting had caught anyone's attention.

"Would you believe me," he said at an interview, "if I told you I've been doing it for about three years?"

A notion like that takes a while to sink in.

"I've gone on and off, but like Augusta I won it playing with my eyes closed every single putt and some of the other wins, too," he added. "I feel like it gives me a little more freedom to feel the stroke. I just let my natural ability take over instead of telling myself what to do."

Clearly, it worked for him. Garcia, trailing through the first two rounds, shot the par-72 Country Club of Jackson in 68-68-66-67 for a total of 269, 19 under. That closing 30-inch birdie putt made him a one-stroke winner over Peter Malnati, who came from five behind with a career-best 63, punctuated by a 30-foot birdie putt at the 17th. Ironically, his lone tour win was in the 2015 Sanderson. He'd finished earlier in this one, leading at 18 under and not convinced it would hold up.

"I feel like I won the tournament," Malnati said. "I probably won't, but I feel like I did, and it's amazing."

Garcia's opening 68 left him four behind Sebastian Munoz, the defending champion, and Jimmy Walker, Kevin Chappell and Charley Hoffman, knotted at 64. All told, there were 16 players at 67 or better. Another 68 left Garcia five behind Keegan Bradley (65) at the halfway point.

Garcia broke through with a flawless 66 in the third round and tied for the lead at 14 under with Cameron Smith (63) and JT Poston (69). Garcia was in strange territory. Not since that 2017 Masters had he had at least a share of the 54-hole lead on the tour. His task for the final round? "Just believing in myself, trusting myself," he said.

And he clearly did, as he demonstrated with two tremendous shots in the final round — that won for him.

In his closing 67, a round punctuated by two bogeys, he came to the par-five 14th two under for the day and two behind. He blasted a five-wood from 260 yards that hit the top collar of a bunker and rolled to within four feet of the hole. He closed his eyes and made the eagle.

He came to the 18th needing a birdie to win.

"I stood up on 18 … I trusted myself," Garcia said. "I aimed down the right side and just hit a hard draw. It gave me the ability to have an eight-iron into the green instead of having a six or something like that."

He put the eight-iron to 30 inches. And closed his eyes and won.

"The perfect ending for an amazing week," Garcia said.

Country Club of Jackson, Jackson, Mississippi — October 1-4
Par 72 (36-36); 7,461 yards — Purse: $6,600,000

1	**Sergio Garcia**	68	68	66	67	269	$1,188,000
2	**Peter Malnati**	70	67	70	63	270	719,400
3	**JT Poston**	66	67	69	70	272	455,400
4	Keegan Bradley	66	65	73	69	273	297,000
	Henrik Norlander	69	70	69	65	273	297,000
6	Cameron Davis	66	73	63	72	274	201,300
	Charley Hoffman	64	69	72	69	274	201,300
	Denny McCarthy	68	67	69	70	274	201,300
	Tyler McCumber	70	69	66	69	274	201,300
	Scott Stallings	67	72	68	67	274	201,300
	Kristoffer Ventura	67	68	68	71	274	201,300
12	Wesley Bryan	72	69	66	68	275	131,010
	Stewart Cink	69	69	72	65	275	131,010
	MJ Daffue	65	69	72	69	275	131,010
	Cheng Tsung Pan	70	69	68	68	275	131,010
	Rory Sabbatini	72	68	66	69	275	131,010
17	Corey Conners	67	70	69	70	276	90,750
	Maverick McNealy	69	71	67	69	276	90,750
	Matthew NeSmith	68	71	68	69	276	90,750
	Chase Seiffert	70	68	69	69	276	90,750

	Brandt Snedeker	70	66	67	73	276	90,750
	Aaron Wise	68	69	67	72	276	90,750
23	Kevin Chappell	64	72	72	70	278	59,070
	Doug Ghim	71	70	67	70	278	59,070
	Zach Johnson	70	71	68	69	278	59,070
	Sebastian Munoz	64	73	70	71	278	59,070
	Camilo Villegas	69	69	74	66	278	59,070
28	Tom Hoge	71	68	70	70	279	46,200
	Sungjae Im	71	70	72	66	279	46,200
	Martin Laird	68	69	72	70	279	46,200
	Doc Redman	70	70	70	69	279	46,200
32	Adam Schenk	69	71	70	70	280	39,380
	Charl Schwartzel	68	73	70	69	280	39,380
	Roger Sloan	67	71	71	71	280	39,380
35	Emiliano Grillo	69	72	71	69	281	35,145
	Bill Haas	69	72	71	69	281	35,145
37	Michael Gligic	65	73	75	69	282	28,710
	Talor Gooch	66	70	74	72	282	28,710
	Brian Harman	70	70	70	72	282	28,710
	Si Woo Kim	72	69	74	67	282	28,710
	Anirban Lahiri	66	70	77	69	282	28,710
	Scottie Scheffler	73	67	72	70	282	28,710
	Cameron Tringale	68	69	72	73	282	28,710
44	Joseph Bramlett	70	71	69	73	283	22,770
	Hank Lebioda	69	71	69	74	283	22,770
46	Ryan Armour	67	72	73	72	284	17,980
	Rafa Cabrera Bello	72	69	71	72	284	17,980
	Kelly Kraft	71	69	73	71	284	17,980
	Jimmy Walker	64	77	71	72	284	17,980
	Kyoung-Hoon Lee	68	73	70	73	284	17,980
	Chez Reavie	70	71	71	72	284	17,980
	DJ Trahan	72	68	71	73	284	17,980
53	William Gordon	72	69	70	74	285	15,609
	Chris Kirk	68	70	75	72	285	15,609
	Grayson Murray	70	71	73	71	285	15,609
	Andrew Putnam	68	71	73	73	285	15,609
57	Beau Hossler	72	69	74	71	286	15,180
	Scott Piercy	70	71	69	76	286	15,180
59	Patton Kizzire	72	69	78	68	287	14,784
	Steve Lewton	68	73	73	73	287	14,784
	Cameron Percy	69	70	74	74	287	14,784
	Richy Werenski	70	71	73	73	287	14,784
63	Jay McLuen	70	71	75	73	289	14,454
64	Vincent Whaley	71	70	73	76	290	14,322
65	JB Holmes	71	68	71	81	291	14,190
66	Wyndham Clark	71	69	74	78	292	14,058

Shriners Hospitals for Children Open

Anybody who could come through that with his mind and his game both still intact, deserved to win. And Martin Laird, in fact, did both gloriously in the Shriners Hospitals for Children Open.

Laird, the 37-year-old Scot, winless for seven years and in the tournament on a sponsor's exemption, was leading by a shot with two holes left when he fired an errant tee shot at the TPC Summerlin's par-three 17th. The ball hit a cart path and ended up 30 yards to the right of the green, with the flag on the right. Where he had basically no shot. But coming from the school of thought that says there is always a shot, Laird hit a chip-and-run that went over the cart path, under the trees and between a set of bunkers and onto the green. The easy part was the 18-foot putt. He sank it for his par.

"That hole owed me one," Laird said, thereby opening a complex tale of debt and redemption.

It developed that Laird had won the 2009 Shriners, in a three-way playoff, and that he had a chance to win the 2010 edition in another three-way playoff until Jonathan Byrd aced the 17th.

And in the 2020 edition, after that spectacular save at the 17th in regulation, he two-putted for a bogey at the 18th and slipped into a tie with Matthew Wolff and Austin Cook at 23 under par. And in his third three-way playoff, he won with a 20-foot birdie on the second extra hole — the 17th.

"To make that putt on 17 honestly was huge in regulation," Laird said, "and then to roll that putt in there to close it out, I mean, obviously, it's pretty special."

The tournament opened with a power display by Bryson DeChambeau, US Open champion, in which he had two-putt birdies on all three par fives and two of the par fours in his leading nine-under 62. He'd have had a 61 if his 15-foot eagle putt from the fringe at the par-five ninth had dropped. "I was not happy it didn't go in," he said, "but I'll take a 62."

The second round turned into a scorekeeper's carnival. Five tied for the lead at 14 under: Laird (63), Patrick Cantlay (65), Peter Malnati (62), Brian Harman (63) and Cook (65). Laird and Malnati both eagled the ninth — Laird from four feet, Malnati from 15.

And Laird and Cantlay tied for the third-round lead, both shooting 65 for 20 under par. Laird eagled the ninth on a 50-foot putt, but Wolff upstaged him with three eagles in a five-hole stretch for a 61. He holed out from 116 yards at the par-four 11th, drove the green at the 301-yard, par-four 15th, and holed an 18-foot putt at the par-five 13th.

"I'm feeling like I can go out there and win any week now," Wolff said.

The fourth round looked like a shootout in the making. And it was. Wolff shot 66 with four birdies and another eagle, this at the par-five 16th. His bid for an outright win was spiked by a bogey at the par-three 14th. Cook also shot 66, posting six birdies but also a bogey at 14. And Laird joined his third three-way playoff with a 68 made up of an eagle, four birdies and three bogeys.

Laird said he couldn't wait to get home. He now has kids who see his old trophies but wonder when he's going to win a new one. "It's going to be nice to take a trophy home for them this time," he said.

TPC Summerlin, Las Vegas, Nevada — October 8-11
Par 71 (35-36); 7,255 yards — Purse: $7,000,000

1	**Martin Laird**	65	63	65	68	261	$1,260,000
2	**Austin Cook**	63	65	67	66	261	623,000
	Matthew Wolff	68	66	61	66	261	623,000
	Laird won playoff at second extra hole						
4	Abraham Ancer	66	66	65	67	264	343,000
5	James Hahn	64	66	67	68	265	259,000
	Peter Malnati	66	62	71	66	265	259,000
	Will Zalatoris	68	64	64	69	265	259,000
8	Patrick Cantlay	63	65	65	73	266	190,750
	Bryson DeChambeau	62	67	71	66	266	190,750
	Si Woo Kim	67	67	63	69	266	190,750
	Matthew NeSmith	66	68	64	68	266	190,750
	Justin Suh	68	65	66	67	266	190,750
13	Sungjae Im	67	63	69	68	267	125,417
	Joaquin Niemann	68	66	67	66	267	125,417
	Webb Simpson	68	67	65	67	267	125,417
	Harold Varner III	63	68	66	70	267	125,417
	Wyndham Clark	67	63	65	72	267	125,417
	Brian Harman	65	63	67	72	267	125,417
19	John Huh	69	66	64	69	268	86,030
	Zach Johnson	65	68	68	67	268	86,030
	Louis Oosthuizen	65	68	71	64	268	86,030
	Scott Piercy	68	65	67	68	268	86,030
	Cameron Tringale	66	66	66	70	268	86,030
24	Tom Hoge	70	64	66	69	269	61,950
	Patton Kizzire	67	68	65	69	269	61,950
	Cameron Smith	70	63	66	70	269	61,950
27	Michael Gligic	65	67	66	72	270	47,950
	Russell Henley	67	67	66	70	270	47,950
	Andrew Landry	64	68	67	71	270	47,950
	Sebastian Munoz	68	67	68	67	270	47,950
	Rob Oppenheim	64	71	65	70	270	47,950
	JT Poston	67	66	66	71	270	47,950
	Adam Schenk	67	67	67	69	270	47,950
34	Emiliano Grillo	64	69	72	66	271	33,483
	Beau Hossler	69	64	73	65	271	33,483
	Matt Kuchar	67	66	72	66	271	33,483
	Sam Burns	67	66	68	70	271	33,483
	Dylan Frittelli	67	64	70	70	271	33,483
	Adam Hadwin	67	68	62	74	271	33,483
	Charles Howell III	69	64	67	71	271	33,483
	Ryan Palmer	67	66	70	68	271	33,483
	Robbyelton	67	67	68	69	271	33,483
43	Joseph Bramlett	68	66	64	74	272	21,665
	Sergio Garcia	66	64	69	73	272	21,665
	Sung Kang	68	65	68	71	272	21,665
	Tom Lewis	67	67	65	73	272	21,665
	Troy Merritt	68	66	70	68	272	21,665
	Kevin Na	66	66	64	76	272	21,665
	Brandt Snedeker	67	68	63	74	272	21,665
	Sepp Straka	65	66	70	71	272	21,665
51	Brice Garnett	65	66	68	74	273	17,570
52	Cameron Davis	65	69	70	70	274	16,674
	Matt Jones	67	67	67	73	274	16,674
	Nate Lashley	63	67	69	75	274	16,674
	Cheng Tsung Pan	68	66	69	71	274	16,674
	Rory Sabbatini	67	66	66	75	274	16,674
57	Denny McCarthy	66	69	68	72	275	16,170
58	Bronson Burgoon	64	68	72	72	276	15,750
	Joel Dahmen	67	68	69	72	276	15,750
	Hunter Mahan	67	68	69	72	276	15,750
	Henrik Norlander	67	65	74	70	276	15,750
	Andrew Putnam	67	67	68	74	276	15,750
63	Chez Reavie	68	64	71	75	278	15,330
64	Stewart Cink	67	63	70	81	281	15,120
	George Markham	70	64	73	74	281	15,120
66	Luke Donald	69	66	72	75	282	14,910

The CJ Cup

"Couldn't be happier," Jason Kokrak said.

And anybody who dreamed a dream so hard and who tried so hard to fulfil it would understand him.

Kokrak came from three shots behind in the final round, shot an eight-under 64, matching the best round of the tournament, and won The CJ Cup at Shadow Creek — his first PGA Tour victory. And Kokrak, 35, had dreamed of this victory for 10 seasons and 233 tournaments.

"It's still setting in," he said. "So very excited. I couldn't be more pleased to get my first win. Ten years out here on the PGA Tour's been a long career so far, so to wait so long for my first win, it's a pretty special thing."

The CJ Cup, a Korean tournament, was moved to Shadow Creek because of the Covid-19 pandemic and the various travel difficulties connected with it.

Kokrak won it in storybook fashion. He shot 70-66-68-64, but trailed through the first three rounds, by as much as six behind Xander Schauffele in the second. And he was three behind Russell Henley going into the final round. And then all those hopes and dreams bubbled over.

But first, Henley ran into rough times. He'd led by three going into the final round but went flat. Then he slipped behind when he bogeyed the par-five seventh just as Kokrak was getting up steam. Henley's hopes ended when he drove over the green and into thick rough at the par-four 11th. The bogey put him four behind. He finished with a 70 and tied for third with Tyrrell Hatton (65), fresh from winning the BMW PGA Championship on the European Tour.

Kokrak, meantime, paired with Schauffele, a good friend, pulled away with four straight birdies on the front nine. And The CJ Cup settled into a shootout between friends on the final nine.

Kokrak started the back with two birdies, from 20 and 18 feet. Schauffele rang up three straight birdies, the last at the 13th, holing out a 45-footer from the thick collar with his putter.

Schauffele then suffered his only bogey of the round at the 16th, where he struggled to escape the heavy rough. He closed with a 66 and finished second by two at 270.

Kokrak was also in trouble at the 16th, going from rough to bunker, but he splashed out to four feet for a par and a one-stroke lead.

Kokrak finished in style. At the par-five 18th, off an excellent drive, he fired his approach to 25 feet and two-putted for his final birdie, a 64 and a 20-under 268 total to win by two.

Then came the question: Did you ever doubt that you would win?

"I think anytime that you've been out here for that length of time, you definitely have doubts in your mind," he said. "As good as my ball-striking is and as hard as I've been working, it was inevitable that it was going to happen. I just tried to go out there today, give myself a lot of opportunities and just let that first win come to me."

And one final question: How do you plan to celebrate your first win?

Said Kokrak: "I think I'll have a nice bourbon and a nice bottle of wine and a nice dinner with my team."

Shadow Creek Golf Course, Las Vegas, Nevada — October 15-18
Par 72 (36-36); 7,527 yards — Purse: $9,750,000

1	**Jason Kokrak**	70 66 68 64	268	$1,755,000
2	**Xander Schauffele**	66 64 74 66	270	1,053,000
3	**Tyrrell Hatton**	65 68 73 65	271	565,500
	Russell Henley	66 68 67 70	271	565,500
5	Talor Gooch	70 65 69 68	272	390,000
6	Joaquin Niemann	72 68 69 66	275	351,000
7	Lanto Griffin	70 68 66 72	276	314,438
	Bubba Watson	74 69 65 68	276	314,438
9	Sebastian Munoz	71 70 67 69	277	282,750
10	Harris English	75 66 69 68	278	263,250
11	Cameron Smith	69 74 68 68	279	243,750
12	Matthew Fitzpatrick	69 68 72 71	280	190,320
	Viktor Hovland	75 66 69 70	280	190,320
	Collin Morikawa	71 65 71 73	280	190,320
	Ian Poulter	69 70 73 68	280	190,320
	Justin Thomas	72 66 68 74	280	190,320
17	Mark Hubbard	70 71 70 70	281	139,035
	Si Woo Kim	69 74 69 69	281	139,035
	Ryan Palmer	68 76 66 71	281	139,035
	Jon Rahm	67 73 69 72	281	139,035
21	Sergio Garcia	71 70 72 69	282	91,956
	Harry Higgs	72 67 70 73	282	91,956
	Danny Lee	71 72 73 66	282	91,956
	Hideki Matsuyama	70 68 70 74	282	91,956
	Robby Shelton	73 70 70 69	282	91,956
	Kevin Streelman	68 70 72 72	282	91,956
	Rory McIlroy	73 69 66 74	282	91,956
28	Abraham Ancer	69 73 70 71	283	57,135
	Daniel Berger	71 70 70 72	283	57,135
	Tyler Duncan	67 71 72 73	283	57,135
	Rickie Fowler	74 68 68 73	283	57,135
	Adam Hadwin	75 69 69 70	283	57,135
	Brian Harman	71 71 71 70	283	57,135
	Billy Horschel	70 70 72 71	283	57,135
	Brooks Koepka	74 68 68 73	283	57,135
	Shane Lowry	72 74 70 67	283	57,135
	Richy Werenski	74 68 70 71	283	57,135
38	Patrick Cantlay	71 72 74 67	284	40,560
	Joel Dahmen	68 75 73 68	284	40,560
	Tom Hoge	73 70 73 68	284	40,560
	Jordan Spieth	74 74 69 67	284	40,560
42	Byeong Hun An	73 73 68 71	285	33,735
	Keegan Bradley	75 70 68 72	285	33,735
	Cameron Champ	74 69 74 68	285	33,735
45	Sungjae Im	78 69 72 67	286	27,885
	Kevin Kisner	77 71 67 71	286	27,885
	Kevin Na	76 66 73 71	286	27,885
48	Hanbyeol Kim	74 69 73 71	287	23,205
	Louis Oosthuizen	70 73 74 70	287	23,205
	Carlos Ortiz	72 71 72 72	287	23,205
51	JT Poston	78 70 71 69	288	21,645
52	Marc Leishman	73 71 70 75	289	20,169
	Seonghyeon Kim	77 70 69 73	289	20,169
	Matt Kuchar	76 68 74 71	289	20,169
	Kyoung-Hoon Lee	78 73 70 68	289	20,169
	Justin Rose	74 72 68 75	289	20,169
	Scottie Scheffler	71 77 71 70	289	20,169
	Brendon Todd	77 73 70 69	289	20,169
59	Tommy Fleetwood	77 71 72 70	290	19,208
	Jaekyeong Lee	77 76 71 66	290	19,208
61	Corey Conners	77 70 72 72	291	18,720
	Andrew Landry	71 69 74 77	291	18,720
	Nick Taylor	71 74 72 74	291	18,720
64	Joohyung Kim	75 71 74 72	292	18,330
65	Jim Herman	78 69 72 75	294	17,843
	Mackenzie Hughes	73 75 69 77	294	17,843
	Brendan Steele	73 79 73 69	294	17,843
	Michael Thompson	75 77 74 68	294	17,843
69	Paul Casey	75 77 67 76	295	17,258
	Dylan Frittelli	74 72 74 75	295	17,258
71	Jeongwoo Ham	79 71 70 76	296	16,965
72	Gary Woodland	73 75 78 71	297	16,770
73	Matthew Wolff	80 73 69 77	299	16,575
74	Adam Long	78 72 72 78	300	16,380
75	Sung Kang	73 71 82 75	301	16,185
76	Alex Noren	77 73 79 76	305	15,990
77	Taehee Lee	75 75 82 74	306	15,795
	Jason Day	70 70 66	WDN	

Zozo Championship

The Zozo Championship at Sherwood was a prime example of PGA Tour golf during the Covid-19 pandemic. The Zozo was originally scheduled for Japan, where the tournament debuted in 2019 as the tour expanded its activities in Asia. (And a dynamite debut it was, won by Tiger Woods, at 43, and tying Sam Snead's record of 82 tour victories.) But because of the pandemic, the 2020 Zozo was relocated to Sherwood Country Club at Thousand Oaks, California.

The 2020 edition opened with the adventures of Sebastian Munoz and ended with another come-from-behind performance by Patrick Cantlay.

Munoz, a Colombian, led the first round with an eight-under 64 that was as wild a ride as he'd ever had in his college golf at North Texas University. He holed out twice for eagles, at the par-four seventh from 168 yards and the par-five 16th from 51, and also made eight birdies and three bogeys.

"Not a normal round," Munoz conceded.

He led by one over Justin Thomas, who shot 29 on the back nine, and England's Tyrrell Hatton, recent winner on the European Tour. Cantlay was three behind with a 67.

Tiger Woods opened the defence of his title the hard way. "As I said, didn't play the par-fives well," he said. In the first round, Woods played them in three-over — a par, a birdie, two bogeys and a double bogey, shot 76 and never was in the running. He would tie for 72nd. To hear the golfers talk, Sherwood's par-fives must have seemed like sitting ducks. There were five of them. "Low scoring's to be expected," Cantlay noted. And he feasted on them — 12 birdies and just one bogey.

Cantlay trailed all the way and was three behind starting the final round, and four behind on the final nine. Then a hot stretch carried him to his third tour victory, and his third coming from behind.

Cantlay hung close on a card of 67-65-68, trailing Munoz by three in the first round, Thomas by two in the second and three through the third.

The Zozo was developing into a battle between Thomas and Spain's Jon Rahm in the final round when Cantlay birdied four of the first six holes. Then at the par-three eighth, he missed the green and took his first bogey of the tournament, on the 62nd hole. But it was only a delay.

He birdied five of seven from the ninth, including three straight — at the par-five 13th, a three-wood second to 45 feet and two putts; at the 14th, a seven-iron and a 17-footer, and at the par-three 15th, a finessed seven-iron over a rocky lagoon to 10 feet for only the fifth birdie there in the final round.

Rahm missed birdies at the last two holes and shot 68. "Just a couple of unlucky moments," he said, of wind shifts. Thomas came up four feet short of the miracle hole-out eagle he needed at 18 to tie. "You're right there and you don't get it done," he said. He birdied for a 69 and tied Rahm at 22 under.

At the 16th, Cantlay made his only bogey on a par-five, his second of the tournament, and parred in for a 65, finishing at 23-under with a 265 total for a one-stroke win.

As to his proclivity for coming from behind to win, Cantlay said: "I would love to start with a big lead and get off to a good start and have an even bigger lead."

Sherwood Country Club, Thousand Oaks, California — October 22-25
Par 72 (36-36); 7,073 yards — Purse: $8,000,000

1	**Patrick Cantlay**	67	65	68	65	265	$1,440,000
2	**Jon Rahm**	68	67	63	68	266	704,000
	Justin Thomas	65	65	67	69	266	704,000
4	Russell Henley	68	72	63	66	269	315,000
	Ryan Palmer	69	65	66	69	269	315,000
	Cameron Smith	67	69	66	67	269	315,000
	Bubba Watson	70	63	68	68	269	315,000
8	Cameron Champ	70	68	65	67	270	232,000
	Corey Conners	69	67	68	66	270	232,000
	Joel Dahmen	68	70	65	67	270	232,000
11	Tony Finau	69	64	69	69	271	184,000
	Dylan Frittelli	66	65	70	70	271	184,000
	Lanto Griffin	66	65	68	72	271	184,000
14	Kevin Kisner	66	67	73	66	272	142,933
	Sebastian Munoz	64	70	66	72	272	142,933
	Patrick Reed	70	63	71	68	272	142,933
17	Daniel Berger	69	68	69	67	273	95,858
	Jason Kokrak	69	65	69	70	273	95,858
	Rory McIlroy	73	67	67	66	273	95,858
	Joaquin Niemann	70	66	68	69	273	95,858
	Alex Noren	67	68	68	70	273	95,858
	Justin Rose	67	67	72	67	273	95,858
	Xander Schauffele	69	72	67	65	273	95,858
	Scottie Scheffler	67	65	69	72	273	95,858
	Webb Simpson	69	65	67	72	273	95,858
26	Matthew Fitzpatrick	69	65	67	73	274	60,880

	Brian Harman	66	68	67	73	274	60,880
28	Tyler Duncan	68	68	72	67	275	50,137
	Shaun Norris	68	73	67	67	275	50,137
	Harris English	66	67	72	70	275	50,137
	Tyrrell Hatton	65	68	76	66	275	50,137
	Hideki Matsuyama	70	71	68	66	275	50,137
	Kevin Na	70	65	69	71	275	50,137
	Kevin Streelman	74	67	70	64	275	50,137
35	Byeong Hun An	74	68	67	67	276	36,680
	Abraham Ancer	67	66	77	66	276	36,680
	Paul Casey	69	71	69	67	276	36,680
	Talor Gooch	74	63	71	68	276	36,680
	Satoshi Kodaira	68	66	70	72	276	36,680
	Carlos Ortiz	72	65	68	71	276	36,680
41	Mark Hubbard	67	70	71	69	277	26,880
	Mackenzie Hughes	67	72	68	70	277	26,880
	Sungjae Im	68	68	69	72	277	26,880
	Takumi Kanaya	70	67	68	72	277	26,880
	Brad Kennedy	72	67	66	72	277	26,880
	Jordan Spieth	70	66	74	67	277	26,880
47	Brendon Todd	69	69	70	70	278	20,053
	Tom Hoge	71	70	69	68	278	20,053
	Viktor Hovland	71	64	71	72	278	20,053
50	Jim Herman	70	65	72	72	279	17,560
	Andrew Landry	69	67	70	73	279	17,560
	Collin Morikawa	71	65	72	71	279	17,560
	Matthew Wolff	69	69	75	66	279	17,560
54	Gunn Charoenkul	73	67	69	71	280	16,480
	Harry Higgs	73	66	73	68	280	16,480
	Matt Kuchar	70	69	70	71	280	16,480
57	Tommy Fleetwood	70	68	74	69	281	16,000
	Rickie Fowler	71	67	73	70	281	16,000
	Richy Werenski	72	61	72	76	281	16,000
60	Jason Day	68	71	69	74	282	15,520
	Jazz Janewattananond	73	66	70	73	282	15,520
	Chan Kim	69	73	67	73	282	15,520
63	Adam Hadwin	75	67	70	71	283	15,040
	Ryo Ishikawa	73	66	70	74	283	15,040
	Nick Taylor	70	68	71	74	283	15,040
66	Mikumu Horikawa	74	74	69	67	284	14,560
	Shugo Imahira	75	64	69	76	284	14,560
	Adam Long	77	72	66	69	284	14,560
69	Billy Horschel	72	67	73	73	285	14,240
70	Marc Leishman	71	73	72	70	286	14,000
	Brendan Steele	72	70	68	76	286	14,000
72	Rikuya Hoshino	68	70	75	74	287	13,600
	Danny Lee	72	76	70	69	287	13,600
	Tiger Woods	76	66	71	74	287	13,600
75	Naoki Sekito	71	80	68	70	289	13,280
76	Phil Mickelson	72	74	67	78	291	13,120
77	Michael Thompson	76	73	72	73	294	12,960

Bermuda Championship

As the veteran Brian Gay was to observe — not so originally, but aptly: "Crazy game."

When the WGC HSBC Championship in Shanghai was cancelled because of the Covid-19 pandemic, that lifted the companion event, the Bermuda Championship, into full status on the PGA Tour. And that, in turn, lifted Brian Gay, on winning the Bermuda, into the 2021 Masters.

"Crazy game," Gay said. "You never know what's going to happen."

Indeed. Gay, 48, had played in over 600 tour events in his 20 years, and had won five times, and this was his first in nearly eight years. This time he was trailing by three coming down the final nine. But he closed with a rush, birdied the 18th, tied Wyndham Clark, and won with a birdie on the first playoff hole.

"I was looking forward to coming back to Bermuda," Gay said. "Tied for third here last year, so I had good feelings."

Any talk of age, however, began with Fred Funk, former PGA Tour fixture, now 64 and playing the PGA Tour Champions. He was paired through the first two rounds with his son, Taylor, 24, a tour player out of the University of Texas. Funk shot 69-72-75-71, three over, and tied for 59th. Taylor missed the cut. "I don't know whether I compete," Funk said, "but making the cut was big."

Gay would shoot the par-71 Port Royal in 70-68-67-64, but after an unpromising start, trailing Peter Malnati (63) by seven strokes. Malnati was a study of a tour golfer in the tough travel of the pandemic days. He'd hoped his wife and his one-year-old son could get to Bermuda for the tournament. Then, when he was playing the 18th he saw them standing there.

"To see them, and then to finish with that birdie," Malnati said. "I'm a happy man."

The Bermuda see-sawed for two rounds. In the wind-whipped second round, Ryan Armour, with a 70, tied Clark (68) for a one-stroke halfway lead at eight under. Gay was four behind. The winds had toned down in the third, and Doc Redman, the 2017 US Amateur champion, seeking his first tour win, shot a 67 and led by one over Armour (70), Clark (70) and Kramer Hickok (69). Gay eagled the par-five 17th for a 67 and was tied at two off the lead.

The final round turned into a duel of two streaking golfers.

Gay, in the group just ahead of Clark, birdied the third, sixth and seventh holes, bogeyed the eighth, and birdied five of the next seven holes. A three-putt bogey at the par-five 17th cost him a tie for the lead. But at the par-four 18th, a gap wedge approach from a sidehill lie left him with a three-footer. He made the birdie for a 64 and a 15-under total of 269.

Clark, chasing his first tour win, birdied seven of 10 holes from the second. Then he bogeyed the par-three 16th out of a bunker, shot 65 and tied Gay at 15 under.

Gay won it on the first playoff hole, the 18th, on a 12-foot putt. Clark missed from seven. “I’m pretty bummed,” Clark said. “I had chances. I just didn’t capitalise.”

Said Gay: “I’ve always known I have the game to compete.”

Port Royal Golf Course, Southampton, Bermuda — October 29-November 1
Par 71 (36-35); 6,828 yards — Purse: $4,000,000

1	**Brian Gay**	70 68 67 64	269	$720,000
2	**Wyndham Clark**	66 68 70 65	269	436,000
	Gay won playoff at first extra hole			
3	**Ollie Schniederjans**	66 70 69 66	271	276,000
4	Stewart Cink	66 74 68 64	272	160,000
	Matt Jones	68 71 66 67	272	160,000
	Denny McCarthy	70 67 72 63	272	160,000
	Doc Redman	65 71 67 69	272	160,000
8	Ryan Armour	64 70 70 69	273	117,000
	David Hearn	68 72 67 66	273	117,000
	Kramer Hickok	67 68 69 69	273	117,000
11	Kiradech Aphibarnrat	71 66 69 68	274	93,000
	Michael Gligic	68 71 69 66	274	93,000
	Anirban Lahiri	68 70 69 67	274	93,000
14	Doug Ghim	64 74 68 69	275	75,000
	Scott Piercy	67 70 72 66	275	75,000
16	Chesson Hadley	68 71 71 66	276	61,000
	Russell Knox	67 74 67 68	276	61,000
	Hank Lebioda	68 72 69 67	276	61,000
	Roger Sloan	67 70 71 68	276	61,000
	Will Zalatoris	69 72 67 68	276	61,000
21	Brice Garnett	68 70 74 65	277	41,960
	Peter Malnati	63 74 70 70	277	41,960
	Maverick McNealy	69 71 69 68	277	41,960
	Andrew Putnam	69 73 67 68	277	41,960
	Sepp Straka	70 70 69 68	277	41,960
26	Mark Anderson	69 70 69 70	278	28,000
	Ryan Brehm	68 74 65 71	278	28,000
	Padraig Harrington	67 71 71 69	278	28,000
	Beau Hossler	71 68 69 70	278	28,000
	Cameron Percy	70 72 71 65	278	28,000
	Adam Schenk	69 71 66 72	278	28,000
	Scott Stallings	68 73 70 67	278	28,000
	Aaron Wise	68 73 69 68	278	28,000
34	William Gordon	69 72 68 70	279	21,800
	Emiliano Grillo	66 72 70 71	279	21,800
	Max Homa	69 71 72 67	279	21,800
37	Rasmus Hojgaard	70 71 70 69	280	19,000
	Seamus Power	69 74 68 69	280	19,000
	Peter Uihlein	72 67 72 69	280	19,000
40	Luke Donald	69 68 71 73	281	15,800
	Branden Grace	73 70 71 67	281	15,800
	Troy Merritt	69 70 71 71	281	15,800
	Vaughn Taylor	65 75 71 70	281	15,800
	Kevin Tway	68 74 69 70	281	15,800
45	Joseph Bramlett	69 73 71 69	282	12,240
	DA Points	70 72 69 71	282	12,240
	DJ Trahan	67 75 72 68	282	12,240
	Johnson Wagner	66 74 69 73	282	12,240
49	Michael Miller	71 72 72 68	283	10,180
	Keith Mitchell	70 73 74 66	283	10,180
	John Senden	68 74 69 72	283	10,180
	Ben Taylor	71 72 70 70	283	10,180
53	Jonathan Byrd	70 73 71 70	284	9,560
	Luke List	68 72 72 72	284	9,560
55	Robert Streb	67 74 72 72	285	9,320
	Camilo Villegas	72 71 71 71	285	9,320
	Danny Willett	67 74 72 72	285	9,320
58	Jason Dufner	71 72 69 74	286	9,160
59	Fred Funk	69 72 75 71	287	9,000
	Patrick Rodgers	68 73 74 72	287	9,000
	Jhonattan Vegas	67 76 75 69	287	9,000
62	Kyoung-Hoon Lee	70 70 76 72	288	8,840
63	Ricky Barnes	71 71 75 72	289	8,720
	Hudson Swafford	67 75 71 76	289	8,720
65	Hunter Mahan	66 75 74 77	292	8,560
	Kyle Stanley	70 73 76 73	292	8,560
67	Matthew Borchert	73 70 75 76	294	8,440
68	Eric Dugas	66 74 82 76	298	8,360

Vivint Houston Open

The Vivint Houston Open was fairly begging for the obvious references to memorable events.

The tournament was returning to Memorial Park after a long absence; it was one of the PGA Tour’s pandemic-forced reschedules; fans were returning at last (although limited), and the winner was former Texas college whiz Carlos Ortiz, who became the first Mexican to win on the tour in 42 years. That’s a fistful of memories.

“Getting a win is amazing, but getting a win here in Texas made it even better,” said Ortiz, 29, who grew up in Guadalajara, played his college golf at North Texas University and lives in Dallas. “There was a bunch of people cheering for me, Latinos and Texans. I’m thankful for all of them.”

As to the return of fans — it wasn’t much, but in the gloom and dreariness of the deadly pandemic, it was a brilliant beacon. The Houston, rescheduled from the spring to early November because of the pandemic, was the first domestic PGA Tour event to have fans since The Players Championship, cancelled after the first round on March 12.

Only 2,000 fans were permitted each day to Memorial Park, but it was a crowd compared to the empty, silent courses of the previous eight months.

"I think that's a big reason why I played well today," said Brandt Snedeker, first-round leader on a five-under-par 65. "I love having fans out here. It's great to hear people excited for good shots and birdies."

The tournament had returned to Houston's public Memorial Park for the first time since 1963. It had been renovated and won the praise of golfers. Said Sam Burns, who led the second and third rounds: "It's not a matter of 'if,' it's a matter of 'when', this golf course will hit you."

If it hit Ortiz, it didn't really hurt him. He hung close for the first three rounds and took the lead in the fourth, shooting 67-68-67-65 for a 13-under 267, outrunning Hideki Matsuyama and world number one Dustin Johnson by two. Matsuyama shot 63, Johnson 65. Johnson was making his first start since the US Open in September, sitting out after a positive coronavirus test.

Pro golf seemed easy for Ortiz at first. He won three times on the Web.com Tour (now the Korn Ferry) in his first year, 2014, gaining membership on the PGA Tour. Unsettled times followed, and he returned to the PGA Tour after the 2018 season. And in this, his 118th start, he became the first Mexican to win on the PGA Tour since Victor Regalado in 1978.

And he survived a severe test on the final back nine.

Johnson, tied for the lead, got stung by his seven-iron approach at the par-five 16th. It left him a tough chip shot, which left him an 18-footer for birdie. He two-putted for par.

Matsuyama birdied 16 and 17, the latter with a 15-footer that tied him for the lead briefly.

Ortiz broke it at the 16th after a six-iron second so pleasing that he was walking just after he hit it. He two-putted from eight feet for a birdie and the lead. Then he locked up the two-shot win at the 18th, holing a 22-footer for a birdie.

"I wasn't really thinking about the other guys, I wasn't worried," Ortiz said. "I knew if I played good I was going to be hard to beat. I knew I was capable of doing that because I know myself, but obviously validating that and then showing it, it definitely gives me more confidence. I'm just happy the way it played out."

Memorial Park Golf Course, Houston, Texas — November 5-8
Par 70 (35-35); 7,021 yards — Purse: $7,000,000

1	**Carlos Ortiz**	67	68	67	65	267	$1,260,000
2	**Dustin Johnson**	72	66	66	65	269	623,000
	Hideki Matsuyama	70	70	66	63	269	623,000
4	Talor Gooch	68	69	71	63	271	343,000
5	Brooks Koepka	72	70	65	65	272	270,375
	Sepp Straka	68	69	66	69	272	270,375
7	Sam Burns	68	65	68	72	273	212,625
	Jason Day	67	68	67	71	273	212,625
	Tyrrell Hatton	71	70	67	65	273	212,625
	Mackenzie Hughes	70	72	68	63	273	212,625
11	Patton Kizzire	69	67	70	68	274	155,750
	Adam Long	68	70	69	67	274	155,750
	Shane Lowry	69	69	68	68	274	155,750
	Aaron Wise	70	66	69	69	274	155,750
15	Viktor Hovland	70	69	68	68	275	113,750
	Russell Knox	69	71	67	68	275	113,750
	Francesco Molinari	70	68	71	66	275	113,750
	Michael Thompson	67	72	67	69	275	113,750
	Harold Varner III	67	71	72	65	275	113,750
20	Maverick McNealy	71	71	67	67	276	82,600
	JT Poston	70	67	70	69	276	82,600
	Dawie van der Walt	70	66	69	71	276	82,600
	Erik van Rooyen	71	69	69	67	276	82,600
24	Scott Brown	69	68	72	68	277	58,450
	Corey Conners	69	67	73	68	277	58,450
	Austin Cook	71	72	68	66	277	58,450
	Tony Finau	69	69	68	71	277	58,450
	Brian Harman	71	69	72	65	277	58,450
29	Russell Henley	69	72	69	68	278	47,950
	Charley Hoffman	71	69	71	67	278	47,950
	Cameron Tringale	70	70	69	69	278	47,950
32	Padraig Harrington	71	68	71	69	279	39,083
	Scott Piercy	68	74	69	68	279	39,083
	Fabian Gomez	70	69	69	71	279	39,083
	Troy Merritt	74	68	69	68	279	39,083
	Scottie Scheffler	67	75	72	65	279	39,083
	Adam Scott	68	69	74	68	279	39,083
38	Erik Barnes	71	72	73	64	280	29,750
	William Gordon	76	67	65	72	280	29,750
	Justin Harding	72	68	72	68	280	29,750
	Satoshi Kodaira	70	69	72	69	280	29,750
	Nate Lashley	73	68	69	70	280	29,750
	Denny McCarthy	69	72	69	70	280	29,750
44	Chris Kirk	73	68	74	66	281	22,750
	Graeme McDowell	69	73	69	70	281	22,750
	Brandt Snedeker	65	71	76	69	281	22,750
	Jhonattan Vegas	73	70	68	70	281	22,750
48	Max Homa	74	68	69	71	282	19,040
	John Huh	73	69	69	71	282	19,040
50	Greg Chalmers	68	73	72	70	283	16,888
	Brice Garnett	74	68	72	69	283	16,888
	James Hahn	71	71	73	68	283	16,888
	Mark Hubbard	69	71	72	71	283	16,888
	Sungjae Im	74	69	73	67	283	16,888
	Zach Johnson	73	70	69	71	283	16,888
	Isaiah Salinda	71	69	75	68	283	16,888
	Brian Stuard	73	69	69	72	283	16,888
58	Lanto Griffin	72	71	71	70	284	15,890
	Kramer Hickok	75	68	68	73	284	15,890
	Cheng Tsung Pan	72	69	73	70	284	15,890

61	Kevin Chappell	70 71 72 72	285	15,540
	Doc Redman	71 70 73 71	285	15,540
63	Matt Jones	69 72 77 68	286	15,330
64	Jamie Lovemark	73 69 70 75	287	15,120
	Kristoffer Ventura	69 69 76 73	287	15,120
66	Scott Harrington	70 72 74 73	289	14,840
	Sean O'Hair	71 69 75 74	289	14,840
68	Cameron Davis	67 76 77 75	295	14,630

The RSM Classic

Can a son of the great flatlands find happiness on a lush Atlantic island in Georgia?

You bet. In a heartbeat and a playoff. Or two playoffs, to be precise.

Thus Robert Streb, born in Oklahoma and living in Kansas, picked up his second PGA Tour victory in the RSM Classic at the Sea Island Resort on St Simons Island. His first victory? Same place, in 2014. Also in a playoff. (It was then called the McGladrey Classic.)

Two wins — on the same golf course? Mere coincidence?

"I don't have a good answer for you," Streb said. "My finishes here are all over the lot, but I do like it here. The greens are always pure and I feel like if you're playing good, you can do well."

In the playoff with hard-closing Kevin Kisner at the Seaside Course's par-four 18th, Streb won on the second extra hole, nearly holing a brilliant pitching wedge from 159 yards. The ball grazed the hole and stopped a foot away. He tapped in the winning birdie.

"Came out perfect, landed soft," Streb said. "I was going to need a little fortune to get close, and I got it."

Cracked Kisner, now 0-5 in extra time: "I just wanted to keep my playoff record intact."

This could be called the Grand Irony Open. In 2014, Streb trailed by five shots heading into the final round, shot 63 to force the playoff, and won. This time, Streb was the leader and Kisner shot 63 to tie and force a playoff. Streb ended the similarity with the exquisite wedge shot and tap-in. The two wins felt differently, however.

"Trying to run in front all day, to me, is sometimes a little hard because you're not necessarily pedal to the metal," Streb said. "Maybe I should have been, but just trying to kill the butterflies the first couple holes and get into it."

Playing the par-72 Plantation Course in the second round and the par-70 Seaside Course in the other three, Streb shot 65-63-67-68 for a 19-under total of 263, and was tied by Kisner's 68 on Plantation followed by 66-66-63.

Streb took the lead in the second round with his flawless performance on the Plantation Course, a nine-birdie 63, matching his career-low. He led by two over Colombia's Camilo Villegas, the sympathy favourite. Villegas, just back after missing a year with a shoulder injury, lost his daughter Mia, not quite two, to cancer in July. "She loved colours and rainbows," he said. He would tie for sixth.

Streb pulled himself out of a shaky start in the third round to post a 67 for a three-stroke lead over Zach Johnson, who birdied three of his last five holes for a 65, and Bronson Burgoon, who birdied five out of six holes coming in for a 67.

In the final round, Streb worked his way to a 68 while Kisner churned away to a flawless 63 to tie. The win settled things for Streb, who had bounced between the Korn Ferry Tour and the PGA Tour since his arrival six years ago. And now the son of the flatlands seemed to have found a home at Sea Island.

"Maybe I should at least come down here in the winter," Streb said. "It's been very good to me."

Sea Island Resort (Seaside), Sea Island, Georgia — November 19-22
Par 70 (35-35); 7,005 yards — Purse: $6,600,000
Plantation (R1&2) par 72 (36-36); 7,060 yards

1	**Robert Streb**	65 63 67 68	263	$1,188,000
2	**Kevin Kisner**	68 66 66 63	263	719,400
	Streb won playoff at second extra hole			
3	**Cameron Tringale**	67 68 67 62	264	455,400
4	Andrew Landry	68 68 65 64	265	297,000
4	Bernd Wiesberger	66 68 68 63	265	297,000
6	Harris English	66 66 72 62	266	215,325
	Zach Johnson	66 67 65 68	266	215,325
	Kyle Stanley	67 65 68 66	266	215,325
	Camilo Villegas	64 66 70 66	266	215,325
10	Corey Conners	67 70 66 64	267	173,250
	Patton Kizzire	65 66 70 66	267	173,250

12	Jason Day	69	67	67	65	268	140,250
	John Huh	69	68	66	65	268	140,250
	Rory Sabbatini	65	72	66	65	268	140,250
15	Keegan Bradley	67	68	67	67	269	113,850
	Bronson Burgoon	68	63	67	71	269	113,850
	Matthew NeSmith	72	63	66	68	269	113,850
18	Doug Ghim	67	71	68	64	270	87,450
	Emiliano Grillo	66	68	65	71	270	87,450
	Chris Kirk	70	67	67	66	270	87,450
	Alex Noren	66	71	68	65	270	87,450
	Scott Piercy	70	66	69	65	270	87,450
23	Wyndham Clark	70	66	70	65	271	55,959
	Lucas Glover	71	68	67	65	271	55,959
	Chesson Hadley	73	65	66	67	271	55,959
	Tyrrell Hatton	69	68	69	65	271	55,959
	Charley Hoffman	68	69	67	67	271	55,959
	Roger Sloan	67	69	71	64	271	55,959
	Henrik Stenson	69	68	71	63	271	55,959
30	Russell Henley	70	69	67	66	272	39,553
	Jim Herman	68	67	69	68	272	39,553
	Bo Hoag	68	71	66	67	272	39,553
	Adam Long	67	68	69	68	272	39,553
	Vaughn Taylor	70	66	71	65	272	39,553
	Branden Grace	70	68	70	64	272	39,553
	Charles Howell III	68	67	72	65	272	39,553
37	Tommy Fleetwood	67	72	67	67	273	28,710
	Matt Kuchar	70	66	67	70	273	28,710
	Nate Lashley	68	67	71	67	273	28,710
	Andrew Putnam	71	68	68	66	273	28,710
	Webb Simpson	68	71	68	66	273	28,710
	Brendon Todd	68	70	67	68	273	28,710
	Matt Wallace	64	71	70	68	273	28,710
44	Matt Jones	67	71	70	66	274	21,450
	Keith Mitchell	69	66	70	69	274	21,450
	Joaquin Niemann	73	66	70	65	274	21,450
	Sepp Straka	71	65	72	66	274	21,450
48	Peter Malnati	65	70	73	67	275	17,952
	Adam Schenk	73	66	70	66	275	17,952
50	Joel Dahmen	74	61	71	70	276	16,401
	Shane Lowry	67	71	71	67	276	16,401
	Ian Poulter	69	69	68	70	276	16,401
	Brian Stuard	74	63	72	67	276	16,401
54	Rafa Cabrera Bello	71	68	70	68	277	15,510
	Kevin Streelman	71	67	69	70	277	15,510
	Josh Teater	73	66	71	67	277	15,510
57	Aaron Baddeley	68	69	69	72	278	15,180
	Sebastian Cappelen	68	71	71	68	278	15,180
59	Graeme McDowell	70	68	70	72	280	14,784
	Sean O'Hair	70	68	69	73	280	14,784
	Rob Oppenheim	73	66	70	71	280	14,784
	JJ Spaun	68	69	74	69	280	14,784
63	Ryan Brehm	72	66	69	76	283	14,388
	Scott Stallings	69	68	78	68	283	14,388
65	Kevin Chappell	71	67	71	76	285	14,190

TaylorMade Pebble Beach Invitational

Kyle Reifers had little reason to be encouraged when he opened the unofficial TaylorMade Pebble Beach Invitational trailing by five shots. But come the fourth round, with Pebble playing fast and firm in November weather, he erased a one-stroke deficit and rolled to a three-stroke victory over Kirk Triplett, of the Champions Tour.

Reifers, 37, took his first lead in the final round, with eagles at the second and third at Pebble, and built it to a four-stroke cushion.

Reifers shot 70-68-69-68 for 275, 13 under par, in posting his third victory since turning pro in 2006. His previous victories were in 2006, in the Charlotte National Open on the Tarheel Tour, followed by his playoff win over Brandt Snedeker in the Chattanooga Classic on the Nationwide Tour (now the Korn Ferry Tour).

Triplett, who won four different events at Pebble — two of them on the Champions Tour — trailed by six after the first round, and entered the fourth trailing Brandon Wu by three. Triplett, who won the event in 2006 when it was known as the Merrill Lynch Open, finished second on 71-70-68-69, 10 under. Wu shot 69-66-71-74 and Germany's Stephan Jeager 65-72-69-74 to tie for third at 280.

LPGA pro Alison Lee was the highest woman finisher, tying for 14th on 72-67-70-79, level par.

The tournament, which began in 1972 as the Hyatt Invitational, has the most diverse field in golf, with 51 players from the PGA Tour, Champions and Korn Ferry tours, and the LPGA Tour. The competition also includes teams of four amateurs, each team playing with a different pro each day. The tournament was played at Pebble Beach, Spyglass Hill and Spanish Bay.

Because of coronavirus pandemic restrictions, fans were not admitted for the first time in the tournament's history.

Pebble Beach Golf Links, Pebble Beach, California
Par 72 (36-36); 6,828 yards
Spyglass Hill (R1-2) par 72 (36-36); 6,960 yards
Links at Spanish Bay (R2-3) par 72 (35-37); 6,821 yards

November 19-22
Purse: $300,000

1	**Kyle Reifers**	70	68	69	68	275	$60,000
2	**Kirk Triplett**	71	70	68	69	278	
3	**Brandon Wu**	69	66	71	74	280	
	Stephan Jaeger	65	72	69	74	280	
5	Taylor Montgomery	74	69	67	71	281	
6	Theo Humphrey	71	67	74	70	282	
	Austin Smotherman	70	67	70	75	282	
8	Ricky Barnes	72	70	70	71	283	
	Esteban Toledo	65	72	75	71	283	
10	Dawie van der Walt	71	73	69	72	285	
11	Austen Truslow	72	69	76	70	287	
	Olin Browne Jr	70	73	73	71	287	
	Paul Barjon	69	69	75	74	287	
14	Taylor Moore	72	76	69	71	288	
	Colt Knost	72	73	72	71	288	
	Alison Lee	72	67	70	79	288	
	Davis Riley	68	76	67	77	288	
18	Jared Wolfe	74	70	72	73	289	
19	Bailey Tardy	76	69	74	71	290	
	Steve Flesch	73	69	75	73	290	
21	Brandon Harkins	67	73	76	76	292	
22	John Mallinger	76	73	70	74	293	
	Martin Flores	72	71	74	76	293	
24	Richard Lee	73	75	74	72	294	
	Dylan Wu	71	75	74	74	294	
	Jin Park	73	75	70	76	294	
	Kevin Dougherty	75	72	70	77	294	
28	Tom Pernice Jr	78	72	71	74	295	
	Olin Browne	70	74	77	74	295	
	Matt Bettencourt	74	70	71	80	295	

Mayakoba Golf Classic

Quick — what's the Norwegian word for "phenom"?

Well, until the translator shows up, "Viktor Hovland" should do.

That's the name of a 23-year-old from the land of the Northern Lights who seemed headed for that rarefied status. Was that a hint — taking the Mayakoba Golf Classic presented by UNIFIN? It was, after all, his second PGA Tour win in 2020 and he had taken both with clutch birdie putts on the final hole. In February, it was the Puerto Rico Open with a 30-footer, and this time, in December, the Mayakoba with a 12-footer.

The Mayakoba, at the par 71 El Camaleon on Mexico's Yucatan coast, was the final official PGA Tour event of the year. Hovland had already qualified for the Sentry Tournament of Champions early in 2021 and he already had a place in the Masters, and he wasn't thinking about phenoms.

"I was shaking there at the end," he said. "I knew I had to make birdie on 18."

Scotland's Russell Knox took the first-round lead on a six-under 65, playing aggressively, he said, despite the brisk Caribbean winds. "I guess it's the tequila and the tacos," Knox offered. Hovland was two back at 67 after a strong finish. He had parred his first nine — the back — with a birdie and a bogey. Then he went four under on his last five holes, starting with an eagle at the fifth, and birdies at the seventh and ninth holes. "Feel good about my game," he said. Not so much in the second round after a two-under 69 consisting of six birdies, all on the front nine, and four scattered bogeys. He had slipped seven off the lead, behind Argentina's Emiliano Grillo, who birdied half the course for a 63 in a round suspended by darkness because of a rain delay.

Grillo would keep a one-shot lead with a 68 in the third round, but now Hovland made his move. He shook off a bogey at the first, strung out nine birdies, and leaped up to third place with a 63. With better chipping and putting, he said, "I don't have to have so many things go my way to shoot a 63".

The final round became a head-to-head clash between Hovland and Aaron Wise three groups ahead. Wise, 24, Rookie of the Year in 2018, started five off the lead but three behind Hovland. And the race was on. Wise gave Hovland something to shoot at, making three birdies and an eagle on the front nine. Hovland had four birdies, and led him by two. Coming in, Wise birdied three straight from the 13th, shot 63, and was in at 19-under 265.

"I hit every shot as good as I could hit it," Wise said. "I just couldn't get them to drop."

Hovland went bogey-birdie-birdie from the 12th and came to his first clutch performance. At the par-four 16th, he saved par with a sensational 40-yard recovery shot from a waste area to four feet. Then the next performance — at 18, he rolled in that 12-footer for his seventh birdie, a 65, a 20-under 264 total and that second victory.

"I don't really feel like I'm honestly very good at those pressure situations," Hovland said. But at the

18th: "I told myself, 'OK, I was able to do it in Puerto Rico, hopefully I can do it today'. But you know, it's still hard."

El Camaleon Golf Club, Playa del Carmen, Mexico
Par 71 (36-35); 7,017 yards

December 3-6
Purse: $7,200,000

1	**Viktor Hovland**	67	69	63	65	264	$1,296,000
2	**Aaron Wise**	67	68	67	63	265	784,800
3	**Tom Hoge**	66	67	65	69	267	424,800
	Adam Long	70	67	63	67	267	424,800
5	Harris English	69	70	66	63	268	266,400
	Lucas Glover	71	65	66	66	268	266,400
	Billy Horschel	70	69	65	64	268	266,400
8	Tony Finau	67	66	69	67	269	203,400
	Emiliano Grillo	66	63	68	72	269	203,400
	Carlos Ortiz	67	69	67	66	269	203,400
	Brendon Todd	67	69	67	66	269	203,400
12	Abraham Ancer	72	67	65	66	270	147,600
	Max Homa	73	67	65	65	270	147,600
	Maverick McNealy	70	71	63	66	270	147,600
	Justin Thomas	72	67	62	69	270	147,600
	Austin Eckroat (A)	69	69	67	65	270	
17	Corey Conners	71	66	68	66	271	117,000
	Patrick Rodgers	70	66	65	70	271	117,000
	Steve Stricker	69	70	65	67	271	117,000
20	Joel Dahmen	68	67	68	69	272	95,400
	John Huh	70	67	70	65	272	95,400
	Jhonattan Vegas	69	70	67	66	272	95,400
23	Daniel Berger	69	70	67	67	273	65,263
	Tyler Duncan	70	67	68	68	273	65,263
	Bo Hoag	68	70	66	69	273	65,263
	Charles Howell III	72	69	67	65	273	65,263
	Vincent Whaley	71	66	69	67	273	65,263
	Russell Knox	65	69	68	71	273	65,263
	Joaquin Niemann	66	70	67	70	273	65,263
30	Chris Baker	68	68	72	66	274	50,400
	Brian Harman	70	69	66	69	274	50,400
32	Keegan Bradley	69	72	68	66	275	43,056
	Brice Garnett	74	65	66	70	275	43,056
	Patton Kizzire	72	68	71	64	275	43,056
	Kevin Streelman	69	71	71	64	275	43,056
	Camilo Villegas	70	66	69	70	275	43,056
37	Sung Kang	70	70	69	67	276	37,440
38	Nate Lashley	67	69	74	67	277	34,920
	Hank Lebioda	71	69	70	67	277	34,920
40	Branden Grace	71	68	69	70	278	29,160
	Brandon Hagy	69	70	69	70	278	29,160
	Satoshi Kodaira	70	70	66	72	278	29,160
	Troy Merritt	70	68	73	67	278	29,160
	Scott Piercy	70	70	68	70	278	29,160
	Rory Sabbatini	69	70	70	69	278	29,160
46	KJ Choi	70	70	69	70	279	20,952
	Doug Ghim	71	69	71	68	279	20,952
	Charley Hoffman	72	66	70	71	279	20,952
	Chris Kirk	69	70	68	72	279	20,952
	Andy Ogletree	69	67	70	73	279	20,952
	Kyle Stanley	68	67	72	72	279	20,952
52	Akshay Bhatia	67	69	70	74	280	17,208
	Rafael Campos	72	68	69	71	280	17,208
	Jason Dufner	69	68	70	73	280	17,208
	Kelly Kraft	70	71	71	68	280	17,208
	Pat Perez	68	72	68	72	280	17,208
	Sepp Straka	73	68	67	72	280	17,208
	Will Zalatoris	72	68	67	73	280	17,208
59	Ryan Brehm	69	67	70	75	281	16,272
	Mark Hubbard	71	67	69	74	281	16,272
	Kyoung-Hoon Lee	69	70	67	75	281	16,272
	Chase Seiffert	69	69	69	74	281	16,272
63	Austin Cook	70	70	70	72	282	15,840
	Xinjun Zhang	72	69	73	68	282	15,840
65	JJ Spaun	70	69	73	71	283	15,552
	Ben Taylor	72	69	72	70	283	15,552
67	Hunter Mahan	68	69	73	74	284	15,336
	Quade Cummins (A)	71	70	74	69	284	
69	Michael Gellerman	70	70	71	75	286	15,192
70	Keith Mitchell	70	70	71	76	287	15,048
71	Harold Varner III	70	71	75	73	289	14,904

QBE Shootout

"The show Harris put on on the back nine was just awesome," Matt Kuchar was saying. "He pulled me aside after 14 and said, 'I think we need two shots to set the new mark'. I said, 'We've got four chances'."

Harris' response was about to rewrite some history.

This was in the final round of the QBE Shootout in December at Tiburon Golf Club, site of 12 two-player teams battling it out in three different competition formats. And old hat to Kuchar and Harris, who with this one — played at better-ball — pretty well in hand, decided to go after some records.

Kuchar noted what Harris did with the four chances to set the new mark.

"He went ahead and went birdie-eagle-birdie to close it out," Kuchar said. "It was fun to watch."

They ran away with the title. They were the first team to win the event three times. They shot a record 37-under-par total of 179, breaking their own previous record of 34 under, and they won by a record nine strokes, breaking their previous record of seven.

Defending champions Rory Sabbatini and Kevin Tway tied for second at 28 under with first-round leaders Kevin Na and Sean O'Hair and the rookie team of Lanto Griffin and Mackenzie Hughes. Sabbatini and Tway closed with a 61, Griffin and Hughes 62, and Na and O'Hair 64.

Na and O'Hair leaped into the first-round lead, posting two eagles and 12 birdies in the scramble format for a 16-under 56. O'Hair credited Na's putting — "It felt pretty easy, watching him make everything he looked at" — and Na credited O'Hair's driving: "A lot of bombs 30, 40 yards ahead of me."

Kuchar and English took over in the alternate-shot second round, riding long birdie runs to an 11-under 61 and a five-stroke lead at 25 under. They birdied the first five holes, then six straight from the 12th. They were a good fit, Harris said. "He does a lot of stuff that I'm not great at, and maybe I do some stuff he's not great at." But there was a caution from Kuchar for the final round, which would be played at better-ball. Birdies would be needed. "Guys are going to shoot some low scores," he said. "Pars aren't going to be helping out very much."

And they got the birdies. They closed with a better-ball of 60. And Kuchar saluted English's birdie-eagle-birdie parade. "It's hard to fathom," said Kuchar, "just how good that golf was."

Tiburon Golf Course, Naples, Florida — December 11-13
Par 72 (36-36); 7,382 yards — Purse: $3,600,000

1	**Harris English/Matt Kuchar**	58	61	60	179	$447,500
2	**Lanto Griffin/Mackenzie Hughes**	58	68	62	188	195,000
	Kevin Na/Sean O'Hair	56	68	64	188	195,000
	Rory Sabbatini/Kevin Tway	59	68	61	188	195,000
5	Cameron Champ/Billy Horschel	59	68	63	190	105,833
	Tony Finau/Louis Oosthuizen	59	68	63	190	105,833
	Brendon Todd/Bubba Watson	62	66	62	190	105,833
8	Marc Leishman/Cameron Smith	62	67	62	191	95,000
9	Daniel Berger/Steve Stricker	60	69	63	192	92,500
10	Ryan Palmer/Harold Varner III	57	71	66	194	90,000
11	Abraham Ancer/Matthew Wolff	62	69	64	195	87,500
12	Sebastian Munoz/Joaquin Niemann	61	69	68	198	85,000

PNC Championship

Team Thomas, Justin and his dad Mike, making their debuts in the celebrated event, blistered the second and final round, birdieing the first seven holes, then birdied the final hole to win the PNC Championship, the long-running, pre-Christmas TV family institution. But Team Woods, also making their debut, had already stolen the show. Not so much Tiger Woods. The other one — little Charlie. His son. Age 11.

On the scoreboard, Tiger and Charlie had finished seventh, five behind Team Thomas. But for the TV viewership and a scattering of fans at the Ritz-Carlton Golf Club in Orlando, this show belonged to Charlie, the youngest ever to play in the event since it began 25 years earlier as the Father-Son Challenge. Charlie upstaged even his dad. Playing from tees perhaps 100 yards ahead, he would hit first, then turn and signal his dad whether his tee shot was good or not. Mostly, Tiger would get a thumbs-up OK and a twirl of the driver. And the ultimate approval — they would use Charlie's tee shot.

The PNC, a two-round, two-day scramble event of 20 teams, began as a father-son, and eventually evolved into a champion-family member pairing such as Annika Sorenstam and dad Tom, and defending champion Bernhard Langer and daughter Jackie.

The Thomases trailed the Kuchars, Matt and Cameron, by four with their first-round 62, then roared through the second, chewing off birdies in bunches — the first seven holes, then three from the ninth, then four from 13 and finally the winner at the last, with dad Mike dropping the five-footer for a 57, a 25-under total of 119 and a one-shot victory.

"More emotional than other victories," Justin said. "I wanted my dad to make that putt so bad."

Vijay Singh and son Qass were second with 60-60 for 24 under. Mark and Shaun O'Meara, and Lee and Daniel Trevino tied for third.

Tiger and Charlie played their final six holes in six under and finished at 20 under after two scores of 62. Not surprisingly, Charlie even swung like his dad. As golf writer Doug Ferguson summed up the like-father, like-son in the Associated Press: "Charlie confidently twirled his club before shots, quickly picked up the tee on his drives and even pumped his fist on the par-five third hole with a three-wood into three feet for eagle."

"I don't really care about my game," Woods said. "I'm just making sure that Charlie has the time of his life. And he's doing that."

Ritz-Carlton Golf Club, Grande Lakes, Orlando, Florida — December 17-19
Par 72 (36-36); 7,106 yards — Purse: $1,085,000

1	**Justin Thomas/Mike Thomas**	62	57	119	$200,000
2	**Vijay Singh/Qass Singh**	60	60	120	80,000
3	**Mark O'Meara/Shaun O'Meara**	62	59	121	53,625
	Lee Trevino/Daniel Trevino	62	59	121	53,625
5	Tom Kite/David Kite	64	58	122	48,500
	Matt Kuchar/Cameron Kuchar	58	64	122	48,500
7	Tiger Woods/Charlie Woods	62	62	124	47,000
8	John Daly/Little John Daly	62	63	125	46,000
9	Jim Furyk/Tanner Furyk	62	64	126	44,500
	Tom Lehman/Sean Lehman	61	65	126	44,500
	Greg Norman/Greg Norman Jr	61	65	126	44,500
12	Lee Janzen/Connor Janzen	67	60	127	43,250
	Bernhard Langer/Jackie Langer John	63	64	127	43,250
14	David Duval/Brady Duval	61	67	128	42,250
	Nick Price/Greg Price	65	63	128	42,250
16	Gary Player/James Throssell	66	63	129	41,500
17	Annika Sorenstam/Tom Sorenstam	65	65	130	41,000
18	Bubba Watson/Wayne Ball	65	67	132	40,500
19	Mark Calcavecchia/Eric Calcavecchia	67	66	133	40,250
20	Padraig Harrington/Paddy Harrington	69	66	135	40,000

Korn Ferry Tour

The Korn Ferry Tour for 2020 could probably be best summed up by the simple little statement at the bottom of the announcement of the new schedule. The irony wasn't intended.

Said the statement: "The Korn Ferry Tour will welcome four new events to the 2020 calendar."

The tour was being successful and planned on becoming more successful. But that was before Covid-19 arrived.

That was in October 2019, when the tour was anticipating the robust new 2020 season.

The ink, metaphorically speaking, was barely dry when what followed was sheer chaos.

Enter the Covid-19 pandemic, rearranging life and the golf landscape with it, including the great shutdown. The Korn Ferry Tour also had shut down for three months, and play resumed early in June.

The PGA Tour was forced into an extensive revision that could be summed up this way: because the Covid-19 pandemic caused the cancellation or postponement of 13 events, no players would lose their eligibility. Which meant that no Korn Ferry players could be "graduated" to the PGA Tour because there were no vacancies, until the following year (at the earliest). Which meant further that the 2020 Korn Ferry season would become the 2020-21 season, with the graduation coming at the end.

Said the PGA Tour's announcement: "The newly created 2020-21 Korn Ferry Tour schedule that will bridge two seasons will conclude with 25 PGA Tour cards awarded at the 2021 WinCo Foods Portland Open presented by KraftHeinz, with an additional 25 cards awarded at the conclusion of the 2021 Korn Ferry Tour Finals."

The acclaimed Will Zalatoris avoided all such complications by vaulting right from the Korn Ferry to the PGA Tour with a Special Temporary Membership because of his strong showing in five starts on the PGA Tour. The special status made him eligible for unlimited sponsor exemptions for the remainder of the 2020-21 PGA Tour season. He gained it through top-10 finishes at the US Open (tie for sixth), Corales Puntacana Resort & Club Championship (tie for eighth), Shriners Hospitals for Children Open (tie for fifth) and a tie for 16th in the Bermuda Championship. And at the US Open, he had the distinction of making a hole-in-one at Winged Foot's par-three seventh in the first round.

Zalatoris' first tour win, and also his first as a pro, came in July at the TPC Colorado Championship. He felt his par save on a 15-foot putt at the seventh was his crucial hole. "If I bogey from 110 yards out," he said, "that kind of ruins my day." Zalatoris shot a three-under 69 for a one-shot victory over Chase Johnson. "It's been probably four years since I've won a golf tournament," he said.

He also had nine other top-10 finishes, and topped the money list with $403,878.

The tour also had two double winners — Jared Wolfe and Davis Riley.

Jared Wolfe scored his first tour win in January, in the Bahamas Great Abaco Classic at Baha Mar, Nassau. He birdied three of the last four holes for a 69 — one of only two scores under 70 — for an 18-under 270 and a four-shot win over Brandon Harkins.

"No argument — it's definitely the biggest win of my career," Wolfe said.

Wolfe posted his second win in the Wichita Open in September. He had to survive some heavy going from both the elements and Taylor Pendrith at Crestview Country Club. Wolfe was leading by a stroke coming to the 18th. He missed the green but saved his par for a 71, a 16-under total of 264 and a one-stroke win when Pendrith missed his 15-footer for a tying birdie.

Davis Riley showed a touch for the dramatic in taking his first Korn Ferry victory in the Panama Championship at the Club de Golf de Panama. He bogeyed the 10th and slid back into a tie. Next came the shot of the tournament. At the par-five 12th, he rolled in a 70-foot putt for an eagle to reclaim the lead. "I knew if I just played solid from there on out, I'd be fine," Riley said. And he did and he was, posting a 69 for a 10-under 270 and a one-stroke win over Roberto Diaz.

Then it was fireworks for his second win when he birdied three of the last four holes in the TPC San Antonio Championship at the Oaks in July. He holed out from a bunker at the 15th, hit his tee shot to 18 inches at the 16th, and then stuck his approach inside two feet at the 18th for a five-under 67 and a two-stroke win over Paul Barjon and Pendrith at 16 under. "I tried to control my breathing," Riley said.

Among other winners:

Seth Reeves, closing with a 64, got the golf right but the fist pump wrong at the Pinnacle Bank

Championship presented by Aetna in Omaha, Nebraska. "I fist-pumped my birdie putt on 18 because I thought it secured a top 10," Reeves said. Top 10, indeed. He discovered that he'd won — and after starting from eight shots behind.

Brandon Wu came from five behind to score his first tour victory at the Korn Ferry Tour Championship presented by United Leasing & Finance in Newburgh, Indiana. "It's almost surreal," he said. "Just over a month and a half ago I was still playing Monday qualifiers."

Final-hole magic: a year earlier, at the WinCo Foods Portland Open, Lee Hodges got up and down for birdie on the 18th, narrowly making it into the top 75 in point standings to retain his eligibility. This time, at the same tournament, he got up and down for birdie again at the 18th for his first Korn Ferry victory and a spot in the US Open. Guillermo Mito Pereira won his first Korn Ferry title, taking the Country Club de Bogota Championship in Colombia by two shots when he eagled the 18th on a 20-foot putt.

2020 SCHEDULE

Bahamas Great Exuma Classic	**Tommy Gainey**
Bahamas Great Abaco Classic	**Jared Wolfe**
Panama Championship	**Davis Riley**
Country Club de Bogota Championship	**Guillermo Mito Pereira**
LECOM Suncoast Classic	**Andrew Novak**
El Bosque Mexico Championship	**David Kocher**
Korn Ferry Challenge	**Luke List**
The King & Bear Classic	**Chris Kirk**
Utah Championship	**Kyle Jones**
TPC Colorado Championship	**Will Zalatoris**
TPC San Antonio Challenge	**Davis Lipsky**
TPC San Antonio Championship	**Davis Riley**
Price Cutter Charity Championship	**Max McGreevy**
Pinnacle Bank Championship	**Seth Reeves**
WinCo Foods Portland Open	**Lee Hodges**
Albertsons Boise Open	**Stephan Jaeger**
Nationwide Children's Hospital Championship	**Curtis Luck**
Korn Ferry Tour Championship	**Brandon Wu**
Lincoln Land Championship	**Brett Drewitt**
Evans Scholars Invitational	**Curtis Thompson**
Wichita Open	**Jared Wolfe**
Savannah Golf Championship	**Evan Harmeling**
Orange County National Championship	**Trey Mullinax**

Bahamas Great Exuma Classic

Sandals Emerald Bay Golf Club, Great Exuma, Bahamas — January 12-15
Par 72 (36-36); 7,001 yards — Purse: $600,000

1	**Tommy Gainey**	66	75	67	69	277	$108,000
2	**John Oda**	69	71	70	71	281	45,000
	Dylan Wu	67	66	76	72	281	45,000
4	George Cunningham	71	69	69	73	282	22,425
	Sean O'Hair	70	71	69	72	282	22,425
	Jose de Jesus Rodriguez	69	72	68	73	282	22,425
	Will Zalatoris	70	74	65	73	282	22,425
8	Davis Riley	71	73	72	68	284	17,700
9	Mark Blakefield	68	78	68	71	285	15,900
	Adam Svensson	69	75	71	70	285	15,900
11	Julian Etulain	70	74	71	71	286	12,378
	Justin Lower	75	72	70	69	286	12,378
	Ryan Ruffels	74	69	70	73	286	12,378
	Ollie Schniederjans	73	71	69	73	286	12,378
	John VanDerLaan	71	75	72	68	286	12,378
16	Dan McCarthy	71	73	69	74	287	9,600
	Augusto Nunez	73	69	74	71	287	9,600
	Will Wilcox	71	73	69	74	287	9,600
19	Brent Grant	73	71	68	76	288	7,575
	Taylor Montgomery	72	74	70	72	288	7,575
	Kevin Roy	70	73	73	72	288	7,575
	Shane Smith	73	74	74	67	288	7,575
23	Kyle Jones	73	70	73	73	289	6,330
24	Roberto Diaz	71	76	74	69	290	5,456
	Robert Garrigus	70	74	75	71	290	5,456
	Greyson Sigg	73	71	75	71	290	5,456

Bahamas Great Abaco Classic

Royal Blue Golf Club, Nassau, Bahamas — January 19-22
Par 72 (36-36); 7,153 yards — Purse: $600,000

1	**Jared Wolfe**	67	69	65	69	270	$108,000
2	**Brandon Harkins**	70	66	66	72	274	54,000
3	**Nick Hardy**	72	65	67	71	275	28,600
	Billy Kennerly	70	66	72	67	275	28,600
	Curtis Thompson	70	65	69	71	275	28,600
6	Greg Yates	72	69	63	73	277	20,700
7	Roberto Diaz	70	68	67	73	278	18,450
	Jack Maguire	66	70	69	73	278	18,450
9	Scott Gutschewski	68	66	71	74	279	14,798
	Grant Hirschman	71	70	64	74	279	14,798
	Kevin Roy	68	68	70	73	279	14,798
	Callum Tarren	70	67	67	75	279	14,798
13	Chip McDaniel	71	66	67	76	280	10,860
	Andrew Novak	67	70	72	71	280	10,860
	Sean O'Hair	74	64	69	73	280	10,860
	Ben Silverman	70	70	68	72	280	10,860
	Will Wilcox	71	64	71	74	280	10,860
18	Dylan Wu	72	69	70	70	281	9,000
19	Daniel Miernicki	72	70	68	72	282	7,575
	Augusto Nunez	72	69	68	73	282	7,575
	Austin Smotherman	70	71	69	72	282	7,575
	TJ Vogel	71	69	69	73	282	7,575
23	Steven Alker	72	68	72	71	283	4,898
	Joshua Creel	69	69	71	74	283	4,898
	Nicolas Echavarria	71	71	67	74	283	4,898
	Richard Johnson	71	66	74	72	283	4,898
	Whee Kim	68	70	68	77	283	4,898
	Alex Prugh	70	70	67	76	283	4,898
	Greyson Sigg	71	69	69	74	283	4,898
	John VanDerLaan	69	70	68	76	283	4,898
	Drew Weaver	66	72	71	74	283	4,898
	Will Zalatoris	69	72	67	75	283	4,898

Panama Championship

Club de Golf de Panama, Panama City, Panama — January 30-February 2
Par 70 (35-35); 7,157 yards — Purse: $625,000

1	**Davis Riley**	67	70	64	69	270	$112,500
2	**Roberto Diaz**	67	70	69	65	271	56,250
3	**Lee Hodges**	69	67	67	69	272	27,734
	Ben Kohles	67	68	69	68	272	27,734
	Max McGreevy	70	63	69	70	272	27,734
	Guillermo Mito Pereira	68	69	65	70	272	27,734
7	Brett Drewitt	67	70	70	66	273	18,542
	Dylan Wu	67	70	67	69	273	18,542
	Nicholas Thompson	66	69	69	69	273	18,542
10	JT Griffin	68	71	70	65	274	13,831
	Luke Guthrie	70	68	68	68	274	13,831
	David Lipsky	67	68	68	71	274	13,831
	Curtis Thompson	68	72	68	66	274	13,831
	Jared Wolfe	66	69	69	70	274	13,831
15	Grant Hirschman	65	69	67	74	275	9,688
	Scott Langley	68	70	69	68	275	9,688
	Ryan Ruffels	65	70	70	70	275	9,688
	Greyson Sigg	64	69	73	69	275	9,688
	Callum Tarren	66	70	69	70	275	9,688
	Chase Wright	71	67	62	75	275	9,688
21	Dawson Armstrong	69	71	71	65	276	7,094
	John Chin	69	71	68	68	276	7,094
	Jack Maguire	71	68	71	66	276	7,094
24	Joey Garber	71	67	71	68	277	5,528
	Taylor Montgomery	69	68	70	70	277	5,528
	Taylor Pendrith	63	68	73	73	277	5,528
	Seth Reeves	67	67	68	75	277	5,528

Country Club de Bogota Championship

Country Club de Bogota (Lagos), Bogota, Colombia — February 6-9
Par 71 (35-36); 7,237 yards — Purse: $700,000
Pacos par 70 (35-35); 6,206 yards

1	**Guillermo Mito Pereira**	65	66	68	64	263	$126,000
2	**Ben Kohles**	66	67	67	65	265	63,000
3	**John Chin**	64	66	68	68	266	42,000
4	Camilo Villegas	64	65	69	69	267	29,050
	Patrick Fishburn	69	65	69	64	267	29,050
6	Kevin Lucas	65	68	68	67	268	22,400
	John VanDerLaan	66	63	66	73	268	22,400
	Brett Drewitt	64	69	67	68	268	22,400
9	Andrew Novak	71	64	70	64	269	17,885
	Will Zalatoris	67	69	63	70	269	17,885
	Trevor Cone	68	64	71	66	269	17,885
12	Augusto Nunez	71	65	67	67	270	13,913
	Davis Riley	69	64	69	68	270	13,913
	Jamie Arnold	68	68	68	66	270	13,913
	Roberto Diaz	64	69	68	69	270	13,913
16	Jack Maguire	68	65	71	67	271	10,500
	Greyson Sigg	70	66	68	67	271	10,500
	Braden Thornberry	70	64	70	67	271	10,500
	Ethan Tracy	67	63	70	71	271	10,500
	Grant Hirschman	68	67	67	69	271	10,500
21	Whee Kim	73	64	69	66	272	7,155
	Conrad Shindler	67	69	70	66	272	7,155
	Brett Stegmaier	67	69	69	67	272	7,155
	Mickey DeMorat	69	65	68	70	272	7,155
	Brent Grant	64	70	70	68	272	7,155
	Scott Gutschewski	71	64	69	68	272	7,155

LECOM Suncoast Classic

Lakewood National Golf Club (Commander), Lakewood Ranch, Florida — February 13-16
Par 72 (36-36); 7,161 yards — Purse: $600,000

1	**Andrew Novak**	69	64	66	66	265	$108,000
2	**John Chin**	68	66	68	64	266	54,000
3	**Taylor Montgomery**	65	69	69	64	267	36,000
4	Chandler Blanchet	69	67	65	67	268	23,500
	David Kocher	71	64	67	66	268	23,500
	Greyson Sigg	66	67	68	67	268	23,500
7	JT Griffin	69	66	67	67	269	17,175
	Jack Maguire	66	66	67	70	269	17,175
	TJ Vogel	66	67	71	65	269	17,175
	Drew Weaver	70	67	66	66	269	17,175
11	Robert Garrigus	70	62	69	69	270	12,015
	Lee Hodges	67	70	68	65	270	12,015
	Taylor Moore	67	68	67	68	270	12,015
	Ben Silverman	67	67	70	66	270	12,015
	Sebastian Vazquez	70	65	67	68	270	12,015
	Dylan Wu	66	69	68	67	270	12,015
17	Eric Cole	68	69	66	68	271	9,000
	Jamie Lovemark	68	69	68	66	271	9,000
	Mike Weir	70	68	68	65	271	9,000
20	Paul Barjon	71	66	70	65	272	6,580
	Alex Chiarella	69	64	68	71	272	6,580
	Joey Garber	68	65	71	68	272	6,580
	Austin Smotherman	67	68	69	68	272	6,580
	Jimmy Stanger	66	70	67	69	272	6,580
	Peter Uihlein	68	64	66	74	272	6,580

El Bosque Mexico Championship

El Bosque Country Club, Leon, Guanajuato, Mexico — February 27-March 1
Par 72 (36-36); 7,762 yards — Purse: $650,000

1	**David Kocher**	70	69	68	69	276	$117,000
2	**Paul Barjon**	71	69	65	71	276	48,750
	Chad Ramey	71	69	70	66	276	48,750
	Kocher won playoff at first extra hole						
4	Dylan Wu	68	69	71	69	277	25,458
	Matt Atkins	68	69	70	70	277	25,458
	Guillermo Mito Pereira	69	63	70	75	277	25,458
7	Sangmoon Bae	69	62	73	74	278	19,988
	Mark Baldwin	71	66	74	67	278	19,988
9	Alex Chiarella	75	69	67	68	279	16,608
	JT Griffin	70	73	67	69	279	16,608
	Jake Knapp	76	67	71	65	279	16,608
12	Brent Grant	73	70	72	65	280	12,919
	KK Limbhasut	73	69	72	66	280	12,919
	Michael Miller	70	72	70	68	280	12,919
	Taylor Moore	72	72	68	68	280	12,919
16	Brad Hopfinger	70	74	70	67	281	8,860
	Nelson Ledesma	73	70	71	67	281	8,860
	Nick Hardy	68	71	69	73	281	8,860
	Theo Humphrey	69	71	69	72	281	8,860
	Kyle Jones	70	72	70	69	281	8,860
	Rick Lamb	69	74	70	68	281	8,860
	Charlie Saxon	72	70	68	71	281	8,860
	John VanDerLaan	73	69	67	72	281	8,860
24	Zhengkai Bai	70	71	68	73	282	5,600
	Harrison Endycott	72	68	70	72	282	5,600
	Augusto Nunez	71	70	67	74	282	5,600
	Seth Reeves	70	72	73	67	282	5,600
	Kyle Reifers	72	66	71	73	282	5,600

Korn Ferry Challenge

TPC Sawgrass (Dye's Valley), Ponte Vedra Beach, Florida — June 11-14
Par 70 (35-35); 6,847 yards — Purse: $600,000

1	**Luke List**	66	70	65	67	268	$108,000
2	**Joseph Bramlett**	69	68	64	68	269	45,000
	Shad Tuten	71	64	67	67	269	45,000
4	Nicholas Lindheim	70	67	67	66	270	24,900
	Kristoffer Ventura	66	68	69	67	270	24,900
6	Lee Hodges	69	65	67	70	271	19,950
	Will Zalatoris	67	68	65	71	271	19,950
8	Theo Humphrey	67	68	67	70	272	17,700
9	Nick Hardy	67	68	68	70	273	16,500
10	Brandon Crick	69	66	68	71	274	13,748
	Vince India	69	70	65	70	274	13,748
	KK Limbhasut	67	68	71	68	274	13,748
	Michael Miller	69	68	67	70	274	13,748
14	Paul Barjon	64	70	70	71	275	9,311
	Ben Kohles	68	66	73	68	275	9,311
	Ryan McCormick	72	65	69	69	275	9,311
	Max McGreevy	72	64	71	68	275	9,311
	Sam Saunders	68	69	70	68	275	9,311
	Austin Smotherman	71	67	67	70	275	9,311
	Dawie van der Walt	67	69	67	72	275	9,311
	Chase Wright	66	69	66	74	275	9,311
22	Justin Lower	68	68	71	69	276	6,810
23	Tommy Gainey	71	67	68	71	277	4,898
	Andres Gonzales	70	65	70	72	277	4,898
	Brandon Harkins	70	67	72	68	277	4,898
	Grant Hirschman	70	69	68	70	277	4,898
	Brad Hopfinger	69	68	70	70	277	4,898
	Scott Langley	66	68	73	70	277	4,898
	Chad Ramey	69	69	71	68	277	4,898
	Jonathan Randolph	73	66	69	69	277	4,898
	Jimmy Stanger	67	70	69	71	277	4,898
	Callum Tarren	68	70	69	70	277	4,898

The King & Bear Classic

World Golf Village (The King & Bear), St Augustine, Florida — June 17-20
Par 72 (36-36); 7,279 yards — Purse: $600,000

1	**Chris Kirk**	66	65	64	67	262	$108,000
2	**Justin Lower**	65	65	67	66	263	54,000
3	**Joseph Bramlett**	68	69	64	64	265	31,500
	Will Zalatoris	65	66	66	68	265	31,500
5	Wes Roach	68	63	67	68	266	22,800
6	Nick Hardy	69	64	67	67	267	16,136
	Brandon Harkins	66	70	67	64	267	16,136
	Vince India	63	66	62	76	267	16,136
	Ben Martin	68	64	68	67	267	16,136
	Ryan McCormick	65	67	68	67	267	16,136
	Chad Ramey	66	68	65	68	267	16,136
	Davis Riley	66	66	68	67	267	16,136
	Jared Wolfe	65	70	63	69	267	16,136
14	Brett Coletta	63	66	70	69	268	11,100
	Taylor Pendrith	65	68	66	69	268	11,100
16	Grant Hirschman	70	68	66	65	269	9,000
	Curtis Luck	68	65	67	69	269	9,000
	Daniel Miernicki	66	68	67	68	269	9,000
	Paul Peterson	70	67	66	66	269	9,000
	Greyson Sigg	71	64	66	68	269	9,000
21	Joshua Creel	71	66	68	65	270	5,951
	Nicolas Echavarria	68	66	69	67	270	5,951
	Scott Gutschewski	68	64	69	69	270	5,951
	Scott Langley	66	68	65	71	270	5,951
	Guillermo Mito Pereira	69	69	67	65	270	5,951
	Braden Thornberry	68	67	64	71	270	5,951
	Drew Weaver	66	66	73	65	270	5,951

Utah Championship

Oakridge Country Club, Farmington, Utah — June 25-28
Par 71 (36-35); 7,045 yards — Purse: $650,000

1	**Kyle Jones**	64	65	67	68	264	$117,000
2	**Daniel Summerhays**	69	65	68	62	264	48,750
	Paul Haley II	67	62	67	68	264	48,750
	Jones won playoff at second extra hole						
4	Will Zalatoris	66	66	67	66	265	29,250
5	Martin Piller	66	65	71	64	266	22,642
	Ollie Schniederjans	68	68	64	66	266	22,642
	Dylan Wu	65	68	69	64	266	22,642
8	John Chin	68	68	65	66	267	16,660
	Brent Grant	68	67	68	64	267	16,660
	Jimmy Stanger	68	64	68	67	267	16,660
	Dawie van der Walt	68	66	63	70	267	16,660
	Mark Blakefield	69	66	67	65	267	16,660
13	Joey Garber	69	65	65	69	268	11,765
	Alex Prugh	66	69	68	65	268	11,765
	Sangmoon Bae	67	69	65	67	268	11,765
	Erik Barnes	68	64	67	69	268	11,765
	Justin Hueber	70	66	65	67	268	11,765
18	Lee Hodges	70	65	66	68	269	7,463
	Whee Kim	67	70	67	65	269	7,463
	Braden Thornberry	66	67	72	64	269	7,463
	Ryan Brehm	70	64	67	68	269	7,463
	Vince India	68	68	67	66	269	7,463
	Jamie Arnold	66	67	68	68	269	7,463
	Paul Peterson	69	68	66	66	269	7,463
	TJ Vogel	64	68	65	72	269	7,463
	Hayden Buckley	66	69	67	67	269	7,463

TPC Colorado Championship

TPC Colorado, Heron Lakes, Berthoud, Colorado — July 1-4
Par 72 (36-36); 7,991 yards — Purse: $600,000

1	**Will Zalatoris**	67	67	70	69	273	$108,000
2	**Chase Johnson**	70	66	75	63	274	54,000
3	**Erik Barnes**	69	69	67	70	275	26,625
	Stephan Jaeger	70	71	68	66	275	26,625
	Taylor Pendrith	68	70	67	70	275	26,625
	Callum Tarren	70	66	70	69	275	26,625
7	Nick Hardy	69	69	72	66	276	18,450
	Augusto Nunez	70	70	68	68	276	18,450
9	Tyson Alexander	70	72	71	64	277	16,500
10	Derek Ernst	71	72	69	66	278	13,278
	Brad Hopfinger	68	72	67	71	278	13,278
	Greyson Sigg	70	72	73	63	278	13,278
	Adam Svensson	71	70	68	69	278	13,278
	Jared Wolfe	72	66	70	70	278	13,278
15	Max Greyserman	71	72	69	67	279	10,500
	Ben Kohles	67	69	72	71	279	10,500
17	Brett Coletta	68	69	74	69	280	7,160
	Stephen Franken	67	71	74	68	280	7,160
	JT Griffin	67	75	69	69	280	7,160
	Lee Hodges	67	71	71	71	280	7,160
	Justin Hueber	73	70	64	73	280	7,160
	David Lipsky	74	69	68	69	280	7,160
	Martin Piller	69	70	72	69	280	7,160
	Davis Riley	67	72	70	71	280	7,160
	Charlie Saxon	71	69	70	70	280	7,160
	Ollie Schniederjans	71	70	73	66	280	7,160

TPC San Antonio Challenge

TPC San Antonio (Canyons), San Antonio, Texas — July 9-12
Par 72 (36-36); 7,106 yards — Purse: $600,000

1	**David Lipsky**	69	66	62	66	263	$108,000
2	**Taylor Pendrith**	67	69	65	66	267	54,000
3	**Paul Barjon**	69	64	65	70	268	31,500
	Paul Haley II	67	70	67	64	268	31,500
5	David Skinns	69	70	66	64	269	22,800
6	Roberto Díaz	71	64	70	65	270	19,950
	Ryan McCormick	69	67	67	67	270	19,950
8	Lee Hodges	68	67	67	69	271	15,923
	Ollie Schniederjans	66	71	66	68	271	15,923
	Adam Svensson	70	68	65	68	271	15,923
	Kristoffer Ventura	68	66	69	68	271	15,923
12	Zecheng Dou	68	69	68	67	272	11,925
	Derek Ernst	68	69	69	66	272	11,925
	Chip McDaniel	70	64	71	67	272	11,925
	Taylor Montgomery	66	71	67	68	272	11,925
16	Joey Garber	70	69	70	64	273	8,443
	Yuwa Kosaihira	70	70	69	64	273	8,443
	Kevin Roy	69	71	64	69	273	8,443
	Shane Smith	70	70	69	64	273	8,443
	Callum Tarren	68	70	67	68	273	8,443
	Ben Kohles	67	69	66	71	273	8,443
	Taylor Moore	69	68	66	70	273	8,443
23	Brett Coletta	70	65	67	72	274	5,675
	Patrick Fishburn	69	67	69	69	274	5,675
	Brad Hopfinger	71	66	70	67	274	5,675
	Greyson Sigg	70	69	65	70	274	5,675

TPC San Antonio Championship

TPC San Antonio (Oaks), San Antonio, Texas — July 15-18
Par 72 (36-36); 7,494 yards — Purse: $600,000

1	**Davis Riley**	70	69	66	67	272	$108,000
2	**Paul Barjon**	67	70	68	69	274	45,000
	Taylor Pendrith	73	67	67	67	274	45,000
4	Austin Smotherman	66	69	70	71	276	27,000
5	Roberto Diaz	71	66	70	70	277	20,100
	Derek Ernst	69	68	67	73	277	20,100
	Whee Kim	71	68	70	68	277	20,100
	Will Zalatoris	77	67	66	67	277	20,100
9	Ben Kohles	70	69	67	72	278	14,298
	Ben Martin	71	69	69	69	278	14,298
	Max McGreevy	67	70	69	72	278	14,298
	Kyle Reifers	71	67	73	67	278	14,298
	Charlie Saxon	70	69	70	69	278	14,298
14	Chandler Blanchet	72	69	70	68	279	10,500
	Joshua Creel	73	67	71	68	279	10,500
	Lee Hodges	71	71	69	68	279	10,500
	Justin Lower	71	69	75	64	279	10,500
18	Max Greyserman	67	71	72	70	280	7,605
	Nick Hardy	73	70	69	68	280	7,605
	Michael Miller	69	71	72	68	280	7,605
	Wes Roach	73	68	70	69	280	7,605
	Ryan Ruffels	71	72	69	68	280	7,605
	Callum Tarren	70	73	69	68	280	7,605
24	Dan McCarthy	69	69	72	71	281	4,832
	Andrew Novak	71	70	72	68	281	4,832
	Chad Ramey	71	70	70	70	281	4,832
	Max Rottluff	73	67	73	68	281	4,832
	Tyrone Van Aswegen	66	74	73	68	281	4,832
	Dawie van der Walt	74	67	69	71	281	4,832
	John VanDerLaan	69	70	70	72	281	4,832
	Jared Wolfe	68	74	70	69	281	4,832

Price Cutter Charity Championship

Highland Springs Country Club, Springfield, Missouri — July 23-26
Par 72 (36-36); 7,115 yards — Purse: $650,000

1	**Max McGreevy**	64	68	71	64	267	$117,000
2	**Jose de Jesus Rodriguez**	66	69	66	67	268	58,500
3	**Chad Ramey**	68	67	67	67	269	39,000
4	Daniel Sutton	66	67	68	69	270	29,250
5	Anders Albertson	72	63	69	67	271	21,775
	Dan McCarthy	66	66	70	69	271	21,775
	Taylor Moore	66	71	67	67	271	21,775
	Austen Truslow	69	70	67	65	271	21,775
9	Michael Arnaud	66	65	70	71	272	15,490
	Jonathan Randolph	67	72	67	66	272	15,490
	Davis Riley	67	70	65	70	272	15,490
	Dylan Wu	68	70	71	63	272	15,490
	Brandon Wu	67	63	68	74	272	15,490
14	Zecheng Dou	68	67	68	70	273	11,700
	Billy Kennerly	67	69	68	69	273	11,700
	Will Zalatoris	67	71	67	68	273	11,700
17	Paul Haley II	69	70	73	62	274	9,425
	Brandon Harkins	71	65	66	72	274	9,425
	Adam Svensson	67	70	68	69	274	9,425
	Greg Yates	70	68	69	67	274	9,425
21	Jamie Arnold	65	70	68	72	275	6,447
	Steve Marino	69	70	70	66	275	6,447
	Robby Ormand	71	68	68	68	275	6,447
	Martin Piller	66	70	71	68	275	6,447
	Andy Pope	69	66	70	70	275	6,447
	Kyle Reifers	69	71	66	69	275	6,447
	John Somers	71	69	70	65	275	6,447

Pinnacle Bank Championship

The Club at Indian Creek, Omaha, Nebraska — July 30-August 2
Par 71 (36-35); 7,581 yards — Purse: $600,000

1	**Seth Reeves**	74	67	68	64	273	$108,000
2	**Tyson Alexander**	69	65	71	69	274	32,100
	Taylor Pendrith	71	70	67	66	274	32,100
	Ryan Ruffels	66	70	65	73	274	32,100
	Nick Voke	70	66	71	67	274	32,100
	Carl Yuan	70	69	67	68	274	32,100
7	Lee Hodges	69	70	67	69	275	18,450
	Greyson Sigg	66	69	72	68	275	18,450
9	Rico Hoey	69	67	68	72	276	15,900
	Michael Miller	70	66	68	72	276	15,900
11	Brandon Crick	67	70	69	71	277	11,010
	Stephen Franken	66	71	66	74	277	11,010
	Theo Humphrey	70	70	68	69	277	11,010
	Jonathan Randolph	73	67	66	71	277	11,010
	Tag Ridings	68	71	69	69	277	11,010
	Austin Smotherman	68	69	69	71	277	11,010
	Jimmy Stanger	72	69	70	66	277	11,010
	Sebastian Vazquez	72	67	71	67	277	11,010
	Cameron Young	67	68	69	73	277	11,010
20	Erik Barnes	69	71	66	72	278	7,300
	Stuart MacDonald	70	68	67	73	278	7,300
	Dylan Wu	71	66	71	70	278	7,300
23	Brent Grant	68	72	69	70	279	5,512
	Nick Hardy	68	72	70	69	279	5,512
	Whee Kim	74	65	68	72	279	5,512
	Nicholas Lindheim	68	70	70	71	279	5,512
	Callum Tarren	69	69	68	73	279	5,512

WinCo Foods Portland Open

Pumpkin Ridge Golf Club (Witch Hollow), North Plains, Oregan — August 6-9
Par 71 (36-35); 7,109 yards — Purse: $800,000

1	**Lee Hodges**	70	64	68	71	273	$144,000
2	**Paul Barjon**	69	67	66	73	275	46,600
	David Lipsky	71	68	71	65	275	46,600
	Chad Ramey	71	70	68	66	275	46,600
	Yechun Yuan	69	67	73	66	275	46,600
6	Will Zalatoris	74	65	68	69	276	27,600
7	Joey Garber	69	66	72	70	277	22,900
	Ollie Schniederjans	72	69	72	64	277	22,900
	Callum Tarren	68	72	71	66	277	22,900
	Tom Whitney	68	70	70	69	277	22,900
11	Anders Albertson	70	65	69	74	278	17,640
	Hayden Buckley	68	70	69	71	278	17,640
	Brett Drewitt	70	71	67	70	278	17,640
14	Evan Harmeling	70	66	76	67	279	12,415
	Brad Hopfinger	69	72	70	68	279	12,415
	Nicholas Lindheim	74	67	68	70	279	12,415
	Guillermo Mito Pereira	74	67	68	70	279	12,415
	Andy Pope	70	71	70	68	279	12,415
	Charlie Saxon	69	64	72	74	279	12,415
	Zach Wright	68	70	71	70	279	12,415
	Cameron Young	69	70	69	71	279	12,415
22	Rick Lamb	73	63	75	69	280	6,762
	David Skinns	71	69	71	69	280	6,762
	Kevin Dougherty	67	69	73	71	280	6,762
	Billy Kennerly	67	68	73	72	280	6,762
	James Nicholas	71	69	68	72	280	6,762
	Augusto Nunez	72	66	72	70	280	6,762
	Taylor Pendrith	68	71	71	70	280	6,762
	Kevin Roy	69	72	69	70	280	6,762
	Ryan Ruffels	71	63	74	72	280	6,762
	Adam Svensson	71	68	70	71	280	6,762
	Austen Truslow	71	66	70	73	280	6,762

Albertsons Boise Open

Hillcrest Country Club, Boise, Idaho — August 13-16
Par 71 (36-35); 6,880 yards — Purse: $1,000,000

1	**Stephan Jaeger**	65	64	65	68	262	$180,000
2	**Dan McCarthy**	67	69	64	64	264	75,000
	Brandon Wu	67	66	63	68	264	75,000
4	Nicholas Lindheim	67	69	65	64	265	41,500
	Justin Lower	65	71	63	66	265	41,500
6	Brad Hopfinger	65	64	68	69	266	30,875
	Charlie Saxon	63	67	70	66	266	30,875
	Jimmy Stanger	65	66	70	65	266	30,875
	Cameron Young	68	66	61	71	266	30,875
10	Alex Chiarella	68	66	65	68	267	25,500
11	Julian Etulain	65	69	67	67	268	19,450
	Paul Haley II	69	66	67	66	268	19,450
	Grant Hirschman	69	67	65	67	268	19,450
	Taylor Pendrith	67	67	68	66	268	19,450
	Davis Riley	65	67	69	67	268	19,450
	Greyson Sigg	67	67	64	70	268	19,450
	Dylan Wu	67	65	69	67	268	19,450
18	Erik Barnes	70	67	64	68	269	13,100
	Nick Hardy	67	69	65	68	269	13,100
	Seth Reeves	66	72	67	64	269	13,100
	Kevin Roy	72	65	63	69	269	13,100
	Will Zalatoris	68	65	70	66	269	13,100
23	Roberto Diaz	67	69	68	66	270	8,938
	Scott Gutschewski	69	65	70	66	270	8,938
	David Lipsky	68	70	65	67	270	8,938
	Max McGreevy	68	68	66	68	270	8,938
	Andrew Novak	67	67	69	67	270	8,938
	Jared Wolfe	66	68	67	69	270	8,938

Nationwide Children's Hospital Championship

Ohio State University Golf Club (Scarlet), Columbus, Ohio — August 20-23
Par 71 (36-35); 7,444 yards — Purse: $1,000,000

1	**Curtis Luck**	68	66	68	71	273	$180,000
2	**Theo Humphrey**	70	67	70	67	274	65,000
	Taylor Montgomery	72	67	67	68	274	65,000
	Cameron Young	66	69	68	71	274	65,000
5	Scott Gutschewski	70	68	70	67	275	32,300
	Nick Hardy	65	74	67	69	275	32,300
	Stephan Jaeger	69	70	70	66	275	32,300
	Jimmy Stanger	65	71	69	70	275	32,300
	Will Zalatoris	69	70	66	70	275	32,300
10	Ollie Schniederjans	71	66	71	68	276	25,500
11	Vince India	69	68	69	71	277	22,050
	Ryan McCormick	71	70	65	71	277	22,050
	Chip McDaniel	69	70	68	70	277	22,050
14	Anders Albertson	70	72	69	67	278	19,000
15	Ben Martin	72	68	68	71	279	17,000
	Peter Uihlein	74	68	67	70	279	17,000
	Kristoffer Ventura	72	68	66	73	279	17,000
18	Erik Barnes	69	67	68	76	280	11,143
	Zecheng Dou	69	69	69	73	280	11,143
	Brad Hopfinger	71	71	69	69	280	11,143
	Justin Hueber	72	69	70	69	280	11,143
	KK Limbhasut	72	70	70	68	280	11,143
	Stuart MacDonald	71	67	75	67	280	11,143
	Guillermo Mito Pereira	71	70	67	72	280	11,143
	Charlie Saxon	67	70	69	74	280	11,143
	David Skinns	68	73	70	69	280	11,143
	Tom Whitney	75	66	70	69	280	11,143

Korn Ferry Tour Championship

Victoria National Golf Club, Newburgh, Indiana — August 27-30
Par 72 (36-36); 7,242 yards — Purse: $1,000,000

1	**Brandon Wu**	67	69	69	65	270	$180,000
2	**Greyson Sigg**	65	69	66	71	271	90,000
3	**Vince India**	70	64	70	68	272	47,667
	Dan McCarthy	69	67	65	71	272	47,667
	Seth Reeves	65	69	68	70	272	47,667
6	Dawie van der Walt	64	71	67	71	273	32,000
	David Lipsky	69	70	64	70	273	32,000
	Max Greyserman	70	67	67	69	273	32,000
9	Zecheng Dou	71	71	67	65	274	26,500
	Taylor Pendrith	68	71	69	66	274	26,500
11	Brandon Harkins	66	70	69	70	275	23,650
12	Ollie Schniederjans	71	68	66	71	276	20,500
	John VanDerLaan	68	71	68	69	276	20,500
	Braden Thornberry	69	73	67	67	276	20,500
15	Justin Lower	67	71	70	69	277	16,500
	Curtis Thompson	70	72	65	70	277	16,500
	Wes Roach	64	73	71	69	277	16,500
	Augusto Nunez	67	69	70	71	277	16,500
19	Tommy Gainey	68	69	71	70	278	12,210
	Adam Svensson	70	68	68	72	278	12,210
	Brad Hopfinger	69	70	67	72	278	12,210
	Will Zalatoris	68	68	72	70	278	12,210
	Andy Pope	68	71	70	69	278	12,210
24	Nicholas Lindheim	66	69	73	71	279	8,616
	Erik Barnes	74	69	68	68	279	8,616
	Nick Hardy	71	70	68	70	279	8,616
	Ben Martin	70	72	72	65	279	8,616
	Davis Riley	73	69	69	68	279	8,616

Lincoln Land Championship

Panther Creek Country Club, Springfield, Illinois — September 3-6
Par 71 (35-36); 7,228 yards — Purse: $600,000

1	**Brett Drewitt**	68	63	69	69	269	$108,000
2	**Harry Hall**	70	63	71	66	270	39,000
	Ben Kohles	66	69	67	68	270	39,000
	Austen Truslow	68	68	64	70	270	39,000
5	Anders Albertson	70	63	66	72	271	21,750
	Dawson Armstrong	71	68	67	65	271	21,750
7	Zecheng Dou	70	65	68	69	272	18,450
	Charlie Saxon	62	67	69	74	272	18,450
9	Brad Brunner	70	67	70	66	273	16,500
10	KK Limbhasut	68	69	68	69	274	14,230
	Trey Mullinax	69	66	72	67	274	14,230
	Kevin Roy	71	68	68	67	274	14,230
13	Hayden Buckley	72	68	64	71	275	11,175
	Whee Kim	67	73	70	65	275	11,175
	Nicholas Lindheim	68	66	70	71	275	11,175
	James Nicholas	69	69	72	65	275	11,175
17	Erik Compton	70	67	69	70	276	8,418
	Spencer Levin	70	70	67	69	276	8,418
	Chip McDaniel	69	67	69	71	276	8,418
	Kyle Reifers	69	67	72	68	276	8,418
	Vincent Whaley	64	68	74	70	276	8,418
22	Jamie Arnold	73	67	65	72	277	5,570
	Brandon Crick	70	65	75	67	277	5,570
	Evan Harmeling	67	72	69	69	277	5,570
	Adam Svensson	71	67	69	70	277	5,570
	TJ Vogel	72	66	68	71	277	5,570
	Peyton White	72	67	72	66	277	5,570
	Corbin Mills	68	71	71	67	277	5,570

Evans Scholars Invitational

Chicago Highlands Club, Glenview, Illinois — September 10-13
Par 72 (36-36); 7,490 yards — Purse: $600,000

1	**Curtis Thompson**	68	65	68	70	271	$108,000
2	**Jimmy Stanger**	69	67	70	66	272	45,000
	Will Zalatoris	69	68	71	64	272	45,000
4	Alex Chiarella	67	68	72	67	274	23,500
	Brad Hopfinger	69	66	72	67	274	23,500
	Max Rottluff	70	67	72	65	274	23,500
7	Paul Barjon	70	66	68	71	275	16,015
	Stephan Jaeger	70	65	69	71	275	16,015
	Trey Mullinax	66	70	68	71	275	16,015
	Guillermo Mito Pereira	74	64	66	71	275	16,015
	Greyson Sigg	69	70	70	66	275	16,015
	Nick Voke	69	67	71	68	275	16,015
13	Nick Hardy	69	71	70	66	276	11,500
	Theo Humphrey	69	67	68	72	276	11,500
	Taylor Pendrith	71	68	71	66	276	11,500
16	Matt Atkins	69	67	71	70	277	9,000
	Hayden Buckley	70	71	67	69	277	9,000
	Brett Drewitt	75	66	66	70	277	9,000
	Justin Hueber	68	71	69	69	277	9,000
	Kevin Roy	73	67	68	69	277	9,000
21	Max Greyserman	69	71	69	69	278	5,951
	Evan Harmeling	72	69	66	71	278	5,951
	David Kocher	68	69	74	67	278	5,951
	Ben Kohles	70	68	73	67	278	5,951
	Taylor Montgomery	71	70	68	69	278	5,951
	Taylor Moore	69	69	70	70	278	5,951
	Braden Thornberry	70	67	70	71	278	5,951

Wichita Open

Crestview Country Club, Wichita, Kansas — September 24-27
Par 70 (35-35); 6,910 yards — Purse: $600,000

1	**Jared Wolfe**	63	65	65	71	264	$108,000
2	**Taylor Pendrith**	65	62	69	69	265	54,000
3	**Dawson Armstrong**	70	66	65	65	266	31,500
	Brad Hopfinger	64	67	67	68	266	31,500
5	Chandler Blanchet	70	65	66	66	267	20,900
	Zecheng Dou	63	68	71	65	267	20,900
	Patrick Fishburn	68	62	71	66	267	20,900
8	Harrison Endycott	69	67	64	68	268	14,370
	Joey Garber	67	66	66	69	268	14,370
	Whee Kim	66	68	65	69	268	14,370
	Ben Kohles	70	64	65	69	268	14,370
	Rick Lamb	71	63	66	68	268	14,370
	Ollie Schniederjans	69	65	68	66	268	14,370
	Braden Thornberry	69	66	68	65	268	14,370
	Noah Norton (A)	68	67	65	68	268	
16	Hayden Buckley	66	68	65	70	269	9,600
	John Chin	68	67	65	69	269	9,600
	Julian Etulain	68	67	63	71	269	9,600
	Chase Johnson	67	66	67	69	269	9,600
	Taylor Montgomery	67	64	65	73	269	9,600
21	Blayne Barber	67	68	68	67	270	6,816
	Trevor Cone	68	63	67	72	270	6,816
	Nick Hardy	66	63	69	72	270	6,816
	Brandon Harkins	67	69	66	68	270	6,816
	Andre Metzger	69	68	66	67	270	6,816

Savannah Golf Championship

The Landings Club (Deer Creek), Savannah, Georgia — October 1-4
Par 72 (36-36); 7,128 yards — Purse: $600,000

1	**Evan Harmeling**	64	67	67	69	267	$108,000
2	**Kevin Dougherty**	65	66	68	68	267	54,000
	Harmeling won playoff at first extra hole						
3	**Brett Coletta**	66	66	69	68	269	25,140
	George Cunningham	65	68	71	65	269	25,140
	Chad Ramey	65	68	69	67	269	25,140
	Austen Truslow	66	71	67	65	269	25,140
	Eric Cole	69	64	67	69	269	25,140
8	Max Greyserman	67	65	68	70	270	17,100
	Harry Hall	69	66	69	66	270	17,100
10	Taylor Montgomery	66	68	67	70	271	14,745
	Brandon Wu	68	66	70	67	271	14,745
12	Zecheng Dou	66	67	70	69	272	12,300
	Scott Gutschewski	70	68	69	65	272	12,300
	Augusto Nunez	68	67	71	66	272	12,300
15	Sangmoon Bae	65	68	67	73	273	9,013
	Roberto Diaz	69	65	69	70	273	9,013
	Whee Kim	69	66	70	68	273	9,013
	Max McGreevy	65	68	71	69	273	9,013
	Brady Schnell	68	66	70	69	273	9,013
	Greyson Sigg	67	68	69	69	273	9,013
	John VanDerLaan	69	66	67	71	273	9,013
22	Erik Compton	68	67	69	70	274	5,728
	Brett Drewitt	71	67	68	68	274	5,728
	JT Griffin	66	70	69	69	274	5,728
	Grant Hirschman	67	71	69	67	274	5,728
	Kyle Jones	64	68	71	71	274	5,728
	Shad Tuten	67	66	72	69	274	5,728

Orange County National Championship

Orange County National Golf Center (Panther Lake), Winter Garden, Florida — October 8-11
Par 71 (35-36); 7,309 yards — Purse: $600,000

1	**Trey Mullinax**	65	65	62	69	261	$108,000
2	**Stephan Jaeger**	64	66	65	67	262	45,000
	Brandon Wu	65	66	66	65	262	45,000
4	Chad Ramey	66	65	67	66	264	24,900
	Greyson Sigg	68	65	67	64	264	24,900
6	George Cunningham	64	66	65	70	265	19,200
	Harry Hall	63	67	66	69	265	19,200
	Brandon Harkins	65	65	67	68	265	19,200
9	Anders Albertson	65	65	67	69	266	15,900
	Stephen Franken	64	64	67	71	266	15,900
11	Erik Barnes	69	67	67	64	267	12,773
	Nicholas Lindheim	69	66	64	68	267	12,773
	Ryan McCormick	67	67	64	69	267	12,773
	Taylor Montgomery	68	65	66	68	267	12,773
15	Alex Chiarella	65	65	66	72	268	8,470
	Brett Coletta	65	68	71	64	268	8,470
	Brandon Crick	69	64	67	68	268	8,470
	Tommy Gainey	64	70	66	68	268	8,470
	Kramer Hickok	65	70	68	65	268	8,470
	David Kocher	69	66	65	68	268	8,470
	Adam Svensson	70	63	67	68	268	8,470
	Callum Tarren	64	71	66	67	268	8,470
	Shad Tuten	63	66	68	71	268	8,470
24	Joey Garber	66	64	67	72	269	5,456
	Rick Lamb	67	68	66	68	269	5,456
	David Lipsky	70	65	67	67	269	5,456

2020 MONEY LIST

1	Will Zalatoris	$403,978
2	Brandon Wu	336,981
3	Davis Riley	333,615
4	Stephan Jaeger	326,482
5	Taylor Pendrith	314,113
6	Lee Hodges	304,646
7	Jared Wolfe	303,547
8	Greyson Sigg	274,402
9	Chad Ramey	249,659
10	Guillermo Mito Pereira	248,404

Mackenzie Tour — PGA Tour Canada

With the Covid-19 pandemic rolling frightfully all over the world, the official announcement out of Toronto in May said it all:

"Due to border restrictions, mandatory quarantines for those entering Canada and gathering restrictions in all provinces because of Covid-19, the Mackenzie Tour – PGA Tour Canada announced Friday that it is canceling its 2020 season."

It would have been the Mackenzie Tour's eighth season, set with 13 tournaments — the most in the tour's history.

"We've weighed all of our options and we came to the realisation that this is the best decision for everyone involved," said Mackenzie Tour executive director Scott Pritchard.

Canada Life stepped in and restored tournament golf with the Canada Life Series — four 54-hole events, two at Bear Mountain Golf & Tennis Resort Community on Vancouver Island and two at TPC Toronto at Osprey Valley. The fields consisted of Canadian professionals, elite amateurs and Mackenzie Tour members regardless of citizenship who were already in Canada.

China's Yi Cao, with his victory in the second Bear Mountain tournament and ties for second, third and eighth in the other three, topped the Canada Line Series points list. This earned him conditional status and six starts on the 2021 Mackenzie Tour and a playing spot in the RBC Canadian Open. He was followed by other winners Albert Pistorius, Evan Holmes and amateur Laurent Desmarchais.

2020 SCHEDULE

Canada Life Series — Bear Mountain (Mountain)	**Evan Holmes**
Canada Life Series — Bear Mountain (Valley)	**Yi Cao**
Canada Life Series — TPC Toronto	**Albert Pistorius**
Canada Life Series Championship	**Laurent Desmarchais** (A)

Canada Life Series — Bear Mountain (Mountain)

Evan Holmes opened the Canada Life Series with a 63 and the understatement of the season."It was nice to get off to that good start," Holmes said. Eight under? A good start? Not that he could coast through the next two rounds, but the three-shot lead over Lawren Rowe plus the feel-good of an eight-under start can inspire a certain level of confidence. And Holmes needed them. He then played the last two rounds in 70-72 on Bear Mountain's par-71 Mountain course for an eight-under-par total of 205 to win by two strokes over Zach Anderson.

Starting off, Holmes birdied his first three holes and four of the first five on his way to that 63. Then he cooled off and was even par for his final two rounds, but it was enough for the narrow win.

Said Holmes: "I couldn't have asked for a better start and I'm looking forward to the other three."

"Chasing Evan all day was good," said Anderson. "I think everyone in the group was tied at minus-eight through three, and then Lawren fell off and me and Evan were battling it out pretty good on the back nine."

Bear Mountain Resort (Mountain), Langford, British Columbia — August 10-12
Par 71 (35-36); 6,849 yards — Purse: C$50,000

1	**Evan Holmes**	63	70	72	205	C$9,000
2	**Zach Anderson**	68	68	71	207	4,250
3	**Yi Cao**	69	69	71	209	2,058
	Derek Gillespie	71	67	71	209	2,058
	Raoul Menard	70	71	68	209	2,058
6	Lawren Rowe	66	68	76	210	1,520
7	Albert Pistorius	71	66	74	211	1,400
8	Jim Rutledge	70	72	70	212	1,300
	Nolan Thoroughgood (A)	75	68	69	212	
10	Chris Crisologo	67	71	75	213	1,150
	Lucas Kim	68	73	72	213	1,150
	Laurent Desmarchais (A)	68	69	76	213	
13	Mark Hoffman	73	71	70	214	1,001
	Brandon Lacasse	72	70	72	214	1,001
	Patrick Murphy	73	72	69	214	1,001
16	Michael Blair	70	75	70	215	863

	Devon Schade	76	68	71	215	863	Tanvir Kahlon	73	72	72	217	641
	Stephen Thomas	70	72	73	215	863	Scott Kerr	79	71	67	217	641
19	Drew Nesbitt	67	77	72	216	783	Doheon Lee	70	69	78	217	641
20	Evan DeGrazia	71	75	71	217	641	Brendan Leonard	71	76	70	217	641
	Kaleb Gorbahn	68	74	75	217	641	Matthew Shubley	70	74	73	217	641

Canada Life Series — Bear Mountain (Valley)

Yi Cao once won coming from way behind back in his native China, and at the Valley course, he won leading from way in front this time.

He preferred winning from the front.

"I have never won going into the final round with a lead," Cao said. "On PGA Tour China, I started eight shots back. So this was a new and fun experience."

Cao shot the Valley course in 67-67-66, tying for the lead in the first round, taking a huge five-shot lead through the second, and winning by eight with a 13-under-par total of 200. Joey Savoie and Albert Pistorios tied for second at 208.

The key to Cao's win was his play on the four par fives. He played them in nine under for the tournament.

"My strategy was to just keep my ball in play with the tee shot," Cao said. "If I have a good chance to reach the green I'll go for it. Otherwise I would stay back and play for the green in three shots.

"Luckily," he added, "my putter worked."

Bear Mountain Resort (Valley), Langford, British Columbia — August 17-19
Par 71 (35-36); 6,807 yards — Purse: C$50,000

1	**Yi Cao**	67	67	66	200	C$9,000	14	Jae Yong Kim	71	71	71	213	929
2	**Albert Pistorius**	70	71	67	208	3,375		Sang Lee	75	70	68	213	929
	Joey Savoie	72	72	64	208	3,375	16	James Allenby	69	73	72	214	784
4	Michael Blair	68	71	70	209	2,000		Troy Bulmer	72	72	70	214	784
5	Lawren Rowe	70	71	69	210	1,675		Derek Gillespie	73	71	70	214	784
6	Marc Casullo	74	70	67	211	1,355		Scott Kerr	67	74	73	214	784
	Callum Davison	72	73	66	211	1,355		Raoul Menard	69	78	67	214	784
	Branson Ferrier	70	74	67	211	1,355	21	Wilson Bateman	73	71	71	215	636
	Andrew Harrison	68	73	70	211	1,355		Mark Hoffman	69	76	70	215	636
	AJ Ewart (A)	70	72	69	211			Jim Rutledge	75	71	69	215	636
11	Russell Budd	69	70	73	212	1,050		Laurent Desmarchais (A)	73	70	72	215	
	Chris Crisologo	73	69	70	212	1,050		Nolan Thoroughgood (A)	69	74	72	215	
	Brandon Lacasse	73	69	70	212	1,050							

Canada Life Series — TPC Toronto

Can anything drop a golfer's heart like three-putting the final hole for a bogey when he was leading?

Thereby hangs the feel-good tale of Albert Pistorius scoring his first professional victory in the Canada Life Series event at TPC Toronto early in September.

Coming down the final nine, four were tied at eight under: the threesome of Pistorius, Yi Cao and Andrew J Funk through the 15th and Callum Davis, playing up ahead. Then Pistorius, a South African living in Canada, birdied the par-five 16th on an eight-footer, and the others bogeyed coming in.

And so Pistorius was leading by two standing on the tee of the par-four 18th, that close to his first win. "There were a lot of thoughts just barging into your mind," he said.

His tee shot was excellent but his wedge second rolled back to 30 feet. And he three-putted for a bogey. But with no scoreboards on the course, he wasn't sure where he stood.

"I thought I was going to be in a playoff," Pistorius said. But he'd shot 71-64-70 for a 205 total, eight under, and had that first win.

"I have to go home and think about this," he said.

TPC Toronto at Osprey Valley (Heathlands), Caledon, Ontario — September 2-4
Par 71 (36-35); 6,810 yards — Purse: C$50,000

1	**Albert Pistorius**	71	64	70	205	C$9,000
2	**Yi Cao**	64	71	71	206	2,917
	Callum Davison	71	67	68	206	2,917
	Andrew Funk	68	67	71	206	2,917
5	Evan Holmes	67	71	69	207	1,675
6	Garrett Rank (A)	68	68	72	208	
7	Chris Crisologo	70	69	70	209	1,460
	Mike Gonko	70	69	70	209	1,460
9	Blair Bursey	66	73	71	210	1,073
	Derek Gillespie	66	74	70	210	1,073
	Jae Yong Kim	69	70	71	210	1,073
	Lucas Kim	70	69	71	210	1,073
	Brendan Leonard	66	69	75	210	1,073
	Patrick Murphy	71	70	69	210	1,073
	Joey Savoie	72	67	71	210	1,073
16	David Byrne	70	67	74	211	803
	Aaron Crawford	71	66	74	211	803
	Zachary Giusti	70	70	71	211	803
	John Regan	66	71	74	211	803
20	Hugo Bernard	77	68	67	212	654
	Mark Hoffman	67	72	73	212	654
	Sameer Kalia	69	71	72	212	654
	James Seymour	69	71	72	212	654
24	Keaton Jones	75	69	69	213	532
	Lawren Rowe	71	70	72	213	532
	Austin Ryan	70	71	72	213	532
	Matthew Scobie	68	71	74	213	532
	Jesse Smith	71	69	73	213	532

Canada Life Series Championship

What more could happen in this 2020 golf season? An amateur winning a professional tournament?

Meet Laurent Desmarchais, 19, Canadian amateur, headed for the University of Tennessee, going wire-to-wire, no less, to take the Canada Life Series Championship at TPC Toronto at Osprey Valley. "I don't even have words right now," Desmarchais said.

"Remarkable" is a word that would serve. He shot the par-71 Heathlands course in 62-67-67 for a 196 total, 17 under, for a one-stroke victory over Callum Davison, the pro who received the $9,000 first prize.

That opening nine-under 62 included an eagle at the par-five first and six birdies in seven holes from the fourth. In the final round, Desmarchais took a two-stroke lead off birdies at 15 and 16. But he missed the green the par-three 17th and bogeyed.

Then he missed the green again at the par-four 18th. He opted to putt from a down slope, left it 10 feet short, then holed the par putt for his one-stroke win.

"I was quite nervous on the last few holes," said Desmarchais. "Just winning this event is huge for my confidence and for my game."

TPC Toronto at Osprey Valley (Heathlands), Caledon, Ontario — September 9-11
Par 71 (36-35); 6,810 yards — Purse: C$50,000

1	**Laurent Desmarchais (A)**	62	67	67	196	
2	**Callum Davison**	66	66	65	197	C$9,000
3	**Sebastian Szirmak**	68	65	65	198	4,250
4	Blair Bursey	65	68	67	200	2,250
	Joey Savoie	64	67	69	200	2,250
6	Brendan Leonard	64	68	69	201	1,675
7	David Sheman	69	65	68	202	1,520
8	Yi Cao	67	69	67	203	1,250
	Albert Pistorius	67	68	68	203	1,250
	John Regan	66	69	68	203	1,250
	Josh Whalen	67	65	71	203	1,250
12	Andrew Funk	67	68	69	204	954
	Mike Gonko	66	69	69	204	954
	Raoul Menard	66	70	68	204	954
	Ziggy Nathu	68	68	68	204	954
	Matthew Scobie	71	67	66	204	954
17	Hugo Bernard	68	63	74	205	803
	Aaron Crawford	68	68	69	205	803
19	PA Bedard	67	69	70	206	708
	Patrick Murphy	72	65	69	206	708
	Kevin Stinson	66	70	70	206	708
22	Cooper Brown	68	70	69	207	591
	Brandon Lacasse	70	66	71	207	591
	Sang Lee	66	70	71	207	591
	Drew Nesbitt	66	66	75	207	591

2020 CANADA LIFE SERIES

1	Yi Cao	930.833	Pts
2	Albert Pistorius	912.500	Pts
3	Evan Holmes	638.000	Pts
4	Laurent Desmarchais (A)	615.000	Pts
5	Callum Davison	594.333	Pts
6	Joey Savoie	433.500	Pts
7	Zach Anderson	326.750	Pts
8	Andrew J Funk	292.833	Pts
9	Lawren Rowe	265.625	Pts
10	Derek Gillespie	260.000	Pts

PGA Tour Latinoamerica

"It was a miracle," was the way Rob Ohno, the PGA Tour's Head of International Tours, tagged this strange thing called the LOCALiQ Series that popped up on the golf radar in the summer of 2020.

Under the onslaught of the Covid-19 pandemic that was ravaging the world, the PGA Tour had to cancel the Mackenzie Tour and the PGA Tour Series – China, and postpone much of the PGA Tour Latinoamerica.

The Latinoamerica circuit had opened as scheduled in March with the Estrella del Mar Open, won by Brazil's Alexandre Roche with a closing 62, and did manage to stage a couple of events at the end of the year. MJ Maguire won the Shell Open and Brandon Matthews the Puerto Plata Open. In the meantime, something had to be conjured out of not much.

The miracle? In about 30 days, finding the golf clubs as hosts, laying out schedules, informing the golfers, gathering an infrastructure, finding sponsorship, and in general cobbling together a functioning tour for ambitious golfers who had suddenly found themselves without golf.

"We weren't sure where we would play or if we even could," Ohno said. But they had created a tour of eight 54-hole events confined to the Southeastern US, where many of the members lived and could reach by driving. And LOCALiQ, a marketing solutions company, became the sponsor.

The LOCALiQ Series began early in August and soon began to look like the private domain of Bryson Nimmer, 24, former Clemson University standout. He swept the first two events.

"Obviously what I'm doing is working," Nimmer was to say. "The biggest thing for me is not being complacent. I'm thrilled to win the first two events. I have to try to win all of them."

In the first LOCALiQ event, the Alpharetta Classic at the Golf Club of Georgia, Nimmer had opened with 68-64 and then was merely trying to bring his three-stroke lead safely home to the par-five 18th. He drove into the fairway, laid up and wedged on, only to see his ball hit and roll in for a birdie, wrapping up a four-shot win with a 62 and a 22-under-par total of 192. "I think it did land a little short," Nimmer noted.

Next, at The Championship at Echelon Golf Club, Nimmer had finished and was watching the end of a tournament he didn't realise he'd already won. He'd signed for 69-65-66 and a total of 200, 16 under, and was watching Argentina's Alejandro Tosti finishing the 18th. "I thought his chip was to tie me," Nimmer said. But Tosti was at 15 under and chipping to save par. As Nimmer was to learn, he had already won.

Stoney Crouch, 26, out of Lipscomb University and a former barista at a coffee shop, had a kind of been-there-done-that ambition — he wanted to shoot 20 under par. "It wasn't that I needed to shoot this number to win," Crouch said. "I just wanted to shoot 20 under." And on a card of 64-66-66 for a total of 196, he did just that in The Classic at Callaway Gardens. And he won as well, beating Hayden Shieh on a three-foot birdie putt at the third extra hole.

They had a name for Cooper Musselman back home at the tracks in Kentucky — long shot. In The Invitational at the Auburn University Club, he started the final round three shots behind Alex Smalley and two behind two-time winner Bryson Nimmer. Musselman shot 67-65-66 for a 198 total, 18 under, and was tied by Nimmer's 63-67-68. Musselman won with a par at the fourth extra hole, two-putting for a four from 30 feet while Nimmer missed from 13 feet. Musselman said the victory was better than his win at the 2017 Kentucky State Open "because the competition is so tough". He added: "It gives me some confidence, for sure."

It seems to have been a touch of home-cookin' for Carson Young in the Jacksonville Championship as the tour swung into Florida. He had won an Unbridled Tour event in June at Hidden Hills, and this time, shooting 63-72-66 for 201, 12 under, he tied with David Pastore and South African Rowin Caron, then won on a 25-foot birdie putt at the first playoff hole. "Two-for-two," Young said. "I guess I just like the way it's set up."

In the final round at The Challenge at Harbor Hills, Finland's Toni Hakula was only trying to get his 60-footer close enough for a stress-free par at the short 16th. "It rolled and rolled and rolled some more," he said, "and it happened to drop in." He also birdied the 18th for a one-stroke win at 17 under on 193 after shooting 66-64-63.

For Justin Doeden, former University of Minnesota star, the Classic at the Club at Weston Hills was the Tale of the Reluctant Wedge. He had 100 yards to the final green. "I've hit a million of those," he said. "But something wouldn't let me take it back. So I backed off, took a deep breath, and hit it to five feet." The birdie gave him his third straight 67, a 15-under-par total of 201 and a victory by two.

Then came the finale in November, the LOCALiQ Series Championship, at TPC Sugarloaf. Dave Pastore, frustrated in the first seven events, seemed set to win the championship, leading by four at the final turn. Then by the 18th, Trace Crowe had a 12-foot birdie try to tie him. But Crowe missed, and Pastore finished his two-putt par for a one-stroke win on 14 under after posting 66-69-68-71.

"I'm very happy with the year," Pastore said. "I was very consistent, and that's what I think really is what players always strive for."

Bryson Nimmer, with the two early wins and a second, easily won the series points race with 1,426.004. His big prize was a start in the 2021 RBC Canadian Open. The championship win lifted Pastore to second, at 1,072.150, and he earned a start in the PGA Tour's 2021 Barbasol Championship.

2020 SCHEDULE

Estrella del Mar Open	**Alexandre Rocha**
Alpharetta Classic*	**Bryson Nimmer**
The Championship — Echelon*	**Bryson Nimmer**
The Classic — Callaway Gardens*	**Stoney Crouch**
The Invitational — Auburn University*	**Cooper Musselman**
Jacksonville Championship*	**Carson Young**
The Challenge — Harbor Hills*	**Toni Hakula**
Classic — Weston Hills*	**Justin Doeden**
LOCALiQ Series Championship*	**David Pastore**
Shell Open	**MJ Maguire**
Puerto Plata Open	**Brandon Matthews**

**LOCALiQ Series event*

Estrella del Mar Open

Estrella del Mar Golf & Country Club, Mazatlan, Mexico — March 5-8
Par 72 (36-36); 7,015 yards — Purse: $175,000

1	**Alexandre Rocha**	65	67	65	62	259	$31,500
2	**Alvaro Ortiz**	66	65	67	64	262	18,900
3	**Rowin Caron**	66	66	65	66	263	10,150
	Raul Pereda	64	67	68	64	263	10,150
5	Alejandro Tosti	62	72	63	67	264	7,000
6	Ryan McCormick	66	67	65	67	265	6,300
7	Juan Jose Guerra	67	69	64	66	266	5,644
	Leandro Marelli	69	67	65	65	266	5,644
9	Cristobal Del Solar	66	70	63	68	267	4,900
	Tano Goya	69	67	65	66	267	4,900
11	Matt Gilchrest	66	66	66	70	268	3,850
	Andreas Halvorsen	68	69	66	65	268	3,850
	Mitchell Meissner	66	66	66	70	268	3,850
	Samuel Stevens	65	66	69	68	268	3,850
15	Piri Borja	69	64	67	69	269	3,063
	Ivan Camilo Ramirez	67	67	70	65	269	3,063
17	Camilo Aguado	66	68	67	69	270	2,450
	Rodolfo Cazaubon	71	66	68	65	270	2,450
	Gonzalo Rubio	66	67	69	68	270	2,450
	Kyle Tate	66	67	68	69	270	2,450
	José Toledo	63	68	69	70	270	2,450
22	Ryan Baca	69	67	68	67	271	1,700
	Rafael Echenique	69	68	68	66	271	1,700
	Jorge Fernandez-Valdes	68	66	69	68	271	1,700
	Joshua Lee	66	70	71	64	271	1,700
	Andres Gallegos	67	68	66	70	271	1,700
	Eric Steger	67	65	70	69	271	1,700

Alpharetta Classic

The Golf Club of Georgia, Alpharetta, Georgia — August 5-7
Par 72 (36-36); 7,020 yards — Purse: $100,000

1	**Bryson Nimmer**	68	64	62	194	$16,000
2	**Hayden Shieh**	69	62	67	198	8,500
3	**Alex Smalley**	65	72	63	200	5,000
4	Carson Young	71	65	65	201	4,000
	Yuxin Lin (A)	67	69	65	201	
6	Stephen Jr Behr (A)	67	67	69	203	
7	Mark Anguiano	66	70	68	204	3,195
	Alex Weiss	66	66	72	204	3,195
9	Chandler Eaton	67	70	68	205	2,227
	Brandon Matthews	66	72	67	205	2,227
	Stanton Schorr	68	70	67	205	2,227
	Justin Suh	68	70	67	205	2,227
	Steven Chervony	69	68	68	205	2,227
	Carson Jacobs	70	68	67	205	2,227
	Blake Olson	64	71	70	205	2,227
	Ryan Snouffer	68	69	68	205	2,227
17	Michael Johnson	70	69	67	206	1,539
	Raul Pereda	69	67	70	206	1,539
	Sean Walsh	67	68	71	206	1,539
	Kyle Wilshire	67	70	69	206	1,539
	Michael Buttacavoli	67	68	71	206	1,539
	Jorge Fernandez-Valdes	66	68	72	206	1,539
23	Matt Hutchins	70	70	67	207	1,117
	Chris Korte	72	65	70	207	1,117
	David Pastore	70	68	69	207	1,117
	Tyler Torano	67	69	71	207	1,117
	Christopher Petefish	66	74	67	207	1,117
	Travis Trace	68	66	73	207	1,117

The Championship — Echelon

Echelon Golf Club, Alpharetta, Georgia — August 11-13
Par 72 (36-36); 7,558 yards — Purse: $100,000

1	**Bryson Nimmer**	69	65	66	200	$16,000
2	**Raul Pereda**	71	66	65	202	5,833
	Alejandro Tosti	66	65	71	202	5,833
	Isaiah Salinda	67	67	68	202	5,833
5	Toni Hakula	68	68	67	203	3,195
	David Pastore	67	67	69	203	3,195
7	Brian Carlson	69	69	66	204	2,286
	Michael Buttacavoli	68	70	66	204	2,286
	Joshua Lee	69	68	67	204	2,286
	Justin Suh	68	69	67	204	2,286
	Christopher Petefish	65	71	68	204	2,286
	Matt Hutchins	69	67	68	204	2,286
	Piri Borja	66	68	70	204	2,286
14	Patrick Cover	67	69	69	205	1,774
	Carson Young	68	66	71	205	1,774
16	David Sanders	72	67	67	206	1,501
	Ian Holt	69	69	68	206	1,501
	Lee Detmer	66	71	69	206	1,501
	MJ Maguire	74	66	66	206	1,501
	Josh Radcliff	70	66	70	206	1,501
21	Rowin Caron	68	70	69	207	1,117
	Kyle Mueller	72	68	67	207	1,117
	Cole Miller	71	66	70	207	1,117
	Garrett May	73	67	67	207	1,117
	Michael Feuerstein	69	72	66	207	1,117
	Spencer Mellon	68	73	66	207	1,117

The Classic — Callaway Gardens

Callaway Gardens Resort (Mountain View), Pine Mountain, Georgia — August 26-28
Par 72 (36-36); 7,057 yards — Purse: $100,000

1	**Stoney Crouch**	64	66	66	196	$16,000
2	**Hayden Shieh**	66	64	66	196	8,500
	Crouch won playoff at third extra hole					
3	**Patrick Cover**	65	69	63	197	5,000
4	Camilo Aguado	64	68	66	198	3,675
	Linus Lilliedahl	64	69	65	198	3,675
6	Tommy Cocha	67	63	69	199	3,040
7	Conner Godsey	66	65	69	200	2,700
	Eric Steger	62	67	71	200	2,700
9	Michael Johnson	66	67	68	201	2,120
	Chris Korte	67	68	66	201	2,120
	Leandro Marelli	69	65	67	201	2,120
	Alex Smalley	69	60	72	201	2,120
	Justin Suh	66	66	69	201	2,120
14	Bryson Nimmer	68	68	66	202	1,775
	Chris Wiatr	65	68	69	202	1,775
16	Grady Brame	68	70	65	203	1,468
	Brendon Doyle	66	68	69	203	1,468
	Cory Howard	69	68	66	203	1,468
	Carson Jacobs	64	67	72	203	1,468
	Brandon Matthews	67	67	69	203	1,468
	Josh Radcliff	68	67	68	203	1,468
22	Blake Kennedy	67	68	69	204	1,115
	Dylan Meyer	64	72	68	204	1,115
	Harrison Rhoades	67	67	70	204	1,115
	Jason Thresher	67	68	69	204	1,115
	Joseph Winslow	66	69	69	204	1,115

The Invitational — Auburn University

Auburn University Club, Auburn, Alabama — September 1-3
Par 72 (36-36); 7,326 yards — Purse: $100,000

1	**Cooper Musselman**	67	65	66	198	$16,000
2	**Bryson Nimmer**	63	67	68	198	8,500
	Musselman won playoff at fourth extra hole					
3	**Alvaro Ortiz**	64	69	66	199	5,000
4	Trace Crowe	65	69	67	201	3,675
	Alex Smalley	66	63	72	201	3,675
6	Brendon Doyle	69	64	69	202	2,710
	David Germann	69	65	68	202	2,710
	Charles Huntzinger	69	64	69	202	2,710
	Travis Trace	67	68	67	202	2,710
10	Eric Ansett	66	69	68	203	2,100
	Peter Creighton	69	67	67	203	2,100
	Andres Gallegos	69	67	67	203	2,100
13	Akshay Bhatia	65	70	69	204	1,699
	Rowin Caron	70	66	68	204	1,699
	Patrick Newcomb	69	67	68	204	1,699
	Josh Radcliff	68	67	69	204	1,699
	David Pastore	69	67	68	204	1,699
	Aaron Terrazas	70	65	69	204	1,699
19	Mookie DeMoss	70	67	68	205	1,335
	Conner Godsey	70	68	67	205	1,335
	Christopher Petefish	67	70	68	205	1,335
	Jacob Solomon	67	70	68	205	1,335
23	Jared Bettcher	70	69	67	206	1,080
	Brian Carlson	68	66	72	206	1,080
	Myles Creighton	71	68	67	206	1,080
	Stoney Crouch	67	71	68	206	1,080
	MJ Maguire	69	68	69	206	1,080
	Motin Yeung	69	68	69	206	1,080

Jacksonville Championship

Hidden Hills Golf Club, Jacksonville, Florida — September 23-25
Par 71 (35-36); 6,892 yards — Purse: :$100,000

1	**Carson Young**	63	72	66	201	$16,000
2	**Rowin Caron**	66	66	69	201	6,750
	David Pastore	67	67	67	201	6,750
	Young won playoff at first extra hole					
4	Camilo Aguado	68	67	67	202	3,032
	MJ Maguire	64	70	68	202	3,032
	Cole Miller	69	65	68	202	3,032
	Chris O'Neill	67	68	67	202	3,032
	Leandro Marelli	66	67	69	202	3,032
	Scott Wolfes	66	67	69	202	3,032
10	Patrick Flavin	68	66	69	203	2,200
11	Justin Doeden	69	69	66	204	1,954
	Garrett May	68	67	69	204	1,954
	Dylan Meyer	68	67	69	204	1,954
	Bryson Nimmer	66	67	71	204	1,954
15	Shotaro Ban	68	68	69	205	1,539
	Andrew Dorn	69	69	67	205	1,539
	Horacio León	68	70	67	205	1,539
	Stanton Schorr	66	70	69	205	1,539
	Brad Gehl	67	68	70	205	1,539
	Toni Hakula	66	69	70	205	1,539
21	Raul Pereda	68	68	70	206	1,171
	Michael Perras	72	66	68	206	1,171
	Hayden Shieh	71	64	71	206	1,171
	Sean Walsh	70	67	69	206	1,171
25	Mike Anderson	70	70	67	207	969
	Eric Ansett	70	69	68	207	969
	Keith Greene	70	68	69	207	969
	Michael Johnson	67	72	68	207	969

The Challenge — Harbor Hills

Harbor Hills Country Club, Lady Lake, Florida — September 30-October 2
Par 70 (34-36); 6,910 yards — Purse: $100,000

1	**Toni Hakula**	66	64	63	193	$16,000
2	**Kyle Wilshire**	67	66	61	194	5,833
	Jorge Fernandez-Valdes	65	64	65	194	5,833
	Cole Miller	62	67	65	194	5,833
5	Piri Borja	65	66	64	195	3,350
6	Michael Johnson	70	64	62	196	3,040
7	Thomas Forster	67	65	65	197	2,800
8	Chris O'Neill	68	67	64	199	2,500
	Alexandre Rocha	70	66	63	199	2,500
10	Brad Gehl	66	69	65	200	1,958
	Ian Holt	65	70	65	200	1,958
	Byron Meth	69	67	64	200	1,958
	Alvaro Ortiz	68	65	67	200	1,958
	Harrison Rhoades	67	64	69	200	1,958
	Carson Young	67	65	68	200	1,958
16	Jason Thresher	67	67	67	201	1,589
	Travis Trace	67	68	66	201	1,589
18	Lee Detmer	69	67	66	202	1,388
	Greg Eason	67	69	66	202	1,388
	David Sanders	71	61	70	202	1,388
	Peyton White	69	64	69	202	1,388
22	Michael Perras	71	64	68	203	1,137
	Joseph Winslow	68	66	69	203	1,137
	Jacob Bergeron	64	67	72	203	1,137
25	Camilo Aguado	70	66	68	204	892
	Patricio Guerra	66	70	68	204	892
	Brandon Matthews	69	66	69	204	892
	Alex Smalley	71	65	68	204	892
	Brian Carlson	65	68	71	204	892
	Tommy Cocha	71	67	66	204	892
	Mookie DeMoss	70	67	67	204	892
	Charlie Netzel	69	68	67	204	892
	Patrick Newcomb	70	68	66	204	892

Classic — Weston Hills

The Club at Weston Hills, Weston, Florida — October 7-9
Par 72 (36-36); 7,069 yards — Purse: $125,000

1	**Justin Doeden**	67 67 67	201	$20,000
2	**Andreas Halvorsen**	72 65 66	203	10,625
3	**Brian Carlson**	69 69 66	204	4,809
	MJ Maguire	72 65 67	204	4,809
	Camilo Aguado	67 70 67	204	4,809
	Brendon Doyle	68 67 69	204	4,809
7	Velten Meyer	68 72 65	205	2,785
	Piri Borja	69 69 67	205	2,785
	Jose Toledo	68 70 67	205	2,785
	Cole Miller	71 66 68	205	2,785
	Jason Thresher	72 65 68	205	2,785
	Scott Wolfes	70 66 69	205	2,785
	Myles Creighton	70 65 70	205	2,785
	AJ Crouch	67 64 74	205	2,785
15	Ian Holt	72 66 68	206	2,094
	Chris Oneill	68 67 71	206	2,094
	Matias Lezcano	66 68 72	206	2,094
18	Alex Smalley	69 69 69	207	1,688
	Raul Pereda	68 70 69	207	1,688
	Dylan Meyer	69 68 70	207	1,688
	Matthew Naumec	68 73 66	207	1,688
	Jorge Fernandez-Valdes	67 69 71	207	1,688
	Andrew Yun	67 69 71	207	1,688
24	Jordan Gumberg	68 70 70	208	1,367
	Hayden Shieh	70 69 69	208	1,367
	David Sanders	71 66 71	208	1,367
	Danny Walker	68 68 72	208	1,367

LOCALiQ Series Championship

TPC Sugarloaf, Duluth, Georgia — November 17-20
Par 72 (36-36); 7,054 yards — Purse: $150,000

1	**David Pastore**	66 69 68 71	274	$24,000
2	**Trace Crowe**	71 66 65 73	275	12,750
3	**Garrett May**	73 65 70 68	276	7,500
4	Brendon Doyle	72 71 66 68	277	6,000
5	Justin Suh	72 68 73 66	279	4,793
	Sean Walsh	71 70 71 67	279	4,793
7	Andreas Halvorsen	70 74 69 68	281	4,125
8	Hayden Shieh	70 71 73 68	282	3,240
	Patrick Newcomb	76 70 67 69	282	3,240
	Andrew Dorn	71 67 71 73	282	3,240
	David Sanders	67 69 74 72	282	3,240
	Carson Young	70 66 72 74	282	3,240
13	Cooper Musselman	75 68 72 68	283	2,550
	Stoney Crouch	68 73 72 70	283	2,550
	Myles Creighton	70 72 70 71	283	2,550
16	Michael Buttacavoli	70 72 75 67	284	1,914
	Alex Smalley	74 71 70 69	284	1,914
	Patrick Flavin	72 73 69 70	284	1,914
	Andres Gallegos	72 72 70 70	284	1,914
	Eric Ansett	72 65 76 71	284	1,914
	Leandro Marelli	71 68 69 76	284	1,914
22	Brandon Matthews	74 77 67 67	285	1,503
	Byron Meth	72 70 72 71	285	1,503
	Chandler Eaton	73 70 70 72	285	1,503
25	Patrick Cover	74 71 70 71	286	1,313
	Joseph Winslow	75 71 67 73	286	1,313
	Michael Perras	72 69 68 77	286	1,313

2020 LOCALiQ SERIES

1	Bryson Nimmer	1,426.000 Pts
2	David Pastore	1,072.150 Pts
3	Carson Young	845.067 Pts
4	Hayden Shieh	757.350 Pts
5	Toni Hakula	707.397 Pts
6	Stoney Crouch	622.767 Pts
7	Justin Doeden	612.230 Pts
8	Cooper Musselman	573.833 Pts
9	Alex Smalley	509.955 Pts
10	Trace Crowe	452.500 Pts

Shell Open

Trump National Doral Golf Club (Golden Palm), Miami, Florida — December 10-13
Par 71 (36-35); 7,012 yards — Purse: $175,000

1	**MJ Maguire**	69	66	66	67	268	$31,500
2	**Andres Gallegos**	67	69	69	65	270	18,900
3	**Chris Wiatr**	67	69	69	67	272	11,900
4	Joshua Lee	72	66	70	65	273	7,700
	Brad Schneider	71	66	69	67	273	7,700
6	Santiago Gomez	66	70	70	69	275	6,081
	Drew Nesbitt	69	69	69	68	275	6,081
8	Ryan Baca	69	72	66	69	276	4,900
	Cyril Bouniol	72	66	70	68	276	4,900
	Leandro Marelli	71	69	68	68	276	4,900
	Raul Pereda	74	64	72	66	276	4,900
12	Rafael Becker	71	70	70	66	277	3,325
	Rowin Caron	69	71	67	70	277	3,325
	Tommy Cocha	70	69	68	70	277	3,325
	Toni Hakula	71	64	75	67	277	3,325
	Patrick Newcomb	72	69	68	68	277	3,325
	Samuel Stevens	67	69	70	71	277	3,325
18	Piri Borja	70	73	68	67	278	2,538
	Brandon Matthews	68	70	70	70	278	2,538
20	Patrick Cover	70	69	72	68	279	2,188
	John Somers	71	67	66	75	279	2,188
22	Rafael Echenique	72	71	68	69	280	1,798
	Alvaro Ortiz	76	66	69	69	280	1,798
	John Clare	67	71	69	73	280	1,798
	Anthony Paolucci	71	72	67	70	280	1,798

Puerto Plata Open

Playa Dorada Golf Course, Puerto Plata, Dominican Republic — December 17-20
Par 71 (36-35); 6,990 yards — Purse: $175,000

1	**Brandon Matthews**	65	65	63	65	258	$31,500
2	**Jacob Bergeron**	67	64	69	63	263	18,900
3	**Brendon Doyle**	65	64	68	67	264	10,150
	Conner Godsey	68	65	67	64	264	10,150
5	Patrick Newcomb	65	66	67	67	265	6,650
	Alejandro Tosti	63	63	71	68	265	6,650
7	MJ Maguire	64	67	69	66	266	5,644
	Leandro Marelli	68	63	68	67	266	5,644
9	Rodolfo Cazaubón	68	69	66	64	267	5,075
10	Camilo Aguado	66	67	68	67	268	4,025
	Tano Goya	68	64	66	70	268	4,025
	Juan Jose Guerra	66	66	69	67	268	4,025
	Trevor Sluman	69	67	68	64	268	4,025
	Scott Wolfes	71	66	64	67	268	4,025
15	Juan Pablo Luna	67	70	64	68	269	3,063
	Thomas Walsh	66	70	66	67	269	3,063
17	Manav Shah	70	66	68	66	270	2,625
	Austin Squires	68	69	67	66	270	2,625
	Aaron Terrazas	68	67	67	68	270	2,625
20	Brad Schneider	68	63	74	66	271	2,115
	Steven Fox	70	67	68	66	271	2,115
	Matias Simaski	68	68	66	69	271	2,115
23	Juan Carlos Benitez	66	67	70	69	272	1,490
	Ricardo Celia	72	64	68	68	272	1,490
	Tommy Cocha	70	67	68	67	272	1,490
	Roland Massimino	67	69	69	67	272	1,490
	Franck Medale	71	66	69	66	272	1,490
	Matt Ryan	69	62	74	67	272	1,490
	Sean Busch	67	69	66	70	272	1,490
	Jeremy Gandon	68	69	66	69	272	1,490
	Alexandre Rocha	68	64	69	71	272	1,490

Cliff Hawkins/Getty Images

Justin Thomas lining up a big year in which he won three times, starting at Kapalua in January.

Micheal Reaves/Getty Images

Ross Kinnaird/Getty Images

Suhaimi Abdullah/R&A

Clockwise from top left: it took seven extra holes before Gaby Lopez won the LPGA's opener; Graeme McDowell with his 11th European Tour title at Royal Greens; Matt Kuchar overcame Justin Rose and himself in Singapore.

Jack Thomas/Getty Images

Cliff Hawkins/Getty Images

David Cannon/Getty Images

Clockwise from top: Min Woo Lee claimed his maiden title at the Vic Open, as sister Minjee had done; amateur Stephanie Kyriacou, 19, won by eight at Bonville; Inbee Park back to her best at the Australian Open.

Rob Carr/Getty Images

A wizard on the greens — Patrick Reed had 45 one-putts in winning the WGC Mexico Championship.

Jed Jacobsohn/Getty Images

Sam Greenwood/Getty Images

Sam Greenwood/Getty Images

Clockwise from top left: Ernie Els claims his first Champions title; a red cardigan for Tyrrell Hatton as the Bay Hill winner; all quiet at the 17th hole at TPC Sawgrass with The Players abandoned in March.

Chung Sung-Jun/Getty Images

Ronald Martinez/Getty Images

Chung Sung-Jun/Getty Images

Clockwise from top left: Hyun Kyung Park feted with flower petals at the KLPGA Championship; So Yeon Ryu won the Korea Open at last; Harold Varner led the way when play resumed on the PGA Tour in June.

Andy Lyons/Getty Images

Rey Del Rio/Getty Images

Andrew Redington/Getty Images

Clockwise from top left: Jon Rahm celebrates at the Memorial; Jim Furyk won his first two starts on the Champions Tour; a guard of honour for Renato Paratore at the Betfred British Masters opening the "UK Swing".

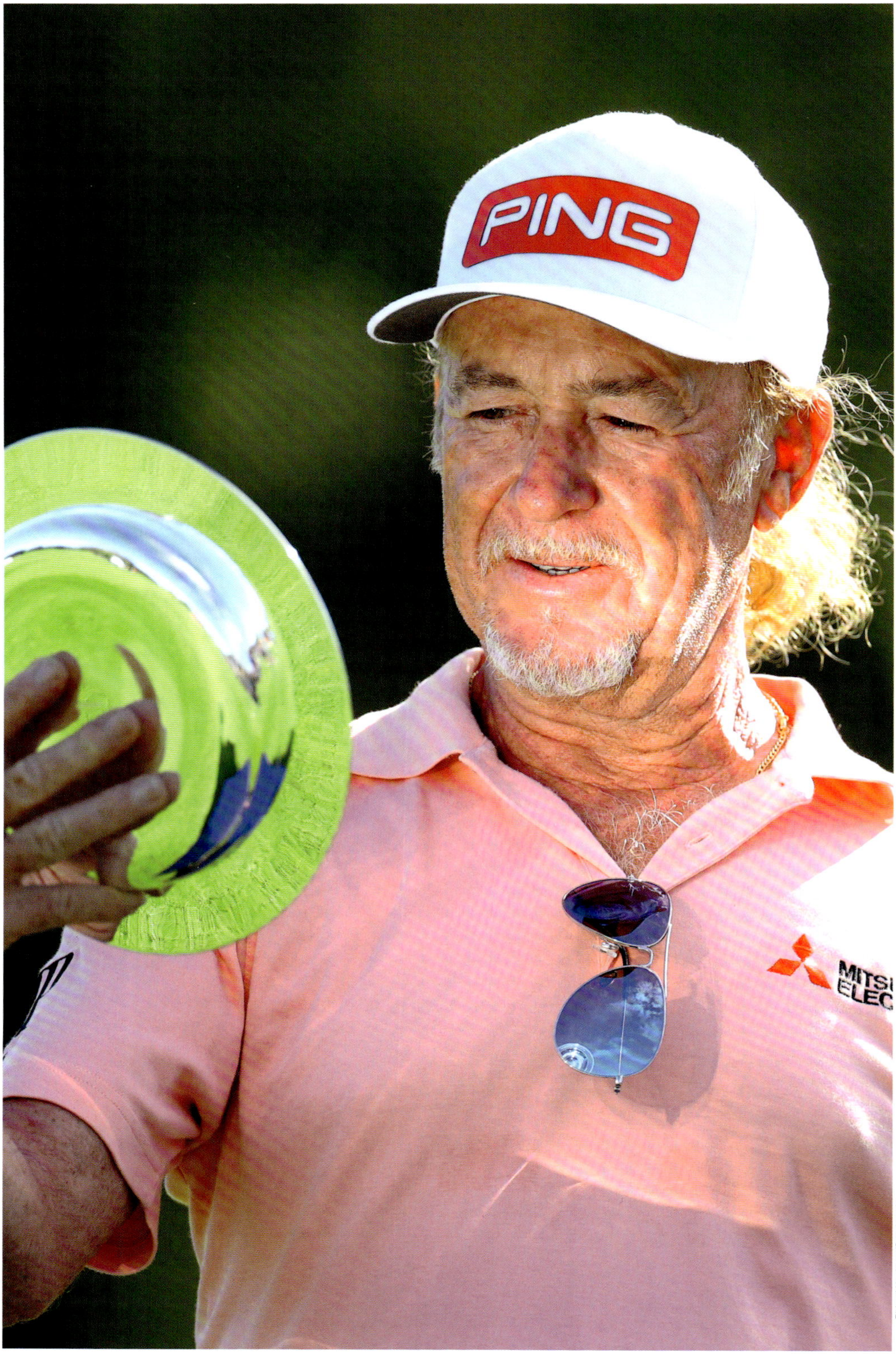

Miguel Angel Jimenez's 707th appearance on the European Tour at the Hero Open set a new record.

European Tour

An extraordinary season ended in suitably remarkable fashion with Lee Westwood becoming the oldest winner of the Harry Vardon Trophy at the age of 47.

It was his third time as the European number one, 20 years after his first. Westwood needed to finish no worse than second on his own at the DP World Tour Championship to win the Race to Dubai but his position behind tournament winner Matthew Fitzpatrick was only confirmed as he sat in the scoring tent at Jumeirah Estates.

It was so tight on the standings that Westwood won by less than 18 points from Fitzpatrick and under 25 points from Patrick Reed, the longtime leader. Fitzpatrick would have done the double but for Laurie Canter having a double bogey at the 17th hole of the final round and falling out of a share of second place. Reed, despite chipping in three times on the final day, had bogeys at the 16th and 17th holes to miss out on becoming the first American ever to win the European order of merit.

Westwood's hopes were shrinking when he went in the water at the 14th for a bogey six and missed a short birdie chance at the next hole. But he birdied the 16th, holed from 15 feet for a par at the 17th and got up and down from a bunker for a birdie at the last.

"I needed a really big finish," Westwood said. "But there are so many permutations that can happen on a day like today. It can all get too confusing if you let it. I'd not really any thoughts of the Race to Dubai until I got into the scoring tent afterwards and looked at it all and realised I've still got a chance."

Westwood added: "The motivation's never changed, really. I get to get up each day and do the job I love. I've always wanted to be a golfer, and I don't want it to end. So I'm prepared to keep working hard and put myself in the line of fire and try and get into contention in tournaments. It's where I'm most comfortable and what I love doing."

Prior to winning the Nedbank Challenge in 2018, Westwood had not won for four years. He started 2020 with his 25th European Tour title in the opening Rolex Series event of the season, the Abu Dhabi HSBC Championship. Consistency was the key as he missed only one cut. When a reliable, accurate long game was most needed, Westwood rose to the occasion. He had a top-10 finish at Valderrama and only just missed doing so at the US Open at Winged Foot. Prior to the final event of the season he had not been able to practice for more than 45 minutes at a time due to a back injury and needed constant physiotherapy throughout the week.

Westwood also supported the European Tour during its restart in the summer, hosting the Betfred British Masters at Close House and skipping the PGA Championship in San Francesco in August. "Lee is the definition of this tour," Fitzpatrick said. "He is a phenomenal player and has been for so long. I can't speak highly enough of him."

Prospects of an 11th appearance in the Ryder Cup, having been a non-playing assistant in 2018, remain a possibility when the match resumes in September 2021. Reflecting on his order of merit titles, Westwood said: "They have all been very different. I guess in 2000, I was winning a lot, but I was still up-and-coming. It was only my seventh year on tour. In 2009, I was honing in on the best-player-in-the-world spot — I needed to win here to win the Race to Dubai, and I managed to do that. And then this one, I'm kind of the more mature player on the European Tour now. It wasn't something I set out to do at the start of the year, but it shows the consistency I've shown. The most satisfying thing is doing it under pressure when it matters."

Fitzpatrick was less concerned about finishing runner-up in the Race to Dubai — he started the final week in 16th position — than securing his first victory for two years. Following five wins in his first four seasons on tour, the 26-year-old Yorkshireman had five second places, plus another on the PGA Tour, before ending his two-year draught. "All I was bothered about this week was winning," he said. Having also won at Jumeirah Estates in 2016, he joined an impressive list of double winners at the end: Henrik Stenson, Rory McIlroy and Jon Rahm.

Reed led the Race to Dubai after winning the WGC Mexico Championship and was only briefly topped by Collin Morikawa's win at the PGA Championship in San Francesco. Reed has been a regular visitor to the European Tour in recent years but Morikawa arrived for his first ever regular event at the DP World Tour Championship with a chance to win the Vardon Trophy.

This reflected the disrupted nature of the tour season, which went quiet after Jorge Campillo won the Qatar Masters in March until July. That 27 events were eventually completed, a number of which were entirely new creations, with a schedule culminating in mid-December was a remarkable achievement, even if many were down to a purse of €1 million. Two events in Austria co-sanctioned with the Challenge Tour led the way. Then came a six-week swing in England and Wales where the next tournament was never more than a three-hour drive away.

A "bio-secure bubble" was created for each tournament with players, caddies and staff undergoing a test before arriving and then remaining strictly on site at the golf course or going directly to their designated hotel. Social distancing, hand sanitising and indoor mask-wearing were pre-requisites. American John Caitlin was withdrawn from the English Championship for stopping off for a meal after a late practice round but redeemed himself later by winning both the Andalucia Masters and the Irish Open.

The tour continued with clusters of events in southern Iberia, back to the UK, the first ever visit to Cypress for back-to-back tournaments and a three-week South African swing co-sanctioned by the Sunshine Tour, where Christian Bezuidenhout was imperious with victories at the Alfred Dunhill Championship and the SA Open.

All four Rolex Series events were won by English players, with Westwood and Fitzpatrick joined by Aaron Rai at the Scottish Open and Tyrrell Hatton at the BMW PGA Championship. Hatton ended the year at 10th on the world rankings having spent much of the year in America where he won for the first time on the PGA Tour at the Arnold Palmer Invitational. Getting to spend Wentworth week at home in Marlow powered the hoodie-wearing Hatton to a four-stroke victory, with Reed finishing tied for third place.

Sami Valimaki became the first player from Finland to win the Sir Henry Cotton Rookie of the Year Award after winning the Oman Open in his sixth start and finishing 11th on the Race to Dubai having contended down the stretch at the DP World Tour Championship. Denmark's Rasmus Hojgaard, half of a pair of twins on tour, was another contender for the award after winning twice on the 2019-20 season, adding his win at the UK Championship to that at the Mauritius Open late in 2019. The 19-year-old was the second youngest to win twice on tour behind Matteo Manassero and won the UK Swing mini order of merit ahead of two-time winner Sam Horsfield. Among those achieving maiden victories were Robert MacIntyre, Callum Shinkwin, Min Woo Lee and Romain Langasque.

At the other end of his career, Miguel Angel Jimenez overtook Sam Torrance's record of 706 appearances on the European Tour. Jimenez said: "I love everything about my life. Golf is my life. You can have a bad game but not a bad day, that's the difference."

The Spaniard showed little sign of wanting to retire but 1999 Open champion Paul Lawrie bowed out of regular European Tour competition at the Scottish Open. "I've had a blast," Lawrie said. "I've been fortunate enough to have been a decent player, to have won a few. The Open was out of this world. I don't want to play in tournaments just making up the numbers. If I'm stopping a young boy coming in and having a game, having a career, I don't want that."

Late in November came the announcement of a "strategic alliance" between the European Tour and the PGA Tour, which took a stake in European Tour Productions and whose commissioner, Jay Monahan, joined the board of the European Tour. Details were thin but cooperation on scheduling and more co-sanctioned events were put forward. Representatives from the Raine Group, proponents of the so-called "Premier Golf League", a Formula 1-style circuit for selected elite players, had previously approached the European Tour offering investment.

Keith Pelley, the chief executive of the European Tour, welcomed the link up with the PGA Tour but denied it would lead to a merge or that his circuit was in financial difficulty, although over 60 employees left the tour during the year. They included retirees John Paramor and Andy McFee, two colossus of the refereeing world with over 80 years combined service to the game.

Alongside the European Tour's return to action was the "Golf for Good" initiative which raised over €1 million for charity. Among the fundraising activities was 2018 Ryder Cup captain Thomas Bjorn's 130-mile walk from Wentworth to Celtic Manor in August which yielded £35,750 for UNICEF UK and the Golf Foundation. The announcement of a full schedule for 2021 saw the return of 18 tournaments that were either postponed or cancelled in 2020.

2020 SCHEDULE

SA Open Championship	**Branden Grace**	*See chapter 14*
Abu Dhabi HSBC Championship	**Lee Westwood**	
Omega Dubai Desert Classic	**Lucas Herbert**	
Saudi International	**Graeme McDowell**	
ISPS Handa Vic Open	**Min Woo Lee**	*See chapter 17*
WGC Mexico Championship	**Patrick Reed**	*See chapter 8*
Oman Open	**Sami Valimaki**	
Commercial Bank Qatar Masters	**Jorge Campillo**	
Magical Kenya Open		*cancelled*
Hero Indian Open		*cancelled*
WGC Dell Technologies Match Play		*cancelled*
Maybank Championship		*cancelled*
GolfSixes Cascais*		*cancelled*
Made in Denmark		*cancelled*
Trophee Hassan II		*cancelled*
Scandinavian Mixed		*cancelled*
BMW International Open		*cancelled*
Open de France		*cancelled*
Austrian Open	**Marc Warren**	
The 149th Open		*postponed to 2021*
Euram Bank Open	**Joel Stalter**	
Betfred British Masters	**Renato Paratore**	
Hero Open	**Sam Horsfield**	
WGC FedEx St. Jude Invitational	**Justin Thomas**	*See chapter 8*
Olympics Men's*		*postponed to 2021*
English Championship	**Andy Sullivan**	
PGA Championship	**Collin Morikawa**	*See chapter 1*
Celtic Classic	**Sam Horsfield**	
ISPS Handa Wales Open	**Romain Langasque**	
D+D Real Czech Masters		*cancelled*
ISPS Handa UK Championship	**Rasmus Hojgaard**	
Omega European Masters		*cancelled*
Estrella Damm Andalucia Masters	**John Catlin**	
Porsche European Open		*cancelled*
Portugal Masters	**George Coetzee**	
Open de Portugal	**Garrick Higgo**	
US Open Championship	**Bryson DeChambeau**	*See chapter 4*
KLM Open		*cancelled*
Dubai Duty Free Irish Open	**John Catlin**	
The Ryder Cup*		*postponed to 2021*
Alfred Dunhill Links Championship		*cancelled*
Aberdeen Standard Investments Scottish Open	**Aaron Rai**	
BMW PGA Championship	**Tyrrell Hatton**	
Scottish Championship	**Adrian Otaegui**	
Mutuactivos Open de Espana		*cancelled*
Italian Open	**Ross McGowan**	
WGC HSBC Champions		*cancelled*
Aphrodite Hills Cyprus Open	**Callum Shinkwin**	
Aphrodite Hills Cyprus Showdown	**Robert MacIntyre**	
Turkish Airlines Open		*cancelled*
Masters Tournament	**Dustin Johnson**	*See chapter 6*

Nedbank Golf Challenge		*cancelled*
Joburg Open	**Joachim B Hansen**	*See chapter 14*
Alfred Dunhill Championship	**Christiaan Bezuidenhout**	*See chapter 14*
Golf in Dubai Championship	**Antoine Rozner**	
SA Open Championship	**Christiaan Bezuidenhout**	*See chapter 14*
DP World Tour Championship	**Matthew Fitzpatrick**	
Volvo China Open*	**Zhang Huilin**	*See chapter 15*
**non-Race to Dubai events*		

Abu Dhabi HSBC Championship

Lee Westwood still has a way to go to match Neil Coles, who is credited with winning professional tournaments in six different decades, from the PGA Assistants' Championship in 1956, the days before the formal European Tour, to the Lawrence Batley Seniors in 2002. But at the age of 46 Westwood showed no signs of slowing down as he won the Abu Dhabi HSBC Championship by two strokes.

In doing so the Worksop golfer matched Des Smyth and Mark McNulty in winning official European Tour events in four different decades and extended his own record for the longest span between victories to almost 24 years. Westwood won the Scandinavian Masters in 1996 for the first of what would become 25 titles with his second Rolex Series win here. His last win had been at the Nedbank Challenge in 2018, his first for over four years. That had been an emotional victory and the tears were not far away this time either. "It's great to know you are still good enough," Westwood said. "I'm ecstatic, and a bit emotional."

Westwood's long game was as impeccable as ever, a hybrid from 260 yards to three feet setting up an eagle at the eighth hole on Saturday. That was the day, with a 65 capped with a birdie at the last, after scores of 69 and 68, that Westwood took a one-shot lead. It was a lead he did not relinquish on the final day. Four birdies in the first eight holes, and another at the 12th, kept him in front though a rare missed putt at the 16th, for only his fourth bogey of the week, meant he took a one-shot lead to the last. A calm birdie four, however, sealed the win with a 67 for a 19-under-par total of 269.

Under pressure on the final day, Westwood's new claw-putting style was tested severely but proved up to the task. "I put in a lot of hard work and felt quite calm on the greens this week and rolled a lot of good putts. That was the key to winning, especially in the desert because the greens are so immaculate, you know that everybody is going to hole their putts."

Tommy Fleetwood, trying to win the event for a third time in four years on his 29th birthday, went out in 30 and matched the 63 of Victor Perez, who eagled the final hole. The pair shared second place with Matthew Fitzpatrick, who did not drop a shot in a 67. Louis Oosthuizen was fifth, two shots further back.

Abu Dhabi Golf Club, Abu Dhabi, United Arab Emirates — January 16-19
Par 72 (36-36); 7,583 yards — Purse: $7,000,000

1	**Lee Westwood**	69	68	65	67	269	€1,047,741
2	**Matthew Fitzpatrick**	68	67	69	67	271	468,783
	Victor Perez	70	70	68	63	271	468,783
	Tommy Fleetwood	71	70	67	63	271	468,783
5	Louis Oosthuizen	69	68	70	66	273	266,547
6	Shaun Norris	64	77	68	65	274	204,311
	Ross Fisher	70	71	66	67	274	204,311
8	Sergio Garcia	67	69	69	70	275	134,845
	Martin Kaymer	68	73	69	65	275	134,845
	Bernd Wiesberger	69	69	65	72	275	134,845
	Scott Jamieson	71	72	67	65	275	134,845
12	Rafa Cabrera Bello	67	68	71	70	276	97,315
	Jack Singh Brar	70	70	68	68	276	97,315
	Paul Waring	71	71	67	67	276	97,315
	Erik van Rooyen	73	68	69	66	276	97,315
	Sam Horsfield	73	69	67	67	276	97,315
17	Branden Grace	68	72	69	68	277	79,838
	Scott Hend	69	70	69	69	277	79,838
	Masahiro Kawamura	69	71	70	67	277	79,838
	Francesco Laporta	71	63	69	74	277	79,838
21	Renato Paratore	64	72	76	66	278	65,379
	Zach Murray	67	72	70	69	278	65,379
	Edoardo Molinari	68	73	68	69	278	65,379
	Andy Sullivan	69	71	68	70	278	65,379
	Sebastian Heisele	70	73	64	71	278	65,379
	Brandon Stone	71	72	66	69	278	65,379
	Gavin Green	73	70	67	68	278	65,379
	Jordan Smith	74	68	67	69	278	65,379
	Joakim Lagergren	75	65	68	70	278	65,379
30	Thomas Pieters	68	70	70	71	279	54,064
	Yuxin Lin	69	70	70	70	279	
	Jack Senior	71	70	66	72	279	54,064

	David Lipsky	73	69	68	69	279	54,064
34	Brooks Koepka	66	75	70	69	280	45,981
	Kurt Kitayama	67	70	68	75	280	45,981
	Zander Lombard	67	71	69	73	280	45,981
	Mike Lorenzo-Vera	68	73	67	72	280	45,981
	Romain Langasque	70	71	67	72	280	45,981
	Patrick Cantlay	71	66	72	71	280	45,981
	Jorge Campillo	71	72	67	70	280	45,981
41	Haotong Li	67	69	74	71	281	40,862
42	Nicolas Colsaerts	69	72	71	70	282	34,576
	Joost Luiten	70	68	73	71	282	34,576
	Kiradech Aphibarnrat	70	73	65	74	282	34,576
	Richie Ramsay	71	69	69	73	282	34,576
	Oliver Fisher	71	70	72	69	282	34,576
	Ashley Chesters	72	69	68	73	282	34,576
	Sean Crocker	72	70	68	72	282	34,576
	Matthias Schwab	74	66	69	73	282	34,576
	Sebastian Soderberg	75	64	73	70	282	34,576
51	Justin Harding	69	73	72	69	283	26,403
	Adri Arnaus	70	67	75	71	283	26,403
	Soren Kjeldsen	70	70	70	73	283	26,403
	Wade Ormsby	71	71	70	71	283	26,403
55	Thomas Detry	69	70	67	78	284	21,374
	David Drysdale	70	71	72	71	284	21,374
	Matthieu Pavon	71	70	72	71	284	21,374
	Justin Walters	73	70	69	72	284	21,374
59	Jason Scrivener	66	74	74	71	285	17,602
	Haydn Porteous	69	71	72	73	285	17,602
	Shubhankar Sharma	71	70	69	75	285	17,602
	Christiaan Bezuidenhout	71	72	72	70	285	17,602
	Jeff Winther	73	70	71	71	285	17,602
64	Matt Wallace	73	70	69	74	286	15,716
65	Thomas Bjorn	71	71	73	72	287	15,088
66	Grant Forrest	74	68	73	73	288	14,459
67	Lucas Herbert	69	69	76	75	289	13,516
	Nacho Elvira	72	67	78	72	289	13,516
69	Andrew Johnston	69	74	72	75	290	11,354
	David Law	70	68	76	76	290	11,354
	Victor Dubuisson	70	73	75	72	290	11,354
	Alexander Bjork	73	70	79	68	290	11,354
73	David Howell	70	72	75	74	291	9,427

Omega Dubai Desert Classic

On Australia Day, Lucas Herbert secured his first professional victory in a dramatic playoff at the Omega Dubai Desert Classic. Herbert's more established compatriot Marc Leishman made it a double for golfers from Down Under later in the day at the Farmers Insurance Open. Herbert, the 24-year-old from Bendigo, had finished runner-up four times, once in his rookie season on the European Tour in 2018 and three times on the PGA Tour of Australasia, once as an amateur.

High winds made the Emirates course particularly tricky on the first and final days, when Herbert and Christiaan Bezuidenhout posted the low rounds of 68. Only two other players broke 70, while overnight leader Ashun Wu, who went three ahead when he chipped in for a birdie on the seventh, dropped into a tie for sixth after a 77. Bryson DeChambeau, the defending champion, tied for the lead during the final round but bogeyed the last four holes to share eighth place after a 76.

Bezuidenhout's only dropped shot came at the 18th when his pitch to the green spun back into the water. The South African holed from 15 feet for a six to post the target at 279, nine under par. Herbert birdied the last two holes to force a playoff as the pair finished two ahead of Arni Arnaus, Tom Lewis and Dean Burmester, whose Uber ride back to the hotel on Wednesday evening was involved in a crash that left him and his family with the odd bruise.

On the first playoff hole at the 18th, Herbert's wild second shot finished 50 yards into the water on the right. But a fine pitch from the drop zone to two feet salvaged a par and on the second extra hole he hit his approach to 20 feet and two-putted for a birdie. Bezuidenhout, who won at Valderrama in 2019, failed to get up and down from thick rough at the back of the green.

"It's the best thing ever," Herbert said before echoing Cam Smith's comments after his countrymen's win at the Sony Open. "There's some pretty awful stuff happening right now in Australia with the fires," he said. "Cam Smith said it a couple weeks ago when he won, and I'd like to say the same thing. Everyone around the world is behind us and hopefully we can keep fighting harder than what I did on the first playoff hole. That's nothing compared to the firefighters and volunteers putting out the fires."

Emirates Golf Club (Majlis), Dubai, United Arab Emirates — January 23-26
Par 72 (35-37); 7,353 yards — Purse: $3,250,000

1	**Lucas Herbert**	69	71	71	68	279	€490,323
2	**Christiaan Bezuidenhout**	73	66	72	68	279	326,885
	Herbert won playoff at second extra hole						
3	**Dean Burmester**	69	68	72	72	281	152,002
	Adri Arnaus	72	68	71	70	281	152,002
	Tom Lewis	73	69	65	74	281	152,002
6	Ashun Wu	69	69	67	77	282	95,614
	Kurt Kitayama	69	70	68	75	282	95,614
	Bryson DeChambeau	70	67	70	76	283	66,096
	Robert MacIntyre	74	70	67	72	283	66,096
	Mike Lorenzo-Vera	74	71	67	71	283	66,096
11	David Lipsky	68	75	71	70	284	48,072
	Eddie Pepperell	69	67	72	76	284	48,072
	Matthieu Pavon	69	71	75	69	284	48,072
	Shane Lowry	72	69	69	74	284	48,072
	Tommy Fleetwood	75	65	69	75	284	48,072
16	Jack Singh Brar	71	71	70	73	285	36,901
	Ian Poulter	71	73	71	70	285	36,901
	Martin Kaymer	72	71	73	69	285	36,901
	Miguel Angel Jimenez	72	74	69	70	285	36,901
	Victor Perez	73	66	67	79	285	36,901
	Grant Forrest	73	68	69	75	285	36,901
	Nacho Elvira	73	70	66	76	285	36,901
23	Viktor Hovland	71	70	71	74	286	31,038
	Sergio Garcia	71	72	70	73	286	31,038
	Louis Oosthuizen	71	72	73	70	286	31,038
	Matthias Schwab	72	72	70	72	286	31,038
27	Romain Langasque	69	69	73	76	287	27,949
	Kalle Samooja	69	74	70	74	287	27,949
	Gavin Green	73	71	70	73	287	27,949
30	Mikko Korhonen	74	71	68	75	288	25,742
	Ryan Fox	76	70	66	76	288	25,742
32	Julien Guerrier	71	74	73	71	289	22,830
	Jordan Smith	72	70	71	76	289	22,830
	Thomas Detry	73	72	72	72	289	22,830
	Tapio Pulkkanen	73	73	72	71	289	22,830
	Scott Jamieson	74	71	69	75	289	22,830
37	Thomas Pieters	67	77	69	77	290	19,417
	Soren Kjeldsen	69	76	65	80	290	19,417
	Erik van Rooyen	70	75	69	76	290	19,417
	Justin Harding	71	73	71	75	290	19,417
	Henrik Stenson	72	70	72	76	290	19,417
	Jeff Winther	76	70	65	79	290	19,417
43	Lorenzo Gagli	75	70	73	73	291	17,063
	Danny Willett	76	70	72	73	291	17,063
45	Robert Karlsson	69	68	79	76	292	15,004
	Adrian Otaegui	72	71	74	75	292	15,004
	Benjamin Hebert	72	73	68	79	292	15,004
	Matthew Fitzpatrick	74	71	69	78	292	15,004
	Alexander Bjork	77	69	72	74	292	15,004
50	Romain Wattel	70	76	76	71	293	11,768
	Padraig Harrington	71	75	73	74	293	11,768
	Gaganjeet Bhullar	73	71	74	75	293	11,768
	David Law	75	71	76	71	293	11,768
	Nicolas Colsaerts	77	69	69	78	293	11,768
	Lee Westwood	78	68	73	74	293	11,768
56	Shaun Norris	69	73	72	80	294	9,414
	Masahiro Kawamura	69	73	75	77	294	9,414
58	Zander Lombard	71	75	74	75	295	7,796
	Sean Crocker	72	72	75	76	295	7,796
	Callum Shinkwin	73	73	70	79	295	7,796
	Richie Ramsay	73	73	73	76	295	7,796
	David Drysdale	74	71	74	76	295	7,796
	Niklas Norgaard Moller	74	72	75	74	295	7,796
	Joachim B Hansen	75	70	74	76	295	7,796
	Jason Scrivener	77	69	73	76	295	7,796
66	Sebastian Heisele	70	69	74	83	296	6,031
	Joost Luiten	72	72	73	79	296	6,031
	Mathiam Keyser	74	68	72	82	296	6,031
	Nino Bertasio	74	70	70	82	296	6,031
70	Sebastian Soderberg	71	75	77	75	298	5,368
71	Aaron Rai	77	69	72	81	299	4,413

Saudi International

Following Lee Westwood's lead, Graeme McDowell became the second vice-captain of the 2018 European team to start a new Ryder Cup year with a victory. McDowell, who lost his card on the PGA Tour in 2018 before winning in the Dominican Republic in 2019, was still ranked outside the world's top 100 before defeating Dustin Johnson by two strokes at Royal Greens and jumping back up to 47th in the world.

On a young course exposed to constantly shifting breezes beside the Red Sea, the 40-year-old McDowell managed his game beautifully. He shared the lead on day one with Gavin Green after a 64, then had a 68 the next day during which he was warned for slow play after taking too long on a shot that followed a brief on-course television interview. He played the rest of the tournament knowing another bad time would result in a one-shot penalty.

A 66 in the third round put him one clear on a day when he had the measure of the grainy greens. "I tell my children we live in a lovely house because their dad can putt," said the 2010 US Open champion. His Sunday playing partner was Victor Dubuisson. The pair had not played together since their successful partnership at the 2014 Ryder Cup. The Frenchman did not have his best day, slipping to a 74 and a tie for sixth place that included Sergio Garcia.

McDowell was two over par for the day when he bogeyed the 13th, one ahead of clubhouse leader Thomas Pieters after a 65, before he holed from 25 feet at the 14th and hit a seven-iron to four feet at the next. Three pars gave the Portrush man a 70 and a 12-under-par total of 268. Defending champion

Johnson eagled the fourth but had only one birdie and was not a threat to McDowell before the American eagled at the last to snatch second place. Phil Mickelson had an early hat-trick of birdies and finished with a 67 to tie for third with Pieters and Green, while world number one Brooks Koepka flickered into life with a 65 on Saturday but closed with a 72.

McDowell's 11th European Tour title came almost six years since his last. "I didn't realise it had been quite that long since I'd won here in Europe. I'm very relieved. It's unusual to win feeling as uncomfortable as I did on a lot of these holes with the tough conditions. The birdies on 14 and 15 were just huge at the time, and it was nice to have that little cushion coming down the last couple. My big goal this year was to be back in the top 50 in the world, back competing in the big tournaments. I'm very excited that it's happened a little faster than I expected. It's been 10 years since I won a US Open, 10 years probably since I played the best golf of my life. I feel like I'm moving back in the right direction."

Royal Greens Golf & Country Club, King Abdullah Economic City, Saudi Arabia — Jan 30-Feb 2
Par 70 (35-35); 7,010 yards — Purse: $3,500,000

1	**Graeme McDowell**	64	68	66	70	268	€529,338
2	**Dustin Johnson**	67	68	68	67	270	352,886
3	**Gavin Green**	64	67	70	70	271	164,096
	Phil Mickelson	66	70	68	67	271	164,096
	Thomas Pieters	70	67	69	65	271	164,096
6	Ross Fisher	66	68	71	68	273	84,102
	Victor Dubuisson	69	65	65	74	273	84,102
	Sergio Garcia	69	68	70	66	273	84,102
	Abraham Ancer	69	70	67	67	273	84,102
	Thomas Detry	73	66	65	69	273	84,102
11	Matthieu Pavon	68	71	67	68	274	56,534
	Dean Burmester	71	68	68	67	274	56,534
13	Shane Lowry	69	67	70	69	275	47,799
	Pablo Larrazabal	69	68	74	64	275	47,799
	Ashun Wu	71	66	68	70	275	47,799
	Martin Kaymer	73	64	73	65	275	47,799
17	Jhonattan Vegas	65	71	71	69	276	40,336
	Brooks Koepka	70	69	65	72	276	40,336
	Jack Senior	71	69	71	65	276	40,336
	Ian Poulter	72	68	65	71	276	40,336
21	Christiaan Bezuidenhout	68	73	67	69	277	34,460
	Richard McEvoy	69	68	71	69	277	34,460
	Richie Ramsay	70	70	69	68	277	34,460
	Stephen Gallacher	70	71	70	66	277	34,460
	Haotong Li	70	71	70	66	277	34,460
	Steven Brown	71	70	69	67	277	34,460
27	Adri Arnaus	65	74	67	72	278	26,534
	Andy Sullivan	66	71	73	68	278	26,534
	Aaron Rai	66	71	71	70	278	26,534
	Ryan Fox	66	75	69	68	278	26,534
	Lucas Herbert	67	71	72	68	278	26,534
	Renato Paratore	68	65	70	75	278	26,534
	Alexander Bjork	68	69	71	70	278	26,534
	David Howell	68	69	71	70	278	26,534
	Adrian Meronk	68	70	70	70	278	26,534
	Benjamin Hebert	71	69	67	71	278	26,534
	Grant Forrest	73	66	66	73	278	26,534
38	Victor Perez	65	65	73	76	279	20,327
	Sebastian Soderberg	65	73	72	69	279	20,327
	Soren Kjeldsen	67	69	73	70	279	20,327
	Sean Crocker	68	68	72	71	279	20,327
	Alexander Levy	69	70	70	70	279	20,327
	Adrian Otaegui	69	71	68	71	279	20,327
44	Henrik Stenson	65	70	70	75	280	15,880
	Francesco Laporta	67	68	72	73	280	15,880
	Joost Luiten	67	72	71	70	280	15,880
	James Morrison	69	68	73	70	280	15,880
	Jeff Winther	69	68	72	71	280	15,880
	Matthias Schwab	69	72	66	73	280	15,880
	Matt Wallace	70	68	71	71	280	15,880
	Sebastian Heisele	70	69	71	70	280	15,880
52	Connor Syme	69	71	69	72	281	12,069
	Maverick Antcliff	70	69	72	70	281	12,069
	Nacho Elvira	72	66	72	71	281	12,069
	Ernie Els	72	69	70	70	281	12,069
56	Marcus Kinhult	67	68	78	69	282	8,604
	Jazz Janewattananond	68	66	76	72	282	8,604
	Fabrizio Zanotti	68	72	69	73	282	8,604
	Justin Harding	68	73	67	74	282	8,604
	Nicolas Colsaerts	69	69	71	73	282	8,604
	Rafa Cabrera Bello	69	70	73	70	282	8,604
	Jordan Smith	71	67	67	77	282	8,604
	Edoardo Molinari	71	69	72	70	282	8,604
	Kalle Samooja	72	68	71	71	282	8,604
	Lorenzo Gagli	73	66	72	71	282	8,604
	Ashley Chesters	73	67	69	73	282	8,604
67	Justin Walters	71	65	75	72	283	6,511
	Gaganjeet Bhullar	74	67	71	71	283	6,511
69	Scott Jamieson	73	67	71	73	284	6,034
70	Antoine Rozner	72	68	69	76	285	5,281
	Nino Bertasio	72	69	72	72	285	5,281
72	Maximilian Kieffer	70	71	67	78	286	4,760
	Masahiro Kawamura	73	68	71	74	286	4,760
74	Sebastian Garcia Rodriguez	67	70	78	72	287	4,754
	Haydn Porteous	72	67	73	75	287	4,754
76	Julien Guerrier	75	65	79	70	289	4,749

Oman Open

A new name announced himself on the European Tour as Finland's 21-year-old Sami Valimaki won the Oman Open in only his sixth appearance. Valimaki beat three-time winner Brandon Stone at the third hole of a playoff after the pair tied on 13-under-par 275 at Al Mouj Golf.

As the wind whipped up on a course that nestles between Muscat Airport and the Gulf of Oman, they were the only survivors from the six-way tie for the lead after 54 holes. First Stone and then

Valimaki birdied the 18th hole from the region of 20 feet for closing scores of 70 to finish one ahead of France's Adrien Saddier, who came from behind with a 69. Of the others to start the last day in a share of the lead, Valimaki's compatriot Mikko Korhonen tied for fourth after a 72, Denmark's Rasmus Hojgaard had a 74, former champion Joost Luiten had a 75 and Callum Shinkwin a 77.

Twice Stone and Valimaki halved the 18th hole in par-fours but on the third occasion, Stone, avoiding the ocean on the right, pulled his approach near the grandstand on the left and failed to get up and down. Valimaki safely two-putted for his maiden victory.

"It's awesome," he said. "There are not many words to say, it's unbelievable. I thought I was going to miss the putt on the last in regulation but thank God it went to the hole and gave me the chance to win the tournament."

Valimaki had recovered from an opening 74 which left him in danger of missing the cut with scores of 67 and 64, while in the final round he came back from a double bogey at the ninth. He only turned professional in 2019 after completing his military service before winning four times on the Pro Golf Tour and then earning his European Tour card at the Qualifying School.

Lorenzo Gagli finished 10th after initially withdrawing from the event on Wednesday after exhibiting flu-like symptoms and self-isolating himself at the hotel on advice from the tournament medical team. His roommate Edoardo Molinari also withdrew and was isolated in another room. But when Gagli's test for coronavirus came back negative on Thursday, the pair were reinstated in the tournament and were paired together in the last group of the day. Molinari finished 50th.

Al Mouj Golf, Muscat, Oman — February 27-March 1
Par 72 (36-36); 7,452 yards — Purse: $1,750,000

1	**Sami Valimaki**	74	67	64	70	275	€265,121
2	**Brandon Stone**	67	71	67	70	275	176,748
	Valimaki won playoff at third extra hole						
3	**Adrien Saddier**	72	68	67	69	276	99,582
4	Guido Migliozzi	66	72	68	71	277	73,493
	Mikko Korhonen	73	67	65	72	277	73,493
6	Rasmus Hojgaard	67	68	70	74	279	44,700
	George Coetzee	68	73	72	66	279	44,700
	Alejandro Canizares	70	69	72	68	279	44,700
	Jordan Smith	70	70	67	72	279	44,700
10	Ross Fisher	68	75	70	67	280	25,711
	Joost Luiten	69	69	67	75	280	25,711
	Lorenzo Gagli	69	70	73	68	280	25,711
	Clement Sordet	70	71	66	73	280	25,711
	Grant Forrest	70	73	69	68	280	25,711
	Antoine Rozner	71	70	70	69	280	25,711
	Martin Kaymer	73	69	67	71	280	25,711
	Connor Syme	73	70	69	68	280	25,711
18	Taehee Lee	67	75	70	69	281	18,612
	Nicolas Colsaerts	69	67	73	72	281	18,612
	Gavin Green	71	70	73	67	281	18,612
	Shaun Norris	72	71	70	68	281	18,612
	Haotong Li	73	69	68	71	281	18,612
	Robin Roussel	75	69	67	70	281	18,612
	Matthew Jordan	77	67	71	66	281	18,612
25	Zander Lombard	68	73	76	65	282	15,589
	SSP Chawrasia	68	75	72	67	282	15,589
	Fabrizio Zanotti	69	70	71	72	282	15,589
	Callum Shinkwin	69	70	66	77	282	15,589
	Paul Waring	70	73	68	71	282	15,589
30	Stephen Gallacher	68	67	74	74	283	12,991
	Adrian Otaegui	68	74	68	73	283	12,991
	Justin Walters	69	74	67	73	283	12,991
	Richard McEvoy	70	68	74	71	283	12,991
	Kalle Samooja	71	65	72	75	283	12,991
	Maximilian Kieffer	72	72	73	66	283	12,991
36	Louis de Jager	69	72	70	73	284	10,658
	Darius van Driel	71	69	72	72	284	10,658
	Thomas Detry	71	72	71	70	284	10,658
	Rikard Karlberg	72	70	71	71	284	10,658
	Marcus Armitage	72	72	71	69	284	10,658
	Robert Rock	73	65	71	75	284	10,658
	Cormac Sharvin	75	67	72	70	284	10,658
43	Victor Dubuisson	68	75	69	73	285	8,431
	Alexander Levy	69	75	71	70	285	8,431
	Jeunghun Wang	71	68	72	74	285	8,431
	Soren Kjeldsen	71	70	73	71	285	8,431
	Benjamin Hebert	71	72	70	72	285	8,431
	Maverick Antcliff	72	71	72	70	285	8,431
	Chris Paisley	73	69	71	72	285	8,431
50	Jeff Winther	69	72	69	76	286	6,681
	Edoardo Molinari	70	72	72	72	286	6,681
	Jamie Donaldson	71	73	71	71	286	6,681
	Ashley Chesters	73	70	74	69	286	6,681
54	Richard Bland	72	71	69	75	287	5,170
	Calum Hill	73	68	74	72	287	5,170
	Ben Stow	73	69	73	72	287	5,170
	Nicolai Hojgaard	73	71	71	72	287	5,170
	Adrian Meronk	73	71	71	72	287	5,170
	James Morrison	74	70	72	71	287	5,170
60	Steven Brown	69	74	71	74	288	4,375
	Johannes Veerman	72	70	73	73	288	4,375
62	Aaron Cockerill	69	73	70	77	289	3,977
	Joel Sjoholm	72	70	71	76	289	3,977
	Lars van Meijel	72	72	71	74	289	3,977
65	Pablo Larrazabal	73	70	74	73	290	3,579
	Darren Fichardt	74	69	73	74	290	3,579
67	Scott Hend	70	72	72	77	291	3,113
	Robin Sciot-Siegrist	70	73	73	75	291	3,113
	Jack Singh Brar	71	73	73	74	291	3,113
	Dean Burmester	73	71	73	74	291	3,113
71	Sean Crocker	72	71	71	78	292	2,386
72	Benjamin Poke	71	73	72	77	293	2,383
73	Andrea Pavan	71	72	70	81	294	2,380
74	Bryce Easton	72	71	75		218	2,374
	Renato Paratore	71	73	74		218	2,374
	Lee Slattery	73	71	74		218	2,374
77	Jean-Baptiste Bonnet	71	73	75		219	2,365
	Peter Hanson	70	74	75		219	2,365
	Andy Sullivan	68	76	75		219	2,365

Commercial Bank Qatar Masters

It took Jorge Campillo 229 events to win his first European Tour event at the Trophee Hassan II in 2019. The wait for a second was far shorter as victory at the Commercial Bank Qatar Masters gave the 33-year-old Spaniard wins in consecutive seasons. But for David Drysdale the wait went on. The 44-year-old Scot was playing his 498th tournament and a little extra besides as he took Campillo to the fifth playoff hole before chalking up a fourth runner-up finish in his 25 years as a professional.

With the tournament moving for the first time to the Jose Maria Olazabal-designed Education City Golf Club in Doha, Campillo joked afterwards: "I have to thank Jose Maria for building a course that suits my game."

The 513-yard 18th hole, usually a par five for regular play but here a par four, appeared to suit Drysdale better. Time after time the Scot knocked a drive down the fairway and then hit a succession of superb seven-iron approaches. It was only a brilliant putting display that brought Campillo the famous pearl trophy.

Campillo, whose solo lead disappeared with a bogey at the 16th and a double at the 17th, saw his putt at the 18th in regulation stop in the jaws of the hole only for Drysdale to miss from 10 feet. Then the first two extra holes were halved in birdies. Each time Campillo knew he needed to hole from longer range — 20 and then 25 feet — with Drysdale, getting ever closer with his approaches, following him in from six and three feet. Eventually, when Campillo birdied again from 20 feet at the fifth extra hole, Drysdale could not match him from a similar range. The pair had produced five birdies between them in the playoff, whereas in regulation play there had only been six all day.

"I'm just so proud right now of the way I played in the playoff," Campillo said. "I hardly missed a shot and I was able to make some putts. It's a great par four, the 18th. A tough hole. David was hitting some great shots into the hole and I had to make some putts. Three birdies out of six on 18 to win is something to be proud of. It was a tough win but I'm glad I pulled it off."

Campillo had rounds of 66, 66, 67 and 72, and Drysdale 67, 69, 64 and 71, as the pair tied on 13-under-par 271. Niklas Lemke, Kalle Samooja and Jeff Winther shared third place, one stroke behind.

Education City Golf Club, Doha, Qatar — March 5-8
Par 71 (36-35); 7,307 yards — Purse: $1,750,000

1	**Jorge Campillo**	66	66	67	72	271	€258,656
2	**David Drysdale**	67	69	64	71	271	172,437
	Campillo won playoff at fifth extra hole						
3	**Jeff Winther**	66	69	65	72	272	80,185
	Niklas Lemke	68	69	70	65	272	80,185
	Kalle Samooja	70	67	66	69	272	80,185
6	Alexander Bjork	70	63	69	71	273	54,319
7	Marcus Kinhult	68	65	73	68	274	35,944
	Chris Paisley	69	70	67	68	274	35,944
	George Coetzee	70	68	69	67	274	35,944
	Pablo Larrazabal	72	67	63	72	274	35,944
	Nino Bertasio	72	69	67	66	274	35,944
12	Lorenzo Gagli	66	70	69	70	275	24,024
	Scott Jamieson	67	68	69	71	275	24,024
	Marcus Armitage	67	71	66	71	275	24,024
	Adrien Saddier	69	70	67	69	275	24,024
	Gavin Green	70	69	71	65	275	24,024
17	Benjamin Hebert	67	70	72	67	276	19,710
	Benjamin Poke	68	67	66	75	276	19,710
	Jack Senior	69	66	68	73	276	19,710
	Thomas Detry	72	66	66	72	276	19,710
21	Joost Luiten	65	68	75	69	277	16,606
	Andy Sullivan	66	66	72	73	277	16,606
	Thomas Pieters	66	70	70	71	277	16,606
	Matthieu Pavon	70	69	69	69	277	16,606
	Matthias Schwab	70	70	67	70	277	16,606
	Jason Scrivener	70	71	70	66	277	16,606
	James Morrison	73	68	68	68	277	16,606
28	Darren Fichardt	67	68	73	70	278	12,742
	SSP Chawrasia	67	69	68	74	278	12,742
	Wilco Nienaber	68	70	69	71	278	12,742
	Fabrizio Zanotti	69	68	71	70	278	12,742
	Lars van Meijel	70	66	71	71	278	12,742
	Matthew Jordan	70	67	69	72	278	12,742
	Justin Harding	70	67	70	71	278	12,742
	Zander Lombard	70	69	70	69	278	12,742
	Jeunghun Wang	70	69	72	67	278	12,742
	Alejandro Canizares	71	69	68	70	278	12,742
38	Sebastian Heisele	68	72	69	70	279	9,933
	Romain Langasque	69	64	74	72	279	9,933
	Jordan Smith	69	69	71	70	279	9,933
	Joakim Lagergren	70	71	68	70	279	9,933
	Sami Valimaki	70	71	65	73	279	9,933
	Sihwan Kim	72	69	69	69	279	9,933
44	Brandon Stone	71	68	72	69	280	8,536
	Stephen Gallacher	72	68	68	72	280	8,536
	Soren Kjeldsen	72	69	68	71	280	8,536
47	Dave Coupland	68	68	77	68	281	7,139
	Oliver Fisher	69	64	76	72	281	7,139
	Renato Paratore	69	71	74	67	281	7,139
	Steven Brown	71	70	70	70	281	7,139
	Haydn Porteous	73	68	71	69	281	7,139
	Oliver Farr	74	64	71	72	281	7,139
53	Nicolai Hojgaard	64	71	73	74	282	5,083
	Carlos Pigem	66	71	72	73	282	5,083
	Ross Fisher	68	73	69	72	282	5,083

	Dean Burmester	69	67	72	74	282	5,083		Gregory Havret	68	71	79	66	284	2,982
	Antoine Rozner	69	69	70	74	282	5,083		Pedro Figueiredo	70	71	71	72	284	2,982
	Maximilian Kieffer	69	71	71	71	282	5,083		Cormac Sharvin	71	69	73	71	284	2,982
	Richie Ramsay	70	71	68	73	282	5,083		Robert Rock	72	69	68	75	284	2,982
	Masahiro Kawamura	76	65	69	72	282	5,083		Julien Guerrier	72	69	75	68	284	2,982
61	Robert MacIntyre	68	72	68	75	283	3,880	72	Yassine Touhami	68	71	71	75	285	2,322
	Taehee Lee	70	70	73	70	283	3,880		David Horsey	69	69	74	73	285	2,322
	Toby Tree	71	69	72	71	283	3,880		Clement Sordet	72	66	74	73	285	2,322
	Sean Crocker	71	70	72	70	283	3,880	75	Hennie du Plessis	72	69	73	73	287	2,315
	Laurie Canter	72	69	69	73	283	3,880		Sebastian Soderberg	74	66	72	75	287	2,315
66	Kyongjun Moon	67	70	75	72	284	2,982	77	Brandon Robinson-Thompson	72	68	72	80	292	2,310

Austrian Open

Four months after being suspended following the Qatar Masters due to the Covid-19 pandemic, the European Tour returned with the Austrian Open at Diamond Country Club, an event co-sanctioned with the Challenge Tour.

No spectators were allowed with only players, caddies and essential staff on site. All personnel undertook daily temperature and symptom checks, social distancing was required and strict hygiene protocols meant only one person per group handled the flagstick.

Everyone also had to pass a Covid-19 test prior to travel to Atzenbrugg, near Vienna, which meant Marc Warren was without his regular caddie Ken Herring, whose test result was not returned in time. Warren was not the only player to carry his own bag but that did not stop the 39-year-old Scot claiming his fourth European Tour title with a one-stroke victory over Germany's Marcel Schneider.

Warren, who holed the winning putt for Great Britain and Ireland at the 2001 Walker Cup at Sea Island and was the rookie of the year on the European Tour five years later, was playing only his second tournament of the year and had not won since the 2014 Made in Denmark tournament. Victory restored his exempt status after finishing 130th and 215th on the Race to Dubai in the previous two years.

"I've played very poorly since my last win," Warren said. "The break has been unfortunate for everyone but it came at a good time for me, spending some time at home with the family and trying to get my game ready to play golf. I came out of it pretty refreshed.

"Carrying my bag this week probably helped tone it down a little, just going out and playing and seeing what happens. The result couldn't have been any better. It's been different not having a caddie, the first time for 15 years or so. I could have done with one of them yesterday, it was brutal, so I'm looking forward to getting a caddie on the bag again."

Warren opened with a 66 to be one behind former winner Joost Luiten but after a 69 in 35-degree heat on Friday fell two behind surprise leader Miguel Angel Jimenez. The 56-year-old Spaniard, six years on from breaking the record as the circuit's oldest winner for the third time, matched the best round of the week with a 65 in his 705th event on the European Tour, one behind Sam Torrance's record.

But in persistent heavy rain on Saturday, Jimenez fell back with a 77 before rallying to finish tied for eighth on Sunday. Warren, battling to keep his gear dry without the help of his caddie, ground out a 70 to share the lead with Germany's Nicolai von Dellingshausen.

Warren added another 70 for a 13-under-par total of 275 while his co-leader came home in 40 for a 76. While Schneider, a 30-year-old German, closed with a 69 to finish on 12 under par, one ahead of Wil Bessling, who matched the best score of the final day with a 66, it was Spain's Sebastian Garcia Rodriguez who put pressure on Warren by eagling the first hole. The pair were tied with two holes to play when Warren holed a steep downhill 15-footer for a birdie at the 17th.

"I was trying to make sure I didn't run it past, tried to get the pace right and fortunately it went right in the middle," Warren said. Garcia Rodriguez found the water at the par-three 18th to close with a double bogey and share fourth place with Darius van Driel and Scots Craig Howie and Connor Syme, who celebrated his 25th birthday on Saturday.

Diamond Country Club, Atzenbrugg, Austria — July 9-12
Par 72 (36-36); 7,458 yards — Purse: €500,000

1	**Marc Warren**	66	69	70	70	275	€76,823
2	**Marcel Schneider**	69	69	69	69	276	49,709
3	**Wil Besseling**	68	69	74	66	277	28,470
4	Sebastian Garcia Rodriguez	70	67	69	72	278	17,782
	Craig Howie	66	69	74	69	278	17,782
	Connor Syme	67	70	69	72	278	17,782
	Darius van Driel	71	65	70	72	278	17,782
8	John Catlin	71	69	71	69	280	8,676
	Thomas Detry	68	71	73	68	280	8,676
	Philip Eriksson	67	73	70	70	280	8,676
8	Miguel Angel Jimenez	68	65	77	70	280	8,676
	Allen John	69	70	70	71	280	8,676
	Oscar Lengden	69	68	73	70	280	8,676
	Christopher Mivis	68	70	72	70	280	8,676
15	Renato Paratore	68	67	75	71	281	6,372
	Joel Statler	68	69	70	74	281	6,372
	Nicolai von Dellingshausen	68	67	70	76	281	6,372
18	Matt Ford	71	68	74	69	282	5,441
	Joost Luiten	65	70	72	75	282	5,441
	Felix Mory	70	68	77	67	282	5,441
	Bernd Ritthammer	74	65	74	69	282	5,441
	Adrien Saddier	70	72	68	72	282	5,441
23	Carlos Pigem	70	69	74	70	283	4,903
	Marcel Siem	73	68	72	70	283	4,903
25	Lorenzo Gagli	72	69	72	71	284	4,361
	Daan Huizing	70	71	73	70	284	4,361
	Oliver Lindell	69	71	70	74	284	4,361
	Jonathan Thomson	68	70	78	68	284	4,361
	Scott Vincent	71	66	72	75	284	4,361
	Jordan Wrisdale	70	69	75	70	284	4,361
31	Matthew Baldwin	71	72	71	71	285	3,751
	Roope Kakko	73	70	71	71	285	3,751
	Deyen Lawson	73	67	74	71	285	3,751
34	Eduardo de la Riva	68	71	76	71	286	3,236
	Rikard Karlberg	72	68	72	74	286	3,236
	Hurly Long	73	70	71	72	286	3,236
	Niklas Norgaard Moller	69	72	77	68	286	3,236
	Lukas Nemecz	70	71	77	68	286	3,236
39	Chase Hanna	72	69	76	70	287	2,757
	Pedro Oriol	71	70	76	70	287	2,757
	Craig Ross	70	70	74	73	287	2,757
	Martin Simonsen	69	71	81	66	287	2,757
	Aron Zemmer	73	68	78	68	287	2,757
44	David Boote	73	70	73	72	288	2,034
	Gregory Bourdy	70	71	76	71	288	2,034
	Todd Clements	75	67	74	72	288	2,034
	Pelle Edberg	71	71	73	73	288	2,034
	Jens Fahbring	72	71	72	73	288	2,034
	Markus Habeler	73	70	71	74	288	2,034
	Nicolai Hojgaard	67	73	71	77	288	2,034
	Moritz Lampert	71	72	70	75	288	2,034
	Ondrej Lieser	72	68	76	72	288	2,034
	Antoine Rohner	74	69	76	69	288	2,034
	Joel Sjohom	71	68	77	72	288	2,034
55	Anton Karlsson	69	72	75	73	289	1,423
	Maximilian Kieffer	70	70	80	69	289	1,423
	Francesco Laporta	73	70	77	69	289	1,423
	Gavin Moynihan	69	74	76	70	289	1,423
	Henric Sturehed	70	70	75	74	289	1,423
	Santiago Tarrio	71	70	77	71	289	1,423
61	David Borda	74	69	72	75	290	1,265
62	Adri Arnaus	70	71	77	73	291	1,130
	Raphael de Sousa	73	69	73	76	291	1,130
	Alexander Knappe	71	69	78	73	291	1,130
	Per Langfors	72	69	77	73	291	1,130
	Robin Roussel	70	72	78	71	291	1,130
67	Enrico Di Nitto	71	72	78	72	293	926
	Joel Girrbach	70	72	76	75	293	926
	Jerome Lando Casanova	69	73	78	73	293	926
	Max Schmitt	72	70	79	72	293	926
71	Scott Henry	69	73	74	79	295	750
72	Lorenzo Scalise	67	75	80	75	297	746
	Robbie van West	71	71	78	77	297	746

Euram Bank Open

Staying in Austria with another co-sanctioned event, the circuit moved up into the Alps at Adamstal where Joel Stalter upgraded his Challenge Tour status into a European Tour winner's exemption. The 28-year-old Frenchman, who played one season on the main circuit in 2017 thanks to his only win on the Challenge Tour the previous year, won by two strokes from Richard Mansell after scores of 65, 65, 68 and 68 for a 14-under-par total of 266.

Despite the teeming rain of the final day, Stalter, who did not touch a golf club for two months during lockdown at home, was able to celebrate the emotional victory with his fiancée Flora, who was caddieing for him.

"This is a special win," he said. "I have been in this situation a few times and was never able to really push through. My girlfriend has done an incredible job. She's definitely part of my success today. It was a horrible day in terms of the conditions. It was tough for everyone, but my girlfriend had her smile on and just kept me going."

The course, which measures under 6,500 yards, yielded plenty of good scoring prior to the final day with Robin Sciot-Siegrist making nine birdies in a third-round 61 to lead by three strokes from Mansell. But Sciot-Siegrist followed a bogey at the seventh with a triple bogey at the ninth, getting into trouble off the tee and then three-putting, and ended with a 75 to share third place with Christofer Blomstrand and Alexander Knappe.

As Sciot-Siegrist played the ninth, fellow Frenchman Statler was birdieing the 10th from four feet to take the lead. He was joined briefly in a tie by Mansell after bogeying the 14th but then claimed a birdie four at the 15th and parred home.

Mansell was playing only his second European Tour event after sharing a van with his caddie on the long drive from Britain to play in the two Austrian events. He had only one birdie at the 14th in a 71. He rued three-putting from 10 feet for a par at the 15th and dropping his second shot of the day at the 16th. "It's difficult to swallow, but I'll be back again," he said. "I know I'll have more chances."

Golf Club Adamstal, Ramsau, Austria — July 15-18
Par 70 (36-34); 6,473 yards — Purse: €500,000

1	**Joel Stalter**	65	65	68	68	266	€76,823
2	**Richard Mansell**	67	66	64	71	268	49,709
3	**Christofer Blomstrand**	65	67	66	71	269	23,408
	Alexander Knappe	66	67	66	70	269	23,408
	Robin Sciot-Siegrist	67	66	61	75	269	23,408
6	Julien Brun	67	64	68	71	270	13,557
	Garrick Higgo	65	69	67	69	270	13,557
	Joost Luiten	65	63	74	68	270	13,557
9	Lorenzo Gagli	70	64	67	70	271	9,580
	Damien Perrier	69	67	66	69	271	9,580
11	Adri Arnaus	66	70	67	69	272	8,044
	Scott Fernandez	71	62	70	69	272	8,044
13	Philip Eriksson	64	66	69	74	273	6,661
	Scott Gregory	66	68	68	71	273	6,661
	Oscar Lengden	68	67	69	69	273	6,661
	Ondrej Lieser	65	73	67	68	273	6,661
	Thomas Rosenmuller	68	67	71	67	273	6,661
18	Daniel Gavins	68	65	66	75	274	5,363
	Deyen Lawson	63	69	72	70	274	5,363
	Oliver Lindell	64	70	69	71	274	5,363
	Mikael Lundberg	72	66	66	70	274	5,363
	Federico Maccario	68	70	70	66	274	5,363
	Scott Vincent,	67	70	72	65	274	5,363
24	Dominic Foos	67	68	72	68	275	4,632
	Sebastian Heisele	71	66	68	70	275	4,632
	Rikard Karlberg	70	67	67	71	275	4,632
	Lukas Nemecz	68	67	68	72	275	4,632
28	Matt Ford	66	70	70	70	276	4,090
	Robin Petersson	69	64	69	74	276	4,090
	Max Schmitt	69	67	68	72	276	4,090
	Nicolai von Dellinghausen	67	70	71	68	276	4,090
32	Niklas Norgaard Moller	70	68	67	72	277	3,547
	Pedro Oriol	68	68	69	72	277	3,547
	Bernd Ritthammer	68	68	67	74	277	3,547
	Chris Robb	68	64	71	74	277	3,547
36	Filippo Bergamaschi	70	67	69	72	278	3,118
	Ricardo Gouveia	67	67	72	72	278	3,118
	Stuart Manley	70	68	67	73	278	3,118
39	David Boote	69	69	72	69	279	2,802
	Edouard Dubois	66	69	68	76	279	2,802
	Felix Mory	68	69	66	76	279	2,802
	Victor Riu	66	71	75	67	279	2,802
43	John Catlin	66	66	72	76	280	2,305
	Jens Dantorp	68	70	70	72	280	2,305
	Enrico Di Nitto	68	70	72	70	280	2,305
	Mateusz Gradecki	67	66	73	74	280	2,305
	Allen John	67	70	72	71	280	2,305
	Hurly Long	69	68	67	76	280	2,305
	Marcel Siem	69	66	76	69	280	2,305
50	Markus Brier	69	68	73	71	281	1,725
	Joel Girrbach	69	68	69	75	281	1,725
	Jonas Kolbing	68	68	72	73	281	1,725
	Haraldur Magnus	70	66	70	75	281	1,725
	Andrew Wilson	65	71	71	74	281	1,725
	Jordan Wrisdale	64	70	73	74	281	1,725
56	Timon Baltl	68	68	71	75	282	1,491
57	Ivan Cantero Gutierrez	69	69	68	77	283	1,378
	Gudmundur Kristjansson	67	66	76	74	283	1,378
	Francesco Laporta	71	66	75	71	283	1,378
	Lukas Lipold	69	66	68	80	283	1,378
61	Hinrich Arkenau	69	67	75	73	284	1,243
	Stanislav Matus	63	71	74	76	284	1,243
63	Marcel Schneider	69	68	71	78	286	1,175
64	Jonathan Thomson	67	69	73	79	288	1,130
65	Santiago Tarrio	65	71	82	71	289	1,085

Betfred British Masters

In the first full European Tour event after lockdown, winner Renato Paratore was greeted at the 18th green at Close House by a video call with his mother back home in Italy and then received a guard of honour from fellow players — socially distanced and with golf clubs raised in an arch.

"It was really amazing," he said. "I didn't expect that from my friends here on tour and it was a really good sensation. These are the moments I love. To see my mama was a big surprise and I was really happy."

A birdie at the 17th hole, greeted with a roar of "vamos", had brought Paratore a victory at the Betfred British Masters by three strokes from Rasmus Hojgaard, whose twin brother Nicolai was an interested spectator over the closing holes at the "behind closed doors" tournament.

Only players, caddies and essential staff and media were permitted on site and had to stay within a "biosecure bubble" of the golf course and the official hotels. All had tested negative for Covid-19, both before travelling and on arrival, and were subject to daily symptom checks. "The tour and Close House have done an amazing job," said tournament host Lee Westwood. "When we turned up on Monday, I was surprised how thorough everything was. I knew we were going to be on lockdown but the testing protocol we have all been through has been a success. I don't think anybody has tested positive so hopefully they will carry on next week."

In his sixth season on tour, although still only 23, Paratore produced an impressive display of front-running after spending lockdown practising in Dubai following six weeks of working out in his DIY gym in his flat before courses re-opened. This was his second title after claiming the Nordea Masters in 2017. He was one behind first-round leader David Law with an opening 65 before he took the lead with a second-round 66 which he matched in Friday's third round.

On a windy final day, South Africa's Justin Harding briefly tied for the lead with a birdie at the third but there was a two-stroke swing at the next hole when the Italian holed from 25 feet. He also birdied the seventh before a run of 62 holes without a bogey came to an end at the short ninth. With the wind at its strongest and behind from the tee, Paratore went over the green and although his chip lipped out, it went five feet past.

He recovered with a birdie four at the 10th but also bogeyed the 11th. Yet he played the last seven holes in one under for a 69 and an 18-under-par total of 266. Hojgaard, who defeated Paratore in a playoff for his maiden title in December 2019, closed with a 70 to finish one ahead of Harding, whose 72 put him one in front of Robert Rock, Andy Sullivan and Dale Whitnell.

"I didn't expect to come back and win my second title after the lockdown," said Paratore. "I have worked really hard over the last year. Both my wins have been tough fought on my part. The European Tour have done a really great job, it is not easy to come back to tournaments with this situation, and they have been good with the restrictions at the golf course and the hotel. It is not easy because you have to do golf club-hotel, hotel-golf club but we have to do this for the benefit of the tour and to play more events."

Andrew Johnson, who admitted his mental struggles with the game in 2019, withdrew after nine holes of the first round saying he had been unsettled by life in the bubble without his family. Miguel Angel Jimenez, who finished tied for 38th, was playing his 706th tournament, tying Sam Torrance's record.

Close House, Heddon-on-the Wall, Newcastle-upon-Tyne — July 22-25
Par 71 (35-36); 6,872 yards — Purse: €1,250,000

1	**Renato Paratore**	65	66	66	69	266	€196,690
2	**Rasmus Hojgaard**	66	67	66	70	269	127,270
3	**Justin Harding**	69	63	66	72	270	72,891
4	Robert Rock	69	66	67	69	271	49,134
	Andy Sullivan	68	69	67	67	271	49,134
	Dale Whitnell	68	64	68	71	271	49,134
7	Oliver Fisher	65	69	70	68	272	34,710
8	Jonathan Caldwell	67	69	67	70	273	27,421
	Ryan Fox	67	67	71	68	273	27,421
10	Jens Fahrbring	68	69	68	69	274	20,739
	Sam Horsfield	70	70	61	73	274	20,739
	Graeme Storm	71	69	67	67	274	20,739
	Ben Stow	67	68	68	71	274	20,739
14	Ashley Chesters	67	66	68	74	275	17,008
	David Horsey	70	69	68	68	275	17,008
	Jeff Winther	70	67	72	66	275	17,008
17	Matthew Jordan	68	68	69	71	276	14,694
	Jack Singh Brar	67	70	72	67	276	14,694
	Clement Sordet	69	67	71	69	276	14,694
	Johannes Veerman	69	71	67	69	276	14,694
21	Pablo Larrazabal	67	71	69	70	277	12,727
	Adrian Meronk	69	68	66	74	277	12,727
	Aaron Rai	69	70	66	72	277	12,727
	Robin Roussel	69	68	69	71	277	12,727
	Jack Senior	71	70	63	73	277	12,727
26	Calum Hill	67	66	72	73	278	11,339
	Rikard Karlberg	69	70	66	73	278	11,339
	Matthieu Pavon	71	69	70	68	278	11,339
29	Laurie Canter	70	68	69	72	279	9,777
	Nacho Elvira	71	68	70	70	279	9,777
	Daan Huizing	73	67	71	68	279	9,777
	Mikko Korhonen	71	69	70	69	279	9,777
	Jason Scrivener	70	69	71	69	279	9,777
	Toby Tree	69	67	74	69	279	9,777
35	Adrian Otaegui	73	65	68	74	280	8,253
	Jordan Smith	69	69	67	75	280	8,253
	Matthew Southgate	70	70	70	70	280	8,253
38	Richard Bland	69	70	66	76	281	6,826
	Paul Dunne	71	70	69	71	281	6,826
	Gonzalo Fdez-Castano	72	69	69	71	281	6,826
	Gregory Havret	70	68	69	74	281	6,826
	Miguel Angel Jimenez	68	71	68	74	281	6,826
	Marcus Kinhult	69	69	74	69	281	6,826
	David Law	64	69	76	72	281	6,826
	Andrea Pavan	69	72	69	71	281	6,826
	Richie Ramsay	69	71	70	71	281	6,826
47	Alexander Bjork	68	72	69	73	282	5,091
	Pedro Figueiredo	66	69	70	77	282	5,091
	Joachim B Hansen	70	70	77	65	282	5,091
	Scott Jamieson	70	69	68	75	282	5,091
	Eddie Pepperell	67	69	69	77	282	5,091
	Benjamin Poke	70	68	71	73	282	5,091
53	Aaron Cockerill	66	71	73	73	283	3,835
	Dave Coupland	70	71	70	72	283	3,835
	Romain Langasque	70	71	69	73	283	3,835
	Niklas Lemke	70	70	69	74	283	3,835
	Alvaro Quiros	69	69	71	74	283	3,835
	Lee Slattery	66	74	74	69	283	3,835
	Lars van Meijel	69	68	69	77	283	3,835
60	Adri Arnaus	70	69	69	77	285	3,124
	Sean Crocker	67	74	69	75	285	3,124
	Guido Migliozzi	71	70	66	78	285	3,124
	Antoine Rozner	72	67	71	75	285	3,124
	Scott Vincent	69	72	68	76	285	3,124
65	Grant Forrest	70	71	71	74	286	2,719
	Garrick Porteous	65	71	70	80	286	2,719
67	Jake McLeod	69	70	71	77	287	2,545
68	Brandon Stone	71	70	79	69	289	2,430
69	Haydn Porteous	71	69	70	80	290	2,314
70	Lee Westwood	70	71	72	79	292	2,198

Hero Open

At the age of 56, Miguel Angel Jimenez celebrated setting a new record for appearances on the European Tour by opening his 707th event with an eight-under-par 64 to lie in second place, two behind his young countryman Sebastian Garcia Rodriguez. Jimenez was applauded on and off the final green at the Forest of Arden by his fellow players and was told by previous record holder Sam Torrance: "It's a record I was very proud of but could not lose it to a better person."

Jimenez said: "It's been a wonderful day. I love everything about my life. Golf is my life. You can have a bad game but not a bad day, that's the difference."

Jimenez finished the Hero Open, a revived English Open that had not been played since 2002 and was only returned to the schedule when a UK swing was created at short notice, went on to finish 34th but it was a younger cohort who contended for the title. Sam Horsfield, a 23-year-old Englishman who grew up in Florida, claimed his maiden victory by one stroke from Belgium's Thomas Detry in an exciting conclusion.

After an opening 68, it was a 63 on Friday that put Horsfield in a tie for the lead. On Saturday he went out in 31 for the second day running to lead by six strokes but came home in 40 for a 71 to see his advantage cut to one. He played the final round with Rasmus Hojgaard, who was the runner-up the previous week, but the 19-year-old Dane slipped down to sixth with a 72.

Instead, Detry charged into contention with a 66. Birdies at the 12th, 13th, 16th and 17th holes put Detry into the lead by one but he rued a three-putt bogey at the final hole. Horsfield responded to losing his lead for the first time over the weekend by hitting a five-wood just off the green at the 17th and claiming a birdie four. Two putts from distance at the long par-three 18th confirmed the win on 18-under-par 270.

Horsfield's talent, long appreciated by Ian Poulter, was first noticed when he shot a 59 at his local club at the age of 13. After a fine college career in the States, Horsfield turned professional in 2017 and won the European Tour Qualifying School by eight strokes. After his first official victory, following a 61 in the third round of the British Masters the previous week, he said: "It's crazy, I can't put it into words. I made a bad bogey on 15, then on 17 hit a great shot, from 233 yards, the wind out of the left.

"With everything that's going on in the world right now, I'm thankful that the European Tour has been able to put on tournaments for us to play. I've been in Orlando for the last three months and felt like my game was right there." Alexander Bjork, Oliver Farr and Chris Paisley tied for third place, four behind the winner.

Forest of Arden Marriott Hotel & Country Club, Meriden, Birmingham — July 30-August 2
Par 72 (36-36); 7,213 yards — Purse: €1,000,000

1	**Sam Horsfield**	68	63	71	68	270	€156,825
2	**Thomas Detry**	67	67	71	66	271	101,475
3	**Alexander Bjork**	68	67	70	69	274	47,786
	Oliver Farr	65	71	67	71	274	47,786
	Chris Paisley	70	68	66	70	274	47,786
6	Rasmus Hojgaard	66	71	66	72	275	25,922
	Maximilian Kieffer	71	69	67	68	275	25,922
	Mikko Korhonen	67	69	67	72	275	25,922
	Matthieu Pavon	69	67	69	70	275	25,922
10	Laurie Canter	67	72	68	70	277	16,052
	Sebastian Garcia Rodriguez	62	69	73	73	277	16,052
	Scott Jamieson	71	71	70	65	277	16,052
	Aaron Rai	71	68	70	68	277	16,052
	Antoine Rozner	68	67	70	72	277	16,052
15	Marcus Armitage	72	68	67	71	278	12,019
	Dave Coupland	68	72	71	67	278	12,019
	Sean Crocker	67	75	66	70	278	12,019
	Jamie Donaldson	72	68	68	70	278	12,019
	Ryan Fox	70	72	68	68	278	12,019
	Julien Guerrier	68	71	71	68	278	12,019
	Robert Rock	71	69	66	72	278	12,019
22	Richard Bland	70	68	67	74	279	9,732
	Ross Fisher	70	71	67	71	279	9,732
	Garrick Porteous	70	72	72	65	279	9,732
	Richie Ramsay	69	68	74	68	279	9,732
	Joel Sjoholm	70	68	68	73	279	9,732
	Matthew Southgate	67	74	69	69	279	9,732
28	Ashley Chesters	66	72	71	71	280	8,072
	Joachim B Hansen	68	71	66	75	280	8,072
	Renato Paratore	70	70	69	71	280	8,072
	Callum Shinkwin	68	69	72	71	280	8,072
	Joel Stalter	67	71	71	71	280	8,072
	Johannes Veerman	75	66	72	67	280	8,072
34	Wil Besseling	67	70	73	71	281	6,405
	Grant Forrest	69	68	72	72	281	6,405
	Benjamin Hebert	69	70	66	76	281	6,405
	David Horsey	71	71	72	67	281	6,405
	Miguel Angel Jimenez	64	72	73	72	281	6,405
	Kalle Samooja	68	69	72	72	281	6,405
	Ben Stow	70	71	71	69	281	6,405
41	Rikard Karlberg	68	71	71	72	282	5,166
	Soren Kjeldsen	70	71	74	67	282	5,166
	Niklas Lemke	70	72	64	76	282	5,166
	Benjamin Poke	72	70	69	71	282	5,166

	Clement Sordet	69	72	72	69	282	5,166		Richard McEvoy	69	72	72	72	285	2,721
	Andy Sullivan	70	70	68	74	282	5,166		Ricardo Santos	70	69	71	75	285	2,721
47	Sihwan Kim	67	71	72	73	283	4,244		Marcel Schneider	73	67	72	73	285	2,721
	Alexander Levy	67	69	74	73	283	4,244		Lee Slattery	70	71	72	72	285	2,721
	Jason Scrivener	69	69	71	74	283	4,244	63	Carlos Pigem	69	69	76	72	286	2,352
	Cormac Sharvin	70	67	73	73	283	4,244		Tapio Pulkkanen	70	71	75	70	286	2,352
51	John Catlin	71	70	72	71	284	3,367	65	Steven Brown	71	71	71	74	287	2,168
	Louis de Jager	74	66	69	75	284	3,367		Steven Tiley	72	67	75	73	287	2,168
	Ben Evans	72	70	71	71	284	3,367	67	Maverick Antcliff	72	70	73	73	288	2,030
	Pablo Larrazabal	64	75	70	75	284	3,367	68	Connor Syme	67	75	74	73	289	1,937
	Darius van Driel	69	71	74	70	284	3,367	69	Thomas Bjorn	71	71	70	78	290	1,845
	Dale Whitnell	69	72	76	67	284	3,367	70	Michael Campbell	71	71	73	77	292	1,753
57	Rhys Enoch	68	72	70	75	285	2,721	71	Gonzalo Fdez-Castano	73	68	68	84	293	1,500
	Romain Langasque	69	72	72	72	285	2,721								

English Championship

It was an emotional and record-breaking way for Andy Sullivan to claim his first victory in almost five years.

Sullivan won three times on the European Tour in 2015, including the Portugal Masters, but not since despite going on to play in the 2016 Ryder Cup. At Hanbury Manor, returning as a tour venue for the first time in over two decades, Sullivan took advantage of heatwave conditions to set a new record low aggregate total of 257, beating the 258 mark of David Llewellyn in 1988 and Ian Woosnam in 1990.

After opening with a 66, on Friday the 33-year-old Englishman set a new course record of 62, coming home in 28 shots with seven birdies. A one-stoke lead was extended to five with a 64 on Saturday that included two eagles after almost holing his tee shot at the first for an albatross. Despite another eagle from Sullivan at the second on the final day, Spain's Adrian Otaegui went out in 31 to cut the lead to two strokes but the Englishman responded with four birdies in the last seven holes for a 65 and a seven-stroke victory at 27 under par. Otaegui completed a 66 to be second with Rasmus Hojgaard in third place after a 64 as the 19-year-old Dane posted his third top-six finish in a row.

Sullivan admitted being close to tears over the final three holes as he thought about those absent, not just family and spectators but his brother-in-law who died in 2018 at the age of 24 and a good friend who died in 2020. "It means a lot to do it for them," Sullivan said. "I'm proud of what I've achieved this week and the manner I've done it.

"It's frustrating that I didn't kick on from 2015 but it's just one of those things. It feels like the weight of the world is lifted off my shoulders that I'm back in the winner's circle. It didn't feel like a seven-shot lead out there. I got on 12 and saw that Adrian was two shots behind and breathing down my neck, and it was just nice that I could keep pressing on with the putter there — it just got hot."

Prior to the tournament, American John Catlin was withdrawn for breaking the Covid-19 protocols by leaving the biosecure bubble and visiting a local restaurant on the Tuesday evening. "I apologise to my fellow players and everyone involved with the tournament this week for this error of judgement. I understand the European Tour's decision and accept the sanction." Catlin was replaced by South Africa's Wilco Nienaber, who went on to finish fourth.

Hanbury Manor Marriott Hotel & Country Club, Ware, Hertfordshire — August 6-9
Par 71 (36-35); 7,042 yards — Purse: €1,000,000

1	**Andy Sullivan**	66	62	64	65	257	€156,825		Scott Vincent	64	70	68	67	269	17,361
2	**Adrian Otaegui**	65	66	67	66	264	101,475	14	Marcus Armitage	68	69	63	70	270	13,007
3	**Rasmus Hojgaard**	65	67	69	64	265	58,118		Louis de Jager	69	66	67	68	270	13,007
4	Wilco Nienaber	68	65	67	66	266	46,125		Jamie Donaldson	67	64	69	70	270	13,007
5	Steven Brown	66	65	66	70	267	39,114		Jason Scrivener	64	69	66	71	270	13,007
6	Dean Burmester	66	63	69	70	268	27,675		Jordan Smith	68	65	67	70	270	13,007
	Min Woo Lee	64	67	70	67	268	27,675	19	Ewen Ferguson	67	70	69	65	271	10,464
	Brandon Stone	65	66	67	70	268	27,675		Ryan Fox	67	67	66	71	271	10,464
9	Nicolas Colsaerts	65	66	68	70	269	17,361		Andrew Johnston	66	65	71	69	271	10,464
	Dave Coupland	69	65	66	69	269	17,361		Oscar Lengden	65	66	70	70	271	10,464
	Sean Crocker	69	67	66	67	269	17,361		Chris Paisley	68	65	70	68	271	10,464
	Scott Jamieson	74	63	68	64	269	17,361		Cormac Sharvin	63	70	69	69	271	10,464

	Connor Syme	65	69	68	69	271	10,464
26	Aaron Cockerill	67	68	68	69	272	8,349
	Oliver Fisher	67	68	69	68	272	8,349
	Nicolai Hojgaard	67	68	69	68	272	8,349
	Romain Langasque	65	70	70	67	272	8,349
	Robin Roussel	67	69	68	68	272	8,349
	Antoine Rozner	67	69	69	67	272	8,349
	Martin Simonsen	65	68	66	73	272	8,349
	Ben Stow	70	67	64	71	272	8,349
34	Laurie Canter	64	65	70	74	273	6,116
	Lorenzo Gagli	68	69	69	67	273	6,116
	Adrian Meronk	66	69	71	67	273	6,116
	Thorbjorn Olesen	66	70	70	67	273	6,116
	Renato Paratore	69	67	69	68	273	6,116
	Andrea Pavan	68	68	67	70	273	6,116
	Richie Ramsay	66	68	69	70	273	6,116
	Johannes Veerman	67	69	70	67	273	6,116
	Marc Warren	68	68	67	70	273	6,116
	Lee Westwood	66	69	68	70	273	6,116
44	Alejandro Canizares	69	64	69	72	274	4,336
	Scott Hend	71	66	70	67	274	4,336
	Miguel Angel Jimenez	66	68	74	66	274	4,336
	Sihwan Kim	67	65	72	70	274	4,336
	Aaron Rai	68	69	68	69	274	4,336
	Ricardo Santos	68	68	69	69	274	4,336
	Jack Senior	65	72	68	69	274	4,336
	Toby Tree	67	67	72	68	274	4,336
	Romain Wattel	65	71	70	68	274	4,336
53	Joachim B Hansen	69	66	70	70	275	3,260
	Justin Harding	67	65	74	69	275	3,260
	Marcel Schneider	67	70	69	69	275	3,260
56	Richard Bland	65	66	73	72	276	2,860
	Thomas Detry	64	72	66	74	276	2,860
	David Drysdale	65	70	70	71	276	2,860
	Bryce Easton	66	69	72	69	276	2,860
	Julien Guerrier	70	67	69	70	276	2,860
61	Matthew Southgate	67	69	69	72	277	2,583
62	Richard McEvoy	70	66	70	72	278	2,491
63	Wil Besseling	70	67	75	67	279	2,352
	Tapio Pulkkanen	70	67	70	72	279	2,352
65	Pablo Larrazabal	69	67	74	71	281	2,122
	Kalle Samooja	67	70	71	73	281	2,122
	Lee Slattery	69	67	71	74	281	2,122
68	Rhys Enoch	66	70	72	74	282	1,891
	David Howell	64	71	73	74	282	1,891
70	Emilio Cuartero Blanco	71	66	73	73	283	1,753
71	David Law	68	68	76	73	285	1,497
	Bernd Ritthammer	69	65	77	74	285	1,497
	Callum Shinkwin	68	67	69	81	285	1,497

Celtic Classic

In winning for the second time in three weeks Sam Horsfield became the first player in the history of the European Tour to miss the cut in-between two victories in three consecutive tournaments. The 23-year-old Englishman, highly rated by fellow Florida resident Ian Poulter, produced a calm and controlled display of front running to win by two strokes from Thomas Detry, who was the runner-up when Horsfield won his maiden title at the Hero Open at the Forest of Arden.

Horsfield opened with a 67 on Celtic Manor's Twenty Ten course, host of the 2010 Ryder Cup, and added a 64 the next day to take the 36-hole lead despite finishing his second round with birdie-birdie-triple bogey-eagle. He vowed not to drop a shot over the weekend and achieved that goal with scores of 68 and 67 for an 18-under-par total of 266. He slipped one behind 54-hole leader Connor Syme, who scored a 63 on Saturday. But after Syme opened with a bogey on Sunday, Horsfield never looked back and had made three birdies in the first seven holes before play was suspended for two hours due to a thunderstorm.

After the resumption, Horsfield kept his clean card to the clubhouse and added a birdie at the 14th. With the light fading fast, he got up and down at the short 17th before holing out in virtual darkness on the 18th green. "I never really felt nervous or felt uncomfortable, maybe because I was in this situation a few weeks ago," he said. "I felt a little more relaxed than last time I did it. The putt at the 17th was huge and gave me a nice cushion down the last.

"After I missed the cut last week I was never concerned. I felt like after your first win and everything that was going on, I felt a little mentally drained and I probably should have decided to take the week off. I just wasn't all there but I knew my game was in good shape so I basically just forgot about last week."

Detry also closed with a 67, while Syme's 71 meant he shared third place with Thomas Pieters and Andrew Johnston, in his second event after returning to the bubble following his retirement after nine holes of the British Masters.

Celtic Manor Resort (Twenty Ten), Newport, Wales — August 13-16
Par 71 (36-35); 7,315 yards — Purse: €1,000,000

1	**Sam Horsfield**	67	64	68	67	266	€156,825
2	**Thomas Detry**	67	66	68	67	268	101,475
3	**Andrew Johnston**	67	66	68	68	269	47,786
	Thomas Pieters	64	68	70	67	269	47,786
	Connor Syme	68	67	63	71	269	47,786
6	John Catlin	68	68	69	65	270	25,922
	David Horsey	68	71	65	66	270	25,922
	Adrian Meronk	66	71	64	69	270	25,922
	Sami Valimaki	71	68	65	66	270	25,922
10	Sebastian Soderberg	66	69	65	71	271	18,450
11	Wil Besseling	67	69	67	69	272	15,898
	Gavin Green	70	69	70	63	272	15,898
	Callum Shinkwin	68	65	69	70	272	15,898
14	Aaron Cockerill	70	69	67	67	273	12,281
	Lorenzo Gagli	67	70	69	67	273	12,281
	Sebastian Heisele	69	70	69	65	273	12,281
	Maximilian Kieffer	69	70	66	68	273	12,281
	Jacques Kruyswijk	70	71	67	65	273	12,281
	Jake McLeod	65	69	69	70	273	12,281
	Adrian Otaegui	69	67	69	68	273	12,281
	Jason Scrivener	69	69	65	70	273	12,281
22	Sean Crocker	68	66	73	67	274	9,871
	Wilco Nienaber	70	67	71	66	274	9,871
	Jack Senior	69	70	66	69	274	9,871
	Jordan Smith	68	68	71	67	274	9,871
	Scott Vincent	69	69	66	70	274	9,871
27	Alexander Bjork	71	70	66	68	275	8,625
	Ross Fisher	72	68	68	67	275	8,625
	James Morrison	67	70	68	70	275	8,625
	Matthew Southgate	67	70	67	71	275	8,625
31	Maverick Antcliff	68	71	70	67	276	6,999
	Steven Brown	67	72	68	69	276	6,999
	Jamie Donaldson	70	70	70	66	276	6,999
	Rhys Enoch	69	66	69	72	276	6,999
	Rikard Karlberg	73	68	69	66	276	6,999
	Aaron Rai	67	70	70	69	276	6,999
	Cormac Sharvin	71	67	65	73	276	6,999
	Dale Whitnell	72	67	69	68	276	6,999
39	Ashley Chesters	72	68	69	68	277	5,351
	Nacho Elvira	66	69	72	70	277	5,351
	Oliver Farr	73	67	69	68	277	5,351
	Scott Hend	75	65	68	69	277	5,351
	Calum Hill	70	68	70	69	277	5,351
	Toby Tree	65	75	69	68	277	5,351
	Justin Walters	70	69	69	69	277	5,351
	Marc Warren	66	72	65	74	277	5,351
47	Adri Arnaus	73	68	65	72	278	3,718
	Dean Burmester	71	68	71	68	278	3,718
	Jonathan Caldwell	68	66	72	72	278	3,718
	Justin Harding	69	71	68	70	278	3,718
	Matthew Jordan	68	66	74	70	278	3,718
	Sihwan Kim	66	70	68	74	278	3,718
	Oscar Lengden	69	69	70	70	278	3,718
	Edoardo Molinari	66	72	70	70	278	3,718
	Martin Simonsen	68	71	70	69	278	3,718
	Andy Sullivan	70	71	66	71	278	3,718
57	Ryan Fox	69	71	68	72	280	2,768
	Francesco Laporta	69	69	70	72	280	2,768
	Guido Migliozzi	66	70	72	72	280	2,768
	Damien Perrier	70	69	71	70	280	2,768
	Joel Sjoholm	68	70	69	73	280	2,768
62	Soren Kjeldsen	70	70	68	73	281	2,491
63	Nicolas Colsaerts	67	73	70	72	282	2,306
	Louis de Jager	71	68	69	74	282	2,306
	Shubhankar Sharma	71	70	70	71	282	2,306
66	Thorbjorn Olesen	71	70	69	73	283	2,030
	Bernd Ritthammer	71	70	76	66	283	2,030
	Julian Suri	72	69	72	70	283	2,030
69	Grant Forrest	72	68	72	72	284	1,845
70	Pablo Larrazabal	70	71	70	74	285	1,626
	Ross McGowan	70	70	71	74	285	1,626
72	Min Woo Lee	69	71	71	76	287	1,497
73	Ben Stow	68	72	73	75	288	1,494
74	Carlos Pigem	70	71	74	74	289	1,491
75	Nino Bertasio	71	69	74		214	1,372

ISPS Handa Wales Open

Competing against several players who were playing on the Twenty Ten course at Celtic Manor for the second week running, Romain Langasque timed his final-round charge to perfection. In claiming the ISPS Handa Wales Open by two strokes, the 25-year-old Frenchman won for the first time on the European Tour.

Langasque was the 2015 British Amateur champion before winning on the Challenge Tour in 2018 and finishing 24th on the Race to Dubai in 2019. He started the last day five strokes off the lead after rounds of 71, 68 and 72 but did not drop a shot in his closing 65 for an eight-under-par total of 276. He moved into contention with three birdies going out, including putts of 30 feet at the third and 20 feet at the sixth.

Overnight leaders Connor Syme, who was ahead after 54 holes in the Celtic Classic before finishing third, and Sebastian Soderberg, 10th the previous week, both had double bogeys at the fifth hole to throw the tournament wide open. Finland's Sami Valimaki, sixth at the Celtic Classic, eagled the ninth hole to get to seven under par but was one over on the way home as a 69 secured second place, one stroke ahead of Matthew Jordan and David Dixon.

Langasque kept up his attack with a birdie at the 11th and another at the 15th, where he drove the green and two-putted. Another 20-footer at the 16th produced his sixth birdie of the day and put him in the lead on his own for the first time. "I'm so happy with how I played on the back nine, I had so many birdie opportunities," he said. "It was one of the first times I did not feel the pressure, I was focusing on every shot. The wait was long but when you come back from five shots and you're in a position like that, it's good. I'm just enjoying my time now."

Ultimately all the other contenders fell away. Soderberg needed to birdie the last hole to force a playoff but his approach with a wedge spun back down the bank in front of the green into the pond. He finished with a triple-bogey eight for a 74 and fifth place, while Syme had a seven at the 18th for a 75 and eighth place.

Syme, along with Langasque and Valimaki, still qualified for the US Open from the UK Swing order of merit. The top 10 after this fifth event earned spots for Winged Foot the following month with double winner Sam Horsfield leading the standings.

Celtic Manor Resort (Twenty Ten), Newport, Wales — August 20-23
Par 71 (36-35); 7,315 yards — Purse: €1,000,000

1	**Romain Langasque**	71	68	72	65	276	€156,825
2	**Sami Valimaki**	70	72	67	69	278	101,475
3	**David Dixon**	70	70	71	68	279	52,121
	Matthew Jordan	69	72	72	66	279	52,121
5	Laurie Canter	71	69	72	68	280	33,026
	James Morrison	73	72	66	69	280	33,026
	Sebastian Soderberg	68	70	68	74	280	33,026
8	Jorge Campillo	75	68	69	69	281	17,712
	Gavin Green	73	71	68	69	281	17,712
	Calum Hill	73	71	68	69	281	17,712
	Haotong Li	72	66	76	67	281	17,712
	Jason Scrivener	70	74	69	68	281	17,712
	Callum Shinkwin	68	75	71	67	281	17,712
	Connor Syme	66	70	70	75	281	17,712
15	Louis de Jager	70	74	70	68	282	12,239
	Ryan Fox	70	74	68	70	282	12,239
	Sebastian Heisele	70	71	73	68	282	12,239
	Liam Johnston	70	68	75	69	282	12,239
	Marcus Kinhult	69	71	72	70	282	12,239
	Thomas Pieters	69	72	69	72	282	12,239
21	Dean Burmester	72	71	68	72	283	10,009
	Mathieu Fenasse	72	70	72	69	283	10,009
	Craig Howie	74	69	69	71	283	10,009
	Daan Huizing	70	73	72	68	283	10,009
	Bernd Ritthammer	75	70	69	69	283	10,009
	Clement Sordet	72	74	68	69	283	10,009
27	Marcus Armitage	74	69	71	70	284	7,795
	Sebastian Garcia Rodriguez	73	70	69	72	284	7,795
	Edoardo Molinari	72	70	68	74	284	7,795
	Chris Paisley	72	74	69	69	284	7,795
	Renato Paratore	69	72	74	69	284	7,795
	Lorenzo Scalise	72	71	74	67	284	7,795
	Marcel Siem	70	74	67	73	284	7,795
	Jordan Smith	66	72	75	71	284	7,795
	Brandon Stone	70	72	70	72	284	7,795
	Dale Whitnell	73	71	72	68	284	7,795
37	Sean Crocker	74	71	71	69	285	5,812
	Andrew Johnston	73	71	70	71	285	5,812
	Masahiro Kawamura	74	70	73	68	285	5,812
	David Law	71	75	69	70	285	5,812
	Adrian Otaegui	71	70	74	70	285	5,812
	Robert Rock	71	69	73	72	285	5,812
	Lars van Meijel	72	74	71	68	285	5,812
44	Nacho Elvira	71	67	74	74	286	4,336
	Justin Harding	70	70	73	73	286	4,336
	Sam Horsfield	73	71	77	65	286	4,336
	Maximilian Kieffer	71	73	70	72	286	4,336
	Jake McLeod	73	71	73	69	286	4,336
	Aaron Rai	70	71	75	70	286	4,336
	Richie Ramsay	73	72	70	71	286	4,336
	Adrien Saddier	71	71	75	69	286	4,336
	Darius van Driel	75	71	69	71	286	4,336
53	Wil Besseling	73	71	73	70	287	3,106
	Aaron Cockerill	73	71	72	71	287	3,106
	Nicolas Colsaerts	71	72	73	71	287	3,106
	Oscar Lengden	72	71	72	72	287	3,106
	Zander Lombard	77	69	68	73	287	3,106
	Damien Perrier	71	75	69	72	287	3,106
59	Matthew Baldwin	74	72	73	69	288	2,629
	Kurt Kitayama	68	74	76	70	288	2,629
	Robert MacIntyre	68	78	72	70	288	2,629
	Daniel Young	73	72	70	73	288	2,629
63	Sihwan Kim	71	67	82	69	289	2,214
	Richard McEvoy	71	74	72	72	289	2,214
	Jack Senior	73	71	71	74	289	2,214
	Cormac Sharvin	73	71	69	76	289	2,214
	Steven Tiley	71	73	74	71	289	2,214
68	Chesters Ashley	69	72	76	73	290	1,759
	Adrian Meronk	73	69	76	72	290	1,759
	Lee Slattery	78	66	79	67	290	1,759
	Scott Vincent	75	71	73	71	290	1,759
72	Niklas Lemke	73	72	70	76	291	1,497
73	Paul Dunne	74	72	73	73	292	1,491
	Anton Karlsson	77	69	70	76	292	1,491
	Matthew Southgate	69	73	80	70	292	1,491
76	Jonathan Caldwell	72	74	71	76	293	1,484
	Oliver Fisher	71	73	71	78	293	1,484

ISPS Handa UK Championship

Martin Kaymer's putt for eagle on the Brabazon's 15th hole at The Belfry lipped out. But his fourth birdie of the day put the 35-year-old German two ahead with three holes to play at the ISPS Handa UK Championship.

A first victory for six years, since the 2014 US Open, would have more than justified his decision to play on the famous Ryder Cup course as part of his preparation for the 2020 US Open. But Kaymer's wait for a victory went on. Although he saved par at the 16th after twice visiting sand, he could not get up and down at the 17th, a bogey six his only dropped shot of the day. At the last a 12-footer for birdie slipped by and he finished third, alongside Benjamin Hebert, one stroke outside a playoff.

Moments after Kaymer had gone two ahead, he was caught by Rasmus Hojgaard, who holed from 15 feet for an eagle at the 17th. The 19-year-old Dane finished with a 65, matching the lowest round of a cool, blustery bank holiday weekend. The exciting young talent, whose twin Nicolai is also on tour, made six birdies, including at the 14th and 16th holes to follow his only dropped shot at the short 12th.

He had started the final round five behind Justin Walters, the South African who had led since opening with a 64 on a rain-affected first day. Walters, two decades Hojgaard's senior, was looking for his maiden victory on the European Tour and overcame a triple bogey at the eighth, caused by an errant drive, with three birdies in the last five holes for a 70 as the pair tied on 14-under-par 274.

Twice in a row, at the 72nd and 73rd holes, Walters holed par putts at the 18th but after missing the green wildly on the second extra hole, he could not do so a third time. Hojgaard's solid pars brought him a second European Tour title in only 15 starts. Only Matteo Manassero had claimed his second win at a younger age. The rookie also finished second, third and sixth during the newly created UK Swing to pip Sam Horsfield at the top of the mini order of merit. He earned £60,000 for charity which he donated to the Danish chapters of Childhood Cancer Foundation and Ronald McDonald House.

"I was a bit surprised that I ended up in a playoff, but it was fun out there," said Hojgaard. "It's hard to describe. It's obviously an amazing feeling to get the wins. It happened really quick. I'm kind of lost for words right now, but it's an amazing feeling."

The Belfry (Brabazon), Sutton Coldfield, West Midlands — August 27-30
Par 72 (36-36); 7,255 yards — Purse: €1,000,000

1	**Rasmus Hojgaard**	73	69	67	65	274	€156,825
2	**Justin Walters**	64	71	69	70	274	101,475
	Hojgaard won playoff at second extra hole						
3	**Benjamin Hebert**	67	69	70	69	275	52,121
	Martin Kaymer	68	72	66	69	275	52,121
5	Craig Howie	68	72	71	65	276	35,701
	Bernd Wiesberger	67	71	73	65	276	35,701
7	Marcus Armitage	70	68	71	68	277	25,369
	Jorge Campillo	69	73	67	68	277	25,369
9	Calum Hill	68	72	72	66	278	19,557
	Andy Sullivan	70	72	69	67	278	19,557
11	Min Woo Lee	71	71	68	69	279	16,421
	Darius van Driel	72	70	71	66	279	16,421
13	Laurie Canter	71	73	65	71	280	14,483
	Marcus Kinhult	68	74	68	70	280	14,483
15	Ben Evans	71	72	70	68	281	13,284
	Aaron Rai	71	72	72	66	281	13,284
17	Thorbjorn Olesen	70	73	71	68	282	12,177
	Lee Westwood	70	71	72	69	282	12,177
19	Richard Bland	70	70	74	69	283	10,609
	Aaron Cockerill	72	69	74	68	283	10,609
	Bryce Easton	72	68	70	73	283	10,609
	Matthew Jordan	69	69	75	70	283	10,609
	Matt Wallace	70	73	72	68	283	10,609
	Paul Waring	70	67	76	70	283	10,609
25	John Catlin	72	72	72	68	284	9,317
	Joachim B Hansen	71	71	69	73	284	9,317
	Wade Ormsby	68	74	73	69	284	9,317
28	Dave Coupland	73	71	70	71	285	8,487
	Ryan Fox	71	67	73	74	285	8,487
	Jack Senior	70	75	71	69	285	8,487
31	Thomas Bjorn	72	69	73	72	286	6,999
	Dean Burmester	70	70	76	70	286	6,999
	Haotong Li	74	71	69	72	286	6,999
	Jake McLeod	71	71	79	65	286	6,999
	Richie Ramsay	75	70	70	71	286	6,999
	Martin Simonsen	74	70	68	74	286	6,999
	Graeme Storm	72	69	71	74	286	6,999
	Scott Vincent	67	72	74	73	286	6,999
39	Jonathan Caldwell	71	74	70	72	287	5,443
	Ross Fisher	68	73	77	69	287	5,443
	Soren Kjeldsen	70	75	70	72	287	5,443
	James Morrison	75	70	72	70	287	5,443
	Julian Suri	68	71	77	71	287	5,443
	Steven Tiley	74	71	70	72	287	5,443
	Marc Warren	69	73	75	70	287	5,443
46	Matthias Schwab	71	72	77	68	288	4,705
47	Nicolas Colsaerts	75	69	74	71	289	4,244
	Garrick Higgo	70	71	75	73	289	4,244
	Masahiro Kawamura	70	75	75	69	289	4,244
	Jeff Winther	69	73	76	71	289	4,244
51	Stephen Gallacher	69	76	68	77	290	3,506
	Tom Gandy	73	68	74	75	290	3,506
	David Horsey	71	72	75	72	290	3,506
	Wilco Nienaber	69	72	76	73	290	3,506
55	David Dixon	68	76	76	71	291	3,044
	Rhys Enoch	68	75	77	71	291	3,044
	Ross McGowan	74	68	75	74	291	3,044
58	Lucas Bjerregaard	73	72	71	76	292	2,721
	Damien Perrier	73	71	76	72	292	2,721
	Joel Sjoholm	67	76	76	73	292	2,721
	Lee Slattery	70	75	81	66	292	2,721
62	Raphael Jacquelin	74	71	73	75	293	2,491
63	Liam Johnston	72	73	76	74	295	2,399
64	Matthieu Pavon	72	72	79	73	296	2,306
	Zander Lombard	75	69	81			WDN
	Eddie Pepperell	74	70	73			WDN

Estrella Damm Andalucia Masters

Becoming only the second American after Tiger Woods, at the 1999 WGC American Express Championship, to win at Valderrama was rather more the sort of headlines that John Catlin would like to make.

A month earlier at the English Championship, Catlin became the first player to be expelled from a tournament for breaking the European Tour's Covid-19 protocols. After a late practice round, Catlin stopped off at a restaurant for dinner, instead of returning straight to his hotel, and was deemed to have exited the bio-secure bubble.

As the circuit moved on to the first event of an Iberian swing at Valderrama, Catlin claimed his maiden tour title at the Estrella Damm Andalucia Masters. The 29-year-old from Sacramento, California, led from wire-to-wire and held off former world number one Martin Kaymer for a one-stroke victory. For the second week running the German was poised to win for the first time since the 2014 US Open but was pipped at the post.

Valderrama, at its immaculate best but exposed to a teasing wind all week, proved a US Open-style test with Catlin's winning score of two over par being the highest for a regular European Tour event since Sandy Lyle won the Volvo Masters at the same venue on three over.

Only five players bettered par on the opening day, with Catlin sharing the lead on 69 with Connor Syme, Jorge Campillo and Guido Migliozzi. Catlin was the only player to post another sub-par round the next day as a 70 gave him a two-stroke lead, an advantage he maintained after a 72 on Saturday despite bogeying the last two holes.

Kaymer followed his Saturday 69 with a 74 that included a double bogey at the ninth and four bogeys. Catlin did not make a birdie in his 75 but it was enough to hang on for the win with a total of 286. Kaymer had led after a two at the 12th but bogeyed three of the last six holes. Catlin made a fine par-save at the 15th to draw level, while Kaymer missed birdie chances at the 16th and 17th holes before finding a bunker at the last. His recovery ran off the green and his chip for a par stopped on the lip.

At the day's hardest hole, Justin Harding had just taken a double bogey after a birdie at the 17th had brought him into a three-way tie for the lead. Harding shared third place with Wil Besseling and Antoine Rozner but Catlin overcame his nerves to finish strongly. He found the green and ran his long approach putt to within inches of the hole.

"I don't think it's quite sunk in but that was my goal at the start of 2019, to win on the European Tour, so to have actually accomplished that is pretty hard to put into words," said Catlin, a four-time winner on the Asian Tour. "The nerves were going nuts the whole of the final round. It's a very difficult course, the greens are firm and fast and the wind was no easier than it has been the previous three days. I managed to make the fairway on 18 and that might have been the difference."

Real Club Valderrama, Sotogrande, Spain — September 3-6
Par 71 (35-36); 7,028 yards — Purse: €1,250,000

1	**John Catlin**	69	70	72	75	286	€196,690
2	**Martin Kaymer**	72	72	69	74	287	127,270
3	**Wil Besseling**	75	72	69	72	288	59,933
	Justin Harding	71	75	71	71	288	59,933
	Antoine Rozner	76	69	73	70	288	59,933
6	Guido Migliozzi	69	74	74	72	289	37,603
	Wilco Nienaber	72	70	76	71	289	37,603
8	Masahiro Kawamura	73	73	74	71	291	27,421
	Connor Syme	69	72	76	74	291	27,421
10	Steven Brown	73	74	74	71	292	19,140
	Jamie Donaldson	72	69	73	78	292	19,140
	Lorenzo Gagli	74	69	71	78	292	19,140
	David Horsey	74	73	72	73	292	19,140
	Sami Valimaki	77	69	69	77	292	19,140
	Johannes Veerman	73	73	72	74	292	19,140
	Lee Westwood	76	73	76	67	292	19,140
17	Jorge Campillo	69	78	72	74	293	14,000
	Joachim B Hansen	74	74	74	71	293	14,000
	Maximilian Kieffer	73	74	76	70	293	14,000
	Romain Langasque	77	73	69	74	293	14,000
	Adrian Otaegui	77	71	68	77	293	14,000
	Alvaro Quiros	72	73	74	74	293	14,000
	Robin Sciot-Siegrist	76	73	75	69	293	14,000
24	Dave Coupland	72	76	71	75	294	11,339
	Ewen Ferguson	73	76	73	72	294	11,339
	Jean-Baptiste Gonnet	75	75	72	72	294	11,339
	Joakim Lagergren	77	72	70	75	294	11,339
	Pablo Larrazabal	71	70	78	75	294	11,339
	Robert MacIntyre	80	69	75	70	294	11,339
	Matthew Southgate	76	73	70	75	294	11,339
31	Thomas Detry	73	72	74	76	295	8,504
	Rasmus Hojgaard	71	79	75	70	295	8,504
	Craig Howie	75	75	71	74	295	8,504
	Wade Ormsby	74	76	75	70	295	8,504

	Victor Perez	76	74	76	69	295	8,504
	Damien Perrier	76	70	78	71	295	8,504
	Marcel Schneider	76	74	73	72	295	8,504
	Bernd Wiesberger	75	71	73	76	295	8,504
	Jeff Winther	77	68	76	74	295	8,504
	Ashun Wu	77	71	72	75	295	8,504
41	Alejandro Canizares	73	70	79	74	296	6,364
	Julien Guerrier	74	74	75	73	296	6,364
	Gregory Havret	75	73	74	74	296	6,364
	Soren Kjeldsen	71	72	74	79	296	6,364
	Alexander Levy	75	75	75	71	296	6,364
	Pedro Oriol	75	72	71	78	296	6,364
	Carlos Pigem	75	73	74	74	296	6,364
48	Pep Angles	70	77	76	74	297	5,091
	Thorbjorn Olesen	72	77	76	72	297	5,091
	Toby Tree	72	77	75	73	297	5,091
	Romain Wattel	74	74	71	78	297	5,091
52	Gonzalo Fdez-Castano	75	71	79	73	298	4,119
	Matthew Jordan	81	69	75	73	298	4,119
	Joost Luiten	79	69	75	75	298	4,119
	Ross McGowan	72	72	75	79	298	4,119
	Paul Waring	73	77	77	71	298	4,119
57	Alexander Bjork	74	73	75	77	299	3,471
	Thomas Bjorn	72	76	74	77	299	3,471
	Alfredo Garcia-Heredia	75	74	74	76	299	3,471
	Jake McLeod	71	73	78	77	299	3,471
	Ben Stow	74	73	71	81	299	3,471
62	Richard Bland	78	72	70	80	300	2,950
	Jonathan Caldwell	73	75	75	77	300	2,950
	Bryce Easton	76	73	76	75	300	2,950
	Robin Roussel	75	71	76	78	300	2,950
66	Grant Forrest	78	72	76	75	301	2,603
	Sebastian Garcia Rodriguez	76	71	75	79	301	2,603
68	Nacho Elvira	77	70	75	80	302	2,314
	Francesco Laporta	76	73	77	76	302	2,314
	Ricardo Santos	78	70	73	81	302	2,314
71	Ben Evans	75	73	78	77	303	1,872
	Adrien Saddier	73	77	76	77	303	1,872
	Max Schmitt	71	75	76	81	303	1,872
74	Raphael Jacquelin	75	73	77	79	304	1,865
	Rikard Karlberg	76	74	78	76	304	1,865
76	Edoardo Molinari	76	73	76	80	305	1,860
77	Jbe' Kruger	74	74	76	82	306	1,857

Portugal Masters

George Coetzee could not have felt more comfortable playing with the lead while winning the Titleist Championship at his home club of Pretoria the previous week. Or more uncomfortable in the final round of the Portugal Masters at Dom Pedro Victoria.

"By far the worst I've felt playing with the lead," said the 34-year-old South African after winning his fifth European Tour event but his first on the European mainland.

It did not show outwardly as Coetzee produced a bogey-free 66 to win by two strokes from Laurie Canter and by three from Tommy Fleetwood and Joakim Lagergren. He had three 66s in the week but a 70 on Friday had left him eight drift of Julien Guerrier before the Frenchman dropped back in the third round and Coetzee went to the top of the leaderboard. Coetzee, who got married in February, spent the lockdown at home practising darts and "keepy uppy" with a football to "test my mental skills".

After losing his overnight one-stroke lead with six pars to start his final round, helped by a brilliant chip from rough at the sixth, Coetzee moved ahead again with birdies at the seventh, eighth and 11th holes. He almost drove into the water at the par-five 12th but recovered with the aid of a fine eight-iron from the rough for his third shot.

Ahead, Fleetwood, 16th in the world, finished strongly with a 64 to set the target at 13 under par. Going 12 under for his last 29 holes, Fleetwood was happy with his preparations for the following week's delayed US Open. Compatriot Canter birdied the 16th and 17th holes before holing a monster par-putt at the last to pip Fleetwood by one and put more pressure on Coetzee. However, Canter was denied a maiden win as the South African birdied the short 16th, where he almost holed his tee shot, and the par-five 17th, to give himself a two-shot cushion at the dangerous 18th, where he produced his best drive of the day. A par left him on a 16-under-par total of 268.

"That was the next step for me really," Coetzee said of winning in Europe for the first time. "I have always had a list of things I wanted to achieve in my career as a golfer. Originally, I never thought I would get as far as winning on the European Tour, so ticking that box a while back was really nice, and then I started to realise that I was a bit comfortable playing back home and I needed to go to the next step and win away from home. I won in Mauritius, which still counts as a Sunshine Tour event, so I still felt like I needed to get off my continent and win something else. So I am just happy that I kind of ticked the box in the right order."

Dom Pedro Victoria Golf Course, Vilamoura, Portugal — September 10-13
Par 71 (35-36); 7,191 yards — Purse: €1,000,000

1	**George Coetzee**	66	70	66	66	268	€156,825
2	**Laurie Canter**	64	72	68	66	270	101,475
3	**Tommy Fleetwood**	68	71	68	64	271	52,121
	Joakim Lagergren	69	69	68	65	271	52,121
5	Masahiro Kawamura	67	71	65	70	273	39,114
6	Sebastian Garcia Rodriguez	70	68	67	69	274	29,981
	Niklas Lemke	70	69	65	70	274	29,981
8	Jorge Campillo	68	71	70	66	275	18,312
	John Catlin	72	69	65	69	275	18,312
	Julien Guerrier	62	66	75	72	275	18,312
	Jason Scrivener	69	68	70	68	275	18,312
	Johannes Veerman	69	68	70	68	275	18,312
	Scott Vincent	70	65	72	68	275	18,312
14	Wil Besseling	70	70	68	68	276	11,882
	Ben Evans	69	71	68	68	276	11,882
	Gonzalo Fdez-Castano	71	69	68	68	276	11,882
	Grant Forrest	72	67	69	68	276	11,882
	Liam Johnston	61	74	70	71	276	11,882
	Matthew Jordan	66	69	74	67	276	11,882
	Rikard Karlberg	72	67	70	67	276	11,882
	Wilco Nienaber	70	65	73	68	276	11,882
	Jack Senior	69	71	72	64	276	11,882
	Brandon Stone	67	70	70	69	276	11,882
24	Alexander Bjork	70	70	68	69	277	9,594
	Martin Simonsen	68	67	73	69	277	9,594
	Dale Whitnell	67	74	66	70	277	9,594
27	Lucas Bjerregaard	67	71	68	72	278	8,487
	Richard Bland	67	70	73	68	278	8,487
	Sihwan Kim	67	66	72	73	278	8,487
	Sebastian Soderberg	66	75	73	64	278	8,487
	Ben Stow	72	69	67	70	278	8,487
32	Alejandro Canizares	70	71	70	68	279	7,242
	Ryan Fox	67	69	75	68	279	7,242
	Adrien Saddier	67	68	73	71	279	7,242
	Paul Waring	67	69	71	72	279	7,242
36	Tom Gandy	69	68	72	71	280	5,904
	Ricardo Gouveia	69	72	69	70	280	5,904
	Adrian Meronk	69	66	72	73	280	5,904
	Guido Migliozzi	67	71	74	68	280	5,904
	Tapio Pulkkanen	70	70	70	70	280	5,904
	Antoine Rozner	68	67	73	72	280	5,904
	Jordan Smith	73	67	71	69	280	5,904
	Toby Tree	73	67	70	70	280	5,904
44	Jamie Donaldson	69	67	74	71	281	4,613
	Rhys Enoch	69	71	71	70	281	4,613
	Garrick Porteous	70	69	69	73	281	4,613
	Alvaro Quiros	73	68	68	72	281	4,613
	Marcel Schneider	69	72	71	69	281	4,613
	Shubhankar Sharma	73	67	70	71	281	4,613
50	Marcus Armitage	68	67	73	74	282	3,390
	Nino Bertasio	67	69	74	72	282	3,390
	Jonathan Caldwell	65	72	75	70	282	3,390
	Bryce Easton	68	72	68	74	282	3,390
	Francesco Laporta	67	70	72	73	282	3,390
	Andres Romero	71	70	70	71	282	3,390
	Ricardo Santos	69	71	72	70	282	3,390
	Julian Suri	69	71	71	71	282	3,390
58	Stephen Gallacher	76	65	71	71	283	2,629
	Pablo Larrazabal	69	71	73	70	283	2,629
	David Law	69	71	70	73	283	2,629
	Thorbjorn Olesen	66	71	73	73	283	2,629
	Max Schmitt	70	71	68	74	283	2,629
	Lars van Meijel	71	70	71	71	283	2,629
64	Tomas Bessa	68	70	75	72	285	2,214
	Steven Brown	68	70	74	73	285	2,214
	Matthew Southgate	69	72	74	70	285	2,214
67	Dave Coupland	72	68	71	75	286	1,983
	Carlos Pigem	72	69	75	70	286	1,983
69	Emilio Cuartero Blanco	70	71	71	75	287	1,845
70	David Drysdale	70	68	77	77	292	1,753

Open de Portugal

With no promotion from the Challenge Tour in 2020 due to the pandemic-curtailed season, Garrick Higgo found an immediate way to gain his European Tour status by winning the Open de Portugal at Royal Obidos, an event co-sanctioned with the Challenge Tour. It was only his seventh start on the European Tour after the 21-year-old South African made his way onto the Challenge Tour through the Sunshine Tour co-sanctioned events at the start of the year.

Higgo, from Stellenbosch, won his second Sunshine Tour title at the Tour Championship in February. His first European Tour victory came by one stroke from Pep Angles, with fellow South African George Coetzee, looking for a Portuguese double after his win the previous week at Dom Pedro Victoria, closing with a 66 to tie Andrew Wilson for third place, four behind the winner.

With play severely delayed on Friday due to thunderstorms, most of the third round was only completed on Sunday morning with Higgo scoring a 66, after rounds of 68 and 70, to lie alongside Angles and one behind local Vitor Lopes, the leader throughout with scores of 65, 71 and 67. But Lopes stalled in the final round with a 72 and fell into a tie for seventh, while Higgo started strongly by going out in 31 with five birdies, including a chip-in at the sixth, his third of the week.

He led Angles by two before moving four clear with a birdie at the 11th, a hole where Angles, in the group behind, took a bogey six. But Angles rallied with birdies at the 12th and then the final three holes for his third 66 of the week. Higgo safely two-putted for birdie at the last, a round of 65 and a 19-under-par total of 269, but then had to wait and watch as Angles narrowly missed from long range for an eagle to tie.

"I thought it was going to be a little bit easier over the last three holes but Pep made it a bit tough.

That birdie on the last was really, really nice," said Higgo, who was over par on only two holes all week, a double bogey at the sixth on day one and a bogey at the 10th in the second round. "It was a bit of a big hit with Covid meaning there isn't any promotion from the Challenge Tour this year, so obviously one of the dual-ranked events is ideal to win because you can get straight on to the European Tour. It's an awesome feeling to get it done."

Royal Obidos Spa & Golf Resort, Obidos, Portugal — September 17-20
Par 72 (36-36); 7,283 yards — Purse: €500,000

1	**Garrick Higgo**	68	70	66	65	269	€78,812
2	**Pep Angles**	72	66	66	66	270	50,996
3	**George Coetzee**	69	70	68	66	273	26,193
	Andrew Wilson	69	67	71	66	273	26,193
5	Jens Dantorp	70	70	67	67	274	17,941
	Carlos Pigem	67	71	68	68	274	17,941
7	Vitor Lopes	65	71	67	72	275	12,749
	Jonathan Thomson	73	67	71	64	275	12,749
9	Maverick Antcliff	70	70	66	70	276	9,828
	Jordan Wrisdale	72	68	66	70	276	9,828
11	Julien Brun	70	72	67	68	277	7,989
	Todd Clements	73	70	69	65	277	7,989
	Ashton Turner	70	69	67	71	277	7,989
14	Harry Ellis	70	70	69	69	278	6,676
	Chase Hanna	70	69	69	70	278	6,676
	Oliver Lindell	74	68	70	66	278	6,676
	Nicolai von Dellingshausen	69	74	68	67	278	6,676
18	David Boote	69	72	66	72	279	5,501
	Pedro Figueiredo	71	73	70	65	279	5,501
	Matt Ford	74	69	72	64	279	5,501
	Nathan Kimsey	69	67	72	71	279	5,501
	Gudmundur Kristjansson	69	72	69	69	279	5,501
	Niklas Norgaard Moller	72	71	68	68	279	5,501
24	Aaron Cockerill	72	71	64	73	280	4,752
	Bjorn Hellgren	74	69	68	69	280	4,752
	Roope Kakko	69	69	72	70	280	4,752
	Ricardo Santos	68	74	71	67	280	4,752
28	Stephen Ferreira	71	71	69	70	281	4,196
	Alexander Knappe	68	71	69	73	281	4,196
	Christopher Mivis	70	72	69	70	281	4,196
	Martin Simonsen	75	69	70	67	281	4,196
32	Damien Perrier	67	73	69	73	282	3,709
	Robin Sciot-Siegrist	69	75	70	68	282	3,709
	Julian Suri	68	77	70	67	282	3,709
35	Hinrich Arkenau	74	70	71	68	283	3,113
	Ricardo Gouveia	69	76	68	70	283	3,113
	Frederic Lacroix	71	74	70	68	283	3,113
	Richard Mansell	73	72	68	70	283	3,113
	Alfie Plant	70	71	69	73	283	3,113
	Benjamin Poke	75	71	68	69	283	3,113
	Christopher Sahlstrom	70	72	73	68	283	3,113
42	Christofer Blomstrand	72	69	71	72	284	2,457
	Jamie Donaldson	70	67	73	74	284	2,457
	Mathieu Fenasse	73	71	67	73	284	2,457
	Dominic Foos	69	71	70	74	284	2,457
	Nicolai Kristensen	75	71	69	69	284	2,457
	Ross McGowan	73	69	70	72	284	2,457
	Bradley Moore	73	72	70	69	284	2,457
49	Tomas Bessa	72	74	72	67	285	1,947
	Jens Fahrbring	72	74	68	71	285	1,947
	Federico Maccario	74	69	70	72	285	1,947
	Santiago Tarrio	72	71	76	66	285	1,947
53	Pelle Edberg	73	73	72	68	286	1,513
	Rhys Enoch	73	71	70	72	286	1,513
	Philip Eriksson	72	69	74	71	286	1,513
	Gonzalo Fdez-Castano	72	71	71	72	286	1,513
	Scott Fernandez	76	69	73	68	286	1,513
	Bradley Neil	71	73	70	72	286	1,513
	Pedro Oriol	74	70	74	68	286	1,513
	Marcel Siem	70	71	70	75	286	1,513
61	Hurly Long	74	72	69	72	287	1,229
	Marco Penge	74	72	70	71	287	1,229
	Bernd Ritthammer	70	74	70	73	287	1,229
	Henric Sturehed	70	76	73	68	287	1,229
65	Raphael de Sousa	72	74	71	71	288	1,020
	Nicolai Hojgaard	73	73	73	69	288	1,020
	Gary King	69	75	72	72	288	1,020
	Robin Petersson	74	70	72	72	288	1,020
	Euan Walker	73	71	72	72	288	1,020
70	Gregory Bourdy	76	70	71	72	289	793
	Kristian Krogh Johannessen	73	71	72	73	289	793
	Martin Ovesen	75	71	70	73	289	793
73	Daniel Young	70	74	72	74	290	744
74	Enrico Di Nitto	73	73	71	74	291	738
	Stuart Manley	73	71	73	74	291	738
	Jesper Sandborg	70	76	70	75	291	738
77	Aron Zemmer	70	71	77	75	293	732

Dubai Duty Free Irish Open

Two starts after winning for the first time on the European Tour at Valderrama, John Catlin added a second victory at the Dubai Duty Free Irish Open. While the 29-year-old American had led from start to finish in sunny Spain, holding off Martin Kaymer in the process, in more challenging conditions at Galgorm Castle he made a late charge with three birdies in the last four holes securing a two-stroke victory over England's Aaron Rai.

Rai was trying to repeat his feat from the 2018 Hong Kong Open when he was a wire-to-wire winner. He was one of three players to open with a 65 and then added a 70 and a 67 before closing with a 70. In contrast, Catlin was four behind after scores of 67, 70 and 69 before a 64 on Sunday took him to a 10-under-par total for 270.

After a delay due to frost in the morning, a number of players contended for the title, including

Thailand's Jazz Janewattananond, who led after birdieing the 13th from three feet until he took a double bogey at the next. He finished third with Australian Maverick Antcliff, who had his first top-10 finish on the European Tour the previous week in Portugal, while Swedes Joakim Lagergren and Oscar Lengden shared fifth place.

Catlin birdied four of the first 10 holes before his only dropped shot of the day at the 13th. But he holed from 18 feet for a birdie at the 15th and hit his approach at the next to four feet for another. His decisive blow was a three-wood from 268 yards which safely found the narrow 18th green and set up a two-putt birdie four. Rai, after birdieing the 17th, needed a four at the last to tie but pulled his second shot into an awful lie in the rough and took four to get down for a bogey.

"So many years of hard work have gone into this moment," Catlin said. "It was my goal to win again at the start of this week and to have accomplished it is something truly special. I had nothing to lose. I was going after every flag, I had good numbers and the greens were soft. That three-wood on 18 was so satisfying. It was 268 yards to the hole, cold and damp. To just hit a big high draw in there like I know I can, under those conditions, really is hard to put into words."

Catlin became the third American to win the title after Ben Crenshaw in 1976 and Hubert Green the following year. The Californian also moved into the world's top-100 for the first time. "To get that monkey off my back at Valderrama really freed me up today to know I could do it," he said.

Galgorm Castle Golf Club, Ballymena, Northern Ireland — September 24-27
Par 70 (34-36); 7,087 yards — Purse: €1,250,000

1	**John Catlin**	67	70	69	64	270	€199,750
2	**Aaron Rai**	65	70	67	70	272	129,250
3	**Maverick Antcliff**	70	65	68	70	273	66,388
	Jazz Janewattananond	68	70	66	69	273	66,388
5	Joakim Lagergren	70	66	71	67	274	45,473
	Oscar Lengden	67	71	66	70	274	45,473
7	Lucas Herbert	71	67	67	70	275	30,315
	Jordan Smith	65	71	70	69	275	30,315
	Fabrizio Zanotti	70	72	70	63	275	30,315
10	Adrian Meronk	71	69	70	66	276	23,500
11	Justin Harding	68	69	69	71	277	20,249
	Scott Hend	68	69	70	70	277	20,249
	Joost Luiten	71	70	69	67	277	20,249
14	Richard Bland	72	67	71	68	278	15,642
	Laurie Canter	73	67	68	70	278	15,642
	Ewen Ferguson	70	67	70	71	278	15,642
	Daan Huizing	70	69	70	69	278	15,642
	Rikard Karlberg	67	75	65	71	278	15,642
	Masahiro Kawamura	74	71	66	67	278	15,642
	Ben Stow	70	75	67	66	278	15,642
	Toby Tree	66	70	69	73	278	15,642
22	Dean Burmester	65	71	68	75	279	13,278
23	Marcus Armitage	69	71	71	69	280	12,749
	Adri Arnaus	73	69	73	65	280	12,749
25	Craig Howie	73	71	68	69	281	11,868
	Robert Rock	69	67	78	67	281	11,868
	Jason Scrivener	73	69	74	65	281	11,868
28	Joachim B Hansen	72	72	68	70	282	10,458
	Calum Hill	70	70	73	69	282	10,458
	Antoine Rozner	73	72	66	71	282	10,458
	Jack Senior	70	73	66	73	282	10,458
	Clement Sordet	70	70	74	68	282	10,458
33	Richie Ramsay	71	74	68	70	283	9,224
	Matthew Southgate	74	70	73	66	283	9,224
35	Alejandro Canizares	71	72	71	70	284	8,254
	David Law	69	69	76	70	284	8,254
	Martin Simonsen	68	75	74	67	284	8,254
	Lars van Meijel	71	71	73	69	284	8,254
39	Steven Brown	71	74	71	69	285	6,698
	Dave Coupland	72	69	73	71	285	6,698
	Sean Crocker	72	67	74	72	285	6,698
	Nacho Elvira	69	71	74	71	285	6,698
	Oliver Farr	70	70	76	69	285	6,698
	Jake McLeod	70	73	74	68	285	6,698
	Garrick Porteous	73	71	71	70	285	6,698
	Robin Sciot-Siegrist	73	72	71	69	285	6,698
	Dale Whitnell	71	72	72	70	285	6,698
48	George Coetzee	71	73	71	71	286	5,288
	Julien Guerrier	68	70	74	74	286	5,288
	Wilco Nienaber	70	72	72	72	286	5,288
51	Lucas Bjerregaard	68	74	70	75	287	4,583
	Mathieu Fenasse	72	72	73	70	287	4,583
	Stephen Gallacher	67	74	70	76	287	4,583
54	Wil Besseling	74	71	73	70	288	3,936
	Jonathan Caldwell	71	70	73	74	288	3,936
	Scott Jamieson	69	76	75	68	288	3,936
	Niklas Lemke	68	74	75	71	288	3,936
58	Aaron Cockerill	75	70	71	73	289	3,584
	Max Schmitt	73	72	73	71	289	3,584
60	James Morrison	72	69	73	76	290	3,290
	Mark Power (A)	74	71	73	72	290	
	Darius van Driel	73	70	75	72	290	3,290
	Romain Wattel	74	71	75	70	290	3,290
64	Damien McGrane	70	74	75	72	291	2,996
	Shubhankar Sharma	72	72	76	71	291	2,996
66	James Sugrue (A)	67	72	73	80	292	
67	Ross McGowan	73	71	76	73	293	2,820
68	Joel Stalter	74	70	74	77	295	2,703
69	Richard McEvoy	72	72	73	79	296	2,526
	Colm Moriarty	75	69	73	79	296	2,526

Aberdeen Standard Investments Scottish Open

From the hunted to the hunter. Aaron Rai led virtually all the way at the Irish Open but was pipped at the 72nd hole by John Catlin. It was a different story at The Renaissance Club. A final round of 64 produced a dramatic leap up the leaderboard before Rai defeated Tommy Fleetwood at the first extra hole to claim the Aberdeen Standard Investments Scottish Open, his first Rolex Series title.

Rai, 25, who won the Hong Kong Open in 2018, had made only seven birdies in the first three rounds and was five behind Robert Rock after 54 holes. He dropped further back with a bogey at the second but then birdied five of the next six holes. At the par-three 12th he almost holed in one but with a two there plus birdies at the 13th and 16th holes, making eight in all for the day and a 64, he set the clubhouse target at 11-under-par 273.

Rock, after a poor front nine, rallied coming home before bogeying the last hole for a 70 to finish one short. Alongside him, Fleetwood played some fine golf holing from 18 feet at both the 11th and the 15th but missing short chances at the 12th, 13th and 16th holes. At the last, however, a 20-footer fell as Fleetwood tied with a 67. There was a further twist in Fleetwood's putting fortunes at the first extra hole, the 18th. Both players faced three-footers for their pars and while Rai holed his, Fleetwood did not.

"It's incredible," said Rai. "I played a lot in Scotland growing up, dreamed of playing in a European Tour event in Scotland. I didn't really see many leaderboards all the way around. I knew we had to play well and knew we had to keep pushing forwards. You have to play some world-class golf to win on tour, but for it to be a Rolex Series with the class of field that was this week is deeply satisfying."

Lee Westwood led the first round with a 62 but a dramatic Saturday saw continuous heavy rain and gale-force winds though, amazingly, play was never halted. Ian Poulter, who had a 73, said it was the worst conditions he had ever played in. Second-round leader Lucas Herbert had a 79 but the Australian bounced back the next day with a 65 to tie for fourth place with Marc Warren.

Fleetwood, who had a 69 on Saturday, said: "I loved every minute of it. It's golf, isn't it? Somebody's got to enjoy it. Let's face it, the money we play for these days, a day like that doesn't do any harm does it? I'd play in it every day if this is what we're doing, so no problems."

Paul Lawrie bowed out after missing the cut. With back issues and a busy off-course life with his foundation and management agency, the 1999 Open champion had decided that his 620th European Tour event would be his last on a regular basis. "I don't want to play in tournaments just making up the numbers," said Lawrie, who turned professional as a five-handicapper in 1986 and went on to win eight times on the European Tour. "That's not what I'm about. If I'm stopping a young boy coming in and having a game, having a career, I don't want that.

"I've been fortunate enough to have been a decent player, to have won a few, and every win is special because I never thought I'd win any to be honest. Never thought I would play in any, never mind win any. The Open was out of this world and to have your name on that is unbelievable. So it's been a great time. I've had a blast."

The Renaissance Club, Gullane, East Lothian, Scotland — October 1-4
Par 71 (36-35); 7,293 yards — Purse: $7,000,000

1	**Aaron Rai**	70	69	70	64	273	€974,353
2	**Tommy Fleetwood**	69	68	69	67	273	630,464
	Rai won playoff at first extra hole						
3	**Robert Rock**	65	67	72	70	274	361,084
4	Lucas Herbert	66	65	79	65	275	264,795
	Marc Warren	70	69	70	66	275	264,795
6	Marcus Kinhult	66	69	71	70	276	171,945
	Ian Poulter	67	66	73	70	276	171,945
	Erik van Rooyen	71	69	71	65	276	171,945
9	Victor Dubuisson	73	68	67	69	277	107,867
	Padraig Harrington	71	70	69	67	277	107,867
	Eddie Pepperell	68	70	71	68	277	107,867
	Kalle Samooja	65	70	74	68	277	107,867
	Matthew Southgate	68	71	71	67	277	107,867
14	David Horsey	70	67	72	69	278	80,814
	Haotong Li	68	70	74	66	278	80,814
	Robert MacIntyre	74	67	68	69	278	80,814
	Victor Perez	69	69	74	66	278	80,814
	Jeunghun Wang	73	68	70	67	278	80,814
19	Alexander Bjork	63	75	72	69	279	65,011
	Grant Forrest	71	66	72	70	279	65,011
	Benjamin Hebert	70	70	69	70	279	65,011
	Joost Luiten	63	72	76	68	279	65,011
	Wade Ormsby	66	70	70	73	279	65,011
	Brandon Stone	69	70	70	70	279	65,011
	Lee Westwood	62	71	76	70	279	65,011
26	Adri Arnaus	75	66	67	72	280	55,309
	Garrick Higgo	72	67	72	69	280	55,309
	Shubhankar Sharma	70	67	76	67	280	55,309
	Andy Sullivan	67	72	69	72	280	55,309

30	Nicolas Colsaerts	68	70	72	71	281	46,712
	Thomas Detry	71	69	77	64	281	46,712
	Ewen Ferguson	69	70	73	69	281	46,712
	Min Woo Lee	66	74	72	69	281	46,712
	Callum Shinkwin	69	70	70	72	281	46,712
	Matt Wallace	70	71	72	68	281	46,712
36	Maverick Antcliff	69	70	75	68	282	37,828
	Sean Crocker	73	68	70	71	282	37,828
	Scott Jamieson	64	73	73	72	282	37,828
	Jordan Smith	70	70	72	70	282	37,828
	Julian Suri	70	70	72	70	282	37,828
	Jeff Winther	71	69	69	73	282	37,828
42	Matthew Fitzpatrick	69	72	72	70	283	30,950
	Gavin Green	70	71	67	75	283	30,950
	Francesco Laporta	71	70	70	72	283	30,950
	Craig Lee	65	71	76	71	283	30,950
	Mike Lorenzo-Vera	68	66	76	73	283	30,950

BMW PGA Championship

Tyrrell Hatton likes his home comforts. Based for most of the year in America, where he won for the first time on the PGA Tour at the Arnold Palmer Invitational, Hatton had been missing his father's Sunday roast lunches. After missing the cut at the US Open, he got to return home to Marlow, 25 minutes from Wentworth, and catch up with the family, as well as having the odd bacon sandwich and a local curry, slightly undoing all his good work in the gym while he was away.

For the BMW PGA Championship, the European Tour's "flagship" event, Hatton could stay at home, as long as throughout the week he commuted directly between there and the course, as those staying in the designated hotels had to do. With the event pushed back to October, it had a feel of the old World Match Play, an autumnal staple of these parts for decades, but lacked the large galleries that the venue usually attracts. Some of those interacting from afar tediously only wanted to complain about Hatton wearing a golf top with a hood — a "hoodie", God forbid — but he had the last laugh when an offer to give away 10 of them attracted over 13,000 replies.

Hatton also came out well of a social media meme of the week where people posted two pictures, with the captions: "How it started," and "How it's going..." Three days before his 29th birthday, Hatton shared a picture of himself at Wentworth as a five-year-old, complete with miniature golf attire, and then with the PGA trophy, the biggest title of his career to date.

"It's been a dream of mine since I was a kid to play the tournament and hopefully win it one day," he said. "I always wanted to be inside the ropes when I grew up. This is just such a massive event, an amazing history with a lot of fantastic players on that trophy. To win here is such a special feeling. It was definitely a goal in my career. I'm very thankful that I managed to get the job done today."

This was his fifth European Tour victory and his third in the Rolex Series. All his wins have come at the same time of year, starting with the Alfred Dunhill Links Championship in 2016 and '17, the Italian Open also in 2017 and the Turkish Airlines Open in 2019. This win took him to a career high of 10th on the world rankings after turning a three-stroke overnight advantage into a four-stroke victory over France's Victor Perez.

It was not straightforward. It never is with Hatton, whose temper can flare in an instant but who has learnt not to let it affect him. Unaware he was three ahead on the last hole, a poor second shot only just cleared the stream well short of the green.

"I was pretty nervous stood on the 18th tee but I thought that was one of the best swings of the day," he said. "When you get around the corner, and you see the green, I guess I was more nervous for the second shot. I think I caught the ground about two inches before the ball and it didn't even get grooves, it was so far out of the toe. I was quite lucky that it got over the hazard to be honest. It is probably the worst shot in the history of the tournament for the champion."

Hatton shared the lead on the opening day with a 66 but a 67 in round two left him one adrift of Shane Lowry, the 2019 Open champion, and Matthew Fitzpatrick, who both had 65s. Fitzpatrick was two clear until he found the water at the eighth, his final hole of the day, and took a double bogey.

Neither Fitzpatrick nor Lowry were able to keep up the challenge over the weekend and Hatton emerged with a three-shot lead on Saturday after a 69. Of his nearest rivals, Perez, after scores of 69, 66 and 70, proved a doughty competitor in the final round. The Frenchman, based in Scotland, birdied the second and eagled the fourth from over 20 feet to tie before adding another birdie at the seventh from only two feet. He saved par on the 10th and then birdied the next two but could not sustain the challenge. He dropped a shot at the 13th and again at the par-five 17th, after blocking his drive into the trees on the right. No birdie at the last meant a 68.

"I knew I had to get off to a quick start," said Perez, who won the Alfred Dunhill Links in 2019. "It was obviously nerve-wracking coming down the stretch. You know you have to execute shots. It didn't really go my way towards the end but obviously I am very pleased."

Hatton needed a two at the fifth to keep pace with Perez but then surged ahead with three birdies in a row from the ninth, including an unlikely 35-footer at the 10th which fell in on its last roll. His only bogey of the day came at the 13th, while a chance at the next refused to drop. "Why did that not turn in?" came the exasperated cry. "That's ridiculous. Can't hit a bad putt."

"I had to manage myself," he said. "Not allow myself to get in my own way." A five-iron approach at the 15th to 12 feet was his finest shot of the round. The putt went in and suddenly the margin was two. Hatton recovered from his ropey second at the last with a pitch-and-putt birdie for a 67 and a 19-under-par total of 269.

Earlier Patrick Reed had eagled the last to finish one behind Perez. The American's concerns about travelling to the event were eased once he was safely ensconced in the bio-bubble of the European Tour. The trip was worth it as the former Masters champion extended his lead at the top of the Race to Dubai. England's Andy Sullivan shared third place after a 65 on Sunday, which included an eagle and six birdies, while Ian Poulter recovered from back spasms on Thursday, when he was close to walking off the course, to take fifth place.

This week marked the retirements from the European Tour of chief referees John Paramor and Andy McFee, with almost 80 years of officiating between them, and tournament director Jamie Birkmyre.

Wentworth Club (West), Virginia Water, Surrey, England — October 8-11
Par 72 (35-37); 7,267 yards — Purse: $7,000,000

1	**Tyrrell Hatton**	66	67	69	67	269	€974,457
2	**Victor Perez**	69	66	70	68	273	630,531
3	**Patrick Reed**	70	68	68	68	274	323,864
	Andy Sullivan	71	69	69	65	274	323,864
5	Ian Poulter	69	70	68	68	275	243,041
6	Eddie Pepperell	67	70	70	69	276	200,624
7	Matthew Fitzpatrick	67	65	76	69	277	147,888
	Joachim B Hansen	68	67	70	72	277	147,888
	Renato Paratore	73	69	68	67	277	147,888
10	Scott Hend	68	69	73	68	278	106,235
	Martin Kaymer	73	68	69	68	278	106,235
	Marcus Kinhult	72	67	71	68	278	106,235
13	Tommy Fleetwood	71	68	67	73	279	84,491
	David Horsey	70	69	67	73	279	84,491
	Shane Lowry	67	65	74	73	279	84,491
	Jordan Smith	72	67	71	69	279	84,491
	Sami Valimaki	72	67	74	66	279	84,491
18	Andrew Johnston	68	71	71	70	280	72,511
	Lee Westwood	70	71	71	68	280	72,511
20	Ross Fisher	72	72	69	68	281	65,776
	Ryan Fox	68	70	73	70	281	65,776
	Masahiro Kawamura	70	69	69	73	281	65,776
	Richie Ramsay	71	71	71	68	281	65,776
24	Steven Brown	75	67	68	72	282	59,614
	Graeme McDowell	73	70	72	67	282	59,614
	Matt Wallace	69	71	72	70	282	59,614
27	Garrick Higgo	69	71	71	72	283	52,735
	Pablo Larrazabal	73	69	66	75	283	52,735
	Thorbjorn Olesen	71	71	71	70	283	52,735
	Matthieu Pavon	71	73	71	68	283	52,735
	Erik van Rooyen	76	68	71	68	283	52,735
32	Adri Arnaus	66	70	74	74	284	44,137
	Victor Dubuisson	72	71	71	70	284	44,137
	Grant Forrest	69	67	76	72	284	44,137
	Joakim Lagergren	69	72	73	70	284	44,137
	Danny Willett	71	71	74	68	284	44,137
37	Michael Bullen	71	72	71	71	285	38,405
	Justin Rose	68	75	72	70	285	38,405
	Matthias Schwab	68	71	78	68	285	38,405
40	Kiradech Aphibarnrat	71	70	72	73	286	34,393
	Christiaan Bezuidenhout	72	72	70	72	286	34,393
	Padraig Harrington	72	71	72	71	286	34,393
	Bernd Wiesberger	70	72	72	72	286	34,393
44	Sean Crocker	72	70	72	73	287	29,807
	Julien Guerrier	72	67	75	73	287	29,807
	Matthew Southgate	70	73	76	68	287	29,807
	Jeunghun Wang	72	70	69	76	287	29,807
48	Thomas Detry	72	71	76	69	288	24,075
	Gavin Green	67	71	74	76	288	24,075
	Alexander Levy	72	68	77	71	288	24,075
	Robert Rock	69	70	72	77	288	24,075
	Kalle Samooja	71	73	73	71	288	24,075
	Shubhankar Sharma	73	70	72	73	288	24,075
54	Nacho Elvira	74	69	76	70	289	19,489
	Wade Ormsby	68	71	74	76	289	19,489
	Tapio Pulkkanen	71	73	74	71	289	19,489
57	Kristoffer Broberg	71	71	69	79	290	18,343
58	Romain Langasque	71	72	77	71	291	17,483
	Robert MacIntyre	73	68	77	73	291	17,483
60	Thomas Aiken	75	68	73	76	292	16,336
	Stephen Gallacher	72	71	74	75	292	16,336
62	Thomas Pieters	72	71	73	77	293	14,903
	Joel Stalter	76	68	77	72	293	14,903
	Fabrizio Zanotti	71	73	75	74	293	14,903
65	David Howell	72	68	80	74	294	13,470
	Soren Kjeldsen	73	71	76	74	294	13,470
67	Oliver Fisher	72	72	72	80	296	12,611

Scottish Championship

In matchplay terms, on a comparison of scorecards, Adrian Otaegui would have beaten Matt Wallace 5 and 4. It would have registered little surprise since the 27-year-old Spaniard's two wins on the European Tour had come at the Paul Lawrie Match Play in 2017 and the Belgian Knockout in 2017. But at the Scottish Championship, played on the Torrance course at Fairmont St Andrews, one of the newer links overlooking the Old Grey Toon, it was pure strokeplay. In those terms, Otaegui delivered an even more convincing win, coming from four behind Wallace to win by four strokes.

Wallace, aiming for this fifth European Tour win and a first for two years, hit his tee shot at the first behind a wall and had to chip out sideways, leading to what was only his second dropped shot of the week. The Englishman did not really get going and a 71 was four strokes higher than his previous highest score.

Otaegui, however, had got his so-so days out of the way with a pair of 70s on Friday and Saturday. In contrast, he opened with a 10-birdie, no-bogey 62 on Thursday and again had 10 birdies on Sunday. His closing 63, containing a solitary bogey at the 10th, gave him a 23-under-par total of 265 and a first strokeplay title. "Stroke play is my favourite way of golf, I think it's the proper way," he said. "You have to play very solidly and very consistently all four rounds, which I think I did.

"I had no expectations this morning. I just wanted to go out there, play well and shoot as well as possible. If you told me I was going to shoot 63 this morning, I wouldn't believe it. Everything went well, I played very well, I was very focused and I holed some good putts. I feel so happy. To be able to win in Scotland, especially here in St Andrews, the home of golf, it means a lot to me."

It was a run of eight birdies in 11 holes from the fifth that saw Otaegui outrun his opponents. Twice he had three birdies in a row and he took the lead on his own at the ninth after going out in 31.

Garrick Porteous, from Bamburgh Castle on the Northumberland coast, tied for the lead on the front nine with three birdies in a row from the fourth. It was only late on that he slipped out of contention, a 71 leaving him tied for fourth, only a second top-10 finish on the European Tour for the 2013 British Amateur champion. Aaron Rai continued his fine form by closing with a 66 to take third place.

Fairmont St Andrews (Torrance), St Andrews, Fife, Scotland — October 15-18
Par 72 (36-36); 7,230 yards — Purse: €1,000,000

1	**Adrian Otaegui**	62	70	70	63	265	€161,925
2	**Matt Wallace**	65	67	66	71	269	104,775
3	**Aaron Rai**	66	67	72	66	271	60,008
4	Chris Paisley	66	71	67	68	272	44,006
	Garrick Porteous	66	69	66	71	272	44,006
6	Adrien Saddier	67	67	71	68	273	33,338
7	Marcus Armitage	70	68	70	66	274	26,194
	Jonathan Caldwell	70	66	68	70	274	26,194
9	Matthew Baldwin	70	72	68	65	275	17,926
	Sean Crocker	70	66	67	72	275	17,926
	Jamie Donaldson	70	70	69	66	275	17,926
	Oliver Farr	73	67	70	65	275	17,926
	Sebastian Soderberg	72	68	70	65	275	17,926
14	Padraig Harrington	66	69	73	68	276	14,288
	Lee Westwood	67	70	72	67	276	14,288
16	Bryce Easton	65	72	72	68	277	11,589
	Ewen Ferguson	67	72	71	67	277	11,589
	Alexander Levy	70	71	70	66	277	11,589
	Eddie Pepperell	68	70	66	73	277	11,589
	Matthew Southgate	69	68	70	70	277	11,589
	Brandon Stone	67	70	70	70	277	11,589
	Ben Stow	70	70	67	70	277	11,589
	Justin Walters	71	69	74	63	277	11,589
	Ashun Wu	67	71	71	68	277	11,589
25	Calum Hill	70	72	66	70	278	9,335
	Matthew Jordan	71	68	68	71	278	9,335
	Martin Simonsen	69	69	68	72	278	9,335
	Paul Waring	68	67	71	72	278	9,335
	Marc Warren	67	69	72	70	278	9,335
30	Wil Besseling	71	69	73	66	279	8,192
	Justin Harding	75	64	73	67	279	8,192
	James Morrison	72	69	69	69	279	8,192
33	Gonzalo Fdez-Castano	67	73	70	70	280	7,191
	David Law	73	67	72	68	280	7,191
	Richie Ramsay	74	68	68	70	280	7,191
	Darius van Driel	72	69	72	67	280	7,191
37	Daniel Gavins	70	68	75	68	281	6,096
	Scott Jamieson	67	75	71	68	281	6,096
	Renato Paratore	68	73	73	67	281	6,096
	Kristoffer Reitan	73	64	74	70	281	6,096
	Shubhankar Sharma	71	72	70	68	281	6,096
	Connor Syme	70	70	69	72	281	6,096
43	Pedro Figueiredo	70	70	72	70	282	4,953
	Sam Horsfield	74	69	68	71	282	4,953
	Craig Howie	70	68	74	70	282	4,953
	Joel Stalter	70	72	71	69	282	4,953
	Lars van Meijel	72	70	70	70	282	4,953
	Oliver Wilson	72	68	75	67	282	4,953
49	Ashley Chesters	72	70	70	71	283	4,191
	Steven Tiley	69	74	73	67	283	4,191
51	SSP Chawrasia	69	69	76	70	284	3,543
	David Drysdale	69	71	73	71	284	3,543
	Tom Gandy	70	73	73	68	284	3,543
	Hurly Long	69	73	73	69	284	3,543
	Adrian Meronk	68	70	74	72	284	3,543
56	Dave Coupland	68	69	75	73	285	3,000

	Robin Petersson	71	71	72	71	285	3,000
	Benjamin Poke	71	71	72	71	285	3,000
	Lorenzo Scalise	71	71	74	69	285	3,000
60	Ben Evans	69	72	75	70	286	2,667
	Jens Fahrbring	72	71	73	70	286	2,667
	Gregory Havret	69	70	77	70	286	2,667
63	Philip Eriksson	73	67	73	74	287	2,429
	Ricardo Santos	71	71	74	71	287	2,429
65	Damien Perrier	70	70	75	73	288	2,238
	Marcel Schneider	73	70	73	72	288	2,238
67	Zach Murray	69	73	72	75	289	2,096
68	Daniel Young	72	71	76	71	290	2,000
69	Joel Sjoholm	72	71	77	73	293	1,905

Italian Open

Perseverance won the day, and the Italian Open, his first title for 11 years, for Ross McGowan.

On Thursday he scored a 66 and was still six behind Laurie Canter's opening 12-under-par 60. It was only at the 16th hole on Sunday, with a holed bunker shot, that McGowan took the lead on his own for the first time. It was also the first time since Thursday morning that Canter did not hold at least a share of the lead, the pair having been tied after 54 holes, three strokes ahead of the pack.

Canter hit back with a birdie from six feet at the short 17th so they were tied again going to the par-five last, where the whole round was encapsulated in one hole. Canter hit a massive drive down the middle of the fairway while McGowan was in the rough. But while Canter finished short left of the green with a tricky chip for his third that came up 10 feet short, McGowan got back in play and then wedged his third to 20 feet over the flag. In went his putt and then Canter, still chasing his first victory at the age of 30, missed his.

Canter closed with 72, 12 higher than his first day's effort, to tie for second place with Nicolas Colsaerts, who birdied the last for a 68. Sebastian Heisle also had a 68 to take fourth place, two behind the winner, while Martin Kaymer and Dean Burmester were among those sharing fifth place.

McGowan, a former English Amateur champion, won the Madrid Masters in 2009 and finished 12th on the Race to Dubai that year. He came close to making the Ryder Cup team in 2010 but lost his card the following year as injuries and loss of form left him in the wilderness before a win on the Challenge Tour in 2019. He followed his opening 66 with scores of 64, 67 and 71 for a 20-under-par total of 268. A front nine of 37 included a double bogey and an eagle back-to-back, while at the 16th he hit a wild tee shot into sand way off line before finding a greenside bunker with his second.

"I can't believe it," McGowan said. "I hit the ball terrible today but luckily the putter kept me in it again.

"The tee shot on 16 was a shocker, the second shot wasn't much better and then I holed the bunker shot so I think that was the one that gave me a bit of belief. Then to roll that putt in at 18 was magical. I didn't really foresee this, my form hasn't been great. But I felt like I was playing better, definitely around the greens. I think I'm going to have to go now and have a nice big glass of red wine and think about what's next."

Chervo Golf Club, San Vigilio di Pozzolengo, Brescia, Italy — October 22-25
Par 72 (36-36); 7,434 yards — Purse: €1,000,000

1	**Ross McGowan**	66	64	67	71	268	€160,650
2	**Laurie Canter**	60	68	69	72	269	81,743
	Nicolas Colsaerts	68	67	66	68	269	81,743
4	Sebastian Heisele	68	67	66	69	270	47,250
5	Adri Arnaus	65	70	67	69	271	29,257
	Dean Burmester	64	68	68	71	271	29,257
	Jonathan Caldwell	67	68	68	68	271	29,257
	Martin Kaymer	69	66	68	68	271	29,257
	Kristoffer Reitan	66	70	70	65	271	29,257
10	Marcus Armitage	67	70	69	66	272	16,939
	Joost Luiten	70	66	68	68	272	16,939
	Damien Perrier	65	71	71	65	272	16,939
	Antoine Rozner	68	71	68	65	272	16,939
14	Emilio Cuartero Blanco	68	68	68	69	273	14,175
	Julien Quesne	66	71	67	69	273	14,175
16	Wil Besseling	65	71	68	70	274	12,049
	Richard Bland	65	70	70	69	274	12,049
	Bryce Easton	68	69	69	68	274	12,049
	Nicolai Hojgaard	67	67	71	69	274	12,049
	Hurly Long	69	69	68	68	274	12,049
	Bernd Wiesberger	67	68	68	71	274	12,049
22	Aaron Cockerill	67	72	69	67	275	9,686
	Louis de Jager	68	68	67	72	275	9,686
	Adrian Meronk	67	71	66	71	275	9,686
	Guido Migliozzi	68	69	73	65	275	9,686
	Adrian Otaegui	67	67	72	69	275	9,686
	Joel Sjoholm	68	70	67	70	275	9,686
	Joel Stalter	73	66	70	66	275	9,686
	Dale Whitnell	68	70	71	66	275	9,686
30	Matthew Jordan	66	72	72	66	276	7,308
	Francesco Laporta	68	70	69	69	276	7,308
	Niklas Lemke	66	71	73	66	276	7,308
	Oscar Lengden	65	71	70	70	276	7,308
	Federico Maccario	70	70	68	68	276	7,308
	Matthieu Pavon	70	65	70	71	276	7,308
	Matthias Schwab	72	68	69	67	276	7,308

	Darius van Driel	71	64	68	73	276	7,308
	Lee Westwood	72	67	69	68	276	7,308
39	Yikeun Chang	70	66	70	71	277	5,576
	Jamie Donaldson	68	69	68	72	277	5,576
	Gonzalo Fdez-Castano	68	69	70	70	277	5,576
	Chris Paisley	69	67	69	72	277	5,576
	Tapio Pulkkanen	67	68	67	75	277	5,576
	Marcel Schneider	69	70	68	70	277	5,576
	Marc Warren	69	68	72	68	277	5,576
46	Toby Tree	68	69	70	71	278	4,725
	Johannes Veerman	70	70	71	67	278	4,725
48	Jorge Campillo	68	71	68	72	279	4,064
	Jens Fahrbring	70	67	68	74	279	4,064
	David Horsey	69	67	74	69	279	4,064
	Scott Jamieson	68	69	71	71	279	4,064
	Matt Wallace	68	68	72	71	279	4,064
53	Robin Roussel	66	68	76	70	280	3,402
	Lars van Meijel	70	69	72	69	280	3,402
55	Maverick Antcliff	70	67	71	73	281	3,024
	Gaganjeet Bhullar	68	69	72	72	281	3,024
	Dave Coupland	69	67	78	67	281	3,024
	Lorenzo Gagli	70	69	72	70	281	3,024
	Nicolai von Dellingshausen	69	68	75	69	281	3,024
60	Eduardo de la Riva	68	72	72	70	282	2,646
	Cormac Sharvin	69	69	69	75	282	2,646
	Daniel Young	68	70	72	72	282	2,646
63	Lorenzo Scalise	67	69	77	70	283	2,410
	Jack Senior	66	72	74	71	283	2,410
65	Renato Paratore	71	69	74	70	284	2,221
	Steven Tiley	68	71	66	79	284	2,221
	Joachim B Hansen	64	69	74			WDN

Aphrodite Hills Cyprus Open

A "one in a million" putt helped Callum Shinkwin win for the first time on the European Tour at the Aphrodite Hills Cyprus Open. The Mediterranean island became the 50th country to stage a tournament on the circuit, with this the first of two events back-to-back at the Aphrodite Hills Resort in Paphos, one of just six courses in the country. The 27-year-old from Watford was simply pleased they had cider available for him to celebrate in style.

Shinkwin was two strokes behind with two holes to play before he birdied the short 17th and then had an eagle at the last. The previous day he had done the same but with a superb second shot to four feet. This time he was in the rough and had to muscle his ball over the water to leave a putt from 54 feet. And in it went. "The thing about holing that putt was there was no chance normally," he said. "It's one in a million that you hole from that distance. My aim was to try and two-putt and I holed it."

A course record of 63, with earlier scores of 67, 66 and 68, gave Shinkwin a 20-under-par total of 264. Finland's Kalle Samooja, also looking for his maiden victory, birdied the final hole for his second 64 of the weekend to tie and force a playoff.

This time Shinkwin found a greenside bunker and came out to eight feet. Samooja, as he had in regulation, ran his long, downhill approach putt five feet past the hole. While Shinkwin stepped in to hole his for a birdie, this time Samooja could not make the one back. "It's been a bit of a shock but it feels great," Shinkwin said after Samooja missed. "It's something I've always wanted to do and now I have."

Another Finn, Sami Valimaki, led by two at the 11th after making six birdies in nine holes but then faded to share sixth place. Jamie Donaldson, the 45-year-old former Ryder Cup player, was looking for his first win in six years having led after 54 holes. He closed with a bogey-free 67 to tie for third place, two shots outside the playoff, with Robert MacIntyre and Garrick Higgo.

Shinkwin won the English Amateur Championship in 2013, beating Matthew Fitzpatrick in the final, but lost a playoff to Rafa Cabrera Bello at the Scottish Open in 2017. He lost his card the following season before getting it back in 2019. Recently, he started working with a new caddie, Sam Robertshawe, who has helped his game on the greens. "He's a great green-reader with his own method," Shinkwin said. "I've trusted him and he's taught me to read greens better."

Aphrodite Hills Resort, Paphos, Cyprus — October 29-November 1
Par 71 (36-35); 6,956 yards — Purse: €1,000,000

1	**Callum Shinkwin**	67	66	68	63	264	€162,563
2	**Kalle Samooja**	70	66	64	64	264	105,188
	Shinkwin won playoff at first extra hole						
3	**Jamie Donaldson**	65	65	69	67	266	49,534
	Garrick Higgo	68	66	67	65	266	49,534
	Robert MacIntyre	68	67	66	65	266	49,534
6	Jason Scrivener	70	66	67	64	267	28,688
	Sami Valimaki	65	67	68	67	267	28,688
	Dale Whitnell	68	68	66	65	267	28,688
9	Adrien Saddier	67	69	66	66	268	21,420
10	Thomas Detry	66	67	67	69	269	18,360
	David Drysdale	65	67	68	69	269	18,360
12	Marcus Armitage	66	64	70	70	270	15,922
	Matthew Jordan	69	67	68	66	270	15,922
14	Aaron Cockerill	69	66	70	66	271	14,057
	Shubhankar Sharma	67	66	69	69	271	14,057
	Jeff Winther	68	68	65	70	271	14,057
17	Wil Besseling	67	67	72	66	272	12,144

	Maximilian Kieffer	69	67	68	68	272	12,144
	Mikko Korhonen	68	70	66	68	272	12,144
	Matthew Southgate	68	69	71	64	272	12,144
21	Dave Coupland	69	68	70	66	273	10,232
	Gregory Havret	69	69	68	67	273	10,232
	Antoine Rozner	71	66	70	66	273	10,232
	Matthias Schwab	67	67	68	71	273	10,232
	Jordan Smith	67	66	68	72	273	10,232
	Julian Suri	70	65	73	65	273	10,232
	Paul Waring	68	69	69	67	273	10,232
28	Sebastian Heisele	68	68	68	70	274	8,367
	Romain Langasque	70	69	67	68	274	8,367
	James Morrison	68	69	66	71	274	8,367
	Thorbjorn Olesen	69	69	65	71	274	8,367
	Robin Sciot-Siegrist	69	67	70	68	274	8,367
	Cormac Sharvin	69	67	72	66	274	8,367
34	Alexander Bjork	69	69	69	68	275	6,639
	Alejandro Canizares	70	66	71	68	275	6,639
	Louis de Jager	68	68	70	69	275	6,639
	Masahiro Kawamura	69	67	73	66	275	6,639
	Ricardo Santos	69	69	71	66	275	6,639
	Johannes Veerman	64	69	70	72	275	6,639
	Mitch Waite	64	70	71	70	275	6,639
41	Maverick Antcliff	69	69	71	67	276	5,164
	Laurie Canter	67	72	72	65	276	5,164
	Lorenzo Gagli	66	69	72	69	276	5,164
	Benjamin Hebert	69	64	75	68	276	5,164
	Calum Hill	69	69	70	68	276	5,164
	Joakim Lagergren	72	67	71	66	276	5,164
	Clement Sordet	66	68	70	72	276	5,164
	Joel Stalter	65	71	68	72	276	5,164
49	Grant Forrest	69	69	71	68	277	4,016
	Richard McEvoy	66	66	77	68	277	4,016
	Matthieu Pavon	71	68	68	70	277	4,016
	Scott Vincent	68	68	70	71	277	4,016
53	Jorge Campillo	69	68	71	70	278	3,270
	Pedro Figueiredo	66	72	70	70	278	3,270
	Joost Luiten	70	68	71	69	278	3,270
	Wilco Nienaber	68	67	79	64	278	3,270
	Alvaro Quiros	68	70	73	67	278	3,270
58	Gonzalo Fdez-Castano	66	70	74	69	279	2,773
	David Horsey	66	69	70	74	279	2,773
	Tapio Pulkkanen	69	70	69	71	279	2,773
	Joel Sjoholm	69	69	71	70	279	2,773
	Andy Sullivan	65	69	69	76	279	2,773
63	Yikeun Chang	73	65	69	73	280	2,438
	Sebastian Soderberg	69	69	71	71	280	2,438
65	Ashun Wu	68	71	72	70	281	2,295
66	Nicolas Colsaerts	69	70	73	71	283	2,152
	Sebastian Garcia Rodriguez	69	68	69	77	283	2,152
68	Carlos Pigem	69	70	74	74	287	1,960
	Haydn Porteous	69	68	74	76	287	1,960

Aphrodite Hills Cyprus Showdown

As any week, you cannot win a tournament on the first day, even as Robert MacIntyre scored a 65 in the second of two weeks at Aphrodite Hills. But by returning the lowest score of the final day, a seven-under-par 64, the 24-year-old Scot was guaranteed his maiden European Tour victory thanks to the unique format of the Cyprus Showdown.

MacIntyre was one of 19 players to qualify for the final day — an 18-hole shootout for the title. After going out in two under, the left-hander from Oban came home in 30 with five birdies, including at the last two holes, to win by one from Japan's Masahiro Kawamura, who played the second nine in 31. Jorge Campillo finished birdie-eagle to take third place on 66, one ahead of Cyprus Open winner Callum Shinkwin, Thomas Detry and Johannes Veerman.

The new format called for the 105-player field to be cut to 32 and ties after 36 holes — exactly 32 players made it on six under — with scores reset for the third round. Then the leading 16 players and ties — 19 made it at three under — contested the final round with scores again reset. However, the leading players from the previous day teed off first so Veerman, who scored 64s on both Friday and Saturday, led the way, recovering from two early bogeys to set the clubhouse target at four under.

Marcus Armitage was on that mark before the threat of lightning briefly interrupted play but took a triple bogey at the 18th after the resumption. MacIntyre returned to hole from 15 feet for a birdie at the 15th as Kawamura birded the 16th from six feet. As the Japanese player birdied the last for his 65, MacIntyre hit his tee shot at the 17th to within two feet before safely finding the 18th green and two-putting from 20 feet for the victory.

"It's unbelievable, it's what I've dreamed of as a wee kid watching Scottish Opens at Loch Lomond," said MacIntyre, who finished runner-up three times in 2019 when he was the rookie of the year. "I've done a lot of work in the last six months, not thinking about winning a golf tournament, just to play my golf. Last year, I was talking and thinking about winning golf tournaments when I was going down the back nine on a Sunday, but this year I've just tried to take my time and let it happen."

MacIntyre admitted he struggled with lockdown in the spring, losing focus after an initial drive to lose weight. "It was in the back of my mind that I'd lost my game a little bit," he said. "I didn't have the motivation for a wee while, I wasn't wanting to play golf and wasn't enjoying it. I finally got the bug back and it's what happens. You start practising more, enjoying it, you could see the smile on my face last week, never mind this week."

Aphrodite Hills Resort, Paphos, Cyprus — October 29-November 1
Par 71 (36-35); 6,956 yards — Purse: €1,000,000

1	**Robert MacIntyre**	65	68	67	64	€200,000
2	**Masahiro Kawamura**	67	67	66	65	110,000
3	**Jorge Campillo**	69	62	68	66	63,000
4	Thomas Detry	66	66	68	67	42,500
	Callum Shinkwin	68	65	66	67	42,500
	Johannes Veerman	67	64	64	67	42,500
7	Gavin Green	70	66	68	68	27,750
	Alexander Levy	67	66	66	68	27,750
9	Steven Brown	68	64	67	69	18,950
	Louis de Jager	68	65	66	69	18,950
	Matthew Jordan	68	68	64	69	18,950
	Niklas Lemke	70	66	66	69	18,950
	Bernd Ritthammer	70	65	65	69	18,950
14	Marcus Armitage	68	68	66	70	16,500
15	James Morrison	68	63	66	71	16,000
16	Richard Bland	69	67	68	72	15,250
	Jonathan Caldwell	72	64	67	72	15,250
18	Sami Valimaki	66	66	67	73	14,500
19	Jamie Donaldson	66	64	65	75	14,250
	MISSED THE 54-HOLE CUT					
20	Nacho Elvira	68	65	69		7,000
	Sebastian Garcia Rodriguez	67	69	69		7,000
	Marcus Kinhult	68	68	69		7,000
	Shubhankar Sharma	67	66	69		7,000
24	David Horsey	67	65	70		7,000
	Romain Langasque	66	66	70		7,000
	Pablo Larrazabal	68	68	70		7,000
	Joost Luiten	67	65	70		7,000
	Antoine Rozner	69	65	70		7,000
	Joel Stalter	71	65	70		7,000
	Ashun Wu	66	69	70		7,000
31	Alexander Bjork	68	66	71		7,000
	Joel Sjoholm	68	68	71		7,000

Golf in Dubai Championship

A late addition to the schedule, the Golf in Dubai Championship on the Fire course at Jumeirah Golf Estates provided the perfect lead in to the DP World Tour Championship on the neighbouring Earth layout the following week. Antoine Rozner had already secured his place in the season's finale but he was glad of making the early trip to Dubai when the 27-year-old rookie claimed his maiden title with a final round of 64 for a two-stroke victory.

Rozner had opened with a 63 but that trailed England Andy Sullivan who had 11 birdies and seven pars in a 61 as the Fire course made its debut on the European Tour. Sullivan, winner of the English Championship, stayed ahead of the field with scores of 66 and 68 but a closing 70 meant a share of second place with Mike Lorenzo-Vera, 65, Francesco Laporta, 66, and Matt Wallace, 68.

Rozner had middle rounds of 69 and 67, posting a final total of 263, 25 under par. He started the final round four behind Sullivan but Rozner followed birdies at the fifth and seventh holes with three more in a row from the ninth. With a fine approach to 10 feet at the 13th, followed by holing the eagle putt, Rozner jumped from one behind Sullivan to one in front.

A bogey at the 15th was regained when the Frenchman got up and down for a three at the short par-four 16th before he two-putted the final green for a seventh birdie of the day. Sullivan, after birdieing the 13th, needed to pick up a shot at the 16th but his drive leaked short right of the green and he ended up with a bogey.

After near-misses in Mauritius at the end of 2019 and at Valderrama in September, Rozner was delighted. "I've been close twice, I couldn't close it out, so I'm just very happy with how I played this week and especially today," he said.

"To get it done in this fashion was a big deal for me. To be honest I had no idea what was going on. I only knew I was the leader when I was on the 18th green. I think that actually helped me a little bit. I knew the game was there. I didn't know it was that good but I'm excited."

Jumeirah Golf Estates (Fire), Dubai, United Arab Emirates — December 2-5
Par 72 (36-36); 7,480 yards — Purse: €1,200,000

1	**Antoine Rozner**	63	69	67	64	263	€160,343
2	**Francesco Laporta**	65	69	65	66	265	62,581
	Mike Lorenzo-Vera	69	66	65	65	265	62,581
	Andy Sullivan	61	66	68	70	265	62,581
	Matt Wallace	63	67	67	68	265	62,581
6	Grant Forrest	66	68	70	63	267	33,012
7	Ross Fisher	63	67	68	70	268	28,296
8	Steven Brown	70	63	69	67	269	19,430
	Joakim Lagergren	67	68	67	67	269	19,430
	Niklas Lemke	66	68	66	69	269	19,430
	Marc Warren	64	70	68	67	269	19,430
	Bernd Wiesberger	70	66	66	67	269	19,430
13	Thorbjorn Olesen	69	64	69	68	270	13,903
	Renato Paratore	68	65	65	72	270	13,903

	Max Schmitt	68	64	68	70	270	13,903
	Clement Sordet	68	70	66	66	270	13,903
	Sami Valimaki	70	68	65	67	270	13,903
18	Rikard Karlberg	65	69	71	66	271	12,167
19	Robert MacIntyre	66	68	66	72	272	11,318
	James Morrison	67	72	67	66	272	11,318
	Sebastian Soderberg	67	69	68	68	272	11,318
22	Sean Crocker	68	66	68	71	273	10,375
	David Horsey	71	67	68	67	273	10,375
	Lorenzo Scalise	65	68	71	69	273	10,375
25	Craig Howie	64	68	70	72	274	9,243
	Thomas Pieters	67	68	68	71	274	9,243
	Bernd Ritthammer	68	67	70	69	274	9,243
	Jordan Smith	69	68	68	69	274	9,243
	Paul Waring	68	68	72	66	274	9,243
30	Matthew Baldwin	71	70	67	67	275	7,546
	Stephen Gallacher	69	69	66	71	275	7,546
	Niall Kearney	71	67	66	71	275	7,546
	Mikko Korhonen	66	69	71	69	275	7,546
	Oscar Lengden	64	69	67	75	275	7,546
	Callum Shinkwin	68	68	71	68	275	7,546
	Danny Willett	67	67	73	68	275	7,546
37	Pep Angles	65	73	71	67	276	5,848
	John Axelsen	66	67	71	72	276	5,848
	Nicolas Colsaerts	72	67	71	66	276	5,848
	Thomas Detry	68	72	66	70	276	5,848
	Jazz Janewattananond	66	70	72	68	276	5,848
	Matthew Jordan	73	68	69	66	276	5,848
	Martin Kaymer	66	71	69	70	276	5,848
	Adrian Otaegui	68	68	69	71	276	5,848
45	Marcus Armitage	68	69	71	69	277	4,622
	Sam Horsfield	68	70	70	69	277	4,622
	Alexander Knappe	70	68	68	71	277	4,622
	Robert Rock	70	70	68	69	277	4,622
	Nicolai von Dellingshausen	70	67	73	67	277	4,622
50	Eddie Pepperell	69	69	71	69	278	3,961
	Aaron Rai	70	69	67	72	278	3,961
52	Hurly Long	70	68	69	72	279	3,419
	Damien Perrier	67	69	72	71	279	3,419
	Robin Sciot-Siegrist	69	72	69	69	279	3,419
	Romain Wattel	71	66	72	70	279	3,419
56	Wil Besseling	73	65	71	71	280	3,065
	Haotong Li	67	72	68	73	280	3,065
58	MJ Keyser	70	69	73	69	281	2,782
	Tapio Pulkkanen	67	69	73	72	281	2,782
	Jack Senior	68	69	72	72	281	2,782
	Euan Walker	71	70	70	70	281	2,782
62	Emilio Cuartero Blanco	69	68	73	72	282	2,405
	Jens Fahrbring	68	70	71	73	282	2,405
	Marcus Kinhult	69	72	71	70	282	2,405
	Andrew Wilson	74	67	70	71	282	2,405
66	Jorge Campillo	66	71	70	76	283	2,169
67	Ewen Ferguson	72	69	73	71	285	2,075
68	Joel Stalter	70	68	70	79	287	1,886
	Steven Tiley	69	71	70	77	287	1,886
	Jordan Wrisdale	72	67	74	74	287	1,886
71	Pedro Oriol	73	68	76	71	288	1,485
72	Ben Evans	71	66	77	76	290	1,482

DP World Tour Championship

Even when he won again, Matthew Fitzpatrick finished as a runner-up as well. When the 26-year-old from Sheffield defended his title at the European Masters in 2018, he had won five times in three years. Since then he had been a runner-up five times on the European Tour and once on the PGA Tour. Breaking that run of near-misses was his prime objective at the DP World Tour Championship and in succeeding in that endeavour he finished second on the Race to Dubai to Lee Westwood, who secured his third order of merit title with an outright second place on the Earth course at Jumeirah Golf Estates.

Winning the tournament, though not without late tension, turned out to be straightforward compared to the destination of the European number one title. Fitzpatrick broke out of a three-way tie for the 54-hole lead with Patrick Reed and Laurie Canter by birdieing the first four holes and then the seventh. Then the former US Amateur champion just had to hang on.

Fitzpatrick started the week 16th on the Race to Dubai and at times was in position to top the list but that plot had several twists to come. Reed entered the final tournament on top of the points list and scored a 64 in the second round to lead by two from Fitzpatrick. But the man hoping to be the first American to be the European number one struggled off the tee over the weekend.

A dazzling short game helped him retain a share of the lead with a 71 on Saturday but a 70 on Sunday left him tied for third with Viktor Hovland. Reed chipped in three times, including at the 15th where he was still in position to be the number one until bogeys at the next two holes. He also chipped in for a birdie at the last but to no avail. Hovland, a week after winning in Mexico, missed a birdie chance at the last which later proved important for Westwood.

The 47-year-old Englishman looked out of contention when he found the water at the 14th for a bogey six and then missed a good chance at the next. But he dug deep to birdie the 16th and the 18th, where he got up and down from a bunker, to get to 14 under par after a 68.

Westwood was only tied for second at that point and Fitzpatrick was on course to do the double until the 17th hole. His only bogey of the day meant he led by one one going to the last but the crucial intervention was Canter's double bogey. Canter fell out of second place and finished in a tie for fifth with Sami Valimaki after a 71. Westwood won the Harry Vardon Trophy by less than 18 points.

"I needed a really big finish," said Westwood, who due to a back injury would not have played had it not been the season-ending event. "But there are so many permutations that can happen on a day like today. It can all get too confusing if you let it. The most satisfying thing is doing it under pressure when it matters." His third order of merit title came 20 years after his first.

Fitzpatrick still needed to par the 18th to secure a one-stroke victory with a 15-under-par total of 273 following scores of 68, 68, 69 and 68. "It was a dream start," he said of those five birdies in the first seven holes. "I managed to pull away and create some distance between me and the rest. The back nine was bit of a grind, if I'm honest. It was just about finishing one hole at a time and just getting through it. But all I was bothered about this week was winning. I turned up here 16th in Race to Dubai so that didn't really enter my head. I just wanted to win this week."

Having also won in 2016, Fitzpatrick joined Henrik Stenson, Rory McIlroy and Jon Rahm as a double winner at the tournament that now boasts a $3 million first prize. "It's one of those few weeks in your career where you're like, it feels really good and I'm playing really well, and you go and win. You can play poorly and win and sometimes you can play amazing and lose. To me this is a week I felt I'm playing really well and I managed to convert it."

Jumeirah Golf Estates (Earth), Dubai, United Arab Emirates — December 10-13
Par 72 (36-36); 7,675 yards — Purse: $8,000,000

1	**Matthew Fitzpatrick**	68	68	69	68	273	€2,481,627
2	**Lee Westwood**	70	68	68	68	274	703,128
3	**Viktor Hovland**	71	69	66	69	275	357,768
	Patrick Reed	70	64	71	70	275	357,768
5	Laurie Canter	71	66	68	71	276	191,085
	Sami Valimaki	69	69	69	69	276	191,085
7	Victor Perez	67	74	69	68	278	144,762
8	Branden Grace	72	66	72	69	279	113,741
	Tyrrell Hatton	69	68	72	70	279	113,741
10	Adri Arnaus	71	68	67	75	281	80,653
	Tommy Fleetwood	69	69	74	69	281	80,653
	Collin Morikawa	72	70	69	70	281	80,653
	Andy Sullivan	71	71	67	72	281	80,653
14	Christiaan Bezuidenhout	71	71	70	70	282	57,123
	Dean Burmester	76	67	72	67	282	57,123
	Sean Crocker	70	76	67	69	282	57,123
	Garrick Higgo	70	77	66	69	282	57,123
	Sungjae Im	75	70	68	69	282	57,123
	Masahiro Kawamura	72	73	70	67	282	57,123
	Martin Kaymer	69	70	71	72	282	57,123
	Adrian Otaegui	75	66	73	68	282	57,123
	Erik van Rooyen	68	73	70	71	282	57,123
23	Tom Lewis	78	68	71	66	283	44,462
	Robert MacIntyre	68	72	66	77	283	44,462
	Wilco Nienaber	79	70	67	67	283	44,462
	Shaun Norris	72	69	71	71	283	44,462
	Kalle Samooja	74	68	71	70	283	44,462
	Brandon Stone	73	71	67	72	283	44,462
29	George Coetzee	71	72	70	71	284	38,879
	Thomas Detry	74	73	69	68	284	38,879
	Matt Wallace	72	71	70	71	284	38,879
32	Marcus Kinhult	76	69	68	72	285	34,536
	Robert Rock	73	73	72	67	285	34,536
	Marc Warren	72	72	68	73	285	34,536
	Danny Willett	72	67	69	77	285	34,536
36	Jamie Donaldson	70	75	69	72	286	28,598
	Thomas Pieters	71	70	75	70	286	28,598
	Antoine Rozner	75	73	70	68	286	28,598
	Callum Shinkwin	70	71	71	74	286	28,598
	Henrik Stenson	70	71	72	73	286	28,598
	Connor Syme	73	73	72	68	286	28,598
	Bernd Wiesberger	76	71	69	70	286	28,598
43	Wil Besseling	72	73	69	73	287	23,989
	Joachim B Hansen	74	72	71	70	287	23,989
	Joost Luiten	71	73	71	72	287	23,989
	Ian Poulter	74	68	71	74	287	23,989
47	Jordan Smith	74	72	71	71	288	21,921
48	Justin Harding	77	69	68	75	289	20,267
	Scott Jamieson	74	70	74	71	289	20,267
	Pablo Larrazabal	73	74	70	72	289	20,267
51	Ross Fisher	73	75	70	72	290	17,785
	Rasmus Hojgaard	76	68	78	68	290	17,785
	Aaron Rai	72	76	73	69	290	17,785
54	John Catlin	75	74	69	73	291	15,441
	Matthieu Pavon	74	76	69	72	291	15,441
	Eddie Pepperell	78	73	69	71	291	15,441
57	Jorge Campillo	72	74	72	74	292	14,063
	Gavin Green	70	78	74	70	292	14,063
	Jazz Janewattananond	70	73	73	76	292	14,063
60	Renato Paratore	75	73	70	75	293	13,235
61	Marcus Armitage	73	74	76	71	294	12,615
	Benjamin Hebert	75	77	70	72	294	12,615
63	Sam Horsfield	77	74	73	72	296	11,995
64	Grant Forrest	75	74	75	75	299	11,581
	Graeme McDowell	73					WDN

2019-20 RACE TO DUBAI

1	Lee Westwood	3,128.0 Pts
2	Matthew Fitzpatrick	3,110.2 Pts
3	Patrick Reed	3,103.7 Pts
4	Tommy Fleetwood	2,182.6 Pts
5	Collin Morikawa	2,096.6 Pts
6	Victor Perez	2,072.9 Pts
7	Christiaan Bezuidenhout	1,874.8 Pts
8	Aaron Rai	1,741.0 Pts
9	Tyrrell Hatton	1,736.5 Pts
10	Louis Oosthuizen	1,646.2 Pts

Challenge Tour

At the end of a necessarily truncated season, Ondrej Lieser finished strongly by winning two tournaments in a row to become the first player from the Czech Republic to be crowned as the Challenge Tour number one. The 29-year-old from Prague won his first title at the Andalucia Challenge de Espana and came to the Grand Final lying sixth on the Road to Majorca Rankings.

Instead of the leading 15 players being granted exemptions for the European Tour as usual, revised conditions meant the top five would be awarded guaranteed starts in certain events on the main circuit in 2021. Lieser needed to move up at least one position on the standings but managed to go all the way to the top of the list with a one-stroke victory at T-Golf and Country Club.

Lieser got himself into contention by posting the only bogey-free round of a windy third day, a 66 leaving him two behind Germany's Alexander Knappe. It was tight on the final day with five players sharing the lead around the turn. Lieser made a brave par-save at the 17th and then got up and down from a bunker at the par-five 18th, holing from six feet, for the winning birdie after a 68 left him on an 11-under-par total of 273. Knappe missed from a similar distance on the final green to force a playoff and so shared runner-up honours with Sweden's Christofer Blomstrand and Spain's Santiago Tarrio.

"It's really emotional for me," Lieser said. "The two putts I holed on 17 and 18 were unbelievable. In those circumstances, with that amount of pressure, I don't even know how I did it."

After seeing other players come off the Pro Golf Tour and achieve at higher levels, Lieser posted his first top 10 on the Challenge Tour in Italy and then won in Cadiz. After making his first bit of history by becoming the first player from his country to win on the circuit, Lieser decided to skip the second tournament at Novo Sancti Petri to spend a week at home in Prague with his wife Michaela and 18-month-old daughter.

"I spoke with my wife already, I was crying at the time," Lieser added after his double triumph in Mallorca. "Four years ago, when I met my wife, my life just turned around. I was close to stopping playing, I wasn't going to play anymore. It's not even my win, it's mostly her win. She gives me the strength, especially mentally, to hold it together.

"When I chose not to play the second event in Cadiz, I was getting messages asking why I wasn't playing. I just said I needed to relax my head a little bit because the Grand Final is the most important thing. I went back home, spent time with the family, flew out here and look where I'm standing now."

Before the disruption to the schedule, the 2020 Challenge Tour started with three events co-sanctioned with the Sunshine Tour. Local favourites JC Ritchie and Christiaan Bezuidenhout claimed two of the titles but the Cape Town Open went to Sweden's Anton Karlsson. After the resumption of the tour, the first two events were co-sanctioned with the main European Tour, seeing victories for Marc Warren at the Austrian Open and Joel Stalter at the Euran Bank Open. In another co-sanctioned event, South Africa's Garrick Higgo won the Open de Portugal.

There was a surprise winner of the Northern Ireland Open, put on with the support of The R&A, when American Tyler Koivisto claimed the title by two strokes. It was the 27-year-old's first appearance on the Challenge Tour, or any OWGR sanctioned event. He had previously played in various mini tours in the States as well as spending three years as a school teacher.

Germany's Hurly Long won the Italian Challenge Open at Castelconturbia in a playoff against countryman Marcel Schneider and England's Matt Ford. Schneider went on to secure second place on the Road to Mallorca and Ford fifth, just pipping Blomstrand by less than 300 points.

Pep Angles was third on the Rankings after the 27-year-old Spaniard won the second of the two successive weeks at Novo Sancti Petri, the Andalucia Challenge de Cadiz. "I've been down the valley of darkness and I came up a little bit, so I'm very happy," Angles said. "What you guys see on the golf course is just the tip of the iceberg. I've been working on different aspects; mind, soul and body to get here and have the calmness inside of me and be able to perform when I need to."

Richard Mansell, runner-up to Lieser in the first event in Cadiz, had to miss the second after he tested positive for Covid. After isolating for 10 days in his hotel room, he arrived on the eve of the Grand Final and still managed to hang on to fourth spot on the points list.

On the tier below the Challenge Tour, there was a notable winner on the Alps Tour, with four-time European Tour winner Matteo Manassero emerging from a devastating loss of form to birdie the final hole for victory at the Toscano Open. His previous win had come at the BMW PGA Championship in 2013.

2020 SCHEDULE

Limpopo Championship	**JC Ritchie**	*See chapter 14*
RAM Cape Town Open	**Anton Karlsson**	*See chapter 14*
Dimension Data Pro-Am	**Christiaan Bezuidenhout**	*See chapter 14*
Austrian Open	**Marc Warren**	*See chapter 12*
Euram Bank Open	**Joel Stalter**	*See chapter 12*
Northern Ireland Open	**Tyler Koivisto**	
Open de Portugal	**Garrick Higgo**	*See chapter 12*
Italian Challenge Open Eneos Motor Oil	**Hurly Long**	
Andalucia Challenge de Espana	**Ondrej Lieser**	
Andalucia Challenge de Cadiz	**Pep Angles**	
Challenge Tour Grand Final	**Ondrej Lieser**	

Northern Ireland Open

Galgorm Spa & Golf Resort, Ballymena, Northern Ireland — September 3-6
Par: 70 (34-36); 6,993 yards — Purse €200,000

1	**Tyler Koivisto**	67	71	62	67	267	€32,000
2	**Kristian Krogh Johannessen**	69	69	66	65	269	22,000
3	**Jens Fahrbring**	71	68	66	65	270	13,000
	Andrew Wilson	71	68	64	67	270	13,000
5	Bjorn Hellgren	68	69	68	66	271	9,000
	Gudmundur Kristjansson	68	67	69	67	271	9,000
7	Garrick Higgo	72	68	67	65	272	6,000
	Santiago Tarrio	69	68	66	69	272	6,000
9	Enrico Di Nitto	68	66	71	68	273	4,600
	Christopher Mivis	69	67	68	69	273	4,600
11	Will Enefer	71	68	69	66	274	3,900
	Benjamin Rusch	71	67	66	70	274	3,900
13	Robert Dinwiddie	69	66	70	70	275	3,100
	Ryan Evans	71	65	71	68	275	3,100
	Scott Fernandez	73	67	69	66	275	3,100
	Scott Gregory	74	68	68	65	275	3,100
	Martin Ovesen	68	68	69	70	275	3,100
	Daniel Young	68	71	69	67	275	3,100
19	JJR Galbraith	70	70	66	70	276	2,300
	Alexander Knappe	71	70	65	70	276	2,300
21	Jens Dantorp	72	69	68	68	277	2,030
	Alfie Plant	67	69	71	70	277	2,030
23	David Borda	71	72	66	69	278	1,800
	Niall Kearney	71	70	68	69	278	1,800
	Per Langfors	70	72	68	68	278	1,800
	Stuart Manley	69	70	69	70	278	1,800
	Richard Mansell	75	63	67	73	278	1,800
	Chris Robb	71	68	70	69	278	1,800
	Mitch Waite	73	69	68	68	278	1,800

Italian Challenge Open Eneos Motor Oil

Golf Club Castelconturbia, Agrate Conturbia, Italy — October 1-4
Par: 72 (36-36); 6,814 yards — Purse: €300,000

1	**Hurly Long**	67	66	70	203	€48,000
2	**Matt Ford**	66	69	68	203	27,000
	Marcel Schneider	67	69	67	203	27,000
	Long won playoff at second extra hole					
4	Matthew Baldwin	66	69	69	204	13,650
	Kristian Krogh Johannessen	68	73	63	204	13,650
	Ondrej Lieser	65	71	68	204	13,650
	Alfie Plant	68	65	71	204	13,650
8	Christofer Blomstrand	71	68	66	205	6,550
	Todd Clements	64	67	74	205	6,550
	Mario Galiano Aguilar	70	70	65	205	6,550
	Ricardo Gouveia	67	72	66	205	6,550
	Scott Gregory	67	70	68	205	6,550
	Benjamin Rusch	70	71	64	205	6,550
14	Bjorn Hellgren	68	69	69	206	4,500
	Stuart Manley	67	71	68	206	4,500
	Richard Mansell	72	69	65	206	4,500
	Lukas Nemecz	69	69	68	206	4,500
	Santiago Tarrio	71	67	68	206	4,500
19	Jens Dantorp	67	72	68	207	3,115
	Manuel Elvira	70	68	69	207	3,115
	Jens Fahrbring	67	71	69	207	3,115
	Nicolai Kristensen	68	71	68	207	3,115
	Robin Petersson	69	69	69	207	3,115
	Christopher Sahlstrom	73	68	66	207	3,115
25	Craig Howie	67	70	71	208	2,640
	Espen Kofstad	72	69	67	208	2,640
	Frederic Lacroix	66	71	71	208	2,640
	Matteo Manassero	66	69	73	208	2,640
	Pedro Oriol	73	66	69	208	2,640

Andalucia Challenge de Espana

Iberostar Real Club de Golf Novo Sancti Petri, Cadiz, Spain — November 5-8
Par: 72 (36-36); 7,064 yards — Purse: €200,000

1	**Ondrej Lieser**	74	70	67	67	278	€32,000
2	**Richard Mansell**	74	67	70	69	280	22,000
3	**Matt Ford**	72	72	69	68	281	13,000
	Pedro Oriol	71	71	68	71	281	13,000
5	Oliver Lindell	68	73	71	70	282	8,133
	Eduard Rousaud (A)	76	72	68	66	282	
	Martin Simonsen	66	69	76	71	282	8,133
	Henric Sturehed	72	69	73	68	282	8,133
9	Christofer Blomstrand	70	69	73	71	283	5,200
	Julien Brun	70	73	72	68	283	5,200
11	Emilio Cuartero Blanco	72	69	72	71	284	3,733
	Jens Dantorp	74	71	69	70	284	3,733
	Philip Eriksson	72	74	68	70	284	3,733
	Bjorn Hellgren	71	77	66	70	284	3,733
	Lukas Nemecz	76	69	70	69	284	3,733
	Nicolai von Dellingshausen	76	70	68	70	284	3,733
17	Scott Fernandez	71	72	69	73	285	2,600
	Angel Hidalgo	75	73	70	67	285	2,600
	Alexander Knappe	73	74	69	69	285	2,600
	Oscar Lengden	70	71	69	75	285	2,600
	Marcel Schneider	78	70	68	69	285	2,600
22	Mario Galiano Aguilar	72	72	71	71	286	1,965
	Ricardo Gouveia	72	74	70	70	286	1,965
	Niall Kearney	72	75	67	72	286	1,965
	Christopher Mivis	69	73	71	73	286	1,965

Andalucia Challenge de Cadiz

Iberostar Real Club de Golf Novo Sancti Petri, Cadiz, Spain — November 11-14
Par: 72 (36-36); 7,064 yards — Purse: €200,000

1	**Pep Angles**	72	67	66	69	274	€32,000
2	**Matthew Baldwin**	72	66	69	68	275	18,000
	Alfredo Garcia-Heredia	69	71	64	71	275	18,000
4	Eduard Rousaud (A)	70	74	66	69	279	
5	Kristian Krogh Johannessen	72	69	72	68	281	10,000
	Allen John	69	71	73	68	281	10,000
	Marcel Schneider	73	66	72	70	281	10,000
8	Hurly Long	71	72	71	68	282	6,400
9	John Axelsen	73	69	73	68	283	4,700
	Christofer Blomstrand	71	70	67	75	283	4,700
	Lukas Nemecz	71	74	68	70	283	4,700
	Santiago Tarrio	70	71	71	71	283	4,700
13	Aron Zemmer	72	71	72	69	284	3,800
14	Emilio Cuartero Blanco	73	70	73	69	285	3,000
	Jens Dantorp	73	70	69	73	285	3,000
	Scott Gregory	71	69	74	71	285	3,000
	Janne Kaske	73	68	73	71	285	3,000
	Niall Kearney	66	71	76	72	285	3,000
	Haraldur Magnus	74	70	70	71	285	3,000
	Niklas Norgaard Moller	70	73	74	68	285	3,000
21	David Boote	71	71	73	71	286	2,012
	Alejandro Del Rey	76	71	67	72	286	2,012
	Ricardo Gouveia	72	70	71	73	286	2,012
	Alexander Knappe	77	69	71	69	286	2,012
	Tyler Koivisto	75	71	69	71	286	2,012

Challenge Tour Grand Final

T-Golf & Country Club, Mallorca, Baleares, Spain — November 19-22
Par: 71 (35-36); 7,053 yards — Purse €350,000

1	**Ondrej Lieser**	70	69	66	68	273	€62,000
2	**Christofer Blomstrand**	68	68	69	69	274	27,333
	Alexander Knappe	68	63	72	71	274	27,333
	Santiago Tarrio	66	70	71	67	274	27,333
5	David Boote	69	68	70	68	275	14,000
	Niklas Norgaard Moller	67	68	69	71	275	14,000
	Robin Petersson	73	66	66	70	275	14,000
8	Kristian Krogh Johannessen	71	65	70	70	276	11,900
9	Enrico Di Nitto	67	68	74	68	277	11,100
10	Harry Ellis	72	67	68	71	278	9,900
	Oscar Lengden	71	66	74	67	278	9,900
12	Julien Brun	73	69	70	67	279	8,300
	Henric Sturehed	72	71	70	66	279	8,300
14	Matt Ford	68	67	73	72	280	6,700
	Bjorn Hellgren	66	67	74	73	280	6,700
16	Alfredo Garcia-Heredia	69	69	71	72	281	4,590
	Craig Howie	70	71	68	72	281	4,590
	Gudmundur Kristjansson	72	68	70	71	281	4,590
	Andrew Wilson	69	73	70	69	281	4,590
	Aron Zemmer	69	69	70	73	281	4,590
21	Matthew Baldwin	67	72	71	72	282	3,412
	Jens Dantorp	69	70	69	74	282	3,412
	Hurly Long	71	71	70	70	282	3,412
	Richard Mansell	66	67	77	72	282	3,412
	Carlos Pigem	70	70	71	71	282	3,412
	Marcel Schneider	70	70	72	70	282	3,412
	Martin Simonsen	70	72	72	68	282	3,412
	Nicolai von Dellingshausen	69	72	73	68	282	3,412

2020 ROAD TO MALLORCA RANKINGS

1	Ondrej Lieser	116,344.6	Pts
2	Marcel Schneider	98,500.3	Pts
3	Pep Angles	92,688.2	Pts
4	Richard Mansell	84,534.2	Pts
5	Matt Ford	69,947.9	Pts
6	Christofer Blomstrand	69,648.8	Pts
7	Santiago Tarrio	65,687.8	Pts
8	Hurly Long	65,241.3	Pts
9	Alexander Knappe	63,811.3	Pts
10	Kristian Krogh Johannessen	59,902.6	Pts

African Sunshine Tour

When it comes to Christiaan Bezuidenhout letting his golf do the talking there is no stutter that can disrupt the eloquence of his game. That became obvious in 2020 when the 26-year-old from Delmas won three times on the Sunshine Tour, capping the year with back-to-back victories at the Alfred Dunhill Championship and the SA Open. By margins of four and five strokes respectively. "To stand here as the SA Open champion is unbelievable," he said. "This is massive for me. It's always been a dream and I wasn't sure when, or if, I would achieve it."

As many now know, aged two Bezuidenhout picked up a can of coke and took a sip without realising it in fact contained rat poison. He almost died and the trauma left a permanent mark on his nervous system. As he grew and started school, a stutter developed. At one point he was prescribed beta blockers but later discovered the medication was banned in sporting circles — something he found out the hard way when he failed a drugs test at the 2014 British Amateur Championship. On appeal, his ban was reduced from two years to nine months.

Someone who had survived all that, had admitted the stutter led to self-doubt in his golf and decided "to accept the fact this is who I am and it's not going to change", was perhaps well suited to coping with the disruption caused by a global pandemic. His season started well. He lost in a playoff at the Dubai Desert Classic but then eagled the last to win the Dimension Data Pro-Am and climb into the world's top 50 for the first time. He was two strokes off the lead at the Players Championship when the season ground to a halt.

Back home he hit balls into a net, not being allowed to play the course he lived on. He set a plan to get into the world's top 30 in 2021. He ended 2020 only just shy of that mark having risen over 50 spots during the year. He only just missed out on his tour card on the PGA Tour but after making his debut at the rescheduled Masters he ended the year in breathtaking fashion. His three European Tour titles have come at impressive venues, Valderrama in 2019 and now Leopard Creek and the Gary Player Country Club at Sun City.

Only Louis Oosthuizen stood higher than Bezuidenhout among South African players on the world rankings. Although without a win in 2020, Oosthuizen finished third at the US Open at Winged Foot, having been runner-up on the defence of his title at the first of two SA Opens that book-ended the year. Branden Grace won at Randpark, immediately achieving his goal of jumping back into the world's top 100. But a horror run in the middle of the year when he missed 12 cuts, and had to withdraw from the Barracuda Championship when in contention due to a positive Covid test, meant he slipped back to where he started the year in rankings terms. His second best result of the year came in his last tournament, a top-10 finish at the DP World Tour Championship.

Dylan Frittelli finished in a tie for fifth place at the Masters, while Garrick Higgo followed his win at the Sunshine Tour Championship, where he was confirmed as the 2019-20 rookie of the year, with a first victory on the European Tour at the Open de Portugal. The Portugal Masters was also kind to a South African visitor with George Coetzee adding to his almost regulation victory at Pretoria Country Club for the Titleist Championship.

JC Ritchie won the Limpopo Championship, the first of three events co-sanctioned with the Challenge Tour early in the year, and claimed the 2019-20 order of merit title. The delayed 2020-21 season finally began with the Rise-Up Series, five new events created in Gauteng. Darren Fichardt won the first, adding to his Eye of Africa PGA title earlier in the year, but the star of the resumption was Daniel van Tonder who won four times in six starts.

He had used lockdown well to slim down on a new diet and work hard on his game. With his wife Abigail keeping him calm as his caddie, van Tonder stuck to his aggressive instincts. Across the two seasons, he had a run of 10 top-10 finishes in a row. His only disappointment was missing the cut at both SA Opens.

Wilco Nienaber, the 2019 SA Amateur champion, turned heads on social media when the 20-year-old professional hit a drive of 439 yards at Randpark during the Joburg Open. He went on to finish runner-up, as he had at the Limpopo Championship, while there were two other top-10 finishes on the European Tour, including at the Andalucia Masters at Valderrama.

2020 SCHEDULE	
SA Open Championship	**Branden Grace**
Eye of Africa PGA Championship	**Darren Fichardt**
Gauteng Team Championship	**Jaco Prinsloo/JC Ritchie**
Limpopo Championship	**JC Ritchie**
RAM Cape Town Open	**Anton Karlsson**
Dimension Data Pro-Am	**Christiaan Bezuidenhout**
Sunshine Tour Championship	**Garrick Higgo**
Betway Championship	**Darren Fichardt**
African Bank Sunshine Tour Championship	**Daniel van Tonder**
Titleist Championship	**George Coetzee**
Vodacom Championship Unlocked	**Daniel van Tonder**
Vodacom Championship Reloaded	**Daniel van Tonder**
Sun Wild Coast Sun Challenge	**Merrick Bremner**
Investec Royal Swazi Open	**Daniel van Tonder**
Time Square Casino Challenge	**Ruan Korb**
Joburg Open	**Joachim B Hansen**
Alfred Dunhill Championship	**Christiaan Bezuidenhout**
SA Open Championship	**Christiaan Bezuidenhout**

SA Open Championship

Leader Louis Oosthuizen, the defending champion and playing host of the SA Open presented by the City of Johannesburg, parred the first seven holes of his final round before making a hole-in-one with a seven-iron at the eighth. But that was about the only thing he holed all day. Although he made only one bogey all week, there was only one birdie on Sunday as a 68 left him in runner-up position, three behind Branden Grace.

Grace came from three behind overnight with a nine-under-par 62, a familiar number for the 31-year-old after he became the first male player to make the score in a major championship at the 2017 Open. A bogey at the second hole was not the start he was looking for but four birdies going out and an eagle at the fourth took him into the lead. Four more birdies in a row from the 11th sealed the much coveted title. Grace recently started working with Brad Faxon on his putting and, in contrast to his compatriot Oosthuizen, holed almost everything he looked at on the greens. "That was remarkable," he said. "I played flawless golf and I can't remember the last time the putter was that hot."

A sixth Sunshine Tour win and a ninth on the European Tour was just the start to 2020 that Grace needed after a poor 2019 campaign during which he failed to make Ernie Els's International Presidents Cup team and fell out of the top 100 in the world. The win earned Grace an exemption into The Open at Royal St George's, along with England's Marcus Armitage, who birdied the last to finish third, and Jaco Ahlers, who shared fourth place with Jack Senior.

But with his son watching on, and his wife celebrating her birthday, winning in front of his home fans meant much to Grace. The national Open was the only one missing from his set of significant home titles after his victories in the Joburg Open in 2012, the Alfred Dunhill Championship in 2014, the Dimension Data Pro-Am in 2015 and the Nedbank Golf Challenge in 2017.

"This is the one I really wanted," said, Grace, who finished on 21 under par with a total of 263 after scores of 64, 70, 67 and 62. "This means so much to any South African, winning on home soil, the guys get so behind you and it's such an emotional feeling. It's the first win with the little one here so he's going to have a photo with the trophy and then it's a good present to my Mrs today, she's a birthday girl."

Randpark Golf Club (Firethorn), Johannesburg, Gauteng — January 9-12
Par 71 (35-36); 7,506 yards — Purse: R17,500,000
Bushwillow (R1&2 only) par 71 (35-36); 7,115 yards

1	**Branden Grace**	64	70	67	62	263	R2,773,750
2	**Louis Oosthuizen**	65	69	64	68	266	1,925,000
3	**Marcus Armitage**	65	72	62	69	268	1,298,500
4	Jack Senior	67	66	69	67	269	791,000
	Jaco Ahlers	66	66	68	69	269	791,000
6	Hennie du Plessis	67	67	69	68	271	457,450
	George Coetzee	65	69	68	69	271	457,450
	JC Ritchie	63	72	67	69	271	457,450
	Jayden Schaper (A)	65	67	69	70	271	
	Andy Sullivan	66	68	67	70	271	457,450
	Martin Rohwer	66	71	64	70	271	457,450
12	Harry Hall	65	68	71	68	272	309,750
13	Maverick Antcliff	67	67	72	67	273	283,500
	Johannes Veerman	62	71	72	68	273	283,500
15	Gavin Green	68	67	71	68	274	231,250
	Lorenzo Scalise	68	69	69	68	274	231,250
	Tapio Pulkkanen	65	66	72	71	274	231,250
	Keith Horne	69	65	69	71	274	231,250
	Nino Bertasio	63	71	69	71	274	231,250
	Min Woo Lee	66	69	67	72	274	231,250
	Jacques Blaauw	69	65	67	73	274	231,250
22	Jean Hugo	70	68	70	67	275	186,375
	Erik van Rooyen	70	68	70	67	275	186,375
	Garth Mulroy	71	65	71	68	275	186,375
	Trevor Fisher Jr	65	67	73	70	275	186,375
	Richard Bland	70	67	67	71	275	186,375
	Connor Syme	66	68	69	72	275	186,375
28	Jaco Van Zyl	70	68	73	65	276	151,813
	Thomas Detry	68	68	74	66	276	151,813
	Clement Sordet	71	67	69	69	276	151,813
	Oliver Farr	68	68	69	71	276	151,813
	Luke Jerling	67	70	68	71	276	151,813
	CJ du Plessis	66	69	69	72	276	151,813
	Juran Dreyer	69	68	67	72	276	151,813
	Peter Karmis	64	70	69	73	276	151,813
36	Casey Jarvis (A)	68	70	72	67	277	
	Rhys Enoch	69	67	73	68	277	122,500
	Hennie Otto	66	71	72	68	277	122,500
	Jeff Winther	65	71	72	69	277	122,500
	Shaun Norris	68	69	70	70	277	122,500
	Mark Williams	67	67	71	72	277	122,500
	Matthew Baldwin	65	70	70	72	277	122,500
	Steve Surry	69	67	68	73	277	122,500
	Thriston Lawrence	67	65	70	75	277	122,500
45	Joachim B Hansen	70	68	71	69	278	101,500
	Dave Coupland	71	67	71	69	278	101,500
	Haydn Porteous	70	66	72	70	278	101,500
	Marc Warren	70	68	65	75	278	101,500
49	Julien Guerrier	68	68	72	71	279	91,000
	Marcel Siem	66	69	72	72	279	91,000
51	Philip Geerts	66	70	75	69	280	77,000
	Gregory Bourdy	70	67	71	72	280	77,000
	Antoine Rozner	66	71	71	72	280	77,000
	Sami Valimaki	67	70	71	72	280	77,000
	James Hart du Preez	71	65	71	73	280	77,000
	Chase Hanna	70	68	69	73	280	77,000
57	Deon Germishuys	70	68	71	72	281	58,800
	Chris Paisley	68	68	72	73	281	58,800
	Rikard Karlberg	70	67	71	73	281	58,800
	Gavin Moynihan	68	69	71	73	281	58,800
	Jonathan Caldwell	70	68	70	73	281	58,800
62	Sam Horsfield	64	68	75	75	282	51,625
	Jarryd Felton	67	71	68	76	282	51,625
64	Matias Calderon	64	72	72	75	283	48,125
	Hurly Long	70	66	70	77	283	48,125
66	Jacques Kruyswijk	66	72	74	72	284	43,750
	Wynand Dingle	68	67	74	75	284	43,750
	Brett Rumford	69	67	70	78	284	43,750
69	Estiaan Conradie	72	66	75	72	285	39,375
	David Micheluzzi	65	72	71	77	285	39,375
71	Rourke van der Spuy	64	74	73	75	286	35,875
	Philip Eriksson	70	68	72	76	286	35,875
73	Ruan de Smidt	66	72	74	75	287	27,975
	Ross Mcgowan	69	68	72	78	287	27,975
75	Daniel Greene	67	66	78	78	289	27,900
76	Christo Lamprecht (A)	70	68	77	77	292	

Eye of Africa PGA Championship

More than a 17th Sunshine Tour title, Darren Fichardt claimed a longed for victory when he won the Eye of Africa PGA Championship. After having to go back to the Qualifying School to regain his European Tour card late in 2019, the 44-year-old South African added his name to the greats listed on the PGA trophy. "I have always wanted to win the PGA Championship of South Africa, and the way I won it was very special. To win in a playoff, when you grind it out for 75 holes, is always awesome," Fichardt said.

Fichardt beat Chile's Matias Calderon at the third extra hole after the pair tied on a 20-under-par total of 268. Fichardt, the joint leader overnight with Jacques Kruyswijk, added a 68 to earlier scores of 65, 70 and 65 to get into the playoff with Calderon, who started four strokes behind but set the clubhouse target with a 64 in which he did not drop a stroke on the Eye of Africa Signature Estate course. Kruyswijk finished one shot behind after a 69, with Thriston Lawrence in fourth place, two shots further back after a 70.

Both Fichardt and Calderon parred the 18th hole on the first two playoff holes but at the third time of asking Calderon made a bogey while Fichardt hit a five-iron to eight feet and holed the putt for a birdie three.

"I had a tough year last year and decided not to touch a club for a few weeks," Fichardt said. "I came out at the South African Open and was a bit rusty, and missed the cut by one. I was thinking, I hope it's not going to be one of those years again. So to win the week after is awesome."

Eye of Africa Signature Golf Estate, Johannesburg, Gauteng — January 16-19
Par: 72 (36-36); 7,210 yards — Purse: R2,000,000

1	**Darren Fichardt**	65	70	65	68	268	R317,000
2	**Matias Calderon**	70	67	67	64	268	221,000
	Fichardt won playoff at third extra hole						
3	**Jacques Kruyswijk**	67	69	64	69	269	139,800
4	Thriston Lawrence	66	66	69	70	271	84,000
5	Daniel van Tonder	67	69	66	70	272	60,000
6	Jaco Ahlers	71	69	64	69	273	55,000
7	MJ Viljoen	70	68	68	68	274	47,500
	JC Ritchie	70	68	68	68	274	47,500
9	Philip Eriksson	66	70	69	70	275	37,500
	Louis de Jager	69	67	68	71	275	37,500
11	Steve Surry	71	70	67	68	276	30,200
12	Toby Tree	70	68	70	69	277	27,800
	Trevor Fisher Jr	67	70	69	71	277	27,800
	Ulrich van den Berg	69	69	68	71	277	27,800
	Andre Nel	71	70	65	71	277	27,800
	Jaco Van Zyl	70	66	69	72	277	27,800
	Bryce Easton	68	66	70	73	277	27,800
	Jake Redman	69	67	68	73	277	27,800
19	Fredrik From	71	68	70	69	278	25,100
	Martin Rohwer	68	70	70	70	278	25,100
21	Oliver Bekker	69	70	70	70	279	24,200
22	James Allan	72	70	70	68	280	22,750
	Hennie Otto	70	67	73	70	280	22,750
	Christiaan Basson	74	67	69	70	280	22,750
	Hennie du Plessis	72	66	71	71	280	22,750
26	Jean Hugo	69	68	74	70	281	21,200
	Tyrone Ferreira	67	69	74	71	281	21,200
	Garrick Higgo	66	75	69	71	281	21,200
29	Luke Jerling	71	70	73	68	282	19,600
	Deon Germishuys	75	67	70	70	282	19,600
	Victor Lange	70	71	68	73	282	19,600
	Kyle Barker	70	67	71	74	282	19,600
	Peter Karmis	71	68	69	74	282	19,600

Gauteng Team Championship

In only the third staging of the Gauteng Team Championship at Dainfern, JC Ritchie and Jaco Prinsloo became the first pair to successfully defend their title. A betterball of 61 followed by a 68 in foursomes put the pair into the lead with a round to play and a betterball 62, for a 25-under-par total of 191, sealed a two-stroke victory over Jaco Ahlers and Vaughn Groenewald, who closed with a 63. Sharing third place on 22 under par were the pairings of Deon Germishuys and Ulrich van den Berg, Kyle Barker and David McIntyre, and Heinrich Bruiners and Andre Nel.

After a bogey at the first hole of the final round, Ritchie and Prinsloo responded with a birdie at the next, six in a row from the fifth, an eagle at the 12th before birdies at the final two holes. "We are very chuffed to have defended this title," said Ritchie. "I think we were expecting a little bit of a charge from the guys who were coming behind us. We played brilliantly together as a team after a tough struggle at the start. But we are happy we managed to turn on the fireworks and bring it home."

Dainfern Country Club, Midrand, Gauteng — January 23-25
Par: 72 (36-36); 7,294 yards — Purse: R1,500,000

1	**JC Ritchie & J Prinsloo**	61	68	62	191	R105,000
2	**J Ahlers & V Groenewald**	62	68	63	193	86,250
3	**D Germishuys & U van den Berg**	64	70	60	194	47,575
	K Barker & D McIntyre	63	69	62	194	47,575
	H Bruiners & A Nel	59	71	64	194	47,575
6	CJ du Plessis & S Wears-Taylor	62	71	62	195	30,750
	O Strydom & D McGuigan	64	70	61	195	30,750
8	S Ferreira & B Follett-Smith	65	68	63	196	21,881
	T Fisher Jr & N Schietekat	62	71	63	196	21,881
	J Van Zyl & D Fichardt	62	69	65	196	21,881
	J Roos & C Basson	61	69	66	196	21,881
12	L Rowe & S Surry	63	69	65	197	18,750
13	G Mulroy & A De Decker	65	68	65	198	16,913
	M Muthiya & A Haig	65	68	65	198	16,913
	H Du Plessis & J Hugo	62	71	65	198	16,913
	D Naidoo & J du Preez	65	69	64	198	16,913
17	J Redman & K Horne	63	71	65	199	14,950
	F From & P Eriksson	66	69	64	199	14,950
	W Dingle & L de Jager	67	68	64	199	14,950
20	K Davidse & D Petersen	63	71	67	201	14,025
	R van der Spuy & T Ryan	64	69	68	201	14025
	A Michael & R Tipping	62	72	67	201	14,025
23	M Palmer & JJ Senekal	65	70	67	202	13,575
24	J Dreyer & L Albertse	65	68	72	205	13,350

Limpopo Championship

It was a double-double for JC Ritchie as history repeated itself at Eurphoria. In 2019 Ritchie won the Gauteng Team Championship with Jaco Prinsloo and a week later claimed the inaugural Limpopo Championship. In 2020, Ritchie and Prinsloo defended their title together before Ritchie also won the Limpopo a week later. "There are not many people who can say they have defended a title, so defending two titles in a row is just something that's crazy special for me," said Ritchie after his fifth official Sunshine Tour victory.

A two-shot victory over Wilco Nienaber was well deserved since the challenge at Euphoria was greater this time with the event now co-sanctioned by the European Challenge Tour with the 204-player field competing over two courses for the first two rounds. Ritchie opened with scores of 66 and 69 before adding twin rounds of 67 on the weekend, during which the 25-year-old did not drop a shot. Starting two behind overnight leader Jacques Kruyswijk, Ritchie took the lead with birdies at the third, fifth and ninth holes before adding two more at the 13th and 16th holes. Nienaber, the 19-year-old rookie, eagled the seventh in a closing 67 to finish three ahead of Kruyswijk, who slipped to a 74, and Hennie du Plessis, who closed with a 70.

"To have the Challenge Tour players coming to play the event this year definitely made defending the title harder and I found myself getting rather nervous on my back nine, but I was able to keep it together well," Ritchie said. "I feel like I played the best golf I possibly could have played this weekend. I could not have played any better out there. To play bogey-free over the weekend is crazy good especially with the conditions. I'm planning to head over to Europe to play some events on the Challenge Tour this year. First though, I think there is quite a party waiting for me at home."

Euphoria Golf & Lifestyle Estate, Modimolle, Limpopo — January 30-February 2
Par 72 (36-36); 7,040 yards — Purse: R3,500,000
Koro Creek Bushveld Golf Estate (R1-2 only) par 72 (36-36); 6,799 yards

1	**JC Ritchie**	66	69	67	67	269	R578,525
2	**Wilco Nienaber**	65	68	71	67	271	403,325
3	**Hennie du Plessis**	65	69	70	70	274	204,218
	Jacques Kruyswijk	67	64	69	74	274	204,218
5	Louis de Jager	67	64	71	73	275	109,500
6	Ross Mcgowan	68	68	71	69	276	100,375
7	Anton Haig	66	73	72	66	277	86,688
	Jens Dantorp	68	71	68	70	277	86,688
9	Daniel van Tonder	63	72	71	72	278	73,000
10	Breyten Meyer	68	68	73	70	279	56,484
	Christopher Mivis	70	69	70	70	279	56,484
	Craig Howie	67	70	71	71	279	56,484
	Neil Schietekat	68	70	69	72	279	56,484
14	Jake Roos	71	70	70	69	280	51,283
	Jbe' Kruger	73	66	68	73	280	51,283
16	Andre Nel	67	73	70	71	281	47,998
	Keenan Davidse	72	68	70	71	281	47,998
	Marcel Schneider	67	70	72	72	281	47,998
	Clement Sordet	68	68	71	74	281	47,998
20	Anthony Michael	68	71	75	68	282	41,286
	Daniel Young	72	69	73	68	282	41,286
	Bernd Ritthammer	66	74	72	70	282	41,286
	Rourke van der Spuy	67	71	73	71	282	41,286
	Mitch Waite	73	68	70	71	282	41,286
	Todd Clements	66	71	73	72	282	41,286
	Jaco Van Zyl	68	68	72	74	282	41,286
	Anton Karlsson	68	68	72	74	282	41,286
	Bryce Easton	67	70	70	75	282	41,286
29	Nicolai Hojgaard	68	73	74	68	283	35,405
	Christiaan Basson	72	68	74	69	283	35,405
	Kyle Barker	67	74	71	71	283	35,405
	Garth Mulroy	67	73	70	73	283	35,405
	Jaco Prinsloo	68	72	70	73	283	35,405
	Stuart Manley	68	73	68	74	283	35,405

RAM Cape Town Open

Sweden's Anton Karlsson achieved his first victory on either the Challenge Tour or the Sunshine Tour with a one-stroke win at the RAM Cape Town Open. The 26-year-old from Uppsala came from three behind in the final round with a 69 at a windy Royal Cape. Propelled by a 64 in the third round, following opening scores of 72 and 69, Karlsson parred the last four holes, including from four feet at the last, to pip South African Garrick Higgo.

Daniel van Tonder led for the first three days but crashed to a 78 in the tricky conditions. Karlsson bogeyed two of the first four holes but took charge by making six birdies in seven holes from the seventh. Another bogey at the 14th, combined with Higgo birdieing the last two holes, made for a tight finish but Karlsson, who had twice lost his card on the European Tour in 2017 and 2019, held firm.

"It was one of the toughest days of golf in my career with the conditions," Karlsson said. "It feels amazing to come out on top and to play some really good golf. My only aim this morning was to go out there and win. I was three shots back and I knew I was playing well after a 64 yesterday. The opening holes were playing tough and I ended up in the wrong places, but I really got it going after that, and from the sixth hole it was probably the best stretch of golf I've ever played."

Left-handed Higgo, the rookie who won the 2019 Sun City Challenge, finished three ahead of Toby Tree, with Harry Ellis, Damien Perrier and Jordan Wrisdale in fourth place.

Royal Cape Golf Club, Wynberg, Cape Town — February 6-9
Par 72 (36-36); 6,065 yards — Purse: R3,500,000
King David Mowbray Golf Club (R1&2) par 72 (36-36); 5,947 yards

1	**Anton Karlsson**	72	69	64	69	274	R590,413
2	**Garrick Higgo**	74	67	67	67	275	411,613
3	**Toby Tree**	67	69	71	71	278	260,378
4	Jordan Wrisdale	73	69	67	70	279	123,546
	Harry Ellis	69	68	70	72	279	123,546
	Damien Perrier	68	73	66	72	279	123,546
7	Allen John	72	68	73	67	280	83,813
	Mitch Waite	69	66	73	72	280	83,813
	Daniel van Tonder	66	67	69	78	280	83,813
10	Robin Petersson	73	70	67	71	281	57,644
	Thriston Lawrence	73	67	69	72	281	57,644
	Daniel Young	72	66	69	74	281	57,644
	Luke Jerling	74	66	64	77	281	57,644
14	Eirik Tage Johansen	73	68	71	70	282	50,660
	Adilson Da Silva	70	72	69	71	282	50,660
	Jonathan Thomson	72	66	70	74	282	50,660
	Jacques Kruyswijk	72	69	67	74	282	50,660
	Wilco Nienaber	71	68	68	75	282	50,660
19	Alex Haindl	74	68	71	70	283	43,536
	Brandon Stone	71	69	72	71	283	43,536
	Deon Germishuys	74	67	71	71	283	43,536
	Clement Sordet	74	68	70	71	283	43,536
	Todd Clements	76	67	67	73	283	43,536
	Enrico Di Nitto	71	69	68	75	283	43,536
	Pedro Oriol	71	69	68	75	283	43,536
	JC Ritchie	68	68	70	77	283	43,536
27	Bernd Ritthammer	70	70	74	70	284	36,133
	Mathieu Fenasse	71	72	71	70	284	36,133
	Euan Walker	75	68	70	71	284	36,133
	Stephen Ferreira	73	68	70	73	284	36,133
	Matthew Baldwin	74	69	68	73	284	36,133
	Aron Zemmer	69	65	76	74	284	36,133
	Neil Schietekat	71	68	71	74	284	36,133
	Louis Albertse	73	68	69	74	284	36,133
	Jean Hugo	70	69	70	75	284	36,133
	Nicolai Kristensen	70	71	68	75	284	36,133

Dimension Data Pro-Am

An eagle at the final hole brought Christiaan Bezuidenhout victory at the Dimension Date Pro-Am at Fancourt. Having led all week, the 25-year-old from Johannesburg was caught by George Coetzee on the final day when a thunderstorm caused a 50-minute delay. After the resumption, Bezuidenhout fell a stroke behind by three-putting the par-three 12th. Coetzee, who made five birdies in the first 11 holes, also birdied the 15th and signed for a bogey-free 66. Bezuidenhout matched the birdie at 15 but needed at least a four at the last to force a playoff. A big drive set up an approach to six feet and he holed the eagle putt.

Bezuidenhout opened with a 61 on the Outeniqua course and added a 67 on The Links as he was joined in the halfway lead by Spain's Santiago Tarrio, who opened with scores of 63 and 64. On the weekend on the Montagu course Bezuidenhout had scores of 69 and 67 for a 25-under-par total of 264 to pip 2016 winner Coetzee by one. Richard Sterne finished third, three behind, after a 66, while Tarrio finished the leading European in fourth place at the third and final event co-sanctioned with the Challenge Tour.

This was Bezuidenhout's second win on the Sunshine Tour but his first since 2016, although his maiden European Tour victory came at the Andalucia Masters in 2019. He had lost out in a playoff at the Dubai Desert Classic the previous month.

"To win it with an eagle on the last is really special," he said. "This is a special event for the South African boys and I've always wanted to put my name on that trophy. I've done it now, so I'm pretty pleased."

Fancourt Hotel & Country Club (Montagu), George, Western Cape — February 13-16
Par 72 (36-36); 6,714 yards — Purse: R6,300,000
The Links (R1-3) par 73 (36-37); 6,638 yards
Outeniqua (R1-3) par 72 (36-36); 6,312 yards

1	**Christiaan Bezuidenhout**	61	67	69	67	264	R951,000
2	**George Coetzee**	65	69	65	66	265	663,000
3	**Richard Sterne**	66	66	69	66	267	419,400
4	Santiago Tarrio	63	64	72	73	272	252,000
5	JC Ritchie	65	70	70	68	273	180,000
6	Daniel van Tonder	69	69	70	66	274	157,500
	Darren Fichardt	66	69	70	69	274	157,500
8	Ugo Coussaud	69	66	71	69	275	120,000
	Louis de Jager	67	70	68	70	275	120,000
	Daniel Hillier	65	68	71	71	275	120,000
11	Martin Simonsen	71	69	68	68	276	84,300
	Oscar Lengden	73	69	64	70	276	84,300
	Dean Burmester	66	68	72	70	276	84,300
	Peter Karmis	72	68	66	70	276	84,300
	Daan Huizing	72	69	65	70	276	84,300
	Alex Haindl	66	71	69	70	276	84,300
	Pep Angles	70	72	65	69	276	84,300
	Rhys Enoch	69	71	66	70	276	84,300
19	Raphael de Sousa	73	67	68	69	277	71,700
	Jack Harrison	73	66	67	71	277	71,700
	Jacques Blaauw	69	70	66	72	277	71,700
	Lorenzo Scalise	68	69	68	72	277	71,700
	Martin Ovesen	67	68	69	73	277	71,700
	Matt Ford	68	67	68	74	277	71,700
25	Trevor Fisher Jr	70	65	74	69	278	63,600
	Craig Howie	69	69	69	71	278	63,600
	Jake Roos	67	68	67	76	278	63,600
	Tom Gandy	68	70	66	74	278	63,600
	Jaco Van Zyl	74	68	66	70	278	63,600
30	Marcel Siem	65	71	73	70	279	59,400
	Aron Zemmer	72	72	64	71	279	59,400

Sunshine Tour Championship

Garrick Higgo rounded out his first season on the Sunshine Tour with a one-stroke victory at the Tour Championship. A second win, which he missed out on two weeks earlier when finishing runner-up at the RAM Cape Town Open, sealed the Bobby Locke Trophy as the rookie of the year for the 21-year-old South African.

Left-handed Higgo was a stroke behind Ockie Strydom after rounds of 67, 70 and 66 and still trailed Thriston Lawrence after going to the turn in 33 at Serengeti Estates. Lawrence went three ahead with an eagle at the 11th before a double bogey at the 16th left him in third place, one ahead of Strydom. Haydn Porteous closed with a 67 to get to 18 under par but Higgo knew he needed to motor on the back nine. He birdied the 11th and 12th holes but missed chances at the next two before dropping his only shot of the day at the 15th. An eagle at the 16th from 15 feet, however, put Higgo on top of the leaderboard at 19-under-par 269 after a second 66 of the weekend.

"I wasn't really expecting to win this one," Higgo admitted. "I knew I had to go for it on the back nine and I did. Then things changed on 16. I'm very proud to win the rookie of the year trophy. It will look really good on my CV and I'm sure there have been big names that have won it before." Higgo finished sixth on the order of merit, which was topped by JC Ritchie, who finished 32nd but was not overhauled by Daniel van Tonder in 10th.

Serengeti Estates, Kempton Park, Gauteng — February 20-23
Par 72 (36-36); 7,096 yards — Purse: R1,500,000

1	**Garrick Higgo**	67	70	66	66	269	R240,000
2	**Haydn Porteous**	67	69	67	67	270	167,400
3	**Thriston Lawrence**	67	68	68	68	271	114,050
4	Ockie Strydom	69	63	70	70	272	82,900
5	Luke Jerling	68	68	68	70	274	66,800
6	Darren Fichardt	73	66	67	69	275	57,550
7	Keith Horne	70	71	64	71	276	48,400
8	MJ Viljoen	73	67	72	65	277	38,425
	George Coetzee	73	67	69	68	277	38,425
10	Daniel van Tonder	70	67	68	73	278	31,875
	Brandon Stone	69	65	70	74	278	31,875
12	Christiaan Basson	68	72	70	69	279	28,200
	Jean-Paul Strydom	66	69	72	72	279	28,200
14	Jacques Kruyswijk	69	68	74	69	280	25,575
	Keenan Davidse	71	68	67	74	280	25,575
16	Martin Rohwer	71	68	72	70	281	23,700
	Deon Germishuys	68	69	70	74	281	23,700
	James Hart du Preez	68	71	68	74	281	23,700
19	Jake Redman	70	71	71	70	282	21,750
	Rhys Enoch	67	75	70	70	282	21,750
	Hennie du Plessis	70	70	69	73	282	21,750
22	Jacques Blaauw	69	70	67	77	283	20,700
23	Jaco Van Zyl	73	71	67	73	284	20,250
24	Merrick Bremner	75	66	73	71	285	19,350
	Daniel Greene	67	72	72	74	285	19,350
	Alex Haindl	72	68	70	75	285	19,350
27	Oliver Bekker	74	70	75	68	287	18,000
	Ruan Conradie	73	70	74	70	287	18,000
	Jean Hugo	72	72	70	73	287	18,000
30	Louis de Jager	76	69	72	71	288	16,950
	Jaco Prinsloo	74	67	72	75	288	16,950

2019-20 ORDER OF MERIT

1	JC Ritchie	R2,162,387
2	Daniel van Tonder	2,043,268
3	Jaco Ahlers	1,902,195
4	George Coetzee	1,722,930
5	Thriston Lawrence	1,377,891
6	Garrick Higgo	1,293,595
7	Christiaan Bezuidenhout	1,140,363
8	Martin Rohwer	1,070,153
9	Louis de Jager	956,940
10	MJ Viljoen	925,564

Betway Championship

Darren Fichardt gradually stepped up his challenge as the Sunshine Tour returned to action after six months with the Betway Championship, the first leg of the new Rise-Up Series created to mark the belated start of the 2020-21 season. All five events were scheduled to be played in Gauteng under a comprehensive risk mitigation strategy due to the Covid-19 pandemic.

At Killarney, Fichardt, who had last played competitively at the European Tour's Qatar Masters in early March, opened with a 73 to be six strokes off the lead. A level-par 70 in the second round meant the 45-year-old was still six adrift going into the final round but a bogey-free 64 with six birdies, starting with three in a row from the eighth and finishing with the winning blow at the last, brought a one-stroke victory on a three-under-par total of 207. Ulrich van den Berg's putt at the last to tie just missed as a 69 secured second place, with overnight leader Alex Haindl finishing third after a 72 alongside Jaco Prinsloo and Ruan Korb.

Fichardt's 64 was the lowest of the tournament as he collected an 18th Sunshine Tour title and his second of the year after winning the Eye of Africa PGA Championship in January. "It looks like I need to take five months off and then play tournaments," said Fichardt. "It was so good to have those butterflies in your stomach going again. Sitting on the couch for five months was tough and I'm really happy to be back.

"After 26 years on tour, lockdown was good in that it gave me time with my family and time to do some focused work in the gym which you can't always do when you're touring every week. I feel I've needed this to give my career a bit more longevity."

Killarney Country Club, Johannesburg, Gauteng — August 19-21
Par 70 (35-35); 6,385 yards — Purse: R600,000

1	**Darren Fichardt**	73	70	64	207	R95,100
2	**Ulrich van den Berg**	70	69	69	208	69,000
3	**Jaco Prinsloo**	71	70	68	209	38,000
	Ruan Korb	68	72	69	209	38,000
	Alex Haindl	70	67	72	209	38,000
6	Adilson Da Silva	70	69	71	210	22,800
7	Jaco Van Zyl	77	69	65	211	17,700
	Martin Rohwer	73	70	68	211	17,700
9	Daniel van Tonder	70	75	68	213	12,500
	Dylan Naidoo	68	76	69	213	12,500
	Jake Roos	73	70	70	213	12,500
	Michael Hollick	69	74	70	213	12,500
	Keith Horne	70	71	72	213	12,500
	Anton Haig	69	69	75	213	12,500
15	Thriston Lawrence	74	72	68	214	9,465
	Heinrich Bruiners	72	73	69	214	9,465
	Dylan Mostert	67	75	72	214	9,465
	Jayden Schaper	73	68	73	214	9,465
19	Nikhil Rama	71	74	70	215	8,220
	Oliver Bekker	75	69	71	215	8,220
	MJ Viljoen	72	71	72	215	8,220
22	Chris Swanepoel	72	72	72	216	7,470
	Wynand Dingle	73	71	72	216	7,470
24	Jaco Ahlers	70	76	71	217	6,492
	Ruan Conradie	73	72	72	217	6,492
	Andrew Williamson	75	70	72	217	6,492
	Hennie O'Kennedy	70	74	73	217	6,492
	Callum Mowat	71	73	73	217	6,492
29	Greg Bentley	70	74	74	218	5,610
	Peter Karmis	72	72	74	218	5,610
	Jake Redman	71	73	74	218	5,610
	Clayton Mansfield	72	70	76	218	5,610

African Bank Sunshine Tour Championship

A "new" slimed down Daniel van Tonder calmly went about his business at Glendower to win the African Bank Sunshine Tour Championship, the second leg of the Rise-Up Series. The 29-year-old claimed his fourth tour title by three strokes after rounds of 67, 70 and 68 for an 11-under-par total of 205. Van Tonder did not drop a stroke in the final round while posting four birdies, at the fifth, seventh, 13th and 15th holes. His co-leaders overnight, Martin Rohwer and Jayden Schaper, both scored 75s to fall into a tie for sixth place. Adilson Da Silva, with a 67, George Coetzee, with a 68, and Neil Schietekat, with a 69, finished as joint runners-up.

"I felt very calm and focused out there and am enjoying myself more. It's a new time, and a new me," van Tonder said. "I decided to use lockdown to my advantage. I used the time to practice hard and make changes in my swing, and also within myself. I've changed the way I eat and I've lost about 20kg. I follow a plan of intermittent fasting and it's made a huge difference. I feel a lot better and have actually gained distance because I'm a bit more supple. So everything feels a bit more consistent now."

Glendower Golf Club, Edenvale, Gauteng — August 26-28
Par: 72 (36-36); 6,962 yards — Purse: R600,000

1	**Daniel van Tonder**	67	70	68	205	R95,100
2	**Adilson Da Silva**	68	73	67	208	51,600
	George Coetzee	71	69	68	208	51,600
	Neil Schietekat	70	69	69	208	51,600
5	Dylan Mostert	70	72	68	210	28,200
6	Deon Germishuys	73	71	68	212	15,857
	Luke Brown	71	72	69	212	15,857
	Louis Albertse	70	70	72	212	15,857
	Darren Fichardt	68	71	73	212	15,857
	Jaco Ahlers	70	68	74	212	15,857
	Martin Rohwer	65	72	75	212	15,857
	Jayden Schaper	67	70	75	212	15,857
13	Tristen Strydom	75	71	67	213	11,100
	Jake Redman	70	71	72	213	11,100
15	Ruan Conradie	69	76	69	214	9,276
	Malcolm Mitchell	73	70	71	214	9,276
	MJ Viljoen	69	73	72	214	9,276
	Thriston Lawrence	72	70	72	214	9,276
	Jake Roos	71	69	74	214	9,276
20	Roberto Lupini	75	70	71	216	7,770
	Heinrich Bruiners	67	77	72	216	7,770
	Jaco Prinsloo	73	70	73	216	7,770
	Oliver Bekker	67	75	74	216	7,770
24	Hayden Griffiths	71	74	72	217	6,870
	Cameron Moralee	71	73	73	217	6,870
26	Riekus Nortje	71	75	72	218	6,150
	Wallie Coetsee	69	76	73	218	6,150
	Dylan Naidoo	73	72	73	218	6,150
	Keagan Thomas	69	74	75	218	6,150
30	Keith Horne	71	75	73	219	5,610
	Jacques Blaauw	70	75	74	219	5,610

Titleist Championship

George Coetzee first played at Pretoria Country Club aged 10. He won. Now aged 34 and long since a member at the club in his hometown, Coetzee continued his winning streak by claiming the Titleist Championship, the third leg of the Rise-Up Series. It was his 11th Sunshine Tour title, four of which have been co-sanctioned with the European Tour. Two of those wins, at the Tshwane Open in 2015 and '18, also came on his home track.

"It's a very special victory because Pretoria Country Club and Titleist have supported me my whole career, so to win with both involved this week is truly special," Coetzee said. "I'm over the moon. It's nice performing well when people expect it. It's really nice to have pulled this off on my home course."

Coetzee was never headed. He shared the lead after an opening 67 and again with a 70 on the second day. But despite bogeys at the first two holes of the final round, he eased away from the field with a 66 for a 13-under-par total of 203. He had eight birdies, five of them in a row from the sixth. In the end he won by four strokes from Tristen Strydom, his co-leader overnight who had a 70, with Jaco Ahlers six back after a 67 and Darren Fichardt one further adrift despite a 65. This was Strydom's best result since winning the Qualifying School in March.

Pretoria Country Club, Waterkloof, Pretoria, Gauteng — September 2-4
Par 72 (36-36); 6,398 yards — Purse: R600,000

1	**George Coetzee**	67 70 66 203	R95,100	16	Anthony Michael	72 76 70 218	8,563
2	**Tristen Strydom**	72 65 70 207	69,000		James Hart du Preez	76 70 72 218	8,563
3	**Jaco Ahlers**	69 73 67 209	48,000		Rupert Kaminski	73 73 72 218	8,563
4	Darren Fichardt	75 70 65 210	37,800		Hennie Otto	74 71 73 218	8,563
5	Pieter Moolman	73 68 71 212	28,200		Keagan Thomas	77 68 73 218	8,563
6	Jaco Prinsloo	74 71 68 213	19,400		Keith Horne	71 73 74 218	8,563
	Deon Germishuys	74 70 69 213	19,400		Martin Rohwer	72 72 74 218	8,563
	Heinrich Bruiners	74 69 70 213	19,400	23	Toto Thimba Jr	76 70 73 219	7,170
9	Wynand Dingle	72 71 71 214	14,700		Malcolm Mitchell	74 70 75 219	7,170
10	Coert Groenewald	73 72 70 215	13,050	25	Riekus Nortje	72 75 73 220	6,170
	Daniel van Tonder	73 71 71 215	13,050		Louis Albertse	80 67 73 220	6,170
12	MJ Viljoen	77 71 69 217	11,100		Michael Hollick	72 73 75 220	6,170
	Kyle Barker	76 70 71 217	11,100		Jared Harvey	74 71 75 220	6,170
	Peetie van der Merwe	73 73 71 217	11,100		Quintin Wilsnach	72 72 76 220	6,170
	Jayden Schaper	71 71 75 217	11,100		Clayton Mansfield	68 72 80 220	6,170

Vodacom Championship Unlocked

Never out of the top 10 so far in four Rise-Up Series events, Daniel van Tonder collected his second win at the Vodacom Championship Unlocked. The 29-year-old came from five strokes behind MJ Viljoen on a final day of strong winds thanks to a daring strategy of keeping to his aggressive approach. After earlier scores of 66 and 70, van Tonder had a 67, tying the best score of the last round, to post a 13-under-par total of 203. No one could beat it, with Viljoen finishing one back after a 73 and Pieter Moolman in third place after a 67 ahead of Louis de Jager, Ulrich van der Berg and Darren Fichardt.

After two early birdies were cancelled out by a pair of bogeys, van Tonder went on a run of five birdies in eight holes from the eighth. Viljoen had taken a double-bogey seven at the second hole as he went out in 39 but an eagle at the 13th reversed his tumble down the leaderboard.

"It was fun out there," said van Tonder at ERPM Golf Club, which dates back to 1903 and is where John Bland was the longtime professional. "I knew that in the wind, five shots back wouldn't be too much to make up. My game is suited to the wind and I play quite aggressively when it's blowing. I've been putting in a lot of hard work and just doing my own thing. My whole game from tee to green feels good, and I think that just comes from all the practice I've been doing. Van Tonder used his victory to raise awareness for mesothelioma, a rare form of cancer with which his wife's grandfather had recently been diagnosed.

ERPM Golf Club, Boksburg, Gauteng — September 23-25
Par 72 (36-36); 6,679 yards — Purse: R600,000

1	**Daniel van Tonder**	66 70 67 203	R95,100		Jacques P de Villiers	73 68 68 209	9,960
2	**MJ Viljoen**	64 67 73 204	69,000		Jake Redman	66 67 76 209	9,960
3	**Pieter Moolman**	69 69 67 205	48,000	18	Oliver Bekker	70 72 68 210	8,520
4	Louis de Jager	69 70 67 206	29,600		Tristen Strydom	69 71 70 210	8,520
	Ulrich van den Berg	69 69 68 206	29,600		Jacques Blaauw	67 70 73 210	8,520
	Darren Fichardt	68 66 72 206	29,600	21	Jake Roos	75 66 70 211	7,620
7	Dylan Mostert	68 69 70 207	18,900		Hayden Griffiths	69 70 72 211	7,620
8	Jaco Ahlers	69 70 69 208	13,450		Luca Filippi	69 70 72 211	7,620
	Luke Jerling	69 69 70 208	13,450	24	Adilson Da Silva	71 71 70 212	6,492
	Coert Groenewald	67 70 71 208	13,450		Andrew Williamson	71 69 72 212	6,492
	Keith Horne	68 69 71 208	13,450		Hennie O'Kennedy	71 68 73 212	6,492
	Paul Boshoff	66 71 71 208	13,450		Teaghan Gauche	72 67 73 212	6,492
	Neil Schietekat	66 70 72 208	13,450		Rupert Kaminski	70 69 73 212	6,492
14	Thriston Lawrence	68 74 67 209	9,960	29	Jayden Schaper	72 69 72 213	5,790
	Kyle Barker	70 72 67 209	9,960		Heinrich Bruiners	72 67 74 213	5,790

Vodacom Championship Reloaded

In eight previous seasons on the Sunshine Tour, Daniel van Tonder had won three times. During the five-event Rise-Up Series which marked the start of the delayed 2020-21 season, van Tonder managed to double his tally of titles. The 29-year-old from Johannesburg dominated the return of tour golf in South Africa with a stunning sequence of results: ninth-first-10th-first-first — the latest victory coming by four strokes at the Vodacom Championship Reloaded at Huddle Park.

Picking up from where he left off in the final round the previous week, van Tonder led outright from wire-to-wire with scores of 63, 66 and 66 for a 21-under-par total of 195. Coming out of lockdown, he recognised his game was built on making lots of birdies but he could do with making fewer mistakes. Here he made only one bogey and while he made 12 birdies, there were also five eagles, two in each of the first two rounds. The one at the ninth in the second round, his final hole of the round, established a three-stroke lead over Jacques Blaauw.

His advantage was never seriously threatened after birdieing the first hole of the final round and adding another eagle at the sixth. About the only thing van Tonder did not scoop during the series was the birdie challenge prize which went to Jaco Ahlers with 79, two more than van Tonder. Ahlers claimed eight of those in a final-round 65 to share second place with Adilson Da Silva, who scored 66, with the pair one ahead of Blaauw.

"It feels amazing," said van Tonder. "I've got the kind of confidence where I don't feel like I need to back down for any shot on the golf course. I feel like if I can make a swing, then there's no shot that's too tough for me. My wife and caddie Abigail plays a big part in that because she keeps me calm on the course and gives me that confidence."

Huddle Park Golf Club, Johannesburg, Gauteng — September 30-October 2
Par 72 (36-36); 6,447 yards — Purse: R600,000

1	**Daniel van Tonder**	63	66	66	195	R95,100
2	**Jaco Ahlers**	67	67	65	199	58,500
	Adilson Da Silva	69	64	66	199	58,500
4	Jacques Blaauw	65	67	68	200	37,800
5	Malcolm Mitchell	65	68	68	201	28,200
6	Ruan Korb	68	66	68	202	22,800
7	Thriston Lawrence	67	69	67	203	15,240
	MJ Viljoen	67	69	67	203	15,240
	Jayden Schaper	66	69	68	203	15,240
	Musiwalo Nethunzwi	65	70	68	203	15,240
	Clayton Mansfield	67	67	69	203	15,240
12	Chris Swanepoel	68	68	68	204	10,812
	Rupert Kaminski	70	66	68	204	10,812
	Matthew Spacey	72	66	66	204	10,812
	Derick Petersen	67	68	69	204	10,812
	Anton Haig	71	63	70	204	10,812
17	Christiaan Basson	64	72	69	205	8,229
	Anthony Michael	67	68	70	205	8,229
	Callum Mowat	67	72	66	205	8,229
	Ulrich van den Berg	69	66	70	205	8,229
	Louis de Jager	64	70	71	205	8,229
	Gideon van der Vyver	70	64	71	205	8,229
	Albert Venter	70	70	65	205	8,229
24	Riekus Nortje	71	67	68	206	6,291
	Quintin Wilsnach	69	66	71	206	6,291
	Hennie Otto	71	67	68	206	6,291
	Nikhil Rama	70	69	67	206	6,291
	Tristen Strydom	69	70	67	206	6,291
	Pieter Moolman	68	67	71	206	6,291
	Michael Hollick	71	68	67	206	6,291

Sun Wild Coast Sun Challenge

From sharing the lead during the second round, Merrick Bremner saw a double bogey and two bogeys in his last three holes drop him four strokes behind in ninth place. Helped by the reassurance of experienced caddie Zack Rasego, alongside the 34-year-old from Pretoria for the first time after years with the likes of Louis Oosthuizen and Branden Grace, Bremner bounced back in the last round to win the Sun Wild Coast Sun Challenge.

Despite the wind getting up at Wild Coast Sun Country Club, Bremner did not drop a shot in a 64 that contained three birdies on each half. A three at the 18th, when the gale was at its height, proved decisive as he won by one stroke from Keenan Davidse and Jacques Blaauw. Finishing, and getting out of the wind, almost an hour ahead of the final groups, Bremner's wait was rewarded with a seventh Sunshine Tour victory. He finished on eight-under-par 202, with Davidse and Blaauw both scoring 68s and Peter Karmis, who made up the trio of 36-hole leaders, a 71.

Bremner admitted being unprepared when the Rise-Up Series started after lockdown as he missed four cuts out of five, but proved he was back on his game by coping with the tricky conditions here. He explained: "It really started gusting quite hard towards the last 30 minutes of the round. It was brutal. I can't explain it. If you mishit it just slightly, the ball just went nowhere. There were crosswinds that just accentuate any mistake you make. You had to be on top of your game and hit quality shots to make a score.

"I gave myself the right opportunities. We were never thinking about keeping bogeys off the card. We were just thinking about giving ourselves as many birdie opportunities as possible."

Wild Coast Sun Country Club, Alfred Nzo, Eastern Cape — October 21-23
Par 70 (35-35); 5,807 yards — Purse: R700,000

1	**Merrick Bremner**	66	72	64	202	R110,950
2	**Keenan Davidse**	69	66	68	203	68,250
	Jacques Blaauw	65	70	68	203	68,250
4	Keith Horne	65	71	68	204	44,100
5	Hennie du Plessis	69	72	65	206	25,200
	Alex Haindl	68	70	68	206	25,200
	Jayden Schaper	67	70	69	206	25,200
	Peter Karmis	67	68	71	206	25,200
9	Ruan Conradie	66	71	70	207	17,150
10	Anthony Michael	68	71	69	208	15,750
11	Christiaan Basson	66	72	71	209	14,700
12	Deon Germishuys	66	73	71	210	12,297
	Ockie Strydom	65	74	71	210	12,297
	Byron Coetzee	70	70	70	210	12,297
	Oliver Bekker	71	69	70	210	12,297
	Callum Mowat	70	71	69	210	12,297
12	Jaco Van Zyl	69	68	73	210	12,297
18	Louis Albertse	64	75	72	211	9,590
	Thriston Lawrence	67	72	72	211	9,590
	Malcolm Mitchell	72	69	70	211	9,590
	Sean Bradley	75	63	73	211	9,590
	Dylan Naidoo	68	74	69	211	9,590
23	Allister de Kock	73	67	72	212	7,868
	Colin Nel	68	70	74	212	7,868
	Ulrich van den Berg	69	72	71	212	7,868
	Luke Jerling	64	73	75	212	7,868
23	Andrew Curlewis	72	70	70	212	7,868
28	Derick Petersen	70	70	73	213	6,755
	Heinrich Bruiners	69	70	74	213	6,755
	Daniel van Tonder	69	72	72	213	6,755
	Jaco Ahlers	68	73	72	213	6,755

Investec Royal Swazi Open

With international borders closed, the Investec Royal Swazi Open had to move to South Africa, as had happened only once before, but the tournament still got to celebrate its 50th anniversary when the Gary Player Country Club at Sun City stepped in to host. Also continuing a fine streak was Daniel van Tonder who won for the fourth time in six starts. The 29-year-old from Johannesburg had won the title in 2014 for his maiden victory and his seventh came by a commanding 18 points under the modified Stableford system.

Only once in seven events since the restart had van Tonder finished outside the top 10 and that was the previous week at Wild Coast. But he was back in the groove at Sun City even if his opening round of 15 points might have been better had it not contained two bogeys and a double. Five birdies and two eagles more than made up for the errors as he led by one point. Another eagle at the 18th hole — the ninth as it is played for the Nedbank Challenge — helped van Tonder to 12 points the next day as he started to streak ahead. Ten points in front after 36 holes, he extended his advantage to 14 in the third round with another solid tally of 11 points. He collected 10 points on the final day, a round highlighted by five birdies in a row from the 12th.

"Each week is different and you have to find something during the week," van Tonder said. "I was struggling with my game in practice but during the tournament I found something, it felt natural and it worked." The win left van Tonder looking forward to the newly announced swing of co-sanctioned events with the European Tour, including a return to Sun City for the SA Open. "All of my titles in my career have come on golf courses that have good greens. Randpark, Leopard Creek Golf Club and the Gary Player Country Club all have very good greens so, yes, I'm looking forward to those tournaments," he said.

Neil Schietekat gave lonely chase to the champion over the last three rounds, scores of 8, 9, 7 and 6 giving him 30 for the week. MJ Viljoen finished one point behind him, with Adilson Da Silva on 28.

Gary Player Country Club, Sun City, North West Province — October 28-31
Par: 72 (36-36); 7,834 yards — Purse: R1,500,000

1	**Daniel van Tonder**	15	12	11	10	48	R206,050
2	**Neil Schietekat**	8	9	7	6	30	143,000
3	**MJ Viljoen**	6	9	5	9	29	96,070
4	Adilson Da Silva	8	7	0	13	28	68,900
5	JC Ritchie	10	6	6	5	27	55,120
6	Jacques Blaauw	5	10	5	6	26	47,190
7	Keenan Davidse	8	-1	9	9	25	39,260
8	Peter Karmis	7	2	3	12	24	29,033
	Oliver Bekker	9	8	1	6	24	29,033
	Anton Haig	4	10	8	2	24	29,033
11	Jake Roos	7	3	7	5	22	24,180
12	Keith Horne	11	-2	4	7	20	22,490
13	Michael Palmer	1	4	4	10	19	21,190
14	Merrick Bremner	-2	5	1	14	18	18,590
	Deon Germishuys	6	4	0	8	18	18,590
	Cameron Moralee	11	1	7	-1	18	18,590
	Jaco Van Zyl	7	7	5	-1	18	18,590
	Dylan Naidoo	4	10	1	3	18	18,590
19	Estiaan Conradie	14	1	-1	3	17	16,770
20	Jaco Ahlers	5	2	6	3	16	16,250
21	Ruan Korb	5	1	3	6	15	15,535
	Ockie Strydom	8	-3	5	5	15	15,535
23	Malcolm Mitchell	-1	4	0	11	14	14,950
24	Anthony Michael	3	3	-1	8	13	14,365
	Desne Van Den Bergh	7	4	1	1	13	14,365
26	Andrew McLardy	0	2	1	8	11	13,780
27	Doug McGuigan	7	-1	1	3	10	13,195
	CJ du Plessis	-2	3	9	0	10	13,195
29	Alex Haindl	10	-7	-4	10	9	12,415
	Jaco Prinsloo	10	-1	4	-4	9	12,415

Time Square Casino Challenge

Ruan Korb timed his maiden victory on the Sunshine Tour to perfection at the Time Square Casino Challenge. By holing from six feet for a birdie on the final hole, the 26-year-old South African, in his second season on tour, upgraded his exemption to gain entry to the next three events, all of them co-sanctioned with the European Tour. Korb beat Anton Haig by one stroke at Wingate Park.

After an opening 67, Korb raced around in 64 shots in the second round to take a two-stroke lead. Haig, who was five behind after 36 holes, made a threatening charge with five birdies and an eagle at the 15th before, at the 17th, he dropped his only shot of a final-round 66. Korb, a member at Wingate for four years earlier in life, also eagled the 15th but then bogeyed the next hole so came to the last in need of the birdie he duly made. A closing 70 left Korb on a 15-under-par total of 201.

"It feels so good. I'm so glad that my days of pre-qualifying for tournaments are over," said Korb, whose previous seven events since the tour's restart had contained two top-six finishes but four missed cuts. "I'm so happy to have pulled it off. I was on the 17th when I saw the leaderboard and that Anton had made par at the last, so I knew I had to make birdie on 18 to win. It was a six-footer, but there were so many thoughts going through my head. I almost cried on the 18th when I made the putt. I haven't felt like that in a very long time. It's such a great feeling."

Deon Germishuys, the first-round leader, tied for third place with Jake Redman, two behind Haig, with Martin Rohwer, Korb's nearest challenger overnight, dropping into a share of fifth place.

Wingate Park Country Club, Pretoria, Gauteng — November 4-6
Par 72 (35-37); 6,740 yards — Purse: R700,000

1	**Ruan Korb**	67	64	70	201	R110,950
2	**Anton Haig**	65	71	66	202	80,500
3	**Jake Redman**	70	65	69	204	50,050
	Deon Germishuys	64	70	70	204	50,050
5	Louis Albertse	70	69	66	205	21,200
	Jacques Blaauw	69	67	69	205	21,200
	Keenan Davidse	66	70	69	205	21,200
	Darren Fichardt	71	64	70	205	21,200
	Anthony Michael	69	66	70	205	21,200
	Oliver Bekker	69	72	64	205	21,200
	Martin Rohwer	67	66	72	205	21,200
12	Rhys Enoch	71	67	68	206	14,000
13	Peter Karmis	67	71	69	207	12,268
	Callum Mowat	67	70	70	207	12,268
	Malcolm Mitchell	65	71	71	207	12,268
	Andre Nel	70	71	66	207	12,268
17	Luke Brown	69	69	70	208	10,313
	Andrew van der Knaap	69	68	71	208	10,313
	Jayden Schaper	71	69	68	208	10,313
20	Jaco Prinsloo	69	70	70	209	9,065
	Desne Van Den Bergh	67	72	70	209	9,065
	Heinrich Bruiners	71	69	69	209	9,065
	Dylan Mostert	69	71	69	209	9,065
24	Chris Cannon	70	68	72	210	7,228
	Jaco Ahlers	72	68	70	210	7,228
	Jbe' Kruger	71	69	70	210	7,228
	Clayton Mansfield	70	70	70	210	7,228
	Thriston Lawrence	69	72	69	210	7,228
	Michael Palmer	69	72	69	210	7,228
	Neil Schietekat	69	72	69	210	7,228
	Christiaan Basson	70	71	69	210	7,228

Joburg Open

The tears came for Joachim B Hansen moments after his maiden victory on the European Tour when he joined a video call with his wife Elisabeth, young son and baby daughter back home in Denmark. Until then the 30-year-old had kept all his wits about him in securing a two-stroke win at the Joburg Open. He needed to in order to see off the challenge of young, big-hitting Wilco Nienaber.

Returning to the Highveld at Randpark in his rookie season on the European Tour, the 20-year-old from Bloemfontein used the near 6,000 feet altitude to his advantage and unleashed a drive of 439 yards during the first round — it did not quite stay on the fairway. He made nine birdies and an eagle during his opening 63 to share the first-round lead with Shaun Norris. Although Jacques Blaauw edged in front on Friday, two rounds of 67 put Nienaber in front again, by one from Hansen, who scored 66, 68 and 64 for the first three days.

It was a duel between the two on Sunday with Nienaber going three ahead with a hat-trick of birdies from the fourth. Hansen got his round going with his second birdie of the day at the 10th, followed by two more at the 12th and 14th holes. Both those were par fives but his young opponent could only makes pars. Hansen, who would not drop a shot all day, made an important save at the 16th when his drive finished in the rough and his second was hampered by an overhanging tree branch and the water between him and the green.

Finally, the pressure told on Nienaber. He finished in the edge of the lake at the short 17th and failed to make his three, while he found sand off the tee at the last and bogeyed again for a 70. Hansen kept his card clean by getting up and down from a greenside bunker with a 67 giving him a 19-under-par total of 265.

"It's quite emotional, this is what we work for," said Hansen, who topped the Challenge Tour in 2018. "It was a fun battle out there with Wilco. I kept the head calm and kept pushing. It was a slow start but finally the birdies came on the back nine. I'm pleased to prove to myself I can win out here."

Nienaber's best result on the European Tour matched his Sunshine Tour best from the Limpopo Championship early in the year. Norris took third place, three strokes behind his compatriot, with Brandon Stone, England's Steve Surry and Canadian Aaron Cockerill sharing fourth spot.

Randpark Golf Club (Firethorn), Johannesburg, Gauteng — November 19-22
Par 71 (35-36); 7,506 yards — Purse: R19,500,00

1	**Joachim B Hansen**	66	68	64	67	265	R2,964,120
2	**Wilco Nienaber**	63	67	67	70	267	1,917,960
3	**Shaun Norris**	63	70	69	66	268	1,098,468
4	Steve Surry	67	71	66	67	271	740,449
	Aaron Cockerill	64	68	71	68	271	740,449
	Brandon Stone	70	68	64	69	271	740,449
7	Lars van Meijel	70	69	67	66	272	424,567
	Bryce Easton	69	69	67	67	272	424,567
	Jacques Blaauw	66	63	73	70	272	424,567
	Richard Bland	67	67	68	70	272	424,567
11	Neil Schietekat	69	67	70	67	273	292,053
	Niklas Lemke	68	66	71	68	273	292,053
	Darren Fichardt	67	69	69	68	273	292,053
	Romain Wattel	68	68	69	68	273	292,053
15	Christiaan Bezuidenhout	68	69	70	67	274	245,848
	Martin Rohwer	69	70	66	69	274	245,848
	Zander Lombard	69	65	70	70	274	245,848
18	Jayden Schaper	67	68	72	68	275	220,565
	Dean Burmester	72	68	65	70	275	220,565
20	Toby Tree	72	68	68	68	276	202,838
	Antoine Rozner	69	70	69	68	276	202,838
	Scott Jamieson	67	70	68	71	276	202,838
23	Matthew Jordan	69	68	72	68	277	178,719
	Lorenzo Scalise	67	70	72	68	277	178,719
	James Hart du Preez	71	67	71	68	277	178,719
	Chase Hanna	69	68	70	70	277	178,719
	Joel Sjoholm	69	71	67	70	277	178,719
	Julian Suri	66	68	71	72	277	178,719
29	Rhys Enoch	65	69	73	71	278	160,411
30	Justin Walters	73	68	70	68	279	144,719
	Marcus Armitage	69	71	70	69	279	144,719
	Oliver Farr	66	68	73	72	279	144,719
	Scott Vincent	69	67	71	72	279	144,719
	Gonzalo Fdez-Castano	65	70	71	73	279	144,719
35	Dale Whitnell	69	71	71	69	280	117,070
	Jonathan Caldwell	69	70	71	70	280	117,070
	Johannes Veerman	64	71	74	71	280	117,070
	Peter Karmis	72	68	69	71	280	117,070
	Jbe' Kruger	68	72	69	71	280	117,070
	Hennie du Plessis	71	70	66	73	280	117,070
	Estiaan Conradie	68	68	71	73	280	117,070
42	Ewen Ferguson	71	68	74	68	281	88,924
	Alvaro Quiros	70	71	71	69	281	88,924
	Yikeun Chang	69	71	72	69	281	88,924
	Louis de Jager	68	69	74	70	281	88,924
	Benjamin Poke	71	70	69	71	281	88,924
	Jake Redman	68	73	68	72	281	88,924
	Matthew Spacey	72	68	69	72	281	88,924
	Jaco Prinsloo	68	72	68	73	281	88,924
	Richard Mcevoy	65	75	68	73	281	88,924
51	Benjamin Follett-Smith	65	72	79	66	282	64,862
	Heinrich Bruiners	70	65	78	69	282	64,862
	Daan Huizing	69	70	74	69	282	64,862
	Ruan de Smidt	69	72	70	71	282	64,862
	Adrian Otaegui	69	70	70	73	282	64,862
56	Anton Haig	69	72	73	69	283	54,052

	MJ Viljoen	69	72	72	70	283	54,052
	Deon Germishuys	67	74	72	70	283	54,052
	Marcel Siem	66	71	73	73	283	54,052
	Grant Forrest	72	68	69	74	283	54,052
61	Jack Harrison	71	70	74	69	284	45,334
	Garrick Higgo	68	71	75	70	284	45,334
	Oliver Wilson	73	68	72	71	284	45,334
	Ryan Lumsden	69	72	71	72	284	45,334
	Steven Brown	71	66	74	73	284	45,334
66	Keith Horne	71	69	73	72	285	37,487
	Ruan Korb	70	70	73	72	285	37,487
	Daniel Greene	71	69	70	75	285	37,487
	Hennie Otto	69	68	73	75	285	37,487
70	Pedro Figueiredo	72	69	73	72	286	30,178
	Richard Joubert	73	67	74	72	286	30,178
	Adilson Da Silva	65	74	73	74	286	30,178
	Louis Albertse	70	69	72	75	286	30,178
74	Sebastian Garcia Rodriguez	70	71	73	73	287	29,058
	Gavin Green	66	71	76	74	287	29,058
76	Jack Senior	68	73	75	72	288	28,920
	Andre De Decker	70	68	76	74	288	28,920
	Daniel van Tonder	69	69	74	76	288	28,920
79	Ockie Strydom	69	72	74	79	294	28,811

Alfred Dunhill Championship

Though still only aged 26, Christiaan Bezuidenhout used his greater experience to seal a four-stroke victory in the Alfred Dunhill Championship at Leopard Creek. It was only in the closing stages at the spectacular venue on the edge of Kruger National Park that Bezuidenhout went clear of the field as a number of young contenders ultimately fell away.

Adrian Meronk, the first player from Poland to lead on the European Tour as he did for the first three rounds, Jayden Schaper, the 19-year-old who finished sixth as an amateur at the SA Open at the start of the year, and Zimbabwe-born American Sean Crocker all topped the leaderboard at times on the final day but ended up sharing second place with veteran Englishman Richard Bland.

Bezuidenhout played the par-37 inward half beautifully over the weekend, coming home in 32 on Saturday to get within three of Meronk's lead, and then drawing away from his challengers with a 34 on Sunday. The tee times on the last day were moved earlier in the morning as a storm was forecast and a gusting wind made scoring tricky. Bezuidenhout, two weeks after making his debut at the Masters, was not immune, following three birdies in the first six holes with a double bogey at the seventh, where he found the water, and a bogey at the next hole.

Schaper led at the turn but suffered a triple bogey at the 10th. Meronk went ahead again only to drop three strokes with sixes at the par-five 13th and the 14th. Bezuidenhout pounced with birdies at the short par-four 11th and the killer blows at the 14th, from 25 feet, and the 15th, from 18 feet. After that he did not put a foot wrong, a 69, following earlier scores of 69, 68 and 68, giving him a 14-under-par total of 274.

Crocker was one behind after a birdie at the 17th but then drove out of bounds at the last when his hooked tee drive bounced off the roof of a buggy. He also later found the water at the island green for a triple-bogey eight. He finished with a 72, matching Bland, who had already closed with a 70, while Schaper also drove out of bounds at the last on the way to a 75 and Meronk found the water to finish off with a 76.

This was Bezuidenhout's third win on the Sunshine Tour and his second of the year following his victory at the Dimension Data Pro-Am. It was also his second European Tour title after he won the Andalucia Open at Valderrama in 2019 and lifted him to a personal best of 41st on the world ranking. "This tournament has been close to my heart since I played it for the first time," he said. "It's always been a tournament I wanted to win and to pull it off today is really special to me. I'm proud of myself to stick in there and to have pulled it off round here. The golf course this week was immaculate."

Leopard Creek Country Club, Malelane, Mpumalanga — November 26-29
Par 72 (35-37); 7,249 yards — Purse: R29,000,000

1	**Christiaan Bezuidenhout**	69	68	68	69	274	R4,579,120
2	**Richard Bland**	67	67	74	70	278	1,787,204
	Sean Crocker	70	68	68	72	278	1,787,204
	Jayden Schaper	69	67	67	75	278	1,787,204
	Adrian Meronk	65	66	71	76	278	1,787,204
6	Robert MacIntyre	72	70	70	67	279	713,265
	Alexander Levy	70	72	68	69	279	713,265
	Scott Jamieson	66	71	72	70	279	713,265
	Marcus Armitage	71	71	67	70	279	713,265
	Adri Arnaus	70	67	69	73	279	713,265
11	Fabrizio Zanotti	71	71	68	70	280	495,622
12	Wilco Nienaber	71	68	72	70	281	463,299
13	Oliver Wilson	69	69	74	70	282	405,387
	Wil Besseling	73	70	68	71	282	405,387
	Matthias Schwab	70	71	68	73	282	405,387
	Calum Hill	71	69	67	75	282	405,387

17	Scott Vincent	72	70	71	70	283	348,372
	Dale Whitnell	70	72	71	70	283	348,372
	Pedro Figueiredo	72	68	69	74	283	348,372
20	Adrian Otaegui	75	68	70	71	284	313,355
	Oliver Farr	70	68	73	73	284	313,355
	Joachim B Hansen	70	64	73	77	284	313,355
23	Masahiro Kawamura	69	73	71	72	285	292,256
	Brandon Stone	71	72	69	73	285	292,256
25	Hennie du Plessis	72	71	71	72	286	259,932
	Richard Mcevoy	71	70	71	74	286	259,932
	Matthew Jordan	69	73	72	72	286	259,932
	Johannes Veerman	71	71	70	74	286	259,932
	Cormac Sharvin	72	72	68	74	286	259,932
	Justin Walters	72	72	72	70	286	259,932
31	Oliver Bekker	73	69	71	74	287	219,528
	David Horsey	69	73	72	73	287	219,528
	Joost Luiten	69	72	73	73	287	219,528
	Robin Roussel	65	71	73	78	287	219,528
35	Jbe' Kruger	69	72	72	75	288	189,225
	Christiaan Basson	69	69	74	76	288	189,225
	Julian Suri	71	69	68	80	288	189,225
	Marcel Siem	69	72	77	70	288	189,225
39	Chris Wood	69	73	72	75	289	164,310
	Sebastian Garcia Rodriguez	68	75	72	74	289	164,310
	Daniel van Tonder	69	70	70	80	289	164,310
	Pablo Larrazabal	74	69	74	72	289	164,310
	Philip Eriksson	74	67	76	72	289	164,310
44	James Kingston	71	68	74	77	290	142,761
	Darius van Driel	73	71	73	73	290	142,761
	Martin Rohwer	74	70	75	71	290	142,761
47	Anthony Michael	76	68	69	78	291	123,906
	Gavin Green	68	74	73	76	291	123,906
	Richard Sterne	71	73	72	75	291	123,906
	Garrick Porteous	71	72	77	71	291	123,906
51	Steve Surry	72	70	72	78	292	105,050
	MJ Viljoen	73	69	74	76	292	105,050
	Steven Brown	69	74	75	74	292	105,050
54	Jaco Van Zyl	70	72	77	74	293	94,276
55	Darren Fichardt	73	70	74	77	294	90,236
	Rourke van der Spuy	74	69	79	72	294	90,236
57	James Hart du Preez	69	74	73	79	295	83,502
	Ockie Strydom	68	70	78	79	295	83,502
	Matthieu Pavon	73	69	79	74	295	83,502
60	Dylan Naidoo	74	69	71	83	297	75,421
	Trevor Fisher Jr	73	71	75	78	297	75,421
	Jean-Paul Strydom	73	71	76	77	297	75,421
63	Ruan Conradie	70	73	75	80	298	70,034
64	Eddie Pepperell	71	71	76	81	299	65,993
	Benjamin Follett-Smith	69	69	81	80	299	65,993

SA Open Championship

Christiaan Bezuidenhout continued right where he left off at Leopard Creek to win the 110th SA Open Championship at Sun City's Gary Player Country Club by a commanding five strokes. Over two of South Africa's most demanding courses he posted 32 under par for eight rounds, while no one had won in successive weeks on the European Tour by four strokes or more on each occasion since Ian Woosnam in 1990.

Bezuidenhout led from start to finish, following three rounds of 67 with a 69 for an 18-under-par total of 270. He was part of a six-way tie for the lead on day one, then Jamie Donaldson caught him after a second round of 63. But by Saturday evening his advantage was five strokes. Donaldson made two birdies in the first three holes on Sunday, while Bezuidenhout had seven pars before hitting his approach at the eighth into the water. He got up and down for a bogey by holing from 18 feet and at that point his lead was down to two.

But the birdies finally came for the 26-year-old as he conjured three in a row to start the run for home. His strong iron-play was illustrated by hitting his tee shot at the short 16th right over the flag, rather than bailing out to the centre of the green, and another birdie fell from eight feet.

Luck was also on the side of the longtime champion elect. At the 17th he appeared to have pulled his tee shot out of bounds only for his ball to take a strange bounce off a cart path, and perhaps the tree tops of the jungle, and landed safely back in play. His approach even had a helpful nudge off the shoulder of a bunker and into the middle of the green.

"It feels amazing," said Bezuidenhout. "It wasn't easy out there and the first nine didn't go my way, but I hung in there. To stand here as the SA Open champion is unbelievable. This is massive for me. It's always been a dream and I wasn't sure when, or if, I would achieve it."

This was his third win in South Africa for the year and his fourth in all, as well as a third European Tour title. It improved his world ranking further to 35th place. "When you go into the final round with a five-shot lead you are expecting to win it, so I did put a bit of pressure on myself. When things didn't go my way on the front nine my caddie just kept me calm, and we did a great job coming in."

Donaldson continued his recent resurgence in form with a 69 to take second place, two ahead of Dylan Frittelli, who returned home after his fifth place at the Masters. Dean Burmester took fourth spot, one behind Frittelli after the pair both scored 71s.

Gary Player Country Club, Sun City, North West Province — December 3-6
Par: 72 (36-36); 7,834 yards — Purse: R19,500,000

1	**Christiaan Bezuidenhout**	67	67	67	69	270	R2,964,120
2	**Jamie Donaldson**	71	63	72	69	275	1,917,960
3	**Dylan Frittelli**	68	68	70	71	277	1,098,468
4	Dean Burmester	67	69	71	71	278	871,800
5	JC Ritchie	70	71	66	72	279	739,286
6	Marcel Siem	74	68	68	70	280	523,080
	Hennie du Plessis	70	70	68	72	280	523,080
	Scott Vincent	72	69	67	72	280	523,080
9	Julien Guerrier	73	69	69	70	281	390,566
10	Connor Syme	72	70	69	71	282	348,720
11	Darren Fichardt	74	73	67	69	283	300,480
	Wilco Nienaber	69	74	68	72	283	300,480
	Joost Luiten	72	67	70	74	283	300,480
14	Calum Hill	77	66	72	69	284	251,078
	Louis de Jager	75	71	69	69	284	251,078
	Ruan Conradie	74	68	72	70	284	251,078
	Matthias Schwab	67	72	72	73	284	251,078
18	Jbe' Kruger	72	73	70	70	285	220,565
	Aaron Cockerill	71	68	72	74	285	220,565
20	Anthony Michael	73	69	75	69	286	197,376
	Steve Surry	72	72	73	69	286	197,376
	Oliver Bekker	70	73	73	70	286	197,376
	Jean-Paul Strydom	76	67	72	71	286	197,376
	Justin Walters	69	72	71	74	286	197,376
25	Ulrich van den Berg	72	74	73	68	287	168,257
	Casey Jarvis (A)	73	74	71	69	287	
	David Law	71	71	73	72	287	168,257
	Richard Sterne	75	69	71	72	287	168,257
	Benjamin Follett-Smith	72	71	71	73	287	168,257
	Jacques Kruyswijk	67	72	71	77	287	168,257
	Ruan Korb	67	72	70	78	287	168,257
32	Brandon Stone	73	68	72	75	288	144,719
	Scott Jamieson	70	74	69	75	288	144,719
	Jaco Ahlers	70	75	68	75	288	144,719
35	Pablo Larrazabal	72	72	75	70	289	124,842
	Deon Germishuys	74	71	74	70	289	124,842
	Luke Brown	71	75	72	71	289	124,842
	Gonzalo Fdez-Castano	70	72	74	73	289	124,842
	Peter Karmis	72	69	73	75	289	124,842
40	MJ Daffue	72	72	76	70	290	104,616
	Rourke van der Spuy	73	72	75	70	290	104,616
	Richard Bland	72	74	73	71	290	104,616
	George Coetzee	73	74	71	72	290	104,616
	Austin Bautista	71	72	74	73	290	104,616
	Sebastian Garcia Rodriguez	72	72	73	73	290	104,616
46	Shaun Norris	75	69	76	71	291	85,436
	Alvaro Quiros	75	70	72	74	291	85,436
	Jacques Blaauw	74	69	73	75	291	85,436
	MJ Viljoen	70	75	70	76	291	85,436
	Aron Zemmer	67	75	72	77	291	85,436
51	Neil Schietekat	69	75	77	71	292	69,744
	Jayden Schaper	73	73	73	73	292	69,744
	Darius van Driel	76	71	72	73	292	69,744
	Pedro Figueiredo	76	68	74	74	292	69,744
55	James Kingston	71	73	77	72	293	59,282
	Martin Rohwer	70	75	76	72	293	59,282
	Shubhankar Sharma	74	73	73	73	293	59,282
58	Matthieu Pavon	68	78	74	74	294	54,052
	Stephen Ferreira	70	76	74	74	294	54,052
	Stanislav Matus	76	71	72	75	294	54,052
61	Michael Palmer	73	73	74	75	295	49,693
	Benjamin Poke	75	69	75	76	295	49,693
63	Matias Calderon	74	73	74	75	296	47,077
64	Daan Huizing	72	74	75	76	297	44,462
	Robin Roussel	72	75	73	77	297	44,462
66	Ockie Strydom	74	70	77	77	298	41,846
67	Jesper Sandborg	73	73	77	78	301	39,231
	Nicolai Hojgaard	72	74	73	82	301	39,231
69	Jean Hugo	74	73	76	79	302	36,616
70	Toby Tree	69	76	79		RTD	34,000
71	Thriston Lawrence	76	70	78		DQ	34,000

Asian Tour

The 2019 Hong Kong Open, the 61st edition of the tournament that was one of the seeds of the Asian Tour, had to be postponed because of political unrest in the streets. And that, it developed, was the easy part of the 2020 Asian Tour season.

The 2019 Hong Kong had been scheduled to lead off the European Tour's new season as a co-sanctioned event at the end of November. But political demonstrations had been boiling over in Hong Kong since June. And so the European Tour cancelled the tournament.

"The safety of our players, staff, stakeholders and everyone involved is our top priority," said European Tour chief executive Keith Pelley.

The Asian Tour then rescheduled the tournament for January 2020. Australian Wade Ormsby stuck to his single-minded game and hoisted the trophy, but he had barely packed it and departed before a new and different kind of threat emerged, not only to golf but to the entire world — the Covid-19 virus. And golf tours around the world soon were postponing tournaments, rescheduling, and painfully cancelling many.

Probably nowhere were the frustrations and the difficulties of the stricken season more clearly shown than at the SMBC Singapore Open in January. The first three finishers — winner Matt Kuchar, and Justin Rose and Jazz Janewattananond — were already exempt for The Open Championship at Royal St George's in July, so the four playing spots available went to teen sensation Joohyung Kim, of Korea, Canada's Richard T Lee, Thailand's Poom Saksansin and Japan's Ryosuke Kinoshita. And then in a cruel irony, a dream of their careers went poof. The Open was later cancelled because of the pandemic.

The Asian Tour finally suspended play in March, after four tournaments were played. They included the New Zealand Open, co-sanctioned with the PGA Tour of Australasia and taken by Brad Kennedy, fittingly enough, in his 25th year on the tour. "Time to get home and spend some more time with my kids and wife," Kennedy said.

With travel restrictions across the region, the Asian Tour was unable to resume later in the year. Two tournaments due to feature on both the Asian and Japan tours were played as part of the Korean PGA Tour. Taehee Lee won the GS Caltex Maekyung Open for the second year running, while Hanbyeol Kim took the Shinhan Donghae Open for his second win of the year. In all there were 11 events on the KPGA circuit with Taehoon Kim winning the KPGA Order of Merit after winning the Genesis Championship and finishing in the top four on three other occasions.

The Volvo China Open, usually co-sanctioned by the Asian Tour and the European Tour, was played in December with a local field only. Huilin Zhang, 31, who finished third on the China Tour Order of Merit in 2019 after picking up his third tour title, won at Genzon by nine strokes from amateur Wenyi Ding. There was only one other event in the country with the China Tour otherwise abandoned for the year due to the pandemic, while the PGA Tour Series — China was cancelled outright.

2020 SCHEDULE

Hong Kong Open	**Wade Ormsby**	
SMBC Singapore Open	**Matt Kuchar**	
New Zealand Open	**Brad Kennedy**	*See chapter 17*
Bandar Malaysia Open	**Trevor Simsby**	
Royal Cup		*cancelled*
Hero Indian Open		*cancelled*
Bangabandhu Cup		*cancelled*
Maybank Championship		*cancelled*
GS Caltex Maekyung Open*	**Taehee Lee**	*(KPGA event)*
Asia-Pacific Diamond Cup		*cancelled*
Kolon Korea Open		*cancelled*
Shinhan Donghae Open*	**Hanbyeol Kim**	*(KPGA event)*
Mercuries Taiwan Masters		*cancelled*
Panasonic Open		*cancelled*

WGC HSBC World Champions		*cancelled*
Volvo China Open*	**Huilin Zhang**	*(China Tour event)*
**non-order of merit event*		

Hong Kong Open

As far as Wade Ormsby was concerned, he was all by himself on the golf course and playing his game. The classical prescription, by the way. Which meant he had to ignore the fact that this was the Hong Kong Open, a jewel on the Asian Tour. He was preaching a mindset.

"I'm not going to play conservative," said Ormsby, 39, a veteran with two previous wins to his credit, and one of them the 2017 Hong Kong Open. "I'll play the course exactly the same way I played it for 10, 15 years, and let them come at me. And if they do," he added, "I'm just going to keep doing my thing."

And Ormsby stuck to his plan. He opened the first round with three straight birdies from the second en route to a one-bogey five-under 65, tying for the lead with Japan's Tomoharu Otsuki. And that was the closest anyone got to him the rest of the way.

Ormsby then rolled into the solo lead he would hold the rest of the way with three 66s across Hong Kong Golf Club for a 17-under total of 263 and a luxurious four-stroke win. His single-minded approach produced an eagle, 21 birdies and six bogeys, a sterling performance for a tournament whose future had seemed iffy. The Hong Kong had been scheduled for late November 2019, but was postponed because of political unrest, and it was reset for mid-January 2020.

In a burst of irony. Ormsby was challenged in the second round by India's SSP Chawrasia, who was about to win the 2017 Hong Kong. Chawrasia led all the way until he triple-bogeyed the ninth in the final round, and after a birdie at the 10th, he bogeyed four of the next five, and Ormsby took the title. This time, Chawrasia shot 63 and climbed to within two of Ormsby. Next came Thailand's Gunn Charoenkul, shooting 65 in the third round, but not getting any closer than two. And finally came Ireland's Shane Lowry, the 2019 Open champion, closing with a 64 and finishing second by four.

"When you get in front," Ormsby said, "there's no point in trying to play defensive."

Hong Kong Golf Club, Hong Kong — January 9-12
Par 70 (34-36); 6,710 yards — Purse: $1,000,000

1	**Wade Ormsby**	65	66	66	66	263	$180,000
2	**Shane Lowry**	69	66	68	64	267	110,000
3	**Gunn Charoenkul**	67	67	65	69	268	63,000
4	Jazz Janewattananond	68	66	67	68	269	50,000
5	Tony Finau	69	69	65	67	270	41,000
6	Rashid Khan	69	69	63	70	271	33,300
7	Charlie Wi	73	68	65	66	272	21,200
	Naoki Sekito	73	67	65	67	272	21,200
	Sadom Kaewkanjana	71	70	64	67	272	21,200
	David Gleeson	66	71	67	68	272	21,200
	Tomoharu Otsuki	65	71	67	69	272	21,200
	Terry Pilkadaris	68	69	64	71	272	21,200
13	Alexander Yang (A)	69	69	67	68	273	
	Yikeun Chang	66	70	68	69	273	14,175
	Travis Smyth	66	68	69	70	273	14,175
	Chan Shih-chang	68	67	67	71	273	14,175
	Taewoo Kim	69	66	66	72	273	14,175
18	Joohyung Kim	67	68	71	68	274	11,850
	Angelo Que	67	68	69	70	274	11,850
	Prom Meesawat	67	68	69	70	274	11,850
	Shiv Kapur	68	66	69	71	274	11,850
22	Jack Harrison	69	68	69	69	275	10,150
	Miguel Tabuena	70	68	68	69	275	10,150
	John Catlin	68	71	67	69	275	10,150
	Paul Peterson	73	67	66	69	275	10,150
	Phachara Khongwatmai	72	69	65	69	275	10,150
	SSP Chawrasia	70	63	69	73	275	10,150
28	Lianwei Zhang	68	71	69	68	276	8,950
	Andrew Martin	72	68	65	71	276	8,950
30	Danthai Boonma	70	71	68	68	277	8,040
	Andrea Pavan	69	69	70	69	277	8,040
	Minchel Choi	71	69	67	70	277	8,040
	Tirawat Kaewsiribandit	72	66	68	71	277	8,040
	Danny Masrin	71	67	65	74	277	8,040

SMBC Singapore Open

Matt Kuchar, in pursuit of the SMBC Singapore Open, kept turning Sentosa Serapong into something of an obstacle course. Obstacles of his own making, it should be noted.

There was that double bogey in the first round, another in the second, and then a whopping triple bogey in the final round.

"I went from the lead to tying for the lead," Kuchar said. Then he went from there to winning comfortably, by three strokes.

Kuchar played the par-71 Serapong in 66-68-62-70 for an 18-under total of 266, beating Justin Rose by three. They were the two highest ranked players in the field — Rose at number nine, Kuchar at 24. Thailand's Jazz Janewattananond, the 2019 champion, tied with Kuchar with nine holes to play, finished third, four back. They were the chief contenders when Thailand's Kosuke Hamamoto, 20, faded after leading after the first round with a 65.

Kuchar's adventures began in his first-round 66. It included an eagle at the par-five seventh and a double bogey at the par-four 13th. In the second round, he doubled-bogeyed his 14th (the fifth hole). And it looked like a real shootout was brewing when Rose shot 66 and tied Kuchar for the lead at eight-under 134. "My round was still quite flat on the front nine," said Rose, after his two-birdie, one-bogey 35. "I knew I had to stay patient." And he did, for a four-birdie 31 coming home.

Kuchar shot a flawless 62 in the third round that would have been the course record but play was under preferred lies.

Then the pièce de résistance of Kuchar's tournament befell him in the fourth round, just as he was getting up steam for the stretch run. He had birdied the fourth, and came to the par-five seventh, which he had already played in eagle-birdie-birdie. This time it was a carnival. His drive ended up against a tree root. He missed trying to punch out. His next hit a cart path and bounced into the leaves, costing him a penalty drop. Eventually, he holed a 10-footer for his triple-bogey eight.

"It was one of my best putts for an eight," Kuchar said.

And he had gone from a plump lead to a tough tie with Jazz, his playing partner. "Just a matter of resettling," he said. And so he did. Kuchar birdied 11, 16 and 18 to outrun a cooling Rose and a faltering Jazz.

"It turned out to be quite a competition," Kuchar said. "Much more of a competition than I was thinking it was going to be."

Sentosa Golf Club (Serapong), Singapore — January 16-19
Par 71 (36-35); 7,403 yards — Purse: $1,000,000

1	**Matt Kuchar**	66	68	62	70	266	$180,000
2	**Justin Rose**	68	66	68	67	269	110,000
3	**Jazz Janewattananond**	67	65	67	71	270	63,000
4	Joohyung Kim	67	66	67	71	271	50,000
5	Richard T Lee	66	69	65	72	272	41,000
6	Poom Saksansin	69	69	70	65	273	30,900
	Ryosuke Kinoshita	70	69	67	67	273	30,900
8	Danny Masrin	69	72	66	68	275	21,667
	Rashid Khan	70	66	69	70	275	21,667
	Miguel Tabuena	68	65	66	76	275	21,667
11	Travis Smyth	69	68	71	68	276	16,283
	Tomoharu Otsuki	69	67	71	69	276	16,283
	Rikuya Hoshino	66	73	68	69	276	16,283
14	Gunn Charoenkul	66	70	73	68	277	14,150
	Kosuke Hamamoto	65	75	68	69	277	14,150
16	Yuta Ikeda	69	71	69	69	278	12,950
	John Catlin	70	69	69	70	278	12,950
18	Minchel Choi	68	74	68	69	279	11,250
	Yuki Inamori	69	68	72	70	279	11,250
	Daijiro Izumida	71	71	67	70	279	11,250
	Danthai Boonma	69	69	69	72	279	11,250
	Mikumu Horikawa	70	70	67	72	279	11,250
23	Henrik Stenson	68	72	74	66	280	10,300
24	Mikiya Akutsu	71	69	72	69	281	9,400
	Kazuki Higa	73	69	68	71	281	9,400
	Johannes Veerman	70	71	69	71	281	9,400
	Ryo Ishikawa	69	73	72	67	281	9,400
	Angelo Que	70	67	77	67	281	9,400
29	Tomoyasu Sugiyama	72	70	69	71	282	8,267
	Tatsuya Kodai	71	71	69	71	282	8,267
	Inhoi Hur	67	72	67	76	282	8,267

Bandar Malaysia Open

It wasn't hard to find the two greatest smiles in Malaysia that March weekend. They beamed like airport beacons.

One was on the face of Trevor Simsby, who finished first in the Bandar Malayasia Open, and the other was on the face of Lo Tien Ming, who finished dead last.

Simsby, 27, from America, had just scored what he termed his biggest victory. And why was Lo smiling? Because he had made his first cut on the Asian Tour. At age 14 — the youngest ever to make the cut on the tour. And the kid stole the show. Lo was one under for the tournament and had to birdie the 18th to make the cut.

"When I saw the cut was two under I was very excited," Lo said. "I had a six-footer for birdie to possibly make the cut, and I did. I'm pretty proud of myself."

Lo, who had played in one tour event earlier, made this cut with 72-70 to be two under par at Kota Permai Golf and Country Club. In the two rounds, he had an eagle, eight birdies and eight bogeys. Lo shot 82 in the third and final round — bad weather had forced the reduction — and finished 74th and last on eight over par.

And Simsby was all aglow with his first Asian Tour victory after beating Andrew Dodt and Jarin Todd in a playoff.

"It was my time this week, I guess," Simsby said, "This is for sure my biggest win of my career." But he didn't see it coming for while.

"The turning point came when I was walking off the 15th hole," said Simsby. "My caddie was saying we were still in it, and I really didn't think so. And then I birdied the 16th, and I knew we had a chance."

Dodt double-bogeyed 15 then birdied 16, and all three parred in and tied at 13 under par on a total of 203: Simsby shooting 69-64-70, Todd 67-66-70 and Dodt 63-68-72.

In the first playoff visit to the par-five 18th, Todd was out on a par and Simsby and Dodt birdied. On the second, Dodt had a 10-footer for birdie, Simsby a five-footer. Dodt missed and Simsby didn't, and had that precious first win, possibly saving a golf career. Simsby had said that if he weren't a golfer, he'd probably be a chef.

"I make," he had said, "a mean lemon chicken."

Kota Permai Golf & Country Club, Shah Alam, Malaysia — March 5-7
Par 72 (36-36); 7,016 yards — Purse: $1,000,000

1	**Trevor Simsby**	69	64	70	203	$180,000
2	**Jarin Todd**	67	66	70	203	86,500
	Andrew Dodt	63	68	72	203	86,500
	Simsby won playoff at second extra hole					
4	Kosuke Hamamoto	67	69	68	204	41,433
	Rikuya Hoshino	68	67	69	204	41,433
	Charlie Wi	69	66	69	204	41,433
7	Naoki Sekito	65	73	67	205	24,800
	Sarit Suwannarut	71	66	68	205	24,800
	Phachara Khongwatmai	66	71	68	205	24,800
10	Chan Shih-chang	70	67	69	206	17,600
	Wade Ormsby	71	65	70	206	17,600
	Richard T Lee	67	68	71	206	17,600
13	Gunn Charoenkul	69	71	67	207	14,483
	Danny Masrin	72	68	67	207	14,483
	Miguel Carballo	70	69	68	207	14,483
16	Danthai Boonma	70	70	68	208	11,383
	Berry Henson	73	67	68	208	11,383
	Chikkarangappa S	68	73	67	208	11,383
	Sunil Jung	74	65	69	208	11,383
	Suradit Yongcharoenchai	69	70	69	208	11,383
	Seungsu Han	71	67	70	208	11,383
	Hiroshi Iwata	68	70	70	208	11,383
	Lawry Flynn (A)	71	66	71	208	
	Mikiya Akutsu	67	68	73	208	11,383
	Adilson Da Silva	72	71	65	208	11,383
26	Panuphol Pittayarat	71	70	68	209	9,100
	Scott Vincent	70	70	69	209	9,100
	Jaco Ahlers	70	71	68	209	9,100
	Pavit Tangkamolprasert	66	73	70	209	9,100
	Liu Yanwei	67	65	77	209	9,100

GS Caltex Maekyung Open

Elysian Gangchon Country Club, Gangwon-do, Korea — August 21-23

Par 70 (35-35); 7,001 yards — Purse: ₩ 1,000,000,000

1	**Taehee Lee**	65	67	67	199	₩160,000,000
2	**Mingyu Cho**	64	68	68	200	67,500,000
	Junseok Lee	68	65	67	200	67,500,000
4	Sungkug Park	69	64	70	203	31,200,000
	Bio Kim	67	68	68	203	31,200,000
	Kyungnam Kang	63	68	72	203	31,200,000
	Doyeob Mun	68	67	68	203	31,200,000
	Sanghun Shin	68	67	68	203	31,200,000
9	Jaekyeong Lee	71	68	65	204	16,457,500
	Keunho Lee	66	71	67	204	16,457,500
	Eunshin Park	69	70	65	204	16,457,500
	Jeunghun Wang	68	69	67	204	16,457,500
13	Dongkyu Jang	73	64	69	206	11,100,000
	Hanbyeol Kim	68	70	68	206	11,100,000
	Wooyoung Cho (A)	67	70	69	206	
16	Bael Jun Kim	73	66	68	207	9,270,000
	Dongseop Maeng	68	72	67	207	9,270,000
	Sungyeol Kwon (A)	68	71	68	207	
19	Jaemin Hwang	70	71	67	208	7,883,333
	Doosik Jung	69	67	72	208	7,883,333
	Junwon Park	70	69	69	208	7,883,333
	Seungyul Noh	68	67	73	208	7,883,333
	Seokhee Jung	70	68	70	208	7,883,333
	Songgyu Yoo	69	70	69	208	7,883,333
25	Junho Hong	71	71	67	209	7,373,333
	Heungchol Joo	72	67	70	209	7,373,333
	Wonjoon Lee	68	71	70	209	7,373,333

Shinhan Donghae Open

Bear's Best CheongNa Golf Club, Incheon, Korea — September 10-13

Par 71 (36-35); 7,238 yards — Purse: ₩ 1,400,000,000

1	**Hanbyeol Kim**	69	68	66	67	270	₩260,303,687
2	**Richard T Lee**	70	67	69	66	272	130,151,843
3	**Minchel Choi**	65	69	71	68	273	70,378,404
	Jeunghun Wang	67	67	71	68	273	70,378,404
	Joungwhan Park	65	70	71	67	273	70,378,404
6	Sungyeol Kwon	66	70	70	68	274	48,228,488
7	Kyongjun Moon	64	65	73	73	275	38,232,104
	Taehee Lee	70	69	69	67	275	38,232,104
	Seunghyuk Kim	70	67	71	67	275	38,232,104
	Yoseop Seo	67	67	70	71	275	38,232,104
11	Minkyu Kim	65	68	72	71	276	27,114,967
	Jeongwoo Ham	71	66	73	66	276	27,114,967
	Seonghyeon Jeon	70	70	66	70	276	27,114,967
	Dongeun Kim	72	66	70	68	276	27,114,967
	Jiho Yang	70	66	71	69	276	27,114,967
16	Junseok Lee	69	68	70	70	277	19,070,860
	Inhoi Hur	71	69	68	69	277	19,070,860
	Eunshin Park	69	67	72	69	277	19,070,860
	Seung Jongheon Park	66	70	70	71	277	19,070,860
20	Todd Baek	70	71	69	68	278	14,822,848
	Changwoo Lee	70	69	68	71	278	14,822,848
22	Soomin Lee	70	70	72	67	279	12,653,651
	Seungyul Noh	64	69	72	74	279	12,653,651
	Taehoon Ok	71	69	72	67	279	12,653,651
	Jaekyeong Lee	68	73	65	73	279	12,653,651

Volvo China Open

Genzon Golf Club, Shenzhen, China — December 10-13

Par 72 (36-36); 7,145 yards — Purse: CN¥2,000,000

1	**Huilin Zhang**	68	67	63	71	269	CN¥350,000
2	**Wenyi Ding** (A)	70	65	72	71	278	
3	**Yanwei Liu**	71	69	71	70	281	203,000
4	Dong Su	71	67	74	71	283	124,000
	Tianlang Guan	67	71	72	73	283	124,000
6	Zecheng Dou	70	71	72	71	284	84,800
7	Xuewen Luo	71	68	73	73	285	70,000
8	Zihao Chen	70	76	67	73	286	55,000
	Yilong Chen	70	71	70	75	286	55,000
	Tianyi Xiong (A)	71	71	73	71	286	
11	Chengyao Ma	68	72	74	73	287	40,800
	Shiyu Fan	72	67	76	72	287	40,800
	Shun Yat Hak	76	69	71	71	287	40,800
	Bo Peng (A)	72	69	75	71	287	
15	Shaocai He	71	73	73	72	289	33,050
	Haimeng Chao	72	70	74	73	289	33,050
	Han Xue	75	72	69	73	289	33,050
	Yue Liu	72	69	72	76	289	33,050
19	Daxing Jin	73	71	71	75	290	29,200
	Jianfeng Ye	70	76	79	65	290	29,200
	Zehao Liu	72	73	68	77	290	29,200
22	Bowen Xiao	76	69	74	72	291	26,333
	Xiaozhong Chen	70	79	71	71	291	26,333
	Qiantong Xie	73	71	72	75	291	26,333
25	Lianwei Zhang	73	72	72	75	292	24,600

2020 ORDER OF MERIT

1	Wade Ormsby	$227,004
2	Trevor Simsby	180,000
3	Brad Kennedy	173,528
4	Jarin Todd	113,417
5	Jazz Janewattananond	113,000
6	Joohyung Kim	108,128
7	Andrew Dodt	92,170
8	Gunn Charoenkul	91,633
9	Charlie Wi	64,513
10	Rashid Khan	62,581

Japan Tour

The coronavirus pandemic nearly wiped out the entire Japan Tour season. Only eight tournaments on the 2020 schedule were played, all but one during the final four months of the year, and three of them were contested in other countries. Matt Kuchar opened the year by winning the Singapore Open but the Shinhan Dongae Open in Korea was played only as part of the KPGA Tour, while the PGA Tour's Zozo Championship moved to the United States at Sherwood Country Club.

Of the five that were held in Japan, the one grabbing the most attention was the venerable Dunlop Phoenix, particularly because of its winner, Takumi Kanaya. The latest sensation on the male golf scene in Japan had, while still in college, won the 2019 Taiheiyo Masters as an amateur and claimed the 2020 Dunlop in his third pro start.

Yuki Inamori won the Japan Open Championship for the second time in three years, edging 41-year-old Hideto Tanihara, who had won 14 tournaments in his impressive career but never a major. Tanihara fell short again in the Golf Nippon Series, finishing in a second-place tie behind winner Chan Kim, one of the few overseas players to be able to compete at the end of the season. Inamori headed the money list at year's end with ¥41,112,558, which was carried over into 2021 with the season extended to the end of the forthcoming year.

Among those events postponed to 2021 was the Olympic Men's Golf competition due to be staged at Kasumigaseki Country Club as part of the Tokyo Games.

2020 SCHEDULE

SMBC Singapore Open	**Matt Kuchar**	*See chapter 15*
Token Homemate Cup		*cancelled*
The Crowns		*cancelled*
Asia-Pacific Diamond Cup		*cancelled*
Kansai Open		*cancelled*
Gateway to The Open Mizuno Open		*cancelled*
Japan Golf Tour Championship		*cancelled*
Dunlop Srixon Fukushima Open		*cancelled*
Japan PGA Championship		*cancelled*
Golf Partner Pro-Am Exhibition Tournament		*cancelled*
Olympics Men's*		*postponed to 2021*
Shigeo Nagashima Invitational		*cancelled*
Rizap KBC Augusta		*cancelled*
Fujisankei Classic	**Rikuya Hoshino**	
Shinhan Donghae Open*	**Hanbyeol Kim**	*KPGA event*
ANA Open		*cancelled*
Panasonic Open		*cancelled*
Vantelin Tokai Classic		*cancelled*
Bridgestone Open		*cancelled*
Japan Open Championship	**Yuki Inamori**	
Zozo Championship*	**Patrick Cantlay**	*See chapter 8*
The Top		*cancelled*
Mynavi ABC Championship		*cancelled*
Mitsui Sumitomo VISA Taiheiyo Masters	**Jinichiro Kozuma**	
Dunlop Phoenix	**Takumi Kanaya**	
Casio World Open		*cancelled*
Golf Nippon Series JT Cup	**Chan Kim**	

**non-Japan Tour money list event*

Fujisankei Classic

The Japan Tour emerged from its pandemic-demanded, nine-month hiatus with the playing of the Fujisankei Classic, one of its oldest tournaments, and provided its followers with an exciting overtime finish to launch its drastically abbreviated season.

Rikuya Hoshino landed the year's first title when he holed a long birdie putt on the third extra hole of the playoff against Mikumi Horikawa on what he dubbed the "monster" Fujizakura Country Club course in Yamanashi. In striking contrast, he had breezed to a five-stroke victory when he scored his first tour win at Fujizakura two years earlier. In between, the 24-year-old pro won the Dunlop SRIXON Fukushima Open in 2019.

He practised a rigorous exercise program during the shutdown to build up his stamina. "My swing got wobbly as I got tired, but now I don't feel fatigue," he explained. "I think my swing change is settling down, too."

With a 69-69 start, Hoshino ran close to the lead as Yushi Ito led the first day with 66 and three players — Koumei Oda, Hiroyuki Nagamatsu and Kodai Ichihara — shared the midway lead at 136. He took over first place on Saturday at eight under par with a six-birdie, two-bogey 67, a shot in front of Ryuko Tokimatsu. Horikawa, who was then six strokes off the pace at two under, produced a bogey-free, seven-under-par 64 on Sunday. His 275 total held up as the lead until Hoshino, who barely offset a double bogey and two bogeys with five birdies, the last at the 17th hole, posted his tying 70 to force the playoff.

Fujizakura Country Club, Fujikawaguchiko, Yamanashi — September 3-6
Par 71 (35-36); 7,566 yards — Purse: ¥110,000000

1	**Rikuya Hoshino**	69	69	67	70	275	¥22,000,000
2	**Mikumu Horikawa**	72	70	69	64	275	11,000,000
	Hoshino won playoff at third extra hole						
3	**Taihei Sato**	71	72	68	65	276	6,380,000
	Ryuko Tokimatsu	72	69	65	70	276	6,380,000
5	Shugo Imahira	73	68	68	68	277	4,400,000
	Takumi Kanaya (A)	72	71	65	69	277	
7	Hirotaro Naito	73	70	67	68	278	3,960,000
8	Tomoyo Ikemura	73	70	68	68	279	3,630,000
9	Tomoharu Otsuki	71	70	69	70	280	3,113,000
	Yuwa Kosaihira	70	70	69	71	280	3,113,000
	Kazuki Higa	70	70	67	73	280	3,113,000
12	Yuta Kinoshita	72	72	68	69	281	2,552,000
	Tadahiro Takayama	72	72	68	69	281	2,552,000
14	Naoto Nakanishi	69	72	71	71	283	1,800,857
	Tomoyasu Sugiyama	73	69	70	71	283	1,800,857
	Takuya Higa	72	71	69	71	283	1,800,857
	Kodai Ichihara	67	69	75	72	283	1,800,857
	Ippei Koike	72	68	70	73	283	1,800,857
	Koumei Oda	70	66	73	74	283	1,800,857
	Koki Shiomi	72	68	69	74	283	1,800,857
21	Hiroyuki Fujita	72	71	70	71	284	1,173,333
	Atomu Shigenaga	75	65	72	72	284	1,173,333
	Ryutaro Nagano	70	72	70	72	284	1,173,333
	Yushi Ito	66	76	69	73	284	1,173,333
	Hiroshi Iwata	72	69	70	73	284	1,173,333
	Ryo Ishikawa	74	65	71	74	284	1,173,333
27	Yusaku Miyazato	68	74	71	72	285	815,571
	Yuki Inamori	71	72	70	72	285	815,571
	Satoshi Kodaira	70	71	73	71	285	815,571
	Taichi Teshima	72	70	73	70	285	815,571
	Yuto Soeda	73	68	71	73	285	815,571
	Ryosuke Kinoshita	68	70	73	74	285	815,571
	Shota Akiyoshi	71	72	67	75	285	815,571

Japan Open Championship

Yuki Inamori had two victories in his fairly productive seven years on the Japan Tour. Nothing unusual about that. He certainly had company in that regard. Unmatched in that category, though, was the fact that both of those victories were in the crown-jewel Japan Open Championship.

The second one was achieved in mid-October in just the second tournament of the Japan Tour's desolate season on Japanese soil when Inamori nipped multi-winner Hideto Tanihara on the Sumire course of Murasaki Country Club in Chiba Prefecture. Inamori's earlier Open win was in 2018.

It all came down to those two players and the final holes. The 41-year-old Tanihara, who had played the previous three seasons on the European Tour, had won 14 times since joining the Japan Tour in 2002, but never one of the majors. At Murasaki, he had moved on top by a stroke over Inamori after 54 holes after Shugo Imahira, 2019's number one money-winner, led the first day with 66 and amateur Riki Kawamoto the second with 67-68. Tanihara had rounds of 72, 64 and 69 for five under, while Inamori posted 70-68-68.

Hideto clung to the lead on Sunday until a bunkered approach at the 17th cost him a bogey and dropped him into a tie with Yuki at four under par. Then, at the 18th, Tanihara overshot the green, Inamori put his approach within birdie range and, with "my heart beating so fast I could hear it", holed out for the victory on a five-under-par total of 275.

"I was a nervous wreck," Inamori admitted afterward. "But I recalled the memory of winning at this major in 2018 and that experience helped me to make the winning birdie."

On the other hand, it was "very disappointing" for Tanihara. "I just couldn't produce the perfect putt and shot at the end. I am regretting the lack of technique."

The popular Ryo Ishikawa closed with a 65 and tied for third place with Hirotaro Naito at 277.

Murasaki Country Club (Sumire), Yokohama, Kanagawa — October 15-18
Par 70 (35-35); 7,317 yards — Purse: ¥157,500,000

1	**Yuki Inamori**	70	68	68	69	275	¥31,500,000
2	**Hideto Tanihara**	72	64	69	71	276	17,325,000
3	**Hirotaro Naito**	70	68	70	69	277	10,001,250
	Ryo Ishikawa	73	67	72	65	277	10,001,250
5	Taiga Sugihara (A)	70	66	74	68	278	
	Riki Kawamoto (A)	67	68	73	70	278	
7	Takumi Kanaya	72	69	69	69	279	6,615,000
8	Rikuya Hoshino	70	73	71	66	280	5,512,500
9	Kei Takahashi	69	72	72	68	281	4,725,000
10	Naoto Nakanishi	70	70	74	68	282	3,517,500
	Shugo Imahira	66	70	76	70	282	3,517,500
	Daijiro Izumida	73	68	70	71	282	3,517,500
13	Hiroyuki Fujita	69	72	74	68	283	2,346,750
	Kazuki Higa	69	71	74	69	283	2,346,750
	Toru Taniguchi	67	71	75	70	283	2,346,750
	Taisei Shimizu (A)	70	72	70	71	283	
	Tomoyo Ikemura	72	65	74	72	283	2,346,750
18	Koumei Oda	70	74	71	69	284	1,795,500
	Yosuke Tsukada	71	69	73	71	284	1,795,500
	Keita Nakajima (A)	69	72	71	72	284	
21	Daisuke Matsubara	72	72	73	68	285	1,502,550
	Takaya Onoda	72	71	73	69	285	1,502,550
	Shota Seki	70	68	75	72	285	1,502,550
	Taisei Yamada	72	71	70	72	285	1,502,550
	Yuto Katsuragawa (A)	67	69	76	73	285	
	Kodai Ichihara	68	69	73	75	285	1,502,550
27	Taichi Teshima	75	69	72	70	286	1,212,750
	Jinichiro Kozuma	72	71	72	71	286	1,212,750
	Atomu Shigenaga	71	72	72	71	286	1,212,750
	Daichi Sato	71	70	73	72	286	1,212,750
	Suzuchiyo Ishida	71	73	70	72	286	1,212,750
	Ren Yonezawa (A)	69	72	71	74	286	
	Tomoharu Otsuki	70	71	71	74	286	1,212,750
	Daiki Imano	68	73	70	75	286	1,212,750
	Ryo Katsumata	70	70	72	74	286	1,212,750

Mitsui Sumitomo VISA Taiheiyo Masters

It was a long time in coming. Jinichiro Kozuma laboured into his eighth season on the Japan Tour, never finishing higher than 33rd on the annual money lists, before breaking through with his first victory — and it took a spectacular final shot to do it.

The 26-year-old pro nearly holed his 230-yard second shot on the par-five 18th hole on the Taiheiyo Club's Gotemba course and tapped in for an eagle three, a 68, an eight-under-par 272 and a one-stroke victory in the highly regarded Mitsui Sumitomo VISA Taiheiyo Masters in mid-November.

"The last four holes were nerve-breaking," exclaimed Kozuma, shaking off a chilly victory shower at the end of the day's cold weather. "My gut was aching with the pressure. But that winning putt was so close I didn't have to worry."

The top of the leaderboard was tightly bunched going into the final round. With his six-under-par 204, Kozuma was tied with amateur Keita Nakajima, who shot a third-round 64 off a front-nine 29. They were a shot behind co-leaders Chan Kim, the 2019 Japan Open champion, and Ryosuke Kinoshita, who had a 63, the week's low round, on the second day.

Kozuma got off to a fast start on Sunday with birdies on three of the first four holes, gave those three strokes back at the sixth and seventh and found himself in a three-way tie with Kinoshita and Nakajima at six under par. Kinoshita, also a non-winner, went ahead with a birdie at the 16th, setting the stage for Kozuma's stunning finish and come-from-behind victory. "I am so happy and at the same time so relieved that I finally won."

Interestingly, as a victor, he joined his sister, Kotono, who won the Munsingwear Tokai Classic on the 2018 Japan LPGA Tour. The only other such brother-sister achievement in Japanese golf history paired Ai and Yusaku Miyazato.

Taiheiyo Club (Gotemba), Gotemba, Shizuoka — November 12-15
Par 70 (35-35); 7,262 yards — Purse: ¥120,000,000

1	**Jinichiro Kozuma**	71	65	68	68	272	¥24,000,000
2	**Ryosuke Kinoshita**	72	63	68	70	273	12,000,000
3	**Keita Nakajima** (A)	71	69	64	70	274	
4	Chan Kim	70	65	68	72	275	8,160,000
5	Todd Baek	68	70	70	68	276	5,280,000
	Takumi Kanaya	69	70	67	70	276	5,280,000
7	Hiroshi Iwata	71	67	70	69	277	4,140,000
	Tomoharu Otsuki	66	70	71	70	277	4,140,000
9	Mikumu Horikawa	69	71	69	69	278	3,660,000
10	Mikiya Akutsu	68	69	71	71	279	3,024,000
	Katsumasa Miyamoto	68	71	69	71	279	3,024,000
	Yuwa Kosaihira	69	66	72	72	279	3,024,000
	Shingo Katayama	72	67	66	74	279	3,024,000
14	Ryo Ishikawa	77	67	66	70	280	2,304,000
	Yuta Ikeda	69	71	67	73	280	2,304,000
16	Tomohiro Kondo	73	69	73	66	281	1,944,000
	Ryuko Tokimatsu	69	72	70	70	281	1,944,000
	Shota Akiyoshi	68	73	69	71	281	1,944,000
19	Koumei Oda	74	68	73	67	282	1,464,000
	Tomoyo Ikemura	72	69	73	68	282	1,464,000
	Tomoyasu Sugiyama	69	74	72	67	282	1,464,000
	Ryuichi Oiwa	75	68	71	68	282	1,464,000
	Tatsuya Kodai	71	73	72	66	282	1,464,000
	Juvic Pagunsan	71	71	69	71	282	1,464,000
25	Naoto Nakanishi	68	70	76	69	283	1,128,000
	Ren Yonezawa (A)	74	71	69	69	283	
27	Shintaro Kobayashi	71	69	74	70	284	984,000
	Taichi Teshima	70	73	72	69	284	984,000
	Gunn Charoenkul	72	72	70	70	284	984,000
	Rikuya Hoshino	75	70	67	72	284	984,000
	Ryutaro Nagano	78	68	72	66	284	984,000

Dunlop Phoenix

Who could have imagined the unprecedented finish that occurred at the Dunlop Phoenix tournament? One senior at one college defeating a junior at another school — both rookie professionals no less — in a four-hole playoff in one of the Japan Tour's most important events.

That's what happened when 22-year-old Takami Kanaya, Japan men's golf's newest shining light, sank the deciding putt to outlast 21-year-old Tomohiro Ishizaka and capture his second tour title a year after winning his first as an amateur in the equally prestigious Taiheiyo Masters when he was the top-ranked amateur in the world.

"I am honoured to have my name listed among the world's legendary players," Kanaya commented. "I knew that if I didn't win my second victory soon, the Taiheiyo win would be considered a fluke." This from a young man who finished seventh and fifth in his only two previous starts as a pro. He became the youngest winner in the Dunlop Phoenix's distinguished history, 88 days younger than his hero, Hideki Matsuyama, who won the title in 2014.

Halfway through the tournament, Ishizaki (67-66) had a one-stroke lead on Kanaya and Gunn Charoenkul. With his own 66, Tomoharu Otsuki overtook Ishizaki Saturday and the two led the way into the final round at Phoenix Country Club with 202s, a shot in front of Kanaya. On Sunday, Kanaya birdied two of the last four holes for a 69 to tie Ishizaka, who was one over par on the final six holes and shot 70 as the pair returned the 13-under-par totals of 271. The two matched scores (par-birdie-birdie) on the first three playoff holes before Kanaya birdied the par-five again with a short putt after Ishizaki found the woods with his tee shot and missed with his birdie chip.

Noting that two other collegians — Keita Nakajima and Ren Yonezawa — tied for eighth and took low-amateur honours, Kanaya remarked: "I guess there is not much difference between professionals and amateurs now. The strongest player wins."

Phoenix Country Club, Miyazaki — November 19-22
Par 71 (36-35); 7,042 yards — Purse: ¥100,000,000

1	**Takumi Kanaya**	68	66	68	69	271	¥20,000,000
2	**Tomohiro Ishizaka**	67	66	68	70	271	10,000,000
	Kanaya won playoff at fourth extra hole						
3	**Yuki Inamori**	67	69	68	68	272	5,800,000
	Tomoharu Otsuki	69	66	66	71	272	5,800,000
5	Chan Kim	67	69	70	67	273	3,800,000
	Ryosuke Kinoshita	69	66	68	70	273	3,800,000
7	Hiroshi Iwata	66	70	72	66	274	3,300,000
8	Ren Yonezawa (A)	71	71	70	63	275	
	Keita Nakajima (A)	68	70	70	67	275	
	Ryo Ishikawa	74	67	67	67	275	2,727,500
	Yuta Ikeda	69	68	69	69	275	2,727,500
	Rikuya Hoshino	68	69	68	70	275	2,727,500
	Gunn Charoenkul	67	67	70	71	275	2,727,500
14	Tatsunori Nukaga	68	70	74	64	276	1,820,000
	Mikumu Horikawa	70	70	69	67	276	1,820,000
	Naoto Nakanishi	67	71	70	68	276	1,820,000
	Tomoyo Ikemura	67	74	67	68	276	1,820,000
	Daijiro Izumida	67	69	70	70	276	1,820,000
	Ryuko Tokimatsu	67	72	67	70	276	1,820,000
20	Kazuki Higa	73	71	67	66	277	1,340,000
	Ryutaro Nagano	67	70	69	71	277	1,340,000
	Justin De Los Santos	71	70	65	71	277	1,340,000
23	Hirotaro Naito	68	69	74	67	278	1,060,000

Koumei Oda	70	69	72	67	278	1,060,000	Shingo Katayama	71	73	66	69	279	840,000
Jinichiro Kozuma	71	69	67	71	278	1,060,000	Shunya Takeyasu	72	71	70	66	279	840,000
Hideto Tanihara	70	67	68	73	278	1,060,000	Taiga Sugihara (A)	69	70	69	71	279	
27 Shugo Imahira	71	69	71	68	279	840,000	Tatsuya Kodai	69	76	71	63	279	840,000

Golf Nippon Series JT Cup

It was worth it!

Despite the hurdles he had to face just to get into the country and be cleared to compete, Chan Kim's determination to play in the few late-season tournaments on the Japan Tour paid off big when he won the significant Golf Nippon Series title, the finale of the pandemic-stricken season.

The 30-year-old Korea-born American, who had four previous tour victories, including the 2019 Japan Open, on his record, worked through visa delays and a two-week quarantine once he arrived in Japan. Finishing fourth and tied for fifth in his only two starts prior to the Nippon Series, Kim holed a five-foot par-putt on final green on the Tokyo Yomiuri Country Club course to snatch a one-stroke victory away from three other contenders.

"I knew I must make it and that made my hands shake," Kim admitted. "I am so glad that I took great effort to come back to my favourite Japan. Being able to win this major is the best highlight of my year."

The lead changed hands each of the first three days. After 54 holes, Hiroshi Iwata was in front by a stroke on seven under par. Yuwa Kosaihira was on six under and Kim shared third place on five under with veteran standout Hideto Tanihara and rookie pro Takumi Kanaya, coming off his victory two weeks earlier in the Dunlop Phoenix.

The contenders were bunched coming into the final holes the last day. First, Tomoharu Otsuki shot 66 and posted 273. Then, Kim birdied the 17th, made the five-foot par-putt at the 18th for a 67 and an eight-under-par total of 272. Finally, playing in the final threesome and tied for the lead with Kim, both Tanihara and Iwata bogeyed the par-three 18th hole, dropping into a second-place tie with Otasuki.

The ¥25-million prize moved Kim into second place on the money list at ¥36,960,00, behind Yuki Inamori and his ¥41,112,558, but all the year's statistics carry over into the 2021 season.

Tokyo Yomiuri Country Club, Inagi, Tokyo — December 3-6
Par 70 (35-35); 7,023 yards — Purse: ¥100,000,000

1 **Chan Kim**	66	66	73	67	272	¥25,000,000	16 Kazuki Higa	74	71	69	69	283	1,850,000
2 **Tomoharu Otsuki**	68	65	74	66	273	7,600,000	Gunn Charoenkul	72	71	70	70	283	1,850,000
Hiroshi Iwata	66	67	70	70	273	7,600,000	18 Tomoyo Ikemura	71	76	70	67	284	1,562,500
Hideto Tanihara	65	73	67	68	273	7,600,000	Tomoyasu Sugiyama	66	74	75	69	284	1,562,500
5 Takumi Kanaya	67	70	68	70	275	4,500,000	Yuta Ikeda	64	77	73	70	284	1,562,500
6 Ryo Ishikawa	67	70	70	69	276	3,550,000	Mikiya Akutsu	66	70	76	72	284	1,562,500
Yuwa Kosaihira	68	64	72	72	276	3,550,000	22 Taihei Sato	70	71	71	73	285	1,400,000
8 Hiroyuki Fujita	68	66	76	68	278	2,925,000	23 Yuki Inamori	68	70	76	72	286	1,300,000
Daijiro Izumida	69	68	71	70	278	2,925,000	Kodai Ichihara	66	80	68	72	286	1,300,000
10 Shugo Imahira	72	69	71	67	279	2,475,000	Koumei Oda	70	74	70	72	286	1,300,000
Ryosuke Kinoshita	68	70	72	69	279	2,475,000	26 Naoto Nakanishi	74	75	74	65	288	1,200,000
Mikumu Horikawa	75	66	69	69	279	2,475,000	27 Jinichiro Kozuma	69	71	76	73	289	1,150,000
Ryuko Tokimatsu	69	70	70	70	279	2,475,000	28 Hirotaro Naito	72	74	69	76	291	1,100,000
14 Todd Baek	68	74	70	68	280	2,100,000	29 Tomohiro Ishizaka	69	73	75	75	292	1,050,000
15 Rikuya Hoshino	69	73	69	70	281	2,000,000	30 Shingo Katayama	74	73	72	74	293	1,000,000

2020-21 MONEY LIST

1	Yuki Inamori	¥41,112,558
2	Chan Kim	36,960,000
3	Takumi Kanaya	36,395,000
4	Rikuya Hoshino	34,968,107
5	Jinichiro Kozuma	27,663,650
6	Hideto Tanihara	26,816,100
7	Tomoharu Otsuki	23,609,857
8	Ryosuke Kinoshita	22,400,270
9	Ryo Ishikawa	20,762,917
10	Mikumu Horikawa	20,159,987

ISPS Handa PGA Tour of Australasia

With Australians battling an unprecedented bushfire crisis over the summer, the year started with their golfers raising funds for the birdies and eagles they made in competition and being inspired to win around the world. Cameron Smith, whose uncle had his home burnt to the ground, won the Sony Open in a playoff in Hawaii for his second PGA Tour title and the first in an individual tournament. "Every birdie putt I had, just meant that little bit more," Smith said. "Rather than kind of wanting to make it, I almost felt like I had to make it."

Smith added: "I realise Australia is doing it tough right now and the focus is probably not on my golf for good reason. But hopefully it gave a few people reason to smile for a moment or two."

Then came an Australia Day double. In Dubai, Lucas Herbert claimed his first European Tour title, also via a playoff. "There's some pretty awful stuff happening right now in Australia with the fires," he said. "Cam Smith said it a couple weeks ago when he won, and I'd like to say the same thing. Everyone around the world is behind us and hopefully we can keep fighting harder than what I did on the first playoff hole. That's nothing compared to the firefighters and volunteers putting out the fires."

Later in the day, in California, Marc Leishman won for the fifth time on the PGA Tour at Torrey Pines. "Seeing Cam Smith win a couple weeks ago, that gave me a bit of determination," Leishman admitted. "The goal was to win." No Australian had won on the PGA Tour in 2019 but then three victories came in quick succession as Adam Scott won the Genesis Invitational in his first start since winning the 2019 Australian PGA.

Meanwhile, back at home, Min Woo Lee won for the first time at the age of 21 in the Vic Open, co-sanctioned with the European Tour. Since the tournament also has a women's event running alongside, older sister Minjee was beside the 18th green in position to be the first to offer a congratulatory hug. Minjee still has the upper hand having won the event twice.

As the domestic circuit continued, Michael Sim and Anthony Quayle won the PGA and Open titles, respectively, in Queensland before Brad Kennedy, who finished third in each of those weeks, claimed a second New Zealand Open title with a two-stroke victory over Herbert.

The win had the 45-year-old reconsidering his plans to retire at the end of the year. "I was looking to hang the boots up at the end of this year, I've been doing it for 25 years and just really wanted to make this year a really positive year to end," said Kennedy, who played for many years in Japan. "I've sacrificed a lot, but also my family has sacrificed a lot, too. I've been pretty selfish over the last 15-20 years playing the game and it just feels now is a good time to get back and watch my girls grow up and spend some time at home."

Of course, at that point, no one knew quite how prophetic his words would become only weeks later as the coronavirus pandemic swept the globe. Although the autumn swing on the PGA Tour of Australasia had been completed, normal service could not be resumed in the spring. Internal boarder restrictions meant the PGA and Open tournaments in Western Australia went ahead with only state residents able to compete. Golfers from Queensland, New South Wales and South Australia could travel to the Northern Territory PGA but could not beat Aaron Pike, who grew up on the course in Palmerston.

None of the three events counted on the ISPS Handa Order of Merit and the 2020 season was extended into the first part of 2021 with some tournaments rescheduled for late January onwards. But the country's major summer golf events had to be cancelled. The Australian Open and the Australian PGA were first postponed to the end of the summer from late November/early December following the relocation of the Masters to November, and then abandoned due to uncertainty over the participation of international players. The Vic Open and the Women's Australian Open due for early 2021 were also cancelled.

"It's unprecedented and a real blow for Australian golf and its fans," said Gavin Kirkman, chief executive of the PGA of Australia in a joint statement with Golf Australia and the WPGA Tour of Australasia. "We have collectively spent months in exhaustive consultation with all relevant authorities and our sanctioning partners to try to find a way to stage all the events safely and at that world-class level to which we've all become accustomed.

"But even with multiple contingency plans, it has reached a point where decisions have to be made and this, regrettably, is the one we've had to take. We look forward to bringing all these tournaments alive again when they return as normal for summer 2021-22."

The men's Australian Open had not missed a year since 1945. James Sutherland, chief executive of Golf Australia, said: "On the advice of relevant domestic government authorities and, with consideration for the global nature of our fields and partners, the call was made with the health and wellbeing of the golfing community as the priority.

"The events rely on significant support from players and tours around the world, so given current quarantine restrictions, we believe the field strength of all the events would be severely compromised. This, in turn, is unsatisfactory for spectators, broadcasters and our events' commercial partners."

The 2021 New Zealand Open, set to be hosted once again in the South Island resort of Queenstown, was also cancelled due to the strict international travel and quarantine restrictions required in a country that had largely eliminated community transmission of Covid-19.

With tours in other parts of the world resuming to a greater or lesser extent, Jason Day finished fourth at the PGA Championship at Harding Park, while Cam Smith almost bookended the year with victories. He was one of the runners-up to Dustin Johnson, five strokes behind, at the Masters and created history by becoming the first player in 84 editions of the tournament at Augusta National to score all four rounds in the 60s.

"I honestly can't believe it," said Smith, who shot 67-68-69-69. "I've got to put it down to just scrambling and digging deep. There were a few times throughout the week where I could have let it slip away, and it didn't.

"It would have been cool to do that and win," Smith added. "I'd take 15 under around here the rest of my career and I might win a couple."

2020 SCHEDULE

ISPS Handa Vic Open	**Min Woo Lee**	
Coca-Cola Queensland PGA Championship	**Michael Sim**	
Isuzu Queensland Open	**Anthony Quayle**	
New Zealand Open	**Brad Kennedy**	
PNG Open		*cancelled*
TX Civil & Logistics WA PGA Championship*	**Jarryd Felton**	
Nexus Risk WA Open*	**Hayden Hopewell** (A)	
Tailor-Made Building Services NT PGA Championship*	**Aaron Pike**	
Gippsland Super 6		*postponed to 2021*
Victorian PGA Championship		*postponed to 2021*
NSW Open		*postponed to 2021*
Australian Open		*cancelled*
Australian PGA Championship		*cancelled*

*non-order of merit event

ISPS Handa Vic Open

Thanks to the men's and women's versions of the ISPS Handa Vic Open being played alongside each other at 13th Beach — with alternating tee times throughout the four days — Min Woo Lee added a special family achievement with his first professional victory coming at the same event his elder sister Minjee claimed hers. "My sister and I winning the same tournament, it's pretty special," Min Woo said. "I've got bragging rights now so it's even better."

Perhaps not yet since Minjee is a two-time Vic Open champion, winning as an amateur in 2014 and as a professional four years later. Although she missed out on a third title, falling two stokes short of a playoff, big sister was able to watch from the edge of the 18th green and offer the first congratulatory hug. "I was super, super proud of him," she said. "It was really cool to be here with him and watch the last two holes."

Min Woo Lee turned professional early in 2019 and only just missed out on his European Tour card but finished the year with a third place at the Australian PGA Championship. This was his 19th European Tour event and a 68 on day three, when the wind started to blow, put him into the lead following earlier scores of 66 and 67. His three-shot lead was bolstered by chipping in for a birdie at the first on Sunday and then two more birdies came at the second and fourth holes.

With the wind getting up again, Lee showed a mature composure by parring until another birdie at the 15th. New Zealand's Ryan Fox produced a remarkable 64, with two eagles, including at the last, to get to 17 under par. Lee's only dropped shot came at the short 17th but the 21-year-old birdied the last for a 68 and a 19-under-par total of 269 to beat Fox by two. Three strokes further back were fellow Australians Marcus Fraser and Travis Smyth, plus France's Robin Sciot-Siegrist.

"It's awesome," Lee said. "I thought coming in I had a really good chance because I was hitting it really good but I think I impressed myself with the game this whole week. I felt really comfortable just because if I did exactly the same as yesterday, I felt pretty hard to stop. I started off really hot out of the gate and it was pretty comfortable those last few holes. It got a bit nervy but I'm pretty proud of the way I finished."

13th Beach Golf Links (Beach), Barwon Heads, Victoria — February 6-9
Par 72 (36-36); 6,778 yards — Purse: A$1,600,000
Creek (R1&2) par 72 (36-36); 6,940 yards

1	**Min Woo Lee**	66	67	68	68	269	A$253,327
2	**Ryan Fox**	67	71	69	64	271	168,882
3	**Robin Sciot-Siegrist**	66	64	76	68	274	78,331
	Travis Smyth	65	67	72	70	274	78,331
	Marcus Fraser	70	65	69	70	274	78,331
6	Jake McLeod	65	68	76	67	276	53,922
7	Sam Horsfield	70	67	73	67	277	37,269
	Darren Beck	69	70	69	69	277	37,269
	Sami Valimaki	69	69	70	69	277	37,269
	Jediah Morgan (A)	66	67	74	70	277	
	Ashley Hall	67	68	71	71	277	37,269
12	Niklas Lemke	70	67	72	69	278	26,452
	Lucas Herbert	70	69	70	69	278	26,452
	Nick Flanagan	67	67	74	70	278	26,452
15	Alejandro Canizares	63	71	76	69	279	21,689
	Daniel Hillier	68	70	72	69	279	21,689
	Zach Murray	66	69	73	71	279	21,689
	Anthony Quayle	75	64	67	73	279	21,689
	Matthew Millar	72	66	68	73	279	21,689
20	Richard Green	70	69	70	71	280	18,801
	Matthew Jordan	72	66	69	73	280	18,801
22	Hideto Tanihara	70	67	73	71	281	16,065
	Cory Crawford	70	68	72	71	281	16,065
	Ben Eccles	68	70	72	71	281	16,065
	Matthew Stieger	67	69	73	72	281	16,065
	Benjamin Poke	68	67	74	72	281	16,065
	Blake Windred	69	69	71	72	281	16,065
	Jarryd Felton	67	67	74	73	281	16,065
	Jason Scrivener	68	71	69	73	281	16,065
	Rikard Karlberg	69	68	70	74	281	16,065
31	Blake Collyer	68	67	74	73	282	13,785
32	Scott Arnold	68	68	72	75	283	13,329
33	Peter Fowler	69	70	71	74	284	12,417
	David Smail	68	69	72	75	284	12,417
	Andrew Martin	66	69	73	76	284	12,417
36	Josh Younger	68	69	73	75	285	11,505
	Lincoln Tighe	69	69	72	75	285	11,505
38	Geoff Ogilvy	67	67	76	77	287	11,049

MISSED THE 54-HOLE CUT

39	Steven Jeffress	67	72	72	211	9,985
	Brad Kennedy	66	72	73	211	9,985
	Luke Toomey	71	68	72	211	9,985
	Sebastian Garcia Rodriguez	68	71	72	211	9,985
	Jonathan Caldwell	67	67	77	211	9,985
	Matthew Griffin	65	68	78	211	9,985
45	Gareth Paddison	67	71	74	212	7,705
	Peter Lonard	69	69	74	212	7,705
	Martin Dive	69	70	73	212	7,705
	Lars van Meijel	68	67	77	212	7,705
	Ashley Chesters	69	67	76	212	7,705
	Wil Besseling	67	69	76	212	7,705
	Derek Ackerman	67	69	76	212	7,705
	Sean Crocker	67	70	75	212	7,705
	Cormac Sharvin	70	67	75	212	7,705
54	Aaron Townsend	69	70	74	213	5,338
	Justin Warren	65	72	76	213	5,338
	Dave Coupland	70	69	74	213	5,338
	Michael Hendry	67	69	77	213	5,338
	Shae Wools-Cobb	67	67	79	213	5,338
	Hugo Leon	68	68	77	213	5,338
	Kevin Yuan	69	68	76	213	5,338
61	Denzel Ieremia	70	68	76	214	4,285
	Stephen Allan	70	65	79	214	4,285
	Brett Rankin	70	67	77	214	4,285
	Aaron Cockerill	66	71	77	214	4,285
65	Daniel Fox	70	68	77	215	3,829
	Nick Cullen	68	71	76	215	3,829
	Andre Lautee (A)	69	67	79	215	
68	Ryan McCarthy	68	71	77	216	3,344
69	Peter Wilson	67	70	80	217	3,340
70	Andrew Evans	66	71	81	218	3,333
	Chang Gi Lee	68	71	79	218	3,333
72	Robbie Morrison	69	70	83	222	3,326

Coca-Cola Queensland PGA Championship

Michael Sim was due to give Scott Arnold a lift back to the Gold Coast, where the Scottish-born Western Australian is now based. The friends still made the journey home from the City Golf Club in Toowoomba but only after Sim had defeated Arnold at the fourth extra hole to win the Coca-Cola Queensland PGA Championship.

The unexpected ending only came about after Brad Kennedy, the longtime leader after an opening 61, dropped four shots on the final three holes. Bogeys at the 16th and 17th holes were followed by a double at the last when Kennedy drove into the trees, took two more to reach the green and then three-putted to miss the playoff by one shot. He closed with a 73 to tie for third place with Michael Hendry, Dimitrios Papadatos and Chang Gi Lee.

Sim, playing alongside Kennedy, thought his chance had gone when he bogeyed the 14th and 15th holes but a birdie at the last tied him with Arnold on 12-under-par 268. Arnold had earlier also birdied the last for a 69 while Sim had scores of 68, 67, 63 and 70. On the fourth playoff hole, Sim missed the green but got up and down for a par while Arnold three-putted for a bogey.

Before Sim checked with the tournament director, he and Kennedy believed Arnold had finished at 13 under par. "He said Scott had actually finished at 12. I thought, 'I've got a chance here'," said the 35-year-old Sim after his second PGA Tour of Australasia title. "I didn't have my best stuff today, I don't really think anyone near the top of the leaderboard did. Everyone kept falling away and it was nice to hit a great eight-iron into the last there in regulation and give myself a chance in the playoff. Everything happened so fast. I never thought I'd be here as the winner and to come away with the trophy is just amazing."

City Golf Club, Toowoomba, Queensland — February 13-16
Par 70 (33-37); 6,562 yards — Purse: A$150,000

1	**Michael Sim**	68	67	63	70	268	A$22,500
2	**Scott Arnold**	70	64	65	69	268	14,250
	Sim won playoff at fourth extra hole						
3	**Michael Hendry**	69	65	67	68	269	7,350
	Dimitrios Papadatos	65	68	67	69	269	7,350
	Chang Gi Lee	67	67	66	69	269	7,350
	Brad Kennedy	61	66	69	73	269	7,350
7	Andrew Dodt	70	68	68	64	270	4,200
	Denzel Ieremia	66	69	65	70	270	4,200
	Anthony Quayle	66	68	63	73	270	4,200
10	Charlie Dann	67	69	69	66	271	2,850
	Jack Munro	70	67	66	68	271	2,850
	Justin Warren	70	66	67	68	271	2,850
	Callan O'Reilly	66	66	68	71	271	2,850
14	Paul Hayden	72	65	72	63	272	1,980
	Jordan Zunic	72	65	71	64	272	1,980
	Lincoln Tighe	71	67	65	69	272	1,980
	Aaron Wilkin	66	69	65	72	272	1,980
	Jamie Hook	66	68	64	74	272	1,980
19	Marcus Fraser	65	70	71	67	273	1,646
	Daniel Fox	70	66	70	67	273	1,646
	Peter Wilson	72	64	70	67	273	1,646
	David Bransdon	67	65	69	72	273	1,646
23	James Marchesani	73	64	72	65	274	1,425
	Steven Jeffress	67	67	72	68	274	1,425
	Michael Wright	68	69	69	68	274	1,425
	Kade McBride	67	66	72	69	274	1,425
	James Nitties	71	65	68	70	274	1,425
	Shae Wools-Cobb	71	67	65	71	274	1,425
	Matias Sanchez	70	67	66	71	274	1,425
	Jason Norris	70	67	65	72	274	1,425
	Douglas Klein	69	67	66	72	274	1,425
	Aaron Townsend	68	66	67	73	274	1,425

Isuzu Queensland Open

Anthony Quayle, who grew up in a small town on the most north-easterly point of the Northern Territory where he built a little six-hole course around his house using old baked bean cans for cups, was delighted to claim his adopted home state's championship as his maiden title on the PGA Tour of Australasia. Quayle won the Isuzu Queensland Open at Pelican Waters by beating South Australian amateur Jack Thompson at the first extra hole of a sudden-death playoff.

The pair shared the 54-hole lead along with New Zealander James Anstiss, who finished three behind. Brad Kennedy and Jake Higginbottom finished two behind in third place as Quayle, who went 67, 69, 67 for the first three days, and Thompson closed with 70s to tie on 15-under-par 273.

Quayle took the lead with four birdies on the front nine but bogeyed the 11th and took a double bogey at the 12th. The 25-year-old, who turned professional in 2017, rallied with birdies at the 15th and 16th holes before another bogey at the last. Moments later, however, Quayle's par at the first playoff hole secured the win over the 21-year-old amateur from The Grange in Adelaide.

"It feels incredible. I've given myself a few chances recently and haven't been able to pull it off and the feeling of frustration or regret walking off the 18th green is definitely not present at the moment," Quayle said. "I felt for a while that my first win would be a pretty difficult one to get done and maybe it was difficult because I thought it into reality."

Pelican Waters Golf Club, Pelican Waters, Queensland — February 20-23
Par 72 (36-36); 6,877 yards — Purse: A$137,500

1	**Anthony Quayle**	67	69	67	70	273	A$20,625
2	**Jack Thompson** (A)	65	70	68	70	273	
	Quayle won playoff at first extra hole						
3	**Brad Kennedy**	65	68	75	67	275	11,344
	Jake Higginbottom	73	63	68	71	275	11,344
5	Steven Jeffress	69	72	69	66	276	5,775
	Josh Armstrong (A)	65	69	73	69	276	
	Richard Green	69	67	71	69	276	5,775
	James Anstiss	69	68	66	73	276	5,775
9	David Bransdon	63	69	74	71	277	4,331
10	Nick Voke	72	69	71	66	278	2,945
	Matthew Millar	68	69	71	70	278	2,945
	Kade McBride	72	68	68	70	278	2,945
	Simon Hawkes	70	69	68	71	278	2,945
	Matias Sanchez	67	72	67	72	278	2,945
	Jarryd Felton	68	68	68	74	278	2,945
16	Andre Lautee (A)	67	72	71	69	279	
	Dylan Perry	68	73	68	70	279	2,063
18	Paul Hayden	73	70	68	69	280	1,684
	Darren Beck	71	71	69	69	280	1,684
	Callan O'Reilly	72	69	69	70	280	1,684
	Nick Cullen	73	71	70	66	280	1,684
	Douglas Klein	70	69	70	71	280	1,684
	Blake Proverbs	69	69	69	73	280	1,684
24	Elvis Smylie (A)	71	68	74	68	281	
	James Nitties	72	68	69	72	281	1,485
	Nathan Barbieri (A)	68	70	69	74	281	
27	Peter Wilson	73	66	72	71	282	1,416
	Blake Windred	70	75	68	69	282	1,416
	Toby Walker (A)	69	71	71	71	282	
	Michael Sim	70	69	71	72	282	1,416
	Matthew Stieger	74	66	69	73	282	1,416

New Zealand Open

Putting behind him the disappointments of the previous two weeks when he finished third on each occasion, Brad Kennedy won the New Zealand Open for the second time at Millbrook. Kennedy had dropped four shots in the final three holes at the Queensland PGA, this time came from two behind with a bogey-free 63 in the final round to beat Lucas Herbert by two strokes. "It's just hard to put into words the emotion I've gone through the last two weeks," Kennedy, 45, said after his fifth win on the PGA Tour of Australasia.

"It felt like I'd lost two events and then to come back and play how I did this week, I think it's going to take a little bit of time to really understand why the things happened for the reasons they did. You just never know in this game. I think I was chasing today which put me in a really good mindset to continue to attack."

Herbert, winner of the Dubai Desert Classic in January, shared the 54-hole lead with Korea's Joohyung Kim and looked in command until a double bogey at the 13th hole. Kennedy, following earlier rounds of 66, 69 and 66, birdied three holes in a row from the 12th and then the 16th to set the target at 21-under-par 264. Herbert produced his own hat-trick of birdies from the 15th to get within one but then missed the green at the par-three 18th and bogeyed for a 67. Nick Flanagan was third after a closing 66 with Kim, who had led from an opening 64, fourth following a 70.

Pernilla Lindberg, a former ANA Inspiration champion, who was in Queenstown to celebrate the first anniversary of her wedding in the famous Southern Island resort, became the first woman to play in the 101-year history of the NZ Open but missed the cut after scores of 80 and 73 on the Millbrook and Hills courses.

Millbrook Golf Resort, Arrowtown, New Zealand | February 27-March 1
Par 71 (35-36); 6,998 yards | Purse: NZ$1,400,000
The Hills (R1&2) par 72; (36-36) 7,176 yards

1	**Brad Kennedy**	66 69 66 63	264	A$240,688			
2	**Lucas Herbert**	66 68 65 67	266	136,390			
3	**Nick Flanagan**	68 68 66 66	268	90,258			
4	Joohyung Kim	64 68 67 70	269	64,183			
5	Harry Bateman	67 69 67 67	270	50,812			
	Michael Hendry	70 66 67 67	270	50,812			
7	Wade Ormsby	65 71 69 66	271	40,783			
	Chan Kim	70 67 65 69	271	40,783			
9	Kieran Muir	70 65 69 68	272	34,766			
	Ryosuke Kinoshita	72 65 66 69	272	34,766			
11	Pavit Tangkamolprasert	70 64 70 69	273	29,417			
12	Jarin Todd	68 72 68 66	274	25,406			
	Jarryd Felton	71 67 67 69	274	25,406			
14	Stephen Allan	69 74 68 64	275	20,191			
	Nick Voke	70 73 67 65	275	20,191			
	Samuel Eaves	73 66 68 68	275	20,191			
	Dimitrios Papadatos	70 68 67 70	275	20,191			
18	Tatsuya Kodai	67 73 73 63	276	14,408			
	KJ Choi	71 67 72 66	276	14,408			
	Shae Wools-Cobb	70 71 67 68	276	14,408			
	Tae Woo Kim	73 68 67 68	276	14,408			
	Mikumu Horikawa	73 67 67 69	276	14,408			
	Ben Eccles	65 68 71 72	276	14,408			
24	Jamie Arnold	70 73 68 66	277	11,009			
	James Anstiss	72 69 68 68	277	11,009			
	Josh Younger	74 69 66 68	277	11,009			
	Jordan Zunic	71 70 67 69	277	11,009			
	Max McCardle	71 70 66 70	277	11,009			
	Zach Murray	68 72 66 71	277	11,009			
30	Terumichi Kakazu	74 68 70 66	278	8,080			
	Blake Windred	73 69 68 68	278	8,080			
	Deyen Lawson	70 72 68 68	278	8,080			
	Bio Kim	74 69 66 69	278	8,080			
	Brendan Jones	70 73 66 69	278	8,080			
	Terry Pilkadaris	66 72 70 70	278	8,080			
	Katsumasa Miyamoto	72 67 69 70	278	8,080			

TX Civil & Logistics WA PGA Championship

Having not played a meaningful competition since the New Zealand Open finished on March 1, Jarryd Felton had low expectations — "I haven't even won a monthly medal," he said — but was keen to improve on his runner-up finish to Darren Beck the previous year at the TX Civil & Logistics WA PGA Championship. Felton did just that by finishing a stroke ahead of 2015 winner Brett Rumford on the Graham Marsh-designed desert course at Kalgoorlie.

With state borders closed due to the pandemic, the event went ahead with a field of 60 comprising local professionals — including former winner Michael Long from New Zealand, a longtime Perth resident — and male and female amateurs, but did not count on the ISPS Handa Order of Merit. Felton, 25, a two-time tour winner, started the third and final round one behind Rumford and Braden Becker but went one in front after Rumford drove out of bounds at the ninth and took a double bogey.

Felton took advantage by birdieing the first five holes of the back nine, the stretch where he stumbled a year earlier to let in Beck. "I holed a nice putt on 12 and for anyone who can remember that's where the disaster started last year," Felton said. "I bogeyed 12 and 13 and Darren went birdie-birdie. I went birdie-birdie this year to open up my round and really push for the win.

"I holed those two putts and I walked to the next tee thinking that maybe someone was looking after me this year. The brain does funny things. It made me remember real quickly about what happened there 12 months ago that's for sure."

Rumford, 44, a six-time European Tour winner, did not back down and matched Felton's homeward 31, chipping in at the last for an eagle. But Felton's 64, equalling the course record, added to earlier scores of 68 and 71, gave him a 13-under-par total of 203. Rumford, who opened with a 65 but suffered a five-putt during a wind-plagued 73 in the second round, closed with a 66 to finish five ahead of Daniel Fox, with Becker a stroke further back.

Kalgoorlie Golf Course, Kalgoorlie, Western Australia | October 8-10
Par 72 (36-36); 7,444 yards | Purse: A$80,000

1	**Jarryd Felton**	68 71 64	203	A$12,496
2	**Brett Rumford**	65 73 66	204	8,080
3	**Daniel Fox**	70 71 68	209	6,064
4	Braden Becker	65 73 72	210	4,448
5	Daniel Hoeve	71 71 69	211	3,712
6	Connor Fewkes (A)	75 70 67	212	
	Scott Strange	71 71 70	212	3,216
	Hayden Hopewell (A)	72 68 72	212	
9	Stephen Dartnall	72 75 67	214	2,920
10	Joseph Owen (A)	72 70 73	215	
11	Tom Addy (A)	73 73 70	216	
12	Haydn Barron (A)	75 74 68	217	
	Michael Hanrahan-Smith (A)	71 74 72	217	
14	Joshua Greer (A)	78 73 67	218	
	Michael Long	75 74 69	218	2,488
	Simon Liddell (A)	75 73 70	218	

	Ben Ferguson	70	74	74	218	2,488
	Adam Brady (A)	73	68	77	218	
19	Cooper Geddes	70	75	75	220	2,136
20	Jose De Sousa (A)	71	78	73	222	
	Ryan Peake (A)	75	74	73	222	
22	Joshua Herrero	75	77	71	223	1,884
	Maddison Tolchard (A)	78	71	74	223	
	Rick Kulacz	76	70	77	223	1,884
25	Ethan Andrews	77	73	74	224	1,240
	Calum Juniper	76	72	76	224	1,240
27	Darren Garrett	71	80	74	225	1,120
	Jordan Jung (A)	82	71	72	225	
29	Stephen Herbert	78	73	75	226	1,040
30	Kirsten Rudgeley (A)	76	77	74	227	
	Blake Windred	69	68	68	278	8,080
	Deyen Lawson	72	68	68	278	8,080
	Bio Kim	69	66	69	278	8,080
	Brendan Jones	73	66	69	278	8,080
	Terry Pilkadaris	72	70	70	278	8,080
	Katsumasa Miyamoto	67	69	70	278	8,080

Nexus Risk WA Open

Hayden Hopewell became the third amateur in five years to win the Nexus Risk Western Australian Open at Royal Fremantle. The 18-year-old, who was the runner-up in the event a year earlier, claimed his third win of the year after successes at the Tasmanian Open and the Western Australian Amateur.

Hopewell beat fellow amateur Haydn Barron by one stroke, with Brody Martin finishing third and Oliver Goss in fourth. Goss, a professional who quit the tour in 2018 and is now the junior development officer at Royal Fremantle, won the WA Open as an amateur in 2012, following in the footsteps of Stephen Leaney (1991) and Terry Gale (1975). Most recently, Curtis Luck, in 2016, and Zach Murray, in 2018, also won the title as an amateur. This tournament did not count on the Order of Merit with only local players able to compete.

Martin led by two from Hopewell with a round to play and was still two in front heading into the back nine. But Hopewell produced a brilliant inward half of 31 with six birdies, including at the last three holes. With few players holding the green at the short 17th on a course playing firm and fast, Hopewell managed to give himself a birdie putt from just inside 25 feet and holed it to trigger a huge roar from the gallery. "That was probably the biggest moment of the tournament, to take a one-shot lead going to the last," Hopewell said. "I had a feeling I was going to hole it. It was the fastest putt on the course, in front of all the crowd and they gave it a good roar so I was quite chuffed with that one."

Hopewell's opening 72 had left him one behind a group of six leaders and then he added rounds of 69 and 68 for a seven-under-par total of 209. Barron also closed with a 68, a birdie at the last forcing Hopewell to follow suit which he did with two putts from 20 feet. Martin came home in one over for a 72.

"It doesn't change anything with my timeline of turning pro but this is a good stepping stone. It's one I wanted to win," Hopewell added. "Last year I had a two-shot lead going into the last round and it was a bit of a different mindset. I had to hold on and play solid golf but this year I was two behind and thought I had to give it my all, leave nothing in the tank. It was more of an aggressive mindset and it paid off."

Royal Fremantle Golf Club, Fremantle, Western Australia — October 16-18
Par 72 (36-36); 6,782 yards — Purse: A$60,000

1	**Hayden Hopewell (A)**	72	69	68	209	
2	**Haydn Barron (A)**	71	71	68	210	
3	**Brody Martin**	71	68	72	211	A$9,882
4	Oliver Goss	71	73	70	214	6,564
5	Jordan Jung (A)	73	74	68	215	
6	Adam Brady (A)	73	72	71	216	
7	Scott Strange	72	75	70	217	5,046
8	Braden Becker	76	74	68	218	3,549
	Simon Liddell (A)	74	76	68	218	
	Rick Kulacz	73	73	72	218	3,549
11	Connor Fewkes (A)	73	73	73	219	
12	Ethan Andrews	75	71	74	220	2,517
	Tom Addy (A)	72	73	75	220	
	Joshua Greer (A)	71	74	75	220	
	Brett Rumford	73	69	78	220	2,517
16	Kirsten Rudgeley (A)	76	75	70	221	
17	Joseph Buttress (A)	77	72	73	222	
18	Gavin Reed	74	76	73	223	1,904
	Cooper Geddes	74	77	72	223	1,904
	Ryan Peake (A)	71	79	73	223	
	Scott Barr	72	74	77	223	1,904
	Darren Garrett	74	71	78	223	1,904
23	Michael Long	77	74	73	224	1,424
	Liam Purslowe (A)	76	74	74	224	
	Stephen Dartnall	77	75	72	224	1,424
	Ben Ferguson	71	74	79	224	1,424
27	Joseph Owen (A)	78	72	75	225	
	Adam Hatch (A)	76	71	78	225	
	Ian Pienaar (A)	80	73	72	225	
	Michael Hanrahan-Smith (A)	79	74	72	225	
	Kim Felton	80	75	70	225	1,260

Tailor-Made Building Services NT PGA Championship

With the major summer tournaments already cancelled, players from Queensland, New South Wales and South Australia ventured up to the Northern Territory for their only remaining event of 2020. But it was a returning local who claimed the alligator skull trophy at the Tailor-Made Building Services NT PGA Championship.

Aaron Pike played, and lived on, the course at Palmerston for 10 years from the age of seven before heading to Queensland. Back in the family home for the week, with his brother as caddie, Pike won his second ISPS Handa Tour title — though it did not count for the Order of Merit — in a playoff against another house guest, Michael Sim.

Sim birdied three of the last four holes to tie Pike but in the playoff suffered a flier from the rough and went out of bounds. Pike, the burly 34-year-old, chipped in for an early eagle but his last birdie came at the 11th hole despite a number of chances. A safe par in the playoff was good enough to add to his 2018 Victorian PGA win. "Winning is always special, winning around here is going to mean that little bit more," Pike said.

"I had my oldest brother Michael caddieing for me so that's something that I'm unlikely to ever get the opportunity to go through again. I had all my family watching so it does mean a little bit more. I made a conscious effort to say to myself that I've played this golf course more than anyone else here, I know what to do around this golf course, let myself make the decision, trust the decision and go from there. Obviously the playoff didn't go Simmy's way but I still had to do my part and had to finish the hole off."

While Sim closed with a 65, Pike had rounds of 68, 66 and 67 as they tied on 12-under-par 201. Amateur Nathan Barbieri, who shared the 36-hole lead with Pike, finished with a 70 to tie for third place, three strokes back, with Deyen Lawson. Barbieri put his plans to turn professional on hold during the pandemic, while Pike, who first came to prominence as an unheralded amateur battling Justin Rose at the 2006 Australian Masters, was robbed of a maiden major appearance at The Open following his third place finish at the 2019 Australian Open.

Palmerston Golf Club, Palmerston City, Northern Territory — October 23-25
Par 71 (36-35); 6,601 yards — Purse: A$70,000

1	**Aaron Pike**	68	66	67	201	A$10,500
2	**Michael Sim**	66	70	65	201	6,650
	Pike won playoff at first extra hole					
3	**Nathan Barbieri** (A)	65	69	70	204	
	Deyen Lawson	68	67	69	204	4,900
5	Justin Warren	68	69	68	205	3,500
6	Anthony Quayle	70	70	66	206	2,870
7	Jediah Morgan (A)	67	69	71	207	
8	Michael Wright	74	67	67	208	2,328
	Jordan Mullaney	72	69	67	208	2,328
10	Lawry Flynn (A)	71	70	68	209	
	Josh Clarke	70	71	68	209	1,838
	Bradley Doherty	71	68	70	209	1,838
13	Kade McBride	72	70	68	210	1,540
	Jack Thompson (A)	68	71	71	210	
15	Dimitrios Papadatos	68	73	70	211	1,208
	Jordan Zunic	71	70	70	211	1,208
	Campbell Rawson	70	70	71	211	1,208
	Peter Martin	70	70	71	211	1,208
19	Blake Windred	72	73	67	212	915
	Simon Viitakangas	72	70	70	212	915
	Jay Mackenzie	69	71	72	212	915
22	Daniel Morgan	72	73	68	213	800
	Charlie Dann	73	75	65	213	800
	Jason Norris	72	68	73	213	800
25	Daniel Gale	73	72	69	214	756
	Jake Hughes (A)	70	69	75	214	
27	Shae Wools-Cobb	73	71	71	215	721
	Karis Davidson	74	70	71	215	721
	Steven Jeffress	71	72	72	215	721
	Christopher Wood	77	69	69	215	721

2020-21 ISPS HANDA ORDER OF MERIT

1	Brad Kennedy	A$269,366
2	Min Woo Lee	253,327
3	Ryan Fox	168,882
4	Lucas Herbert	162,841
5	Nick Flanagan	116,710
6	Marcus Fraser	79,977
7	Travis Smyth	78,331
8	Michael Hendry	63,450
9	Jake McLeod	54,822
10	Harry Bateman	50,812

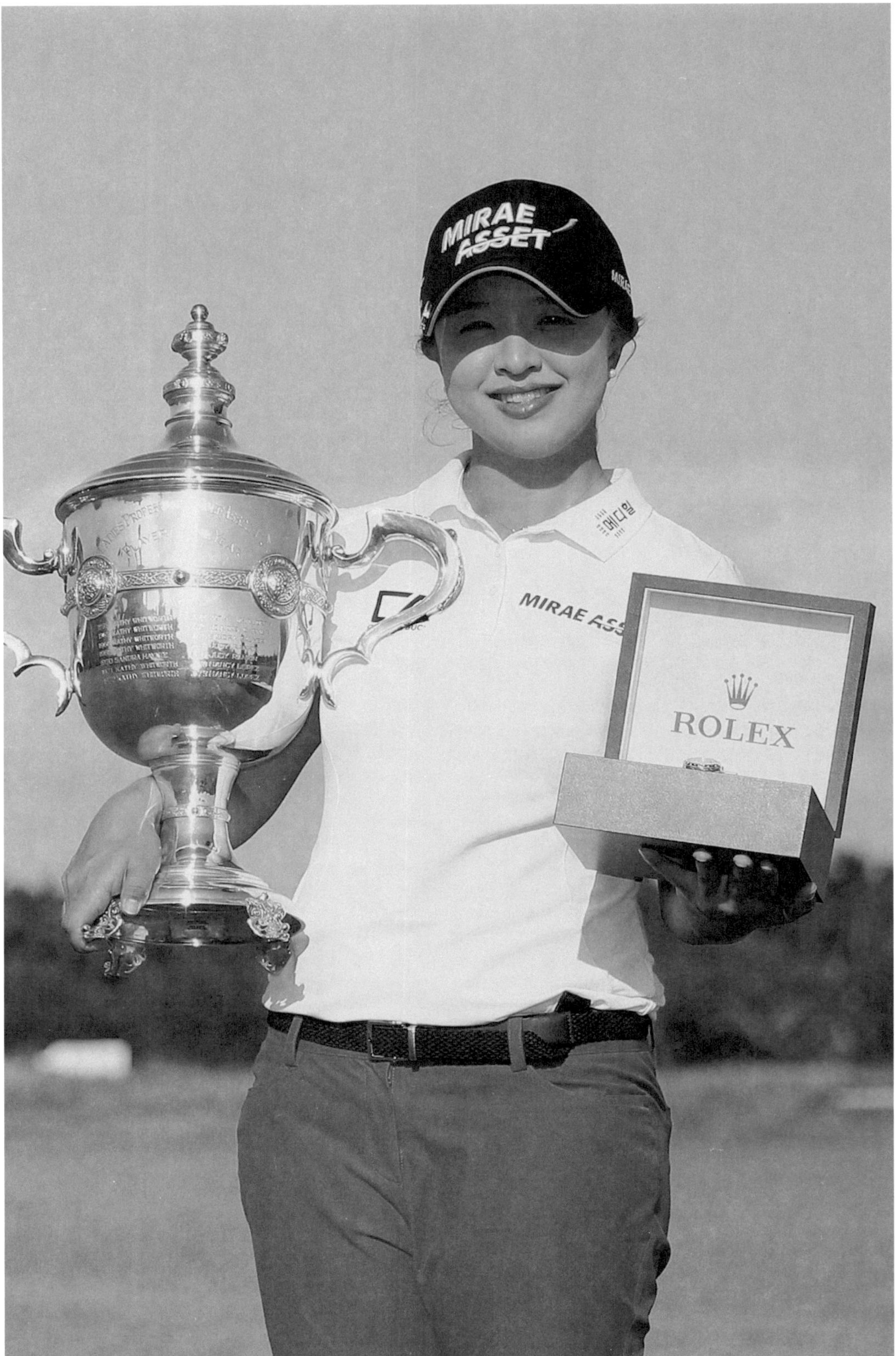

Michael Reeves/ Getty Images

LPGA Tour

A sense of the excitement building for 2020 on the LPGA Tour came early on. Japan's Nasa Hataoka was a runner-up at the first two events in Florida in January. After losing a playoff along with Hataoka to Gaby Lopez at the Diamond Resorts Tournament of Champions, Inbee Park won the Australian Open, the second of two stops Down Under. In an Olympic year, Park was getting ready to defend her Gold medal at the Tokyo Games, where Hataoka was looking forward to leading the challenge of the home nation. Yet, of course, neither that nor the International Crown team event scheduled for London would take place.

The LPGA were one of the first circuits to be disrupted by the coronavirus pandemic as a three-week swing in Asia in late February and March was cancelled. After Park's win in Adelaide it would take 166 days for the tour for resume, the longest break in the LPGA's history. If the organisation's celebrations for its 70th anniversary did not go to plan, there was no better tribute to the spirit of the founders than its return in the second half of the year.

Tournaments were rescheduled and new ones created. Sponsors whose events could no longer take place committed funds to boost those that did. There were no mass galleries, but television viewing figures were up. Four of the five major championships took place and if there was no one dominant player, there were plenty of moments to savour in a season when that alone meant something special.

However, Sei Young Kim, winning her first major title at the KPMG Women's PGA Championship, was the clear Rolex Player of the Year. After a commanding victory at Aronimink, the Korean claimed her 12th LPGA win at the Pelican Championship. No player has won more on tour since her debut in 2015.

She set up a grandstand finish to the season, deep into December, with Jin Young Ko. Kim had the chance to overtake Ko at the top of the Rolex Rankings as the paired duelled over the weekend at the CME Group Tour Championship. But Ko prevailed to retain her world number one spot. After spending most of the year at home in Korea, Ko played only four times in the States. She finished second at the US Women's Open to qualify for the season-ending tournament and then won the huge $1.1 million first prize at Tiburon six days later to head the money list for the second year running.

It was a hugely impressive performance. Kim and others may be pushing her hard but Ko was not ready to relinquish her place at the top of the women's game.

"She did a great job," Kim said of her compatriot on the last day of the season. "I tried to chase her but I couldn't. I'm disappointed I could not play well today but I'm really happy I got Player of the Year, that's really awesome." Ko's thoughts turned to the downpayment she could now afford for the house she was planning to buy in Texas.

Although the Evian Championship could not go ahead, nor the usual late season return to Asia, the AIG Women's Open was the only major to be contested outside the United States. Strict bio-secure protocols were in place for the trip to the Home of Golf, first for the ASI Scottish Open, where Stacy Lewis collected her first victory as a mother, and then Royal Troon's staging of the Women's Open.

If the weather on the west coast of Scotland was dramatic, even more so was Sophia Popov's victory as the 304th ranked player in the world. It came after losing her status as an LPGA member by a stroke at Q Series in 2019 and years of health issues that were finally diagnosed as Lyme Disease.

Her incredible story was followed by Mirim Lee chipping in three times in the final round of the ANA Inspiration, then winning in a playoff against Brooke Henderson and Nelly Korda. Lee was ranked 94th on the Rolex Rankings, which turned out to be the same position as her fellow Korean A Lim Kim when, playing in a major and in America for the first time, she won the US Open at Champions thrillingly by birdieing the last three holes.

When the regular tour resumed in late July, it did so with the hastily arranged Drive On Championship at Inverness, host in 2021 to the Solheim Cup. Danielle Kang won and said: "I am so thankful for this inaugural championship on our brand new schedule. I love the decisions made by the commissioner and the entire LPGA staff, how safe they have made it for us and doing all the extra steps with all the protocols that mean we are able to play."

Kang claimed the Toledo double a week later at the Marathon Classic after outlasting Lydia Ko.

She then missed out on the playoff at the Scottish Open the week after by a single shot. There was also a runner-up finish at the second Drive On event at Reynolds Lake Oconee. Kang finished the season by winning the Vare Trophy for the lowest stroke average among players who had played enough rounds.

Austin Ernst and Ally McDonald claimed, respectively, a long awaited second win and a maiden title, while at the Volunteers of America Classic Angela Stanford won for the first time since the 2018 Evian, for the first time in her home state of Texas and for the first time in front of her parents. McDonald, who held off Kang and Philippine big-hitter Bianca Pagdanganan at the Lake Oconee Drive On event, ended the season playing under her married name of Ewing, having arranged a scaled back wedding during the lockdown.

English golfers won back-to-back for the first time since 1996 when Georgia Hall won at the Cambia Portland Classic, her first title in America and second in all, and Mel Reid won her first LPGA title at the ShopRite Classic.

Procedural issues came to the fore after Popov's victory. As a non-member she did not receive the full major exemption, while she missed the very next major with her status as the AIG Women's Open champion only kicking in for the 2021 ANA Inspiration. Her Troon win also did not collect official Race to the CME points so despite consistent play for the rest of the season the German did not qualify for the Tour Championship.

Mike Whan, the LPGA commissioner, had said the regulations may need looking at but would not be changed mid-season. At the end of the season, Whan said: "Quite frankly, you can't rattle me this year on weekly issues because we won the war."

By announcing a schedule for 2021 of 34 events with increased prize money of over $75 million, Whan had done just that. Only 42 of 7,200 Covid tests had been positive. Testing and all the other protocols cost $3.5 million but all the tournaments that were lost in 2020 were due to return to the schedule. Whan himself exhibited the make-do-and-mend spirit of the year by filling in for a day as an on-course commentator at Lake Oconee when Golf Channel were short staffed.

"We can all agree that 2020, while certainly not the 70th anniversary year that we expected, was a year that we will never forget," Whan said. "As we look back at the year, I am amazed at how our partnerships have actually grown during this trying time. We added sponsorship sales and we proved that professional golf can be played safely for all involved. And our fans responded. Social engagement is up more than 40 per cent and TV viewership is up more than 30 per cent over last year. As we look to 2021, we are recapturing the momentum that we had at the beginning of 2020 and we are excited about our future."

But in the first week of 2021, Whan announced he would be leaving his position after 11 years. The LPGA's longest serving commissioner had taken over at a rocky moment for the circuit and managed to increase the number of tournaments by 50 per cent, prize money by 85 per cent, TV coverage by 150 per cent and revenue by 100 per cent.

"I think he saved the LPGA," said Hall of Famer Juli Inkster. "It was in dire straits when he took over. The players, they lost their trust. I think the LPGA was very close to folding, and he brought it back to life and now it's thriving."

2020 SCHEDULE

Diamond Resorts Tournament of Champions	**Gaby Lopez**	
Gainbridge LPGA	**Madelene Sagstrom**	
ISPS Handa Vic Open	**Hee Young Park**	*See chapter 22*
ISPS Handa Women's Australian Open	**Inbee Park**	*See chapter 22*
Honda LPGA Thailand		*cancelled*
HSBC Women's World Championship		*cancelled*
Blue Bay LPGA		*cancelled*
Volvik Founders Cup		*cancelled*
Lotte Championship		*cancelled*
HUGEL-AIR PREMIA LA Open		*cancelled*
LPGA Mediheal Championship		*cancelled*
Pure Silk Championship		*cancelled*

Dow Great Lakes Bay Invitational		*cancelled*
Evian Championship		*cancelled*
Olympics Women's*		*postponed to 2021*
LPGA Drive On Championship	**Danielle Kang**	
Marathon Classic	**Danielle Kang**	
ASI Ladies Scottish Open	**Stacey Lewis**	*See chapter 19*
AIG Women's Open	**Sophia Popov**	*See chapter 2*
UL International Crown*		*cancelled*
Walmart NW Arkansas Championship	**Austin Ernst**	
CP Women's Open		*cancelled*
ANA Inspiration	**Mirim Lee**	*See chapter 3*
Cambia Portland Classic	**Georgia Hall**	
Kia Classic		*cancelled*
Meijer LPGA Classic		*cancelled*
ShopRite LPGA Classic	**Mel Reid**	
KPMG Women's PGA Championship	**Sei Young Kim**	*See chapter 5*
LPGA Drive On — Reynolds Lake Oconee	**Ally McDonald**	
Buick LPGA Shanghai		*cancelled*
BMW Ladies Championship		*cancelled*
Taiwan Swinging Skirts		*cancelled*
Toto Japan Classic*	**Jiyai Shin**	*See chapter 20*
Pelican Women's Championship	**Sei Young Kim**	
Volunteers of America Classic	**Angela Stanford**	
US Women's Open	**A Lim Kim**	*See chapter 7*
CME Group Tour Championship	**Jin Young Ko**	

**non-Race to the CME Globe event*

Diamond Resorts Tournament of Champions

It took seven extra goes on the par-three 18th hole at Tranquilo before Gaby Lopez claimed her second LPGA title at the Diamond Resorts Tournament of Champions. The 26-year-old Mexican holed from 25 feet for a birdie to defeat Nasa Hataoka, who missed from 10 feet to keep the playoff going. Inbee Park dropped out on the third extra hole.

The 197-yard hole, ranked the hardest for the week and requiring a three or four-hybrid depending on the wind, was good to Lopez. Including the playoff, she made three birdies there, the same as the other 25 players in the field put together. Lopez holed from 18 feet for a two on the 72nd hole to post a 66 and, after rounds of 65, 69 and 71, a 13-under-par total of 271. Hataoka matched her with a 68 while Park, the overnight leader by two strokes, had a 71.

Park, starting the season early in an attempt to qualify for the Olympics and defend her Gold medal, had a rare three-putt at the 18th at the end of the third round and then found the water on the third extra hole in the playoff. Meanwhile, Hataoka, looking to lead the home nation at the Tokyo Games, and Lopez matched each other par for par until darkness halted proceedings after five extra holes. Lopez then triumphed on the second playing of the 18th on Monday morning.

"I proved to myself that I can win in any situation. My first win was in the lead, and now my second win was coming from behind," said Lopez. "Being able to put all those moments together and recall them while I'm walking on the fairway here and try to stay patient. I think that's what I proved to myself the most. It was my ability to stay in the moment."

Hall of Fame pitcher John Smoltz successfully defended his title in the celebrity section of the event, which in 2019 had produced higher viewing figures in the USA than the US Women's Open.

Four Seasons Golf & Sports Club Orlando (Tranquilo), Lake Buena Vista, Florida — January 16-20
Par 71 (34-37); 6,645 yards — Purse: $1,200,000

1	**Gaby Lopez**	65	69	71	66	271	$180,000
2	**Nasa Hataoka**	66	69	68	68	271	127,649
	Inbee Park	65	68	67	71	271	127,649
	Lopez won playoff at seventh extra hole						
4	Mi Jung Hur	69	70	70	63	272	74,933
	Brooke M Henderson	67	66	72	67	272	74,933
6	Annie Park	68	73	68	64	273	54,681
7	Lexi Thompson	66	71	69	68	274	42,935
	Sei Young Kim	66	69	67	72	274	42,935
9	Celine Boutier	66	69	69	71	275	36,049
10	Nelly Korda	73	67	69	67	276	32,808
11	Moriya Jutanugarn	68	71	73	65	277	30,377
12	Cydney Clanton	69	69	69	71	278	26,624
	Angela Stanford	65	72	70	71	278	26,624
	Danielle Kang	63	73	71	71	278	26,624
15	Amy Yang	68	69	76	66	279	22,844
	Jessica Korda	70	68	71	70	279	22,844
17	Jasmine Suwannapura	68	73	69	70	280	21,062
18	Brittany Lincicome	71	72	70	68	281	19,685
	Georgia Hall	70	71	71	69	281	19,685
20	Cheyenne Knight	68	70	74	70	282	18,632
21	Marina Alex	66	81	68	68	283	17,984
22	Pernilla Lindberg	70	73	73	68	284	17,336
23	Bronte Law	69	73	72	72	286	16,688
24	Eun-Hee Ji	74	67	76	70	287	15,756
	In Gee Chun	71	71	73	72	287	15,756
26	Ariya Jutanugarn	75	76	73	68	292	14,906

Gainbridge LPGA

As the LPGA returned to Boca Raton for the first time in over three decades with the inaugural Gainbridge LPGA at Boca Rio, a number of players got to stay at home. It was an out-of-towner who won, however, albeit another Florida resident in Sweden's Madelene Sagstrom, who in 2021 will be able to play in the Diamond Resorts Tournament of Champions at her home club in Lake Buena Vista. The previous week she had been a spectator at the winners-only event.

Sagstrom's maiden victory came by one stroke from Japan's Nasa Hataoka, who finished runner-up for the second week running after losing out in the playoff to Gaby Lopez at Tranquilo. Hataoka led by one with two to play but Sagstrom hit an eight-iron to three feet at the short 17th for a birdie and then holed from eight feet for a par at the last while Hataoka three-putted, missing from inside four feet.

Sagstrom had led by two overnight but made two bogeys in the first five holes. She rallied by holing a bunker shot at the 10th and birdieing the next as well, before Hataoka birdied the 15th and 16th holes.

"It doesn't matter how you start," Sagstrom said. "If you just continue fighting, things can go your way. And I just told myself, 'Keep fighting, keep fighting'."

The 27-year-old Sagstrom, who in her rookie season of 2017 was picked as a wild card for the Solheim Cup by Annika Sorenstam, opened with a 72 but then produced a brilliant 62 the next day. Following that low round with a 67 the next day helped the Swede feel she already "had beaten my own demons".

A closing 70 gave her a 17-under-par total of 271. Hataoka had a 69, as did Danielle Kang, who finished third, two ahead of Celine Boutier. With Sagstrom's regular caddie unavailable for the week, she was aided by her boyfriend's father, Alan Clarke, who was on vacation in Florida and promptly retired from caddieing duties after the victory.

Boca Rio Golf Club, Boca Raton, Florida — January 23-26
Par 72 (36-36); 6,701 yards — Purse: $2,000,000

1	**Madelene Sagstrom**	72	62	67	70	271	$300,000
2	**Nasa Hataoka**	72	64	67	69	272	185,623
3	**Danielle Kang**	72	67	65	69	273	134,656
4	Celine Boutier	71	67	67	70	275	104,167
5	Sei Young Kim	68	69	67	73	277	83,843
6	Moriya Jutanugarn	72	67	67	72	278	63,009
	Cydney Clanton	72	64	69	73	278	63,009
8	Yui Kawamoto	68	73	69	69	279	45,563
	Klara Spilkova	72	68	68	71	279	45,563
	Jessica Korda	66	73	69	71	279	45,563
11	Charley Hull	75	68	69	68	280	34,578
	Cristie Kerr	72	71	69	68	280	34,578
	Xiyu Lin	69	72	67	72	280	34,578
	Jennifer Song	72	64	72	72	280	34,578
15	Lexi Thompson	73	68	69	71	281	27,236
	Carlota Ciganda	69	66	75	71	281	27,236
	Georgia Hall	70	71	68	72	281	27,236
	Brooke M Henderson	72	68	68	73	281	27,236
19	Morgan Pressel	75	69	72	66	282	21,380
	Caroline Masson	74	70	71	67	282	21,380
	Jennifer Kupcho	77	67	70	68	282	21,380
	Jodi Ewart Shadoff	71	71	71	69	282	21,380
	Austin Ernst	71	70	70	71	282	21,380
	Dana Finkelstein	70	71	70	71	282	21,380
	Jaye Marie Green	73	66	70	73	282	21,380
	Bronte Law	73	66	70	73	282	21,380
27	Lindsey Weaver	69	71	72	71	283	17,987
28	Eun-Hee Ji	73	70	73	68	284	15,976

	Nelly Korda	71	69	75	69	284	15,976
	Mariah Stackhouse	74	69	71	70	284	15,976
	Pernilla Lindberg	73	68	73	70	284	15,976
	Stacy Lewis	71	70	72	71	284	15,976
33	Kristen Gillman	74	70	70	71	285	13,821
	Brittany Altomare	76	69	68	72	285	13,821
35	Lauren Stephenson	73	72	72	69	286	10,874
	Lindy Duncan	72	71	74	69	286	10,874
	Jing Yan	74	71	71	70	286	10,874
	Marina Alex	75	69	72	70	286	10,874
	Haeji Kang	74	71	70	71	286	10,874
	Patty Tavatanakit	68	75	72	71	286	10,874
	Yealimi Noh	74	71	69	72	286	10,874
	Maria Fernanda Torres	74	68	71	73	286	10,874
	Chella Choi	70	72	71	73	286	10,874
	Stephanie Meadow	71	72	68	75	286	10,874
45	Jasmine Suwannapura	74	68	74	71	287	7,738
	Yu Liu	73	71	71	72	287	7,738
	Albane Valenzuela	75	68	72	72	287	7,738
	Mariajo Uribe	73	69	72	73	287	7,738
	In Gee Chun	71	73	69	74	287	7,738
	Brittany Lincicome	75	67	70	75	287	7,738
	Angela Stanford	70	70	71	76	287	7,738
52	Megan Khang	72	72	75	69	288	6,199
	Anna Nordqvist	75	69	74	70	288	6,199
	Alison Lee	76	69	71	72	288	6,199
	Mel Reid	71	73	72	72	288	6,199
	Pajaree Anannarukarn	74	71	70	73	288	6,199
	Angel Yin	75	65	73	75	288	6,199
58	Mi Hyang Lee	73	72	73	71	289	5,209
	Gerina Piller	75	69	72	73	289	5,209
	Mind Muangkhumsakul	75	68	70	76	289	5,209
	Linnea Strom	71	70	72	76	289	5,209
62	Jane Park	70	73	75	73	291	4,878
63	Hee Young Park	72	72	78	71	293	4,675
	Tiffany Chan	74	69	77	73	293	4,675
	Sakura Yokomine	70	73	73	77	293	4,675
66	Anne van Dam	73	71	76	74	294	4,472
67	Ariya Jutanugarn	71	73	77	74	295	4,319
	Ryann O'Toole	72	72	76	75	295	4,319
69	Jillian Hollis	70	73	77	76	296	4,167
70	Daniela Darquea	73	71	78	78	300	4,066
71	Ally McDonald	74	70	79	78	301	4,015

LPGA Drive On Championship

After being on hiatus since February, the LPGA returned after an absence of 166 days, the longest fallow period in its history, with a newly recreated event, the Drive On Championship, funded partly by contributions from sponsors whose events were cancelled. Many overseas players did not enter while Marina Alex, before travelling to Toledo, and Gaby Lopez, after arriving on site, withdrew after testing positive for Covid-19 as the event observed similar new protocols to other tours. No spectators were on the course at Inverness, which lived up to its reputation as a four-time venue for the men's US Open with only five players finishing under par for 54 holes.

Danielle Kang, who had not competed since January, displayed the sort of form that brought her victory at the KPMG Women's PGA Championship at Olympia Fields to secure her fourth title by one stroke from Celine Boutier. Kang led from wire-to-wire, opening with a 66 but was joined at the top of the leaderboard after 36 holes by Boutier and Jodi Ewart Shadoff following a 73 in teeming rain.

A final grouping of an American and two Europeans was a preview of the 2021 Solheim Cup, due to be played at Inverness. Kang led for much of Sunday, which started wet and then turned sunny, with birdies at the second, fourth and 11th holes. But her only dropped shot of the day at the 13th meant Boutier, who hit the flagstick when birdieing the short 12th, tied for the lead with her third birdie in four holes at the 14th.

The Frenchwoman dropped a shot at the 15th when her short par putt lipped out, and as Kang parred her way home, Boutier again lipped out from six feet at the last as she tried to force a playoff. Kang finished on seven-under-par 209 after a 70, while Boutier had a 71 and Shadoff a 75 to fall to fifth place. Minjee Lee took third place with a 70 and Japanese rookie Yui Kawamoto was fourth.

"I'm really happy that I got to pull it off after leading the first day and the second day," said Kang. "I wanted to close it out and it came down to the last hole, last putt. It was a really good battle out there, and it's pretty cool. I kept telling myself, stick to the game plan to play aggressive and play my game."

Kang added: "I am so thankful for this inaugural championship on our brand new schedule. I love the decisions made by the commissioner and the entire LPGA staff, how safe they have made it for us and doing all the extra steps with all the protocols that mean we are able to play."

Inverness Club, Toledo, Ohio
Par 72 (36-36); 6,852 yards

July 31-August 2
Purse: $1,000,000

1	**Danielle Kang**	66	73	70	209	$150,000
2	**Celine Boutier**	68	71	71	210	91,269
3	**Minjee Lee**	69	73	70	212	66,209
4	Yui Kawamoto	70	71	72	213	51,218
5	Jodi Ewart Shadoff	67	72	75	214	41,225
6	Gemma Dryburgh	73	72	71	216	25,834
	Brittany Lang	72	72	72	216	25,834
	Mina Harigae	71	72	73	216	25,834
	Sarah Burnham	70	72	74	216	25,834
	Sarah Schmelzel	72	69	75	216	25,834
11	Megan Khang	74	73	70	217	16,499
	Caroline Masson	72	72	73	217	16,499
	Anne van Dam	71	73	73	217	16,499
	Kelly Tan	71	72	74	217	16,499
	Lee-Anne Pace	68	74	75	217	16,499
16	Lexi Thompson	73	72	73	218	12,742
	Perrine Delacour	73	71	74	218	12,742
	Carlota Ciganda	70	74	74	218	12,742
	Amy Olson	69	73	76	218	12,742
20	Kendall Dye	74	75	70	219	10,131
	Alena Sharp	78	69	72	219	10,131
	Madelene Sagstrom	73	74	72	219	10,131
	Brittany Altomare	74	72	73	219	10,131
	Azahara Munoz	73	73	73	219	10,131
	Austin Ernst	73	72	74	219	10,131
	Jasmine Suwannapura	74	70	75	219	10,131
	Hee Young Park	70	73	76	219	10,131
28	Xiyu Lin	76	74	70	220	6,862
	Paula Reto	73	77	70	220	6,862
	Albane Valenzuela	73	77	70	220	6,862
	Lydia Ko	69	80	71	220	6,862
	Jenny Shin	75	73	72	220	6,862
	Sarah Kemp	73	75	72	220	6,862
	Cydney Clanton	72	76	72	220	6,862
	Bianca Pagdanganan	74	73	73	220	6,862
	Angel Yin	74	73	73	220	6,862
	Min Seo Kwak	73	74	73	220	6,862
	Lizette Salas	74	72	74	220	6,862
	Ashleigh Buhai	71	75	74	220	6,862
40	Nelly Korda	76	74	71	221	4,293
	Charlotte Thomas	73	77	71	221	4,293
	Kris Tamulis	71	79	71	221	4,293
	Jennifer Song	74	75	72	221	4,293
	Christina Kim	74	74	73	221	4,293
	Kim Kaufman	72	76	73	221	4,293
	Anna Nordqvist	72	75	74	221	4,293
	Isi Gabsa	76	70	75	221	4,293
	Jiwon Jeon	73	73	75	221	4,293
	Cristie Kerr	73	73	75	221	4,293
	Yu Liu	73	72	76	221	4,293
51	Andrea Lee	78	72	72	222	2,998
	Amy Yang	73	77	72	222	2,998
	Jessica Korda	75	73	74	222	2,998
	Stephanie Meadow	74	74	74	222	2,998
	Morgan Pressel	73	74	75	222	2,998
	Brittany Lincicome	73	74	75	222	2,998
	Haley Moore	72	75	75	222	2,998
	Pei-Yun Chien	73	73	76	222	2,998
	Mel Reid	74	71	77	222	2,998
60	Haeji Kang	76	74	73	223	2,424
	Gerina Piller	76	74	73	223	2,424
	Dana Finkelstein	70	79	74	223	2,424
	Jennifer Kupcho	72	76	75	223	2,424
64	Katelyn Dambaugh	76	74	74	224	2,249
	Celine Herbin	75	75	74	224	2,249
	Clariss Guce	75	73	76	224	2,249
67	In Gee Chun	77	73	75	225	2,036
	Stacy Lewis	77	73	75	225	2,036
	Cheyenne Woods	75	75	75	225	2,036
	Robynn Ree	74	76	75	225	2,036
	Linnea Johansson	72	76	77	225	2,036
	Marissa Steen	74	73	78	225	2,036
73	Klara Spilkova	75	75	76	226	1,911
	Ruixin Liu	75	74	77	226	1,911
75	Angela Stanford	74	76	77	227	1,864
	Lindsey Weaver	73	75	79	227	1,864
77	Jennifer Chang	77	73	78	228	1,817
	Mariah Stackhouse	75	73	80	228	1,817

Marathon Classic

In five previous appearances in the Marathon Classic, at the height of her powers, Lydia Ko won twice, in 2014 and 2016, and also finished third, seventh and 20th. In the four years since the second of those victories at Highland Meadows, the 23-year-old New Zealander had won only once, at the 2018 Mediheal Championship. Back on familiar territory, Ko opened with a 64, her lowest score at the venue, to tie Drive On champion Danielle Kang for the first-round lead.

Ko then birdied the first four holes on Friday and posted a 65 to lead by one from Jodi Ewart Shadoff before a Saturday 68 gave her a four-stroke lead over Kang, who had gone 67-70 on the second and third days.

Fast forward to the 12th hole on Sunday, where a bogey dropped Kang five behind Ko with six to play. Inspired rather than perturbed when informed of her situation by her caddie, Kang responded by birdieing the next two holes. "That put me in a matchplay mentality, it was crucial. I hit some great shots coming in," said Kang.

Kang parred home, including the twin par-five finishing holes for a 68 and a 15-under-par total of 269. That she claimed the Toledo double — the first back-to-back wins on the LPGA since Shanshan Feng in 2017 — with a one-stroke victory was due to a sudden collapse from former world number one Ko. Having dropped five strokes in the previous 67 holes, Ko lost four over the closing five holes with bogeys at the 14th and 16th holes and a double-bogey seven at the last.

After missing the green on the right and receiving a drop from a cart path, Ko skulled her chip over the green and from the rough on the other side saw her next chip rebound from the fringe into a bunker. She missed from 10 feet to force a playoff.

After a shocking finale, Ko was sanguine in her reaction. "I think I have to see the positives," she said. "I'm pretty sure I'm going to be disappointed and go, 'Oh, man, I should have done this over that.' I would've loved to be the one holding the trophy. But I think there are so many positives from the week, and I feel overall more confident in my game. Obviously, not the finish that I had envisioned but Danielle played great today. Every time she made a mistake she fought back with a birdie, so credit to her."

Shadoff, who went 63-73 on Friday and Saturday, closed with a 67 to tie Ko for second place, one ahead of Minjee Lee, who had a 68.

"I mean, there are really no words, to be honest," Kang said of what happened to Ko on the 18th. "As a competitor, friend, I mean, she'll bounce back and she's a great player and she's proven to be one of the best players in the world."

For herself, after working hard with her coach Butch Harmon in Las Vegas, Kang said: "I won two weeks in a row, so that's good. I'm really proud of all the work that I did during the off time, all the work that I did with Butch and all the workouts that I put in. I really utilised that time, and I'm proud to come out during this quarantine and be able to execute my game the way I wanted to."

Highland Meadows Golf Club, Sylvania, Ohio — August 6-9
Par 71 (34-37); 6,555 yards — Purse: $1,700,000

1	**Danielle Kang**	64	67	70	68	269	$255,000
2	**Jodi Ewart Shadoff**	67	63	73	67	270	133,555
	Lydia Ko	64	65	68	73	270	133,555
4	Minjee Lee	68	67	68	68	271	86,874
5	Andrea Lee	67	71	73	65	276	54,244
	Marina Alex	69	71	69	67	276	54,244
	Emma Talley	72	66	69	69	276	54,244
	Yu Liu	70	68	69	69	276	54,244
9	Stacy Lewis	69	71	72	65	277	27,129
	Kendall Dye	72	70	68	67	277	27,129
	Patty Tavatanakit	71	66	72	68	277	27,129
	Pernilla Lindberg	71	70	67	69	277	27,129
	Kelly Tan	70	68	70	69	277	27,129
	Maria Fassi	67	66	75	69	277	27,129
	Carlota Ciganda	68	68	71	70	277	27,129
	Cydney Clanton	67	70	69	71	277	27,129
	Sophia Popov	66	70	70	71	277	27,129
	Maria Fernanda Torres	70	68	67	72	277	27,129
	Lindsey Weaver	68	69	67	73	277	27,129
20	Dottie Ardina	72	70	69	67	278	18,138
	Xiyu Lin	68	72	70	68	278	18,138
	Stephanie Meadow	69	69	72	68	278	18,138
	Jenny Shin	66	72	71	69	278	18,138
	Pei-Yun Chien	68	72	66	72	278	18,138
25	Jennifer Song	68	72	72	67	279	13,909
	Sarah Schmelzel	71	69	70	69	279	13,909
	Alena Sharp	72	67	71	69	279	13,909
	Lindy Duncan	69	69	72	69	279	13,909
	Jessica Korda	70	70	69	70	279	13,909
	Matilda Castren	71	66	72	70	279	13,909
	Ally McDonald	66	75	67	71	279	13,909
	Elizabeth Szokol	70	68	70	71	279	13,909
	Lizette Salas	73	64	70	72	279	13,909
34	Cheyenne Knight	67	76	69	68	280	10,637
	Jiwon Jeon	70	71	71	68	280	10,637
	Austin Ernst	68	73	71	68	280	10,637
	Lee Lopez	69	71	71	69	280	10,637
38	Caroline Masson	69	72	70	70	281	8,174
	Kim Kaufman	70	73	67	71	281	8,174
	Brittany Altomare	70	72	68	71	281	8,174
	Cristie Kerr	70	70	70	71	281	8,174
	Amy Yang	71	67	72	71	281	8,174
	Nelly Korda	67	73	69	72	281	8,174
	Kristen Gillman	67	67	75	72	281	8,174
	Mariah Stackhouse	68	74	65	74	281	8,174
	Paula Reto	70	67	69	75	281	8,174
47	Annie Park	70	71	72	69	282	6,102
	Megan Khang	65	69	78	70	282	6,102
	Isi Gabsa	68	74	68	72	282	6,102
	Jing Yan	70	68	72	72	282	6,102
	Lexi Thompson	70	66	73	73	282	6,102
	Christina Kim	68	70	70	74	282	6,102
53	Haru Nomura	70	72	72	69	283	5,000
	Alison Lee	70	72	72	69	283	5,000
	Youngin Chun	70	73	67	73	283	5,000
	Louise Ridderstrom	70	70	70	73	283	5,000
	Haley Moore	70	69	71	73	283	5,000
	Jasmine Suwannapura	69	69	70	75	283	5,000
59	Angel Yin	66	74	77	67	284	4,125
	Cheyenne Woods	72	71	71	70	284	4,125
	In Gee Chun	71	72	71	70	284	4,125
	Bianca Pagdanganan	69	67	77	71	284	4,125
	Haeji Kang	71	70	70	73	284	4,125
	Amy Olson	69	71	68	76	284	4,125
65	Albane Valenzuela	71	72	70	72	285	3,771
	Katherine Kirk	71	66	71	77	285	3,771
67	Angela Stanford	67	76	72	71	286	3,517
	Anna Nordqvist	72	69	72	73	286	3,517
	Lauren Stephenson	73	69	70	74	286	3,517
	Ashleigh Buhai	71	71	70	74	286	3,517
71	Lee-Anne Pace	73	70	73	71	287	3,305
	Morgan Pressel	70	71	73	73	287	3,305
	Ruixin Liu	69	74	70	74	287	3,305
74	Charlotte Thomas	68	75	74	72	289	3,201
	Linnea Johansson	69	72	74	74	289	3,201
76	Daniela Darquea	72	71	72	75	290	3,141
77	Brittany Lincicome	72	71	77	71	291	3,062
	Sierra L Brooks	74	69	72	76	291	3,062
	Maia Schechter	71	72	70	78	291	3,062

Walmart NW Arkansas Championship

"I'm trying to birdie every hole out there," said Austin Ernst after her second successive 65 at Pinnacle. On the final day at the Walmart NW Arkansas Championship, Ernst looked as if she would do just that. She birdied the first three holes, had six in an outward nine of 31, notched her eighth of the day at the 12th hole to take the lead for the first time and her 10th at the 18th after her eagle putt lipped out. A final round of 63 gave the 28-year-old a 20-under-par total of 193 and a two-stroke victory over Anna Nordqvist.

"I knew I needed a really low score," Ernst said. "I thought at the beginning of the week that 20 under would win and that's what I got to. But you knew that out here, you needed to attack and you couldn't be afraid and couldn't just kind of middle-the-green it all day. I didn't officially know where I stood, but I assumed I got the lead pretty early on in the back nine. I just knew I needed to attack and make a lot of birdies coming in."

Ernst, a Solheim Cup player in 2017, had gone six years and 143 starts since her maiden victory at the Cambia Portland Classic in 2014. Five runner-up finishes in the meantime included one at Pinnacle in 2018, the year she was also runner-up at the Evian Championship. "I feel great," Ernst said. "It hasn't fully sunk in, but to get my second win out here, I always knew that I could win more than one. To actually do it means a lot."

Nordqvist's supply of birdies ran low on Sunday. The Swede had opened with a 64 and added a 62 on Saturday to be 16 under par. She had missed only one green in two days. Sei Young Kim, in her first appearance on the LPGA since early in the year, was one behind but both players posted 69s in the final round. Kim finished tied for fifth with Jenny Shin, while Angela Stanford, after a 65, and Nelly Korda, with a 67, shared third place. Nordqvist stayed in front despite only two birdies on the front nine but her driving faltered down the stretch and bogeys at the 12th and 14th holes followed. A birdie at the 16th meant she could still tie with an eagle at the last but she settled for a par.

Pinnacle Country Club, Rogers, Arkansas — August 28-30
Par 71 (36-35); 6,438 yards — Purse: $2,300,000

1	**Austin Ernst**	65	65	63	193	$345,000
2	**Anna Nordqvist**	64	62	69	195	201,031
3	**Angela Stanford**	66	66	65	197	129,324
	Nelly Korda	67	63	67	197	129,324
5	Jenny Shin	67	63	68	198	82,548
	Sei Young Kim	65	64	69	198	82,548
7	Inbee Park	67	67	65	199	58,334
	Katherine Kirk	65	68	66	199	58,334
9	Linnea Strom	67	68	65	200	46,777
	Kristy McPherson	68	66	66	200	46,777
11	Carlota Ciganda	68	68	65	201	37,448
	Pernilla Lindberg	69	66	66	201	37,448
	Jodi Ewart Shadoff	67	67	67	201	37,448
	Mi Hyang Lee	67	67	67	201	37,448
15	Morgan Pressel	70	67	65	202	28,249
	Yealimi Noh	68	69	65	202	28,249
	Charlotte Thomas	68	67	67	202	28,249
	Maria Fassi	67	67	68	202	28,249
	Caroline Hedwall	69	64	69	202	28,249
	Esther Lee	64	69	69	202	28,249
21	Pajaree Anannarukarn	68	71	64	203	21,887
	Emma Talley	70	68	65	203	21,887
	Lindsey Weaver	70	67	66	203	21,887
	Patty Tavatanakit	69	68	66	203	21,887
	Caroline Masson	68	69	66	203	21,887
	In Gee Chun	67	70	66	203	21,887
	Annie Park	69	67	67	203	21,887
28	Minjee Lee	69	70	65	204	14,833
	Lydia Ko	71	67	66	204	14,833
	Cheyenne Knight	70	68	66	204	14,833
	Matilda Castren	70	68	66	204	14,833
	Haeji Kang	70	68	66	204	14,833
	Robynn Ree	70	67	67	204	14,833
	Nasa Hataoka	68	69	67	204	14,833
	Maria Fernanda Torres	65	72	67	204	14,833
	Azahara Munoz	71	65	68	204	14,833
	Chella Choi	70	65	69	204	14,833
	Jasmine Suwannapura	68	67	69	204	14,833
	Stacy Lewis	66	68	70	204	14,833
	Jackie Stoelting	64	70	70	204	14,833
41	Nicole Broch Larsen	70	70	65	205	9,780
	Alexa Pano (A)	72	67	66	205	
	Jeong Eun Lee	69	70	66	205	9,780
	Ally McDonald	68	71	66	205	9,780
	Caroline Inglis	71	67	67	205	9,780
	Brittany Lang	70	68	67	205	9,780
	Moriya Jutanugarn	67	70	68	205	9,780
	Ruixin Liu	68	65	72	205	9,780
49	Christina Kim	71	69	66	206	7,301
	Georgia Hall	71	69	66	206	7,301
	Brooke Matthews (A)	70	69	67	206	
	Kelly Tan	70	68	68	206	7,301
	Brooke M Henderson	71	66	69	206	7,301
	Jennifer Chang	70	67	69	206	7,301
	Aditi Ashok	69	68	69	206	7,301
	Cydney Clanton	69	68	69	206	7,301
	Gemma Dryburgh	69	67	70	206	7,301
	Danielle Kang	69	66	71	206	7,301
59	Brittany Lincicome	70	70	67	207	5,746
	Lindy Duncan	69	71	67	207	5,746
	Angel Yin	70	69	68	207	5,746
	Gaby Lopez	68	71	68	207	5,746
	Stephanie Meadow	65	72	70	207	5,746
64	Jaye Marie Green	73	67	68	208	5,228

	Lizette Salas	66	72	70	208	5,228		Bianca Pagdanganan	70	68	72	210	4,329
66	Yui Kawamoto	72	68	69	209	4,843		Bronte Law	70	68	72	210	4,329
	Min Seo Kwak	71	69	69	209	4,843		Mina Harigae	65	73	72	210	4,329
	Cristie Kerr	71	68	70	209	4,843	77	Leona Maguire	71	69	72	212	4,132
	Sarah Schmelzel	69	70	70	209	4,843	78	Gerina Piller	71	69	73	213	4,054
	Jing Yan	66	72	71	209	4,843		Dana Finkelstein	66	73	74	213	4,054
71	Haru Nomura	70	70	70	210	4,329	80	Isi Gabsa	67	72	75	214	3,951
	Sarah Kemp	69	71	70	210	4,329		Ashleigh Buhai	68	70	76	214	3,951
	Esther Henseleit	69	70	71	210	4,329							

Cambia Portland Classic

Due to wildfires in the Pacific Northwest which made for hazardous air quality early in the week, the Cambia Portland Classic was reduced from 72 to 54 holes with a start on Friday instead of Thursday. Practice was allowed from late on Wednesday morning and a thunderstorm during the first round helped clear the air but, in the end, 54 holes were not enough. It took two extra holes for Georgia Hall, the 2018 British Open champion, to win her second LPGA title.

Hall defeated South Africa's Ashleigh Buhai in a playoff after the pair tied on 12-under-par 204. Buhai started the final day seven behind overnight leader Mel Reid, who had scored a 65 on Saturday, her 33rd birthday, to lead defending champion Hannah Green by two strokes. Reid fell back to fifth place with a 74 and Green was 12th after a 73, but Buhai produced a strong challenge when she birdied four of the last five holes for a 65. Hall, after rounds of 70 and 66, made an early bogey on Sunday but twice posted a hat-trick of birdies from the fifth and 10th holes.

But with few leaderboards on the course, Hall was unaware she was leading when she came to the last. Her approach sailed into the back bunker and she took three to get down for a 68. "I was pretty nervous the last nine holes and I never looked at the leaderboard once, so I had no idea where I was," she said. "I didn't know I was leading. To bogey the last, I was quite upset about that. I had to refigure myself and get back to try and win that playoff."

It was Hall's first playoff but she drew on her matchplay pedigree, even after missing a six-footer for birdie at the 18th. Moving to the first for the second extra hole, both players missed the green and Hall faced a six-footer again. This time she holed it for her par, while Buhai, from a similar distance, missed, leaving the South African still seeking her first LPGA victory.

Weeks after triumphing at Royal Lytham in 2018, Hall was leading after 54 holes at Columbia Edgewater but finished runner-up to Marina Alex. "That did enter my mind. I didn't want to come second again," said Hall. "This course suits me.

"After I won the British, I just wanted to win again really badly, especially in America. I always knew it would be harder the longer it went on, so for me to win, it's a relief that I've won in America. I was quite nervous the last six or seven holes, so it was a buildup of emotions. And then bogeying the last and getting in a playoff, it was a buildup and then just really happy tears at the end."

Columbia Edgewater Country Club, Portland, Oregon — September 18-20
Par 72 (36-36); 6,467 yards — Purse: $1,750,000

1	**Georgia Hall**	70	66	68	204	$262,500		Amy Yang	69	66	72	207	25,854
2	**Ashleigh Buhai**	71	68	65	204	152,337		Hannah Green	66	68	73	207	25,854
	Hall won playoff at second extra hole						17	Angela Stanford	71	68	69	208	19,984
3	**Moriya Jutanugarn**	70	68	67	205	97,999		Angel Yin	70	68	70	208	19,984
	Yealimi Noh	67	69	69	205	97,999		Chella Choi	69	68	71	208	19,984
5	Robynn Ree	71	69	66	206	45,098		Celine Boutier	69	67	72	208	19,984
	Inbee Park	70	70	66	206	45,098		Amy Olson	67	68	73	208	19,984
	Caroline Masson	67	73	66	206	45,098	22	Eun-Hee Ji	70	71	68	209	17,515
	Mariah Stackhouse	69	70	67	206	45,098		Emma Talley	70	70	69	209	17,515
	Cheyenne Knight	69	69	68	206	45,098	24	Kelly Tan	74	70	66	210	15,638
	Jasmine Suwannapura	68	70	68	206	45,098		Jennifer Song	73	67	70	210	15,638
	Mel Reid	67	65	74	206	45,098		Sophia Popov	71	69	70	210	15,638
12	Danielle Kang	72	70	65	207	25,854		Hinako Shibuno	71	69	70	210	15,638
	Yu Liu	69	71	67	207	25,854	28	Mi Hyang Lee	75	67	69	211	12,606
	Lizette Salas	69	70	68	207	25,854		Christina Kim	73	69	69	211	12,606

	Austin Ernst	72	70	69	211	12,606
	Ilhee Lee	72	69	70	211	12,606
	Leona Maguire	71	69	71	211	12,606
	Maria Fassi	70	69	72	211	12,606
	Gaby Lopez	67	69	75	211	12,606
35	Matilda Castren	73	69	70	212	9,460
	Charlotte Thomas	71	71	70	212	9,460
	Alana Uriell	71	71	70	212	9,460
	Sarah Schmelzel	72	69	71	212	9,460
	Gigi Stoll	71	70	71	212	9,460
	Perrine Delacour	69	72	71	212	9,460
	Carlota Ciganda	71	68	73	212	9,460
42	Minjee Lee	70	74	69	213	6,867
	Alena Sharp	71	72	70	213	6,867
	Jennifer Chang	69	74	70	213	6,867
	Lydia Ko	73	69	71	213	6,867
	Dottie Ardina	70	72	71	213	6,867
	Andrea Lee	70	72	71	213	6,867
	Kristen Gillman	71	70	72	213	6,867
	Azahara Munoz	68	72	73	213	6,867
	Pornanong Phatlum	68	72	73	213	6,867
51	Mina Harigae	73	71	70	214	5,004
	Sarah Kemp	73	71	70	214	5,004
	Bronte Law	71	73	70	214	5,004
	Anna Nordqvist	72	71	71	214	5,004
	Mirim Lee	70	73	71	214	5,004
	Mo Martin	68	74	72	214	5,004
	Esther Lee	70	71	73	214	5,004
	Megan Khang	73	67	74	214	5,004
	Jeong Eun Lee	73	67	74	214	5,004
60	Lauren Coughlin	73	71	71	215	4,045
	Cydney Clanton	66	77	72	215	4,045
	Nanna Koerstz Madsen	70	71	74	215	4,045
	Brittany Lincicome	70	71	74	215	4,045
64	Wichanee Meechai	73	71	72	216	3,628
	Lauren Stephenson	71	72	73	216	3,628
	Linnea Johansson	71	72	73	216	3,628
	Madelene Sagstrom	74	68	74	216	3,628
	Bianca Pagdanganan	70	72	74	216	3,628
	Jodi Ewart Shadoff	74	65	77	216	3,628
70	Tiffany Joh	74	70	73	217	3,274
	Juli Inkster	74	70	73	217	3,274
	Ryann O'Toole	73	70	74	217	3,274
	Pei-Yun Chien	72	71	74	217	3,274
74	Jaye Marie Green	74	70	74	218	3,150
	Haru Nomura	74	70	74	218	3,150
76	Isi Gabsa	71	73	75	219	3,072
	Casey Danielson	69	75	75	219	3,072
78	Kendall Dye	75	69	76	220	2,975
	Maia Schechter	73	71	76	220	2,975
	Laetitia Beck	72	72	76	220	2,975

ShopRite LPGA Classic

From the number of players and caddies who doused the winner in various beverages on the 18th green of the Bay course at Seaview, it was clear Mel Reid was a popular first-time champion at the ShopRite Classic.

It had been a long time coming for the 33-year-old from England. There was the standout amateur career; then six wins on the LET between 2010-17; three Solheim Cup appearances for Europe. But there were also dark times such as the death of her mother in a traffic accident at a tournament in Germany in 2012. It took Reid until 2017 to get status on the LPGA. In 2019, poor form meant nobly swapping a potential playing berth in the Solheim at Gleneagles for a vice-captain role, while Suzann Pettersen made a triumphant last appearance as a player.

In August 2020, Reid started working with sports psychologist Howard Falco and a last piece of the jigsaw slotted into place. From battling through the halfway cut on the number at the AIG Women's Open, she finished seventh at the ANA Inspiration and then fifth at the Portland Classic. But a two-shot lead with a round to play had got away. When Reid edged in front by one at the same stage in Atlantic City, with rounds of 68, 64 and 66, she was determined not to fold again. Certainly not after reading on social media that she was going to choke on the final day.

"After Portland, I wanted to redeem myself," Reid said. "I read a tweet yesterday and it was probably one of the only bad tweets that I got saying 'she'll choke'. It gave me a bit of motivation. I know it sounds stupid, but probably the best thing I could have read. I was definitely not letting that happen.

"The older you get in this game you do create a few scars. But being 33 years old and lifting this trophy when I had some young players behind me, it goes to show, I guess, that I like adversity. I'll always be a fighter and try and fight my way through things. I'm so happy and relieved that I got it done, for myself and my team."

After two early birdies, bogeys at both the sixth and seventh holes put Reid one behind Jennifer Song. But Reid then birdied four of the next five holes and went four clear of Song and Jennifer Kupcho, who rallied after a double bogey at the eighth. A fist pump accompanied a crucial 15-foot par save at the 15th but a dropped shot at the short 17th, combined with tap-in birdies for Song and Kupcho, meant the lead was down to two.

A six-iron from the rough that crept onto the green at the par-five 18th settled the issue. A birdie gave Reid a 67 and a 19-under-par total of 265. Kupcho also birdied to claim second place with a 68 while Song was third after a 69. Nasa Hataoka and Nelly Korda finished fourth and fifth.

After Georgia Hall's win at the Portland Classic, this was the first time since Trish Johnson and Caroline Pierce in 1996 that two English players had won successive LPGA tournaments.

Seaview Dolce Hotel (Bay), Galloway, New Jersey — October 1-4
Par 71 (37-34); 6,190 yards — Purse: $1,300,000

1	**Mel Reid**	68	64	66	67	265	$195,000
2	**Jennifer Kupcho**	69	65	65	68	267	114,323
3	**Jennifer Song**	65	69	65	69	268	82,933
4	Nasa Hataoka	64	67	70	69	270	64,155
5	Nelly Korda	68	70	68	66	272	51,638
6	Mina Harigae	68	70	69	66	273	34,112
	Ashleigh Buhai	66	71	70	66	273	34,112
	Brooke M Henderson	68	70	65	70	273	34,112
	Ryann O'Toole	64	71	67	71	273	34,112
10	Christina Kim	69	65	72	68	274	23,576
	Katherine Kirk	66	69	70	69	274	23,576
	Brittany Altomare	66	71	67	70	274	23,576
13	Maria Fassi	70	71	69	65	275	18,276
	Jessica Korda	68	71	68	68	275	18,276
	Lexi Thompson	67	72	68	68	275	18,276
	Megan Khang	69	70	67	69	275	18,276
	Ally McDonald	69	67	68	71	275	18,276
18	Minjee Lee	70	69	70	67	276	14,167
	Brittany Lang	68	69	72	67	276	14,167
	Sei Young Kim	69	71	68	68	276	14,167
	Anne van Dam	67	68	69	72	276	14,167
	Georgia Hall	67	67	70	72	276	14,167
	Kelly Tan	68	69	65	74	276	14,167
24	Leona Maguire	71	69	70	67	277	11,955
	Moriya Jutanugarn	67	70	68	72	277	11,955
	Xiyu Lin	70	69	65	73	277	11,955
27	Sung Hyun Park	72	66	74	66	278	9,662
	Hinako Shibuno	68	72	69	69	278	9,662
	Tiffany Joh	70	70	68	70	278	9,662
	Yu Liu	68	68	72	70	278	9,662
	Yealimi Noh	69	70	68	71	278	9,662
	Gaby Lopez	72	65	70	71	278	9,662
	Amy Olson	67	66	73	72	278	9,662
	Mi Hyang Lee	63	69	72	74	278	9,662
35	Pajaree Anannarukarn	70	72	72	65	279	7,386
	Sarah Schmelzel	70	72	67	70	279	7,386
	Stacy Lewis	70	70	68	71	279	7,386
	Jenny Shin	66	70	72	71	279	7,386
	Jodi Ewart Shadoff	68	69	68	74	279	7,386
40	Yui Kawamoto	70	70	71	69	280	6,259
	Lindy Duncan	66	74	71	69	280	6,259
	Alena Sharp	72	66	71	71	280	6,259
43	Cheyenne Knight	73	69	70	69	281	4,876
	Lindsey Weaver	71	71	70	69	281	4,876
	Na Yeon Choi	72	69	71	69	281	4,876
	Anna Nordqvist	72	69	71	69	281	4,876
	In Gee Chun	68	67	77	69	281	4,876
	Min Seo Kwak	69	73	69	70	281	4,876
	Pornanong Phatlum	67	73	71	70	281	4,876
	Emma Talley	70	67	73	71	281	4,876
	Celine Boutier	68	65	74	74	281	4,876
	Sophia Popov	69	68	69	75	281	4,876
53	Cristie Kerr	72	67	70	73	282	4,005
54	Lizette Salas	69	72	71	71	283	3,693
	Gerina Piller	68	73	71	71	283	3,693
	Charlotte Thomas	69	70	72	72	283	3,693
	Ayako Uehara	71	71	68	73	283	3,693
58	Stephanie Meadow	70	72	70	72	284	3,255
	Cydney Clanton	67	73	72	72	284	3,255
	Matilda Castren	68	69	73	74	284	3,255
61	Hee Young Park	67	73	74	71	285	2,973
	Carlota Ciganda	72	70	69	74	285	2,973
	Austin Ernst	68	71	72	74	285	2,973
	Kristen Gillman	67	70	74	74	285	2,973
65	Lauren Stephenson	63	75	73	75	286	2,816
66	Tiffany Chan	71	70	74	72	287	2,660
	Hannah Green	73	69	70	75	287	2,660
	Annie Park	70	72	70	75	287	2,660
	Haeji Kang	68	69	73	77	287	2,660
70	Elizabeth Szokol	71	70	73	74	288	2,488
	Pernilla Lindberg	69	72	73	74	288	2,488
72	Andrea Lee	71	70	70	78	289	2,441
73	Nicole Broch Larsen	70	71	76	73	290	2,379
	Albane Valenzuela	73	69	73	75	290	2,379
	Linnea Strom	69	68	75	78	290	2,379
76	Dana Finkelstein	69	73	72	78	292	2,320

LPGA Drive On Championship — Reynolds Lake Oconee

All the changes required to keep playing golf in 2020 added up to a major blessing for Ally McDonald when she got to celebrate her maiden victory on her 28th birthday with her parents alongside. Usually, in October, McDonald would be in Asia but the revamped LPGA schedule offered a second Drive On Championship at Reynolds Lake Oconee in Georgia, the closest event to the family home in Mississippi. "It's the best birthday present ever," said McDonald, who got married during the hiatus earlier in the year in a ceremony with limited attendance.

At the Jack Nicklaus-designed Great Waters course, LPGA players enjoyed performing in front of a gallery of sorts as home owners watched from their back yards and many took to their boats to view the closing holes from the lake, cheering and honking along as McDonald held off Danielle Kang by one shot.

McDonald, who impressed at the 2019 Solheim Cup after coming into the US team as a late injury replacement for Stacy Lewis, hit the top of the leaderboard on Friday and opened up a four-shot advantage on the back nine on Saturday. She ended up one ahead of young Philippine star Bianca

Pagdanganan and two in front of Kang before again going four ahead with three birdies in a row after the turn on Sunday.

But a bogey at the 13th, along with Kang birdieing the same hole and the 14th, meant the lead was only one. Suddenly it was three again as Kang dropped a shot at the 15th and McDonald birdied the 16th thanks to a fine approach. Not so fast. Three-putting the 17th put her two ahead at the par-five last.

Kang, after a long debate about firing at the green from a dubious lie in the rough, laid up and then very nearly holed out for an eagle. A birdie for a 68 meant Kang was denied a second Drive On title as McDonald secured a winning par. The big-hitting Pagdanganan, who averaged nearly 300 yards off the tee, birdied the last two holes after 16 pars to finish third — her best finish in only her seventh start — while former world number one Ariya Jutanugarn, who threatened on the front nine, recorded her first top-10 finish for a year in sixth place.

"I've never doubted my ability, but I've definitely questioned whether I would be able to win out here. It's really hard to win out here," said McDonald, who had rounds of 66, 68, 69 and 69 for a 16-under-par total of 272. "I've hung in there and tried to stick to my process since day one. That was able to get me in the winner's circle today. I'm really thankful." Towards the end of the season, the winner switched to playing under her married name of Ewing.

Reynolds Lake Oconee (Great Waters), Greensboro, Georgia — October 22-25
Par 72 (36-36); 6,664 yards — Purse: $1,300,000

1	**Ally McDonald**	66	68	69	69	272	$195,000
2	**Danielle Kang**	65	70	70	68	273	115,184
3	**Bianca Pagdanganan**	68	67	69	70	274	83,557
4	Mina Harigae	72	68	68	67	275	58,332
	Carlota Ciganda	73	65	68	69	275	58,332
6	Ariya Jutanugarn	67	69	72	69	277	39,099
	Katherine Kirk	72	65	70	70	277	39,099
8	Matilda Castren	69	69	73	67	278	28,273
	Lydia Ko	71	70	68	69	278	28,273
	Brittany Altomare	71	67	70	70	278	28,273
11	Mel Reid	69	68	73	69	279	22,859
	Pernilla Lindberg	68	69	72	70	279	22,859
13	Su Oh	71	72	69	68	280	18,918
	Brittany Lincicome	72	70	70	68	280	18,918
	Gaby Lopez	70	71	70	69	280	18,918
	Megan Khang	71	70	68	71	280	18,918
17	Stacy Lewis	70	71	71	69	281	15,682
	Hannah Green	74	68	68	71	281	15,682
	Angel Yin	72	67	70	72	281	15,682
20	Liz Nagel	73	73	65	71	282	13,748
	Sarah Schmelzel	72	71	68	71	282	13,748
	Lindsey Weaver	67	72	72	71	282	13,748
	Chella Choi	69	69	72	72	282	13,748
24	Austin Ernst	75	72	67	69	283	11,171
	Marissa Steen	68	72	74	69	283	11,171
	Lexi Thompson	71	74	68	70	283	11,171
	Elizabeth Szokol	71	70	72	70	283	11,171
	Jennifer Song	65	75	71	72	283	11,171
	Lindy Duncan	71	71	68	73	283	11,171
	Yealimi Noh	72	69	69	73	283	11,171
31	Andrea Lee	75	68	72	69	284	9,144
	Mariah Stackhouse	70	75	68	71	284	9,144
	Jennifer Kupcho	70	71	71	72	284	9,144
34	Amy Olson	72	73	75	65	285	7,168
	Moriya Jutanugarn	75	69	73	68	285	7,168
	Xiyu Lin	74	69	73	69	285	7,168
	Stephanie Meadow	74	70	71	70	285	7,168
	Cheyenne Knight	72	72	70	71	285	7,168
	Lauren Coughlin	69	75	70	71	285	7,168
	Brittany Lang	71	70	73	71	285	7,168
	Christina Kim	71	70	72	72	285	7,168
	Cristie Kerr	73	70	69	73	285	7,168
43	Gerina Piller	72	75	70	69	286	5,373
	Jenny Shin	71	76	70	69	286	5,373
	Robynn Ree	70	70	74	72	286	5,373
	Maria Fassi	73	71	69	73	286	5,373
	Celine Boutier	69	70	74	73	286	5,373
48	Eun-Hee Ji	72	70	74	71	287	4,525
	Haeji Kang	71	75	69	72	287	4,525
	Caroline Masson	71	73	71	72	287	4,525
	Pornanong Phatlum	74	70	70	73	287	4,525
52	Morgan Pressel	71	76	73	68	288	3,910
	Azahara Munoz	75	72	71	70	288	3,910
	Angela Stanford	72	72	74	70	288	3,910
	Daniela Darquea	72	73	72	71	288	3,910
	Alena Sharp	70	69	73	76	288	3,910
57	Patty Tavatanakit	72	71	75	71	289	3,406
	Sophia Popov	72	71	74	72	289	3,406
	Perrine Delacour	69	70	76	74	289	3,406
60	Minjee Lee	70	73	75	72	290	2,964
	Jing Yan	75	70	72	73	290	2,964
	Yu Liu	76	69	71	74	290	2,964
	Kristen Gillman	70	75	71	74	290	2,964
	Wichanee Meechai	73	72	70	75	290	2,964
	Kelly Tan	70	71	74	75	290	2,964
	Esther Lee	71	72	71	76	290	2,964
67	Haley Moore	71	75	72	73	291	2,680
	Jessica Korda	74	67	77	73	291	2,680
69	Ashleigh Buhai	72	74	77	69	292	2,533
	Leona Maguire	74	72	73	73	292	2,533
	Annie Park	74	71	73	74	292	2,533
72	Alana Uriell	71	76	76	71	294	2,459
73	Brianna Do	72	74	76	73	295	2,428
74	Anne van Dam	74	70	76	77	297	2,396
75	Jiwon Jeon	72	75	78	73	298	2,367
76	Linnea Johansson	73	73	74	79	299	2,337
77	Yujeong Son	76	71	77	77	301	2,293
	Julieta Granada	74	73	75	79	301	2,293

Pelican Women's Championship

In a battle of the two most recent winners on tour, the new major champion, Sei Young Kim, came out on top by beating Ally McDonald by three strokes at the inaugural Pelican Women's Championship. Since winning the KPMG Women's PGA, Kim had returned to Korea for an emotional reunion with family and friends, albeit the first fortnight of her four-week stay was spent self-isolating in her bedroom at her parents' home.

A few days' practice in Texas enabled Kim to regain the magic from Aronimink. The LPGA's return to the Tampa area at Pelican, recently revamped and reopened in Belleair, was delayed from May but the November date allowed club members to spectate, including the Augusta National chairman Fred Ridley, a week after overseeing the rescheduled Masters.

After AIG Women's Open champion Sophia Popov led the way on Thursday with a six-under-par 64, Kim topped the leaderboard on Friday after scores of 67 and 65. Her own 64 on Saturday put the 27-year-old Korean five ahead of McDonald. The Drive On champion from Lake Oconee was only one behind after holing-in-one at the 12th with a pitching wedge from 132 yards, her first ace in LPGA competition, but Kim responded with four birdies in a row from the 14th.

Far from resting on her laurels after claiming a longed for major, Kim's desire to improve included watching *The Last Dance*, the Michael Jordan documentary. Though her lead, after briefly expanding to six, was cut to three at the turn on Sunday, Kim overcame her weakest display of the week, holing from 18 feet for a birdie at the 14th and taking a five-shot lead to the final hole. McDonald birdied the last for a 68 to take second place, two ahead of Stephanie Meadow, who matched her third place finish from her professional debut at the 2014 US Open.

Kim failed to get up and down at the 18th, a 70 leaving her on 14-under-par 266, and was swiftly doused in champagne, the proper stuff, by her fellow players. With her 12th LPGA win, Kim now ranked third among Koreans, behind only Se Ri Pak and Inbee Park, while this was her fourth multi-win season out of six.

"I'm very happy to win my 12th tournament, and after winning the major, it means a lot to me," Kim said. "Ally was going really good, it could be she chase me. When I turned after the ninth hole, I had a little bit of pressure before I made the birdie. After hole 14, little more comfortable and then good feeling back."

Pelican Golf Club, Belleair, Florida — November 19-22
Par 70 (35-35); 6,353 yards — Purse: $1,500,000

1	**Sei Young Kim**	67	65	64	70	266	$225,000
2	**Ally McDonald**	67	66	68	68	269	135,214
3	**Stephanie Meadow**	69	65	68	69	271	98,088
4	Austin Ernst	71	68	65	68	272	68,477
	Lydia Ko	70	67	66	69	272	68,477
6	Jessica Korda	69	73	67	64	273	40,346
	Angela Stanford	70	68	70	65	273	40,346
	Jennifer Song	68	70	70	65	273	40,346
	Brooke M Henderson	68	70	66	69	273	40,346
10	Ashleigh Buhai	66	72	70	67	275	29,982
11	Elizabeth Szokol	69	66	70	71	276	27,760
12	Caroline Masson	69	70	70	68	277	25,095
	Mel Reid	73	70	65	69	277	25,095
14	Jodi Ewart Shadoff	68	71	74	65	278	22,801
15	Brittany Altomare	72	70	69	68	279	19,396
	Amy Olson	70	71	70	68	279	19,396
	Hee Young Park	68	73	68	70	279	19,396
	Sophia Popov	64	70	75	70	279	19,396
	Minjee Lee	68	69	67	75	279	19,396
20	Sarah Schmelzel	70	73	71	66	280	15,282
	Perrine Delacour	70	71	71	68	280	15,282
	Andrea Lee	71	70	70	69	280	15,282
	In Gee Chun	71	69	70	70	280	15,282
	Robynn Ree	69	69	72	70	280	15,282
	Lindsey Weaver	69	68	71	72	280	15,282
	Mi Jung Hur	70	69	68	73	280	15,282
27	Angel Yin	72	71	73	66	282	11,654
	Maria Fassi	73	70	71	68	282	11,654
	Lindy Duncan	71	70	72	69	282	11,654
	Lexi Thompson	70	70	73	69	282	11,654
	Xiyu Lin	71	74	67	70	282	11,654
	Nanna Koerstz Madsen	72	70	70	70	282	11,654
	Alena Sharp	68	71	71	72	282	11,654
34	Jenny Shin	70	73	72	68	283	9,106
	Bianca Pagdanganan	73	69	72	69	283	9,106
	Nasa Hataoka	71	71	72	69	283	9,106
	Jin Young Ko	72	71	69	71	283	9,106
	Nicole Broch Larsen	73	69	69	72	283	9,106
39	Yealimi Noh	71	72	70	71	284	7,699
	Cristie Kerr	72	69	72	71	284	7,699
	Cheyenne Knight	70	70	73	71	284	7,699
42	Jeongeun Lee[6]	73	69	77	66	285	6,681
	Madelene Sagstrom	72	71	71	71	285	6,681
	Jeong Eun Lee	71	70	73	71	285	6,681
	Kristen Gillman	70	71	70	74	285	6,681
46	Hannah Green	73	72	71	70	286	5,436
	Brittany Lincicome	69	72	75	70	286	5,436
	Su Oh	71	72	72	71	286	5,436
	Annie Park	73	69	73	71	286	5,436
	Daniela Darquea	73	69	72	72	286	5,436

	Tiffany Joh	70	71	71	74	286	5,436
	Megan Khang	70	70	70	76	286	5,436
53	Sierra L Brooks	74	71	71	71	287	4,442
	Eun-Hee Ji	70	70	76	71	287	4,442
	Gerina Piller	76	69	70	72	287	4,442
	Sarah Jane Smith	69	72	73	73	287	4,442
	Leona Maguire	72	72	69	74	287	4,442
58	Stacy Lewis	76	69	74	70	289	3,746
	Jaye Marie Green	68	74	76	71	289	3,746
	Mi Hyang Lee	71	73	73	72	289	3,746
	Maria Fernanda Torres	69	71	75	74	289	3,746
	Jennifer Kupcho	75	70	69	75	289	3,746
63	Sarah Burnham	77	68	73	72	290	3,405
	Pernilla Lindberg	74	71	73	72	290	3,405
	Haeji Kang	68	73	75	74	290	3,405
66	Sung Hyun Park	74	70	77	70	291	3,220
	Mina Harigae	72	70	77	72	291	3,220
68	Jackie Stoelting	73	71	75	73	292	3,109
69	Tiffany Chan	73	72	75	73	293	2,998
	Morgan Pressel	73	71	76	73	293	2,998

Volunteers of America Classic

When Yealimi Noh had a double bogey at the 18th hole on Saturday, she fell back into a tie for the lead with two US Open champions, Inbee Park and So Yeon Ryu. Seven further players were a stroke behind on a crowded leaderboard at the Volunteers of America Classic. Among them were world number one Jin Young Ko and Texas's Angela Stanford. On Sunday at Old American, less than an hour from her home in Fort Worth, it was Stanford who left the rest behind with a burst of four birdies in five holes on the back nine.

A bogey at the last did not prevent a two-stroke victory for the recently turned 43-year-old Stanford, a first win since the Evian Championship in 2018. A drop in form had followed and Stanford briefly wondered if her career was complete but having rededicated herself to the game she added not just a seventh title but a first in her home state and in front of her parents. "Honestly, I never thought I would," she said of the emotional home win.

After three birdies in a row from the sixth, Stanford made her move with birdies at the 13th and 14th holes, the latter where she had a double bogey on Saturday. Then she added two more birdies at the 16th and 17th holes. It was at the 17th in the third round that she had ignited her challenge by chipping in, validation of the hard work on her short game.

"Not many people at 42 are going to say, I want to learn how to chip the ball properly," said Stanford. "I just felt like if I'm getting close to the end of my career, I don't want to leave any stone unturned. I want to find out, if I chip it the best I can, if I putt it the best I can, if I hit it the best I can, what am I capable of before I'm done. I really think it boils down to passion. I just love trying to get better."

Only Catriona Matthew, 42, and Cristie Kerr, 40, had won in their 40s in the last 10 seasons. Stanford closed with a 67, the low round of the day, after scores of 71, 69 and 70 for a seven-under-par total of 277. In contrast to Stanford, in her 20th year on tour, Noh was in contention as a 19-year-old rookie. She was delighted to play alongside two of her heroes in Park and Ryu, with all three scoring 70 to tie for second place. On the eve of the rescheduled US Open in Houston, Ryu had 17 pars and a birdie at the 18th, while Ko also had a 70 to be fifth.

Old American Golf Club, The Colony, Texas — December 3-6
Par: 71 (35-36); 6,517 yards — Purse: $1,750,000

1	**Angela Stanford**	71	69	70	67	277	$262,500
2	**So Yeon Ryu**	72	72	65	70	279	120,709
	Inbee Park	72	68	69	70	279	120,709
	Yealimi Noh	72	66	71	70	279	120,709
5	Jin Young Ko	71	69	70	70	280	71,533
6	Anna Nordqvist	70	68	73	70	281	53,758
	Charley Hull	68	74	68	71	281	53,758
8	Lindsey Weaver	71	68	73	70	282	40,752
	Kristen Gillman	73	71	66	72	282	40,752
10	Madelene Sagstrom	71	69	71	72	283	35,116
11	Su Oh	73	70	72	69	284	28,630
	Jennifer Kupcho	69	73	70	72	284	28,630
	Kelly Tan	73	68	71	72	284	28,630
	Brittany Lang	70	71	71	72	284	28,630
	Nasa Hataoka	72	69	69	74	284	28,630
16	Xiyu Lin	78	67	70	70	285	22,601
	Moriya Jutanugarn	73	70	71	71	285	22,601
	Jeongeun Lee[6]	73	73	66	73	285	22,601
19	Austin Ernst	72	72	73	69	286	19,249
	Minjee Lee	75	70	71	70	286	19,249
	Sarah Kemp	75	69	70	72	286	19,249
	Linnea Strom	71	70	71	74	286	19,249
	Jessica Korda	69	69	72	76	286	19,249
24	Hannah Green	75	67	72	73	287	17,168
25	Caroline Masson	78	71	71	68	288	14,502
	Katherine Kirk	74	76	67	71	288	14,502
	Leona Maguire	72	74	70	72	288	14,502
	Yu Liu	73	70	73	72	288	14,502
	Cheyenne Knight	71	73	71	73	288	14,502
	Tiffany Chan	72	76	66	74	288	14,502

	Jasmine Suwannapura	73	72	68	75	288	14,502
	Pornanong Phatlum	69	71	70	78	288	14,502
33	Sung Hyun Park	72	70	75	72	289	11,116
	Ryann O'Toole	74	74	68	73	289	11,116
	Nanna Koerstz Madsen	81	67	67	74	289	11,116
	Lindy Duncan	76	71	68	74	289	11,116
	Sophia Popov	71	73	71	74	289	11,116
38	Celine Boutier	79	69	70	72	290	9,035
	Annie Park	72	71	75	72	290	9,035
	Alana Uriell	76	71	70	73	290	9,035
	Megan Khang	70	74	73	73	290	9,035
	Mi Jung Hur	71	72	74	73	290	9,035
43	Ally Ewing	70	76	74	71	291	7,387
	Robynn Ree	75	72	71	73	291	7,387
	Emma Talley	74	73	71	73	291	7,387
	Sarah Schmelzel	76	71	70	74	291	7,387
	Perrine Delacour	74	71	71	75	291	7,387
48	Sarah Jane Smith	78	72	68	74	292	6,221
	Jodi Ewart Shadoff	72	75	71	74	292	6,221
	Stacy Lewis	75	71	72	74	292	6,221
	Patty Tavatanakit	76	67	74	75	292	6,221
52	Pernilla Lindberg	75	75	72	71	293	5,289
	Jenny Coleman	79	71	71	72	293	5,289
	Nicole Broch Larsen	72	77	72	72	293	5,289
	Andrea Lee	73	74	72	74	293	5,289
	In Gee Chun	73	70	75	75	293	5,289
	Morgan Pressel	73	70	75	75	293	5,289
58	Stephanie Meadow	75	73	74	72	294	4,444
	Chella Choi	75	71	75	73	294	4,444
	Pajaree Anannarukarn	73	75	72	74	294	4,444
	Gaby Lopez	76	71	69	78	294	4,444
62	Ariya Jutanugarn	72	76	76	71	295	4,075
	Amy Olson	74	75	71	75	295	4,075
	Jing Yan	75	72	73	75	295	4,075
65	Amy Yang	76	74	70	76	296	3,858
	Mel Reid	73	74	71	78	296	3,858
67	Jeong Eun Lee	74	74	77	72	297	3,642
	Ayako Uehara	79	71	72	75	297	3,642
	Cydney Clanton	74	71	76	76	297	3,642
70	Lauren Stephenson	73	75	76	74	298	3,425
	Brittany Altomare	73	73	73	79	298	3,425
	Gerina Piller	70	75	73	80	298	3,425
73	Jaye Marie Green	75	74	72	79	300	3,338
74	Haley Moore	73	76	76	78	303	3,295
75	Ashleigh Buhai	78	69	79	78	304	3,255
76	Bianca Pagdanganan	78	72	78	77	305	3,214

CME Group Tour Championship

Jin Young Ko's timing was almost as perfect as her golf as the world number one ended the season with a five-stroke victory at the CME Group Tour Championship. Ko spent most of the year in Korea and only returned to America for the last four events of the season. She finished 34th and fifth in her first two outings and then second at the US Open before, in Naples, claiming the largest first prize of the season of $1.1 million. And so, Ko led the money list for the second year running.

Ko was not even qualified for the season-ending event until she put in a late charge to finish as a runner-up in Houston on Monday. For 2020 only, the CME field was expanded to 72 players, including two sponsor's invitations but neither was granted to Ko, nor Sophia Popov, whose victory at the AIG Women's Open did not count on the points list. "I still can't believe am I here," Ko said. "And then I won this tournament, so just I want to thank to God."

Over the weekend there was a duel for the title and the top spot on the Rolex Rankings between Ko and Sei Young Kim, who have known each other since school days. Kim led by three during Saturday's play but ended the third round only one stroke ahead. Ko closed that gap at the first hole on Sunday. She led briefly before a bogey at the ninth, but when Kim dropped a shot at the 11th, Ko holed an important par putt to go ahead for good.

She closed out the tournament in dominant fashion with three birdies in a row from the 12th and five in the last seven holes. At the last her caddie Dave Brooker said a previous employer, Lorena Ochoa, always believed that a professional should finish a tournament in style. Ko did by holing for a three from 10 feet and blowing a kiss to the sky. "That was my motivation for my last putt," Ko said. "I would say just thank you Dave and Lorena."

Another motivation was her plan to buy a house in Frisco, Texas. "I needed money to buy the house," she said. "I can buy it now."

Ko's closing 66, after rounds of 68, 67 and 69, gave the 25-year-old an 18-under-par total of 270. Kim closed with a 72 to tie for second place with Hannah Green, the Australian celebrating her birthday with a bogey-free 67. Mina Harigae was fourth after a 68, while Lydia Ko and Lexi Thompson shared fifth place having both scored 65s during the week.

"She did a great job today," Kim said of her compatriot. "I tried to chase her but I couldn't." Kim, winner of the KPMG Women's PGA and the Pelican Championship, did do enough to overtake Inbee Park and claimed the Rolex Player of the Year title. "I'm disappointed I could not play well today but I'm really happy I got Player of the Year, that's really awesome."

Although Kim had the lowest stroke average for the season, she did not play enough rounds to qualify for the Vare Trophy, which was claimed by Danielle Kang.

Tiburon Golf Club, Ritz Carlton Golf Resort, Naples, Florida — December 17-20
Par 72 (36-36); 6,556 yards — Purse: $3,000,000

1	**Jin Young Ko**	68	67	69	66	270	$1,100,000
2	**Hannah Green**	69	68	71	67	275	209,555
	Sei Young Kim	67	69	67	72	275	209,555
4	Mina Harigae	70	69	69	68	276	117,279
5	Lydia Ko	74	65	69	69	277	82,319
	Lexi Thompson	65	71	71	70	277	82,319
7	Brooke M Henderson	73	68	66	71	278	52,021
	Austin Ernst	69	69	69	71	278	52,021
	Georgia Hall	69	69	68	72	278	52,021
10	Ariya Jutanugarn	72	70	71	67	280	37,162
	Anna Nordqvist	68	72	70	70	280	37,162
	Cristie Kerr	68	74	66	72	280	37,162
13	Brittany Lincicome	72	71	71	67	281	27,839
	So Yeon Ryu	71	73	69	68	281	27,839
	Madelene Sagstrom	72	72	68	69	281	27,839
	Perrine Delacour	70	71	68	72	281	27,839
	Charley Hull	72	69	66	74	281	27,839
	Minjee Lee	68	73	66	74	281	27,839
19	Christina Kim	73	72	69	68	282	21,970
	Celine Boutier	71	71	70	70	282	21,970
	Nelly Korda	72	66	74	70	282	21,970
	Cheyenne Knight	71	72	68	71	282	21,970
23	Jenny Shin	73	72	68	70	283	18,832
	Gaby Lopez	71	71	70	71	283	18,832
	Katherine Kirk	72	68	72	71	283	18,832
	Xiyu Lin	71	72	66	74	283	18,832
	Sarah Schmelzel	71	69	69	74	283	18,832
28	Jennifer Kupcho	70	72	70	72	284	16,638
	Cydney Clanton	70	68	72	74	284	16,638
30	Jessica Korda	75	74	70	66	285	14,671
	Danielle Kang	71	75	70	69	285	14,671
	Amy Yang	73	73	69	70	285	14,671
	Yealimi Noh	73	69	70	73	285	14,671
	Caroline Masson	67	71	74	73	285	14,671
35	Brittany Altomare	73	73	71	69	286	12,661
	Jodi Ewart Shadoff	70	73	70	73	286	12,661
	Inbee Park	71	71	71	73	286	12,661
38	Nasa Hataoka	73	70	75	69	287	10,782
	Azahara Munoz	73	75	69	70	287	10,782
	Stephanie Meadow	70	76	69	72	287	10,782
	Linnea Strom	74	71	70	72	287	10,782
	Megan Khang	67	71	75	74	287	10,782
	Moriya Jutanugarn	70	73	69	75	287	10,782
44	Carlota Ciganda	68	74	77	69	288	9,340
	Mirim Lee	73	73	69	73	288	9,340
46	Alena Sharp	73	76	76	64	289	8,129
	In Gee Chun	73	74	75	67	289	8,129
	Stacy Lewis	71	75	74	69	289	8,129
	Lizette Salas	71	72	76	70	289	8,129
	Jennifer Song	74	70	74	71	289	8,129
	Robynn Ree	74	72	69	74	289	8,129
	Leona Maguire	73	72	69	75	289	8,129
53	Emma Talley	72	74	74	70	290	6,806
	Lindsey Weaver	74	74	70	72	290	6,806
	Sarah Kemp	72	73	73	72	290	6,806
	Jasmine Suwannapura	70	74	73	73	290	6,806
	Andrea Lee	71	72	73	74	290	6,806
	Nanna Koerstz Madsen	66	77	73	74	290	6,806
59	Pernilla Lindberg	76	74	68	73	291	6,107
	Mel Reid	74	73	70	74	291	6,107
61	Maria Fassi	68	76	78	70	292	5,757
	Anne van Dam	71	77	72	72	292	5,757
	Ashleigh Buhai	69	77	70	76	292	5,757
64	Maria Fernanda Torres	76	75	69	73	293	5,582
65	Kelly Tan	72	74	72	76	294	5,495
66	Yu Liu	74	77	69	75	295	5,407
67	Hee Young Park	73	76	71	76	296	5,320
68	Bianca Pagdanganan	73	79	76	69	297	5,189
	Angela Stanford	75	72	76	74	297	5,189
70	Kristen Gillman	75	77	72	75	299	5,058
71	Brittany Lang	76	78	75	74	303	4,971
72	Natalie Gulbis	77	78	77	80	312	4,927

2020 MONEY LIST

1	Jin Young Ko	$1,667,925
2	Sei Young Kim	1,416,993
3	Inbee Park	1,377,799
4	Danielle Kang	897,872
5	Nasa Hataoka	854,024
6	Austin Ernst	771,092
7	Amy Olson	763,832
8	Minjee Lee	724,273
9	Lydia Ko	677,545
10	Brooke M Henderson	648,604

Gregory Shamus/Getty Images

A Toledo double as Danielle Kang won the LPGA's first two events after the season resumed in August.

David Cannon/Getty Images

Mark Runnacles/Getty Images

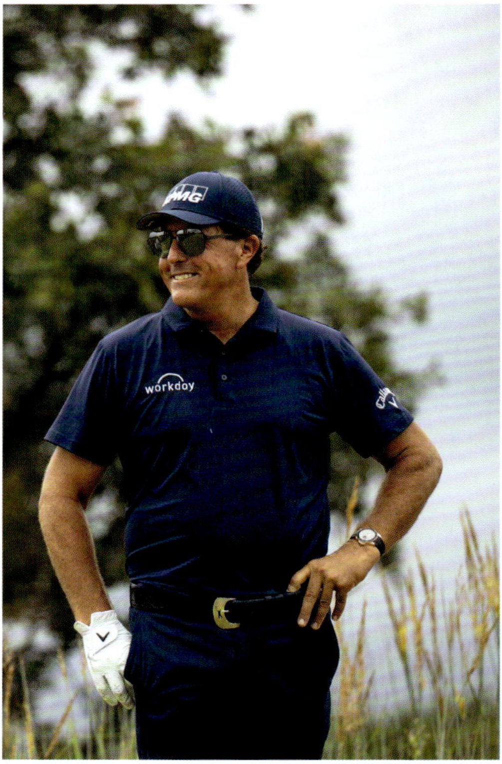

Brett Carlsen/Getty Images

Clockwise from top: the Rose Series Grand Final at Wentworth was abandoned due to a wildfire; two out of two for Phil Mickelson on the Champions Tour; Stacy Lewis won for the first time as a mother in Scotland.

Jamie Sabau/Getty Images

A hole-in-one helped Jerry Kelly on the way to victory at the Bridgestone Senior Players.

Ross Kinnaird/Getty Images

Octavio Passos/Getty Images

Atsushi Tomura/Getty Images

Clockwise from top left: Dane Rasmus Hojgaard, 19, earned his second tour title at The Belfry; American John Catlin, 29, had the first of two wins at Valderrama; Filipino Yuka Saso, 19, won two in a row in Japan.

Sean M Haffey/Getty Images

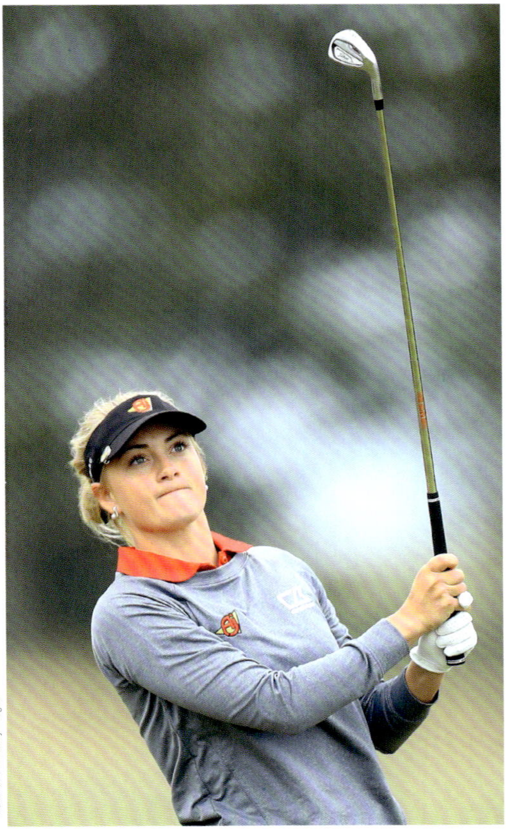

David Cannon/Getty Images

David Cannon/Getty Images

Clockwise from top: 2009 Open champion Stewart Cink won in Napa with son Reagan as caddie; Daniel van Tonder won four out of six events on the Sunshine Tour; Julia Engstrom won twice on the Ladies European Tour.

Richard Heathcote/Getty Images

Ross Kinnaird/Getty Images

Ross Kinnaird/Getty Images

Clockwise from top: a lone spectator, with bovine friends, at the Irish Open; Japan's Takami Kanaya won in his third start as a pro at the Dunlop Phoenix; a maiden win for Robert MacIntyre at the Cyprus Showdown.

Ladies European Tour

Christopher Pike/Getty Images

Micheal Cohen/Getty Images

Clockwise from top left: Emily Kristine Pedersen leading the way in Europe with four wins; Minjee Lee winning under floodlights in Dubai; Mel Reid soaking in a memorable first LPGA victory in Atlantic City.

Warren Little/Getty Images

Francois Nel/Getty Images

Clockwise from top left: three wins in 2020 for Japanese rookie Ayaka Furue, 20; and South Africa's Christiaan Bezuidenhout, 26; while England's Lee Westwood, 47, earned a third Race to Dubai title in December.

Ladies European Tour

Emily Kristine Pedersen could be forgiven for thinking she was living in a parallel universe in 2020. "It's been a strange year for all of us with Covid and everyone's saying it's such a bad year," said the 24-year-old Dane, "but I'm here having the best year ever, so it's a little weird. I'm just really happy."

Pedersen started the year outside the top 500 on the Rolex Rankings after a turbulent couple of years. She ended it by winning three times in a row and securing the Race to Costa del Sol title with a tournament to spare. "I can't believe what's happened this season," she said. "I was confident I could get back to where I was but I couldn't imagine that it would be like this."

A British and European Amateur champion, Pedersen was the LET rookie of the year in 2015. When she was picked for the 2017 Solheim Cup by Annika Sorenstam, it appeared a natural progression for an undoubted young star. But she lost all three matches she played in Des Moines and her confidence faltered for the first time. "I think maybe I wasn't ready," she later admitted. "I was upset and it knocked me. My focus changed. I put all my energy in to proving to myself, and to others, that I was good enough to be on the team."

Pedersen subsequently lost her LPGA card and continued to struggle for form after returning to the LET in 2019. "I needed to mature and see the difference between Emily the golfer and Emily the person," she said. "I worked hard with a psychologist to make that clear. When I played badly, I thought I wasn't a good human being and I doubted I'd ever be back."

Seventh place at the South African Open was a positive step but then came lockdown. Challenged by her coach to improve her game, Pedersen had time and motivation to work hard. In June she won a Danish ECCO Tour event with a largely male field including rising star Rasmus Hojgaard.

Her best ever LPGA result came when she was involved in the playoff won by Stacy Lewis at the ASI Scottish Open. She was 11th at the AIG Women's Open and then won for the first time in five years on the LET at the Tipsport Czech Open. A six-shot lead had dwindled to one with two to play but Pedersen birdied the 17th and then holed from 80 feet for an eagle at the last.

Two weeks later she was third in Switzerland but an opening 82 at the Dubai Moonlight Classic brought a forthright reminder from family members that the Race to Costa del Sol was not yet guaranteed. Her response was extraordinary, matching Marie-Laure de Lorenzi as the only other player to win three tournaments in a row on the LET.

She came from three behind with five to play to beat major champion Georgia Hall in a playoff at the Saudi International and then took the individual honours, as well as guiding her team to victory, in a second tournament at Royal Greens. She completed the hat-trick with a four-stroke in the Andalucia Costa del Sol Open de Espana.

It was only after the winning putt had been holed, her position as European number one long since confirmed, that the tears came in talking about her father, who was caddieing for her at Guadalmina. "He got me into golf and he has been a big supporter the whole way," she said. "He kept me going when I was down and I was really happy to go through something really positive with him because he is right beside me off the course and, now, he has been there on it."

There was another emotional victory at the AIG Women's Open at Royal Troon for Sophia Popov, the German whose promising career was stalled by Lyme disease. Popov had not won anything as a professional until three wins arrived on a mini tour in Arizona when the tours had come to a halt. She then belied her status as the 304th ranked player in the world to produce a remarkably assured performance and claim a major on the same links as Bobby Locke, Arnold Palmer, Tom Watson and, most recently, Henrik Stenson.

The season started in optimistic fashion with the Ladies European Tour having been taken under the umbrella of the LPGA and Alexandra Armas returning as chief executive. The first of two tournaments in Australia saw 19-year-old amateur Stephanie Kyriacou win at Bonville by a staggering eight strokes. Kyriacou then turned professional and topped the standings for rookie of the year despite her win not counting on the points list.

Kyriacou was third on the Race to Costa del Sol, behind runner-up Julia Engstrom, another teenager. The Swede, who was the rookie of the year in 2018, earned her maiden title at the New South Wales

Open and then claimed the Lacoste Open de France later in the year.

There were also top-five finishes on the order of merit for Belgium's Manon De Roey and Finland's Sanna Nuutinen reflecting their consistent seasons, while England's Alice Hewson won on her first appearance as an LET member at the South African Open in March, the last event completed before the tour went into hiatus. Hewson also won the unofficial Rose Ladies Series Grand Final after the final round at Wentworth had to be abandoned due to a wildfire encroaching on the course.

Play resumed with the Scottish Open and the AIG Women's Open in August before Pedersen won in the Czech Republic. Wales's Amy Boulden claimed her maiden victory at the Swiss Open six years after claiming rookie of the year honours.

Australia's Minjee Lee defeated Celine Boutier in a playoff under the lights at the Dubai Moonlight Classic but then Pedersen raced away with the rest of the season. The Dane also triumphed in the inaugural LET Break Par Challenge with an unrivalled 13 eagles, worth five points each, and 158 birdies. She finished ahead of everyone else by 54 points despite De Roey banking 40 points for an albatross at the Czech Open. Pedersen donated the €5,000 prize to the Pink Cup Breast Cancer Foundation.

2020 SCHEDULE

Geoff King Motors Australian Ladies Classic	**Stephanie Kyriacou** (A)	*See chapter 22*
Women's NSW Open	**Julia Engstrom**	*See chapter 22*
Investec South African Women's Open	**Alice Hewson**	
Lalla Meryem Cup		*cancelled*
La Reserva de Sotogrande Invitational		*cancelled*
Jabra Ladies Open		*cancelled*
Mediterranean Ladies Open		*cancelled*
Rose Ladies Series Grand Final*	**Alice Hewson**	
Evian Championship		*cancelled*
ASI Ladies Scottish Open	**Stacy Lewis**	
AIG Women's Open	**Sophia Popov**	*See chapter 2*
Tipsport Czech Ladies Open	**Emily Kristine Pedersen**	
VP Bank Swiss Ladies Open	**Amy Boulden**	
Lacoste Ladies Open de France	**Julia Engstrom**	
Ladies European Thailand Championship		*cancelled*
Omega Dubai Moonlight Classic	**Minjee Lee**	
Aramco Saudi Ladies International	**Emily Kristine Pedersen**	
Saudi Ladies Team International	**Emily Kristine Pedersen**	
Andalucia Costa del Sol Open de Espana	**Emily Kristine Pedersen**	

**non-Race to Costa del Sol event*

Investec South African Women's Open

After finishing fifth at the Qualifying School in January, Alice Hewson won her first event as a member of the LET at the Investec South African Women's Open. Even more remarkable was the background to the tournament at Westlake in Cape Town. The event was completed even as the Players Championship was abandoned after 18 holes, other tournaments cancelled around the world including the LET's first visit to Saudi Arabia the following week, plus the Masters and the ANA Inspiration both being postponed indefinitely due to the coronavirus pandemic.

There was not much social distancing on the leaderboard in the final round as seven players shared the lead at times and 13 finished within three of the winner. Olivia Cowan started with a three-stroke lead but closed with a 77 to fall into a tie for seventh. Hewson had two birdies and two bogeys in the first 11 holes but then claimed a crucial birdie at the 13th. She parred the last five holes, including at the 18th when she drove into the trees and was still in trouble in the rough for her third, before holing from seven feet to win by one stroke.

The 22-year-old from Hemel Hempstead, the reigning European Amateur champion who turned professional in September 2019, had scores of 70, 70 and 71 for a five-under-par total of 211. Emma Nilsson birdied two of the last three holes to share runner-up honours with South African Monique Smit, who parred the last 10 holes to leapfrog Stacy Bregman to win the Sunshine Ladies Tour order of merit.

"I couldn't have hoped for a better start," said Hewson. "Growing up as a kid, all I could ever dream of was playing on the Ladies European Tour and to come and win my first event, the feeling is indescribable."

Hewson added: "I think it was definitely the right decision that we continued playing this week and it's also the right decision that future tournaments have been cancelled. Everyone was already here and there is a very low risk here so it was nice to be able to play some golf, because we don't know how long it's going to be now before we will again."

Westlake Golf Club, Cape Town, South Africa — March 12-14
Par 72 (36-36); 6,298 yards — Purse: €200,000

1	**Alice Hewson**	70	70	71	211	€30,000
2	**Monique Smit**	70	71	71	212	15,000
	Emma Nilsson	69	72	71	212	15,000
4	Manon Gidali	72	72	69	213	7,467
	Manon De Roey	75	68	70	213	7,467
	Kelsey Macdonald	70	70	73	213	7,467
7	Agathe Sauzon	72	72	70	214	4,550
	Julia Engstrom	71	72	71	214	4,550
	Emily Kristine Pedersen	73	70	71	214	4,550
	Maha Haddioui	72	71	71	214	4,550
	Meghan MacLaren	73	69	72	214	4,550
	Valdis Thora Jonsdottir	72	70	72	214	4,550
	Lucrezia Colombotto Rosso	69	71	74	214	4,550
	Olivia Cowan	69	68	77	214	4,550
15	Ashleigh Buhai	70	73	72	215	3,600
16	Lejan Lewthwaite	73	74	69	216	3,350
	Johanna Gustavsson	73	73	70	216	3,350
18	Laura Fuenfstueck	70	75	72	217	3,050
	Lee-Anne Pace	71	73	73	217	3,050
	Mireia Prat	71	73	73	217	3,050
	Karolin Lampert	78	71	68	217	3,050
22	Hannah McCook	73	72	73	218	2,700
	Jane Turner	74	70	74	218	2,700
	Maria Hernandez	73	71	74	218	2,700
25	Casandra Hall	72	76	71	219	2,353
	Anna Magnusson	75	71	73	219	2,353
	Tiia Koivisto	72	74	73	219	2,353
28	Karoline Lund	77	70	73	220	2,070
	Sian Evans	73	73	74	220	2,070
30	Laura Gomez Ruiz	77	70	74	221	1,890
	Becky Brewerton	76	72	73	221	1,890
	Stacy Lee Bregman	74	75	72	221	1,890
	Maiken Bing Paulsen	73	77	71	221	1,890

Rose Ladies Series Grand Final

A wildfire encroaching on Wentworth from Chobham Common made for an unfortunate, unintentionally dramatic, ending to the Rose Ladies Series. The Grand Final was designed as a three-day event, starting at Justin Rose's home club of North Hants, continuing to The Berkshire and culminating on the West course at Wentworth. The final round had to be abandoned with players evacuating the course as firefighters battled to bring the blaze under control.

Alice Hewson, who won the South African Open in March, was declared the winner on five under par after her rounds of 67 at North Hants and then 70 on the Blue course at The Berkshire. Charley Hull, who claimed the order of merit and £20,000 bonus, was one stroke behind after a 65 on the second day, with two-time winner Georgia Hall and Liz Young sharing third place.

Young had created the unofficial series to give LET players a chance to play competitive golf while the main tour was halted. Young had not competed since the Kenya Open the previous December and organised a one-day event at her home club of Brokenhurst Manor, where she lost a playoff to Hull. Justin and Kate Rose stepped in to provide funding for a series of seven 18-hole events, plus the Grand Final.
The weekly winners, who each earned £5,000, in June and July were:

Brokenhurst Manor — Charley Hull
Moor Park — Meghan MacLaren
The Buckinghamshire — Gemma Dryburgh
Royal St George's — Gemma Dryburgh
JCB Golf & Country Club — Gabriella Cowley
Bearwood Lakes — Georgia Hall
The Shire London — Georgia Hall

This marked the first time professional women's events had been staged at Royal St George's and on the West course at Wentworth.

R1 *North Hants Golf Club* par 71 (36-35)
R2 *The Berkshire Golf Club* (Blue) par 71 (36-35)
R3 *Wentworth Club* (West) — abandoned

August 5-7
Purse: £10,000

1	**Alice Hewson**	67 70	137	£10,000		Sian Evans	71 74 145
2	**Charley Hull**	73 65	138		12	Felicity Johnson	76 71 147
3	**Georgia Hall**	73 68	141			Gabriella Cowley	76 71 147
	Liz Young	72 69	141			Cara Gainer	77 70 147
5	Inci Mehmet	72 72	144			Sophie Powell	74 73 147
	Meghan MacLaren	76 68	144			Emily Price (A)	76 71 147
	Whitney Hillier	71 73	144		17	Keely Chiericato	77 71 148
	Hannah Burke	74 70	144			Charlotte Thompson	74 74 148
9	Annabel Dimmock	74 71	145		19	Hayley Davis	79 70 149
	Rachel Drummond	74 71	145			Amy Boulden	78 71 149

Aberdeen Standard Investments Ladies Scottish Open

Stacy Lewis became a winner for the first time as a mother when she claimed only her second victory in six years at the ASI Ladies Scottish Open. Lewis gave birth to daughter Chesnee in 2018 who was watching, along with dad Gerrod Chadwell, as mum added to her achievements in Scotland.

Lewis won five matches out of five at the Curtis Cup at St Andrews in 2008 and five years later won the Women's Open also at the Home of Golf. At the Renaissance Club, near North Berwick, Lewis won a four-way playoff at the first extra hole with a 24-foot birdie-putt on the 18th green.

"I have been trying to get a trophy from the day she was born. That's been my goal," said Lewis after FaceTiming with her husband and daughter.

Greater patience since becoming a mother helped on the course as Lewis hummed Chesnee's favourite song, Taylor Swift's "Shake it Off", in a final round that extended over five and a quarter hours. Lewis had stated after the third round that her greatest challenge would be staying in rhythm when the pace of play was so slow, knowing she would once again be playing alongside compatriot Jennifer Song and Spain's Azahara Munoz.

The group was put on the clock on the 11th hole in the final round when Lewis promptly had a double bogey but she fought in typical fashion to close with a 72 and, after earlier rounds of 71, 66 and 70, join the playoff at five-under-par 279. Munoz, who was disqualified at the Marathon Classic after forgetting to sign her scorecard in the third round, began the week by holing a seven-iron for an eagle at the first hole on Thursday. She led by one after 54 holes but went out in 40 before two birdies coming home for a 73 also put her in the playoff. Song slipped out of contention with a back nine of 39 strokes.

Lewis's fellow Texan Cheyenne Knight also made the playoff with a 70, helped by a birdie at the 16th when her overhit chip hit the flagstick and stopped dead. Denmark's Emily Pedersen set the five-under target with a 68. Her compatriot Nanna Koerstz Madsen posted the round of the week with a 65 to finish one behind, sharing fifth place with Danielle Kang, whose quest for a third title in a row came up just short despite three birdies in four holes on the back nine.

Knight had the chance to extend the playoff from 10 feet but her birdie putt slipped by, handing Lewis the victory and a place in the US Women's Open in her hometown of Houston. Lewis called for a more aggressive policy on slow play, including penalty strokes rather than fines, adding: "It shouldn't take that long to play. I knew it was going to; that's the sad part, you know it's going to take that long. I do think an effort needs to be made across the board to play faster, because obviously I wasn't watching it on TV, but I'm sure it couldn't have been fun to watch on TV. There's only so much the announcers can talk about to fill time."

The Renaissance Club, Gullane, East Lothian, Scotland
Par 71 (36-35); 6,464 yards

August 13-16
Purse: $1,500,000

1	**Stacy Lewis**	71	66	70	72	279	€190,323
2	**Emily Kristine Pedersen**	68	74	69	68	279	76,729
	Cheyenne Knight	72	68	69	70	279	76,729
	Azahara Munoz	68	69	69	73	279	76,729
	Lewis won playoff at first extra hole						
5	Nanna Koerstz Madsen	69	71	75	65	280	39,545
	Danielle Kang	71	71	69	69	280	39,545
7	In Gee Chun	71	71	70	69	281	29,511
	Xiyu Lin	72	71	69	69	281	29,511
	Amy Olson	68	71	71	71	281	29,511
	Jennifer Song	68	70	70	73	281	29,511
11	Andrea Lee	69	71	73	69	282	25,970
12	Kylie Henry	71	75	69	68	283	23,019
	Harukyo Nomura	72	70	72	69	283	23,019
	Nasa Hataoka	73	69	70	71	283	23,019
	Lydia Ko	70	72	67	74	283	23,019
16	Hannah Green	72	72	70	70	284	20,362
	Minjee Lee	68	73	70	73	284	20,362
18	Celine Boutier	70	73	74	68	285	18,533
	Moriya Jutanugarn	74	69	73	69	285	18,533
	Leona Maguire	72	72	71	70	285	18,533
	Manon De Roey	73	70	70	72	285	18,533
22	Charley Hull	74	72	72	68	286	14,418
	Brittany Lang	73	73	71	69	286	14,418
	Anna Nordqvist	70	72	74	70	286	14,418
	Brittany Altomare	70	73	73	70	286	14,418
	Anne Van Dam	72	71	72	71	286	14,418
	Emma Talley	73	71	71	71	286	14,418
	Yu Liu	71	70	69	76	286	14,418
29	Kelly Tan	73	72	73	69	287	10,565
	Amy Yang	71	72	74	70	287	10,565
	Nicole Broch Larsen	67	73	74	73	287	10,565
	Daniela Holmqvist	72	71	71	73	287	10,565
33	Megan Khang	76	71	73	68	288	8,046
	Yujeong Son	71	74	74	69	288	8,046
	Klara Spilkova	69	73	74	72	288	8,046
	Charlotte Thomas	71	74	71	72	288	8,046
	Gerina Piller	70	72	72	74	288	8,046
	Eleanor Givens	74	71	69	74	288	8,046
39	Alice Hewson	74	72	74	69	289	6,138
	Lee-Anne Pace	70	77	73	69	289	6,138
	Ashleigh Buhai	74	70	75	70	289	6,138
	Austin Ernst	71	72	75	71	289	6,138
	Katherine Kirk	72	73	73	71	289	6,138
	Ariya Jutanugarn	73	70	73	73	289	6,138
	Kristen Gillman	71	73	71	74	289	6,138
	Annie Park	76	70	69	74	289	6,138
	Caroline Inglis	71	71	72	75	289	6,138
48	Sanna Nuutinen	74	69	78	69	290	5,430
	Johanna Gustavsson	70	71	76	73	290	5,430
	Sandra Gal	69	74	73	74	290	5,430
51	Jasmine Suwannapura	73	74	72	72	291	5,134
	Georgia Hall	73	72	70	76	291	5,134
53	Meghan MacLaren	73	71	73	75	292	4,898
	Olivia Cowan	68	71	73	80	292	4,898
55	Yealimi Noh	71	74	77	71	293	4,603
	Pernilla Lindberg	71	76	73	73	293	4,603
	Christina Kim	73	73	72	75	293	4,603
58	Haley Moore	74	71	77	72	294	4,131
	Lindsey Weaver	70	76	76	72	294	4,131
	In-Kyung Kim	75	72	75	72	294	4,131
	Jennifer Chang	73	74	73	74	294	4,131
	Cydney Clanton	72	75	73	74	294	4,131
63	Lizette Salas	73	73	77	72	295	3,718
	Muni He	72	73	75	75	295	3,718
65	Tvesa Malik	71	74	79	72	296	3,541
66	Hannah Burke	72	75	73	77	297	3,423
67	Becky Morgan	73	73	74	78	298	3,128
	Camilla Lennarth	74	71	73	80	298	3,128
69	Gemma Dryburgh	69	75	73	82	299	2,597
70	Michele Thomson	78	69	79	76	302	2,360

Tipsport Czech Ladies Open

When golf courses opened in Denmark after lockdown, Emily Kristine Pedersen won an ECCO Tour event in June comprised mainly of male players, including emerging talent Rasmus Hojgaard. On the same day that 19-year-old Hojgaard won his second European Tour title at the ISPS Handa UK Championship, Pedersen claimed her second LET victory at the Tipsport Czech Ladies Open.

Although Pedersen had led throughout, the 24-year-old Dane still needed a dramatic finish to clinch a four-stroke win. Her career low score of 63 put her two clear of the field on the first day at Beroun, while a 65 the following day meant she was six in front with a round to play. But a third bogey of a rainy final day at the 16th hole, meant Pedersen was only leading by one shot, the smallest margin since the opening afternoon. She responded by hitting a wedge to 10 feet at the 17th for a birdie and then, having reached the par-five 18th in two over the water, she holed from 80 feet for a stunning climax.

"That was a bonus," she said. "It was a bit of luck holing one that far, but it was nice to hole it, I'll definitely remember it. I wasn't thinking about the score until after 16 and I was told I was one ahead so the birdie at 17 was really crucial for me." Her coach, who was acting as her caddie for the week, had told that he would quit if she laid up in front of the water at the last. A closing 71 left Pedersen on 17-under-par 199, while the woman who had put most pressure on her, Christine Wolf, had a bogey-free 67 to be 13 under par. Sanna Nuutinen was third and Lucrezia Colombotto Rosso fourth.

Having been the LET rookie of the year in 2015 when she won the Hero Indian Open, Pedersen had to wait five years for her second victory. After a debut for Europe in the Solheim Cup in 2017, her form deserted her, meaning a loss of status on the LPGA tour. But her fortunes improved dramatically in Scotland, where Pedersen lost a playoff to Stacy Lewis and then finished 11th at the AIG Women's Open. This victory extended her lead at the top of the Race to Costa del Sol.

"It feels good to be back, the last two to three years have been hard, I've had doubts about whether I would compete again and I am so happy my coach didn't quit on me, my friends didn't quit on me, my boyfriend and my family, because it's been tough, I've been tough on myself and had to figure out what needed to be done. It feels so good to be back."

Golf Club Beroun, Na Veselou, Beroun, Czech Republic — August 28-30
Par 72 (36-36); 6,225 yards — Purse: €200,000

1	**Emily Kristine Pedersen**	63	65	71	199	€30,000
2	**Christine Wolf**	67	69	67	203	18,000
3	**Sanna Nuutinen**	66	68	70	204	12,000
4	Lucrezia Colombotto Rosso	66	69	70	205	9,000
5	Stephanie Kyriacou	69	71	66	206	6,333
	Marianne Skarpnord	69	69	68	206	6,333
	Manon De Roey	65	71	70	206	6,333
8	Karolin Lampert	70	70	67	207	4,800
	Cloe Frankish	65	74	68	207	4,800
	Pia Babnik	70	67	70	207	4,800
11	Johanna Gustavsson	69	69	70	208	4,300
	Kim Metraux	68	69	71	208	4,300
13	Klara Spilkova	70	70	69	209	3,700
	Maria Hernandez	70	70	69	209	3,700
	Becky Morgan	70	69	70	209	3,700
	Caroline Rominger	70	68	71	209	3,700
17	Rachael Taylor	70	72	68	210	3,200
	Laura Fuenfstueck	71	72	67	210	3,200
	Camille Chevalier	66	71	73	210	3,200
20	Olafia Kristinsdottir	67	74	70	211	2,800
	Olivia Cowan	71	70	70	211	2,800
	Tvesa Malik	70	72	69	211	2,800
	Sara Kouskova (A)	72	72	67	211	
	Leonie Harm	65	74	72	211	2,800
	Carly Booth	69	70	72	211	2,800
26	Gabriella Cowley	70	71	71	212	2,290
	Katja Pogacar	68	73	71	212	2,290
	Linette Littau Durr Holmslykke	69	71	72	212	2,290
	Felicity Johnson	72	67	73	212	2,290
30	Elina Nummenpaa	72	70	71	213	1,920
	Marta Sanz Barrio	70	71	72	213	1,920
	Patricia Sanz Barrio	71	69	73	213	1,920
	Lydia Hall	72	72	69	213	1,920

VP Bank Swiss Ladies Open

When a maiden victory finally arrived for Amy Boulden, the 27-year-old from Wales achieved it in style with a three-stroke victory at the VP Bank Swiss Ladies Open.

After an opening 70 at Holzhausern, Boulden did not drop a shot during rounds of 65 and 64 for a 17-under-par total of 199. One behind Finland's Sanna Nuutinen, who was looking to do a Swiss double after winning in the country on the LET Access Series the previous week, Boulden birdied the first hole to share the lead and added three more in an outward 31. It was a run of four birdies in five holes at the start of the back nine that put Boulden clear of the field and she finished calmly with four pars.

Australian rookie Stephanie Kyriacou also produced a strong charge with a 65 to take second place, while the limited gallery allowed at the event closely followed the fortunes of 25-year-old left-hander Kim Metraux. The Swiss rookie shared the first-round lead and on the last day had an eagle and three bogeys in the first five holes before a run of five birdies in a row from the ninth. She finished with a 68 to tie for third place with Nuutinen, who closed with a 70, and order of merit leader Emily Kristine Pedersen, who had a 68. Metraux's younger sister, right-hander Morgane, also an LET rookie, finished in 11th place.

Boulden, after a glittering amateur career, was the LET rookie of the year in 2014, when she had four top-10 finishes, including a second, a third and a fourth. But only four more top 10s followed and none since 2017 as her form dipped. But she won the Qualifying School at the start of 2020 to regain her card and benefitted during lockdown of having the undivided attentions of her boyfriend, the coach Liam James.

"My goals this year were to put myself in contention again," Boulden said. "I am really happy with how I handled the pressure and how I put my foot down on the gas when I needed to. I'm thrilled and really excited to get that first LET win. I am obviously overwhelmed. I'm looking forward to playing more like this and being in these positions more often."

Golfpark Holzhausern, Rotkreuz, Switzerland — September 10-12
Par 72 (35-37); 6,312 yards — Purse: €200,000

1	**Amy Boulden**	70	65	64	199	€30,000
2	**Stephanie Kyriacou**	71	66	65	202	18,000
3	**Kim Metraux**	66	70	68	204	9,400
	Emily Kristine Pedersen	71	65	68	204	9,400
	Sanna Nuutinen	66	68	70	204	9,400
6	Maha Haddioui	70	65	70	205	6,200
7	Annabel Dimmock	73	67	67	207	5,600
8	Liz Young	72	66	70	208	5,000
9	Laura Fuenfstueck	72	70	67	209	4,700
	Silvia Banon	73	68	68	209	4,700
11	Luna Sobron Galmes	74	69	67	210	4,100
	Morgane Metraux	72	69	69	210	4,100
	Becky Morgan	69	72	69	210	4,100
	Camille Chevalier	71	68	71	210	4,100
15	Lucrezia Colombotto Rosso	70	73	68	211	3,433
	Maiken Bing Paulsen	72	70	69	211	3,433
	Chloe Williams	70	71	70	211	3,433
18	Anaelle Carnet	72	73	67	212	2,950
	Florentyna Parker	73	71	68	212	2,950
	Pia Babnik	74	69	69	212	2,950
	Celine Herbin	72	70	70	212	2,950
	Julia Engstrom	71	70	71	212	2,950
	Meghan MacLaren	70	70	72	212	2,950
24	Isabella Deilert	74	70	69	213	2,500
	Manon De Roey	71	71	71	213	2,500
	Whitney Hillier	71	70	72	213	2,500
27	Rachael Taylor	72	74	68	214	1,980
	Karolin Lampert	70	74	70	214	1,980
	Johanna Gustavsson	70	73	71	214	1,980
	Patricia Sanz Barrio	75	68	71	214	1,980
	Marianne Skarpnord	70	72	72	214	1,980
	Harang Lee	70	72	72	214	1,980
	Kylie Henry	72	69	73	214	1,980

Lacoste Ladies Open de France

With the best round of the week at the Lacoste Ladies Open de France, a seven-under-par 64 on day two at Golf du Medoc, Julia Engstrom took a four-stroke lead. The 19-year-old Swede needed all of it in the final round before securing a one-shot victory over former champion Celine Herbin and Argentina's Magdalena Simmermacher.

It was her second title of the year, with her maiden LET win coming at the NSW Open prior to the shutdown of the tour.

Engstrom opened with a 70 to be two shots off the lead and then her challenge sparked into life when she holed an eight-iron from 133 yards at the eighth hole in the second round. Four more birdies followed that day and two came early in the final round but she would go three over par for the rest of the round, a 72 giving her a seven-under-par total of 206.

Simmermacher set the target at six under with a bogey-free 66, which resulted in her best ever finish on tour. Herbin, the winner in 2015, put pressure on the leader with birdies at the ninth and 10th holes before a three-putt bogey at the short 17th. That put Engstrom back to two in front and the Swede hit a fine seven-iron to the heart of the green to ensure a par. A bogey at the last did not affect the result.

"It's been the perfect week, I love this place," said the Swede, who was the rookie of the year in 2018 but had struggled while leading during the 2019 season. "I came out here with a good feeling and obviously yesterday's hole-in-one was a highlight, but the 17th hole was extremely important for me today. It was nerve-wracking at the end, but I am relieved to get it done.

"It was a fight out there today, Celine was pushing me hard and I could see she was making birdies so I just tried to keep my head cold. This win was different, it is harder to defend. I've been in the lead and lost before so for me to get a win with the lead is a huge confidence boost."

Golf du Medoc (Chateaux), Le Pian Medoc, France — September 17-19
Par 71 (36-35); 6,341 yards — Purse: €200,000

1	**Julia Engstrom**	70	64	72	206	€27,600
2	**Magdalena Simmermacher**	69	72	66	207	13,800
	Celine Herbin	72	66	69	207	13,800
4	Florentyna Parker	70	70	69	209	8,280
5	Stephanie Kyriacou	74	68	68	210	6,624
6	Kylie Henry	73	69	69	211	5,152
	Astrid Vayson De Pradenne	73	69	69	211	5,152
	Charlotte Thompson	68	72	71	211	5,152
9	Noora Komulainen	71	71	70	212	4,452
10	Joanna Klatten	72	71	70	213	3,864
	Cloe Frankish	73	69	71	213	3,864
	Becky Morgan	70	71	72	213	3,864
	Luna Sobron Galmes	71	70	72	213	3,864
	Tvesa Malik	70	68	75	213	3,864
15	Emily Kristine Pedersen	73	69	72	214	3,054
	Eleanor Givens	71	71	72	214	3,054
	Karolin Lampert	71	70	73	214	3,054
	Anne-Charlotte Mora	70	70	74	214	3,054
	Marianne Skarpnord	71	69	74	214	3,054
20	Manon De Roey	70	74	71	215	2,530

	Noemi Jimenez Martin	70	74	71	215	2,530	26 Whitney Hillier	71	73	72	216	2,010
	Meghan MacLaren	72	72	71	215	2,530	Kim Metraux	73	70	73	216	2,010
	Gabriella Cowley	68	75	72	215	2,530	Annabel Dimmock	73	70	73	216	2,010
	Lee-Anne Pace	71	72	72	215	2,530	Lucie Malchirand (A)	68	73	75	216	
	Sian Evans	72	68	75	215	2,530	Anne-Lise Caudal	71	69	76	216	2,010

Omega Dubai Moonlight Classic

A thrilling, late-night finish to the Omega Dubai Moonlight Classic saw Minjee Lee hole a 20-foot birdie-putt to win a playoff against Celine Boutier at the first extra hole. Under floodlights on the Faldo course at Emirates, Lee celebrated with a fist pump before lifting the famous coffee pot trophy.

"I couldn't really see the break too well," said the 24-year-old Australian, "but I thought it would be about two cups outside the right and luckily I hit it hard enough and it dropped. It feels pretty special to be here playing at night-time — it's been a really fun week."

At ninth on the Rolex Rankings, Lee was the highest ranked player in the field of 56 but had to go to a 55th hole to claim her maiden title on the Ladies European Tour, and her first anywhere since her fifth LPGA win at the LA Open in April 2019.

The first two rounds were played with a pro-am shotgun format in day and night sessions. The final round was also a shotgun start so that everyone played under the lights although both Lee and Boutier were in the two groups that finished at the 18th. As were Nuria Iturrioz, the defending champion, and Caroline Hedwall, who both had putts to join the playoff. They finished one stroke back with Germany's Laura Fuenfstueck.

Hedwall led after the first two rounds, helped by holing in one at the 17th with a six-iron from 162 yards during a 65 on the first evening. The Swede started the final round with three bogeys on the front nine but rallied for a 72, while Iturrioz had a 67 and Fuenstueck a 70. Boutier went in front thanks to birdies at the second, third and fifth holes before two more at the 10th and the 13th. The French Solheim Cup player led by two before finding the water with her second at the 16th and taking a bogey six on the way to a 68.

Lee, who opened slowly with a 72 before a 65 on the second day, birdied the second and then the 10th and 14th holes but dropped a shot at the 15th. But following Boutier's bogey at the 16th, Lee claimed a four at the same hole to tie on 10-under-par 206 with a 69. "This year has been tough but this is a nice way to close it out," Lee said. "Playing night golf was certainly memorable."

Emirates Golf Club (Faldo), Dubai, United Arab Emirates — November 4-6
Par 72 (36-36); 6,274 yards — Purse: €260,000

1	**Minjee Lee**	72	65	69	206	€36,266	17 Olivia Cowan	70	75	68	213	4,055
2	**Celine Boutier**	67	71	68	206	21,760	Alison Muirhead	69	74	70	213	4,055
	Lee won playoff at first extra hole						Stephanie Kyriacou	71	71	71	213	4,055
3	**Laura Fuenfstueck**	67	70	70	207	11,363	Sanna Nuutinen	76	65	72	213	4,055
	Nuria Iturrioz	69	71	67	207	11,363	21 Celine Herbin	76	70	68	214	3,638
	Caroline Hedwall	65	70	72	207	11,363	Muni He	74	70	70	214	3,638
6	Aditi Ashok	75	69	64	208	7,156	23 Lucrezia Colombotto Rosso	75	70	71	216	3,445
	Meghan MacLaren	69	67	72	208	7156	Karolin Lampert	71	70	75	216	3,445
8	Kelsey Macdonald	72	69	68	209	5,996	25 Becky Morgan	74	74	69	217	3,203
	Bronte Law	70	70	69	209	5,996	Christine Wolf	72	72	73	217	3,203
10	Lydia Ko	68	70	72	210	5,294	27 Tvesa Malik	75	75	69	219	2,909
	Kylie Henry	75	72	63	210	5,294	Beth Allen	72	74	73	219	2,909
	Georgia Hall	72	73	65	210	5,294	Gabriella Cowley	74	71	74	219	2,909
	Alison Lee	72	68	70	210	5,294	30 Marianne Skarpnord	76	75	69	220	2,563
14	Johanna Gustavsson	70	70	71	211	4,581	Julia Engstrom	76	73	71	220	2,563
	Kim Metraux	69	70	72	211	4,581	Alice Hewson	74	75	71	220	2,563
16	Emilie Paltrinieri (A)	74	69	69	212							

Aramco Saudi Ladies International

Asked what she missed about the Ladies European Tour when away competing in America, Georgia Hall pointed to friends such as Emily Kristine Pedersen. The 24-year-olds have known each other for half their lives but Hall may have seen a little too much of the Dane at Royal Greens as Pedersen twice birdied the 18th hole on Sunday to win the inaugural Aramco Saudi Ladies International at the first extra hole.

Hall led the way with an opening 65 before Pedersen went ahead on day two. She was tied with Wales's Lydia Hall on 10 under par after 54 holes with Georgia Hall one behind. It was the English major winner who played the steadiest golf on an increasingly breezy final day beside the Red Sea. She went out in two under par and responded to a bogey at the 12th with a third birdie of the round at the 13th.

Pedersen had a topsy turvy day with four birdies and four bogeys before a double at the 12th where her attempted escape from a fairway bunker hit the face and fell back into the sand. She was soon three behind with five to play and Lydia Hall was the main chaster until a triple bogey at the 14th.

At the same hole, Pedersen hit close to get one shot back before Georgia Hall, who holed a good par-putt at the 15th, missed the green at the short 16th and dropped one there. At the par-five 18th — where Anna Nordqvist took a nine after twice finding the water to fall from third to 11th — Pedersen hit a superb three-wood to set up an eagle putt from the back of the green.

"I knew I had to make a birdie and I just kind of felt the shot," said Pedersen. "It was one of the best shots I've ever hit."

Hall laid up but then hit a fine pitch to 10 feet. While Pedersen came up short from 12 feet, her birdie, for a 72 and a 10-under-par total of 278, forced Hall to hole her putt for the win but it missed on the right. A 71 meant a playoff, the pair finishing two ahead of Caroline Hedwall, who fought back after an opening 77, and three ahead of Anne van Dam.

In the playoff at the 18th, Pedersen missed the green on the right but Hall's second came up short in the water. Hall said: "I had 170 to the front and the ball was sitting up well, I got underneath my four-iron and it got caught high in the face. Emily hit a fantastic chip and that's where I lost it."

Pedersen, from thick rough with little room on the green, left herself only a tap-in for her third LET win and a second of the season, virtually securing her place at the top of the Race to Costa del Sol. "I'm really proud that I got it back twice," she said. "I feel like I was out of it at the start of the front nine, then again at the start of the back nine but I kept fighting back."

Royal Greens Golf & Country Club, King Abdullah Economic City, Saudi Arabia — November 12-15
Par 72 (36-36); 6,319 yards — Purse: $1,000,000

1	**Emily Kristine Pedersen**	67	68	71	72	278	€127,170
2	**Georgia Hall**	65	73	69	71	278	76,302
	Pedersen won playoff at first extra hole						
3	**Caroline Hedwall**	77	65	70	68	280	50,868
4	Anne van Dam	74	69	70	68	281	34,335
	Stephanie Kyriacou	71	73	68	69	281	34,335
6	Charley Hull	74	71	68	69	282	22,890
	Laura Fuenfstueck	73	66	73	70	282	22,890
	Luna Sobron Galmes	74	66	72	70	282	22,890
	Lydia Hall	66	71	69	76	282	22,890
10	Morgane Metraux	73	75	68	67	283	18,736
11	Marianne Skarpnord	73	70	72	70	285	16,311
	Eleanor Givens	72	69	72	72	285	16,311
	Tonje Daffinrud	69	72	71	73	285	16,311
	Aditi Ashok	73	70	69	73	285	16,311
	Anna Nordqvist	71	69	69	76	285	16,311
16	Kim Metraux	71	72	73	70	286	13,717
	Alison Muirhead	75	70	71	70	286	13,717
	Carly Booth	72	68	72	74	286	13,717
	Esther Henseleit	71	68	71	76	286	13,717
	Celine Herbin	72	70	67	77	286	13,717
21	Julia Engstrom	72	73	71	71	287	12,632
22	Olivia Cowan	73	75	70	70	288	11,869
	Magdalena Simmermacher	70	74	73	71	288	11,869
24	Whitney Hillier	71	76	71	71	289	10,979
	Nobuhle Dlamini	69	76	72	72	289	10,979
26	Lucrezia Colombotto Rosso	72	75	74	69	290	8,902
	Noora Komulainen	75	74	69	72	290	8,902
	Sanna Nuutinen	77	69	72	72	290	8,902
	Marta Sanz Barrio	76	71	70	73	290	8,902
	Agathe Sauzon	72	73	70	75	290	8,902
	Laura Davies	70	73	71	76	290	8,902
	Ursula Wikstrom	67	76	71	76	290	8,902

Saudi Ladies Team International

Emily Kristine Pedersen continued her fine form at Royal Greens to make a clean sweep of the titles in Saudi Arabia.

The Saudi Ladies Team International, starting just two days after Pedersen defeated Georgia Hall in a playoff at the Aramco event, was a late addition to the schedule with a two-in-one format. Pedersen's victory in the individual event, by two strokes from Stephanie Kyriacou, Anne van Dam and Luna Sobron Galmes, ensured the 24-year-old Dane won the Race to Costa del Sol with one tournament to spare. For good measure she also captained her team to victory.

After scores of 69 and 66, Pedersen came from one behind Sobron Galmes with a closing 67 in which she did not drop a stroke. Four birdies in an outward 32 put her clear of the field and another at the 13th sealed her third win of the season, and fourth in all, with a 14-under-par aggregate of 202. Kyriacou, the 19-year-old Australian rookie, chipped in at her last hole, the ninth, to set a new course record of 63 and set the clubhouse mark, where she was joined by van Dam, after a 67, and Sobron Galmes with a 70. Charley Hull took fifth place.

"I have loved the course," said Pedersen. "It sets up well for me and it's been a good 10 days. I can't believe what's happened this season."

For the team event, each of the 36 captains could select another player and were then allocated a third professional and one amateur. Pedersen selected Scotland's Michele Thompson, with South African Casandra Hall and English amateur Matt Selby completing their line-up. With two scores counting on each hole, their team finished on 40 under par after rounds of 129, 132 and 131, pipping by one stroke the teams of Kyriacou and Manon De Roey.

Tied for the lead at the final hole, both Hall and Pedersen gave themselves birdie putts from 12 feet with 21-year-old Hall holing the winning putt. Pedersen missed but needed it neither for the team or individual glory. Hall, playing in her first LET event outside South Africa, said: "It's definitely one of the biggest putts of my career. I felt like I was letting the team down a little bit to that point. I thought Emily would hole hers on 18 but I thought let's give it the best shot I can and all those hours of practising paid off."

Royal Greens Golf & Country Club, King Abdullah Economic City, Saudi Arabia — November 17-19
Par 72 (36-36); 6,284 yards — Purse: $500,000 ($300,000 team, $200,000 ind)

1	**Emily Kristine Pedersen**	69	66	67	202	€21,066
2	**Stephanie Kyriacou**	71	70	63	204	10,040
	Anne van Dam	69	68	67	204	10,040
	Luna Sobron Galmes	69	65	70	204	10,040
5	Charley Hull	70	69	68	207	5,560
6	Eleanor Givens	72	68	68	208	4,556
	Georgia Hall	75	65	68	208	4,556
8	Ursula Wikstrom	75	67	67	209	3,784
	Johanna Gustavsson	68	72	69	209	3,784
10	Esther Henseleit	75	66	69	210	3,475
	Sanna Nuutinen	66	72	72	210	3,475
12	Liz Young	71	71	69	211	3,089
	Caroline Hedwall	72	69	70	211	3,089
	Kelsey Macdonald	70	70	71	211	3,089
15	Laura Davies	72	70	70	212	2,749
	Lee-Anne Pace	72	72	68	212	2,749
17	Sarah Schober	73	69	71	213	2,656
18	Sophie Hausmann	70	71	73	214	2,449
	Maiken Bing Paulsen	71	74	69	214	2,449
	Manon Gidali	72	72	70	214	2,449
	Karolin Lampert	72	72	70	214	2,449
	Stina Resen	69	75	70	214	2,449
23	Olivia Cowan	73	74	68	215	2,192
24	Harang Lee	75	74	67	216	1,854
	Nuria Iturrioz	77	69	70	216	1,854
	Marta Sanz Barrio	76	71	69	216	1,854
	Marianne Skarpnord	74	70	72	216	1,854
	Annabel Dimmock	69	73	74	216	1,854
	Celine Herbin	72	69	75	216	1,854
	Franziska Friedrich	70	74	72	216	1,854

TEAM COMPETITION

1	**Emily Kristine Pedersen**	129	132	131	392	€27,386
	Michele Thomson					27,386
	Casandra Hall					27,386
	Matt Selby (A)					
2	Stephanie Kyriacou	136	133	124	393	14,114
	Pia Babnik					14,114
	Manon Gidali					14,114
	Abdulwahed Al Qasem (A)					
	Manon De Roey	135	130	128	393	14,114
	Eleanor Givens					14,114
	Linette Littau Durr Holmslykke					14,114
	Ahmed El Mehelmy (A)					
4	Inci Mehmet	134	138	123	395	9,269
	Jenny Haglund					9,269
	Marta Sanz Barrio					9,269
	Scott Peddie (A)					
5	Lee-Anne Pace	131	136	129	396	6,741
	Nicole Garcia					6,741
	Elia Folch					6,741
	Albert Venter (A)					

Andalucia Costa del Sol Open de Espana

Only once before in the history of the Ladies European Tour had a player won three individual tournaments in a row.

Marie-Laure de Lorenzi achieved the feat in 1989 and over three decades later Emily Kristine Pedersen matched the Frenchwoman's achievement. The 24-year-old Dane's totally dominant season, having already secured the Race to Costa del Sol title before making the journey from the Middle East to southern Spain, ended in style with victory at the Andalucia Costa del Sol Open de Espana. Her fourth individual win of the season came by a commanding four strokes from local Nuria Iturrioz as Pedersen continued her stunning form at Guadalmina.

Iturrioz led for the first two rounds and 17 holes of the third. Then Pedersen took over. Torrential rain on Thursday meant Pedersen completed a 68 and added a second-round 71 on Friday. She was three behind Iturrioz, who opened 66-70. Pedersen was not yet at her best, making two bogeys and a double in the first two rounds. Over the weekend, she did not drop a shot. The pivotal moment came at the par-five 18th on Saturday when she launched her favourite hybrid onto the green and holed from 30 feet to leapfrog into the lead over Iturrioz with a 68 to a 72.

On Sunday Pedersen chipped in for a birdie at the fourth, but although she missed a number of chances, her lead grew to four when Iturrioz had her second bogey of the day at the 11th. Both players were to finish quickly, however, with five birdies in the last seven holes. Pedersen's run started with driving behind a tree at the short par-four 12th before hitting a superb chip-and-run recovery to two feet. "That was the turning point," she said. "It felt like fate and made me believe I could win again."

She also birdied the 14th and the last three holes for a 66 and a 15-under-par total of 273. Iturrioz closed with a 69 to finish four ahead of 22-year-old compatriot Ana Pelaez, who recorded the best ever finish by an amateur in the Open de Espana. Her third place, achieved with weekend scores of 68 and 67, was even more commendable as she dealt with the nerves of playing with Guadalmina club member and former champion Azahara Munoz, who finished tied for sixth.

Victory was all the sweeter for Pedersen, who struggled for form in recent years, as her father was caddieing for her for the first time. "It was very special with my Dad here," said the new European number one. "He got me into golf and he has been a big support the whole way, he kept me going when I was down and it is really big for me to have him here and win this amazing trophy. He is right beside me off the course and now, he has been there on it."

Real Club de Golf Guadalmina (South), Marbella, Spain — November 26-29
Par: 72 (35-37); 6,329 yards — Purse: €600,000

1	**Emily Kristine Pedersen**	68	71	68	66	273	€90,000
2	**Nuria Iturrioz**	66	70	72	69	277	51,629
3	**Ana Pelaez** (A)	75	71	68	67	281	
4	Sanna Nuutinen	67	73	74	68	282	29,828
	Maha Haddioui	72	71	67	72	282	29,828
6	Cloe Frankish	72	76	69	66	283	17,383
	Azahara Munoz	74	71	69	69	283	17,383
	Manon Gidali	71	73	69	70	283	17,383
9	Maiken Bing Paulsen	76	70	69	69	284	13,889
	Luna Sobron Galmes	70	70	71	73	284	13,889
11	Marianne Skarpnord	73	75	70	67	285	12,551
	Laura Fuenfstueck	73	70	72	70	285	12,551
	Kelsey Macdonald	68	71	73	73	285	12,551
14	Meghan MacLaren	75	68	72	71	286	11,550
15	Olivia Cowan	73	73	72	69	287	10,229
	Karolin Lampert	70	75	71	71	287	10,229
	Manon De Roey	71	75	70	71	287	10,229
18	Alice Hewson	68	76	75	69	288	9,760
19	Esther Henseleit	71	75	72	71	289	9,375
	Kylie Henry	72	72	71	74	289	9,375
	Annabel Dimmock	75	73	67	74	289	9,375
22	Harang Lee	74	75	71	70	290	8,373
	Kim Metraux	75	74	72	69	290	8,373
	Eleanor Givens	77	75	67	71	290	8,373
	Sarah Schober	73	76	69	72	290	8,373
	Johanna Gustavsson	75	71	71	73	290	8,373
27	Tonje Daffinrud	73	71	73	74	291	6,622
	Christine Wolf	75	73	71	72	291	6,622
	Ursula Wikstrom	78	74	67	72	291	6,622
30	Maria Hernandez	74	75	71	72	292	5,428
	Felicity Johnson	74	71	74	73	292	5,428
	Aditi Ashok	77	75	69	71	292	5,428
	Celine Herbin	70	75	76	71	292	5,428

2020 RACE TO COSTA DEL SOL

1	Emily Kristine Pedersen	1,249.35	Pts
2	Julia Engstrom	415.70	Pts
3	Stephanie Kyriacou	323.78	Pts
4	Manon De Roey	317.45	Pts
5	Sanna Nuutinen	312.56	Pts
6	Azahara Munoz	272.96	Pts
7	Nuria Iturrioz	256.02	Pts
8	Georgia Hall	255.37	Pts
9	Anne van Dam	234.46	Pts
10	Laura Fuenfstueck	233.17	Pts

Japan LPGA Tour

Already distinctive for its plethora of young stars in recent seasons, the Japan LPGA Tour added an exclamation point to the disrupted 2020 campaign when a 19-year-old finished the year atop the money list and was followed by a 20-year-old who, with three victories, had the most wins in the season and a 21-year-old, who won two of the year's three major titles.

Number one was Yuka Saso, a Filipino-Japanese newcomer, who won the second and third tournaments of her rookie season. She never yielded the money lead, posting five other top 10s and finished worse than 14th only three times during the 14-tournament season that, after a single June event, began in earnest in mid-August. Saso won just short of ¥100 million in what was less than half of the normal season.

Number two was Ayaka Furue, another rookie who won as an amateur in 2019. Following a September win, she finished her first pro season in a flourish, winning twice, then placing second, in the final three tournaments.

Number three was Erika Hara, who latched onto the Japan Women's Open and Japan LPGA Tour Championships in her third year on the circuit.

Once again, the number one spot eluded Jiyai Shin, the 32-year-old South Korean star who has won 26 events in Japan and more times — 79 internationally — than any active female player but never the Japan LPGA Tour's top position. Because of the pandemic and injury problems, she missed the first six tournaments but still won twice in her eight starts. Ai Suzuki, the leading money-winner twice in the previous three years who won seven times in 2019, went winless in 2020, losing in her best chance to Ayaka Watanabe in a playoff in the season opener.

Hinako Shibuno, who made such a splash in 2019 winning four times in Japan and capturing the AIG Women's Open, played only six times on the JLPGA, missing the cut twice, as she did on the defence of her British title at Royal Troon. After a quiet initial spell in America, Shibuno finished the season on an uptick. She was fifth and third in the last two events of the JLPGA season and then returned to the States where she was the longtime leader at the US Women's Open before finishing fourth.

In the race to represent Japan at the delayed Tokyo Olympics, Nasa Hataoka led the way at year's end, followed by Shibuno, Furue and Suzuki.

2020 SCHEDULE

Daikin Orchid Ladies		*cancelled*
Meiji Yasuda Life Ladies Yokohama Tire		*cancelled*
T-Point Eneos Ladies		*cancelled*
AXA Ladies		*cancelled*
Yamaha Ladies Open		*cancelled*
Studio Alice Ladies Open		*cancelled*
Vantelin Ladies Open KKT Cup		*cancelled*
Fujisankei Ladies Classic		*cancelled*
Panasonic Open Ladies		*cancelled*
World Ladies Championship Salonpas Cup		*cancelled*
Hoken no Madoguchi Ladies		*cancelled*
Chukyo TV Bridgestone Ladies Open		*cancelled*
Resort Trust Ladies		*cancelled*
Yonex Ladies		*cancelled*
Ai Miyazato Suntory Ladies Open		*cancelled*
Nichirei Ladies		*cancelled*
Earth Mondahmin Cup	**Ayako Watanabe**	
Shiseido Anessa Ladies Open		*cancelled*
Nipponham Ladies Classic		*cancelled*
Samantha Thavasa & GMO Internet Girls Collection		*cancelled*

Daito Kentaku Eheyanet Ladies		*cancelled*
NEC Karuizawa 72	**Yuka Saso**	
CAT Ladies		*cancelled*
Nitori Ladies	**Yuka Saso**	
Golf 5 Ladies	**Sakura Koiwai**	
JLPGA Championship Konica Minolta Cup	**Saki Nagamine**	
Descente Ladies Tokai Classic	**Ayaka Furue**	
Miyagi TV Cup Dunlop Ladies Open		*cancelled*
Japan Women's Open	**Erika Hara**	
Stanley Ladies	**Mone Inami**	
Fujitsu Ladies	**Jiyai Shin**	
Nobuta Group Ladies Masters		*cancelled*
Mitsubishi Electric/Hisako Higuchi Ladies	**Yuna Nishimura**	
Toto Japan Classic	**Jiyai Shin**	
Itoen Ladies	**Ayaka Furue**	
Daio Paper Elleair Ladies Open	**Ayaka Furue**	
JLPGA Tour Championship Ricoh Cup	**Erika Hara**	

Earth Mondahmin Cup

Professional golf flickered to life in Japan at the end of June with the 72-hole Earth Mondahmin Cup tournament after the coronavirus pandemic-demanded cancellation of the first 16 tournaments on the 2020 Japan LPGA Tour and the absence of galleries wasn't the only thing that was abnormal about it.

Rainy weather pestered play early and late, forcing the event to the first Monday finish on the tour since the 1997 Japan Women's Open. Even then, it took an extra hole for Ayaka Watanabe to defeat reigning number one Ai Suzuki in a battle of 26-year-olds at Camelia Hills Country Club in Sodegaura City, Chiba. Before that, as happened during much of the 2019 season, players still in or barely out of their teens snatched the headlines.

On the first day, after a rain-delayed start, 19-year-old Filipino-Japanese Yuka Saso shared the lead with Mayu Hamada and Tsugumi Miyazaki with six-under-par 66s. Although she and the others yielded the lead to 21-year-old Mizuki Tanaka (68-67) on the second day, she remained in contention the rest of the way.

With a 70 for 11 under par, Tanaka retained a three-shot lead on Saturday over 18-year-old Mao Saigo and 20-year-old Ayaka Furue, who turned pro late in the 2019 season after winning the Fujitsu Ladies.

Watanabe and Suzuki, with 71s, were next, two back, and, after heavy rain forced the postponement to Monday, they dueled down the back stretch as Tanaka slipped to a 73. Each made two late birdies to close out with 68s and matching 277s.

Watanabe then picked up her fourth tour victory and first in five years with a 12-foot putt on the first playoff hole against the seven-time winner of 2019. What of the youngsters? Tanaka tied for third, Saso and Saigo tied for fifth and Furue slipped to a tie for 27th.

Camellia Hills Country Club, Sodegaura City, Chiba — June 25-29
Par 72 (36-36); 6,622 yards — Purse: ¥240,000,000

1	**Ayaka Watanabe**	69	69	71	68	277	¥43,200,000
2	**Ai Suzuki**	68	70	71	68	277	21,120,000
	Watanabe won playoff at first extra hole						
3	**Miki Sakai**	68	73	68	69	278	15,600,000
	Mizuki Tanaka	68	67	70	73	278	15,600,000
5	Erika Hara	68	73	71	67	279	8,640,000
	Mao Nozawa	70	69	72	68	279	8,640,000
	Yuka Saso	66	74	71	68	279	8,640,000
	Momoko Osato	69	70	71	69	279	8,640,000
	Mao Saigo	70	71	67	71	279	8,640,000
10	Aoi Ohnishi	69	73	71	67	280	4,240,000
	Lala Anai	73	68	71	68	280	4,240,000
	Nanoko Hayashi	70	73	69	68	280	4,240,000
13	Mika Miyazato	71	73	70	67	281	3,240,000
	Yuting Seki	71	74	67	69	281	3,240,000
	Sakura Koiwai	68	72	71	70	281	3,240,000
	Mone Inami	68	74	69	70	281	3,240,000
17	Hikari Tanabe	75	70	69	68	282	2,136,000
	Yui Kawamoto	71	71	71	69	282	2,136,000
	Mayu Hamada	66	74	72	70	282	2,136,000

	Minami Hiruta	68	73	71	70	282	2,136,000	Eimi Koga	69	74	71	71	285	1,387,200
	Mami Fukuda	71	71	70	70	282	2,136,000	Miki Uehara	69	76	69	71	285	1,387,200
	Ayaka Furue	73	69	66	74	282	2,136,000	Yuri Yoshida	74	71	69	71	285	1,387,200
23	Hiroko Azuma	70	73	71	69	283	1,704,000	Yuka Yasuda	73	72	68	72	285	1,387,200
	Ririna Staiano	73	71	72	67	283	1,704,000	Mio Kotaki	70	74	72	69	285	1,387,200
	Haruka Kudo	71	68	72	72	283	1,704,000	Ji-Hee Lee	71	67	74	73	285	1,387,200
	Reika Usui	68	71	70	74	283	1,704,000	Minami Katsu	73	68	71	73	285	1,387,200
27	Nana Suganuma	68	72	70	74	284	1,584,000	Tsugumi Miyazaki	66	74	71	74	285	1,387,200
28	Seira Oki	67	75	72	71	285	1,387,200	Ritsuko Ryu	71	70	70	74	285	1,387,200

NEC Karuizawa 72

After an eight-week absence in precautionary response to the coronavirus pandemic, the Japan LPGA Tour resumed action with the NEC Karuizawa 72 tournament in Nagano and another teenager joined the remarkable number of very young players in the circuit's winner's circle in recent years.

This time it was 19-year-old Yuka Saso, the Filipino-Japanese player who contended in the earlier Earth Mondahmin tournament in her first pro start after a world-spanning amateur career capped by a gold medal in the Asian Games. Saso, whose family moved from the Philippines to Tokyo when she was five, fired a final-round 63 and rolled to a four-stroke victory on the Karuizawa 72 Golf North course in mid August, becoming the first-ever Filipino victor on the Japan LPGA Tour.

Yuka, whose long-term ambitions are clearly indicated by a sponsoring-company's sword business embroidered on her golf caps, got off to a fast start with a seven-birdie 65 in the first round, taking a two-stroke lead over Yoko Maeda, Serena Aoki and Haruka Kudo. An even-par 72 on Saturday dropped her a shot behind Mao Saigo (68-68) and Miyu Goto (70-66), but she regained the lead quickly on Sunday with an outgoing 31, her closest pursuers then being Maiko Wakabayashi and Saiki Fujita.

Any hopes they had dissolved when Saso eagled the par-five 16th hole en route to the 63 and a 16-under-par total of 200. Wakabayashi (64) and Fujita (66) tied for second on 12 under.

Karuizawa 72 Golf (North), Karuizawa, Nagano — August 14-16
Par 72 (36-36); 6,710 yards — Purse: ¥80,000,000

1	**Yuka Saso**	65	72	63	200	¥14,400,000		Mika Miyazato	68	71	71	210	976,000
2	**Maiko Wakabayashi**	71	69	64	204	6,320,000		Shina Kanazawa	68	70	72	210	976,000
	Saiki Fujita	70	68	66	204	6,320,000		Pei-Ying Tsai	68	69	73	210	976,000
4	Chie Arimura	69	70	66	205	4,800,000		Miyu Goto	70	66	74	210	976,000
5	Mao Saigo	68	68	70	206	4,000,000	22	Ai Suzuki	70	71	70	211	720,000
6	Minami Hiruta	69	70	68	207	3,000,000		Aoi Ohnishi	69	71	71	211	720,000
	Ayano Yasuda	68	69	70	207	3,000,000		Kana Nagai	68	71	72	211	720,000
8	Asako Fujimoto	75	64	69	208	2,200,000	25	Rei Matsuda	69	72	71	212	672,000
	Rumi Yoshiba	70	67	71	208	2,200,000		Anna Kono	71	70	71	212	672,000
10	Yuna Takagi	69	71	69	209	1,456,000		Tsugumi Miyazaki	68	71	73	212	672,000
	Mamiko Higa	71	69	69	209	1,456,000	28	Serena Aoki	67	74	72	213	600,000
	Yoko Maeda	67	71	71	209	1,456,000		Shiho Oyama	72	69	72	213	600,000
	Karen Tsuruoka	69	69	71	209	1,456,000		Haruka Kudo	67	72	74	213	600,000
14	Ayaka Furue	70	72	68	210	976,000		Saki Nagamine	68	71	74	213	600,000
	Yuting Seki	69	72	69	210	976,000		Erika Kikuchi	72	67	74	213	600,000
	Miki Sakai	71	70	69	210	976,000		Fumika Kawagishi	68	69	76	213	600,000
	Nozomi Uetake	72	68	70	210	976,000							

Nitori Ladies

The accomplishments grew more impressive tournament by tournament as 19-year-old Yuka Saso followed her fifth-place finish and victory in her first two starts on the Japan Tour with another convincing win her third time out in the Nitori Ladies event in Hokkaido.

The young Filipino-Japanese player came from slightly behind in scoring the first win, but she all but led from the start at Otaru Country Club. Her opening 67 trailed only the 65 of Satsuki Oshiro, who was never a factor the rest of the way. Saso moved a shot in front of Hikaru Yoshimoto (69-68) with a 69 to be eight under par on the second day and, although squandering a four-stroke lead during the round, retained that one-shot margin Saturday with a 68. Sakura Koiwai was the only player within four strokes of the leader after a 66. The field was reduced to 34 players with a rare 54-hole cut at 215, one under par.

Koiwai, herself only 22 and a first-time winner in 2019, had her best chance early on Sunday when Saso double-bogeyed the second hole, but Yuka rang up four birdies on the next seven holes to regain the lead. She established the final two-shot margin with another birdie at the 12th hole, bogeyed the 15th and parred in for a 71 and a 13-under-par total of 275. That fattened her money total to a remarkable total of nearly ¥60 million.

Koiwai, with her 72 for 11 under par, finished eight strokes ahead of third-placed Kana Mikashima, Ji-Hee Lee and Mayu Hamada.

Otaru Country Club, Hokkaido — August 27-30
Par 72 (36-36); 6,695 yards — Purse: ¥200,000,000

1	**Yuka Saso**	67	69	68	71	275	¥36,000,000
2	**Sakura Koiwai**	68	71	66	72	277	17,600,000
3	**Kana Mikashima**	72	71	71	71	285	12,000,000
	Ji-Hee Lee	70	72	69	74	285	12,000,000
	Mayu Hamada	68	71	70	76	285	12,000,000
6	Saki Nagamine	73	71	69	73	286	7,000,000
	Shiho Oyama	69	72	71	74	286	7,000,000
	Chie Arimura	70	75	65	76	286	7,000,000
9	Sae Ogura (A)	70	69	75	73	287	
	Yuna Nishimura	71	70	72	74	287	4,500,000
	Mao Nozawa	69	73	71	74	287	4,500,000
12	Miyu Shinkai	70	74	70	74	288	3,160,000
	Ayaka Watanabe	70	73	71	74	288	3,160,000
	Momoko Osato	71	71	72	74	288	3,160,000
	Mizuki Ooide	71	74	69	74	288	3,160,000
	Saiki Fujita	72	70	71	75	288	3,160,000
	Sumika Nakasone	74	72	66	76	288	3,160,000
18	Seira Oki	69	69	74	77	289	2,460,000
19	Saki Asai	71	71	72	76	290	1,920,000
	Yuri Yoshida	74	70	69	77	290	1,920,000
	Ayako Kimura	73	71	71	75	290	1,920,000
	Shina Kanazawa	68	71	73	78	290	1,920,000
	Pei-Ying Tsai	69	70	76	75	290	1,920,000
	Yuka Yasuda	71	71	69	79	290	1,920,000
	Hinano Muguruma (A)	70	69	69	82	290	
26	Ritsuko Ryu	70	73	71	77	291	1,640,000
	Serena Aoki	74	72	69	76	291	1,640,000
	Minami Hiruta	73	72	70	76	291	1,640,000
	Yuting Seki	72	73	70	76	291	1,640,000
30	Kana Nagai	74	71	70	77	292	1,520,000
	Hikaru Yoshimoto	69	68	71	84	292	1,520,000

Golf 5 Ladies

Sakura Koiwai made up for a pair of near-misses when she continued the run of young winners on the Japan LPGA Tour with a whopping six-stroke victory in the Golf 5 Ladies tournament.

Two years earlier in the Golf 5, then a 20-year-old rookie, Koiwai lost on the third hole of a playoff against powerhouse Jiyai Shin and she came to the 2020 Golf 5 off a second-place finish behind teen sensation Yuka Saso. In between, she scored her maiden victory with a tournament-record score in the 2019 Samantha Thavasa tournament.

Sakura set another tournament record on Gifu Golf 5 Club's Mizunami course this time around. Three strokes behind Rumi Yoshiba's opening 65 after 18 holes, she played the final 36 holes in 13 under par. The Hokkaido native who swung her first golf club at the age of eight, made her lone bogey amid eight birdies and a back-nine 30 on Saturday, moving atop the field with a 65 to be 11 under par, two strokes ahead of Mamiko Higa.

She was never challenged on Sunday with her bogey-free 66 and record 199 total, 17 under par. The runners-up started the day too far behind. Ayaka Furue, the 20-year-old rookie who won the 2019 Fujitsu Ladies as an amateur, matched Koiwai's 66 to join Ayaka Watanabe, the Earth Mondahmin winner in the June opener, in second place, Watanabe shooting 67 for her 205 total.

Golf 5 Club (Mizunami), Ibaraki, Gifu — September 4-6
Par 72 (36-36); 6,571 yards — Purse: ¥60,000,000

1	**Sakura Koiwai**	68	65	66	199	¥10,800,000
2	**Ayaka Furue**	71	68	66	205	4,740,000
	Ayaka Watanabe	70	68	67	205	4,740,000
4	Min Young Lee[2]	69	69	68	206	3,300,000
	Mamiko Higa	70	65	71	206	3,300,000
6	Nozomi Uetake	69	70	68	207	2,100,000
	Erika Hara	73	66	68	207	2,100,000
	Eri Okayama	68	70	69	207	2,100,000
9	Mika Miyazato	69	69	70	208	1,350,000
	Minami Hiruta	68	69	71	208	1,350,000
11	Pei-Ying Tsai	68	72	69	209	996,000
	Yuting Seki	69	71	69	209	996,000

	Saiki Fujita	70	70	69	209	996,000
	Shina Kanazawa	72	69	68	209	996,000
	Hikari Kawamitsu	72	68	69	209	996,000
16	Mayu Hamada	70	70	70	210	756,000
	Rumi Yoshiba	65	73	72	210	756,000
	Momo Yoshikawa	68	70	72	210	756,000
19	Yoko Maeda	72	69	70	211	538,800
	Miki Sakai	72	69	70	211	538,800
	Chae-Young Yoon	69	72	70	211	538,800
	Naruha Miyata	72	68	71	211	538,800
	Yuka Yasuda	73	68	70	211	538,800
	Hikari Tanabe	69	72	70	211	538,800
	Sayaka Takahashi	69	72	70	211	538,800
	Mizuki Tanaka	66	73	72	211	538,800
	Miyuu Yamashita	67	71	73	211	538,800
	Kokone Yoshimoto	69	69	73	211	538,800
29	Mi-Jeong Jeon	74	66	72	212	408,000
	Ai Suzuki	70	71	71	212	408,000
	Hikaru Yoshimoto	69	72	71	212	408,000
	Yu Tajima	72	68	72	212	408,000
	Kana Mikashima	68	73	71	212	408,000
	Yuka Saso	71	71	70	212	408,000
	Rie Tsuji	73	66	73	212	408,000
	Yuna Takagi	72	70	70	212	408,000
	Karin Takeyama	72	67	73	212	408,000
	Kana Nagai	71	68	73	212	408,000
	Rei Matsuda	73	69	70	212	408,000

Japan LPGA Championship Konica Minolta Cup

Saki Nagamine was already looking for a third victory when she wrapped up her second in the Japan LPGA Championship and hugged the Konica Minolta Cup in mid-September at JFE Setonaikai Golf Club in Okayama.

"There was a gap between my first and second wins" — the Fujisankei in April of 2018 — "but I want to achieve the third win soon," said the 25-year-old veteran of six seasons on the Japan LPGA Tour, blaming the gap primarily on her short stick. "I simply lacked the skill, especially the putting. I had several chances to win. What I couldn't make was putting."

Nagamine, who won the Fujisankei in a playoff, barely avoided another overtime session at Setonaikai. She stayed close for three rounds as Serena Aoki and Min Young Lee[2] the first day, Hee-Kyung Bae the second and Yuna Nishimura the third exchanged first place. The lead remained bunched through the front nine on Sunday before Nagamine went in front to stay with birdies at the 10th and 11th holes.

Even though she then bogeyed the 12th and 16th holes with nary a birdie the rest of the way, she squeezed out a one-stroke victory with her 69 and 12-under-par 276. She edged Na-Ri Lee (67), Ayako Kimura (69) and Hikari Tanabe (71) with their 277s.

Stunned by what she had just achieved, Nagamine confessed: "I still don't feel like I won the championship, but I'm thrilled."

JFE Setonaikai Golf Club, Okayama, Hyogo — September 10-13
Par 72 (36-36); 6,640 yards — Purse: ¥200,000,000

1	**Saki Nagamine**	69	70	68	69	276	¥36,000,000
2	**Na-Ri Lee**	70	70	70	67	277	14,533,333
	Ayako Kimura	67	71	70	69	277	14,533,333
	Hikari Tanabe	69	70	67	71	277	14,533,333
5	Hee-Kyung Bae	69	67	70	72	*278*	10,000,000
6	Sakura Koiwai	68	71	68	72	279	8,000,000
7	Shina Kanazawa	69	72	70	70	281	6,500,000
	Yuna Nishimura	70	68	67	76	281	6,500,000
9	Haruka Morita	73	72	69	68	282	3,920,000
	Erika Kikuchi	68	73	71	70	282	3,920,000
	Serena Aoki	66	76	70	70	282	3,920,000
	Sayaka Takahashi	70	68	69	75	282	3,920,000
13	Eri Joma	68	72	71	72	283	2,640,000
	Ritsuko Ryu	69	72	70	72	283	2,640,000
	Teresa Lu	67	72	71	73	283	2,640,000
	Min Young Lee[2]	66	74	68	75	283	2,640,000
	Yuka Saso	68	70	69	76	283	2,640,000
18	Ayaka Furue	70	73	71	70	284	1,780,000
	Mi-Jeong Jeon	68	72	73	71	284	1,780,000
	Shiho Oyama	70	75	67	72	284	1,780,000
	Mika Miyazato	70	74	67	73	284	1,780,000
22	Eri Fukuyama	71	74	69	71	285	1,480,000
	Anna Kono	70	75	69	71	285	1,480,000
	Mao Saigo	69	73	71	72	285	1,480,000
	Miyuki Takeuchi	71	69	70	75	285	1,480,000
	Nana Yamashiro	70	72	68	75	285	1,480,000
27	Ayano Yasuda	71	73	71	71	286	1,300,000
	Minami Hiruta	71	74	71	70	286	1,300,000
	Yuri Yoshida	68	73	72	73	286	1,300,000
	Saki Asai	69	75	69	73	286	1,300,000

Descente Ladies Tokai Classic

Just as Ayaka Furue's victory as a 19-year-old amateur in the 2019 Fujitsu Ladies tournament was not a huge surprise, neither was her first win as a 20-year-old professional in the Descente Ladies Tokai Classic.

The brilliant youngster had a tie-for-second and three other top-20 finishes in the previous five events before she nailed win number two with a pinpoint wedge shot in a playoff in the Descente Ladies Tokai Classic in mid-September. The victim of Furue's shot that wound up a foot from the cup on the first extra hole was 28-year-old Hiroko Azuma, who has laboured since 2012 on the Japan LPGA Tour with moderate success but without a victory.

It was a remarkable week for Furue on Shin Minami Aichi Country Club's Mihama course as she played all 54 holes without a bogey, just the eighth player in 30 years to have accomplished that feat on the tour. Among the others were worldwide stars Annika Sorenstam and Paula Creamer.

Furue began with a 66, tied with three others, including Ai Suzuki, a stroke behind Pei-Ying Tsai. Azuma shot a 65 Saturday as Furue posted 67 and joined her atop the standings at 11 under par. Tsai managed only a 71 and dropped into third place, four strokes behind the leaders. Both Furue and Azuma shot 68s on Sunday, each holing clutch birdie putts of consequence on the 18th green to force the playoff with their 15-under-par totals of 201.

Reflecting on her young career, Furue remarked: "It's so cool that I can't think I'm just 20 years old."

Shin Minami Aichi Country Club (Mihama), Aichi — September 18-20
Par 72 (36-36); 6,456 yards — Purse: ¥80,000,000

1	**Ayaka Furue**	66	67	68	201	¥14,400,000
2	**Hiroko Azuma**	68	65	68	201	7,040,000
	Furue won playoff at first extra hole					
3	**Pei-Ying Tsai**	65	71	69	205	5,600,000
4	Saiki Fujita	66	71	69	206	4,800,000
5	Shoko Sasaki	69	71	67	207	3,333,333
	Naruha Miyata	67	72	68	207	3,333,333
	Miki Sakai	67	71	69	207	3,333,333
8	Yuka Saso	68	73	67	208	1,876,000
	Mone Inami	68	70	70	208	1,876,000
	Sumika Nakasone	70	68	70	208	1,876,000
	Ai Suzuki	66	71	71	208	1,876,000
12	Mayu Hamada	70	69	70	209	1,384,000
	Ji-Hee Lee	70	65	74	209	1,384,000
14	Mi-Jeong Jeon	72	70	68	210	1,024,000
	Serena Aoki	69	71	70	210	1,024,000
	Lala Anai	71	69	70	210	1,024,000
	Kana Mikashima	71	72	67	210	1,024,000
	Asuka Kashiwabara	72	67	71	210	1,024,000
	Chie Arimura	68	70	72	210	1,024,000
	Mika Miyazato	70	68	72	210	1,024,000
21	Ayako Kimura	70	71	70	211	744,000
	Saki Nagamine	70	70	71	211	744,000
	Miyu Shinkai	71	72	68	211	744,000
	Yuna Nishimura	70	69	72	211	744,000
25	Momoko Osato	73	68	71	212	680,000
	Seon Woo Bae	69	73	70	212	680,000
	Kana Nagai	69	71	72	212	680,000
	Shina Kanazawa	69	69	74	212	680,000
29	Teresa Lu	72	70	71	213	608,000
	Ayaka Watanabe	70	72	71	213	608,000
	Kokone Yoshimoto	66	76	71	213	608,000
	Min Young Lee[2]	71	72	70	213	608,000
	Ayano Yasuda	71	69	73	213	608,000

Japan Women's Open Championship

The second victory in her young career came much more easily for Erika Hara than her first one a year earlier and carried much greater significance.

The 21-year-old captured the coveted Japan Women's Open Championship by four strokes in sharp contrast to the 2019 Resort Trust when she had to go two sudden-death playoff holes against number one Ai Suzuki before picking up her maiden win.

Hara, one of a cluster of young players on the Japan LPGA Tour dubbed the Golden Generation, was a contending presence from the start in the year's prestigious major at The Classic Golf Club in Miyawaka City. She opened with a four-under-par 68 that included seven birdies on the back nine. She was tied for third place behind veteran South Korean Na-Ri Lee (64) and Sakura Koiwai (66), the Golf 5 tournament winner a month earlier who would turn out to be Hara's lone challenger of any consequence at the end.

In fact, Koiwai, another member of the Golden Generation, took over the lead Friday with a 69, despite a bogey and double bogey, as Lee tumbled with a 76 and Hara moved into second place with her 70. The leading two then exchanged places the next day, Erika firing a seven-birdie 66 for 12 under par, four shots ahead of Sakura, whose faulty front-nine 39 with a double bogey and two bogeys led to a 73.

Hara started fast Sunday with a first-hole birdie for the third day in a row, made four more with a bogey for a 68 and her winning total of 272, 16 under par. Koiwai never got closer than the final four-stroke margin, but she finished four ahead of third-placers Momoko Ueda and Sumika Nakasone.

Hara had an unusual description of her feelings after the big win. "I'm happy. I'm really happy, but I don't really feel it."

The Classic Golf Club, Miyawaka City, Fukuoka — October 1-4
Par 72 (36-36); 6,761 yards — Purse: ¥112,500,000

1	**Erika Hara**	68	70	66	68	272	¥22,500,000
2	**Sakura Koiwai**	66	69	73	68	276	12,375,000
3	**Momoko Ueda**	68	73	70	69	280	7,143,750
	Sumika Nakasone	72	74	65	69	280	7,143,750
5	Minami Hiruta	72	70	73	66	281	4,331,250
	Na-Ri Lee	64	76	73	68	281	4,331,250
7	Erika Kikuchi	70	72	71	70	283	2,925,000
	Lala Anai	70	71	70	72	283	2,925,000
	Kokone Yoshimoto	69	73	69	72	283	2,925,000
10	Teresa Lu	71	72	69	72	284	2,137,500
11	Au-Reum Hwang	75	71	70	69	285	1,762,500
	Yuna Nishimura	74	70	71	70	285	1,762,500
	Ji-Hee Lee	73	72	69	71	285	1,762,500
14	Maria Shinohara	75	72	73	66	286	1,226,250
	Yuka Saso	73	70	73	70	286	1,226,250
	Ayaka Furue	73	70	73	70	286	1,226,250
	Akie Iwai (A)	73	69	72	72	286	
	Ai Suzuki	73	69	72	72	286	1,226,250
	Ayaka Watanabe	74	69	70	73	286	1,226,250
	Miki Sakai	71	69	71	75	286	1,226,250
21	Min Young Lee[2]	74	71	73	69	287	951,750
	Saki Asai	71	71	73	72	287	951,750
	Kana Mikashima	70	72	73	72	287	951,750
	Mone Inami	75	70	70	72	287	951,750
	Eri Okayama	73	68	73	73	287	951,750
26	Mirai Hamasaki (A)	73	71	73	71	288	
	Asako Fujimoto	73	73	71	71	288	821,250
	Yumi Narisawa	72	74	71	71	288	821,250
	Mizuki Ooide	71	70	75	72	288	821,250
	Sayaka Takahashi	69	75	72	72	288	821,250
	Mao Nozawa	70	73	72	73	288	821,250
	Pei-Ying Tsai	70	73	72	73	288	821,250

Stanley Ladies

Bad weather of all denominations has affected tournament play in many ways over the years around the world, but never as it did two years running at the Japan LPGA Tour's Stanley Ladies tournament.

In 2019, Typhoon Hagibis forced officials to settle for an unprecedented 27-hole tournament and Ah-Reum Hwang's weird winning total of 100. Remarkably, in 2020, another typhoon disrupted Stanley play at Tomei Country Club, this time bringing about cancellation of Saturday's second round and the season's first 36-hole finish.

The beneficiary was Mone Inami, who emerged from a three-way playoff with her second tour victory. The 21-year-old, playing in her second full season, and South Korea's Seon Woo Bae were bunched on level par 72 in a six-woman, eighth-place tie after the first round. But they were just a stroke out of the lead, shared in bulk by seven others on 71.

After Typhoon number 14 wiped out Saturday's play, the pair shot 67s on Sunday, Inami birdieing three of her last four holes, and tied Saki Asai, who tacked a 68 onto her opening 71 to forge the 139 deadlock and playoff. Inami then birdied again at the first extra hole, holing a 13-foot putt for the win as Bae parred and Asai picked up.

Interestingly, Mone, who sat out three tournaments, had been concentrating on improving her putting at the urging of her father, using a new intensive practice drill. "They say the second win is the most difficult," Imani said afterwards. "I set a goal of getting at least one win before the start of the season." Goal achieved.

Tomei Country Club, Susano, Shizuoka — October 9-11
Par 72 (36-36); 6,572 yards — Purse: ¥100,000,000

1	**Mone Inami**	72	67	139	¥13,500,000
2	**Seon Woo Bae**	72	67	139	5,925,000
	Saki Asai	71	68	139	5,925,000
	Inami won playoff at first extra hole				
4	Na-Ri Lee	71	69	140	4,500,000
5	Mamiko Higa	75	67	142	2,327,142
	Ayaka Furue	74	68	142	2,327,142
	Erika Hara	76	66	142	2,327,142

	Sakura Koiwai	72 70	142	2,327,142		Nozomi Uetake	76 68	144	602,500
	Lala Anai	72 70	142	2,327,142		Sumika Nakasone	72 72	144	602,500
	Miyuu Yamashita	71 71	142	2,327,142	25	Mi-Jeong Jeon	75 70	145	510,000
	Naruha Miyata	71 71	142	2,327,142		Min Young Lee[2]	76 69	145	510,000
12	Yuka Saso	75 68	143	990,000		Pei-Ying Tsai	74 71	145	510,000
	Ayako Kimura	76 67	143	990,000		Kana Mikashima	74 71	145	510,000
	Shoko Sasaki	74 69	143	990,000		Sayaka Takahashi	73 72	145	510,000
	Ritsuko Ryu	73 70	143	990,000	30	Chae-Young Yoon	75 71	146	426,562
	Au-Reum Hwang	73 70	143	990,000		Ji-Hee Lee	76 70	146	426,562
	Jiyai Shin	73 70	143	990,000		Yu Tajima	76 70	146	426,562
	Hina Arakaki	71 72	143	990,000		Rei Matsuda	74 72	146	426,562
19	Yuna Nishimura	75 69	144	602,500		Saiki Fujita	77 69	146	426,562
	Kana Nagai	75 69	144	602,500		Hikaru Yoshimoto	73 73	146	426,562
	Maria Shinohara	76 68	144	602,500		Saki Nagamine	77 69	146	426,562
	Momoko Ueda	74 70	144	602,500		Miyu Shinkai	71 75	146	426,562

Fujitsu Ladies

It didn't take Jiyai Shin long to start making up for lost time on the Japan LPGA Tour.

Playing in just her third event of the season after the pandemic and recuperation from surgery on her right wrist and left elbow delayed her arrival in Japan, Shin again lived up to her reputation as the "Final-Round Queen" in the Fujitsu Ladies tournament. She came from a stroke off the pace on the last day and landed her 25th title in Japan and 58th of her splendid international career. The ¥18 million prize jumped her over the ¥1 billion total-earnings in her 207th start, the fastest in tour history.

"I didn't expect to win so quickly," the 32-year-old admitted. "This year's course setting was the most difficult I've ever seen. I'm glad I was able to play well. I liked my short game the last three days."

The scoring on the Tokyu Seven Hundred Club course in Chiba Prefecture was demanding all week. Shin opened with a two-under-par 70, two behind leader Seon Woo Bae, playoff loser to Mone Inami the previous Sunday. Saki Asai, at five under par, took over first place on a cold, rainy Saturday with a 67. Hana Wakimoto, with 69, had the only other sub-70 round. Shin moved into the runner-up position with another 70, this time abetted by her 12th hole-in-one at the par-three fourth.

Asai faded to a 73 on Sunday and the issue remained in doubt until Shin scored back-to-back birdies at the 15th and 16th holes, a cushion for the bogey that followed at the 17th. Her 69 for a seven-under-par total of 209 gave her a two-stroke victory over Bae (70) and Ayaka Furue, the Descente winner in September, who closed with 66, the week's lowest round.

Tokyu Seven Hundred Club, Chiba — October 16-18
Par 72 (36-36); 6,659 yards — Purse: ¥100,000,000

1	**Jiyai Shin**	70 70 69	209	¥18,000,000	17	Ha Neul Kim	74 73 69	216	1,170,000
2	**Ayaka Furue**	74 71 66	211	7,900,000		Teresa Lu	69 76 71	216	1,170,000
	Seon Woo Bae	68 73 70	211	7,900,000		Mayu Hamada	71 74 71	216	1,170,000
4	Mamiko Higa	69 75 68	212	4,625,000	20	Kana Nagai	69 77 71	217	940,000
	Yuna Nishimura	73 71 68	212	4,625,000		Yuri Yoshida	70 76 71	217	940,000
	Mi-Jeong Jeon	71 71 70	212	4,625,000		Ayaka Watanabe	73 73 71	217	940,000
	Saki Asai	72 67 73	212	4,625,000		Asuka Ishikawa	73 71 73	217	940,000
8	Asuka Kashiwabara	70 74 69	213	2,750,000	24	Au-Reum Hwang	72 76 70	218	870,000
	Mone Inami	69 73 71	213	2,750,000		Seira Oki	77 73 68	218	870,000
10	Yuka Saso	70 74 70	214	1,935,000		Ayano Yasuda	70 74 74	218	870,000
	Hana Wakimoto	73 69 72	214	1,935,000	27	Akira Yamaji	69 78 72	219	780,000
12	Minami Katsu	71 75 69	215	1,570,000		Rumi Yoshiba	71 77 71	219	780,000
	Ai Suzuki	73 73 69	215	1,570,000		Ji-Hee Lee	70 78 71	219	780,000
	Lala Anai	71 74 70	215	1,570,000		Eri Okayama	75 71 73	219	780,000
	Erika Kikuchi	72 73 70	215	1,570,000		Shiho Oyama	73 73 73	219	780,000
	Sakura Koiwai	70 74 71	215	1,570,000		Sumika Nakasone	74 76 69	219	780,000

Mitsubishi Electric/Hisako Higuchi Ladies

Lessons learned in a near-miss earlier in the season helped Yuna Nishimura capture a victory in just her 10th start and join the parade of young winners on the 2020 Japan LPGA Tour.

The 20-year-old rookie gained some knowledge after failing to hold onto the lead in the final round of the Japan LPGA Championship in mid-September, explaining:

"I was nervous. I regret that I was too conscious of the score. Also I may have played too defensively. The next time I played in the final group, I swore that I would attack. Today, I think I was able to control not only my management but also my feelings."

Nishimura's one-stroke victory did not come easily. Instead it was spectacular. She entered the final round in third place, but six shots behind Minami Katsu, who led the first two days at Musashigaoka Golf Club in Saitama Prefecture with a pair of 67s in a bid for her fifth tour title. Yuna still trailed by four at the turn after Katsu eagled the ninth, but Minami made nothing but pars on the back nine and Nishimura unleashed a five-birdie 31 finish, the last birdie with a five-foot putt for the win on the final green. She closed with a 65 for a total of 205, 11 under par, while Katsu carded a 72 for 10 under.

In the first 10 tournaments of the season, Yuka Saso (19) won twice and Nishimura and Ayaka Furue (both 20), Erika Hara and Mone Inami (both 21) and Sakura Koiwai (22) finished on top.

Musashigaoka Golf Club, Hanno, Saitama — October 30-November 1
Par 72 (36-36); 6,585 yards — Purse: ¥80,000,000

1	**Yuna Nishimura**	69	71	65	205	¥14,400,000
2	**Minami Katsu**	67	67	72	206	7,200,000
3	**Seon Woo Bae**	71	71	67	209	5,600,000
4	Akira Yamaji	71	73	67	211	4,000,000
	Sumika Nakasone	70	72	69	211	4,000,000
	Shina Kanazawa	70	71	70	211	4,000,000
7	Jiyai Shin	68	71	73	212	2,800,000
8	Sayaka Takahashi	71	70	72	213	2,200,000
	Miyuu Yamashita	69	71	73	213	2,200,000
10	Ji-Hee Lee	71	72	71	214	1,406,666
	Mone Inami	72	71	71	214	1,406,666
	Momoko Ueda	69	73	72	214	1,406,666
	Mi-Jeong Jeon	71	71	72	214	1,406,666
	Erika Hara	76	70	68	214	1,406,666
	Chae-Young Yoon	69	72	73	214	1,406,666
16	Ayaka Watanabe	69	75	71	215	938,666
	Erika Kikuchi	74	71	70	215	938,666
	Ai Suzuki	72	73	70	215	938,666
	Yuka Yasuda	75	69	71	215	938,666
	Eri Okayama	75	68	72	215	938,666
	Mami Fukuda	75	68	72	215	938,666
22	Mayu Wakui (A)	70	74	72	216	
	Kumiko Kaneda	72	74	70	216	760,000
	Yuna Takagi	70	72	74	216	760,000
	Ayaka Furue	75	71	70	216	760,000
26	Ayaka Matsumori	71	73	73	217	728,000
27	Chie Arimura	71	73	74	218	661,714
	Kana Mikashima	71	74	73	218	661,714
	Hana Wakimoto	70	73	75	218	661,714
	Teresa Lu	73	73	72	218	661,714
	Min Young Lee2	73	73	72	218	661,714
	Nana Yamashiro	72	74	72	218	661,714
	Ayako Kimura	73	68	77	218	661,714

Toto Japan Classic

Jiyai Shin's sentimental victory in the limited-field Toto Japan Classic had the earmarks of the talented champion that she is — faultless play from the start and a blazing spurt at the finish.

The 32-year-old South Korean star, playing in just her fifth tournament of the abbreviated season, went the event's entire 54 holes without a bogey and, just when she needed it, closed eagle-birdie to score her second win in three weeks and pick up her 26th title in Japan (59th overall). Those three strokes gave her that margin of victory over Yuka Saso, the 19-year-old Filipino-Japanese money list leader with two earlier-season wins, who closed with a nine-birdie 63.

Shin went in front on the second day on the Minori course of the Taiheiyo Club after sitting just a shot behind the 65s of first-round leaders Saiki Fujita and Seon Woo Bae. With a 65 of her own to go 13 under on Saturday, Shin moved a stroke in front of Ayako Kimura (68-64) as Fujita and Bae mustered only 70s.

Clad in black attire on Sunday — a Korean tradition — in memory of her mother on the 17th anniversary of her death in a traffic accident, Shin arrived at the 17th tee three under par for the day. Looking at the scoreboard, the Korean said, "I saw Saso catch a birdie at 18 and line up with me" at 16 under par. Shin promptly reached the green in two on the par-five hole, ran in the 18-foot eagle putt, scored her 17th birdie putt of the week on the 18th for a 66 and a 19-under-par total of 197, and won by three strokes.

Because of the pandemic, the tournament, normally co-sponsored with the US LPGA Tour, was without any of its overseas players.

Taiheiyo Club (Minori), Ibaraki — November 6-8
Par 72 (36-36); 6,554 yards — Purse: ¥160,000,000

1	**Jiyai Shin**	66	65	66	197	¥24,000,000
2	**Yuka Saso**	70	67	63	200	14,637,920
3	**Mi-Jeong Jeon**	69	68	65	202	8,481,066
	Maiko Wakabayashi	67	69	66	202	8,481,066
	Nasa Hataoka	69	67	66	202	8,481,066
6	Ai Suzuki	68	70	65	203	4,634,666
	Min Young Lee[2]	67	66	70	203	4,634,666
	Ayako Kimura	68	64	71	203	4,634,666
9	Yuna Nishimura	69	67	68	204	3,272,000
	Saiki Fujita	65	70	69	204	3,272,000
	Seon Woo Bae	65	70	69	204	3,272,000
12	Nozomi Uetake	67	70	68	205	2,716,800
	Mone Inami	69	68	68	205	2,716,800
14	Momoko Osato	66	73	68	207	2,267,600
	Yuka Yasuda	72	67	68	207	2,267,600
	Rumi Yoshiba	69	67	71	207	2,267,600
	Mao Saigo	68	67	72	207	2,267,600
18	Chie Arimura	72	69	67	208	1,846,400
	Erika Hara	68	72	68	208	1,846,400
	Mao Nozawa	69	71	68	208	1,846,400
	Hikari Tanabe	69	69	70	208	1,846,400
	Sakura Koiwai	70	68	70	208	1,846,400
23	Mizuki Ooide	71	70	68	209	1,475,885
	Lala Anai	70	70	69	209	1,475,885
	Eri Okayama	70	70	69	209	1,475,885
	Saki Asai	71	69	69	209	1,475,885
	Reika Usui	67	72	70	209	1,475,885
	Au-Reum Hwang	72	67	70	209	1,475,885
	Mami Fukuda	68	70	71	209	1,475,885
30	Miyu Shinkai	72	70	68	210	1,161,600
	Hinako Shibuno	71	69	70	210	1,161,600
	Sayaka Takahashi	68	74	68	210	1,161,600
	Saki Nagamine	72	71	67	210	1,161,600
	Yuting Seki	69	69	72	210	1,161,600

Itoen Ladies

Ayaka Furue had good reason to remark that she "never hated playoffs" after scoring her second victory of the season in the Itoen Ladies tournament. Both wins for the 20-year-old standout required extra effort, this time three holes to defeat the experienced Miki Sakai. Her Descente Tokai Classic triumph in September ended on the first overtime hole.

With the victory, Furue, who also posted two seconds among her nine top-20 finishes in her first full pro season, joined veteran Jiyai Shin and 19-year-old Yuka Saso as the only double winners of the truncated season. It moved her into position to be one of the serious challengers to front-running Saso for the season's money title, prompting her to say: "I want to be the prize queen someday."

Furue carried a share of the lead into the final round at the Great Island Club in Chonan, Chiba Prefecture, having followed her opening 69 with a seven-birdie 65 to match Hikaru Yoshimoto (68-66) on 10 under par. Ha Neul Kim, the first-round leader, dropped two back. Sakai, 29, whose only two tour victories came in 2014, was three behind in a tie for sixth place. On Sunday, Miki shot the day's best round — 67 — and had a two-stroke lead through 13 holes before Furue birdied the 14th and 16th holes to overhaul her and finish with 70 for her equaling 12-under-par total of 204.

After both players halved the first two playoff holes, Furue hit the flagstick with her approach from 161 yards on the third and tapped in for the win, her third to go with the Descente and the 2019 Fujitsu Ladies while still an amateur.

Great Island Club, Chonan, Chiba — November 13-15
Par 72 (36-36); 6,741 yards — Purse: ¥100,000,000

1	**Ayaka Furue**	69	65	70	204	¥18,000,000
2	**Miki Sakai**	69	68	67	204	8,800,000
	Furue won playoff at third extra hole					
3	**Seon Woo Bae**	69	69	68	206	6,000,000
	Chae-Young Yoon	68	68	70	206	6,000,000
	Bo Mee Lee	71	65	70	206	6,000,000
6	Nana Suganuma	68	69	70	207	3,750,000
	Ha Neul Kim	65	71	71	207	3,750,000
8	Mami Fukuda	70	69	69	208	2,750,000
	Hikaru Yoshimoto	68	66	74	208	2,750,000
10	Haruka Kudo	70	70	69	209	1,925,000
	Mika Miyazato	67	70	72	209	1,925,000
12	Min Young Lee[2]	68	72	70	210	1,550,000
	Ai Suzuki	70	70	70	210	1,550,000
	Eri Okayama	71	69	70	210	1,550,000
	Mamiko Higa	69	70	71	210	1,550,000
	Saki Nagamine	71	68	71	210	1,550,000
17	Minami Katsu	70	70	71	211	1,040,000
	Mone Inami	71	69	71	211	1,040,000
	Yoko Maeda	68	71	72	211	1,040,000

	Na-Ri Lee	68	71	72	211	1,040,000
	Megumi Kido	70	69	72	211	1,040,000
	Shiho Oyama	69	69	73	211	1,040,000
23	Mi-Jeong Jeon	71	70	71	212	820,000
	Teresa Lu	70	71	71	212	820,000
	Erika Kikuchi	70	71	71	212	820,000
	Seira Oki	71	71	70	212	820,000
	Chie Arimura	69	71	72	212	820,000
	Hinako Shibuno	70	73	69	212	820,000
	Yuri Yoshida	74	69	69	212	820,000
	Nana Yamashiro	76	63	73	212	820,000

Daio Paper Elleair Ladies Open

The remarkable dominance of young players on the Japan LPGA Tour was further emphasised when 20-year-old Ayaka Furue won for the third time in 2020 with a smooth victory in the Daio Paper Elleair Ladies Open in the shortened season's next-to-last tournament.

With that, she and Yuka Saso, the 19-year-old Filipino-Japanese who won back-to-back, early-season events, had bagged five of the 13 events and four of the other 2020 winners were 22 or younger.

As things turned out, the battle for the Daio Paper Elleair title came down primarily to those two young players. Both opened with six-under-par 65s at Elleair Golf Club at Matsuyama, Ehime Prefecture, Furue coming off her Sunday victory in the Itoen Ladies. They shared the lead with 20-year-old Yuna Nishimura, winner of the Mitsubishi three weeks earlier.

Furue (71) slipped a stroke behind Saso and Nishimura (70s) on Friday, then surged two shots in front of Saso (67) on Saturday with a flawless, seven-birdie 64 to be 13 under par. A three-putt on the first hole on Sunday started Saso on her way to a 73 as Furue built a six-stroke lead with four birdies and a bogey in the first 10 holes. That gave her all the cushion she needed as she coasted home with seven pars and a closing bogey for a 69, a 15-under-par total of 269 and a three-stroke victory. Reputed veteran Min Young Lee[2] finished with a 66 to snag second place, three shots ahead of Saso and Erika Kikuchi.

"The third win was really strong," Ayaka summarised. "I was conscious of winning."

Elleair Golf Club, Matsuyama, Ehime — November 19-22
Par 71 (35-36); 6,545 yards — Purse: ¥100,000,000

1	**Ayaka Furue**	65	71	64	69	269	¥18,000,000
2	**Min Young Lee[2]**	68	71	67	66	272	8,800,000
3	**Erika Kikuchi**	68	72	65	70	275	6,500,000
	Yuka Saso	65	70	67	73	275	6,500,000
5	Hinako Shibuno	68	73	69	66	276	5,000,000
6	Sakura Koiwai	70	68	71	69	278	2,811,666
	Maiko Wakabayashi	71	70	67	70	278	2,811,666
	Minami Katsu	68	68	71	71	278	2,811,666
	Momoko Ueda	73	68	66	71	278	2,811,666
	Kana Nagai	73	66	67	72	278	2,811,666
	Ayaka Watanabe	71	68	67	72	278	2,811,666
12	Sayaka Takahashi	74	68	70	67	279	1,670,000
	Miyuki Takeuchi	72	69	70	68	279	1,670,000
	Ji-Hee Lee	68	71	69	71	279	1,670,000
15	Ai Suzuki	71	72	69	68	280	1,320,000
	Rumi Yoshiba	71	70	70	69	280	1,320,000
	Bo Mee Lee	68	73	70	69	280	1,320,000
	Yuna Nishimura	65	70	71	74	280	1,320,000
19	Sumika Nakasone	72	70	71	68	281	980,000
	Yuri Yoshida	71	69	74	67	281	980,000
	Kana Mikashima	70	71	71	69	281	980,000
	Momoko Osato	72	72	67	70	281	980,000
23	Megumi Kido	72	70	72	68	282	870,000
	Shiho Oyama	72	69	73	68	282	870,000
	Na-Ri Lee	69	69	72	72	282	870,000
	Teresa Lu	73	70	67	72	282	870,000
	Seon Woo Bae	71	67	71	73	282	870,000
28	Yui Kawamoto	74	69	70	70	283	770,000
	Maria Shinohara	69	71	72	71	283	770,000
	Anna Kono	68	73	70	72	283	770,000
	Mika Miyazato	74	70	73	66	283	770,000
	Kokone Yoshimoto	70	72	69	72	283	770,000

JLPGA Tour Championship Ricoh Cup

It seemed appropriate that a young player such as Erika Hara would win the final tournament of the Japan LPGA season. The 22-year-old Hara, a member of the sizeable Golden Generation of young Japanese female stars on the tour, never trailed as she added the JLPGA Tour Championship to the Japan Women's Open Championship she won in October and rose to third place on the final money list behind 19-year-old Yuka Saso and 20-year-old Ayaka Furue.

Both of them were among Hara's closest pursuers throughout a hard-playing weekend at Miyazaki Country Club, as Furue, who made a remarkable four eagles in her unsuccessful bid for a third straight and fourth victory of the season, closed fast but fell two strokes short in second place. Saso's bid died with a last-round 75, but she wrapped up the money title with ¥93,891,170, ¥3 million ahead of Furue.

"I think I've taken a big first step in my golf life," observed Hara after winning the Tour Championship and Ricoh Cup. She pointed out that "I didn't have a track record in my amateur days".

Her "first big step" at Miyazaki came Thursday when she eagled the second hole on her way to a 67 and a lead she never relinquished. She shot 68 on Friday to move two strokes in front of Furue (66 with two of the eagles), recent winner Yuna Nishimura (also 66) and Hinako Shibuno (69), making only her sixth start in Japan around playing on the US LPGA Tour.

On a Saturday when Saso, with 69, was the only player to break 70, Hara's 71, for 10 under par, kept her a shot ahead of Nishimura, three in front of Saso and six ahead of Furue, who mounted the biggest challenge on Sunday. Aided by her fourth eagle, she was five under par before two late bogeys killed her bid. Hara also bogeyed twice in the stretch after getting a big break when an errant tee shot on the 13th hole that bounced out of the woods into play turned into a birdie. She shot a 72 for a 10-under-par total of 278 and won the third title of her two-year pro career, finishing two strokes ahead of Furue, who closed with 68.

Miyazaki Country Club, Miyazaki — November 26-29
Par 72 (36-36); 6,543 yards — Purse: ¥120,000,000

1	**Erika Hara**	67	68	71	72	278	¥30,000,000
2	**Ayaka Furue**	71	66	75	68	280	17,400,000
3	**Hinako Shibuno**	68	69	74	71	282	9,548,000
	Momoko Ueda	69	69	70	74	282	9,548,000
	Yuna Nishimura	71	66	70	75	282	9,548,000
6	Kana Mikashima	69	69	73	73	284	4,638,000
	Mamiko Higa	71	69	71	73	284	4,638,000
	Minami Hiruta	69	71	70	74	284	4,638,000
	Yuka Saso	70	70	69	75	284	4,638,000
10	Ayaka Watanabe	70	74	71	71	286	1,413,600
	Seon Woo Bae	69	73	72	72	286	1,413,600
	Mi-Jeong Jeon	71	69	73	73	286	1,413,600
	Ai Suzuki	69	71	72	74	286	1,413,600
	Ji-Hee Lee	69	69	73	75	286	1,413,600
15	Mone Inami	71	71	72	74	288	792,000
16	Min Young Lee[2]	74	73	74	68	289	684,000
17	Jiyai Shin	72	67	75	76	290	642,000
	Sakura Koiwai	69	70	75	76	290	642,000
19	Ayako Kimura	70	72	77	72	291	612,000
20	Mao Nozawa	74	76	71	71	292	588,000
	Erika Kikuchi	75	70	74	73	292	588,000
	Yui Kawamoto	70	77	72	73	292	588,000
23	Sumika Nakasone	76	71	73	73	293	558,000
	Chie Arimura	71	75	72	75	293	558,000
25	Na-Ri Lee	73	75	74	72	294	522,000
	Hikari Tanabe	73	76	71	74	294	522,000
	Shina Kanazawa	71	73	75	75	294	522,000
	Mayu Hamada	70	70	74	80	294	522,000
29	Saki Asai	75	69	81	70	295	492,000
30	Miki Sakai	73	74	74	76	297	474,000
	Saki Nagamine	72	73	75	77	297	474,000

2020 MONEY LIST

1	Yuka Saso	¥93,891,170
2	Ayaka Furue	90,502,992
3	Erika Hara	70,722,208
4	Sakura Koiwai	62,886,208
5	Ayaka Watanabe	60,259,965
6	Saki Nagamine	49,871,162
7	Yuna Nishimura	47,964,000
8	Jiyai Shin	47,553,250
9	Ai Suzuki	36,777,182
10	Seon Woo Bae	32,369,350

Korea LPGA Tour

Jin Young Ko spent most of the year at home in Korea and ended it intending to buy a house in Texas to use as a base when her campaign in America resumes in full. She remained the number one on the Rolex Rankings throughout but only just ahead of Sei Young Kim thanks to a head-to-head victory at the CME Group Tour Championship in December.

Ko only went to America at the end of the year but it was worth it. She was second at the US Women's Open and then claimed her only win of the year. She began 2020 nursing an ankle injury back to full fitness and by the time she intended to head to the States in March the world's tours were grinding to a halt.

That included the KLPGA. After one tournament at the end of 2019, the season could not resume as planned and instead got underway with the KLPGA Championship in May, a full month before the PGA Tour returned in June. Broadcasters around the world were grateful to show some live sport as Hyun Kyung Park claimed her maiden win and got a hug from her caddie only because he was her father. Fellow players feted Park with flower petals thrown from the requisite two metres.

Social distancing was mandatory, masks had to be worn by players before and after rounds and by caddies throughout. There were frequent thermal screenings and extensive sanitisation. There was no crowd, of course, and media were restricted to the first and 10th tees.

"I was surprised to see so many cameras at the first tee, feeling as if I was seeing a gallery," said Sung Hyun Park, one of those players who remained at home when they would usually be playing in America. "From the second tee, it became all quiet and you could hear every little sound. It felt a little boring, yet refreshing." Park fell from second to 10th on the world rankings during a lacklustre year so maybe she was one of the players affected by the lack of atmosphere.

Although there were further cancellations and gaps on the schedule, the high level of competition on offer no doubt benefitted those players who played internationally later in the year. Ko did not play until the third tournament back and finished in the top 10 in four of her six events, a second place at the KB Financial Group Star Championship being her best. She missed three of the four LPGA major championships but made up for lost time at the end of the year.

"I don't regret not playing at majors so far this year," Ko said at the KB Star event. "I am not getting caught up in results this year. Winning tournaments and being world number one is important, but what I am doing now is investing for the future. To make sure I will stay competitive for a long time, I am working on my body and my swing."

Concentrating on practising and exercising allowed Ko to stay close to home. "Given that health and safety are the most important things, this was an unavoidable choice," she said. "My parents were worried that something might happen to me, and I am their only daughter. I couldn't just leave them behind."

Even without Ko adding to her two majors from 2019, it was another extraordinary year for Korean players at the game's biggest tournaments. There is none bigger than the US Women's Open, where A Lim Kim birdied the last three holes to claim a stunning upset at Champions in Houston. The KLPGA's longest hitter only found form at the end of the domestic season, finishing in the top 10 at the last four tournaments before winning on her first ever international major appearance.

A Lim was ranked 94th in the world at the time, as was Mirim Lee when she chipped in three times before winning the ANA Inspiration in a playoff against Brooke Henderson and Nelly Korda. And Sei Young Kim finally broke through at the highest level with a dominating performance at the KPMG Women's PGA Championship, a final round of 63 at Aronimink seeing Kim finish five ahead of Inbee Park.

Sei Young might not have dethroned Ko at the top of the Rolex Rankings, but she did earn Player of the Year honours on the LPGA where she also won the Pelican Women's Championship. Her season was set up, however, by some strong outings at home. She finished in the top six in three of her four events. The nearest she came to winning was losing a playoff at the Lotte Cantata Open to Hyo Joo Kim.

Hyo Joo, the 2014 Evian champion, enjoyed playing on the KLPGA so much she stayed for the entire season, topping both the money list and, one of her main goals, the stroke average table on 69.57.

As well as the playoff win over Sei Young, she also claimed the last domestic major of the year, the KB Star Championship, by a hefty eight strokes from Ko. Her last wins before this year came in 2016.

Hyo Joo Kim finished runner-up at the Kia Motors Korea Women's Open, just pipped to the coveted title by So Yeon Ryu. The former US Open champion had waited over a decade to win her national championship and on doing so she donated the first prize of ₩250 million, just over $200,000, to Covid-19 relief funds.

"Since this tournament has a lot of meaning to me," Ryu said, "I thought that I may be able to play better if I had a positive goal." Back in February, after finishing runner-up at the Vic Open, Ryu had also donated part of her prize money to bushfire relief in Australia.

On returning to competition in America at the end of the year, Ryu revealed of her Korea Open victory: "I almost like felt satisfied with my 2020 season after I won the tournament."

Having not played regularly at home since the start of her career, Ryu added: "That was so weird playing the KLPGA Tour, because people literally were seeing me and going to judge which tour is better. So when I play really bad, people started to say, 'Oh, maybe KLPGA Tour is tougher to compete in.'

"I almost feel like I should play well to represent the LPGA Tour well. So that was one of the biggest challenges for me when I played an KLPGA event."

The issue was played out for real on the course at the unofficial annual team event matching those Koreans based on the LPGA and the Japan LPGA against the youngsters on the domestic KLPGA Tour. For the second year running, the KLPGA took the honours at the Orange Life Champions Trophy.

Jeongeun Lee[6] had dominated the KLPGA before heading to America in 2019 and becoming the US Open champion and the LPGA Rookie of the Year. In 2020 she played extensively back on the KLPGA and contended often but without winning, although she did have back-to-back runner-up finishes.

As well as Hyo Joo Kim, Hyun Kyung Park won twice, her second title coming at the IS Dongseo Busan Open after a five-hole playoff against Hee Jeong Lim when the final round was washed out. And Na Rin An followed her maiden victory at the Autech Championship, when a 10-shot lead with a round to play was whittled down to two before she birdied the final two holes, with a win at the Hana Financial Group Championship to claim the biggest first prize of the season of ₩300 million. Lim was a regular contender at the top of the leaderboard but could not add to her three wins as a rookie in 2019.

Rookie of the Year for 2020 was Hae Ran Ryu, who successfully defended her title at the Jeju Samdasoo Masters. When she won the event in 2019 she was a member of a lower tier circuit and the victory granted her membership of the main tour for 2020. The 19-year-old was a presence all season and finished second on the money list, just ahead of Ha Na Jang, who won for the ninth year running on either the KLPGA or LPGA circuits. Jang finished in the top three at each of the last three events of the season.

The undisputed star of the 2019 season, Hye Jin Choi, had to wait until the final tournament of the year, the SK Telecom ADT CAPS Championship, to gain her first win of 2020. A year earlier she had won five times but she still had a remarkable 2020, finishing in the top 10 in 14 of her 16 completed tournaments. That meant she again topped the Player of the Year points list, an award she had secured the week before she won the final event.

2020 SCHEDULE

Lotte Rent a Car Ladies Open		*cancelled*
Nexen Saint Nine Masters		*cancelled*
Kyochon Honey Ladies Open		*cancelled*
NH Investment and Securities Championship		*cancelled*
Doosan Match Play Championship		*cancelled*
KLPGA Championship	**Hyun Kyung Park**	
E1 Charity Open	**So Young Lee**	
Lotte Cantata Ladies Open	**Hyo Joo Kim**	
S-Oil Championship		*abandoned*

Kia Motors Korea Women's Open	**So Yeon Ryu**	
BC Card Hankyung Ladies Cup	**Ji Yeong Kim**[2]	
McCol Yongpyong Resort Open	**Min Sun Kim**[5]	
Asiana Airlines Open		*cancelled*
MY Munyoung Queens Park Championship		*cancelled*
IS Dongseo Busan Open	**Hyun Kyung Park**	
Jeju Samdasoo Masters	**Hae Ran Ryu**	
Orange Life Champions Trophy*	**KLPGA**	
Dayouwinia MBN Ladies Open	**Min Ji Park**	
HighOne Resort Ladies Open		*cancelled*
Hanwha Classic		*cancelled*
KG Edaily Ladies Open		*cancelled*
All for You Renoma Championship		*cancelled*
OKSavingsBank Se Ri Pak Invitational		*cancelled*
Fantom Classic	**Song Yi Ahn**	
Autech Carrier Championship	**Na Rin An**	
Hite Jinro Championship		*cancelled*
KB Financial Group Star Championship	**Hyo Joo Kim**	
Huencare Ladies Open	**So Mi Lee**	
BMW Ladies Championship		*cancelled*
SK Networks Seokyung Ladies Classic	**Ha Na Jang**	
Hana Financial Group Championship	**Na Rin An**	
SK Telecom ADT CAPS Championship	**Hye Jin Choi**	

**non-tour event*

KLPGA Championship

When Hyun Kyung Park won her maiden title she was allowed to hug her caddie since he was her father. Otherwise social distancing and plenty of other Covid protocols, including the absence of spectators, were in place as professional golf returned with the KLPGA Championship at Lakewood, just north of Seoul.

Having delayed the start of their season, the Korean circuit was able to get going in May, ahead of most other tours around the world, and did so with one of their major events.

With the country's stars not away playing overseas, the field included world number three Sung Hyun Park, who missed the cut, while Sei Young Kim was 46th and US Women's Open champion Jeongeun Lee[6] tied for 15th. Instead, it was another of the young talents on the home tour, ranked 92nd in the world, who triumphed.

Seon Woo Bae led for the first two days with rounds of 67 and 65 but a 72 in the third round let Hee Jeong Lim head to the top of the leaderboard with a 64, in which she birdied five of the first seven holes. Hyun Kyung Park improved steadily all week with rounds of 69, 68 and then two 67s. After three early birdies on Sunday, followed by her only dropped shot of the day at the ninth, Park took control of the tournament with three birdies in a row from the 11th. She parred in to finish on 17 under par with a total of 271 to complete a one-stroke victory.

Bae, 68, birdied two of the last three holes to share second place with Lim, who scored 71. So Young Lee had a 65 to tie for fourth with Hyo Joo Kim, who closed with a 64.

As rookie in 2019, the 20-year-old Park finished 23rd on the money list but could not quite close out a first title. "I was so disappointed not to have been part of that winners' group last year," she said. "I am so happy that I got the first win out of the way in the first tournament of the year." In a new style of celebration appropriate for the pandemic, fellow competitors threw flower petals at Park and her father as they left the 18th green.

Lakewood Country Club, Yangju, Gyeonggi — May 14-17
Par 72 (36-36); 6,540 yards — Purse: ₩3,000,000,000

1	**Hyun Kyung Park**	69	68	67	67	271	₩220,000,000
2	**Seon Woo Bae**	67	65	72	68	272	108,042,207
	Hee Jeong Lim	72	65	64	71	272	108,042,207
4	So Young Lee	71	71	67	65	274	64,542,207
	Hyo Joo Kim	72	68	70	64	274	64,542,207
6	Ji Su Kim	70	71	68	66	275	48,042,207
7	Da Been Heo	70	66	73	68	277	39,042,207
	Mi Jeong Gong	70	70	67	70	277	39,042,207
9	Ree An Kim	73	69	67	69	278	29,422,207
	Ji Sun Kang	73	68	70	67	278	29,422,207
	Chae Yoon Park	73	68	68	69	278	29,422,207
	Ye Sung Jun	72	69	71	66	278	29,422,207
	Hye Jin Choi	69	73	67	69	278	29,422,207
	Ye Jin Kim	71	71	69	67	278	29,422,207
15	Jeongeun Lee[6]	73	70	72	64	279	27,642,207
	Bo Mi Kwak	71	73	69	66	279	27,642,207
	Ji Hyun Oh	73	68	67	71	279	27,642,207
	Se Lin Hyun	67	70	68	74	279	27,642,207
19	Min Ji Park	72	70	69	69	280	26,742,207
	Ha Na Jang	72	72	68	68	280	26,742,207
	Ga Young Lee	75	68	67	70	280	26,742,207
	Hyo Rin Lee	69	72	69	70	280	26,742,207
	Ga Eun Song	69	70	70	71	280	26,742,207
	A Yean Cho	68	72	69	71	280	26,742,207
25	Seul Gi Jeong	73	69	69	70	281	25,842,207
	U Ree Jun	71	69	70	71	281	25,842,207
	Ran Hong	69	71	70	71	281	25,842,207
	Char Young Kim[2]	67	69	74	71	281	25,842,207
29	Hyeon Ji Kim[3]	72	71	70	69	282	25,212,207
	Yeon Ju Jung	69	73	70	70	282	25,212,207
	Hyeon Ji Ryu	72	71	68	71	282	25,212,207

E1 Charity Open

Returning to the scene of her last victory at South Springs in Icheon helped So Young Lee end her two-year winless streak. Lee won three times in 2018, including the All For You Championship at South Springs, but was a runner-up three times in 2019. In the E1 Charity Open, Lee went wire-to-wire to win by two strokes from rookie Hae Ran Ryu for her fifth title in all.

"I feel great to play well to pick up another win at South Springs," Lee said, "and it feels great to win early in the season. I hope I could win one or two more victories if I could play despite the Covid-19 situation."

Taking advantage of fine weather at the start of the second tournament after the KLPGA got underway in 2020, Lee opened with a 65. The 22-year-old posted another seven birdies on Friday although two bogeys added up to a 67. They turned out to be the only dropped shots of her week. Although there were only five more birdies over the weekend, the key to her win was not making any more bogeys.

"It was frustrating because I made a lot of pars from the third round, but I was able to win by not losing my confidence," said Lee.

After a 70 on Saturday, the pack were close enough to challenge on the final day so a par save from 10 feet at the eighth was an example of how Lee kept her nerve. She had birdied the seventh and then two-putted the 13th for a three at the drivable par four to stay one ahead despite Ryu holing out from a greenside bunker for an eagle at the same hole. A wedge from Lee to a foot at the 16th took her two ahead as Ryu missed from six feet. Lee's 69 gave her a 17-under-par total of 271, with Ryu closing with a 69 to finish three ahead of So Yi Kim and Hee Jeong Lim.

South Springs Country Club, Icheon, Gyeonggi — May 28-31
Par 72 (36-36); 6,501 yards — Purse: ₩800,000,000

1	**So Young Lee**	65	67	70	69	271	₩160,000,000
2	**Hae Ran Ryu**	67	67	70	69	273	92,000,000
3	**So Yi Kim**	70	69	68	69	276	52,000,000
	Hee Jeong Lim	68	68	69	71	276	52,000,000
5	Ye Rim Choi	70	67	66	74	277	32,000,000
6	Eun Bin Lim	71	68	70	69	278	22,000,000
	Min Ji Park	71	68	70	69	278	22,000,000
	Na Rin An	71	68	68	71	278	22,000,000
	Hye Lim Jo	71	68	67	72	278	22,000,000
10	Hye Jin Choi	69	71	70	69	279	10,580,000
	Ha Na Jang	68	70	69	72	279	10,580,000
	Eun Soo Jang	67	68	73	71	279	10,580,000
	Min Kyung Choi	67	70	71	71	279	10,580,000
14	Shin Sil Bang[A]	71	68	73	68	280	
	Bo Ah Kim	71	70	71	68	280	8,320,000
	Jung Min Lee	70	73	68	69	280	8,320,000
	Ye Sung Jun	72	69	69	70	280	8,320,000
	Eun Woo Choi	68	69	72	71	280	8,320,000
	Da Yeon Lee	74	66	71	69	280	8,320,000
	Seon Woo Bae	74	69	69	68	280	8,320,000
21	Seung Yeon Lee	72	69	70	70	281	7,080,000
	Min Song Ha	67	73	72	69	281	7,080,000
	Su Bin Park	71	69	69	72	281	7,080,000
	Jeongeun Lee[6]	67	71	67	76	281	7,080,000
25	Ji Hyun Lee[2]	69	71	69	73	282	6,520,000
	Da Won Kweon	71	71	68	72	282	6,520,000

27	Ju Yeon In	70 68 74 71	283	6,053,333	Ye Nah Hwang	69 73 72 69	283	6,053,333
	Gi Ppuem Lee	69 67 75 72	283	6,053,333	Yun Ji Jeong	72 69 70 72	283	6,053,333
	Yoon Kyung Heo	73 69 69 72	283	6,053,333	Hyun Soo Kim	71 69 73 70	283	6,053,333

Lotte Cantata Ladies Open

On the week that she was due to defend her title at the US Women's Open before it was postponed until December, Jeongeun Lee[6] finished tied for eighth at the Lotte Cantata Ladies Open. That left her five strokes outside a playoff that featured two other LPGA stars in Hyo Joo Kim, winner of the 2014 Evian Championship, and Sei Young Kim, a 10-time winner on the US circuit.

At the first extra hole, the par-five 18th, Hyo Joo pitched to nine feet, while Sei Young, who had found the green in two, putted up to four feet. In a dramatic conclusion, Hyo Joo made her birdie putt while her opponent missed.

Hyo Joo Kim's first win on the KLPGA came as an amateur on the same course at Sky Hill on Jeju Island in 2012. This was her 11th win on the circuit to go with her three LPGA victories but she had not won on either tour since 2016. "It's been a long time since my last win," she said. "Last night my father told me that if I shot five under par, I'd go to a playoff and if I hit six under par I would win. And it became true. It made me shudder throughout the playoff but I'm very happy to win."

Both Kims started three strokes behind a trio of leaders on Sunday but scored 67s to tie on 18 under par. Hyo Joo, who had earlier scores of 66, 68 and 69, reckoned she had added around 40 yards of distance thanks to a new exercise and diet regime over the extended winter break. She bogeyed the opening hole but then matched her namesake birdie for birdie until a two-shot swing went in her favour at the short 14th.

Sei Young got back on level terms with a birdie at the 15th and the pair birdied the last to edge one ahead of Ji Hyun Oh. While Oh closed with a 70, her overnight co-leaders Jin Seon Han and Ran Hong, posted rounds of 73 and 74 respectively. In her first tournament of the year, world number one Jin Young Ko finished tied for 45th.

Lotte Sky Hill Jeju Country Club, Jeju Island — June 4-7
Par 72 (36-36); 6,373 yards — Purse: ₩800,000,000

1	**Hyo Joo Kim**	66 68 69 67	270	₩160,000,000		Hyun Kyung Park	68 69 70 70	277	8,940,000
2	**Sei Young Kim**	70 62 71 67	270	92,000,000	17	So Yi Kim	76 62 71 69	278	7,760,000
	Hyo Joo Kim won playoff at first extra hole					Ji Yeong Kim[2]	69 70 71 68	278	7,760,000
3	**Ji Hyun Oh**	65 66 70 70	271	64,000,000		Seul Ki Lee	65 69 75 69	278	7,760,000
4	Jin Seon Han	63 67 70 73	273	40,000,000		Eun-Hee Ji	63 72 70 73	278	7,760,000
5	Jeong Mee Hwang	71 68 67 68	274	28,000,000	21	Se Lin Hyun	65 72 72 70	279	6,800,000
	Min Ji Park	68 70 66 70	274	28,000,000		Ju Yeon In	67 68 72 72	279	6,800,000
	Ran Hong	71 67 62 74	274	28,000,000		Jeong Min Cho	70 66 70 73	279	6,800,000
8	Jeongeun Lee[6]	68 71 69 67	275	16,000,000		Bo Ah Kim	67 71 68 73	279	6,800,000
	So Young Lee	68 68 69 70	275	16,000,000		Han Sol Ji	66 68 73 72	279	6,800,000
	Hye Jin Choi	71 63 70 71	275	16,000,000	26	Su Yeon Jang	68 70 74 68	280	6,160,000
11	Hee Jeong Lim	68 70 67 71	276	10,400,000		Seon Woo Bae	66 69 74 71	280	6,160,000
	Ha Na Jang	67 69 69 71	276	10,400,000		Seo Jin Park	67 71 70 72	280	6,160,000
13	So Mi Lee	66 69 75 67	277	8,940,000		Ina Yoon (A)	67 72 73 68	280	
	Na Rin An	69 69 71 68	277	8,940,000		Yealimi Noh	66 71 71 72	280	6,160,000
	Da Yeon Lee	68 69 71 69	277	8,940,000		Yewon Lee (A)	65 72 70 73	280	

S-Oil Championship

After an opening 64 at Elysian Jeju Country Club, Hye Jin Choi had hopes of defending her title at the S-Oil Championship. Choi, 20, was the player of the year in 2019 with five victories, taking her tally in a brief career to nine. But she was hoping to do something she had not previously achieved. "I'd really love to defend my title for once," Choi said. "I claimed two out of five wins on Jeju Island last year. The country club here suits my game."

Choi had nine birdies and a bogey playing alongside the playoff contenders from the previous week, Hyo Joo Kim and Sei Young Kim, who had rounds of 69 and 68 respectively.

But Choi's hopes were dashed as heavy rain and wind over the weekend meant that not even a second round could be completed. The tournament was abandoned, the reduced payout was unofficial and Choi had to wait to get back into the winner's circle.

Elysian Jeju Country Club, Jeju Island — June 12-14
Par 72 (36-36); 6,489 yards — Purse ₩700,000,000

1	Hye Jin Choi	64	₩94,500,000	10	Jin Joo Hong	67	6,305,833
2	U Ree Jun	65	36,750,000		Hyo Rin Lee	67	6,305,833
	So Mi Lee	65	36,750,000		Ga Young Lee	67	6,305,833
	Yeon Ju Jung	65	36,750,000		Ji Su Kim	67	6,305,833
	Je Yeong Lee	65	36,750,000		Chae Yoon Park	67	6,305,833
6	Bo Ah Kim	66	14,437,500		Seung Yeon Lee	67	6,305,833
	Ha Na Jang	66	14,437,500		Min Song Ha	67	6,305,833
	Gyeol Park	66	14,437,500		Na Rin An	67	6,305,833
	Gi Ppuem Lee	66	14,437,500		Hae Ran Ryu	67	6,305,833

Kia Motors Korea Women's Open

As if So Yeon Ryu needed any more motivation to win her national championship for the first time, she decided to donate the first prize of ₩250 million, a little more than $200,000, to Covid-19 relief funds in her country.

"I thought of donating since last night," Ryu said. "Since this tournament has a lot of meaning to me and I thought that I may be able to play better if I had a positive goal, I came up with it last night.

"Before the awards ceremony, I called my mom. I told her that I'm going to make the announcement so don't get too surprised. She was just as happy I was. All the competitions KLPGA golfers are currently playing are like a bonus for us. We only have to come and hit the ball, but a lot of people are continuing to struggle. This donation is going towards funding Covid-19 recovery."

A selfless act was rewarded with a one-stroke victory over Hyo Joo Kim at the Kia Motors Korea Women's Open. Ryu, just short of her 30th birthday, had waited more than a decade for a victory in her home Open, although she had collected plenty of national titles having won the US Open in 2011, the Canadian Open in 2014 and the Japan Open in 2018. But it was also a long wait for any win, since the one in Japan was her last anywhere and her last on the KLPGA was in 2015. This was her 10th victory on her home circuit.

Ryu had not played a tournament since the Australian Open in February four months earlier. "It's been a while since I competed in a tournament, so I did want to win," Ryu said. "But rather than being greedy, I just told myself to do my job. I was glad that I didn't lose my focus until the end."

Ryu had five birdies in seven holes in her bogey-free opening round of 66. That put her one behind Jin Young Ko's 65 as the world number one teed up for only the second time all year. Ko faded to finish in sixth place but Ryu had four birdies in a row in round two for a 67 to take the lead at 11 under par. It was more of a battle over the weekend as she added scores of 71 and 72 for a 12-under-par total of 276.

On Sunday at Bear's Best CheongNa Golf Club Ryu had 16 pars, including the entire back nine, and only one birdie and one bogey. Kim, the winner of the Lotte Cantata Open a fortnight earlier, had two early birdies in her 70 to finish two ahead of 2019 number one Hye Jin Choi, who also closed with a 70. Sei Young Kim and Ji Hyun Oh shared fourth place.

Bear's Best CheongNa Golf Club, Incheon, Gyeonggi — June 18-21
Par 72 (36-36); 6,929 yards — Purse: ₩1,000,000,000

1	**So Yeon Ryu**	66	67	71	72	276	₩250,000,000
2	**Hyo Joo Kim**	70	69	68	70	277	100,000,000
3	**Hye Jin Choi**	69	69	71	70	279	75,000,000
4	Ji Hyun Oh	68	66	71	75	280	40,000,000
	Sei Young Kim	68	69	73	70	280	40,000,000
6	Jin Young Ko	65	72	73	72	282	30,000,000
7	Hae Rym Kim	70	67	73	73	283	22,500,000
	A Yean Cho	70	73	69	71	283	22,500,000
9	Min Ji Park	73	71	72	68	284	14,164,000
	Hae Ran Ryu	73	69	70	72	284	14,164,000
	Han Sol Ji	70	71	72	71	284	14,164,000
	Jeongeun Lee[6]	71	69	73	71	284	14,164,000
	Ji Young Park	69	71	72	72	284	14,164,000
14	Eun Hye Jo	72	73	71	70	286	10,840,000
	Gi Ppuem Lee	70	73	71	72	286	10,840,000
	Seon Woo Bae	70	72	74	70	286	10,840,000
	Eun Soo Jang	69	74	73	70	286	10,840,000
	Min Young Lee[2]	66	75	71	74	286	10,840,000
	Yeun Jung Seo	73	65	74	74	286	10,840,000
20	Woo Jeong Kim	71	74	74	68	287	8,508,888
	Jeong Hwa Lee[2]	70	70	74	73	287	8,508,888
	Jin Seon Han	70	71	72	74	287	8,508,888
	Yu Jin Sung	67	74	72	74	287	8,508,888
	Yun Ji Jeong	73	71	69	74	287	8,508,888
	Ji Hyun Lee[2]	70	74	71	72	287	8,508,888
	U Ree Jun	71	70	73	73	287	8,508,888
	Hee Jeong Lim	68	72	72	75	287	8,508,888
	Na Rin An	71	69	74	73	287	8,508,888
29	Ye Jin Kim	72	72	74	70	288	7,160,000
	Eun-Hee Ji	71	72	73	72	288	7,160,000
	Song Yi Ahn	70	69	75	74	288	7,160,000
	Chae Yoon Park	72	71	66	79	288	7,160,000

BC Card Hankyung Ladies Cup

Having recorded seven runner-up finishes since her only win on the KLPGA Tour in 2017, Ji Yeong Kim[2] claimed her second title at the BC Card Hankyung Ladies Cup. Kim birdied the second extra hole of a playoff to defeat Min Ji Park after the pair both had a par on the first extra hole at Fortune Hills.

Kim, 24, was one of the first round leaders after an opening 65 but So Mi Lee took over at the top of the leaderboard for rounds two and three as she posted 68-66-67. Kim had a 71 on day two but rebounded with a pair of 67s to finish on 18 under par with a total of 270. She had four birdies in a row from the second and, following her only bogey of the day at the 12th, birdied the next two before parring home to force the playoff. Park scored 69-68-67-66, her seventh birdie of the final round coming at the 18th to set the clubhouse target.

Lee slowed down on the final day for a 71 to finish in a tie for third place, two strokes outside the playoff. She needed a birdie at the last to continue to extra holes herself but bogeyed instead to join Na Rin An (69) and Han Sol Ji (66) on 16 under par. Hyo Joo Kim, a week after finishing runner-up at the Korea Women's Open, shared the first-round lead and was only three strokes behind when she was forced to withdraw after the third round.

Practice rounds on the day before the tournament started were cancelled after it emerged that an amateur who had played at Fortune Hills the previous Friday had tested positive for Covid-19 and a club caddie had been a close contact. After extensive sanitisation the event began as scheduled on the Thursday.

Fortune Hills Country Club, Pocheon, Gyeonggi — June 25-28
Par 72 (36-36); 6,605 yards — Purse: ₩700,000,000

1	**Ji Yeong Kim**[2]	65	71	67	67	270	₩140,000,000
2	**Min Ji Park**	69	68	67	66	270	80,500,000
	Kim won playoff at second extra hole						
3	**Na Rin An**	68	68	67	69	272	39,666,667
	Han Sol Ji	65	70	71	66	272	39,666,667
	So Mi Lee	68	66	67	71	272	39,666,667
6	Ye Rim Choi	71	68	68	66	273	24,500,000
7	So Young Lee	69	67	67	71	274	21,000,000
8	Chae Yoon Park	68	68	70	69	275	17,500,000
9	Mi Jeong Gong	74	67	65	70	276	12,250,000
	Da Yeon Lee	69	69	68	70	276	12,250,000
11	Ji Hyun Kim	67	70	71	69	277	8,627,500
	Yu Jin Sung	70	71	68	68	277	8,627,500
	Seon Woo Bae	71	69	67	70	277	8,627,500
	Ji Hyun Oh	71	68	67	71	277	8,627,500
15	Jung Min Lee	71	71	68	68	278	7,420,000
	Julie Kim	72	69	66	71	278	7,420,000
	Ga Eun Song	68	70	67	73	278	7,420,000
18	So Yi Kim	67	70	72	70	279	6,790,000
	Ji Hyun Lee[2]	68	71	71	69	279	6,790,000
	Gi Ppuem Lee	74	67	69	69	279	6,790,000
21	A Lim Kim	67	70	72	71	280	6,160,000
	Hae Rym Kim	71	71	71	67	280	6,160,000
	So Hyeon Ahn	69	69	72	70	280	6,160,000
	Seung Hui Ro	70	73	66	71	280	6,160,000
	Yeun Jung Seo	69	71	67	73	280	6,160,000
26	Ha Na Jang	72	69	69	71	281	5,600,000
	Su Jin Lee[3]	71	71	67	72	281	5,600,000

Da Been Heo	71	70	67	73	281	5,600,000	Jeong Min Cho	73	70	70	68	281	5,600,000
Yul Lin Hwang	69	73	70	69	281	5,600,000	Min Song Ha	70	70	68	73	281	5,600,000
Su Yeon Jang	69	72	71	69	281	5,600,000							

McCol Yongpyong Resort Open

Twice she three-putted in the last six holes but Min Sun Kim[5] hung on to win the McCol Yongpyong Resort Open at Birch Hill Golf Club in Pyeongchang. The 25-year-old, appropriately, won her fifth title on the KLPGA but first for three years. She won once a year after arriving as a rookie in 2014 but had gone winless in both 2018 and 2019.

After an opening 68, Kim scored 66 in the second round to take the lead and then closed with a 70 for a 12-under-par total of 204. An early bogey-birdie exchange was followed by four birdies in a row from the eighth hole. Thoughts of a straightforward run for home immediately evaporated as Kim missed her par putt at the 12th. She three-putted again for bogey at the 15th but the blow was cushioned by the fact So Young Lee had bogeyed the same hole moments before.

Lee finished with three pars for a 68 to finish one behind in a tie for second place with Yu Jin Sung, who also scored a 68 after a birdie at the 18th hole. Seung Hui Ro, Seul Ki Lee and Se Lin Hyun all shared fourth place, three behind the winner. Ryu, the first-round co-leader on 66, fell from second after 36 holes to seventh with a closing 73.

Birch Hill Golf Club, Yongpyong Resort, Pyeongchang — July 3-5
Par 72 (36-36); 6,434 yards — Purse: ₩600,000,000

1	**Min Sun Kim**[5]	68	66	70	204	₩120,000,000		Ju Yeon In	72	71	69	212	5,497,500
2	**Yu Jin Sung**	70	67	68	205	58,500,000		Yu-Ju Chen	75	66	71	212	5,497,500
	So Young Lee	69	68	68	205	58,500,000		Jeongeun Lee[6]	73	68	71	212	5,497,500
4	Seung Hui Ro	66	71	70	207	25,000,000		Jin Joo Hong	70	69	73	212	5,497,500
	Seul Ki Lee	68	67	72	207	25,000,000		Min Ji Park	67	74	71	212	5,497,500
	Se Lin Hyun	71	65	71	207	25,000,000		Da Been Heo	69	69	74	212	5,497,500
7	Hye Jin Choi	71	66	71	208	16,500,000	25	Woo Jeong Kim	72	71	70	213	4,395,000
	Hae Ran Ryu	66	69	73	208	16,500,000		A Lim Kim	71	72	70	213	4,395,000
9	Han Sol Ji	69	68	72	209	10,500,000		Ha Na Jang	70	73	70	213	4,395,000
	Ye Sung Jun	71	67	71	209	10,500,000		Gyeol Park	69	71	73	213	4,395,000
11	Hae Rym Kim	68	73	69	210	7,395,000		Ji Su Kim	69	68	76	213	4,395,000
	Bo Ah Kim	71	69	70	210	7,395,000		So Mi Lee	69	71	73	213	4,395,000
	Ga Young Lee	71	73	66	210	7,395,000		So Yi Kim	72	71	70	213	4,395,000
	Ji Yeong Kim[2]	70	68	72	210	7,395,000		Hee Jeong Lim	75	68	70	213	4,395,000
15	Min Kyung Choi	70	72	69	211	6,420,000		Hyun Kyung Park	75	69	69	213	4,395,000
	Ji Hyun Kim	68	72	71	211	6,420,000		Hye Lim Jo	68	71	74	213	4,395,000
17	Ji Young Park	73	67	72	212	5,497,500		Ka Ram Choi	69	71	73	213	4,395,000
	Chae-Young Yoon	74	68	70	212	5,497,500		Cho Hui Kim	70	69	74	213	4,395,000

IS Dongseo Busan Open

Hyun Kyung Park became the first player to win for a second time during the season while surviving torrential rain at Stone Gate Country Club which saw the inaugural IS Dongseo Busan Open reduced to 36 holes. Although Park needed five more to defeat Hee Jeong Lim in a playoff.

Friday's play was washed out entirely and the tournament was pushed to a Monday finish to maintain 54 holes of competition. Saturday's first round was notable for Jeongeun Lee[6] making an albatross — the seventh in KLPGA history — at the fifth hole from 208 yards although the US Open champion would finish only 63rd in the end.

Lim took the lead with a 64 before adding a 67 on Sunday for a 13-under-par total of 131. Park, after an opening 65, followed up with a 66 to tie Lim. Park made six birdies, three in a row from the fourth, and did not drop a shot despite the continuing rain. "Even before I teed up, it started raining," Park said. "But I had good memories playing in the rain, so I was able to play a little more comfortably."

More heavy rain led to Monday's third round being abandoned with Park and Lim heading out onto the saturated course for a three-hole aggregate playoff. Each player parred the 16th, 17th and 18th holes before heading into sudden-death with two birdies at the 18th. At the 18th again for the fifth extra hole, Park hit her approach next to the hole, while Lim missed for her three from long range.

Both rookies in 2019, Lim had won three times while Park, 20, had to wait until this year's KLPGA Championship for her maiden title in May. Lim had been a runner-up on that occasion as well.

"I still can't believe that I was able to achieve my goal of picking up another win this quickly," Park said. "Since this win was made in such bad conditions, I feel happier and it is more meaningful."

Min Ji Park finished in third place, two strokes behind, while Sei Young Kim was among those tying for sixth place.

Stone Gate Country Club, Gijang, Busan July 10-13
Par 72 (36-36); 6,491 yards Purse: ₩1,000,000,000

1	**Hyun Kyung Park**	65 66	131	₩200,000,000	
2	**Hee Jeong Lim**	64 67	131	115,000,000	
	Park won playoff at fifth extra hole				
3	**Min Ji Park**	67 66	133	80,000,000	
4	Ji Sun Kang	69 66	135	50,000,000	
5	Ji Hyun Kim	68 68	136	40,000,000	
6	Da Yeon Lee	70 67	137	23,083,333	
	So Young Lee	70 67	137	23,083,333	
	Char Young Kim[2]	69 68	137	23,083,333	
	Ree An Kim	69 68	137	23,083,333	
	Yu Jin Sung	68 69	137	23,083,333	
	Sei Young Kim	67 70	137	23,083,333	
12	Ji Hyun Oh	71 67	138	11,042,857	
	Ye Jin Kim	69 69	138	11,042,857	
	Na Rin An	66 72	138	11,042,857	
	Seung Hui Ro	71 67	138	11,042,857	
	Seo Jin Park	66 72	138	11,042,857	
	Bo Ah Kim	65 73	138	11,042,857	
	Hee Won Jung	66 72	138	11,042,857	
19	Jeong Mee Hwang	70 69	139	9,016,667	
	Hae Ran Ryu	71 68	139	9,016,667	
	Eun Soo Jang	70 69	139	9,016,667	
	Hae Rym Kim	65 74	139	9,016,667	
	Han Sol Ji	69 70	139	9,016,667	
	Eun-Hee Ji	66 73	139	9,016,667	
25	Ji Su Kim	70 70	140	7,950,000	
	Yun Ji Jeong	70 70	140	7,950,000	
	Jeong Min Cho	70 70	140	7,950,000	
	Hyo Rin Lee	72 68	140	7,950,000	
	Bo Mi Kwak	67 73	140	7,950,000	
	Chae Yoon Park	68 72	140	7,950,000	
	Hye Lim Jo	69 71	140	7,950,000	
	Woo Jeong Kim	69 71	140	7,950,000	

Jeju Samdasoo Masters

When Hae Ran Ryu won the Jeju Samdasoo Masters in 2019 she was competing on the Jump Tour, two tiers below the main circuit. The win gave her status as a rookie on the KLPGA Tour for 2020 when the 19-year-old successfully defended her title at Saint Four.

She did it the hard way as well, beating US Open champion Jeongeun Lee[6] by three strokes over 72 holes. The previous year the event had been scheduled for 54 holes but the last round was washed out with Ryu declared the winner.

Here Ryu led from start to finish, sharing the first-round lead with a 65 before adding a 67 and another 65 to lead by five strokes after 54 holes. Lee closed that gap by two as Ryu parred the first seven holes before the defending champion's patience was rewarded with five birdies, and only one bogey, in the last 11 holes. Ryu's 68 gave her a 23-under-par total of 265 — she dropped only two shots all week — while Lee's bogey-free 66 left her two ahead of Hee Jeong Lim, who had lost out in a playoff at the previous tournament.

"It was just that I wasn't making birdies earlier in the round," Ryu reflected. "Rather than feeling rushed, I became more calm, because there were still more holes to play and I told myself to look from the wider view." She took the same mature attitude to her bogey at the 13th. "Rather than feeling rushed, I felt calmer and I didn't feel bad about it."

Ryu added: "Ahead of this tournament, I told myself to have fun. I'm really happy to finish strong. Also, it's not a usual thing for a defending champion to defend the title. So I feel very thankful and honoured to do it."

Hyo Joo Kim and Ha Na Jang shared fourth place with a strong field seeing Jin Young Ko, Inbee Park and So Yeon Ryu all finishing in the top 20.

Saint Four Golf and Resort, Cheju, Jeju Island — July 30-August 2
Par 72 (36-36); 6,500 yards — Purse: ₩800,000,000

1	**Hae Ran Ryu**	65	67	65	68	265	₩160,000,000
2	**Jeongeun Lee[6]**	68	68	66	66	268	92,000,000
3	**Hee Jeong Lim**	72	67	64	67	270	64,000,000
4	Hyo Joo Kim	68	69	67	67	271	36,000,000
	Ha Na Jang	67	68	68	68	271	36,000,000
6	A Yean Cho	66	67	71	68	272	28,000,000
7	Hye Jin Choi	69	69	67	68	273	24,000,000
8	Min Sun Kim[5]	70	69	68	67	274	20,000,000
9	Ji Yeong Kim[2]	68	72	70	65	275	12,933,333
	So Young Lee	65	70	72	68	275	12,933,333
	Bo Mee Lee	69	67	69	70	275	12,933,333
12	Da Been Heo	68	72	70	66	276	9,546,667
	Seo Jin Park	68	70	68	70	276	9,546,667
	Jin Seon Han	66	69	69	72	276	9,546,667
15	Inbee Park	68	70	70	69	277	8,160,000
	Ga Young Lee	70	66	71	70	277	8,160,000
	So Yeon Ryu	69	69	70	69	277	8,160,000
	Jung Min Lee	68	70	69	70	277	8,160,000
	Seon Woo Bae	67	66	72	72	277	8,160,000
20	Gyeol Park	73	69	67	69	278	6,992,000
	Ju Yeon In	72	68	69	69	278	6,992,000
	Jin Young Ko	69	71	67	71	278	6,992,000
	Yoon Kyung Heo	70	70	67	71	278	6,992,000
	Han Sol Ji	69	67	68	74	278	6,992,000
25	Eun Woo Choi	71	67	68	74	280	6,160,000
	So Hyun Bae	71	68	70	71	280	6,160,000
	Yeun Jung Seo	71	66	72	71	280	6,160,000
	So Mi Lee	75	65	70	70	280	6,160,000
	Hyun Ju Yoo	68	70	68	74	280	6,160,000
	Min Ji Park	70	67	71	72	280	6,160,000

Orange Life Champions Trophy

The youngsters of the domestic Korea LPGA Tour retained the Orange Life Champions Trophy Inbee Park Invitational against a team of overseas-based Korean players. Traditionally, an "LPGA" team, the overseas side were missing some of the US-based players such as Danielle Kang, Minjee Lee and Lydia Ko but featured a number of players who would otherwise have been playing in Japan, such as captain Jiyai Shin.

With various tours around the world rescheduled due to the pandemic, this event at Blue One The Honors Country Club in Gyeongju was brought forward to August from its usual end-of-year date. However bad weather on the Saturday meant the foursomes series was abandoned after only two matches were able to tee off.

The "home" team took a three-point advantage after the opening fourballs with only Hyo Joo Kim and Eun-Hee Ji salvaging a win for the overseas side. Sunday's singles were shared 6-6 giving the KLPGA a 10½-7½ victory and a second win in a row.

Young stars Hae Ran Ryu, Hyun Kyung Park and Hee Jeong Lim, who defeated Jeongeun Lee[6] 2 and 1, all record two wins out of two, while at the top of the order Ji Hyun Oh dispatched Shin 5 and 4. There was a late victory for 2020 Korea Open champion So Yeon Ryu over 2019 KLPGA number one Hye Jin Choi but the overall result had by then been decided.

Sponsors Orange Life donated ₩120 million on behalf of the two 13-player squads to support Covid-19 vaccine development efforts.

Blue One The Honors Country Club, Gyeongju — August 7-9
Par 72 (36-36); 6,484 yards

FRIDAY FOURBALLS
Hee Jeong Lim & So Young Lee defeated So Yeon Ryu & Seon Woo Bae 2 and 1
Min Ji Park & Ji Yeong Kim[2] defeated Inbee Park & Min Young Lee[2] 3 and 2
Hyun Kyung Park & Hye Jin Choi defeated Na Yeon Choi & Mi Hyang Lee 3 and 2
A Lim Kim & Hae Ran Ryu defeated Jiyai Shin & Jeongeun Lee[6] by 1 hole
Ji Hyun Oh & Ye Rim Choi halved with Ha Neul Kim & Min Jung Hur
Ji Hyun Kim & So Mi Lee lost to Hyo Joo Kim & Eun-Hee Ji 4 and 3
Points — KLPGA 4½ LPGA 1½

SATURDAY FOURSOMES — abandoned
Ji Hyun Oh & Ji Hyun Kim versus Inbee Park & Na Yeon Choi
Hyun Kyung Park & So Mi Lee versus Ha Neul Kim & Min Jung Hur
Hye Jin Choi & Ji Yeong Kim[2] versus So Yeon Ryu & Jeongeun Lee[6]

Ye Rim Choi & Hae Ran Ryu versus Bo Mee Lee & Mi Hyang Lee
Hee Jeong Lim & Min Ji Park versus Eun-Hee Ji & Hyo Joo Kim
Da Yeon Lee & So Young Lee versus Min Young Lee[2] & Seon Woo Bae

SUNDAY SINGLES
Ji Hyun Oh defeated Jiyai Shin 5 and 4
So Mi Lee halved with Na Yeon Choi
Ye Rim Choi lost to Ha Neul Kim by 1 hole
Hae Ran Ryu defeated Min Jung Hur 4 and 3
Min Ji Park lost to Hyo Joo Kim by 1 hole
Da Yeon Lee lost to Min Young Lee[2] 2 and 1
Ji Yeong Kim[2] halved with Mi Hyang Lee
Hyun Kyung Park defeated Bo Mee Lee by 1 hole
Hee Jeong Lim defeated Jeongeun Lee[6] 2 and 1
So Young Lee halved with Eun-Hee Ji
Hye Jin Choi lost to So Yeon Ryu 3 and 1
A Lim Kim halved with Seon Woo Bae
Points — KLPGA 6 LPGA 6

FINAL RESULT — KLPGA 10½ LPGA 7½

Dayouwinia MBN Ladies Open

For a second strokeplay tournament in a row the defending champion won on the KLPGA, and Jeongeun Lee[6] was the runner-up. Min Ji Park doubled up at the Dayouwinia MBN Ladies Open with a wire-to-wire victory to finish two strokes ahead of Lee. It was a fourth tour title for the 24-year-old Park.

Sharing the lead on each of the first two days with rounds of 66 and 69, Park edged ahead only in the closing stages on Sunday with a 68 to finish at 13-under-par 203. A crowded leaderboard saw her co-leaders overnight fall away, Rae Hyeon Ku closing with a 71 to tie for third place, while Ga Eun Song had a 76 to fall all the way down to 30th.

Hyo Joo Kim, with a 67, and Ha Na Jang (69) were among the big names to make a move in the final round to join the tie for third place but it was Lee who created the biggest stir. The US Open champion made six birdies in seven holes from the fourth to the 10th to get to 11 under par. Lee parred her way to the clubhouse to set the clubhouse target after a bogey-free 66 but Park still had work to do. She made a vital par save at the 13th, then birdied the 15th from six feet and the 17th from 20 feet to provide her two-shot cushion.

Dayou Montvert Country Club, Pocheon, Gyeonggi — August 14-16
Par 72 (36-36); 6,525 yards — Purse: ₩700,000,000

1	**Min Ji Park**	66	69	68	203	₩140,000,000
2	**Jeongeun Lee[6]**	72	67	66	205	80,500,000
3	**Hyo Joo Kim**	69	70	67	206	35,875,000
	Ye Rim Choi	70	67	69	206	35,875,000
	Ha Na Jang	68	69	69	206	35,875,000
	Rae Hyeon Ku	67	68	71	206	35,875,000
7	Chae Yoon Park	71	68	68	207	17,500,000
	Na Kyung Lee	71	67	69	207	17,500,000
	Se Lin Hyun	66	71	70	207	17,500,000
10	Hye Jin Choi	70	68	70	208	8,878,333
	Hee Jeong Lim	70	72	66	208	8,878,333
	Song Yi Ahn	71	68	69	208	8,878,333
	Hae Rym Kim	72	68	68	208	8,878,333
	Hyun Kyung Park	70	69	69	208	8,878,333
	So Mi Lee	67	69	72	208	8,878,333
16	A Lim Kim	70	69	70	209	7,245,000
	Hee Won Na	68	69	72	209	7,245,000
	Da Been Heo	72	67	70	209	7,245,000
	Ga Young Lee	72	66	71	209	7,245,000
20	Ye Sung Jun	71	71	68	210	6,160,000
	Keun Yeong An	72	69	69	210	6,160,000
	Hae Ran Ryu	70	71	69	210	6,160,000
	Ji Su Kim	71	69	70	210	6,160,000
	Ju Young Park	69	72	69	210	6,160,000
	Eun Bin Lim	70	68	72	210	6,160,000
	Min Kyung Choi	69	68	73	210	6,160,000
	Ji Young Park	72	67	71	210	6,160,000
	Shi Hyun Ahn	74	65	71	210	6,160,000

	Mi Jeong Gong	68	70	72	210	6,160,000
30	Jeong Mee Hwang	70	70	71	211	5,460,000
	Han Sol Ji	68	73	70	211	5,460,000
	Seon Woo Bae	69	71	71	211	5,460,000
	Julie Kim	68	73	70	211	5,460,000
	Yun Ji Jeong	71	69	71	211	5,460,000
	Ju Yeon In	70	70	71	211	5,460,000
	Ga Eun Song	67	68	76	211	5,460,000

Fantom Classic

Song Yi Ahn had no idea she was leading the Fantom Classic by a stroke as she arrived at the 18th green at South Links Yeongam. She had a 20-foot birdie putt and ran it almost two feet past the hole.

"I did not even think about winning. I guess that it was all about making me relaxed," said Ahn. "If I had known that I was leading by one stroke, I would not have made such an aggressive putt."

Nervelessly, Ahn holed out for her par but she only realised it was the winning putt when she was immediately drenched in water by her fellow players.

This was Ahn's second KLPGA victory. It arrived 10 months after her first, at the end of 2019, which had taken 10 years on tour to arrive. Scores of 68, 69 and 69 gave the 30-year-old a 10-under-par total of 206 as she finished one ahead of a group of five players. Woo Jeong Kim's late bogey at the 17th had opened the door for the unaware Ahn, while runner-up honours were also shared by Ha Na Jang, Su Yeon Jang, Chae Yoon Park and Da Been Heo.

Overnight leader So Mi Lee (66-69) faded to a 74 on the final day to fall into a tie for 10th place. Ahn started three strokes behind and first took the lead with her third birdie of the day at the 10th hole. But a bogey at the 13th resulted in a seven-way tie for the lead and it was probably for the best that Ahn's caddie told her to concentrate on her own game. Her approach to five feet for a birdie at the 14th got her to the winning score but it was not until after she parred the last that the winner was made aware of her success.

South Links Yeongam Country Club (Kyle Phillips), Jeollanam — September 25-27
Par 72 (36-36); 6,454 yards — Purse: ₩600,000,000

1	**Song Yi Ahn**	68	69	69	206	₩120,000,000
2	**Su Yeon Jang**	70	69	68	207	38,400,000
	Ha Na Jang	71	67	69	207	38,400,000
	Chae Yoon Park	71	69	67	207	38,400,000
	Da Been Heo	72	68	67	207	38,400,000
	Woo Jeong Kim	69	69	69	207	38,400,000
7	Ju Yeon In	70	70	68	208	15,000,000
	Yeon Ju Jung	70	69	69	208	15,000,000
	Hee Jeong Lim	71	67	70	208	15,000,000
10	Na Rin An	71	68	70	209	7,935,000
	Hye Jin Choi	70	70	69	209	7,935,000
	Seung Yeon Lee	70	69	70	209	7,935,000
	So Mi Lee	66	69	74	209	7,935,000
14	Ji Hyun Oh	72	71	67	210	6,450,000
	Shin Sil Bang (A)	71	68	71	210	
	Min Ji Park	71	68	71	210	6,450,000
	Ina Yoon (A)	71	68	71	210	
	Hae Ran Ryu	67	70	73	210	6,450,000
	Seung Hui Ro	67	69	74	210	6,450,000
20	A Lim Kim	73	69	69	211	5,760,000
	Yu Jin Sung	76	65	70	211	5,760,000
	Hyo Joo Kim	73	67	71	211	5,760,000
23	Ji Young Park	71	69	72	212	5,220,000
	Hae Rym Kim	73	68	71	212	5,220,000
	Ji Won Shin[2]	77	64	71	212	5,220,000
	Chae Lin Yang	72	70	70	212	5,220,000
	Hye Lim Jo	68	71	73	212	5,220,000
28	So Young Lee	71	72	70	213	4,800,000
	Jeongeun Lee[6]	72	71	70	213	4,800,000
	Bo Ah Kim	72	70	71	213	4,800,000
	So Hye Park	71	69	73	213	4,800,000
	So Yi Kim	70	68	75	213	4,800,000

Autech Carrier Championship

How does a 10-stroke lead with a round to play get reduced to two with three holes left?

"I was very nervous on the final round since I didn't have any experience in winning the tournament," said Na Rin An. "I think that's why my play didn't work out the way I wanted it to."

It was not just some wobbly play by the unproven leader but a brilliant charge from rookie Hae Ran Ryu, who made nine birdies for a 63, that produced some unexpected tension late in proceedings. Yet in the nick of time, An birdied the last two holes at Sejong Field to secure a four-stroke victory at the Autech Carrier Championship.

An, 24, had been on the KLPGA since 2017 but never finished better than 36th on the money list. After the first round at Sejong her 70 left her five strokes behind Gyeol Park. However, a 65 by An on Friday put her into the lead by three strokes and, remarkably, she repeated the feat the next day to go 10 shots clear. The wind that posed problems for everyone else in the field was no match for An's precise iron-play.

Lying in second place after 54 holes was Jin Young Ko (72-66-72). The Rolex Rankings number one was playing for only the fourth time all year and had remained in Korea instead of competing in the KPMG Women's PGA on the same week. Ko closed with a 71 to share third place with Hee Jeong Lim, nine strokes adrift of the winner.

Instead it was the 19-year-old Ryu who put the most pressure on An in the final round although playing alongside superstar Ko, dressed in all white to An's all-black outfit, may have been a contributory factor in the leader's nerves. An bogeyed the third hole and then had a long run of pars before further dropped shots at the 12th and 13th holes. A birdie at the next helped settle An and then she finished in style at the last two holes.

Sejong Field Golf Club, Yeongi, Sejong City — October 8-11
Par 72 (36-36); 6,676 yards — Purse: ₩800,000,000

1	**Na Rin An**	70	65	65	72	272	₩144,000,000
2	**Hae Ran Ryu**	70	74	69	63	276	88,000,000
3	**Hee Jeong Lim**	73	69	70	69	281	52,000,000
	Jin Young Ko	72	66	72	71	281	52,000,000
5	Ha Na Jang	73	68	73	68	282	32,000,000
6	Hyun Kyung Park	74	70	73	66	283	22,000,000
	Hye Jin Choi	72	73	69	69	283	22,000,000
	Jin Seon Han	71	74	71	67	283	22,000,000
	Gyeol Park	65	73	74	71	283	22,000,000
10	Min Kyung Choi	71	75	69	69	284	12,000,000
11	A Lim Kim	76	73	66	70	285	10,060,000
	Han Sol Ji	71	72	72	70	285	10,060,000
	Ji Hyun Oh	72	70	72	71	285	10,060,000
	Min Song Ha	72	74	68	71	285	10,060,000
15	So Mi Lee	72	73	74	67	286	8,693,333
	Hyo Moon Kim	71	74	70	71	286	8,693,333
	Hyo Rin Lee	73	73	71	69	286	8,693,333
18	Yun Ji Jeong	72	75	70	70	287	7,893,333
	Seung Yeon Lee	75	70	70	72	287	7,893,333
	Woo Jeong Kim	73	71	72	71	287	7,893,333
21	Se Lin Hyun	73	71	75	69	288	7,160,000
	Hee Won Na	72	70	73	73	288	7,160,000
	Hyo Joo Kim	73	68	73	74	288	7,160,000
	Ju Yeon In	73	71	71	73	288	7,160,000
25	So Yeon Ryu	73	73	75	68	289	6,640,000
	Jeong Hwa Lee[2]	74	70	73	72	289	6,640,000
	Mi Jung Hur	75	69	74	71	289	6,640,000
28	Min Sun Kim[5]	76	71	74	69	290	6,440,000
	Jeongeun Lee[6]	68	76	74	72	290	6,440,000
30	So Hye Park	71	75	74	71	291	6,200,000
	So Hyeon Ahn	75	72	75	69	291	6,200,000
	So Yi Kim	71	76	68	76	291	6,200,000
	Sae Ro Mi Kim	73	73	75	70	291	6,200,000

KB Financial Group Star Championship

Hyo Joo Kim was rewarded for remaining in her homeland rather than returning to the LPGA circuit in America by winning her second title of the year at the KLPGA's last major of the season.

It was a dominating performance at the KB Financial Group Star Championship as the 25-year-old beat Jin Young Ko by eight strokes. The pair were the only players to finish under par in tricky conditions at Black Stone in Icheon.

"I'm so glad I won the final major this season," Kim said. "My goal was to have one win this year, but it's really good to have two wins."

In June Kim won the Lotte Cantata Open in a playoff over Sei Young Kim, who in the week before the KB Star won her first LPGA major at the KPMG Women's PGA. Prior to the Lotte, Hyo Joo had not won anywhere since 2016. Now she brought her tally of tour titles up to 12 and was planning to finish the season at home. "Another goal for this year is to get the award for low scoring average," Kim said.

For the second week running a player was 10 strokes ahead with a round to play. Kim (66-69-69) set up her victory by being the only player to record three scores under par on the first three days. Her performance on Saturday was particularly impressive as she extended her lead by seven shots.

She only managed one birdie in a closing 75, for a nine-under-par total of 279, but no one could put any pressure on the leader. Ko, who started 12 shots behind, had a 71 — one of only three sub-par rounds on the final day — as the world number one recorded her best result of the season to date and her second top-three finish in successive weeks.

Of the four players who shared second place overnight, Jeongeun Lee[6] finished best with a 74 meaning she shared third place with Jung Min Lee (72) and Ju Young Pak (71).

Black Stone Golf Club, Icheon, Gyeonggi — October 15-18
Par 72 (36-36); 6,702 yards — Purse: ₩1,200,000,000

1	**Hyo Joo Kim**	66	69	69	75	279	₩240,000,000
2	**Jin Young Ko**	71	69	76	71	287	138,000,000
3	**Jung Min Lee**	74	72	70	72	288	68,000,000
	Ju Young Pak	66	76	75	71	288	68,000,000
	Jeongeun Lee[6]	76	68	70	74	288	68,000,000
6	Mi Jung Hur	71	69	74	75	289	42,000,000
7	Ha Na Jang	66	76	75	73	290	27,000,000
	Han Sol Ji	72	71	74	73	290	27,000,000
	Hye Jin Choi	70	72	73	75	290	27,000,000
	Hee Jeong Lim	72	72	70	76	290	27,000,000
11	So Mi Lee	75	71	68	77	291	16,200,000
12	Da Yeon Lee	72	72	73	76	293	14,640,000
	Na Rin An	72	74	74	73	293	14,640,000
14	A Yean Cho	76	74	72	73	295	13,680,000
15	Min Ji Park	77	74	76	69	296	12,450,000
	Hyo Rin Lee	75	75	72	74	296	12,450,000
	Min Sun Kim[5]	72	73	77	74	296	12,450,000
	Hae Ran Ryu	69	75	74	78	296	12,450,000
19	Hye Lim Jo	73	78	74	72	297	10,640,000
	Song Yi Ahn	75	76	72	74	297	10,640,000
	Bo Mi Kwak	73	76	71	77	297	10,640,000
	Julie Kim	71	70	80	76	297	10,640,000
	Jeong Mee Hwang	72	74	76	75	297	10,640,000
	Woo Jeong Kim	73	76	73	75	297	10,640,000
25	Hyun Kyung Park	69	70	79	80	298	9,540,000
	Hyun Soo Kim	72	73	75	78	298	9,540,000
27	Yewon Lee (A)	70	77	79	73	299	
	Seul Gi Jeong	78	72	77	72	299	9,160,000
	Ye Sung Jun	71	74	78	76	299	9,160,000
	Yeon Ju Jung	73	74	74	78	299	9,160,000

Huencare Ladies Open

So Mi Lee had been close before. In her rookie season in 2019 she had two runner-up finishes. In the opening event of the 2020 season at the end of 2019 she was second again. And she was lying second after round one of the the S-Oil Championship when the tournament was abandoned and the results made unofficial.

So the 21-year-old was ready to make her breakthrough at the Huencare Ladies Open, a new tournament played at South Links Yeongam. Lee won by one stroke from Bo Ah Kim but the focus was also on Hye Jin Choi, who led for the first two days.

The nearest Choi had come to winning in 2020 came when she was leading after the first round of that abandoned S-Oil Championship. A far cry from her five-win season in 2019. When would the next victory come? Yet her consistency was remarkable. This would be her 12th top-10 finish in 13 completed events.

Choi's 67 on Thursday put her one ahead of Lee, U Ree Jun, who would later fall away, and, showing a first glimpse of form in a while, A Lim Kim. Friday's play was scrubbed when high winds made it impossible to complete play and the event was reduced to a 54-hole affair.

A 71 on Saturday kept Choi one ahead of Lee, who also had a 71, but on Sunday Choi made only one birdie in a level-par 72 to tie for third place with Hae Ran Ryu (67) and Da Yeon Lee (69).

Bo Ah Kim, after two 71s, proved the strongest challenger in the final round, making an eagle at the fifth and then birdieing four of the last five holes to set the clubhouse target at eight under par after a 66. So Mi Lee picked up an early birdie and then three in five holes around the turn before a bogey at the 13th. She holed from 20 feet for a birdie at the next to get back to nine under par and then bravely parred in. A closing 68 gave her a total of 207 and her first tour title.

South Links Yeongam Country Club (Kyle Phillips), Jeollanam — October 22-25
Par 72 (36-36); 6,420 yards — Purse: ₩800,000,000

1	**So Mi Lee**	68	71	68	207	₩144,000,000
2	**Bo Ah Kim**	71	71	66	208	88,000,000
3	**Da Yeon Lee**	72	69	69	210	45,333,333
	Hae Ran Ryu	72	71	67	210	45,333,333
	Hye Jin Choi	67	71	72	210	45,333,333
6	Julie Kim	70	75	66	211	26,000,000
	Yun Ji Jeong	69	73	69	211	26,000,000
8	A Lim Kim	68	72	72	212	20,000,000
9	Seul Ki Lee	69	73	71	213	14,000,000
	Song Yi Ahn	70	72	71	213	14,000,000

11	Hee Jeong Lim	70	73	71	214	10,960,000
12	Hyun Soo Kim	70	76	69	215	8,930,000
	Ji Hyun Kim	72	71	72	215	8,930,000
	Min Kyung Choi	72	72	71	215	8,930,000
	Chae Lin Yang	72	72	71	215	8,930,000
	A Yean Cho	72	74	69	215	8,930,000
	Hyo Rin Lee	71	72	72	215	8,930,000
	Yeun Jung Seo	71	74	70	215	8,930,000
	Na Kyung Lee	69	72	74	215	8,930,000
20	Seung Hyun Lee	76	72	68	216	7,160,000
	So Young Lee	73	74	69	216	7,160,000
	Seung Hui Ro	71	75	70	216	7,160,000
	Su Yeon Jang	73	72	71	216	7,160,000
	Ran Hong	69	75	72	216	7,160,000
	Seul Gi Jeong	72	73	71	216	7,160,000
26	You Min Hwang (A)	70	78	69	217	
	Ju Young Pak	72	75	70	217	6,368,000
	Hyun Kyung Park	75	73	69	217	6,368,000
	Gi Ppuem Lee	71	74	72	217	6,368,000
	Ji Hyun Kim[2]	73	73	71	217	6,368,000
	Da Been Heo	71	75	71	217	6,368,000

SK Networks Seokyung Ladies Classic

There is no messing with Ha Na Jang in the autumn. With a two-stroke victory at the SK Networks Seokyung Ladies Classic, Jang posted her 17th career victory — 13 in Korea, five on the LPGA with her previous win at the 2019 BMW Ladies Championship counting on both tours — and nine of them have arrived from September to the end of the year.

"I had a faith that I do well in autumn, so I played with confidence and that led to a good result," Jang said.

In fact, having withdrawn from her previous tournament, October had not been kind to the 28-year-old. Fortunately, this event finished on November 1. "I had a lot happening in October," Jang said. "I got injured a lot and my uncle passed away. But as I started a new month, I got off to a strong start. I've had a lot to overcome, and today I finally picked up a win. It makes today the happiest day for me. I think my uncle who passed away last week helped me from heaven."

This win meant Jang had won each year, on either the KLPGA or LPGA circuits, for nine years in a row. Jang was seven behind first-round leader Julie Kim's 65 but she was sharing the lead after 54 holes with scores of 72, 68 and 70. While co-leader Min Kyung Choi slipped back with a 75, Jang battled her way to a 71 and a seven-under-par total of 281. She had one bogey and a third birdie of the day at the 14th from five feet put her two ahead.

"Overall, I had a really tough day," Jang said. "I had quite a number of birdie chances but wasn't able to make them. With so many difficulties, once the round was over, I felt relieved."

Hyo Joo Kim made a charge on the back nine with an eagle at the 10th and the birdies at 13 and 16 for a 70 to share second place with U Ree Jun (70), Ji Hyun Kim (70) and Min Ji Park, who had the lowest round of the final day with a 68.

Pinx Golf Club, Seogwipo, Jeju Island
Par 72 (36-36); 6,638 yards

October 29-November 1
Purse: ₩800,000,000

1	**Ha Na Jang**	72	68	70	71	281	₩160,000,000
2	**Hyo Joo Kim**	70	72	71	70	283	57,000,000
	U Ree Jun	70	72	71	70	283	57,000,000
	Min Ji Park	69	75	71	68	283	57,000,000
	Ji Hyun Kim	72	70	71	70	283	57,000,000
6	Da Been Heo	69	70	72	74	285	26,000,000
	Min Kyung Choi	69	71	70	75	285	26,000,000
8	Hye Jin Choi	70	73	72	71	286	20,000,000
9	A Lim Kim	77	69	70	71	287	11,664,000
	Jeong Mee Hwang	68	77	72	70	287	11,664,000
	Hae Ran Ryu	68	74	73	72	287	11,664,000
	A Yean Cho	72	72	72	71	287	11,664,000
	Julie Kim	65	72	75	75	287	11,664,000
14	Chae Yoon Park	72	73	70	73	288	9,120,000
15	Yoon Kyung Heo	75	76	70	68	289	8,160,000
	Min Sun Kim[5]	68	72	77	72	289	8,160,000
	Han Sol Ji	72	70	75	72	289	8,160,000
	Ree An Kim	71	72	71	75	289	8,160,000
	Hee Jeong Lim	67	74	74	74	289	8,160,000
20	Ga Young Lee	68	75	70	77	290	7,360,000
21	Jeongeun Lee[6]	70	77	72	72	291	7,080,000
	Bo Ah Kim	73	74	73	71	291	7,080,000
23	Hae Rym Kim	73	71	72	76	292	6,613,333
	Se Lin Hyun	74	73	72	73	292	6,613,333
	Yun Ji Jeong	76	72	71	73	292	6,613,333
26	Ju Young Pak	75	76	73	69	293	6,112,000
	Na Yeon Choi	74	74	73	72	293	6,112,000
	Gyeol Park	74	71	78	70	293	6,112,000
	Na Rin An	74	74	73	72	293	6,112,000
	Hee Won Na	70	74	73	76	293	6,112,000

Hana Financial Group Championship

A month after claiming her maiden victory on the KLPGA, Na Rin An won again at the Hana Financial Group Championship at Sky 72 in Incheon.

Instead of the 10-shot lead she almost let slip at the Autech Championship, this time An had to battle high winds and cold weather before securing a three-stroke victory over Ha Na Jang, who was heading for a second win in successive weeks.

Jang was at the top of the leaderboard for each of the first three days, sharing the first-round lead with Jin Young Ko on 68 and then adding another 68 before a 73 on Saturday. After 54 holes, Jang was tied with Min Ji Park (70-67-72) and An, who followed a pair of 69s with a 71.

An posted another 71 on Sunday, one of the few sub-par rounds on a day of difficult conditions. A birdie at the second from five feet put her into the lead and another at the ninth, from 27 feet, increased her advantage to two shots at the turn. Then it was a question of hanging on. Her only blip came with a dropped shot at the 17th but at the same hole Jang had a double bogey to fall three behind. An finished on eight under par with a total of 280, while Jang closed with a 74 and Park a 77 to tie for third with Da Yeon Lee (72).

"A month ago, I picked up my first-ever win," An, 24, said. "I'm very happy to pick up my second win this quickly. I'll work even harder. At the Autech, I didn't have any experience so I got really nervous. Of course, I was nervous today, but I tried to keep my focus on playing my own game. And I think that worked out well."

So Yeon Ryu and A Lim Kim shared fifth place with Fantom Classic winner Song Yi Ahn, while Ko, in her last tournament before retuning to America and the conclusion of the LPGA season, was eighth. Hye Jin Choi tied for 17th, only her second finish outside the top 10 all season, but such was her consistency that she sealed the points-based Player of the Year award with a tournament to go — and without having won.

Sky 72 Golf Club (Ocean), Incheon, Gyeonggi — November 5-8
Par 72 (36-36); 6,474 yards — Purse: ₩1,500,000,000

1	**Na Rin An**	69	69	71	71	280	₩300,000,000
2	**Ha Na Jang**	68	68	73	74	283	172,500,000
3	**Da Yeon Lee**	71	72	71	72	286	97,500,000
	Min Ji Park	70	67	72	77	286	97,500,000
5	A Lim Kim	74	66	73	74	287	52,500,000
	Song Yi Ahn	70	72	70	75	287	52,500,000
	So Yeon Ryu	72	70	72	73	287	52,500,000
8	Jin Young Ko	68	75	73	72	288	33,750,000
	So Mi Lee	73	70	71	74	288	33,750,000
10	Yoon Kyung Heo	73	70	71	75	289	22,500,000
11	Hyo Joo Kim	73	70	74	73	290	18,950,000
	A Yean Cho	74	72	71	73	290	18,950,000
	Han Sol Ji	69	71	77	73	290	18,950,000
14	Eun Woo Choi	70	73	77	71	291	17,100,000
15	So Yi Kim	72	72	74	74	292	16,125,000
	Woo Jeong Kim	69	78	66	79	292	16,125,000
17	Min Sun Kim[5]	70	76	76	71	293	14,775,000
	Hye Jin Choi	69	72	77	75	293	14,775,000
	Seo Jin Park	69	73	73	78	293	14,775,000
	Su Yeon Jang	73	74	69	77	293	14,775,000
21	Jung Min Lee	76	73	72	73	294	13,350,000
	Ga Young Lee	73	72	75	74	294	13,350,000
	Min Song Ha	72	73	72	77	294	13,350,000
	Min Kyung Choi	70	70	74	80	294	13,350,000
25	Ji Sun Kang	71	77	74	73	295	12,375,000
	Yeon Ju Jung	77	70	76	72	295	12,375,000
	Hyo Rin Lee	72	74	74	75	295	12,375,000
	Hye Lim Jo	75	70	77	73	295	12,375,000
29	Eun Soo Jang	74	73	74	75	296	11,775,000
	Hyun Kyung Park	74	72	76	74	296	11,775,000
	Ji Yeong Kim[2]	75	69	77	75	296	11,775,000
	Na Yeon Choi	73	70	75	78	296	11,775,000

SK Telecom ADT CAPS Championship

Finally. The only thing missing from Hye Jin Choi's season was a victory.

She had five in 2019 but had to wait until the very last tournament of the season to claim her first of 2020 at the SK Telecom ADT CAPS Championship.

Choi had already retained her Player of the Year title the previous week thanks to a season that saw the 21-year-old finish in the top 10 in 14 of her 16 completed tournaments. She was also leading the S-Oil Championship when it was abandoned after one round and deemed unofficial.

Everything came together for Choi at La Vie est Belle Country Club. For two days she was a stroke behind Song Yi Ahn, who opened 65-69 while Choi went 66-69. But on Sunday the Fantom Classic winner crashed to a 79 and finished outside the top 20.

Choi took the lead with an eagle at the fifth hole and got to 13 under par before dropping a shot at the 16th. With a 69, Choi finished on a 12-under-par total of 204. Hae Ran Ryu, the undisputed rookie of the year, made a strong challenge in also getting to 13 under before two bogeys in the last four holes, including at the last.

Ryu finished alone in second place after a 68, one ahead of Hyo Joo Kim, 69, and Ha Na Jang, 68, who finished in the top three for the third week running. Ryu's second place lifted her into second on the money list, behind Kim, who also topped the stroke average table.

La Vie est Belle Country Club, Chuncheon, Gangwon — November 13-15
Par 72 (36-36); 6,747 yards — Purse: ₩1,000,000,000

1	**Hye Jin Choi**	66	69	69	204	₩200,000,000
2	**Hae Ran Ryu**	68	69	68	205	115,000,000
3	**Ha Na Jang**	70	68	68	206	65,000,000
	Hyo Joo Kim	70	67	69	206	65,000,000
5	Woo Jeong Kim	66	70	71	207	37,500,000
	Da Been Heo	68	68	71	207	37,500,000
7	A Lim Kim	71	67	70	208	27,500,000
	Julie Kim	70	68	70	208	27,500,000
9	Ji Yeong Kim2	70	72	68	210	20,000,000
10	Yu Jin Sung	74	67	70	211	12,242,857
	Min Kyung Choi	68	72	71	211	12,242,857
	Ji Sun Kang	75	68	68	211	12,242,857
	Han Sol Ji	71	68	72	211	12,242,857
	Min Ji Park	71	67	73	211	12,242,857
	Hae Rym Kim	69	68	74	211	12,242,857
	Na Rin An	70	66	75	211	12,242,857
17	So Mi Lee	69	72	71	212	9,700,000
	Ga Young Lee	68	72	72	212	9,700,000
	Da Yeon Lee	73	71	68	212	9,700,000
	Hye Lim Jo	73	68	71	212	9,700,000
21	Se Lin Hyun	72	70	71	213	8,144,444
	So Yeon Park	73	73	67	213	8,144,444
	Min Song Ha	72	69	72	213	8,144,444
	Ye Rim Choi	69	74	70	213	8,144,444
	Gyeol Park	70	70	73	213	8,144,444
	Jung Min Lee	72	69	72	213	8,144,444
	Ji Young Park	71	72	70	213	8,144,444
	Song Yi Ahn	65	69	79	213	8,144,444
	Yeon Ju Jung	71	67	75	213	8,144,444
30	Hee Jeong Lim	72	73	69	214	7,175,000
	Jae Hee Kim	73	71	70	214	7,175,000
	So Yi Kim	71	73	70	214	7,175,000
	Ji Hyun Oh	76	66	72	214	7,175,000

2019-20 MONEY LIST

1	Hyo Joo Kim	₩797,137,207
2	Hae Ran Ryu	628,313,540
3	Ha Na Jang	624,492,207
4	Na Rin An	607,265,476
5	Min Ji Park	593,346,564
6	Hye Jin Choi	538,273,873
7	Hyun Kyung Park	529,093,833
8	Hee Jeong Lim	526,064,428
9	So Young Lee	411,418,040
10	So Mi Lee	402,020,540

WPGA Tour of Australasia

As a 19-year-old amateur, Stephanie Kyriacou did not have much of a plan despite leading the Australian Ladies Classic at Bonville by two strokes with a round to play. "I don't really have a post-round routine," she said, "I will just go home and relax, not do too much, have a big dinner and come out and do it all again tomorrow."

She did it all again and then some the next day. Kyriacou not only posted her fourth score in the 60s but birdied seven of the first 10 holes, including five in a row, and went on to win by eight strokes at 22 under par. Ayean Cho, the highest ranked player in the field as the world number 35, was the runner-up but scooped the first prize of just under A$60,000.

This was the first time, remarkably, that the amateur from St Michael's Golf Club in Sydney, who started playing golf at the age of four and came through the Jack Newton Junior Programme, had been in contention in a professional tournament. "I'm lost for words and still on cloud nine," Kyriacou said. "I think everything was going my way today. I was pretty confident going into the last round and got off to a good start. After the five birdies in a row, I played a bit more defensive, because I assumed I had a bit of a lead by then. On the last hole, I was thinking about what would happen, but I told myself to get a par and then worry about it."

Two days later Kyriacou decided to turn professional and take up her status as a winner on both the renamed WPGA Tour of Australasia and the Ladies European Tour. Australian golfing royalty Karrie Webb declared: "Steph's win will be a huge boost of confidence — the sky is the limit for her. She looked like she was playing a different course to everyone else at Bonville. It seemed the hole was as big as a bucket. Now she doesn't have to play for her card and has two years to get comfortable playing professional golf."

When Kyriacou went to Europe later in the year, with her father Nick along as her caddie, she looked pretty comfortable. She made the cut at the AIG Women's Open, then finished in the top five at five of her next six events, including runner-up spots at the Swiss Open and the Saudi Team International. At the latter, she closed out the event with a course record of 63 at Royal Greens before deciding to skip the final tournament of the season in order to return home for the first time in four months. She had already secured the LET Rookie of the Year award, ahead of South African Open winner Alice Hewson, and third place on the Race to Costa del Sol, despite her Bonville win not counting for either ranking.

"Even though Covid is here, I've had my best year ever," Kyriacou said. "Obviously, I managed to win at the start of the year and then coming over here for what I thought was two events, then my flight got cancelled, which meant I ended up staying in Europe and I played well so I was stoked about that, then it got cancelled again so the break between France and Dubai was tough but then I played good again, so I guess everything happens for a reason.

"I hadn't thought about the Rookie of the Year title until my friend told me about it and then was like that's cool, it would be great to win. It's a once in a lifetime opportunity to play for the award and I'm so happy with my year."

Minjee Lee finished the year as the leading Australian on the Rolex Rankings in eighth position having earlier topped her home Order of Merit for 2019-20. In the two LPGA events played Down Under, Lee was sixth at the Vic Open, sharing honours as the leading home players with Su Oh and Robyn Choi, and was 25th a week later at the Australian Open. A two-time winner of the Vic Open, Lee missed out on a playoff by two strokes but was beside the 18th green as her brother, Min Woo, won his first professional title.

Lee went on to record her highest finish in a major when she was third at the AIG Women's Open at Royal Troon and then the Western Australian claimed her first LET victory in the Dubai Moonlight Classic, holing from 20 feet under the floodlights at the first extra hole to defeat Celine Boutier in a playoff.

Royal Adelaide saw Inbee Park, having just been voted the greatest player of the previous decade, back to her best with the putter as she claimed her 20th LPGA title at the Australian Open. After receiving the Patricia Hodges Bowl, featuring champions such as Annika Sorenstam, Karrie Webb and

Laura Davies, Park said: "It's a great honour to put my name among these legends in golf and hopefully later, everybody looks at those names, and maybe my name, and thinks that it is their honour to be on there." Hannah Green was the leading Australian in 13th place.

Hee Young Park won the Vic Open after a four-hole playoff against compatriots Hye Jin Choi and So Yeon Ryu to claim her first LPGA title for more than six years, while Sweden's Julia Engstrom earned her maiden LET title at the Women's NSW Open.

Queensland's Robyn Choi started the year by winning the Qualifying Tournament and her high finish at the Vic Open helped her into second place on the Order of Merit, ahead of Belgium's Manon De Roey, who was runner-up to Engstrom at Dubbo and won the Aoyuan International Moss Vale Pro-Am.

In the Pro-Am section of the tour, Dottie Ardina became the first overseas player to win the ClubCar Series since its inception in 2007. Ardina, from the Philippines, was involved in playoffs at both of the two 36-hole events. In the first, at Moss Vale, she lost at the second extra hole when De Roey holed out from a greenside bunker. But a few days later Ardina claimed the Ballarat Icons ALPG Pro-Am by beating China's Xiyu Lin and Scot Kylie Henry at the first extra hole with an eight-iron to inside three feet for the winning birdie. Celine Herbin, from France, was runner-up to Ardina on the points list. Germany's Laura Fuenfstueck and England's Holly Clyburn won the opening two 18-hole events.

Although travel restrictions to Australia meant the main co-sanctioned events in early 2021, including the Australian and Vic Opens, had to be cancelled, the ALPG moved to align itself ever more closely with the PGA of Australia. From now on the ALPG Tour would become known as the WPGA Tour of Australasia. "We are extremely excited to leverage the strength of the world-renowned PGA brand and create a strong, bold and aspirational platform to elevate women's professional golf," ALPG chief executive Karen Lunn said.

"As the ALPG we celebrate a proud history dating back to 1972 when our founding members started the women's tour here in Australia, and this next step will ensure the future of our game is structured in a way that provides women golfers with even greater opportunities moving forward. We are proud to adopt the 'W' mark, which has become a powerful symbol in women's sport the world over. The WPGA Tour of Australasia will sit proudly alongside the PGA Tour of Australasia representing the tournament playing arms of the professional game in our territory."

2020 SCHEDULE

Windaroo Lakes Pro-Am	**Laura Fuenfstueck**
Findex Yamba Pro-Am	**Holly Clyburn**
Aoyuan International Moss Vale Pro-Am	**Manon De Roey**
Ballarat Icons ALPG Pro-Am	**Dottie Ardina**
ISPS Handa Vic Open	**Hee Young Park**
ISPS Handa Women's Australian Open	**Inbee Park**
Geoff King Motors Australian Ladies Classic	**Stephanie Kyriacou (A)**
Women's NSW Open	**Julia Engstrom**

Aoyuan International Moss Vale Pro-Am

Moss Vale Golf Club, Moss Vale, New South Wales — January 28-29
Par 73 (36-37); 5,805 yards — Purse: A$30,000

1	**Manon De Roey**	71	69	140	A$4,500.00
2	**Dottie Ardina**	68	72	140	3,000
	De Roey won playoff at second extra hole				
3	**Paige Stubbs**	70	71	141	2,250
4	Mizuki Oide	70	73	143	1,500
	Stephanie Na	71	72	143	1,500
	Whitney Hillier	72	71	143	1,500
7	Isabell Gabsa	70	74	144	1,050
	Hannah Hellyer	71	73	144	1,050
	Celine Herbin	75	69	144	1,050
10	Diksha Dagar	70	75	145	780
	Ingrid Gutierrez Nunez	72	73	145	780
	Nuria Iturrios	72	73	145	780
13	Alejandra Llaneza	76	70	146	660
14	Koto Ishiyama	71	76	147	498
	Luna Sobron Galmes	72	75	147	498
	Nadine White	72	75	147	498
	Astha Madan	74	73	147	498
	Laura Gonzalez Escallon	77	70	147	498
19	Megan Osland	72	76	148	345
	Gemma Dryburgh	74	74	148	345
	Robyn Doig	74	74	148	345
	Rebecca Kay	74	74	148	345

Ballarat Icons ALPG Pro-Am

Ballarat Golf Club, Ballarat, Victoria — February 1-2
Par 72 (36-36); 5,639 yards — Purse: A$30,000

1	**Dottie Ardina**	69	70	139	A$4,500
2	**Kylie Henry**	69	70	139	2,625
	Xiyu Lin	70	69	139	2,625
	Ardina won playoff at first extra hole				
4	Elmay Viking	67	73	140	1,500
	Alejandra Llaneza	68	72	140	1,500
	Luna Sobron Galmes	70	70	140	1,500
7	Felicity Johnson	67	75	142	1,050
	Kim Kaufman	69	73	142	1,050
	Laura Gonzalez Escallon	70	72	142	1,050
10	Stephanie Na	69	74	143	750
	Nina Pegova	73	70	143	750
	Holly Clyburn	73	70	143	750
	Marianne Skarpnord	73	70	143	750
14	Soo Jin Lee	70	74	144	480
	Christine Wolf	71	73	144	480
	Ingrid Gutierrez Nunez	71	73	144	480
	Laura Fuenfstueck	72	72	144	480
	Manon De Roey	72	72	144	480
	Tonje Daffinrud	72	72	144	480
20	Whitney Hillier	71	74	145	318
	Diksha Dagar	71	74	145	318
	Yae Eun Hong	72	73	145	318
	Celine Herbin	74	71	145	318

ISPS Handa Vic Open

Married to a Korean music executive and living in Los Angeles, when Hee Young Park failed to retain her card at the end of the 2019 season she almost gave up the game. Her husband helped persuade the 32-year-old to return to the eight-round Q Series and Park never looked back. She finished second in Pinehurst and then claimed her first LPGA title for six and a half years, and a third in all, at the ISPS Handa Vic Open. It took four extra holes, however, before Park defeated Hye Jin Choi and So Yeon Ryu in a playoff.

At the event where men and women play alongside each other, two-time champion Minjee Lee missed out on the playoff by two strokes but was able to stand by the 18th green and watch her brother Min Woo win his first professional title. With the wind ever increasing on the Beach course at 13th Beach, overnight leader Ayean Choi, the 2019 KLPGA rookie of the year, and Madelene Sagstrom, one behind and attempting to win for the second tournament running after her Gainbridge victory in Florida, both scored 81 to leave the event wide open.

Hye Jin Choi, the KLPGA number one in 2019, scored a 69, helped by four birdies in a row early in the day, to set the clubhouse target at eight under par with a total of 281. Park birdied the par-five 18th for a 73 to force a tie and Ryu, 72, made it a three-way Korean affair by saving par at the last after driving into the hazard.

Ryu dropped out of the playoff at the second extra hole but decided to donate half of her prize money, around A$65,000, to the Australian bushfire relief fund. Park and Choi both birdied the 18th three times in a row but Choi drove into the trees on the right on the fourth extra hole and ended up hitting into the hazard on the left with her third. A par for Park secured the victory.

"This is payback for my family and my husband," Park said. "I wasn't going to go to Q school because I thought my game was gone. But I finished second and that gave me some confidence. I just want to have the rookie-year feeling, you know? Back to refreshed."

13th Beach Golf Links (Beach), Barwon Heads, Victoria — February 6-9
Par 72 (36-36); 6,354 yards — Purse: A$1,600,000
Creek (R1&2) par 73 (36-37); 6,307 yards

1	**Hee Young Park**	68	68	72	73	281	A$240,000
2	**Hye Jin Choi**	69	68	75	69	281	130,980
	So Yeon Ryu	71	70	68	72	281	130,980
	Park won playoff at fourth extra hole						
4	Leona Maguire	69	69	74	70	282	76,888
	Linnea Strom	66	69	76	71	282	76,888
6	Su Oh	73	68	74	68	283	48,073
	Robyn Choi	70	65	77	71	283	48,073
	Minjee Lee	69	67	74	73	283	48,073
9	Christina Kim	67	70	77	70	284	35,327
	Alena Sharp	68	69	70	77	284	35,327
11	Wichanee Meechai	72	69	74	70	285	27,447
	Ally McDonald	68	65	81	71	285	27,447
	Hannah Green	69	73	71	72	285	27,447
	Tiffany Joh	67	73	73	72	285	27,447
	Pei-Ying Tsai	68	68	73	76	285	27,447

16	Ho Yu An (A)	70	71	72	73	286	
	Yu Liu	70	71	72	73	286	21,667
	Perrine Delacour	69	69	75	73	286	21,667
	Ayean Cho	69	66	70	81	286	21,667
20	Anne van Dam	71	71	73	72	287	18,121
	Cheyenne Knight	67	75	73	72	287	18,121
	Dottie Ardina	70	70	75	72	287	18,121
	Jin Hee Im	69	70	75	73	287	18,121
	Stephanie Meadow	67	70	74	76	287	18,121
	Madelene Sagstrom	65	67	74	81	287	18,121
26	Peiyun Chien	65	74	76	73	288	14,166
	Jenny Coleman	72	70	72	74	288	14,166
	Yealimi Noh	71	70	73	74	288	14,166
	Maria Fernanda Torres	72	67	75	74	288	14,166
	Jeong Eun Lee	71	70	72	75	288	14,166
	Emma Talley	73	66	73	76	288	14,166
	Pornanong Phatlum	67	70	74	77	288	14,166
33	Sarah Kemp	71	67	76	75	289	11,803
	Min A Yoon	71	66	77	75	289	11,803
35	Ssu-Chia Cheng	71	71	71	77	290	10,847
	Dana Finkelstein	67	73	72	78	290	10,847
37	Haeji Kang	65	71	77	78	291	10,224
38	Stephanie Kyriacou (A)	68	73	73	79	293	
39	Suzuka Yamaguchi	70	72	73	79	294	9,809
40	Kelly Tan	72	70	73	80	295	9,393

MISSED THE 54-HOLE CUT

Manon De Roey	72	70	74	216	8,146
Alana Uriell	70	72	74	216	8,146
Hee Jeong Lim	70	71	75	216	8,146
Xiyu Lin	67	72	77	216	8,146
Klara Spilkova	67	71	78	216	8,146
Jeongeun Lee[6]	68	69	79	216	8,146
Haley Moore	66	71	79	216	6,691
Inbee Park	70	72	75	217	6,691
Tiffany Chan	70	70	77	217	6,691
Cydney Clanton	68	69	80	217	6,691
Jennifer Song	75	67	76	218	5,756
Charlotte Thomas	74	68	76	218	5,756
Karine Icher	70	68	80	218	5,756
Jasmine Suwannapura	69	67	82	218	5,756
Pajaree Anannarukarn	74	68	77	219	5,070
Mina Harigae	69	73	77	219	5,070
Lauren Stephenson	70	70	79	219	5,070
Pavarisa Yoktuan	67	72	80	219	5,070
Matilda Castren	68	74	78	220	4,572
Andrea Lee	74	68	79	221	4,572
Dani Holmqvist	69	73	79	221	4,323
Linnea Johansson	70	69	83	222	4,156
Karis Davidson	73	69	81	223	4,032
Mel Reid	72	69	82	223	4,032
Jiwon Jeon	69	69	86	224	3,907

ISPS Handa Women's Australian Open

She was voted the LPGA's player of the previous decade but Inbee Park showed no sign of slowing down as she started the 2020s with her 20th LPGA title at the ISPS Handa Women's Australian Open. The 31-year-old Korean was back to her best at Royal Adelaide and led by as many as six strokes on the final day before securing a three-shot win over Amy Olson.

Park started the season as early as possible in order to claim a place in the Republic of Korea's Olympic team. Needing to move up the Rolex Rankings to be among the top-four Koreans, Park lost a playoff at the Diamond Resorts Tournament of Champions and then made a rare trip Down Under, much to the delight of her longtime Australian caddie Brad Beecher. Her accurate play and rejuvenated putting were perfectly suited to the fast-running course. Only on the back nine on Sunday, with an ample lead and the wind strengthening, did the odd par putt miss.

"My putter really hasn't been working the last couple of years," said Park, who had not won since the 2018 Founders Cup. "I felt like I was hitting the ball just fine, just the putter was different. So, I was trying to get that putter back and this week has been a really great putting week. Those clutch putts have been going in."

Park had rounds of 67, 69, 68 and 74 for a 14-under-par total of 278. Ayean Cho, the 19-year-old in the final group for the second week running, had a 77 to tie for sixth with Cristie Kerr, whose 69 was the only sub-70 score on Sunday. Olson closed with a 70 while Perrine Delacour was third after a 73, with Yu Liu and Marina Alex in fourth.

After receiving the Patricia Hodges Bowl, featuring champions such as Annika Sorenstam, Karrie Webb and Laura Davies, Park said: "It's a great honour to put my name among these legends in golf and hopefully later, everybody looks at those names, and maybe my name, and thinks that it is their honour to be on there."

Royal Adelaide Golf Club, Adelaide, South Australia — February 13-16
Par 73 (37-36); 6,681 yards — Purse: A$1,900,000

1	**Inbee Park**	67	69	68	74	278	A$285,000
2	**Amy Olson**	68	72	71	70	281	173,020
3	**Perrine Delacour**	72	70	67	73	282	125,514
4	Yu Liu	73	67	70	73	283	87,623
	Marina Alex	68	70	70	75	283	87,623
6	Cristie Kerr	76	67	72	69	284	51,627
	Mi Hyang Lee	71	69	72	72	284	51,627
	Celine Boutier	70	69	70	75	284	51,627
	Ayean Cho	69	69	69	77	284	51,627
10	Lizette Salas	70	70	73	72	285	35,680
	Jodi Ewart Shadoff	66	70	77	72	285	35,680
	Christina Kim	70	73	68	74	285	35,680
13	Pavarisa Yoktuan	72	70	73	71	286	25,766
	Stephanie Meadow	70	72	70	74	286	25,766
	Ashleigh Buhai	71	69	72	74	286	25,766
	Ally McDonald	70	70	72	74	286	25,766
	Hannah Green	69	71	72	74	286	25,766
	Jillian Hollis	68	69	75	74	286	25,766
	Brittany Altomare	70	70	71	75	286	25,766
	Maria Fassi	73	67	70	76	286	25,766
21	Lindsey Weaver	73	73	71	70	287	19,893
	Kristen Gillman	69	72	76	70	287	19,893
	Nicole Broch Larsen	71	71	70	75	287	19,893
	Elizabeth Szokol	71	69	70	77	287	19,893
25	Nanna Koerstz Madsen	73	72	73	70	288	15,546
	Anna Nordqvist	71	71	75	71	288	15,546
	Yuka Saso	75	71	70	72	288	15,546
	Jane Park	71	73	72	72	288	15,546
	Minjee Lee	70	72	74	72	288	15,546
	Erika Hara	74	69	72	73	288	15,546
	Georgia Hall	70	72	73	73	288	15,546
	Azahara Munoz	74	70	70	74	288	15,546
	Madelene Sagstrom	69	70	71	78	288	15,546
34	Hee Jeong Lim	72	72	75	70	289	11,415
	Stacy Lewis	70	74	75	70	289	11,415
	Pajaree Anannarukarn	72	74	71	72	289	11,415
	Ho Yu An (A)	69	72	76	72	289	
	Robyn Choi	72	70	74	73	289	11,415
	Jeongeun Lee[6]	67	74	74	74	289	11,415
	So Yeon Ryu	71	69	71	78	289	11,415
41	Anne van Dam	73	73	74	70	290	8,756
	Gemma Dryburgh	71	74	72	73	290	8,756
	Jasmine Suwannapura	70	72	74	74	290	8,756
	Kim Kaufman	69	73	73	75	290	8,756
	Nelly Korda	69	73	72	76	290	8,756
	Hee Young Park	73	70	70	77	290	8,756
	Xiyu Lin	73	70	70	77	290	8,756
48	Albane Valenzuela	74	71	76	70	291	6,711
	Jiyai Shin	75	71	74	71	291	6,711
	Hye Jin Choi	71	75	73	72	291	6,711
	Mel Reid	72	71	74	74	291	6,711
	Kelly Tan	69	73	75	74	291	6,711
	Lauren Stephenson	72	70	74	75	291	6,711
	Dottie Ardina	70	70	75	76	291	6,711
55	Cheyenne Knight	73	71	76	72	292	5,305
	Ayako Uehara	73	72	72	75	292	5,305
	Mind Muangkhumsakul	70	72	75	75	292	5,305
	Yealimi Noh	71	69	75	77	292	5,305
	Wei-Ling Hsu	69	73	72	78	292	5,305
	Peiyun Chien	71	71	71	79	292	5,305
	Pornanong Phatlum	72	71	69	80	292	5,305
62	Julieta Granada	73	72	73	75	293	4,452
	Dana Finkelstein	73	71	74	75	293	4,452
	Cydney Clanton	76	70	71	76	293	4,452
	Alana Uriell	72	72	73	76	293	4,452
	Andrea Lee	72	74	70	77	293	4,452
67	Pernilla Lindberg	70	72	79	73	294	4,073
	Wichanee Meechai	73	70	75	76	294	4,073
	Jing Yan	69	77	71	77	294	4,073
70	Katherine Kirk	73	73	75	74	295	3,726
	Beatriz Recari	71	74	76	74	295	3,726
	Min A Yoon	73	73	73	76	295	3,726
	Daniela Darquea	74	70	75	76	295	3,726
	Esther Henseleit	72	72	72	79	295	3,726
	Giulia Molinaro	71	74	69	81	295	3,726
76	Ryann O'Toole	72	72	76	76	296	3,556
77	Charlotte Thomas	74	72	77	74	297	3,489
	Na Yeon Choi	69	76	76	76	297	3,489
79	Charlotte Heath (A)	76	70	74	79	299	
80	Tonje Daffinrud	70	73	84	73	300	3,422
81	Karis Davidson	75	71	79	78	303	3,379

Geoff King Motors Australian Ladies Classic

Following in the footsteps of Minjee Lee and Aaron Baddeley, Stephanie Kyriacou claimed her first professional title while still an amateur. The 19-year-old from Sydney, ranked 90th on the World Amateur Golf Rankings, swept aside her professional opponents to win the Geoff King Motors Australian Ladies Classic at Bonville by no less then eight strokes.

Kyriacou had missed the cut in her two previous appearances in the event but this time collected four scores in the 60s, starting with a 69 and following with a 63 on Friday. Lying third at the halfway stage, Kyriacou scored another 69 on Saturday to take a two-stroke lead over previous frontrunner Lauren Stephenson. While the American closed with a 75 on Sunday to tie for fifth place with Anne van Dam, Kyriacou ran away with the trophy.

After a birdie at the second, she added five more in a row from the fourth. Out in 29, Kyriacou went 10 strokes ahead with a birdie at the 10th and 11 in front with her eighth gain of the day at the 15th. Her only dropped shot came at the next as she finished with a 65 for a 22-under-par total of 266. Korea's Ayean Cho forgot her final-round woes of the previous fortnight to claim second place thanks to an eagle and two birdies in the last five holes. Sweden's Linnea Strom was third and Scotland's Gemma Dryburgh fourth.

"I'm lost for words and still on cloud nine," Kyriacou said. "I think everything was going my way today. I was pretty confident going into the last round and got off to a good start. After the five birdies in a row, I played a bit more defensive, because I assumed I had a bit of a lead by then. On the last hole, I was thinking about what would happen, but I told myself to get a par and then worry about it."

Although she had to forego the winner's prize money, two days later Kyriacou decided to turn professional in order to take up her winner's status on the LET and ALPG circuits.

Bonville Golf Resort, Bonville, New South Wales — February 20-23
Par 72 (35-37); 6,332 yards — Purse: A$395,000

1	**Stephanie Kyriacou** (A)	69	63	69	65	266	
2	**Ayean Cho**	67	64	73	70	274	A$59,250
3	**Linnea Strom**	71	66	72	66	275	35,550
4	Gemma Dryburgh	67	71	67	72	277	23,700
5	Anne van Dam	70	68	68	72	278	15,998
	Lauren Stephenson	66	64	73	75	278	15,998
7	Julia Engstrom	70	70	70	69	279	11,653
	Johanna Gustavsson	70	71	69	69	279	11,653
9	Manon De Roey	69	70	71	70	280	9,875
10	Charlotte Thomas	69	68	73	71	281	9,480
11	Esther Henseleit	72	72	71	67	282	8,098
	Tiia Koivisto	73	72	69	68	282	8,098
	Celine Herbin	71	70	72	69	282	8,098
	Marianne Skarpnord	72	68	72	70	282	8,098
	Kylie Henry	73	68	71	70	282	8,098
	Breanna Gill	67	73	70	72	282	8,098
17	Astrid Vayson De Pradenne	69	77	69	68	283	6,369
	Mireia Prat	73	72	70	68	283	6,369
	Hye Ji Lee	67	71	73	72	283	6,369
	Pia Babnik	70	70	67	76	283	6,369
21	Leona Maguire	68	73	71	72	284	5,701
	Hana Lee	70	71	71	72	284	5,701
	Lina Boqvist	68	70	69	77	284	5,701
24	Aditi Ashok	69	75	69	72	285	5,056
	Pei-Ying Tsai	70	68	72	75	285	5,056
	Meghan MacLaren	70	68	70	77	285	5,056
27	Cassie Porter (A)	70	71	74	71	286	
	Sanna Nuutinen	72	70	73	71	286	4,197
	Elina Nummenpaa	71	72	72	71	286	4,197
	Katja Pogacar	72	74	66	74	286	4,197
	Ayaka Sugihara	73	67	70	76	286	4,197

Women's NSW Open

Having lost a seven-stroke lead in the final round of the Kenya Open, the last event of the 2019 season, Julia Engstrom knew Manon De Roey's five-shot advantage going into the last day of the Women's NSW Open at Dubbo was far from insurmountable. It took Engstrom 17 holes to get level with the Belgian but then the 18-year-old Swede, Rookie of the Year in 2018, produced a stroke of genius at the last to secure her maiden victory.

At the 193-yard par-three, Engstrom hit a five-iron to two feet for a winning birdie. "I bogeyed 18 in all three previous rounds and I decided that this time, I was not going to bogey it," she said. "I hit a great shot and I didn't realise how close it was until I heard the reaction from the crowd. It was amazing and a great finish to a great week. I've been close a few times and I've been waiting for a win, but you never know if it is going to happen."

De Roey took the lead on Friday with a course-record 64 and then added a 66 in the third round. But she dropped four strokes in the last six holes, including bogeys at the last two holes, to finish two behind after a 75. Engstrom, who made only one bogey all day, gained two strokes in a front nine of 34, and after two players birdied the 12th she made five pars before her closing birdie. Steady returns of 69, 69, 68 and 68 gave her a 14-under-par total of 274.

Camilla Lennarth was third while Thailand's Atthaya Thitikul, already a two-time LET winner at the age of 17, finished in a tie for fourth place on her professional debut. Stephanie Kyriacou, the amateur winner in Bonville, also turned professional but missed the cut.

Dubbo Golf Club, Dubbo, New South Wales — February 27-March 1
Par 72 (36-36); 6,277 yards — Purse: A$345,870

1	**Julia Engstrom**	69	69	68	68	274	A$51,880
2	**Manon De Roey**	71	64	66	75	276	31,128
3	**Camilla Lennarth**	68	69	70	70	277	20,752
4	Aditi Ashok	73	68	70	67	278	14,008
	Atthaya Thitikul	70	69	70	69	278	14,008
6	Katja Pogacar	71	69	68	72	280	10,722
7	Pia Babnik	73	70	66	73	282	9,166
	Diksha Dagar	69	68	71	74	282	9,166
9	Kylie Henry	72	72	72	68	284	7,955
	Soo Jin Lee	72	69	71	72	284	7,955
	Michele Thomson	67	71	73	73	284	7,955
12	Maha Haddioui	71	72	73	69	285	6,940

	Agathe Sauzon	70	67	78	70	285	6,940
	Esther Henseleit	70	74	68	73	285	6,940
15	Olivia Cowan	68	71	74	73	286	6,260
16	Gemma Dryburgh	67	73	75	72	287	5,914
17	Sanna Nuutinen	75	71	70	72	288	5,655
	Leonie Harm	72	71	70	75	288	5,655
19	Amy Boulden	72	71	76	70	289	5,309
	Breanna Gill	69	73	72	75	289	5,309
21	Valdis Thora Jonsdottir	72	74	72	72	290	4,617
	Chloe Williams	72	74	72	72	290	4,617
	Sarah Kemp	72	71	74	73	290	4,617
	Laura Gonzalez Escallon	72	73	72	73	290	4,617
	Hannah Burke	72	76	71	71	290	4,617
	Whitney Hillier	73	73	74	70	290	4,617
	Grace Kim (A)	72	71	70	77	290	
28	Meghan MacLaren	75	74	68	74	291	3,666
	Noora Komulainen	74	72	73	72	291	3,666
	Celine Herbin	72	69	75	75	291	3,666

2019-20 ORDER OF MERIT

1	Minjee Lee	A$63,618
2	Robyn Choi	62,917
3	Manon De Roey	54,129
4	Hannah Green	53,212
5	Su Oh	48,072
6	Anne van Dam	42,714
7	Gemma Dryburgh	39,392
8	Dottie Ardina	33,005
9	Peiying Tsai	32,502
10	Zhang Weiwei	26,250

PGA Tour Champions

By May, with the strange, new Covid-19 pandemic gathering awful momentum, PGA Tour Champions officials were scrambling. Simple postponements meant nothing. This wasn't merely bad weather they were dealing with. Tournaments were being postponed and cancelled. Eventually, only 15 of the originally scheduled 27 would be played. Four of the five senior majors were cancelled — the KitchenAid Senior PGA Championship, US Senior Open, The Senior Open and the Regions Tradition. (The only one played, the Bridgestone Senior Players Championship, was won by Jerry Kelly, his first senior major.)

Something severe was happening and something severe had to be done.

The answer came on May 14, 2020: A combined 2020-2021 schedule.

Said PGA Tour Champions President Miller Brady: "While we won't have a Charles Schwab Cup champion in 2020, we feel that the combined schedule for 2020-21 is the best solution for everyone. We have created solutions that best serve our members and our tournament communities."

There would be adjustments: The 2020 tournament fields would increase from 78 to 81; the three Charles Schwab Cup Playoffs events would also be converted into 81-player fields, and the Charles Schwab Cup Championship reduced from 72 to 54 holes. And fans would not be permitted.

The tour had been shut down following the Hoag Classic in mid-March and — following cancellations and reschedulings — resumed the first week of August with the Ally Challenge.

And strangely enough, the Champions Tour got a big boost of attention because of the pandemic. But it took a weird confluence of circumstances and timing.

It was all because Phil Mickelson was looking for a game, and ended up playing on the Champions Tour. And while his name may have been the brightest on the marquee, the tour got two other big bursts of star power — Ernie Els and Jim Furyk.

Mickelson's path to the Champions Tour: He had missed the cut on the PGA Tour's Northern Trust late in August, but he still wanted a game. He badly wanted to tune up for the coming US Open, postponed from June to September because of the pandemic. The nearest game was the Charles Schwab Series at Ozarks National — on the Champions Tour. So Mickelson, newly 50 and now eligible for senior play, entered the Schwab.

"Yeah, I haven't been called 'young' in a long time," Mickelson said of his reception. "I'm hopeful to play in some more, too, but I also want to use this as a way to get sharp for the regular tour and for the majors."

He shot 61 in the first round and rolled to a four-stroke win. In his only other tour start, he won the Dominion Energy Charity Classic in October, in a tuneup for the rescheduled Masters.

Els and Furyk also had come of age. Els, with four majors and 19 PGA Tour victories, had joined the Champions in January, and Furyk, with one major and 17 wins, joined in May.

All three won twice in 2020, with Furyk and Mickelson joining Bruce Fleisher, from 1999, as the only three players to win their first two starts. Furyk won the Ally Challenge and the PURE Insurance Championship, and Mickelson the Schwab Series Ozarks and the Dominion Energy. Els' two wins were widely separated. His first, the Hoag Classic in March, was his first win on any tour since 2013 and his first on a PGA Tour-sanctioned event since 2012. Then in October the South African won the SAS Championship.

"I gotta be satisfied," Els said. "It was nice to win again. As a rookie to have had the year I've had so far, I'm very satisfied."

Furyk said he'd been uncertain about committing to the Champions Tour, but "coming out here and having some success, seeing golf courses that are 7,000 yards, I kind of like the atmosphere. I've been enjoying it."

Miguel Angel Jimenez also won twice, lifting his victory total to 10 since joining the tour in 2014. He beat two Hall of Famers, Fred Couples and Els, in a playoff in the opener, the Mitsubishi Electric Championship, then won the Sanford International by a stroke.

"No, no, no nerves, no nerves," Jimenez said, on winning the Mitsubishi. "You feel the tension, but no nerves."

And on the return of fans to the tour — a limited number at the Sanford: "It's amazing. Now we have the start of getting back to life, you know."

Elsewhere among the champions:

The amazing Bernhard Langer, 63, continued to roll. He won the Cologuard Classic, his 41st tour victory, nearing Hale Irwin's record 45. Along with 12 top-10 finishes, he led the 2020 money list with almost $1.5 million in 15 starts.

Colin Montgomerie returned from the shutdown reporting, "I've lost a little weight." Actually, some 40 pounds, down to 198, after rigorous dieting and exercise. "I've felt good about it," Monty said. "Sometimes you lose rhythm and timing when you lose weight and all the swing goes. But I've hit a lot of balls and got the swing back."

Kevin Sutherland was becoming the tour's playoff scourge. He'd won four tour titles, and three of them by playoffs — but two of them not so ordinary. In 2019, he won the Rapiscan Systems Classic in a seven-hole playoff over Scott Parel, forced into a second day by darkness. (Later in 2019, he beat Parel in another playoff, just two holes, in the Principal Charity Classic.) Then Sutherland closed out the 2020 schedule in the Charles Schwab Cup Championship, beating Paul Broadhurst in a nine-hole playoff that was forced over two days by darkness. His principal concern that Sunday evening: "I've got to go find a hotel."

2020 SCHEDULE

Mitsubishi Electric Championship	**Miguel Angel Jimenez**	
Morocco Championship	**Brett Quigley**	
Chubb Classic	**Scott Parel**	
Cologuard Classic	**Bernhard Langer**	
Hoag Classic	**Ernie Els**	
Rapiscan Systems Classic		*cancelled*
Mitsubishi Electric Classic		*cancelled*
Insperity Invitational		*cancelled*
KitchenAid Senior PGA Championship		*cancelled*
American Family Insurance Championship		*cancelled*
Mastercard Japan Championship		*cancelled*
US Senior Open Championship		*cancelled*
The Senior Open presented by Rolex		*postponed to 2021*
Ally Challenge	**Jim Furyk**	
Bridgestone Senior Players Championship	**Jerry Kelly**	
Dick's Sporting Goods Open		*cancelled*
Charles Schwab Series — Big Cedar Lodge	**Shane Bertsch**	
Boeing Classic		*cancelled*
Charles Schwab Series — Ozarks National	**Phil Mickelson**	
Shaw Charity Classic		*cancelled*
Principal Charity Classic		*cancelled*
Sanford International	**Miguel Angel Jimenez**	
PURE Insurance Championship	**Jim Furyk**	
Regions Tradition		*cancelled*
Ascension Charity Classic		*cancelled*
SAS Championship	**Ernie Els**	
Dominion Energy Charity Classic	**Phil Mickelson**	
TimberTech Championship	**Darren Clarke**	
Charles Schwab Cup Championship	**Kevin Sutherland**	

Mitsubishi Electric Championship

This one was worth a big cigar. A big, big cigar.

And a man who can rip a shot into the rocks and watch it bounce back to safety is a man ready to light up.

The Mitsubishi Electric Championship, opening the PGA Tour Champions 2020 season in mid-January, turned into a Hall of Fame Derby. Early in the final nine, four members of the World Golf Hall of Fame were tied for the lead at 12 under — Bernhard Langer, Fred Couples, Retief Goosen and Ernie Els, the last making his tour debut.

But along came a party crasher — Spain's free-spirited Miguel Angel Jimenez, famed for capping off a win with a good cigar and a fine wine. Jimenez, perhaps a Hall of Famer himself someday, then won in a playoff against Couples and Els.

"I said to my caddie, 'The winning score is going to be 15 under par and we need to hurry up and make birdie'," offered Jimenez, coming down the homestretch. "Make three birdies in a row, 14 under par, and then here we are."

Close enough. Jimenez, two strokes behind starting the final round, birdied three straight from the 13th and wrapped up a card of 64-71-67 to tie Couples and Els at 14-under 202 at Hawaii's par-72 Hualalai.

Jimenez beat Els with a 12-foot birdie putt on the second visit to the playoff hole, the par-four 18th. Couples had bowed out with a bogey on the first visit, missing a three-foot par putt.

Els opened his new career with a 72, eight behind co-leaders Jimenez and Bernhard Langer. "Pretty disappointing," Els said. "Believe it or not, after all these years, I felt like a rookie and ... a little out of place." He joined the tie with a pair of 65s.

The shot of the tournament was Jimenez's tee shot at the par-three 17th in the final round. He watched it sail left, and then bounce off the lava — and back into a bunker. He saved par.

"I was very, very lucky," Jimenez said.

A lei was slipped over his head at the championship ceremony. He raised the beautiful flowers.

"Well, now here we are," Jimenez said, smiling hugely. "It looks nice and sexy."

Hualalai Golf Club, Ka'upulehu-Kona, Hawaii — January 16-18
Par 72 (36-36); 7,053 yards — Purse: $1,800,000

1	**Miguel Angel Jimenez**	64	71	67	202	$310,000
2	**Fred Couples**	67	68	67	202	170,000
	Ernie Els	72	65	65	202	170,000
	Jimenez won playoff at second extra hole					
4	Retief Goosen	67	73	64	204	101,000
	Wes Short Jr	70	67	67	204	101,000
6	Doug Barron	68	71	66	205	72,250
	Paul Broadhurst	70	66	69	205	72,250
	Bernhard Langer	64	70	71	205	72,250
9	Woody Austin	65	68	73	206	50,750
	Marco Dawson	67	69	70	206	50,750
	Scott McCarron	67	69	70	206	50,750
12	Joe Durant	66	72	69	207	38,250
	Steve Flesch	70	70	67	207	38,250
	Scott Parel	69	70	68	207	38,250
15	Jeff Maggert	69	72	67	208	31,156
	Colin Montgomerie	71	70	67	208	31,156
	Kenny Perry	66	75	67	208	31,156
	Kevin Sutherland	74	68	66	208	31,156
19	Davis Love III	74	66	69	209	24,458
	Mark O'Meara	73	67	69	209	24,458
	Ken Tanigawa	67	70	72	209	24,458
22	Brandt Jobe	68	71	71	210	21,125
	Jerry Kelly	70	70	70	210	21,125
	Rocco Mediate	72	71	67	210	21,125
25	Bart Bryant	70	73	68	211	17,594
	John Daly	69	68	74	211	17,594
	Sandy Lyle	71	71	69	211	17,594
	Gene Sauers	68	77	66	211	17,594
29	Vijay Singh	70	70	72	212	15,500
30	Fred Funk	71	70	72	213	14,500
	Jay Haas	71	73	69	213	14,500
	Tom Watson	69	75	69	213	14,500
33	Tom Pernice Jr	70	70	74	214	13,500
34	Tom Lehman	71	71	73	215	12,750
	Jeff Sluman	72	71	72	215	12,750
36	Kirk Triplett	72	71	73	216	12,000
37	Hale Irwin	72	74	72	218	11,500
38	Mark Calcavecchia	73	76	74	223	11,000

Morocco Champions

Brett Quigley, a native Rhode Islander from the northeastern coast of the US, found himself playing golf in Morocco, on the northwestern coast of Africa, and somehow immersed in a kind of stranger-in-paradise sensation.

"Just incredible," said Quigley, who had never been to Morocco. "I had a peace all week. I wouldn't say I was nervous until the last hole here on my second putt, but just felt comfortable here in Marrakech."

This was Quigley after winning the historic Morocco Champions, the first PGA Tour Champions strokeplay event in Africa. It was also his first win since the 2001 Arkansas Classic on what is now the Korn Ferry Tour.

The Morocco, played at Samanah Golf Club, a Jack Nicklaus course at Marrakech, drew a field of 66, including Bernhard Langer, Colin Montgomerie, Tom Lehman and Miguel Angel Jimenez.

And Quigley, 50, in his second Champions start, came from behind in the final round to edge two-round leader Stephen Ames. Quigley shot 69-66-66 for a 15-under-par total of 201 and won by one.

Quigley's chances seemed dim in the first round. His 69 left him six behind Ames' course record-tying 63 that included a charge on the par fives — an eagle and three birdies. "I capitalised with my putting," Ames said.

It was in Quigley's flawless second-round 66 that he noticed his surprising and pleasant state of mind. "We were shooting the breeze, talking sports and golf and being here," he said, playing with fellow Rhode Islander Billy Andrade. "Then all of a sudden I was five under on the front nine." That's also when he reached the leaderboard — in a way. The board didn't say "Quigley", it said "Brett". He guessed they didn't have a "Q". Ames cooled to a 69 and led him by three in the final round.

In the final round, Quigley quickly staked his claim to the title with a birdie-birdie-eagle burst from the second. Ames went bogey-bogey-birdie over the same stretch. Quigley kept control with two clutch putts, a 20-footer that saved par at 13 and a 40-footer for birdie at the par-three 14th. Quigley bogeyed 15 and parred in for his 66 to win by one, and Ames bogeyed 14 and 15 and birdied 16 and 17 and shot 70.

Quigley wondered if having been off for years with an injury was the key to his victory. "I think I was happier to be here," he said. "When you try too hard, you grip too tight and you want it too much."

Samanah Golf Club, Marrakech, Morocco — January 30-February 1
Par 72 (36-36); 7,369 yards — Purse: $2,000,000

1	**Brett Quigley**	69	66	66	201	$320,000		Tom Pernice Jr	68	71	70	209	37,050
2	**Stephen Ames**	63	69	70	202	176,000	17	Retief Goosen	67	73	70	210	30,000
3	**Doug Barron**	71	66	68	205	131,000		Kent Jones	69	69	72	210	30,000
	Scott Parel	68	68	69	205	131,000		Scott McCarron	71	65	74	210	30,000
5	Woody Austin	69	71	66	206	82,867	20	Marco Dawson	72	68	71	211	24,000
	Jose Maria Olazabal	67	68	71	206	82,867		Larry Mize	71	69	71	211	24,000
	Bernhard Langer	67	68	71	206	82,867		Tommy Tolles	73	70	68	211	24,000
8	Rod Pampling	68	68	71	207	60,000		Kirk Triplett	70	67	74	211	24,000
	Kevin Sutherland	68	70	69	207	60,000	24	Billy Andrade	69	72	71	212	18,286
10	Paul Broadhurst	71	70	67	208	48,000		Miguel Angel Jimenez	70	72	70	212	18,286
	Stephen Leaney	70	68	70	208	48,000		Sandy Lyle	71	69	72	212	18,286
	Duffy Waldorf	72	68	68	208	48,000		Roger Chapman	70	68	74	212	18,286
13	Darren Clarke	71	68	70	209	37,050		Jerry Kelly	69	70	73	212	18,286
	Colin Montgomerie	67	69	73	209	37,050		Jesper Parnevik	70	69	73	212	18,286
	Mark O'Meara	71	68	70	209	37,050		Ken Tanigawa	68	70	74	212	18,286

Chubb Classic

Legend and lore can say what they want about the wrist, but as Scott Parel demonstrated to his own satisfaction and success at the Chubb Classic, it's all in the thumb.

"I changed my thumb a little bit on my grip," Parel said. "The club doesn't feel in the right spot, so I made a little adjustment, made my thumb on top of the club, and then from there on I hit every line I was looking at."

And then there was the putting. "My speed was great today," he said. "When you make that 12-footer on the first hole, it gives you a little confidence ... I mean, my putting was really good."

It all added up to a card of 64-69-63 at the par-71 Classics at Lely for his third Champions Tour win by two over Bob Estes.

Parel's opening 64, which tied him with Doug Barron for a one-shot lead, was made up of eight birdies and a bogey that had him thanking his stars. "I lost the ball in the palm tree," Parel said. "And I chipped in for a five. It could be six or seven, easily."

A buffeting stretch of three bogeys over four holes heading into the turn held Parel to the 69 in the second round, three off the lead. Australia's Stephen Leaney, with his second 65, took the top spot, one ahead of Langer, and was needled with the question of how he might do under the pressure with such as Langer and Fred Couples in pursuit. Said Leaney, "I have won 16, 17 times in the world."

Parel wasted no time crashing the party in the final round. He birdied the first two holes, added two others, and took the lead with another at the 10th as Langer bogeyed the eighth and ninth. He was up by two, and was untouched the rest of the way in his flawless eight-birdie 63. He shot a 17-under 196 total.

"You start to wonder how many more times are you're going to get in contention," Parel said. "So for me to be in contention and to finish the job — very happy."

The Classics at Lely Resort, Naples, Florida — February 14-16
Par 71 (35-36); 6,843 yards — Purse: $1,600,000

1	**Scott Parel**	64	69	63	196	$240,000
2	**Bob Estes**	67	67	64	198	140,800
3	**Kevin Sutherland**	70	63	67	200	105,600
	Bernhard Langer	65	66	69	200	105,600
5	Chris DiMarco	68	64	69	201	66,133
	Marco Dawson	67	67	67	201	66,133
	Stephen Leaney	65	65	71	201	66,133
8	Fred Couples	67	65	70	202	51,200
9	Brandt Jobe	66	69	68	203	37,067
	Stephen Ames	69	67	67	203	37,067
	Brett Quigley	69	67	67	203	37,067
	Tom Lehman	71	69	63	203	37,067
	Woody Austin	66	71	66	203	37,067
	David Toms	69	68	66	203	37,067
15	Tim Petrovic	66	68	70	204	28,000
	Retief Goosen	69	68	67	204	28,000
17	Fred Funk	65	67	73	205	21,947
	Kent Jones	69	66	70	205	21,947
	Mark Brooks	66	69	70	205	21,947
	Rod Pampling	69	67	69	205	21,947
	Doug Barron	64	72	69	205	21,947
	Darren Clarke	71	69	65	205	21,947
23	Scott Verplank	67	68	71	206	16,032
	John Daly	68	67	71	206	16,032
	Ken Tanigawa	65	69	72	206	16,032
	Jeff Maggert	70	68	68	206	16,032
	Robert Karlsson	69	68	69	206	16,032
28	Tom Byrum	71	67	69	207	12,672
	Ken Duke	70	69	68	207	12,672
	Wes Short Jr	67	71	69	207	12,672
	Billy Andrade	68	70	69	207	12,672
	Jerry Kelly	68	70	69	207	12,672

Cologuard Classic

Bernhard Langer wrapped up his 41st victory on the PGA Tour Champions with a crackling good finish. Just four from Hale Irwin's record 45. He'd trailed by four strokes entering the last round, made nine birdies, shot an eight-under 65 and won by two. And the first question was, where would he rank this round in his career?

"It was very much up there," Langer said, without hesitating. Then he added an exception. "Certainly the first 17 and a half holes," he allowed. "That six-iron on the last wasn't a lot of quality."

This would be his approach shot to Tucson National's par-four 18th. It was a bit off and cost him a bogey — his only bogey of the day. In fact, his first in 38 holes. Those nine birdies were wonderful. But that six-iron ate at him.

He had to stay out of the water at 18, he explained, so "hit a great three-wood off the tee," he said, "and had a six-iron in there, which was not a very good shot. But almost chipped in and almost holed the putt. But almost doesn't count."

Brett Quigley, who won his first tour title in the Morocco Champions a month ago, opened the Cologuard with 64-68, and led Robert Karlsson by a stroke in the first round, then Fred Couples by two in the second and noted, "I'm just playing golf, I'm just trying to keep it simple."

Langer was not in an entirely promising position. With his 68-68 start at the par-73 course, he trailed by four in each of the first two rounds. And with the challengers facing him — Quigley, Couples and Miguel Angel Jimenez, among others — his prospects didn't brighten.

But he lit up the final round from the start, with birdies at the first three holes. He added two more on the front nine, then made four on the back, before that offending bogey at 18. Did he ever think about Hale Irwin's record? he was asked..

Another smile. "I don't think about it," he said. "But I get reminded of it just about every week. We don't live and die for records," he noted, "but it's fun to have a couple of them."

So Langer loves that 41st win. Even so, he'd give anything for another crack at that six-iron.

Omni Tucson National (Catalina), Tucson, Arizona — February 28-March 1
Par 73 (36-37); 7,238 yards — Purse: $1,700,000

1	**Bernhard Langer**	68	68	65	201	$255,000
2	**Woody Austin**	69	68	66	203	149,600
3	**Rod Pampling**	67	68	70	205	112,200
	Brett Quigley	64	68	73	205	112,200
5	Fred Couples	68	66	72	206	70,267
	Miguel Angel Jimenez	69	66	71	206	70,267
	Steve Stricker	67	71	68	206	70,267
8	Robert Karlsson	65	71	71	207	54,400
9	John Daly	67	71	70	208	36,975
	Glen Day	67	70	71	208	36,975
	Ken Duke	73	68	67	208	36,975
	Lee Janzen	69	71	68	208	36,975
	Stephen Leaney	69	70	69	208	36,975
	Larry Mize	72	67	69	208	36,975
	Kevin Sutherland	72	67	69	208	36,975
	Scott Verplank	70	68	70	208	36,975
17	Mark O'Meara	69	69	71	209	27,200
18	Bart Bryant	71	66	73	210	21,902
	Bob Estes	73	70	67	210	21,902
	Jeff Maggert	70	71	69	210	21,902
	Jesper Parnevik	71	72	67	210	21,902
	Kenny Perry	76	67	67	210	21,902
	Gene Sauers	72	68	70	210	21,902
	Olin Browne	70	68	73	211	16,252
	Darren Clarke	70	71	70	211	16,252
	David Frost	72	72	67	211	16,252
	Colin Montgomerie	73	68	70	211	16,252
	David Toms	71	69	71	211	16,252
29	Paul Broadhurst	73	70	69	212	12,852
	Thongchai Jaidee	69	73	70	212	12,852
	Jose Maria Olazabal	71	73	68	212	12,852
	Tim Petrovic	72	70	70	212	12,852
	Willie Wood	70	71	71	212	12,852

Hoag Classic

Ernie Els was listening to the silence coming from the last green.

That was big-hitting Fred Couples up ahead, always smooth and dangerous. They were closing out the Hoag Classic at Newport Beach Country Club, and Els, now 50 and in his third start on the PGA Tour Champions, had that first victory almost in hand.

"I was listening to the crowd," Els said.

The Hoag had turned into a real scramble coming down the final homestretch. Els had entered the last round with a one-stroke lead. There was a five-way tie at one point, and Els even lost the lead at another, and then there was a three-way tie.

"Freddie's a hometown man," Els said. "There wasn't any big roar, so I knew he didn't make birdie. So I saw Robert Karlsson hit it over the green and he didn't make birdie. So then I just had to survive."

Els had lost in a playoff to Miguel Angel Jimenez in his tour debut in the season-opener, the Mitsubishi Electric Championship, then tied for 34th in his second start, the Cologuard Classic.

"I didn't want to mess this one up," he said.

He didn't. He birdied the par-five 18th, wrapping up a card of 66-64-67 for a 16-under-par total of 197 and a two-stroke win over Couples (66), who parred the last in quiet, and Karlsson (66) and Glen Day (64).

Said Couples, trying to win the event for the third time: "I butchered the two par fives coming in." Parred them, that is. "Other than that, I had a really, really good round."

First-round leader David Morland IV was a Monday qualifier of the toughest kind. An intense California brush fire was roaring near Goose Creek, finally forcing a halt to play and the evacuation of players. Scores had to be phone-videoed in for a match of cards. Morland then opened with a 10-under 61. "Nice stroll in the park," the Canadian said.

And Els was an uncomfortable winner. "I didn't have that free-flowing feeling," he said. "I had to work hard for it and that's a good thing, to work hard for something. You don't want something falling in your lap."

Newport Beach Country Club, Newport Beach, California — March 6-8
Par 71 (35-36); 6,575 yards — Purse: $1,800,000

1	**Ernie Els**	66	64	67	197	$270,000
2	**Fred Couples**	67	66	66	199	132,000
	Glen Day	70	65	64	199	132,000
	Robert Karlsson	68	65	66	199	132,000
5	Scott McCarron	63	68	69	200	86,400
6	Jay Haas	67	67	67	201	72,000
7	David Morland IV	61	70	71	202	61,200
	Kevin Sutherland	69	68	65	202	61,200
9	Scott Dunlap	67	72	64	203	50,400
10	Ken Duke	63	69	72	204	43,200
	Steve Flesch	66	72	66	204	43,200
	David McKenzie	68	68	68	204	43,200
13	Chris DiMarco	66	67	72	205	35,100
	Miguel Angel Jimenez	66	68	71	205	35,100
15	Jesper Parnevik	68	70	68	206	30,600
	Kenny Perry	68	71	67	206	30,600
	Kirk Triplett	70	65	71	206	30,600
18	Paul Broadhurst	70	70	67	207	23,190
	Darren Clarke	71	69	67	207	23,190
	Bob Estes	71	69	67	207	23,190
	Tim Herron	69	70	68	207	23,190
	John Huston	68	69	70	207	23,190
	Ken Tanigawa	66	66	75	207	23,190
24	Michael Allen	70	72	66	208	16,457
	Scott Parel	70	70	68	208	16,457
	Tommy Armour III	72	67	69	208	16,457
	Woody Austin	67	71	70	208	16,457
	Doug Barron	71	68	69	208	16,457
	Billy Mayfair	66	71	71	208	16,457
	Gene Sauers	70	65	73	208	16,457

Ally Challenge

It was merely a date on the golf schedule, July 31-Aug 2, and the name Ally Challenge was on the board, and the world of golf rejoiced. This was the return of golf, shut down after the first week of March by the Covid-19 pandemic. There would be no fans, none of the usual trappings of golf. But golf was back.

The question was, how would the golfers feel after some five months without competition? There was plenty of practice, but no real competition.

"All of us are in the same boat," said Billy Andrade. "You don't know coming out of the gate, how you're going to play."

And if there was such a thing as homecookin' in golf, the chap over there with the white apron and chef's hat is Jim Furyk, holding court at Warwick Hills for the Ally Challenge.

Warwick Hills hosted the old Buick Open on the PGA Tour. Furyk won it in 2003, was runner-up twice and shot par or better in 59 out of his 60 rounds when the tournament was a fixture on the PGA Tour. Now he'd turned 50, and the course was hosting the Ally Challenge on the Champions Tour.

The winner? Jim Furyk, and in his debut on the Champions Tour. Furyk also kept his Warwick Hills par-or-better record intact, shooting 68-66-68, and took the lead in the final round to win by two with a 14-under-par total of 202. Brett Quigley (71) bogeyed his last two holes and tied for second with Retief Goosen (66).

"It feels good," said Furyk, with his first victory since the RBC Heritage in 2015 on the PGA Tour. "So just excited to be able to come out here first week and play so well and get a win."

Furyk turned 50 while the Champions Tour had been discontinued because of the Covid-19 pandemic.

"I guess the one thing I did miss all week was the fans," Furyk said. "Miss the rowdiness at 17 ..."

Furyk launched his return to the par-72 Warwick Hills with a 68, as Tommy Armour III and Andrade shared the first-round lead with 66s. Bernhard Langer made six birdies in 12 holes, then stumbled to two bogeys and shot 67. Quigley shot 69 and spoke of the pressure he put on himself. "I was trying to shoot 20 under on the front nine," he said.

The chase tightened in the second round. Quigley, playing his regular game, took the lead with a 64, and Furyk moved to within a shot with a 66. "I'm looking forward to getting in the mix, having some nerves," Furyk said. "I've got a lot of experience to fall back on, but it will still be a little new."

Furyk got his wish in the final round. Quigley wobbled down the back nine to two bogeys, then two birdies, and closed with two bogeys for a 71, tying for second at 12 under with Retief Goosen, who eagled the first, then had an active three-bogey 66. Furyk fell back on that experience for a flawless four-birdie 68.

Furyk noted he was the 19th player to win their first event on the Champions Tour. "It sounds so ordinary," he said. "Wow. I'm amazed. It felt pretty darn hard to do."

Warwick Hills Golf & Country Club, Grand Blanc, Michigan — July 31-August 2
Par 72 (36-36); 7,085 yards — Purse: $2,000,000

1	**Jim Furyk**	68	66	68	202	$300,000
2	**Retief Goosen**	69	69	66	204	160,000
	Brett Quigley	69	64	71	204	160,000
4	Chris DiMarco	70	70	65	205	98,000
	Rod Pampling	68	69	68	205	98,000
	Wes Short Jr	67	69	69	205	98,000
7	Jerry Kelly	69	68	69	206	64,000
	Bernhard Langer	67	70	69	206	64,000
	Tom Lehman	70	68	68	206	64,000
10	Woody Austin	68	68	71	207	46,000
	Glen Day	69	66	72	207	46,000
	Kevin Sutherland	69	68	70	207	46,000
	Carlos Franco	70	64	73	207	46,000
14	Joe Durant	71	68	69	208	34,000
	Fred Funk	71	67	70	208	34,000
	Jeff Maggert	71	67	70	208	34,000
	Scott Parel	70	69	69	208	34,000
	Kirk Triplett	70	68	70	208	34,000
19	Bob Estes	68	70	71	209	23,000
	Tim Herron	73	66	70	209	23,000
	Scott Hoch	70	70	69	209	23,000
	Kenny Perry	72	68	69	209	23,000
	Tim Petrovic	70	69	70	209	23,000
	David Toms	68	70	71	209	23,000
	Tommy Armour III	66	68	75	209	23,000
	Dudley Hart	71	69	69	209	23,000
27	Doug Barron	68	73	69	210	15,886
	Paul Broadhurst	75	67	68	210	15,886
	Angel Cabrera	70	72	68	210	15,886
	KJ Choi	72	68	70	210	15,886
	Ernie Els	69	69	72	210	15,886
	Rocco Mediate	72	69	69	210	15,886
	Mike Weir	70	69	71	210	15,886

Bridgestone Senior Players Championship

Happiness is — making double bogey on the last hole and winning anyway.

Meet Jerry Kelly, one really happy gentleman. Well, with reservations.

"It was hard to go crazy after doubling the last hole," he said.

Kelly had double-bogeyed Firestone South's par-four 18th, and despite that wound, he won the Bridgestone Senior Players Championship, his first major on the Champions Tour, by two strokes. He had the cushion because six holes earlier, his perfect soft-cut five-iron at the par-three 12th rolled obediently into the cup.

The ace gave Kelly the final control, and the closing double bogey merely reduced his winning margin to two strokes over Scott Parel. Kelly shot the four-round tournament in 68-70-70-69, a three-under 277.

"Just to have a major is huge for me," Kelly said.

The tournament opened on the gallop. Fully five players tied for the first round lead at two-under 68 — Miguel Angel Jimenez, Wes Short Jr, Steve Stricker, Rod Pampling and Kelly. Paul Broadhurst, with a 69, was the only other player to break par, and Fred Couples and Bernhard Langer were at 70.

Kelly's 70 in the second round gave him the lead to nurse the rest of the way, though Parel would cut it to one with his 67 in the third. "I did get some lucky breaks," Parel said, "but you're not going to get a whole lot of luck out there."

In the final round, both had two early birdies, and Kelly went two ahead when Parel bogeyed the sixth. It was one when Kelly bogeyed the 11th. Then came Kelly's ace at the 12th, followed by Parel's bogey at 13.

It came down to Kelly's crash at Firestone's par-four 18th. Kelly went from a fairway bunker off a tree into the rough, then reached in three and three-putted from 40 feet for his only double bogey of the tournament, and a 69.

Said Parel: "I was very happy with how I played today. Just — it was Jerry's day."

Kelly's ace at 12 created a family issue. He decided it put him one ahead of his mother, an eight-handicap golfer in her time. "So my mom's got some work to do right now," he said.

Firestone Country Club (South), Akron, Ohio — August 13-16
Par 70 (35-35); 7,400 yards — Purse: $3,000,000

1	**Jerry Kelly**	68	70	70	69	277	$450,000
2	**Scott Parel**	71	71	67	70	279	264,000
3	**Miguel Angel Jimenez**	68	74	69	69	280	197,250
	Colin Montgomerie	72	69	68	71	280	197,250
5	Woody Austin	73	69	67	73	282	123,500
	Ernie Els	71	73	68	70	282	123,500
	Rod Pampling	68	73	75	66	282	123,500
8	Fred Couples	70	75	68	70	283	90,000
	Kevin Sutherland	74	72	69	68	283	90,000
10	Tom Gillis	71	71	72	71	285	69,000
	Dudley Hart	75	69	74	67	285	69,000
	Bernhard Langer	70	73	71	71	285	69,000
	Mike Weir	72	70	71	72	285	69,000
14	Joe Durant	76	69	71	70	286	55,500
	Robert Karlsson	70	71	72	73	286	55,500
16	Paul Broadhurst	69	76	74	68	287	48,000
	Stephen Leaney	76	76	66	69	287	48,000
	Gene Sauers	74	73	70	70	287	48,000
19	Scott Dunlap	72	71	69	76	288	38,250
	Kenny Perry	70	74	68	76	288	38,250
	Dicky Pride	71	71	72	74	288	38,250
	Willie Wood	73	70	71	74	288	38,250
23	Doug Barron	76	71	72	70	289	30,750
	Darren Clarke	75	70	72	72	289	30,750
	Steve Stricker	68	73	73	75	289	30,750
	Duffy Waldorf	70	74	72	73	289	30,750
27	Jay Haas	73	75	71	71	290	27,300
28	Tom Byrum	75	72	73	71	291	23,760
	Marco Dawson	72	73	74	72	291	23,760
	Retief Goosen	75	75	70	71	291	23,760
	Scott McCarron	71	75	78	67	291	23,760
	Brett Quigley	73	72	72	74	291	23,760
33	Billy Andrade	72	74	75	71	292	17,100
	Paul Goydos	78	72	73	69	292	17,100
	Brandt Jobe	76	74	72	70	292	17,100
	Kent Jones	76	76	70	70	292	17,100
	Billy Mayfair	78	73	68	73	292	17,100
	Jesper Parnevik	80	72	69	71	292	17,100
	Steve Pate	73	76	73	70	292	17,100
	Tim Petrovic	74	70	78	70	292	17,100
	Ken Tanigawa	72	73	76	71	292	17,100
	David Toms	76	75	72	69	292	17,100
43	Tom Lehman	75	76	73	69	293	13,200
	Vijay Singh	73	74	72	74	293	13,200
45	Ken Duke	74	74	72	74	294	11,700
	Lee Janzen	71	79	76	68	294	11,700
	Shaun Micheel	71	71	74	78	294	11,700
48	Stephen Ames	73	75	77	70	295	9,600
	David McKenzie	75	71	76	73	295	9,600
	Larry Mize	77	71	74	73	295	9,600
	Wes Short Jr	68	83	72	72	295	9,600
52	Tim Herron	71	76	78	71	296	7,425
	John Huston	71	78	72	75	296	7,425
	Jeff Maggert	76	76	71	73	296	7,425
	Jeff Sluman	77	77	67	75	296	7,425
56	Chris DiMarco	78	76	69	74	297	6,300
	Carlos Franco	72	79	75	71	297	6,300
	David Morland	76	75	72	74	297	6,300
59	Bob Estes	74	74	75	75	298	5,550
	Esteban Toledo	75	75	73	75	298	5,550
61	Kirk Triplett	77	74	72	76	299	5,100
62	Glen Day	76	78	73	73	300	4,350
	Steve Flesch	73	73	74	80	300	4,350
	David Frost	76	74	75	75	300	4,350
	Loren Roberts	72	74	74	80	300	4,350
66	Mark O'Meara	74	82	70	75	301	3,600
67	Mark Calcavecchia	76	79	76	71	302	3,150
	Rocco Mediate	78	77	73	74	302	3,150
69	Joey Sindelar	75	76	75	77	303	2,820
70	Angel Cabrera	78	77	81	68	304	2,550
	John Daly	72	79	82	71	304	2,550
72	Frank Lickliter II	81	74	75	75	305	2,280
73	Olin Browne	74	77	75	81	307	2,100
74	Dan Forsman	78	78	74	79	309	1,980
75	Tom Pernice Jr	77	78	80	78	313	1,860
76	Blaine McCallister	82	84	77	78	321	1,740

Charles Schwab Series — Big Cedar Lodge

"I've always had a hard time saying what my most special moment in golf is," Shane Bertsch said.

Then he answered his own question and underlined it when his eagle putt dropped in the playoff for the Charles Schwab Series at Bass Pro Shops Big Cedar Lodge.

"Without a doubt," Bertsch could finally say, "it was that putt on the first playoff hole."

Bertsch, 50, a three-time winner on the Korn Ferry Tour, won the Bass in his second Champions start, and he did it in heavy traffic, in a four-way playoff with Kenny Perry, Glen Day and Bernhard Langer. And he did it after what he called the "thinking" had started bothering him in the final round. He tied for the first-round lead with Tom Lehman at seven-under 64 at the par-71 Buffalo Ridge, then shot another 64 in the second round and led by four going into the final round.

"I don't think I've ever had a four-stroke lead going into the final day," he said. He was paired with Langer and Perry, and led both by four. Day was three groups ahead. Then came the "thinking".

"I was pretty comfortable this morning really, but missed a little putt on the first hole for birdie and started thinking," Bertsch said. "Miss another little one on the third hole. You start thinking. It really is hard to win that way. I hit some goofy shots and some poor putts, and I just kept hanging in there."

Bertsch birdied the fourth, bogeyed the seventh and eighth, birdied 14 and bogeyed 15 for a one-over 72 and a 13-under-par total of 200.

Perry was leading by one at the 18th, but drove into rough on the left under the trees, bogeyed for a 68 and fell into a playoff with Langer (68), Day (66) and Bertsch.

The playoff began — and ended — at the par-five first hole. Bertsch drove to near the back edge of a bunker, reached the green, and faced a 20-foot downhill putt.

"It had probably two feet of break," Bertsch said. "It was pretty quick. It took its time getting there. I really had a good feeling because I just felt like everything had gone the wrong way today and something had to go right. And it did."

Big Cedar Lodge (Buffalo Ridge), Ridgedale, Missouri — August 19-21
Par 71 (35-36); 7,036 yards — Purse: $3,000,000

1	**Shane Bertsch**	64	64	72	200	$450,000
2	**Glen Day**	67	67	66	200	219,500
	Bernhard Langer	68	64	68	200	219,500
	Kenny Perry	67	65	68	200	219,500
	Bertsch won playoff at first extra hole					
5	Tom Byrum	68	70	63	201	131,250
	Vijay Singh	67	66	68	201	131,250
7	Ernie Els	68	68	66	202	102,000
	Steve Stricker	67	68	67	202	102,000
9	Darren Clarke	66	67	70	203	81,000
	Wes Short Jr	66	66	71	203	81,000
11	Scott Dunlap	70	69	65	204	58,286
	Robert Karlsson	69	69	66	204	58,286
	David McKenzie	69	70	65	204	58,286
	KJ Choi	68	69	67	204	58,286
	Tom Lehman	64	71	69	204	58,286
	Colin Montgomerie	68	66	70	204	58,286
	Scott Parel	69	65	70	204	58,286
18	Fred Couples	69	68	68	205	40,800
	Retief Goosen	70	65	70	205	40,800
	Gene Sauers	72	68	65	205	40,800
	Duffy Waldorf	67	67	71	205	40,800
22	Lee Janzen	68	72	66	206	33,900
	Kent Jones	67	72	67	206	33,900
24	Paul Goydos	70	70	67	207	28,680
	Miguel Angel Jimenez	69	71	67	207	28,680
	Rocco Mediate	68	69	70	207	28,680
	Jesper Parnevik	68	67	72	207	28,680
	Tim Petrovic	66	69	72	207	28,680
29	Marco Dawson	67	69	72	208	22,200
	Jay Haas	70	67	71	208	22,200
	Brandt Jobe	72	69	67	208	22,200
	Jerry Kelly	70	67	71	208	22,200
	Kirk Triplett	75	66	67	208	22,200
	Scott Verplank	73	64	71	208	22,200

Charles Schwab Series — Ozarks National

Champions Tour — meet Phil Mickelson.

Who needed no introduction.

And who entered the Champions Tour laughing, with a 10-under-par 61 in the first round of the Charles Schwab Series at Ozarks National, and who rolled from there to a four-stroke win.

"It's a lot of fun," Mickelson said, in his debut on the 50-and-older tour. "It's a fun environment. And it's fun to see a lot of the guys I grew up watching, and played with them for a number of years. I was a little nervous, too, because I wanted to come out and play well. I was playing really well."

Mickelson's appearance at the Ozarks in August was largely by happenstance. He had turned 50 two months earlier, in June, but he intended to stay with the PGA Tour. Then he missed a cut, and felt he needed some more real competition to get ready for the upcoming US Open, rescheduled from June to September because of the Covid-19 pandemic. The Schwab fit, and so he jumped in.

He got the tune-up, but he wasn't seriously challenged as he posted 61-64-66 for a total of 191, 22 under. He won by four over Tim Petrovic, who also closed with a 66.

Mickelson already had a target in the first round. Australia's David McKenzie played earlier in the first round and shot a 62. Mickelson's 61 had one blemish, a bogey at the ninth. He raced through the back nine with six birdies, five consecutively from the 13th.

"We have a lot of golf left," Mickelson cautioned. He managed a one-bogey 64 in the second round, but at 17 under had widened his lead to four over Tim Petrovic (65) and Rod Pampling (65).

Petrovic had played with Mickelson on the PGA Tour. "Told him I was happy he came out and played, hang with the old guys," Petrovic said. "Now he's one of the old guys, a young 50."

Mickelson's closing 66 was marked by two noteworthy points. It was his only two-bogey round, and he eagled number five, which happened to be a par four. A 340-yard drive and a 30-foot putt did the trick.

Said Petrovic: "We're like, 'OK, all right. That's enough'."

And Mickelson's report card on himself and his tune-up: "There was a lot of good and there was some things I identified that I've got to work on. Being able to play and compete here was very helpful for me rather than shutting it down for a couple weeks."

Big Cedar Lodge (Ozarks National), Ridgedale, Missouri — August 24-26
Par 71 (36-35); 7,036 yards — Purse: $3,000,000

1	**Phil Mickelson**	61	64	66	191	$450,000
2	**Tim Petrovic**	64	65	66	195	264,000
3	**Kevin Sutherland**	66	68	63	197	216,000
4	Robert Karlsson	66	67	65	198	177,000
5	Rocco Mediate	64	66	69	199	131,250
	Steve Stricker	66	66	67	199	131,250
7	KJ Choi	64	67	69	200	91,500
	Ernie Els	65	69	66	200	91,500
	Brandt Jobe	65	69	66	200	91,500
	Jeff Maggert	69	68	63	200	91,500
11	Rod Pampling	64	65	72	201	69,000
	David Toms	66	68	67	201	69,000
13	Ken Duke	66	67	69	202	58,500
	Mike Weir	65	69	68	202	58,500
15	Mark Calcavecchia	66	68	69	203	48,000
	Marco Dawson	66	70	67	203	48,000
	Retief Goosen	68	65	70	203	48,000
	Gene Sauers	67	69	67	203	48,000
	Kirk Triplett	70	65	68	203	48,000
20	Paul Broadhurst	69	71	64	204	34,100
	Chris DiMarco	70	68	66	204	34,100
	Kent Jones	68	69	67	204	34,100
	Bernhard Langer	65	68	71	204	34,100
	Billy Mayfair	70	65	69	204	34,100
	David McKenzie	62	70	72	204	34,100
26	Doug Barron	71	66	68	205	27,300
	Joe Durant	69	69	67	205	27,300
	Tom Lehman	68	68	69	205	27,300
29	Bob Estes	65	74	67	206	23,175
	John Huston	66	71	69	206	23,175
	Scott Parel	66	72	68	206	23,175
	Scott Verplank	71	68	67	206	23,175

Sanford International

The Sanford International in mid-September was a celebration of golf — the first tournament admitting fans since the suspension for the Covid-19 pandemic. The precautions were everywhere at Minnehaha Country Club — hand-sanitiser stations, temperature checks, free masks, a ban on autographs.

And Miguel Angel Jimenez, the moustachioed, pony-tailed Spanish golfer-philosopher, held a celebration of his own on winning the Sanford.

"How am I going to celebrate?" said Jimenez. "We start already. We have some wine here — it's my favourite drink. Nice cigar... The short period you're going to be here in this world, enjoy yourself."

Jimenez went wire-to-wire at the par-70 Minnehaha, tying in his first two rounds of 65-66, then closing with a 65 for a 14-under-par total of 196 and a one-stroke victory over Steve Flesch.

Jimenez was hardly a flamenco whiz, but he might have done some heel-banging on the par-five 12th. "That hole," he marvelled, after playing it eagle-birdie-eagle, "is beautiful. Five under par in three days, and especially today, after hitting a beautiful drive into the wind, I have 230 yards to the hole, right to the flag, and five-foot putt. Knock it in."

The tournament had opened on a sombre note, with John Daly revealing he was being treated for bladder cancer. "I never thought I would see me getting to 50," the 54-year-old Daly said. He shot 68-66-68 and tied for 12th.

Jimenez opened with a 65, tying for the lead with David Toms and Dicky Pride in the rain. "Keep working and enjoy yourself on the golf course — that's the main thing," he said. He had a busy second-round 66, birdieing three of the last four holes. Steve Stricker, winner of the inaugural Sanford in 2018, shot 64 and tied Jimenez at nine under, and Darren Clarke rocketed 31 spots on his 62 to tie for third.

In the finale, Flesch eagled the 16th, shot 63, finished second by a stroke, and was pleased by his recovery from shoulder surgery. "I'm playing golf instead of worrying about how I feel," he said.

Jimenez had the last word, and it was on the return of fans. "It's amazing," he said. "Now we have the start of getting back to life, you know."

Minnehaha Country Club, Sioux Falls, South Dakota
Par 70 (34-36); 6,729 yards

September 11-13
Purse: $1,800,000

1	**Miguel Angel Jimenez**	65	66	65	196	$270,000
2	**Steve Flesch**	66	68	63	197	158,400
3	**Bernhard Langer**	68	65	65	198	118,350
	Steve Stricker	67	64	67	198	118,350
5	Scott Parel	71	66	62	199	85,500
6	Jerry Kelly	66	68	66	200	68,400
	David Toms	65	68	67	200	68,400
8	Glen Day	69	64	68	201	49,500
	Ernie Els	68	68	65	201	49,500
	Brandt Jobe	69	66	66	201	49,500
	Scott McCarron	68	66	67	201	49,500
12	Paul Broadhurst	66	71	65	202	34,560
	Darren Clarke	70	62	70	202	34,560
	John Daly	68	66	68	202	34,560
	Tim Herron	71	66	65	202	34,560
	Dicky Pride	65	69	68	202	34,560
17	Woody Austin	68	65	70	203	23,288
	Shane Bertsch	71	68	64	203	23,288
	Robert Karlsson	67	68	68	203	23,288
	Bob May	70	66	67	203	23,288
	Rocco Mediate	70	68	65	203	23,288
	Rod Pampling	70	63	70	203	23,288
	Tim Petrovic	71	65	67	203	23,288
	Kevin Sutherland	68	64	71	203	23,288
25	Fred Couples	68	64	72	204	16,416
	Colin Montgomerie	70	67	67	204	16,416
	Brett Quigley	70	68	66	204	16,416
	Scott Verplank	73	66	65	204	16,416
	Ken Tanigawa	70	68	66	204	16,416
30	Michael Allen	70	64	71	205	12,996
	Jay Haas	68	69	68	205	12,996
	Jeff Maggert	69	66	70	205	12,996
	David McKenzie	68	68	69	205	12,996
	Dudley Hart	70	67	68	205	12,996

PURE Insurance Championship

Jim Furyk had come of age and taken his loopy swing to the PGA Tour Champions and was quick to join some exclusive company. It was a matter of putting just the right spin on things.

Furyk beat Jerry Kelly on the first playoff hole in the PURE Insurance Championship at Pebble Beach in September, thereby joining Bruce Fleisher as the only players to win their first two starts on the Champions Tour. Furyk won in his debut in the Ally Championship the previous month. Fleisher won his first two in 1999.

The key to Furyk's victory was how well and how fast he learned his lesson at Pebble's sun-kissed par-five 18th. In the final round, he'd hit a gap wedge in and could see how firm the green was. The ball kicked forward. He parred and tied Kelly. So in the playoff, he said, "with it not playing quite as long, it was kind of a perfect go-ahead-and-hit-sand-wedge. I knew I could spin it."

Kelly hit his approach to 10 feet and Furyk stuck his to three feet. Kelly pulled his putt, and Furyk holed his for the win.

The playoff came within a whisker of being a three-way affair. Ernie Els, who had duelled Furyk from the start, just missed a two-footer for par at the 18th.

After an early birdie-bogey exchange in the opening round, Furyk ran off eight birdies over 13 holes for an eight-under 64 and led by one. "A great golf course in front of me and two more days," he said. Els tied for second with a 65 that included a hole-in-one at the par-three 12th, his third ace of the season. "I should go to the casino," Els mused.

Els battled stiff winds for a 70 in the second round and took the lead by one over Dicky Pride (70) and by two over Furyk, who closed bogey-double bogey for a 73.

Furyk was looking at his target in the final round. Kelly had closed with a 65 and was leading at 12-under 204. Furyk went five under on the first six holes, including an eagle at the par-five second, for a 67 to tie Kelly.

Then came his decisive sand-wedge spin in the playoff.

"I knew it was going to be a fight," Furyk said, "and I knew I had to make birdie."

Pebble Beach Golf Links, Pebble Beach, California
Par 72 (36-36); 6,864 yards

September 18-20
Purse: $2,200,000

1	**Jim Furyk**	64	73	67	204	$330,000
2	**Jerry Kelly**	71	68	65	204	193,600
	Furyk won playoff at first extra hole					
3	**Ernie Els**	65	70	70	205	158,400
4	Retief Goosen	69	68	70	207	117,950
	Mike Weir	73	65	69	207	117,950
6	Steve Flesch	70	69	69	208	83,600
	Robert Karlsson	69	72	67	208	83,600
8	Kent Jones	68	73	68	209	66,200
	Bernhard Langer	68	73	68	209	66,200

10	Cameron Beckman	65 72 73	210	50,600		Stephen Leaney	65 72 75	212	27,500
	Marco Dawson	70 70 70	210	50,600		Scott Parel	68 72 72	212	27,500
	Gene Sauers	68 71 71	210	50,600		Tim Petrovic	71 70 71	212	27,500
	Kevin Sutherland	68 71 71	210	50,600		Vijay Singh	71 71 70	212	27,500
14	Woody Austin	74 69 68	211	38,500	25	Billy Andrade	69 72 72	213	19,617
	Doug Barron	66 73 72	211	38,500		Brandt Jobe	75 67 71	213	19,617
	KJ Choi	71 71 69	211	38,500		Jesper Parnevik	72 73 68	213	19,617
	Tim Herron	70 74 67	211	38,500		Scott Verplank	70 70 73	213	19,617
18	Paul Broadhurst	71 69 72	212	27,500		Jay Haas	71 69 73	213	19,617
	Fred Couples	70 67 75	212	27,500		Dicky Pride	66 70 77	213	19,617
	Scott Dunlap	70 71 71	212	27,500					

SAS Championship

Going into the final round of the SAS Championship, Ernie Els had his work more or less cut out for him. Actually, more, and by a great deal.

Els, a rookie, would score his second Champions Tour win in the October tournament, but the chances weren't looking great. Els had shot Prestonwood in 70-68, six under, and was going into the final round three strokes behind a threesome tied at nine under — Woody Austin, seeking his fifth tour win; Darren Clarke, the 2011 British Open champion, hungry for his first, and the redoubtable Colin Montgomerie, a seven-time winner. A stroke behind them was Bernhard Langer, going for his 42nd tour victory. In addition, Els was tied with fellow rookie Jim Furyk, who had won his first two starts and was going for a record third.

A host of things had to fall into place for Els in the final round. Furyk, for example, had to cool off. A pair of par fours had kept him at bay. He bogeyed number five all three times, and he played the 16th in birdie-double bogey-bogey. Langer was undone early in the first six holes. He birdied the first, then had three straight bogeys, a par, and a double bogey.

The path ahead of Els also cleared. Clarke shot a five-bogey 74, Austin a 72 with two birdies and two bogeys, and Monty had three birdies and a bogey for a 70 and finished second.

Els figured he'd need a 64 to win. "There were so many guys bunched," he said. "I was coming from six under. I reckoned 14 under may be a good score." He had a tough start, a bogey at the third. Then from the sixth on, he played the 13 holes in seven under for a 66, and a 12-under-par tally of 204 to beat Monty by one, after Monty missed the final green.

Els had finished birdie-birdie, and with an ironic memory. A few weeks earlier, in the PURE Championship, he missed a playoff when he missed a two-foot par putt at the last. This time, in the rain, he holed a 40-footer for birdie at the last to win.

Said Els: "Figure that one out."

Prestonwood Country Club, Cary, North Carolina — October 9-11
Par 72 (35-37); 7,137 yards — Purse: $2,100,000

1	**Ernie Els**	70 68 66	204	$315,000	19	Steve Flesch	75 65 71	211	28,455
2	**Colin Montgomerie**	68 67 70	205	184,800		Rod Pampling	74 69 68	211	28,455
3	**Vijay Singh**	70 66 70	206	151,200	21	Wes Short Jr	71 68 73	212	25,095
4	Woody Austin	66 69 72	207	90,300		Mike Weir	71 71 70	212	25,095
	Robert Karlsson	73 66 68	207	90,300	23	Tom Byrum	70 72 71	213	20,580
	Gene Sauers	67 73 67	207	90,300		Marco Dawson	68 71 74	213	20,580
	David Toms	69 67 71	207	90,300		Glen Day	71 69 73	213	20,580
	Kirk Triplett	68 70 69	207	90,300		Scott Dunlap	72 71 70	213	20,580
9	Jim Furyk	70 68 70	208	56,700		Rocco Mediate	71 73 69	213	20,580
	Scott Parel	69 69 70	208	56,700		Scott Verplank	73 67 73	213	20,580
11	Cameron Beckman	70 68 71	209	46,200	29	Paul Broadhurst	71 71 72	214	15,210
	Darren Clarke	69 66 74	209	46,200		John Daly	72 69 73	214	15,210
	Kevin Sutherland	69 68 72	209	46,200		Dudley Hart	72 70 72	214	15,210
14	Tim Herron	69 68 73	210	35,700		Lee Janzen	72 67 75	214	15,210
	Brandt Jobe	69 72 69	210	35,700		Jesper Parnevik	72 70 72	214	15,210
	Jerry Kelly	72 67 71	210	35,700		Kenny Perry	69 70 75	214	15,210
	Bernhard Langer	70 66 74	210	35,700		Carlos Franco	70 71 73	214	15,210
	Dicky Pride	72 67 71	210	35,700					

Dominion Energy Charity Classic

Phil Mickelson had his game plan, but in golf, the best laid plans …

"I'm trying man — I'm trying to attack," Mickelson insisted. "I'm trying to get after this course, but it's hard to do from the rough."

This was his frustration in the Dominion Energy Charity Classic at the Country Club of Virginia, so rain-heavy that the first round had to be folded onto the second on Saturday.

Mickelson finally got his game in synch. Coming from three strokes behind in the final round, he was doing things like driving the green at the 274-yard, par-four 15th and reaching the par-five 16th in two, and two-putting both for birdies. He shot 68-66-65 for a 17-under 199 total and a three-stroke victory over fellow left-hander Mike Weir.

Mickelson thus became the second player of the year and third overall to win his first two starts on the Champions Tour. Jim Furyk had done it earlier in 2020, and Bruce Fleisher in 1999.

But it was a duel. Weir opened with 68-63 and a three-stroke lead over Mickelson (68-66). "I'm super-happy with the way I played today," Weir said. "Let's just keep the pedal down."

Said Mickelson: "I let a lot of shots go, but I'm in a good position."

They had turned it into their private chase. Retief Goosen and Brandt Jobe were tied at five behind, and Bernhard Langer and Wes Short Jr were at six back.

Weir closed with a three-birdie, two-bogey 71 and finished at 14-under 202. Mickelson's only flaw in the final round was a bad drive that cost him a bogey. "And I was lucky to get away with it," he said. Then he finished with four of his eight birdies for his closing 65.

Paul Goydos finished third with an eight-birdie 65. Langer tied for fourth, for his tour-best 10th top 10; Robert Karlsson had an albatross at the 18th and tied for ninth after a 64, and Jim Furyk eagled 15 and 16 and shot 69.

Mickelson, 50, still had this image problem. He was using the Champions Tour for tuning up for majors on the PGA Tour — earlier the Ozarks event for the US Open, and now, in October, the Dominion for the rescheduled Masters.

The problem? "If I win, well, I'm supposed to," he said, "and if I don't? Oh my gosh — what happened?"

The solution? Win.

Country Club of Virginia (James River), Richmond, Virginia — October 16-18
Par 72 (36-36); 7,025 yards — Purse: $2,000,000

1	**Phil Mickelson**	68	66	65	199	$300,000
2	**Mike Weir**	68	63	71	202	176,000
3	**Paul Goydos**	70	68	65	203	144,000
4	Brandt Jobe	68	68	68	204	107,000
	Bernhard Langer	67	70	67	204	107,000
6	KJ Choi	72	67	66	205	72,000
	Retief Goosen	68	68	69	205	72,000
	Kenny Perry	71	70	64	205	72,000
9	Ernie Els	72	66	68	206	54,000
	Robert Karlsson	72	70	64	206	54,000
11	Wes Short Jr	69	68	70	207	46,000
	Kevin Sutherland	69	72	66	207	46,000
13	Doug Barron	73	66	69	208	39,000
	Jim Furyk	71	68	69	208	39,000
15	Paul Broadhurst	70	70	69	209	34,000
	Tom Byrum	71	70	68	209	34,000
	Dicky Pride	73	69	67	209	34,000
18	Tim Herron	75	68	67	210	26,400
	Miguel Angel Jimenez	74	69	67	210	26,400
	Kent Jones	72	71	67	210	26,400
	Jerry Kelly	74	69	67	210	26,400
	Rod Pampling	72	69	69	210	26,400
23	Michael Allen	72	71	68	211	19,600
	Steve Jones	72	69	70	211	19,600
	Jeff Maggert	70	69	72	211	19,600
	Scott Parel	69	70	72	211	19,600
	Joey Sindelar	68	72	71	211	19,600
	Vijay Singh	72	72	67	211	19,600
29	Woody Austin	74	70	68	212	14,800
	Bob Estes	76	68	68	212	14,800
	Steve Flesch	71	69	72	212	14,800
	Colin Montgomerie	72	70	70	212	14,800
	Steve Pate	69	72	71	212	14,800
	Kirk Triplett	71	71	70	212	14,800

TimberTech Championship

Darren Clarke's timing was magnificent — exit laughing and cheering your head off!

"Maybe one of these days I am going to have one," the bearded Northern Irishman, 52, had said earlier in the TimberTech Championship at the Old Course at Broken Sound. He meant a win. But not one of these days. Right now. His visa was expiring. This was his last chance.

Prospects didn't look rosy after he opened with a three-under 69, five behind co-leaders Jim Furyk and John Daly. (Daly was in his fourth start since revealing he was battling cancer. "Tired all the time," he said. "Proud of myself. I only smoked six cigarettes today.")

Clarke's prospects looked even less rosy in the second round when he forgot the rule on preferred lies under wet conditions. "Second hole, down the middle of the fairway," he said. "Marked it, picked it up. Oops. One-shot penalty straightaway."

The error set up his first extraordinary play of the day. Even with the penalty, he escaped a blot on his card. "Anyway," he said, "hit it over the back of the green, chipped it in for par." The other extraordinary point came at the par-five 18th — an eight-iron to three feet and an eagle. That gave him a flawless 10-under 62 and tied him with Sweden's Robert Karlsson (66) for the lead at 13 under.

Clarke just missed another eagle at the 18th in the final round, from 30 feet, but he tapped in for birdie and a 68, taking his first Champions Tour win with 17-under 199, a stroke ahead of Furyk (68), who missed an eagle from 20 feet, and Bernhard Langer (67), tying for second.

"It's great to finally win one," Clarke said. "I wouldn't be working this hard if I didn't think I could still win." And so it would be a great trip home. This was his first victory since the 2011 Open Championship.

"Well, the last victory I had, I was drunk for a week," Clarke said, "so this time I won't be."

Broken Sound Club (Old), Boca Raton, Florida — October 30-November 1
Par 72 (36-36); 6,807 yards — Purse: $2,000,000

1	**Darren Clarke**	69	62	68	199	$300,000
2	**Jim Furyk**	64	68	68	200	160,000
	Bernhard Langer	65	68	67	200	160,000
4	Miguel Angel Jimenez	68	67	66	201	119,000
5	Robert Karlsson	65	66	71	202	87,500
	Gene Sauers	69	65	68	202	87,500
7	Steve Flesch	67	70	66	203	64,000
	Kent Jones	67	66	70	203	64,000
	Tim Petrovic	67	68	68	203	64,000
10	Cameron Beckman	67	66	71	204	44,400
	Stephen Leaney	70	66	68	204	44,400
	Vijay Singh	69	67	68	204	44,400
	Kirk Triplett	69	70	65	204	44,400
	Duffy Waldorf	65	71	68	204	44,400
15	Joe Durant	66	69	70	205	32,000
	Retief Goosen	67	69	69	205	32,000
	Brett Quigley	66	71	68	205	32,000
	David Toms	67	70	68	205	32,000
	Dicky Pride	71	68	66	205	32,000
20	Jose Maria Olazabal	70	69	67	206	26,200
21	Chris DiMarco	69	71	67	207	22,160
	Scott Hoch	67	69	71	207	22,160
	Scott Parel	65	68	74	207	22,160
	Kevin Sutherland	67	69	71	207	22,160
	Kenny Perry	70	70	67	207	22,160
26	Doug Barron	69	72	67	208	15,273
	Olin Browne	68	69	71	208	15,273
	John Daly	64	73	71	208	15,273
	Ernie Els	69	69	70	208	15,273
	Dudley Hart	67	71	70	208	15,273
	Brandt Jobe	72	70	66	208	15,273
	Jerry Kelly	68	72	68	208	15,273
	David McKenzie	69	69	70	208	15,273
	Rod Pampling	69	65	74	208	15,273
	Jeff Sluman	67	72	69	208	15,273
	Tom Pernice Jr	69	67	72	208	15,273

Charles Schwab Cup Championship

Kevin Sutherland can read more that just greens. How about the future?

In the Charles Schwab Cup Championship, the final tournament on the Champions Tour's virus-wracked 2020 schedule, early in November, he had just taken a hefty five-stroke lead through the second round. But Sutherland, 56, who had won the event in 2017, also at Phoenix Country Club, refused to be tempted into a bright view.

"You know," Sutherland offered, "the way this course is, someone's probably going to shoot seven or eight or nine under par tomorrow, so I might have to shoot something at least three or four under par to win."

The next day, England's Paul Broadhurst, who had started six behind Sutherland, shot that eight under, a flawless 63. So Sutherland had to shoot at least three under to win. But he didn't. He shot a two-under 69 and tied Broadhurst at 15-under 198. Sutherland had shot 65-64-69, and Broadhurst 67-68-63. There would be a playoff.

For added eerie: Sutherland had won twice earlier in playoffs. In June 2019, he beat Scott Parel on the second extra hole of the Principal Charity Classic. But in March of that year, in the Rapiscan Systems Classic, he beat Parel in a seven-hole playoff — spread over two days, because of darkness.

This playoff would start at the par-four 17th, go to the par-five 18th, and alternate, as needed. And they proceeded to battle in pars through six holes, a duel stopped by darkness. The next morning, in the chill desert air, at the 17th, Sutherland two-putted from 30 feet for his par, and Broadhurst chipped to four feet and tied him. At the 18th, Sutherland holed a 25-footer for the first playoff birdie. Broadhurst matched him from six feet. Back to 17, the ninth playoff hole: Broadhurst was just short of the green, but got up and down for his par. Sutherland lofted his 163-yard approach to four feet. He made the birdie for his only win of the year and his fourth Champions title — and third by playoff.

"Kevin hit the shot on the ninth extra hole ... a great shot into a couple of feet," Broadhurst said. "I thought I hit a good shot, but it just hung up in the cold breeze and came up a yard short."

For Sutherland, familiarity was the key. "I've always hit good iron shots here," he said. "I think it's a good eye for me."

Phoenix Country Club, Phoenix, Arizona — November 6-9
Par 71 (36-35); 6,763 yards — Purse: $2,500,000

1	**Kevin Sutherland**	65	64	69	198	$375,000
2	**Paul Broadhurst**	67	68	63	198	220,000
	Sutherland won playoff at ninth extra hole					
3	**Woody Austin**	67	69	65	201	180,000
4	Wes Short Jr	68	66	69	203	148,750
5	Fred Couples	67	71	66	204	91,750
	Glen Day	69	69	66	204	91,750
	Ernie Els	68	70	66	204	91,750
	Retief Goosen	70	69	65	204	91,750
	Bernhard Langer	70	70	64	204	91,750
10	Paul Goydos	64	75	66	205	60,000
	Tom Lehman	68	67	70	205	60,000
	Corey Pavin	69	67	69	205	60,000
13	Jim Furyk	68	68	70	206	47,500
	Mark O'Meara	67	70	69	206	47,500
	Gene Sauers	70	69	67	206	47,500
16	Doug Barron	68	73	66	207	35,357
	Shane Bertsch	67	73	67	207	35,357
	Ken Duke	69	69	69	207	35,357
	Brandt Jobe	64	73	70	207	35,357
	Jerry Kelly	71	71	65	207	35,357
	Jose Maria Olazabal	71	68	68	207	35,357
	Rod Pampling	69	71	67	207	35,357
23	Mark Brooks	65	72	71	208	26,250
	Steve Flesch	67	73	68	208	26,250
	Kenny Perry	71	68	69	208	26,250
26	Billy Mayfair	67	70	72	209	23,250
	Jerry Smith	69	71	69	209	23,250
28	Stephen Ames	67	72	71	210	18,563
	KJ Choi	65	74	71	210	18,563
	Bob Estes	72	68	70	210	18,563
	Fred Funk	69	71	70	210	18,563
	Lee Janzen	70	72	68	210	18,563
	Robert Karlsson	70	71	69	210	18,563
	Jeff Maggert	70	69	71	210	18,563
	David Toms	70	72	68	210	18,563

2020-21 CHARLES SCHWAB CUP MONEY LIST

1	Bernhard Langer	$1,493,737
2	Ernie Els	1,466,838
3	Kevin Sutherland	1,226,807
4	Miguel Angel Jimenez	1,120,079
5	Scott Parel	1,031,908
6	Jerry Kelly	980,978
7	Jim Furyk	933,200
8	Woody Austin	876,401
9	Robert Karlsson	862,768
10	Retief Goosen	775,224

European Legends Tour

The European Tour's senior administrators dealt with the present and the future during the overwhelming 2020 coronavirus pandemic, cancelling its entire Staysure Tour season and creating a new name and distinctive format for the 2021 campaign. The kingpin Senior Open, presented by Rolex, was immediately rescheduled for July 22-25, 2021, at the prestigious Sunningdale Golf Club, its intended 2020 site.

In announcing the Staysure Tour cancellation on June 19, Mark Aspland, head of the circuit, explained: "This decision was not taken lightly. We had to recognise the additional risk associated with the age demographic of the Staysure Tour membership, alongside the challenges of implementing the requisite health strategy across the multiple territories we play in." The tour staged tournaments in 13 countries in 2019.

Two months later, the European Tour unveiled a new name for its senior wing — Legends Tour — and an unprecedented restructuring, primarily the formation of a joint venture agreement with Staysure founder and Group CEO Ryan Howsam. The insurance company executive acquired a majority equity share of the circuit and will now oversee its commercial activities, while the regular tour staff continue to handle the regular tournament operations. Howsam's leadership position is a first ever for an individual in major tournament golf. His goal, he stated, was to utilise the "as yet untapped commercial potential of the Legends Tour".

The new format put an increased focus on three-day, pro-am play and the creation of a "Legends Club" and an amateur Order of Merit that will determine players eligible for spots in the circuit's season-ending climax tournament. It also included plans for Celebrity Pro-Ams, linking legendary golfers with legendary figures of other sports, music and entertainment.

Eight of European senior golf's most prominent players were designated "as the Tour's first official ambassadors who will play a key role in outlining the Tour's vision in the months to come". The announcement added: "The ambassadors will also be a central part of growing the popular alliance format which gives amateurs the chance to play alongside some of golf's great names in tournament conditions."

Named as ambassadors were six former Ryder Cup captains — Darren Clarke, Mark James, Paul McGinley, Colin Montgomerie, Ian Woosnam and American Tom Lehman — along with 1999 Open champion Paul Lawrie and 2005 US Open champion Michael Campbell.

2020 SCHEDULE	
Murhof Legends - Austrian Senior Open	*cancelled*
KitchenAid Senior PGA Championship	*cancelled*
Senior Italian Open	*cancelled*
Arras Open Senior Hauts de France	*cancelled*
Farmfoods European Legends Links Championship	*cancelled*
US Senior Open Championship	*cancelled*
The Senior Open presented by Rolex	*postponed to 2021*

Japan PGA Senior Tour

Things were quite different on the Japan Senior Tour in 2020 and it wasn't just the disruptions caused by the coronavirus pandemic. A season earlier, Thailand stars Prayad Marksaeng and Thaworn Wiratchant scored four victories between them, were factors in nearly every tournament and finished one-two on the final money list. In 2020, they weren't even in Japan, thanks to the perils of the health crisis.

Instead, the victories in the eight tournaments that were played in the latter part of the year were spread among eight men, including Eiji Mizoguchi, who won twice in 2019. Three were first-time senior winners.

Akira Teranishi, who had single wins in each of the previous three seasons, captured the Japan Senior Open Championship in decisive fashion, finishing five strokes in front of Hiroo Okamo, who had two other runner-up showings during the abbreviated season. Teranishi headed the money list with ¥19,019,464, a shade ahead of Norio Shinozaki, who had a victory and a pair of second-place finishes.

In the other major championship, Masayoshi Nakayama had to win a playoff to bag the Japan PGA Senior title in a tournament shortened to 54 holes when a massive power outage wiped out the third round.

2020 SCHEDULE

Nojima Champion Cup Hakone		*cancelled*
Ryosen More Surprise Cup		*cancelled*
Starts Senior		*cancelled*
Sumaiida Cup		*cancelled*
Fancl Classic		*cancelled*
ISPS Handa Corona Ni Katsu!	**Shinsuke Yanagisawa**	
ISPS Handa Corona! Professional Golfer 100th Anniversary	**Toru Suzuki**	
Maruhan Cup Taiheiyo Club	**Norio Shinozaki**	
Sports Promotion Hiroshima Senior		*cancelled*
Komatsu Open		*cancelled*
Japan Senior Open Championship	**Akira Teranishi**	
Kumamoto Aso Senior Open		*cancelled*
Japan PGA Senior Championship	**Masayoshi Nakayama**	
Trust Group Cup Sasebo Senior Open		*cancelled*
Fukuoka Senior Open		*cancelled*
Fujifilm Senior Championship		*cancelled*
Cosmohealth Cup Senior	**Yoshinori Mizumaki**	
Fubon Yeangder Senior Cup		*cancelled*
Iwasaki Shiratsuyu Senior	**Eiji Mizoguchi**	
Kanehide Senior Okinawa Open	**Masayuki Kawamura**	

ISPS Handa Corona Ni Katsu!

The pandemic-delayed Japan Senior Tour finally came alive on the final days of July with a new 36-hole event — the ISPS Handa Corona Ni Katsu! tournament in Shizuoka.

Shinnosuke Yanagisawa rode a first-round 64 to a three-stroke victory at Asagiri Country Club, picking up his third Senior Tour title to go with wins in the 2017 ISPS Handa Cup Philanthropy and 2019 Hiroshima Senior tournaments.

Yanagisawa was flawless the first day as he racked up an eagle and six birdies for the eight-under-par 64, but it only gave him a one-shot lead on Masayuki Kawamura, who also was bogey-free with his seven-birdie 65. However, he had three strokes on the rest of the field and eased home on Sunday with a six-birdie 67 and total of 131. Kawamura could only muster a 69 and no other serious threats developed. Norio Shinzaki, with a pair of 67s, tied Kawamura for second place.

Asagiri Country Club, Shizuoka — July 30-31
Par 72 (36-36); 6,863 yards — Purse: ¥30,000,000

1	**Shinsuke Yanagisawa**	64 67	131	¥5,000,000
2	**Norio Shinozaki**	67 67	134	1,875,000
	Masayuki Kawamura	65 69	134	1,875,000
4	Masayoshi Yamazoe	72 63	135	975,000
	Yoichi Shimizu	70 65	135	975,000
	Akira Teranishi	70 65	135	975,000
	Toru Taniguchi	68 67	135	975,000
8	Hideki Kase	68 68	136	700,000
	Eiji Mizoguchi	68 68	136	700,000
10	Takeshi Sakiyama	71 66	137	508,333
	Ryoken Kawagishi	70 67	137	508,333
	Katsumi Kubo	69 68	137	508,333
13	Koichi Kasimura	71 67	138	450,000
14	Kazuhiro Takami	72 67	139	375,000
	Masayoshi Nakayama	70 69	139	375,000
	Yoshinobu Tsukada	70 69	139	375,000
	Toru Suzuki	70 69	139	375,000
	Mamoru Osanai	69 70	139	375,000
19	Kunihiko Masuda	73 67	140	290,000
	Shoichi Kuwabara	71 69	140	290,000

ISPS Handa Corona! Professional Golfer 100th Anniversary

Toru Suzuki emerged from a three-man battle in the stretch run with the title in the ISPS Handa Corona! Professional Golfer 100th Anniversary tournament. He won by a stroke with his 19-under-par 197 over Tsukasa Watanabe and Kiyoshi Murota, the all-time wins leader on the Japan Senior Tour.

The 54-year-old Suzuki, an eight-tournament winner on the Japan Tour earlier in his career, never trailed at Akagi Golf Club in Gunma Prefecture, but had Watanabe on his heels a shot behind each day as he opened with a sparkling 64 and followed with 65 in Saturday's round. Murota, seeking his 21st victory on the circuit and first in two seasons, joined the fray on Sunday.

At the turn, Suzuki (35) and Watanabe (34) shared the lead, but just a stroke ahead of Murota, who was out in 32. Suzuki inched a shot in front with a birdie at the 11th hole. Murota matched it, all three birdied the par-five 13th and Murota caught Suzuki with another birdie at the 14th.

Toru birdied the 16th to regain the lead and held on with a par at the final hole after a Murota par and a Watanabe birdie. It was his fourth senior win, complementing three he won in a five-tournament stretch in late 2018.

Akagi Golf Club, Gunma — August 21-23
Par 72 (36-36); 7,010 yards — Purse: ¥55,000,000

1	**Toru Suzuki**	64 65 68	197	¥10,000,000
2	**Kiyoshi Murota**	66 67 65	198	4,200,000
	Tsukasa Watanabe	65 65 68	198	4,200,000
4	Mitsutaka Kusakabe	68 65 67	200	2,250,000
5	Masayoshi Yamazoe	68 68 65	201	1,950,000
6	Hiroo Okamo	69 68 65	202	1,516,666
	Keiichiro Fukabori	67 70 65	202	1,516,666
	Takeshi Sakiyama	67 67 68	202	1,516,666
9	Kiyoshi Maita	71 66 66	203	1,118,750
	Shinichi Akiba	65 72 66	203	1,118,750
	Yoshinobu Tsukada	69 65 69	203	1,118,750
	Hitoshi Kato	66 68 69	203	1,118,750
13	Jiro Minamizaki	69 69 66	204	831,250
	Naoyuki Tamura	67 71 66	204	831,250
	Takenori Kamobayashi	68 67 69	204	831,250
	Akira Teranishi	65 68 71	204	831,250
17	Shoichi Kuwabara	71 68 66	205	637,500
	Norio Shinozaki	71 68 66	205	637,500
	Hidezumi Shirakata	69 70 66	205	637,500
	Satoshi Higashi	69 69 67	205	637,500
	Masayuki Kawamura	69 67 69	205	637,500
	Mamoru Osanai	71 64 70	205	637,500
	Kazuhiro Fukunaga	67 68 70	205	637,500
	Naoki Okaji	69 65 71	205	637,500

Maruhan Cup Taiheiyo Club Senior

For Norio Shinozaki the second victory of his long career came much more easily than his first one 13 years ago on the Japan Tour but had one familiar aspect — a playoff.

Shinozaki had to fight through 77 holes, the last five in overtime, before winning the ANA tournament in 2007. The second time, playing in his first full season on the Japan Senior Tour, the 50-year-old pro only needed one extra hole to land the two-day Maruhan Cup Taiheiyo Club Senior title, defeating Yoshinobu Tsukada, 51, after the two newly minted seniors tied with 36-hole 135s.

Both trailed Hiroyuki Fujita after the opening round on the Gotemba course at the Taiheiyo Club. Fujita, 51, a 16-times winner who is still active on the Japan Tour, teed it up at the Taiheiyo Club while the regular circuit remained idle because of the pandemic. He shot 65 in his debut round on Saturday, a shot ahead of Tsukada and Hiroshi Okashige and three in front of Shinozaki.

While Fujita was shooting 72 en route to a six-way tie for third place on Sunday, Shinozaki and Tsukada moved in front and dueled down the stretch. Norio birdied the last two holes for 67 to tie Yoshinobu, who closed with seven straight pars and 69. Shinozaki only needed a par on the first hole of the playoff when Tsukada bogeyed the par-five 18th.

Taiheiyo Club (Gotemba), Shizuoka — August 29-30
Par: 72 (36-36); 7,327 yards — Purse: ¥50,000,000

1	**Norio Shinozaki**	68	67	135	¥10,000,000
2	**Yoshinobu Tsukada**	66	69	135	5,000,000
	Shinozaki won playoff at first extra hole				
3	**Tsuyoshi Yoneyama**	71	66	137	1,966,666
	Masayoshi Yamazoe	69	68	137	1,966,666
	Masayuki Kawamura	69	68	137	1,966,666
	Shoichi Kuwabara	69	68	137	1,966,666
	Hiroo Okamo	66	71	137	1,966,666
	Hiroyuki Fujita	65	72	137	1,966,666
9	Mamoru Osanai	71	67	138	1,300,000
10	Akira Teranishi	72	67	139	1,050,000
	Hideki Kase	71	68	139	1,050,000
12	Ryoken Kawagishi	71	69	140	875,000
	Yoshinori Mizumaki	70	70	140	875,000
	Masahiro Kuramoto	70	70	140	875,000
	Kyoji Hirota	67	73	140	875,000
16	Hiroshi Tominaga	72	69	141	700,000
	Taichi Teshima	71	70	141	700,000
	Katsuyoshi Tomori	71	70	141	700,000
19	Hidezumi Shirakata	72	70	142	424,166
	Masahiro Yamasaki	71	71	142	424,166
	Toshimitsu Izawa	71	71	142	424,166
	Masayoshi Nakayama	71	71	142	424,166
	Katsumi Kubo	71	71	142	424,166
	Yuzo Oyama	71	71	142	424,166
	Seiki Okuda	70	72	142	424,166
	Gregory Meyer	70	72	142	424,166
	Naoyuki Tamura	69	73	142	424,166
	Keiichiro Fukabori	69	73	142	424,166
	Masami Ito	68	74	142	424,166
	Koichi Kasimura	68	74	142	424,166

Japan Senior Open Championship

Akira Teranishi paid his fourth annual visit to the winner's circle of the Japan Senior Tour in mid-September, this time picking up the Japan Senior Open Championship, the circuit's most prestigious title, and doing so in most impressive fashion.

The 54-year-old pro, who posted single victories in each of his previous three seasons, led the field from the opening day at Naruo Golf Club and finished things off with a five-stroke victory margin over runner-up Hiroo Okamo. At 275, he was the only player under par for the week.

He started smoothly with a five-birdie 65, two shots in front of veteran Ryoken Kawagishi and widened the gap to five on Friday with a 69 for 134, then trailed most closely by Okamo and Hiroyuki Fujita at 139. Despite a wild-and-wooly 72 — the product of an eagle, a birdie, a double bogey and a six on the par-three fourth hole — he remained on top after the third day, at 206 two shots ahead of Okamo and Kawagishi.

Teranishi was never threatened on Sunday even though he went out in one-over-par 36, salvaging a par at the ninth hole, which he double bogeyed on Saturday, barely escaping the pond with an errant tee shot. Birdies at 13, 14 and 17 led to his final-round 69 and five-shot margin on Okamo, who mustered only a single birdie in a 72 round.

"It's been four years since I envisioned winning the Japan Senior Open at Naruo," proclaimed Teranishi afterwards. "I was more particular about winning the championship at Naruo than anywhere else in order to make my dream come true."

Naruo Golf Club, Hyogo
Par 70 (35-35); 6,616 yards

September 17-20
Purse: ¥60,000,000

1	**Akira Teranishi**	65	69	72	69	275	¥12,000,000
2	**Hiroo Okamo**	69	70	69	72	280	6,600,000
3	**Ryoken Kawagishi**	67	74	67	73	281	4,620,000
4	Yoshinobu Tsukada	71	70	73	68	282	2,355,000
	Taichi Teshima	69	73	69	71	282	2,355,000
	Shinichi Akiba	68	72	70	72	282	2,355,000
	Norio Shinozaki	74	67	68	73	282	2,355,000
8	Keiichiro Fukabori	73	67	73	70	283	1,440,000
	Mamoru Osanai	70	71	69	73	283	1,440,000
10	Gregory Meyer	72	71	72	69	284	1,095,000
	Toru Suzuki	73	67	69	75	284	1,095,000
12	Masayoshi Yamazoe	72	69	73	71	285	948,000
13	Kiyoshi Murota	74	73	73	66	286	789,000
	Hiroyuki Fujita	70	69	70	77	286	789,000
15	Toru Taniguchi	73	69	75	71	288	684,000
	Toshimitsu Izawa	70	73	71	74	288	684,000
17	Hiroya Kamide	74	75	69	71	289	572,400
	Hidezumi Shirakata	70	74	72	73	289	572,400
	Tsuyoshi Yoneyama	72	70	73	74	289	572,400
	Yoshinori Mizumaki	70	76	68	75	289	572,400
	Taku Yamanaka	69	76	68	76	289	572,400
22	Hisashi Sawada	76	71	70	73	290	492,000
	Masayuki Kawamura	73	71	71	75	290	492,000
	Takeshi Sakiyama	71	73	71	75	290	492,000
25	Yoichi Shimizu	73	70	77	71	291	456,000
	Kazuhiro Takami	71	76	68	76	291	456,000
	Seiki Okuda	75	71	69	76	291	456,000

Japan PGA Senior Championship

Speaking of dreams coming true, as Akira Teranishi did after winning the Japan Senior Open two weeks earlier:

"Actually, last week I had a dream of winning this tournament," professed Masayoshi Nakayama after capturing the Japan PGA Senior Championship, the other major on the Japan Senior Tour. "I'm happy. Oh, I'm about to cry," said the 52-year-old pro after prevailing in a playoff against Yoichi Shimizu and landing the first national tournament title of his career.

The overtime finish capped a week during which a major power outage wiped out the Saturday round, resulting in a 54-hole tournament. Tsutomu Higa commanded the field the first two days with 67-69 for 136, as Nakayama and Shimizu moved into second place at 138 with 66 and 65 respectively after weak starts (72 and 73) on Thursday.

"Higa-san wasn't very good (on early holes) so I thought it would be match play between me and Shimizu," said Nakayama, recapping the final round. So it was as the two put together three-birdie 69s, Masayoshi going ahead with his third at the 17th and Yoichi matching it at the 18th for a total of 207. Nakayama won with a par on the first extra hole.

Summit Golf Club, Ishioka City, Ibaraki
Par 72 (36-36); 7,019 yards

October 8-11
Purse: ¥50,000,000

1	**Masayoshi Nakayama**	72	66	69	207	¥10,000,000
2	**Yoichi Shimizu**	73	65	69	207	5,000,000
	Nakayama won playoff at first extra hole					
3	**Hiroo Okamo**	75	71	64	210	3,500,000
4	Toru Suzuki	73	71	67	211	1,720,000
	Eiji Mizoguchi	68	75	68	211	1,720,000
	Katsunori Kuwabara	70	71	70	211	1,720,000
	Keiichiro Fukabori	70	70	71	211	1,720,000
	Tsutomu Higa	67	69	75	211	1,720,000
9	Mitsutaka Kusakabe	72	70	70	212	1,150,000
10	Takenori Kamobayashi	73	70	70	213	1,050,000
11	Hideki Kase	71	77	66	214	950,000
	Takeshi Sakiyama	73	72	69	214	950,000
	Akira Teranishi	73	71	70	214	950,000
14	Toshimitsu Izawa	73	75	67	215	708,571
	Yuji Igarashi	74	73	68	215	708,571
	Gregory Meyer	72	75	68	215	708,571
	Yoshinobu Tsukada	72	74	69	215	708,571
	Hiroyuki Fujita	74	71	70	215	708,571
	Ikuo Shirahama	71	71	73	215	708,571
	Norio Shinozaki	71	71	73	215	708,571
21	Masahiro Yamasaki	76	72	68	216	512,000
	Shigeru Harimoto	70	77	69	216	512,000
	Koichi Kasimura	74	72	70	216	512,000
	Naoyuki Tamura	72	74	70	216	512,000
	Ryoken Kawagishi	73	71	72	216	512,000

Cosmohealth Cup Senior

Yoshinori Mizumaki displayed longevity with his victory in the Cosmohealth Cup Senior tournament. Nine years after scoring his first of three wins on the Japan Senior Tour, the 62-year-old Mizumaki broke from a four-way, second-place tie to register a two-stroke victory in the new event at Ogose Golf Club in Saitama in mid-November.

The first round belonged to Akira Teranishi, who opened with a six-under-par 66 as he tried to add the Cosmohealth title to the Japan Senior Open Championship he won in September. A stroke back, Mizumaki shared second place with Shigeru Nonaka, Gregory Meyer and Yutaka Hagawa.

Mizumaki seized the lead early in the Sunday round with a birdie at the second hole where Teranishi found water, bogeyed and never recovered the top spot, finishing in a tie for seventh with a 73. Mizumaki countered a bogey at the third with a birdie at the ninth and secured his lead with three birdies around a bogey in the middle of the back nine. His 69 for an eight-under-par total of 136 gave him the two-shot margin over Toshimitsu Izawa, Hiroo Okamo, Norio Shinozaki, Meyer and Nonaka, all of whom except Shinozaki birdied the final hole.

Ogose Golf Club, Saitama
Par 72 (36-36); 7,015 yards

November 13-14
Purse: ¥20,000,000

1	**Yoshinori Mizumaki**	67	69	136	¥3,600,000
2	**Norio Shinozaki**	71	67	138	1,072,000
	Toshimitsu Izawa	70	68	138	1,072,000
	Hiroo Okamo	68	70	138	1,072,000
	Gregory Meyer	67	71	138	1,072,000
	Shigeru Nonaka	67	71	138	1,072,000
7	Tsukasa Watanabe	70	69	139	555,000
	Hiroshi Tominaga	69	70	139	555,000
	Yutaka Hagawa	67	72	139	555,000
	Akira Teranishi	66	73	139	555,000
11	Ryoken Kawagishi	69	71	140	400,000
	Toru Suzuki	68	72	140	400,000
	Hidezumi Shirakata	68	72	140	400,000
14	Kohki Idoki	72	69	141	282,400
	Kazuhiro Takami	69	72	141	282,400
	Seiki Okuda	68	73	141	282,400
	Shinsuke Yanagisawa	68	73	141	282,400
	Ikuo Shirahama	68	73	141	282,400
19	Naoya Sugiyama	73	69	142	214,000
	Katsunori Kuwabara	70	72	142	214,000
	Katsunari Takahashi	70	72	142	214,000
	Mamoru Osanai	70	72	142	214,000

Iwasaki Shiratsuyu Senior

Eiji Mizoguchi, who ended a five-season victory drought on the Japan Senior Tour with two wins in 2019, didn't wait nearly as long to capture a third one. The 55-year-old pro, who also sports two titles from his earlier years on the Japan Tour, bagged the Iwasaki Shiratsuyu Senior in late November, scoring a playoff victory over veteran American Gregory Meyer. He was the seventh straight different winner in the eerie season.

He and Meyer, 57, who was seeking his fourth win on the tour, wound up in a tie for the lead on a windy Sunday on Ibusuki Golf Club's Kaimon course after two-day leader Taichi Teshima (65-74 for 139) faded from contention. Mizoguchi started the final round two off the lead and Meyer was four back.

Finishing first, the American posted a solid, five-birdie 67 for 210 on Sunday and Mizoguchi, knowing he needed it, birdied the last hole for the 69 that forged the tie and forced the playoff. After both bunkered their second shots on the par-five playoff hole and Meyer missed his birdie putt from 13 feet, Mizoguchi holed from eight feet for the win.

Ibusuki Golf Club, (Kaimon), Kagoshima
Par 72 (36-36); 7,151 yards

November 27-29
Purse: ¥60,000,000

1	**Eiji Mizoguchi**	71	70	69	210	¥12,000,000
2	**Gregory Meyer**	70	73	67	210	5,700,000
	Mizoguchi won playoff at first extra hole					
3	**Keiichiro Fukabori**	71	73	67	211	3,900,000
4	Shigeru Nonaka	71	73	68	212	2,490,000
	Akira Teranishi	68	74	70	212	2,490,000
6	Norio Shinozaki	73	71	69	213	1,620,000
	Masahiro Yamasaki	67	76	70	213	1,620,000

	Ryoken Kawagishi	67	74	72	213	1,620,000
	Satoshi Higashi	68	72	73	213	1,620,000
10	Naoyuki Tamura	74	74	66	214	1,115,000
	Yutaka Hagawa	74	72	68	214	1,115,000
	Koichi Kasimura	71	73	70	214	1,115,000
	Yoichi Shimizu	68	75	71	214	1,115,000
	Hiroo Okamo	67	76	71	214	1,115,000
	Taichi Teshima	65	74	75	214	1,115,000
16	Katsumi Kubo	72	76	67	215	840,000
	Toru Taniguchi	74	70	71	215	840,000
	Shinichi Akiba	72	72	71	215	840,000
19	Katsunori Kuwabara	74	72	70	216	678,000
	Yoshinori Mizumaki	71	74	71	216	678,000
	Toru Suzuki	74	69	73	216	678,000

Kanehide Senior Okinawa Open

"I don't want to step on the same rut." So thought Masayuki Kawamura on his way to his first Japan Senior Tour victory in the Kanehide Senior Okinawa Open. He was remembering that he bogeyed the last two holes of the same tournament in 2019 to lose by a stroke to Taichi Teshima. "I'm a whole year dragging that regret," he said. "I wanted revenge."

He did bogey the 18th hole at Kanehide Kise Country Club again on the last day for 71 and five-under-par 139, but had enough of a cushion to finish two strokes in front of runner-up Hiroo Okamo, who closed with a 67, the week's low round. It was Okamo's third second-place finish of the season.

The 53-year-old Kawamura, whose wife was his caddie, was just a shot higher than the 67 on Saturday when, amid strong winds and rain, he took only 22 putts in a five-birdie, one-bogey 68, the only sub-70 round of the day. The bogey occurred on the second hole. Kawamura then went 33 straight holes — 31 pars and two birdies — before the other bogey on the final green.

Akira Teranishi, the Japan Senior Open champion, topped the shortened season's money list with ¥19,019,464, nosing out Norio Shinozaki and his ¥18,500,987. Shinozaki had a win and two second-place finishes in 2020.

Kanehide Kise Country Club, Kise, Okinawa
Par 72 (36-36); 7,193 yards

December 4-5
Purse: ¥27,000,000

1	**Masayuki Kawamura**	68	71	139	¥4,500,000
2	**Hiroo Okamo**	74	67	141	2,250,000
3	**Yoshinori Mizumaki**	74	68	142	1,375,000
	Hidezumi Shirakata	70	72	142	1,375,000
5	Ken Hayano	75	68	143	931,250
	Satoshi Higashi	74	69	143	931,250
	Toshimitsu Izawa	72	71	143	931,250
	Taichi Teshima	71	72	143	931,250
9	Ikuo Shirahama	71	73	144	675,000
10	Toru Suzuki	73	72	145	575,000
11	Takeshi Oyama	73	73	146	487,500
	Kazuhiro Fukunaga	71	75	146	487,500
13	Masayoshi Nakayama	77	70	147	412,500
	Kiyoshi Maita	77	70	147	412,500
	Katsumi Kubo	74	73	147	412,500
	Gregory Meyer	73	74	147	412,500
17	Yoichi Shimizu	78	70	148	325,000
	Kohki Idoki	73	75	148	325,000
	Kiyoshi Murota	72	76	148	325,000
20	Mitsutaka Kusakabe	79	70	149	232,916
	Shigeru Nonaka	78	71	149	232,916
	Norio Shinozaki	77	72	149	232,916
	Shinichi Akiba	76	73	149	232,916
	Kazuhiro Takami	74	75	149	232,916
	Masami Ito	74	75	149	232,916

2020 MONEY LIST

1	Akira Teranishi	¥19,019,464
2	Norio Shinozaki	18,500,987
3	Hiroo Okamo	18,158,650
4	Eiji Mizoguchi	15,399,380
5	Toru Suzuki	15,090,500
6	Masayoshi Nakayama	12,215,166
7	Yoshinobu Tsukada	10,175,571
8	Masayuki Kawamura	10,076,666
9	Gregory Meyer	9,509,737
10	Keiichiro Fukabori	9,193,832

Jamie Squire/Getty Images